ORIGINS OF MADNESS
Psychopathology in Animal Life

Other Titles of Interest

BOYDEN A.
Perspectives in Zoology

CORSON S. A.
Ethology and Nonverbal Communication in Mental Health

MELLETT P. G.
Learning and Psychosomatic Approach to the Nature and Treatment of Illness

PRICE K. P. and GATCHEL R. J.
Clinical Applications of Biofeedback: Appraisal and Status

ORIGINS OF MADNESS
Psychopathology in
Animal Life

edited by

J. D. KEEHN

*Department of Psychology,
Atkinson College, York University*

PERGAMON PRESS
Oxford · New York · Toronto · Sydney · Paris · Frankfurt

U.K.	Pergamon Press Ltd., Headington Hill Hall, Oxford OX3 0BW, England
U.S.A.	Pergamon Press Inc., Maxwell House, Fairview Park, Elmsford, New York 10523, U.S.A.
CANADA	Pergamon of Canada, Suite 104, 150 Consumers Road Willowdale, Ontario M2J 1P9, Canada
AUSTRALIA	Pergamon Press (Aust.) Pty. Ltd., P.O. Box 544, Potts Point, N.S.W. 2011, Australia
FRANCE	Pergamon Press SARL, 24 rue des Ecoles, 75240 Paris, Cedex 05, France
FEDERAL REPUBLIC OF GERMANY	Pergamon Press GmbH, 6242 Kronberg-Taunus, Pferdstrasse 1, Federal Republic of Germany

Copyright © 1979 J. D. Keehn

First edition 1979

British Library Cataloguing in Publication Data

Origins of madness.
1. Psychology, Pathological   2. Animals, Habits and behavior of
1. Keehn, J D
591.2   QL785   78-41152

ISBN 0-08-023725-8

Printed and bound in Great Britain by
William Clowes (Beccles) Limited, Beccles and London

Contents

Section X, ENVIRONMENTAL CONTROL OF ANOMALOUS
          BEHAVIOUR

Section XI, TREATMENT OF ABNORMAL ANIMALS

Preface

My aim in preparing this volume is to familiarize experimental and clinical workers with each other's contributions to the study of abnormal behaviour in animals and its bearing on human psychopathology. The readings were chosen from numerous reports of natural and experimental behavioural abnormalities in animals, many of which are surveyed in the introduction. The final selections come from over 30 books and professional journals in the fields of abnormal and comparative psychology, clinical and experimental veterinary medicine, and psychiatry.

The relevant literature divides naturally into two broad classes, one to do with behavioural peculiarities exhibited by animals themselves, and how these peculiarities might be dealt with, the other to do with the use of animals in the analysis of human abnormal behaviour. The first class includes behavioural abnormalities of animals in the wild or under circumstances of confinement, as in laboratories, circuses, households and zoos, where the abnormalities appear without intention. Many examples of this class are mentioned in the introduction and others appear among the individual readings. The second class is primarily concerned with laboratory creations of animal models of human psychopathologies, although it also includes a body of research on normal psychological processes that might bear on psychopathological functioning.

Most of the book is organized according to the second class of investigations, where possible models of neuroses, psychoses, addictions, personality disorders, psychophysiological disorders and disorders of childhood are illustrated with animals. In other parts of the book animal and human psychopathologies are compared and some treatments of animal disorders are described, which should make the readings valuable for veterinary and psychiatric practitioners as well as for other students of animal behaviours.

I am grateful to Mary Hudecki, Susan Partridge and Gary MacDonald for assistance in the acquisition of difficult sources, and to Marilyn Weinper and Rhonda Strasberg for help with correspondence and the efficient preparation of the manuscript. Special thanks are due to Professor P. L. Broadhurst of Birmingham University for providing research facilities during my sabbatical year.

J.D.K.
Toronto
September 1978

Introduction
The Psychopathology of Animal Life

Psychology began as the study of human mentality but modern theories of behaviour depend on experiments with animals. Most of these experiments investigate normal behaviour, but abnormal behaviour in animals is not uncommon. There are reports of neurosis in farm animals (Croft, 1951); hysteria in battery hens and caged baboons (Sanger and Hamdy, 1962; Startsev, 1976); pica in cattle, sheep, horses and birds (Stainton, 1943); intromission phobia in the bull (Fraser, 1957); pseudopregnancy in the rat, and other psychosomatic disturbances in cats, dogs and pigs (Chertok and Fontaine, 1963).

There are cases of agitated depression and self-mutilation in monkeys (Mitchell, 1968; Tinkelpaugh, 1928); sexual inversions in fishes and birds (Morris, 1952, 1955); ulcers in gibbons (Stout and Snyder, 1957); repetitive tics in horses and bears (Brion, 1964; Levy, 1944); compulsive pacing in caged wild animals (Hediger, 1950) and head-banging and stereotyped movements in monkeys and apes (Davenport and Menzel, 1963; Levison, 1970). As well, there are accounts of emotional disturbances in cats and dogs (Mitchell, 1953; Pavlov, 1927), and personality dysfunctions in wild and captive chimpanzees (Hebb, 1947; van Lawick-Goodall, 1971).

Some of these animal's abnormalities are as distinctly pathological as human mental illnesses, and a respectable body of research on comparative psychopathology exists (Brion and Ey, 1964; Broadhurst, 1960, 1973; Dinsmoor, 1960; Finger, 1944; Fox, 1968; Kimmel, 1971; Krushinskii, 1962; Maser and Seligman, 1977; Patton, 1951; Shagass, 1975; Zubin and Hunt, 1967). The clinical and research reports that follow are selected from that research.

In part the selections are organized to conform with the traditional psychiatric system of classification, firstly because some spontaneous abnormalities in animals have been given psychiatric labels and secondly because many animal abnormalities are laboratory creations designed as models of human psychiatric disorders. However, an organization on this basis cannot be adhered to completely owing to the uncertain status of diagnosis in general (Kendell, 1975) and to the low reliability of diagnosis in particular cases (Tinbergen, 1974). The models are meant to suggest how natural abnormalities might occur and how normal desirable behaviour might be restored.

Exemplary models are those of Pavlov (1961), who deduced from the behaviour of dogs that neurosis is a disorder of personality caused by conflicting cortical neural impulses, and of Wolpe (1958, 1967), who concludes from the behaviour of cats that neurosis is a disorder of learning, treatable by reconditioning. Pavlov's and Wolpe's models are neurophysiological and learning theory models of neurotic illness respectively; over the range of psychopathologies Zubin and Hunt (1967) have identified genetic, developmental, and internal-environment models as well. Examples of these

1

models are included in the following selections, although not all alternative models are represented in every case. Thus, with alcoholism, six animal models have been implied or suggested: a nutritional model (Richter, 1941), a genetic model (Eriksson, 1968), a neuro-physiological model (Myers, 1972), a pharmacological model (Kalant, 1970), a reinforcement model (Keehn, 1969) and an adjunctive behaviour model (Gilbert, 1976), but they are not all represented among the selections.

In the case of depression, however, adult psychotic depression and separation depression in infants are both represented, as also are proponents of learning and biochemical theories of depression in the first case, and of mother-separation and sensory-deprivation in the second. But these selections do not all appear in a single section. Nor are stereotyped animal behaviours all included in a single psychiatric category, because it seems wiser to illustrate variables in control of particular activities than to insist that these activities model particular human mental illnesses.

Over the years since Pavlov (1927) described experimental neurosis in dogs, changes have occurred in the aspirations of students of comparative psychopathology. At first, the methods of Pavlov were extended to create experimental neuroses in the monkey and the cat (Masserman, 1943), the pig, the sheep and the goat (Liddell, 1944). Abnormalities induced in the rat were mainly stereotyped fixations (Maier, 1949) and audiogenic seizures (Patton, 1951), which are also found in rabbits (Antonitis, Cary, Sawin and Cohen, 1954) and mice (Kruchinskii, 1962).

Additional studies with rats concerned themselves with experimental analogues of Freudian psychodynamic mechanisms, such as displacement of aggression (Miller, 1939), reaction formation and regression (Mowrer, 1940; Sanders, 1937), and effects on adult behaviour of restricted infant feeding (Hunt, 1941). Now, Freudian mechanisms are no longer attributed to rats, and experimental neurosis is not thought to mimic the natural human disorder (Hunt, 1964). Liddell (1956) acknowledges that a "basic semantic problem can be avoided by admitting that there cannot be a *psychodynamics of animal behaviour*" (italics in original), and Broadhurst (1973), commenting in 1973 on his review of thirteen years before, wrote:

> "In 1960 it seemed sufficient to explore the extent of the evidence for an experimental neurosis in the strict sense, that is to say, to decide if evidence for a clear-cut animal analogue of a clinical disease entity of some sort existed. The answer, not surprisingly, it now seems, was 'No'. No animal preparation that convincingly mimicked such entity could be provided by experimental psychology for the study of etiology, prognosis or therapy."

(Broadhurst, 1973, p. 745)

Although the pioneering demonstrations of Pavlov, Liddell, Masserman, Maier, and Gantt (1944) may be unacceptable as experimental examples of neurosis, the number of human disabilities for which animal analogues have been described has grown to include catatonic, paranoid and depressive psychosis (Ellinwood, Sudilovsky and Nelson, 1972; Newton and Gantt, 1968; Seligman, 1975); infantile autism (Harlow and Harlow, 1971); drug and alcohol addiction (Gilbert, 1976); psychopathic aggression (Ulrich, Dulaney, Kucera and Colasacco, 1972); masochism (Mitchell, 1969); psychosomatic disorders (Miller, 1975), and inadequate or inappropriate sexual performance (Harlow, 1965; Ward, 1972). Some of these disabilities have been created intentionally, as with self-administration of drugs (Thompson and Schuster, 1964); gastric ulcerations (Sines and McDonald, 1968); essential hypertension (Herd, Morse, Kelleher and Jones, 1969); chronic inebriation (Keehn, 1969); and alcohol-dependence (Falk, Samson and

Winger, 1972; Pieper and Skeen, 1972); but others have emerged as more general effects of impoverished early environments (Harlow and Harlow, 1971; Scott and Senay, 1973).

Unlike clinical investigations with humans, in all these studies with animals *"originating situations* must take precedence over *resulting symptoms"* (Liddell, 1956, p. 59). Liddell continues:

> "Because of man's incredibly complicated cognitive machinery, his neurotic symptoms may exhibit a bewildering diversity. Nevertheless, our emotionally disturbed animals under careful observation show many of the same or closely similar symptoms. The physician is in a much better position, however, to explore and analyse his psychoneurotic patient's symptomatology than is the behaviorist in the case of his experimentally neurotic animal. When it comes to analyzing the *originating situations* . . . the shoe is on the other foot. The behaviorist can *create and rigorously control* the situations in which experimental neuroses originate."

In such cases, isolation of circumstances responsible for the afflictions of experimental animals are not only useful guides to the sources of human disabilities but also suggest ways of preventing or alleviating spontaneous disorders found in animals (Hebb, 1947; Meyer-Holzapfel, 1968; Tuber, Hothersall and Voith, 1974) and man. Suggestions of this kind are to be found in Section XI. Examples of spontaneous and experimental originations of animal abnormalities that resemble some human psychopathologies appear in Section I, which also contains suggestions for the humane conduct of experiments with animals.

The selections in Section II exhibit the *originating situation* versus *resulting symptom* dichotomy as it appears in the problem of psychiatric diagnosis with humans and the experimental analysis of behaviour in animals. The same dichotomy is present in the selections of Sections III through IX, which are arranged according to the usual psychiatric categories, and in those of Section X, which concentrate on situational determinants of behaviour.

Some selections in Sections V and X exhibit abnormal behaviours that are not particularly pathological in their topographies although they are unexpected on the basis of normal psychological law. The law of effect (Thorndike, 1911) predicts that behaviours which produce food for a hungry animal, or behaviours that end an aversive state of affairs, are learned. It does not predict that a hungry rat fed small meals at suitable intervals will drink polydipsic quantities of liquid (Falk, Samson and Winger, 1972; Keehn and Matsunaga, 1971), or that rats may freeze into stereotyped positions instead of avoiding electric shocks (Davis and Kenney, 1975). These behaviours are beyond the law of effect (Keehn, 1972) and so must reshape the form of this basic psychological law (Jenkins, 1975). If this means that laws of the normal derive from abnormal behaviours so much the better: it was a great event for psychology when Freud applied theoretical propositions deduced from neurotically abnormal humans to the "psychopathology of everyday life" (Freud, 1900).

Abnormal behaviour is not unlawful and there is a need for free trade between specialists in normal and abnormal psychology. As Sidman (1960) has put it:

> "The clinical psychologist need no longer seek his experimental foundations among demonstrations of behavioral chaos. The experimentalist, too, would do well to cultivate an interest in pathology as a source of insight into normal behavioral processes."

The selected articles that follow are offered in the hope that the psychopathology of animal life will help the clinical and experimental analyses of behaviour unite to find a common body of psychological law that will assist psychiatrists, psychologists and veterinarians in serving humans and animals in distress.

REFERENCES

Antonitis, J. J., Cary, D. D., Sawin, P. B. and Cohen, C. Sound induced seizures in rabbits, *Journal of Heredity*, 1954, **45**, 279-84.

Brion, A. Les tics chez animaux, *In* A. Brion & H. Ey (Eds.), *Psychiatrie Animale*, Paris: Desclée de Brouwer, 1964.

Brion, A. & Ey, H. (Eds.), *Psychiatrie Animale*, Paris: Desclée de Brouwer, 1964.

Broadhurst, P. L. Abnormal animal behaviour, *In* H. J. Eysenck (Ed.), *Handbook of Abnormal Psychology*, London: Pitman, 1960, 726-63.

Broadhurst, P. L. Animal studies bearing on abnormal behaviour, *In* H. J. Eysenck (Ed.), *Handbook of Abnormal Psychology* (2nd ed.), London: Pitman, 1973, 721-54.

Chertok, L. and Fontaine, M. Psychosomatics in veterinary medicine, *Journal of Psychosomatic Research*, 1963, **7**, 229-35.

Croft, P. G. Some observations on neurosis in farm animals, *Journal of Mental Science*, 1951, **97**, 584-8.

Davenport, R. K. and Menzel, E. W. Stereotyped behavior of the infant chimpanzee, *Archives of General Psychiatry*, 1963, **8**, 99-104.

Davis, H. and Kenney, S. Some effects of different test cages on response "strategies" during leverpress escape, *Psychological Record*, 1975, **25**, 535-43.

Dinsmoor, J. A. Abnormal behavior in animals, *In* R. H. Waters, D. A. Rethlingshafer & W. E. Caldwell (Eds.), *Principles of Comparative Psychology*, New York: McGraw-Hill, 1960, 289-324.

Ellinwood, E. H., Sudilovsky, A. and Nelson, L. Behavioral analysis of chronic amphetamine intoxication, *Biological Psychiatry*, 1972, **4**, 215-30.

Eriksson, K. Genetic selection for voluntary alcohol consumption in the albino rat, *Science*, 1968, **159**, 739-41.

Falk, J. L., Samson, H. H. and Winger, G. Behavioral maintenance of high concentrations of blood ethanol and physical dependence in the rat, *Science*, 1972, **177**, 811-13.

Finger, F. W. Experimental behavior disorders in the rat, *In* J. McV. Hunt (Ed.), *Personality and the Behavior Disorders*, New York: Ronald, 413-30.

Fox, M. W. (Ed.), *Abnormal Behavior in Animals*, Philadelphia: Saunders, 1968.

Fraser, A. F. Intromission phobia in the bull, *Veterinary Record*, 1957, **69**, 621-3.

Freud, S. The psychopathology of everyday life, *In* J. Strachey (Ed.), *The Standard Edition of the Complete Psychological Work of Sigmund Freud* (Vol. 6.), London: Hogarth, 1960.

Gantt, W. H. Experimental Basis for Neurotic Behavior: Origin and development of artificially produced disturbances of behavior in dogs, New York: Hoeber, 1944.

Gilbert, R. M. Drug abuse as excessive behaviour, *Canadian Psychological Review*, 1976, **17**, 231-40.

Harlow, H. F. Sexual behavior in the rhesus monkey, *In* F. A. Beach (Ed.), *Sex and Behavior*, New York: Wiley, 1965, 234-65.

Harlow, H. F. and Harlow, M. K. Psychopathology in monkeys, *In* H. D. Kimmel (Ed.), *Experimental Psychopathology: Recent Research and Theory*, New York: Academic Press, 1971, 203-29.

Hebb, D. O. Spontaneous neuroses in chimpanzees: theoretical relations with clinical and experimental phenomena, *Psychosomatic Medicine*, 1947, **9**, 3-16.

Hediger, H. *Wild Animals in Captivity*, London: Butterworth, 1950.

Herd, J. A., Morse, W. H., Kelleher, R. T. and Jones, L. G. Arterial hypertension in the squirrel monkey during behavioral experiments, *American Journal of Physiology*, 1969, **217**, 24-29.

Hunt, H. F. Problems in the interpretation of 'experimental neurosis', *Psychological Reports*, 1964, **15**, 27-35.

Hunt, J. McV. The effects of infant feeding-frustration upon adult hoarding in the albino rat, *Journal of Abnormal and Social Psychology*, 1941, **36**, 338.

Jenkins, H. M. Behavior theory today: a return to fundamentals, *Mexican Journal of Behavior Analysis*, 1975, **1**, 39-54.

Kalant, H. Cellular effects of alcohols, *In* R. E. Popham (Ed.), *Alcohol and Alcoholism*, Toronto: University of Toronto Press, 1970.

Keehn, J. D. 'Voluntary' consumption of alcohol by rats, *Quarterly Journal of Studies on Alcohol*, 1969, **30**, 320-29.

Keehn, J. D. Schedule-dependence, schedule-induction and the Law of Effect, *In* R. M. Gilbert & J. D. Keehn (Eds.), *Schedule Effects: Drugs, Drinking and Aggression*, Toronto: University of Toronto Press, 1972, 65-94.

Keehn, J. D. and Matsunaga, M. Attenuation of rats' alcohol consumption by trihexyphenidyl, *In* O. Forsander & K. Erikssen (Eds.), *Biological Aspects of Alcohol Consumption*, Helsinki: Finnish Foundation for Alcohol Studies, 1972.

Kendell, R. E. *The Role of Diagnosis in Psychiatry*, Oxford: Blackwell, 1975.

Kimmel, H. D. (Ed.) *Experimental Psychopathology,* New York: Academic Press, 1971.

Krushinskii, L. V. *Animal Behavior: Its Normal and Abnormal Development,* New York: Consultants Bureau, 1962.

Levison, C. A. The development of head-banging in a young rhesus monkey, *American Journal of Mental Deficiency,* 1970, **75,** 323-8.

Levy, D. M. Animal psychology in its relation to psychiatry, *In* F. Alexander & H. Ross (Eds.), *Dynamic Psychiatry,* Chicago: University of Chicago Press, 1952, 483-507.

Liddell, H. S. Conditioned reflex method and experimental neurosis, *In* J. McV. Hunt (Ed.), *Personality and the Behavior Disorders,* New York: Ronald, 1944, 389-412.

Liddell, H. S. *Emotional Hazards in Animals and Man,* Springfield: Thomas, 1956.

Maier, N. R. F. *Frustration: The Study of Behavior without a Goal,* New York: McGraw-Hill, 1949.

Maser, J. D. and Seligman, M. E. P. *Psychopathology: Experimental Models,* San Francisco: Freeman, 1977.

Masserman, J. H. *Behavior and Neurosis,* Chicago: University of Chicago Press, 1943.

Meyer-Holzapfel, M. Abnormal behavior in zoo animals, *In* M. W. Fox (Ed.), *Abnormal Behavior in Animals,* Philadelphia: Saunders, 1968, 476-503.

Miller, N. E. Experiments relating Freudian displacement to generalization of conditioning, *Psychological Bulletin,* 1939, **36,** 516-17.

Miller, N. E. Applications of learning and biofeedback to psychiatry and medicine, *In* A. M. Freedman, H. I. Kaplan & B. J. Sadock (Eds.), *Comprehensive Textbook of Psychiatry* (Vol. 1), (2nd Ed.), Baltimore: Williams & Wilkins, 1975, 349-65.

Mitchell, G. Persistent behavior pathology in rhesus monkeys following early social isolation, *Folia Primatologica,* 1968, **8,** 132-47.

Mitchell, J. M. A psychosis among cats, *Veterinary Record,* 1953, **65,** 254.

Mitchell, W. M. Observations on animal behavior and its relationship to masochism, *Diseases of the Nervous System,* 1969, **30,** 124-9.

Morris, D. Homosexuality in Ten-spined sticklebacks (*Pygosteus pungitius L.*), *Behaviour,* 1952, **4,** 75-113.

Morris, D. The causation of pseudofemale and pseudomale behaviour: a further comment, *Behaviour,* 1955, **8,** 46-56.

Mowrer, O. H. An experimental analogue of "regression" with incidential observations on "reaction formation", *Journal of Abnormal and Social Psychology,* 1940, **35,** 56-87.

Myers, R. D. Brain mechanism involved in volitional intake of ethanol in animals, *In* O. Forsander & K. Eriksson (Eds.), *Biological Aspects of Alcohol Consumptions,* Helsinki: Finnish Foundation for Alcohol Studies, 1972, 173-85.

Newton, J. E. O. and Gantt, W. H. History of a catatonic dog, *Conditional Reflex,* 1968, **3,** 45-61.

Patton, R. A. Abnormal behavior in animals, *In* C. P. Stone (Ed.), *Comparative Psychology,* (3rd Ed.), New York: Prentice-Hall, 1951, 458-513.

Pavlov, I. P. *Conditioned Reflexes,* London: Oxford University Press, 1927.

Pavlov, I. P. *Psychopathology and Psychiatry: Selected Works,* Moscow: Foreign Languages Publishing House, 1961.

Pieper, W. H. and Skeen, M. J. Induction of physical dependence on ethanol in rhesus monkeys using an oral acceptance technique, *Life Sciences,* 1972, **11,** 989-97.

Richter, C. P. Alcohol as food, *Quarterly Journal of Studies on Alcohol,* 1941, **1,** 650-62.

Sanders, M. J. An experimental demonstration of regression in the rat, *Journal of Experimental Psychology,* 1937, **21,** 493-510.

Sanger, V. L. and Hamdy, A. H. A strange fright/flight behavior pattern (hysteria) in hens, *Journal of American Veterinary Medical Association,* 1962, **140,** 455-9.

Scott, J. P. & Senay, E. C. (Eds.) *Separation and Depression: Clinical and Research Aspects,* Washington: American Association for the Advancement of Science, 1973.

Seligman, M. E. P. *Helplessness,* San Francisco: Freeman, 1975.

Shagass, C. Experimental neurosis, *In* A. M. Freedman, H. I. Kaplan & B. J. Shadok (Eds.), *Comprehensive Textbook of Psychiatry* (Vol. 1), (2nd Ed.), Baltimore: Williams & Wilkins, 1975, 428-45.

Sidman, M. Normal sources of pathological behavior, *Science,* 1960, **132,** 61-68.

Sines, J. O. and McDonald, D. G. Irritability of stress-ulcer susceptibility in rats, *Psychosomatic Medicine,* 1968, **30,** 390-4.

Stainton, H. Addiction in animals, *British Journal of Inebriaty,* 1943, **41,** 24-31.

Startsev, V. G. *Primate Models of Human Neurogenic Disorders,* Hillsdale: Erlbaum, 1976.

Stout, C. and Snyder, R. L. Ulcerative colitis-like lesion in Siamang gibbons, *Gastroenterology,* 1969, **57,** 256-61.

Thompson, T. and Schuster, C. R. Morphine self-administration food-reinforced and avoidance behavior in rhesus monkeys, *Psychopharmacologia,* (Berl.), 1964, **5,** 87-94.

Thorndike, E. L. *Animal Intelligence,* New York: Hafner, 1965.

Tinbergen, N. Ethology and stress diseases, *Science,* 1974, **185,** 20-27.

Tinklepaugh, O. L. The self-mutilation of a male macacus rhesus monkey, *Journal of Mammalogy,* 1928, **9,** 293-300.

Tuber, D. S., Hothersall, D. and Voith, V. L. Animal clinical psychology: A modest proposal, *American Psychologist*, 1974, **29**, 762-6.

Ulrich, R., Dulaney, S., Kucera, T. and Colasacco, A. Side-effects of aversive control, *In* R. M. Gilbert & J. D. Keehn (Eds.), *Schedule Effects: Drugs, Drinking and Aggression*, Toronto: University of Toronto Press, 1972, 203-242.

van Lawick-Goodall, J. *In the Shadow of Man*, Boston: Houghton Mifflin, 1971.

Ward, I. L. Prenatal stress feminizes and demasculinizes the behavior of males, *Science*, 1972, **175**, 82-84.

Wolpe, J. *Psychotherapy by Reciprocal Inhibition*, Stanford: Stanford University Press, 1958.

Wolpe, J. Parallels between animal and human neuroses, *In* J. Zubin & H. Hung (Eds.), *Comparative Psychopathology*, New York: Grune & Stratton, 1967, 305-13.

Zubin, J. & Hunt, H. F. (Eds.) *Comparative Psychopathology: Animal and Human*, New York: Grune & Stratton, 1967.

Section I

ANIMAL AND HUMAN PSYCHOPATHOLOGY

1. Psychosomatics in Veterinary Medicine

L. CHERTOK and M. FONTAINE

Journal of Psychosomatic Research, 1963, **7**, 229-35. Copyright 1963 by Pergamon Press.
Reprinted by permission.

LEON J. SAUL [24] has recently written "Veterinary medicine should be a rich field for psychosomatic studies. It has been relatively neglected. . . . Psychosomatic medicine has still much to learn from the direct clinical observation of animals." Brouwers [6] the well known Belgian veterinarian also writes that, "Mental factors . . . play their part in veterinary medicine just as in human medicine. The peacock which spreads its tail does so not from pride, but to excite the females. The secretion of prolactin is started off in the pigeon by the sight of the female pigeon sitting on her eggs or feeding her young. In the female parrot, the sight of the nest starts off the laying of eggs, withdrawal from the nest quickly stops it. What effect does domestication have on mammals which enjoy free choice of partners? In birds like the parrot, free choice of partner is an important factor in successful mating. With the exception of the street dog and the cat on the tiles, all mammals must, over a long period, experience frustration. Fear by inhibitory reflex action, can stop laying in birds,—hens, parrots, and canaries—and reduce the yield of milk in cows. This happens after some operation such as vaccination, tuberculination or disinfestation. Fear, on the other hand, can be held to be responsible, through stimulatory reflex action, for some cases of miscarriage and premature birth."

Experimental studies carried out on certain species of domestic animals, particularly carnivores, have shown that disorders of behaviour and sometimes functional and organic disorders may be produced by influencing "mental" activity. These findings have not so far been applied to veterinary practice. Veterinary practice, however, provides careful observations which raise the question of the existence of psychosomatic animal medicine. To accept the existence of mental life in animals implies the possibility of psychosomatic disturbances. But how can these be delimited?

We are concerned with organic or functional disturbances whose origin, onset or persistence is influenced by emotional (relational or situational) factors. The plan of presentation which we have adopted is necessarily schematic and arbitrary. We shall first of all consider certain states which appear to be of hysterical origin and then consider the somatic disorders which follow emotional traumata and which constitute the post-emotional neuroses. We shall next review the various organismic systems the integrity of which may be impaired by emotional factors; problems relating to sexual functioning and reproduction; mention some aspects of animal surgery and fully consider therapy.

HYSTERICAL DISORDERS

The examples of collective epilepsy [9, 22, 23] among dogs shows that there is an element of imitation [14] and suggestion in the onset of attacks, and this may be regarded as analogous to collective hysteria [10]. Hystero-epilepsy is a mental state [21] which in animals produces convulsive symptoms which may overlap with certain epileptic elements. Cases are known, particularly in horses and dogs, in which the revival in memory of some series of events produced by the sight of an object or by the conjunction of some circumstances results in a convulsive attack resembling an epileptic fit [7. p. 499; 11]. The element of memory is beyond doubt, but in interpreting it, we must take account of the possible "conditioning" of the subject. The signs of a female in heat may be expressed in an exaggerated way, prolonged and renewed in an abnormal manner [15]. This nymphomania is common among cats, and it would be hard to deny a relational factor in its genesis. In fact, the affective relations between the nymphomaniac and the humans about her who lavish their affectionate attention on her are partly responsible for the violent, disordered and sometimes convulsive excitement of female cats in heat [6, 11]. The same phenomena occur independently of the states of the oestrous cycle, and the relational element may by itself be the occasion of hystero-epileptic fits in female cats.

POST-EMOTIONAL NEUROSES

There is a whole series of disorders [12] immediately consequent upon an emotional assault experienced by the animals—anorexia, nausea, vomiting, urinating, defecating, colic, attacks of tachycardia, polypnoea, muscular contractions, piloerections, changes in the iris, disturbance of the blood leucocyte values and blood standard values. These, trivial though they may be, may nevertheless continue after the cause has ceased. This is the case, for example, with dogs which have lost a master to whom they were very attached, or which have changed their habitat [1, 20]. Loss of hair without any lesion of the skin, or even alopecia, may continue for several days after an emotional assault in horses, dogs and cats [16].

OTHER "PSYCHOSOMATIC" DISTURBANCES

Asthma

In animals we do not find precisely the same kind of asthma as in man, but we can nevertheless compare with it the bronchial spasms which induce gross respiratory disturbances through attacks of dyspnoea, sometimes accompanied by bronchial exudate. These spasmodic attacks may be precipitated by an apparently insignificant emotion, by a minimal stimulus, often of a particular and specific nature, as it were, in its tendency to produce the symptom. It may be remembered that Seitz [25] with cats separated from the mother at the age of two weeks, found attacks of bronchial spasm which he compares to the symptoms of bronchial asthma in human beings.

Metabolic and Endocrine Disorders

Nervous pedigree bitches which have been continuously cajoled may, on reaching adulthood, show irregularities of genital functioning, when they show signs of an obesity out of relation to their appetite. The clinical picture reminds one of the adiposo-genital syndrome with obesity, involution of the sexual organs and frigidity. This state is often preceded by psycho-endocrine events such as nervous lactation and nervous pregnancy. The organic disturbance then develops. It is not unusual to find, with obesity, the development of a polyuro-polydipsic syndrome [4] accompanied by an increase of blood cholesterol, which can be cured by the administration of hypoglycemia-inducing sulfonamides. The development of these disorders may proceed in an unexpected way towards diabetes mellitus. Very often, with the same bitches, after a series of nervous lactations, mammary tumors form, sometimes of a malignant nature.

Gastric and Duodenal Ulcers

Peptic ulcers are very rare in animals. A few cases have been found in cats, cattle and pigs, which can be considered as neuro-vascular disorders, without any apparent psychological contribution. Although ulcers due to constraint can be produced experimentally in several species of laboratory animals [3, 5] and pigs [17], it is remarkable that no comparable pathological manifestations have been known to occur spontaneously in domestic animals except in pigs during transportation [17].

Oesophagospasm and Cardiospasm

We are completely ignorant about the possible importance of emotional factors in neuro-vegetative dystonia of the oesophagus in carnivores and equidae.

Dyspepsia and Anorexia

Therapeutic experience may sometimes indicate a mental factor in persistent refusal to eat in dogs and cats, especially after a period of anorexia initially justified by some lesion which has later disappeared, while the antipathy to food remains. A change of the people about the animal, the presence of a new animal to share the meal, or a change of environment and habitat may effect a return of appetite. In carnivores, digestive disturbances accompanied by halitosis, nausea, vomiting and intestinal sluggishness may also sometimes benefit by a change in the emotional climate in which the animals live. We have noted the cessation of pyloric spasms in cats as a consequence of a change of habits and environment.

Arterial Hypertension

Hypertensive disease is rare in animals and its clinical manifestations poor, and no psychological factor can be assumed in its origin.

Affections of the Skin

Besides the post-emotional alopecia already considered, we must take into account, in the field of dermatology, the special circumstances in which eczemas may arise in dogs. Very often, dogs of an excitable breed suffering from eczema live a sedentary life, subject to the excessive solicitude of their masters.

The Mobilization of the Third Eyelid of the Cat

The mobilization of the third eyelid of the cat, or procidentia of the nictitating membrane may indicate a vagal attack. We have observed the following case where this procidentia was due to psychological factors. An adult cat, when fondled by its mistress, showed a very marked procidence of the nictitating membrane and later, this procidence became permanent. In spite of treatment (which in cases of procidence of the nictitating membrane is generally successful in restoring the third eyelid to its normal position) and in particular in spite of the administration of sympathomimetics, the disorder continued until the cat was separated from its owner. The procidentia of the nictitating membrane at once disappeared. The cat was then kept in the hospital for a fortnight. During this period, the animal was seen again by its mistress, and immediately the third eyelid again protruded. It was possible to produce this phenomenon at will during a long period. Only the complete separation of the cat from the environment in which it had been in the habit of living allowed a cure to take place.

Enuresis

Some carnivores may urinate at the wrong time from emotional causes. The cases described in the literature and those which we have been able to observe concern animals which want to draw attention to themselves in this way [13, p. 170]. It is not a matter of incontinence from anatomical causes, where the act is passive and involuntary, but of active emission of urine. Is it unconscious, like the urination of the child which takes place during deep sleep? But we must take into consideration the fact that the subject may act in two different ways. It may adopt the usual posture and urinate entirely voluntarily, or it may seem to be quite unconscious of the act, and consequently fail to adopt the usual posture for urinating. In the first case, it seems as if the animal were motivated by the conscious desire to indicate its presence. In the second case, the subject appears to act without realising it.

Neuro-muscular System

In canine and feline medicine, intermittent states of paroxysmal hypotonia remind one of cataplexy. We do not, however, know the sensations experienced by the animal, and the only basis for comparison with human medicine is the similarity of the clinical facts. Is it possible that some light might be shed upon the etiology of infectious diseases by a study of the psychological aspects of behaviour? We may point out the role of psychological factors in the appearance of symptoms of infections in carnivores and especially in the expression of nervous symptoms during encephalomyelitis in dogs. A change of habits and environment aggravates the disease. On the other hand, attentive care reduces the symptoms.

SEXUALITY AND REPRODUCTIVE FUNCTION

In the different manifestations of sexuality, psychological disorders may have repercussions on behaviour and on the somatic forms of expression of this behaviour. Although we have spoken of nymphomania in cats, a typical example, we must not forget the state of frigidity to which, as much for the male as for the female, the environment in which the subject lives makes its contribution. Thus, for example, the presence of the male intensifies the symptoms of heat in females. This is clear enough in the bovine species; it has been remarked that the presence and preparation of the bull effects an increase in the tone of the cow's uterus before intercourse has actually started. The impotence which afflicts males used for artificial insemination seems determined to some extent by a psychological factor. The animals seem to miss the effect of fresh air, of life in the herd, and the proximity of a female. It is sometimes enough to return the bull to the presence of females for his sexual power to be revived again and for his impotence to disappear [19].

PSEUDO-PREGNANCY

The pseudo-pregnancy* observed in domestic animals is a psychological [13, p. 171] and somatic disorder of infertile females which imitates the different aspects of pregnancy during the post-oestrous phase. There are many synonyms for it—imaginary pregnancy, false pregnancy, nervous pregnancy, maternity psychosis. The disorder is common among bitches, especially of small, nervous breeds. It is rarer among cats, and exceptional among mares and heifers. The females affected, females which have not been fertilized during their last period in heat, show the signs of imminent littering at the end of the luteal period (8 weeks in bitches, 11 months in mares). The belly is heavy, frequently the uterus is palpable, the vulva is swollen and a phlegm-like liquid comes out of the vagina, and the nipples, hypertrophied, become functional with the start of milk secretion.

The organic disorders observed are always accompanied by an important psychological change which drives the animal to imitate the behaviour of pregnant females ready to litter. The bitch is anxious and reacts abruptly, with unaccustomed vivacity, to external attractions. She may be aggressive or bad-tempered, or in a state of permanent defence in relation to the environment. She seems to be seeing phantoms and this may be of some influence in her behaviour. She looks for material for a nest, collects the oddest articles in order to take possession of and adopt them. Certain females with imaginary pregnancy go so far as to simulate the preparations for the labour. In all these cases, this state ends in copious lactation, identical to that of bitches which have given birth to young. The so-called nervous lactation may, in addition, exist alone, without a pseudo-pregnancy, and seems to be a minor form of these post-oestrous manifestations.

PARTURITION

The question of the role of psychological factors in pain during labour in female domestic animals has formed the object of an inquiry by one of the present writers [8]. Veterinarians were approached, with a view to interpreting the sensations experienced by the animal in the course of dropping her young. Opinion does not seem to be unanimous on the intensity of the pain experienced by the animals, and in all cases we must distinguish between the perception of contractions, and dropping proper, i.e. the passage of the foetus into the pelvis. The behaviour of the animal is, in these two cases, modified by the psychological state. In fact, the more the animals are considered to be delicate and nervous, the more evident the manifestations during labour are. Moreover, small domestic animals or laboratory animals have a more marked tendency to express overtly the sensations experienced during labour, the more subject they have been to attention from the people around them.

ANIMAL SURGERY

In surgical practice it is interesting to note that anxious, panic-stricken or maltreated animals, or those excited by strong conflict, are liable during either the anaethesia or

---

* Pseudo-pregnancy had also been studied experimentally [2, 26].

the operation to very severe neuro-vegetative disturbances, which may produce death by shock.

THERAPY

Can therapeutics provide any arguments for the reality of psychological factors? There is no specific, codified psychotherapy, but we can count as a psychotherapeutic element the benefits obtained by a change of environment and a change in the people around those animals which have disorders analogous to those to which we have referred. It is also sometimes possible to modify depressive behaviour by bringing back an object or person whose disappearance has frustrated the animal. We may thus take into account a genuine, individual relational psychotherapy, practiced by those keepers whose successes are greater than others in their profession. Medication itself emphasizes the role of psychological factors in the determination of some disorders. Thus meprobamate may have a beneficial effect on nymphomania in cats, on nervous lactation and pregnancy, on fits of bronchial spasm, on potomania in carnivores, on anorexia and dyspnoea, and on the whole series of post-emotional neuroses and disorders considered to be of hysterical origin.

SUMMARY

Direct observation in animals has shown that a series of organic and functional disturbances occur as a result of situational stress arising from alterations in interpersonal relationships. Changes in situation and in interpersonal relationship may improve or cure the animal.

Thus, psychosomatic studies in animals provide a new field of investigation. It might shed some light on the biological sources of sympathy. A good deal is known about interpersonal relationship on the psychological level (transference), but little about the somatic basis of these relationships. Smell, for example, is one of the mediators; the work in this field was summarized by Kalogerakis [27]. Physical attraction between individuals certainly exists. The interpersonal relationship between humans and animals and among animals themselves is probably on a more somatic level, and this might be a field for future study. Moreover, from a strictly psychosomatic point of view it would be valuable to study why some animals, just as with some human beings, react to stress or conflicts by behavioural change, and others by somatic or functional disturbances.

REFERENCES

1. Arouch. Reference quoted by [7], p. 520.
2. Ball, J. Demonstration of a quantitative relation between stimulus and response in pseudopregnancy in the rat. *Amer. J. Physiol.* **107**, 698-703 (1934).
3. Bonfils, S., Liefooche, X., Dubrasquet, M. and Lambling, A. Ulcère expérimental de contrainte du rat blanc. *Rev. franc. Etud. clin. biol.* **5**, 571-581 (1960).
4. Brion, A. and Fontaine, M. Syndromes polyuriques et diabète insipide chez les animaux domestiques. *Thérapie,* **14**, 506-513 (1959).
5. Brodie, D. A. and Hanson, H. M. A study of the factors involved in the production of gastric ulcers by the restraint technique. *Gastroenterology* **38**, 353-360 (1960).
6. Brouwers, J. Le rôle du système nerveux en pathologie génétale. *Ann. Med. Vet.* **44**, 245-270 (1956).
7. Cadeac, C. *Encyclopedie veterinaire.* Vol. 8. Pathologie interne. 2nd Ed. J. B. Bailliere, Paris (1914).
8. Chertok, L. *Psychosomatic methods in painless childbirth*—history, theory and practice. Trans. by D. Leigh, Pergamon Press (1959).
9. Cornish, Bowden and Badcock. Specific hysteria in dogs. Report of the Meeting at Dog Owners Club (1928). (Quoted by [22] p. 207).

10. Fontaine, M. and Leroy, Cl. Epilepsie de groupe, in *Psychiatrie animale,* edited by H. Ey (to be published).
11. Fontaine, M. and Leroy, Cl. Hystérie, in *Psychiatrie animale,* edited by H. Ey (to be published).
12. Fontaine, M. and Leroy, Cl. Névroses post-émotionnelles, in *Psychiatrie animale,* edited by H. Ey (to be published).
13. Frauchiger, F. and Frankhauser, R. *Die nervenkrankheiten Underer Hunde.* Hans Huber, Bern (1949).
14. Griffiths. Reference quoted by [18], p. 543.
15. Grobon. De l'hysterie chez les chats. *Rev. Vet.* **32**, 172-178 (1907).
16. Guilhon, J. L'Alopécie post-émotionnelle, in *Psychiatrie animale,* edited by H. Ey (to be published).
17. Le Bars, H., Tournut, J. and Calvet, H. Production d'ulcerations gastriques chez le porc. *C. R. Acad. Sci.* **255**, 3501-3503 (1962).
18. Liegeois. *Traité de pathologie médicale des animaux domestiques.* Duculot, Gembloux, Belgium (1949).
19. Parez, M. Le taureau d'insemination artificielle. Thèse Doct. Vet. Alfort (1953).
20. Pierquin. *Traité de la folie des animaux.* Vol. 1. Huzard, Paris (1839).
21. Prime, R. Hysteria and epileptoid seizures in dogs. *Vet. Rec.* **9**, 32 (1929).
22. Rossi, P. La maladie de la peut chez le chien (Fright disease). *Rev. Gen. Med. Vet.* **40**, 201-223 (1931).
23. Saint Paul, J. Maladie de la peur chez le chien. Thèse Doct. Vet. Toulouse (1950).
24. Saul, L. J. Psychosocial medicine and observation of animals. *Psychosom. Med.* **XXIV**, 58-61 (1962).
25. Seitz, F. D. Philip. Infantile Experience and Adult Behaviour in Animal Subjects: II. Age of separation from the mother and adult behaviour in the cat. *Psychosom. Med.* **XXI**, 353-378.
26. Swingle, W., Seay, P., Perimutt, J., Collins, E. J., Barlow, G. J. and Fedor, E. J. An experimental study of pseudopregnancy in the rat. *Amer. J. Physiol.* **167**, 586 (1951).
27. Kalogerakis, M. G. The role of olfaction in sexual development. *Psychosom. Med.* XXV, **5**, 420-432 (1963).

2. Zoological Garden and Mental Hospital*

H. F. ELLENBERGER[1]

Canadian Psychiatric Association Journal, 1960, 5, 136-49. Reprinted by permission.

INTRODUCTION

The starting point for this paper was the studies of the effects of closed communities on their occupants. These studies were stimulated by the movement for the reform of Mental Hospitals which developed in certain countries of Western Europe after World War II.

There are two ways of studying the means of improving Mental Hospitals. One is simply to make improvements and through trial and error determine which reforms are efficient and which are not. This pragmatic method is the preferred way in Anglo-Saxon countries. The second, which of course does not exclude the first, is to investigate the negative factors of Mental Hospitals, so that once these negative factors are well defined they can be eliminated. This second, rational method has been used largely in France.

The French coined a word, *aliénisation,* which designates the phenomenon that patients' stay in Mental Hospitals often aggravates the mental disease instead of curing it. In other words, it is the sum total of the negative factors of the Mental Hospital milieu on the patients.

Aliénisation includes a wide range of psychopathological, neurotic, psychotic and psychopathic reactions. Some of them are relatively close to the normal, such as the "enracinement", i.e. "nestling" of recovered patients in the Mental Hospitals; at the other extreme are the most advanced stages of emotional regression and infantilism. That these conditions are artifacts has also been demonstrated by the fact that they hardly appear in the institutions using the method of "aktivere Therapie" of Hermann Simon in Germany or the "total push therapy' or other good programs of intensive therapy combined with a good occupational therapy.

It is interesting to compare these negative manifestations of Mental Hospital milieu with negative manifestations occurring in other types of closed communities. A surprisingly large amount of information is to be found in widely scattered places.

In monasteries and convents observations have been made for maybe 20 centuries. In the fifth century AD there seems to have been a widespread epidemic of "acedia" in monasteries in the West. "Acedia" was a consuming boredom combined with doubt about one's religious vocation. This epidemic was put to an end largely through a reform by St. Benedict who introduced systematic work in the monasteries (1). This reform may be mentioned as an outstanding example of the success of work therapy.

In regard to prisons, we possess a flourishing literature on "prison psychoses" (2).

* Paper read on Oct. 21, 1959, at a meeting of the psychiatric section of the Montreal Medico-Chirurgical Society.

[1]Asst. Prof. of Psychiatry, McGill University, Montreal.

Nineteenth century psychiatrists distinguished between: 1) Immediate morbid reaction such as "Zuchthausknall" (a short-lived, violent state of furious agitation), prison stupor, the Ganser syndrome, etc. 2) Chronic conditions with systematic delusions such as systematized delusion of persecution, delusion of being innocent, delusion of being pardoned, etc.; and unsystematic psychotic conditions more or less similar to schizophrenia. The focus today in prison psychiatry seems to be rather on the study of anti-social reactions such as the so-called "prison code", and on the more subtle effects of the prison on its inmates. One of the general findings has been that cellular confinement is more inducive of severe psychosis and emotional regression, whereas the group life in prison is more inducive of anti-social behaviour.

In regard to military prison camps, a Swiss physician, Adolf Vischer, visited camps of French, English and German prisoners of war during World War I and gave a classical description of "Stacheldrahtkrankheit", i.e. "barbed-wire disease" (3). The emotional life becomes poorer, the patient becomes lethargic, cannot concentrate, becomes irritable, hypochondriacol, etc. Vischer analyzed the pathogenic factors of this neurosis, which he ascribed to three factors that must coincide, namely: 1) internment, 2) for unlimited, unknown duration, 3) in the forced presence of a group.

Incidentally, Arthur Kielholz in Switzerland was the first to point out that this neurosis also existed in certain remote and isolated Mental Hospitals, not only in patients but also at times in nurses and young residents (4).

In regard to TB sanatoriums, another condition was described, not by a physician but by a writer, Thomas Mann, in his famous novel *Der Zauberberg*. A German psychiatrist, Hellpach, pointed out the actual existence of this neurosis of which Thomas Mann had given a literary description (5). In the "Zauberberg" disease the patients of the TB sanatorium are fascinated, so to speak, by the thought of death and by the revelation of a new world. There is a certain similarity between this condition and one found in a few expensive, private mental sanatoriums, where the surroundings are those of an exclusive country club, providing rich intellectual food, sometimes as rich as the meals served there and where the milieu is pervaded with a burning concern with psychiatric and psychoanalytical problems.

In hospitals for children and in nurseries a condition had been described in the 1890's by a school of German and Austrian pediatrists, Pfaundler, Freund (6), Czerny, etc. who called it "hospitalism". Freund's definition of hospitalism was: "The sum total of noxious influences of all kinds produced by the crowding of healthy and sick infants in hospitals". Certain infants lost weight, faded away and died in spite of the best dietetic and hygienic conditions and these pediatricians ascribed it to the lack of emotional stimulation, monotony and lack of exercise. These investigations, however, did not receive the attention they deserved, but today hospitalism has been re-discovered and wrapped in a psychoanalytical cloak with prodigious success.

Studies also have been made of homes for children, orphanages, etc., some of which are well known, such as Goldfarb's study (7).

Among studies of Old Folks homes special mention is due to those performed in Basel, Switzerland, by a team of a psychiatrist, a psychologist and a sociologist, Vittiger, Jaffé and Vogt: "Alte Menschen im Altersheim" (8). Although the establishment investigated is considered one of the best, the conclusion is not particularly cheerful. These authors emphasized the high percentage lack of adaptation, the difficulty of taking roots in their new setting, and difficulty in tolerating the presence of other people.

In each one of the above mentioned and in other milieu we learn something which can be applied to the understanding of the negative factors in Mental Hospitals. One may wonder where the zoo will fit in this picture. It may seem farfetched, indeed, to compare the psychopathology of the Zoological Garden with these various settings. There is a wide gap between the human and the animal personality. However, the great French naturalist Buffon said, that "if there were no animals, human nature would be far more incomprehensible to us". To be sure, we are perfectly aware of the difficulties of such comparative studies. Two kinds of pitfalls are to be avoided: One is the "anthropomorphic fallacy". This, for instance, is the case of most people seeing a lion in a cage, imagining this lion as a noble warrior in shameful captivity, dreaming nostalgically of his native forest. The other could be called the "zoomorphic fallacy". Many behaviourist psychologists do not seem to be aware of it. Recently, for instance, a psychologist made a study of frustration in white rats and applied the findings directly to problems of international politics.

We will try to keep to the straight and narrow path. There are psychobiological manifestations in higher animals which can be compared with those in man; a close critical study of these manifestations may help us to see more clearly certain phenomena in the normal and the sick human mind. Before we go further we should make a short review of the history of the Zoological Garden.

HISTORY OF THE ZOOLOGICAL GARDEN

Contrary to what is generally believed, the zoo is an extremely old institution (9). Francis Galton, a century ago, gathered abundant evidence from a great number of primitive people from all over the world, showing that these people liked to keep pet animals, sometimes in great numbers. It is known, for instance, that African potentates before the discovery of their country often kept large collections of wild animals of all kinds (10).

There were large animal parks in all the ancient Asiatic kingdoms, Assyria, Babylonia and so on. They reached their peak in ancient Persia, whose kings throughout their empire kept a number of these parks, which in Persian were called *paradeisos*.

A *paradeisos* was an extremely large park, enclosed with walls, with a monumental door and exclusively reserved for the king and his favourites. In this beautiful garden animals, especially wild animals, lived in relative liberty and most of them probably eventually became tame. The "Garden of Eden" in the Bible is nothing but an idealized picture of a Persian *paradeisos*. After the downfall of Persia the *paradeisos* survived for some time in Central and Eastern Asia, but at the same time another type of garden developed in other parts of the world, strangely enough also in pre-Columbian America. It was a garden where animals lived in cages or small enclosures side by side. The most remarkable of these gardens was the one of the Aztecs in their capital Tenochtitlan, i.e. Mexico. From the wondrous descriptions by the Spanish conquerors we see it as a zoological garden of fabulous size, richness and perfection, and it is doubtful whether it has ever been equalled. Incidentally, it included not only every species of mammals, birds and reptiles known to the ancient Mexicans, but also a large collection of abnormal human beings, midgets, hunchbacks, albinos, etc.

In Europe the most famous zoo was for a long time that of Louis XIV in Versailles, where he collected animals from all over the world and where a large team of artists and scientists were at work. Unfortunately this remarkable institution declined during the reign of Louis XV. When the French Revolution broke out, the new government decided to institute a model zoo and, interestingly enough, the Natural History Society of Paris appointed a committee of 3 members to study the project; one of its members was none other than the famous Pinel, who at the same time was concerned with the reform of the notorious Bicêtre asylum, where he removed the chains of the insane. The result of the efforts was the founding of the "Jardin des Plantes" in Paris, which served as a model for all other institutions of its kind in the 19th century. Contrary to all previous institutions, it was intended for the education of the public and the idea expanded rapidly all over the world till today the zoo is regarded as an integral part of our culture.

A new period in the history of the zoo was inaugurated when the great German merchant of wild animals, Carl Hagenbeck, opened his park at Stellingen outside Hamburg, Germany. The cages and narrow enclosures of previous zoos were replaced by larger spaces, resembling as much as possible the animal's natural habitat. Cages were dispensed with. It was found that the biological and psychological conditions of the zoo animals greatly improved, and this is perhaps one of the facts which led the zoologists to a closer study of the psychopathology of captive animals.

The biology and psychopathology of zoo animals have been objects of much investigation in the last few decades. Among these pioneers we must mention the works of Hediger (11), director of the zoo in Zürich, Dr. Meyer-Holzapfel (12) in Bern, and Grzimek (13) in Frankfurt, Germany.

To their surprise, psychologists learned that from a scientific point of view lions and tigers could be as interesting as rats and mice. The interest of the psychopathology of zoo animals for the psychiatrist has been steadily increasing. I was probably one of the first to attract attention to this point in a paper published in "L'Evolution Psychiatrique" in 1953. Since that time, at least two studies have been published to my knowledge. One by Balthasar Stachelin of Zürich: A study of a ward of chronic schizophrenic patients, where the psychopathology was easily interpreted in terms of the concepts elaborated by Hediger in his studies of animal psychopathology (14). Another study by Racamier in France comes to similar conclusions (15).

COMPARATIVE PSYCHOPATHOLOGICAL SYNDROMES

From the enormous amount of data on the psychopathology of zoo animals we want to pick four points to elaborate on here:

1. The trauma of captivity
2. The nestling process
3. The syndromes produced by social competition and frustrations
4. Emotional deterioration

To all these manifestations we find parallels in the Mental Hospital. We expect that a study of the common denominators between the psychology of man and of the higher animals will help us to differentiate better between disease itself and the other exogenous factors.

It is a natural tendency of a psychiatrist to ascribe *all* the clinical symptoms he observes in the mental patient to the disease proper. In the situation of a prison psychiatrist it is much easier because he has to deal with people who were non-psychotic when they arrived in the prison, but even in that case it is often far from easy to make a diagnosis between whether it is a reactive condition, or a mental illness proper which would have developed spontaneously anyhow.

1. The Trauma of Captivity

The emotional disturbances occurring in animals after they are removed from their natural element are extremely severe. Carl Hagenbeck gave an excellent study of these emotional disturbances and devised a system of treatment (16). He contended that it is useless to try to have an animal adjust to captivity before the effects of this trauma are removed.

Whereas Hagenbeck thought of trauma mainly in physiological terms, Hediger (17) emphasized mainly psychological trauma resulting from the sudden change from one mode of life to another one, completely different. In its native habitat the animal is extremely narrowly integrated in a space-time system and also in a system of social relationships within a group of the same species. For instance, one of the most basic and imperative instincts, as it has been shown, is the "territory instinct", i.e. each animal appropriates for himself a certain amount of space which he considers his own and he marks its limitations in ways varying for the different species, and he jealously and fiercely defends it from other animals of the same species. For an animal it is a severe trauma to be dispossessed from his territory. Furthermore, unlike the animal at liberty, the captured animal is neither able to flee from his enemy, nor to attack him and this helpless situation results in a state of anxiety, feverish agitation and stereotypic movements and sometimes the animal may even inflict severe wounds upon itself, often to the point of causing its death, which should not be interpreted as suicide.

According to Hediger there are three main pictures of trauma in captivity: 1) Attacks of acute agitation, at times extraordinarily violent, often resulting in severe wounds, or in death. 2) A prolonged stupor, and 3) a kind of hunger strike which also can result in the death of the animal if it is not forcibly fed.

According to Hediger the trauma of captivity dominates the whole psychopathology of zoo animals. It is more severe the older the animal is. Most animals, when captured as adults, are never able to overcome it. Most young animals are able to overcome it with more or less difficulty. Many zoo animals, for instance most lions, have been born in captivity—sometimes for several generations. However, even these animals may show an extenuated type of trauma when transferred from one zoo to another or even from one cage to another in the same zoo.

Coming back to human psychopathology we find similar manifestations. Certain criminals can, when brought into prison, show that violent manifestation called "Zuchthausknall" or fall into a stuporous condition. Among mental patients, the majority do not show any "trauma of commitment". However, it may develop in a few patients, mostly in acute psychotics who, as it were, are deprived of their ego, and the more it is so, the more their condition is comparable to that of the captured animal.

It seems that in certain psychotic patients the trauma of commitment can be extraordinarily severe and dominate the whole psychopathology, especially if the commitment has been accomplished in a brutal or unethical way. A clinical observation demonstrates this:

A 30 year old man in the South-East of the US, married and father of a small child, had for 2 or 3 years troubles of schizophrenic nature. His family decided to have him committed to a Mental Hospital. He was taken to see his brother-in-law, who was a surgeon, under the pretext of having a blood-test, which in reality was an intravenous injection with a powerful sedative. A waiting ambulance took the patient to the airport, where a plane, which had also been hired in advance, took him to a midwestern city, where his commitment to an institution had been pre-arranged. When the patient finally regained consciousness he discovered that he was 1,400 miles away from home, in a "mad-house" and that his family had already gone back by plane. For several years the mental attitude of this patient was completely dominated by the shock of what he—not without reason—called his kidnapping. His rage against his wife, his brother-in-law and the psychiatrists, whom he erroneously regarded as accomplices in trapping him, was manifested in delusional ideas of persecution, which dominated his morbid state, probably much more than the mental disturbances which had preceded his commitment.

This is certainly an exceptional case. However, for many psychotic patients the circumstances of commitment, the transportation to the hospital, the upsetting of daily routine constitute a serious and long-lasting shock, the symptoms of which should not be confused with the symptoms of the mental disease proper.

2. The Nestling Process

Whereas the preceding sydrome—the trauma of captivity—is always pathological, the following syndrome, which we may call the nestling process, is considered *normal* if it occurs in the zoo animal, but *abnormal* if it occurs in a Mental Hospital patient.

Since the process is much clearer in animal psychology, let us consider first how it occurs in an animal in the zoo. The drive to possess an "individual territory" of one's own is one of the most basic drives in animals. The captured animal has been dispossessed of its natural territory but is ready to appropriate another one, if it has the chance to do so. One of the fundamental rules of zoo psychology is to bring the newly arrived animal to transform its cage or enclosure into a "territory". How this process takes place may be illustrated by an instance borrowed from Hediger (18):

The tiger Griedo, bought from the zoo in Philadelphia, arrived at the zoo in Zürich on April 9th, 1957. He was to be mated with the tigress Fatma. But Griedo was upset, stayed in a corner of his cage, was shy with his keeper, and not at all interested in Fatma. The 25th of June, 1957, two and a half months after his arrival, the tiger made his "proprietor's tour" of his cage, the periphery of which he "marked" with squirts of urine, in the same way in which a tiger in liberty "marks" the limits of his individual territory. The next day there was a remarkable change in the animal, he felt at home, and his attitude toward the tigress underwent a change and so, as a result, some months afterwards Fatma brought into this world a new little tiger.

In this particular case the process was very clear-cut, but it could easily have been overlooked if Hediger and the keepers had not been watching very closely.

As a general rule, for most species, an animal which has been captured at an adult age will never succeed in performing this "appropriation" of his cage or enclosure. If the animal has been caught at a younger age it will be less difficult. It will be still easier if it is a matter of a transfer from one zoo to another, as in the case of the tiger Griedo.

The effects of this appropriation are manifold: Since the "prison" is now transformed into an "individual territory", the animal will not try to escape. Mannteufel (19), a scientist of the Moscow Zoo, says that certain zoo animals could easily jump over the fences or demolish the walls of their enclosure if they wanted to, but they simply do not think of it. Barriers are more often made to protect the animals from the public than the reverse. Many animals even refuse to leave their cage when one wants them to do so. Finally, there are countless stories of escaped zoo animals going back voluntarily to the zoo.

Mannteufel (20) tells of a she-wolf from the Moscow zoo, whose name was Kashirka. She had been brought in a taxi to an institution at the other end of Moscow. At the door of the institution she escaped, to the greatest annoyance of the zoologists. She ran through the whole city, in the midst of crowds of pedestrians who believed her to be an Alsatian dog, straight to the gates of the zoo and from there to her enclosure and sat down in front of the door, waiting for the keeper to let her in.

Lorenz Hagenbeck (21) tells that during the bombardment of Hamburg in June 1943, the Stellingen Park was set on fire, many animals escaped, but almost all of them came back spontaneously and the others were easy to bring back. He adds that to his knowledge the same occurred in all other bombed zoos in Germany.

Thus, an animal escaped from the zoo is not at all what the public imagines: a prisoner regaining liberty. It is rather a kind of "displaced person", eager to get back to its home.

Another consequence of the same process is the following: the animal which has been rather shy before, will now defend its new territory fiercely against any intruder or supposed aggressor. Therefore, in our anthropocentric viewpoint, it will become more "dangerous". A deer, for instance, can be a very "nice" animal as long as you feed it over the hedge of its enclosure; however, if you try to get into the enclosure, it will perhaps become "nasty" and attack you. And by its attacking you it will prove that it has successfully accomplished the process of adjustment and transformed its prison into a territory.

Let us go back now, from the zoo to the Mental Hospital. Do we observe anything comparable to this process of adjustment through the acquirement of a "territory"? It would seem that it is so, if we think of a phenomenon which has been studied very carefully in France by Gustave Daumézon, who called it "L'enracinement du malade guéri à l'asile", i.e. the "taking roots' in the asylum of a patient who has recovered (22). In English the same phenomenon has been called "nestling".

This may occur in a mental patient, no matter what was the initial diagnosis. The problem is not in the clinical diagnosis, but in the personality of the patient. He is a passive individual, lacking in drive and ambition, lethargic, without a sound social integration. He may be a bachelor, or a widower, has often no definite occupation, his economic status is precarious. During the first period of his stay in the hospital nothing peculiar is seen. But as soon as the eventuality of a discharge is mentioned, something goes wrong; his discharge is postponed. Sometimes a severe relapse occurs just the day before the planned discharge. If the patient is discharged, you can be sure that he will be back soon for a second commitment. Such patients can succeed in spending their whole life in a Mental Hospital.

We may interpret such cases by saying that the patient acquired a "territory" in the Mental Hospital. Some people will perhaps object that it is not the same because the animal in the zoo has no choice, whereas the "nestling" patient has a choice but "chooses captivity" rather than freedom. However, there is perhaps more similarity, because the "nestling" patient mostly is a man who has no home; now he has created a home for himself in the Mental Hospital and when he is discharged he is like an escaped lion who has no place to go, except back to the cage.

The "nestling" process has been investigated among patients who recovered spontaneously. Among chronic mental patients it is much more difficult to recognize it. It would be very rewarding to ascertain to what extent the nestling contributes to make the disease chronic by hampering its recovery or, on the contrary, whether the inability to nestle does not increase the sufferings of certain chronic patients.

Of course the "nestling" process does not exist only in Mental Hospitals. Recently, two American surgeons, Gatto and Dean, described exactly the same picture in a military hospital (23).

The syndrome also exists in TB sanatoriums. A literary example is that of Hans Castorp, the hero of Thomas Mann's novel *Der Zauberberg*. It even occurs at times in prison, although much more infrequently (24). In Old Folks homes the trouble is rather that the individual *cannot* perform the "nestling" process and transform his room in the home to a "territory".

This brings us to wonder about the factors that favour or impede the development of the "nestling" process. We could single out three factors: 1) *The individual factor*. In human beings the characteristics have been extremely well analysed by Daumézon, as mentioned before. 2) *The factor of age*. The older the individual, the more difficult is the "nestling" process. This rule seems to be valid for human beings as well as for animals. 3) *The factor of milieu*. Zoologists have shown that the more an animal enclosure resembles the animal's natural habitat, the easier is the appropriation. Thanks to this knowledge the biological and emotional conditions of zoo animals have improved considerably in the last few decades. In regard to Mental Hospitals, Daumézon has shown that the "nestling" process is favoured by oldfashioned hospitals, holding on to tradition, whereas the process is hampered by a strict hospital atmosphere with an intensive therapeutic program.

One main difference between the zoo and the Mental Hospital is that the "nestling" process is "normal" and "desirable" in a zoo animal, but highly undesirable in a Mental Hospital patient, whenever there is the slightest chance of recovery.

However, it has been said that when there is a high probability that the mental disease will not be cured, the "nestling" process should be encouraged. This, at least, was the teaching of Professor Klaesi of Bern, who divided his Mental Hospital in two sharply separated parts, the "Heilanstalt" and the "Pflegeanstalt". The "Heilanstalt" had a strict hospital character and the patients were told from the beginning that they were only temporarily there. The "Pflegeanstalt" was considered a home for permanent patients and it was made as attractive as possible for them, with curtains, flowers, pictures on the walls, pet animals, etc.

3. The Syndromes Produced by Social Competition and Frustrations

Any living being, at least among higher species, can thrive only if put in an adequate social setting. Grzimek emphasized that it is not enough to put a number of monkeys in a cage. If that is done there will be terrific fights in certain cages, with large numbers of casualties. In other cages the monkeys will live in peace with each other. Why the difference? If the proportion of males is too great, they will fight with each other for the females and not only the males but the females too will be wounded and die and finally almost the whole lot will be exterminated. In order to be at peace there must be a small number of adult males, a larger number of females and a group of babies and young animals (25).

There is also the phenomenon of "social rank" which has been investigated by the pioneer work of the Norwegian zoologist, Thorleif Schjelderup-Ebbe (26). In any group of mammals or birds a social hierarchy is spontaneously established. At the top is a dominating *animal alpha,* who takes the best part of the food, of the females, the best resting place and demands from all the other animals certain gestures and signs of submission. After him comes the second highest in the rank, the *animal beta,* who acts in the same way towards the other animals except the animal alpha. At the bottom comes the *animal omega,* a paria who has no privileges at all and has to submit to all the others. Parallel to this social rank there often exists a kind of hierarchy of maltreatment, biting, clawing, pecking and so on. For instance, among hens exists the "pecking order": hen No. 1 pecks all the other hens and is pecked by no one. Hen No. 2 is pecked only by No. 1 and pecks all the others except No. 1 and so on. The last one does not peck any and is pecked by all.

Grzimek (25) has emphasized the fact that social rank and pecking order are much more strict and despotic among zoo animals than among a group of the same species in nature. In a monkey group at liberty the animals of inferior social rank have certain means of protecting themselves, for instance, by creeping around in the periphery of the group or hiding between trees. In the open space of a monkey cage they can not do this but are constantly under the watching eye of the despot; they are deprived of food, bitten and tormented, sometimes killed by the others. The situation of these unfortunate animals could be compared to that of a shy, honest man put in prison with hardened criminals. And to be sure, there is nothing so similar to the animal system of "social rank" and "pecking order" than the spontaneous self-organization of convicts in a prison with its "prison code".

This is not all. To this internal system of inequalities one must add another one. Hediger (27) has emphasized how the attitude of the public toward the animals is completely irrational. There are in the zoos "star-attractions", i.e. animals getting all attention and food from the visitors, which infuriates the animals in the neighbouring cages who are less favoured. The same is true when keepers, as it often occurs, favour a special animal.

Let us go back to the Mental Hospital. Do these data have any relevance for Mental Hospitals? Perhaps more than we think. The phenomenon of social rank can be found in Mental Hospitals under various forms. Baruk has described instances where, in a male ward containing a number of psychopaths, social competition established itself in a form not very different from what it would be in a prison (28). Another picture has been described in female wards with many regressed schizophrenic persons, by Balthasar Staehelin in Zürich (14). It is, indeed, surprising to read Staehelin's findings and to see how closely these interpersonal relationships of chronic schizophrenics on a ward resemble what Hediger described among animals.

In most cases, however, these phenomena of social rank, competition and pecking order are more or less masked by other phenomena, i.e. rivalry between old-timers and newly arrived patients, or the privileges of patients who have personal contact with the administration, help from outside and so on. These situations are made more complex by the interplay of the personal sympathies and antipathies of the staff. Henri Baruk (28) in France made a special study of these phenomena of social injustice among ward patients and contended that part of the delusions and hallucinations of chronic ward patients are the result of the oppression of the weaker patients and of the favouritism shown by the staff. Baruk claims that he observed a noticeable reduction of delusions and hallucinations after such conditions had been improved; this was the starting point of what Baruk called his "Psychiatrie Morale".

In order to eliminate these noxious effects of social competition and frustrations, several methods can be used. The first one, used by Esquirol and the ancient alienists, was to perform the so-called ''classification'' of patients, i.e. grouping them in such a way that they would not harm each other. The second one, emphasized by Baruk, consists in paying special attention to the social frustrations of patients in order to remove or compensate them. The third one, very much in favour today, consists in a good program of individualized occupational and recreational therapy.

4. Emotional Deterioration

Emotional deterioration as a result of captivity has been extensively studied in the field of prison psychopathology. In Mental Hospitals it is much more difficult because the physician has a natural tendency to confuse these symptoms with the clinical picture of the disease proper. However, some of the old pioneers had already noticed this point. Pinel, for instance, speaking of the insane who were tied with iron fetters, said that it was impossible to distinguish between the disease itself and the aggravation resulting from the use of the chains. More recently, in the wake of World War I, Hermann Simon in Germany proclaimed that many so-called catatonic symptoms were secondary products of pathogenetic milieu factors. Symptoms such as deep emotional regression and infantilism, pseudodementia, catatonic gestures and a large part of the agitation, aggressiveness, even of the delusions and hallucinations are included by some French psychiatrists in what they call *aliénisation*.

What can we learn from the zoo psychopathology in this regard? Symptoms of emotional deterioration in captive animals have been known for a long time but were not made the object of systematic investigation until our time.

Among the manifestations of emotional suffering and deterioration in captive animals, some are probably subjective and can only be guessed. Konrad Lorenz (29) has written about the hidden sufferings and the secret emotional deterioration in caged birds, turtles and other pet animals. He also infers that intelligent, vivacious animals such as monkeys, wolves, foxes and so on must suffer much more deeply than a lion who is a basically lazy animal, or an eagle who is a thoroughly stupid bird. However, since animals can not speak to us and tell us of their sufferings we have to rely on objective symptoms whenever they appear. One common manifestation is depression, which is one of the symptoms of the trauma of captivity. Yerkes, for instance, described the miserable condition of a monkey who had been spoiled as the pet animal in a family, but when getting older and more difficult to keep was given to a zoo, where the animal fell into depression with inertia, apathy and soon died. But depression can occur in other circumstances also, for instance from lack of mental stimulation.

Among the various specific symptoms of emotional deterioration in zoo animals we will mention only two:

1) *Stereotypic movements.* For instance, a bear will constantly nod his head, a chained elephant moves his head back and forth, a tiger will trot back and forth in his cage, a hyena makes a figure 8 and so on. Hediger (30) has been the first to show that these stereotypic movements were psychopathological reactions to captivity. After him, Dr. Meyer-Holzapfel (12) made a systematic investigation and showed that in the most severe cases these stereotypic movements occurred in animals who had been either chained or kept in too narrow a space.

2) *Coprophagia.* Another manifestation is coprophagia in chimpanzees and other big monkeys. Carl Stemmler (31) has shown that coprophagia, which is unknown under

natural conditions, is a reaction to certain conditions of captivity, sometimes to an unbalanced diet, but mostly stems from psychological factors. It always increases in the wintertime when the monkeys do not see so many visitors. Monkeys are nosy animals, always eager to look at people and to be amused by them and when deprived of this spectacle they fall into boredom. On the other hand, in good weather the monkeys are let out to climb trees, play in the grass and dig in the earth, all of which occupy them, but in bad weather they are kept inside and coprophagia is likely to reappear.

We cannot enlarge upon other manifestations of emotional deterioration. Let it be said only that these manifestations are multiform and each one of them can probably be determined by a variety of pathogenic factors.

To conclude our comparison of the psychopathological syndromes. This comparison might help us to distinguish more accurately certain exogenous elements which may interfere in the picture of mental disease:

1. The trauma of commitment with its immediate and long-lasting effects
2. The nestling process in recovered and non-recovered patients
3. The noxious effects of social competition and the frustrations of group life
4. The emotional deterioration produced by various other factors in the setting

GENERAL COMPARISON

We should terminate with a few statements of a more general nature, pertaining to a general comparison between the two settings as a whole, the Zoological Garden and the Mental Hospital.

As we have seen, zoos are an age-old institution but until about a century ago they were reserved for kings, princes and a few privileged people. With Louis XIV they became places for scientific research but they were still private institutions. Then the French Revolution brought a new idea; the zoo should also be a place for the education of the people, but it was not long before that ideal became distorted. The zoo became— at least for a great part—a place of amusement for a large public which included many benevolent people but also quite a few malevolent ones. It is absolutely no exaggeration to say that the role of the keepers consists more in protecting the animals from the public than the reverse.

Here are, for instance, a few excerpts of a book written by a former keeper in the Moscow Zoo, Vera Hegi (32):

"(Among the spectators) mixed a host of the embittered, of people dissatisfied with the world and with themselves, carrying everywhere their rancors and their grudges. Under the pretext of getting something for their money they woke up with a stick the sleeping lion or demanded that the bear should perform some tricks in exchange for a few lousy bits of food."

"The whole day long a huge crowd, quarrelsome and noisy, milled around the cages. The multitude, which would have been seized with a deadly panic if seeing at a distance one of these animals in liberty, revelled in seeing them disarmed, humiliated and vilified. They avenged themselves for their own cowardice by mocking the animals, shouting at them; and the protests of the keepers were cut off with this reply: 'I have paid for it'."

This was the picture of the public during a period of social upheaval and disorganization. No doubt the average public of the zoo is, on the whole, more kind. However, it is surprising what you learn from a talk with old zoo keepers. The average, kind attitude of the public is the result of a long-time effort of education of the public, in connection with a never-ending vigilance by the personnel. As soon as this watch is slackened the public starts teasing the animals, sometimes in a very mean way.

Now let us shift to the history of the Mental Hospital. Here we find the reverse of what was the case with the zoo. Until about the end of the XVIIIth century many Mental Hospitals were open to a large public. Here are a few details about the famous hospital Bedlam in London in the middle of the XVIIIth century, taken from reliable sources:

> On each side of the big gate was a column topped with a grotesque statue of Madness. A visit to Bedlam was one of the great amusements of the Londoners, especially on a Sunday. According to Robert Reed (33), it has been estimated that Bedlam received an average of 300 visitors a day. The visitors went through the two gates called the Penny-Gates, because the entrance fee was one penny. The sums paid by the visitors were one of the main sources of revenue for the hospital.
>
> The visiting gentleman disposed of his sword, strolled everywhere he wished throughout the lobbies, looked in every cell, spoke to the patients, made fun of them. Some visitors would bring them liquor.
>
> One of Hogarth's paintings, ''The Rake's Progress'', shows the rake in a miserable cell in Bedlam with two fashionable ladies looking at him as if he was a peculiar animal. According to Robert Reed, certain of the patients attracted the crowds more than others, probably the manics who were the ''star-attractions'', and it seemed on the whole that the patients in Bedlam looked more ''mad'' and agitated than our present day patients.
>
> But most surprising is the fact that a large proportion of the patients actually recovered and left Bedlam. In his book about Bedlam, Reed says that this institution played in London life of the XVIIIth century exactly the part of the zoo in our time.

This brings us to mention a problem of vast importance, which we have not the time now to discuss—the problem of the attitude toward mental patients.

A German anthropologist, John Koty (34), compiled a remarkable material of the attitude toward old people, crippled people, etc., including mental patients, throughout the world. The striking fact is how this attitude differs from one population to another. We also know that the attitude toward animals differs according to population.

Recently, there has been attempts made to find some rules—at least concerning animals. What underlies the attitude of people toward animals? The zoo, of course, is an excellent place for such research. Hediger has developed a concept—*Schauwert* (27), ''show value''—of an animal. The financial success of a zoo depends on the *Schauwert* of its animals, which is not related at all to zoology proper, nor to the rarity and scientific interest of animals, or to their commercial value or utility to man. Neither is it based on esthetics, but on certain completely irrational factors, whose investigation is still at its beginning.

This research, I think, could instigate a similar research in Mental Hospitals. We are beginning to realize that the attitude of each of us to the various mental patients is completely irrational. We find certain mental patients sympathetic, unsympathetic, indifferent, or we have an ambivalent attitude, and we simply do not know why. When we come to know more about these unconscious attitudes and motivations, it might help us to work out better methods of individual and collective therapy in Mental Hospitals.

BIBLIOGRAPHY

1. Revers, Wilhelm: *Die Psychologie der Langeweile.* Meisenberg, Verlag Anton Hein, 1949.
2. Nitsche, Paul and Wilmanns, Karl: *The History of the Prison Psychosis.* Engl. trans. New York, Nervous and Mental Disease Monographs Series, No. 13, 1912.
3. Vischer, A. L.: *Die Stacheldraht-Krankheit.* Zürich, Rascher, 1918.
4. Kielholz, Arthur: Probleme der Führung in der Anstalt. *Die Irrenpflege,* vol. 23, 1944, p. 201-207, 221-232.
5. Hellpach, W.: Die Zauberberg-Krankheit. *Die medizinische Welt,* vol. 1-2, 1927, p. 1341, 1425, 1465.
6. Freund, Walther: Ueber den Hospitalismus der Säuglinge. *Ergebnisse der inneren Medizin und Kinderheilkunde,* vol. 6, 1910, p. 333-368.
7. Goldfarb, W.: Psychological Privation in Infancy and Subsequent Adjustment. *American Journal of Orthopsychiatry,* vol. 15, 1945, p. 247-255.
8. Vettiger, G., Jaffé, A., Vogt, A.: *Alte Menschen im Altersheim.* Basel, B. Schwabe, 1951.
9. Loisel, Gustave: *Histoire des Ménagcries.* Paris, Doin & Laurens, 1912, 3 vol.
10. Galton, Francis: Domestication of Animals. (1865). In: *Inquiry into Human Faculties.* London, Dent, 1911.
11. Hediger, H.: *Wildriere in Gefangenschaft.* Basel, B. Schwabe, 1942.
12. Holzapfel, Monika: Die Entstehung eini er Bewegungsstereotypien bei gehaltenen Säugern und Vögeln. *Revue suisse de Zoologie,* vol. 46, 1939, p. 567-580.
13. Grzimek, Bernhard: Gefangenhaltung von Tieren. *Studium Generale,* vol. 3, 1950, p. 1-5.
14. Staehelin, Balthasar: Gesetzmässigkeiten im Gemeinschaftsleben schwer Geisteskranker. *Schweizer Archiv für Neurologie und Psychiatrie,* vol. 72, 1953, p. 277-298.
15. Racamier, P. C.: Introduction à une sociopathologie des schizophrènes hospitalisés. *L'Evolution Psychiatrique,* No. 1, 1957, p. 47-91.
16. Hagenbeck, Carl: *Beasts and Men,* Engl. trans. London, Longmans and Green, 1909.
17. Hediger, H.: Freiheit und Gefangenschaft im Leben des Tieres. *Ciba-Zeitschrift,* vol. 5, No. 54, 1938, p. 1850-1861.
18. Hediger, H.: *Neue Zürcher Zeitung,* March 16th, 1958.
19. Mannteufel, P.: *Tales of a Naturalist.* Engl. trans. Moscow, Foreign Languages Publ. House, p. 19-21.
20. Mannteufel, P.: loc. cit., p. 49-50.
21. Hagenbeck, Lorenz: *Animals are my Life.* Engl. trans. London, The Bodley Head, 1956.
22. Daumézon, Gustave: L'enracinement des malades guéris à l'asile. *L'Hygiène Mentale,* vol. 36, 1946-1947, p. 59-71.
23. Gatto, L. and Dean, H.: The "Nestling" Military Patient. *Military Medicine,* vol. 117, 1955, p. 1-26.
24. Boven, W.: D'un prisonnier par vocation. *Revue médicale de la Suisse romande,* vol. 63, 1943, p. 859-865.
25. Grzimek, Bernhard: loc. cit., p. 1-5.
26. Schjelderup-Ebbe, Thorleif: Beiträge zur Sozialpsychologie des Haushuhns. *Zeitschrift für Psychologie und Physiologie der Sinnesorgane,* vol. 88, 1922, p. 225-264.
27. Hediger, H.: Vom Schauwert der Tiere. *Atlantis,* 1955, p. 348-352.
28. Baruk, Henri: *Psychiatrie Morale.* Paris, Presses Universitaires de France, 1945.
29. Lorenz, Konrad: *King Solomon's Ring.* Engl. trans. New York, Crowell, 1952, p. 53-64.
30. Hediger, H.: Ueber Bewegungsstereotypien bei gehaltenen Tieren. *Revue suisse de Zoologie,* vol. 41, 1934, p. 349-356.
31. Stemmler-Morath, Carl: Die Koprophagie, eine Gefangenschaftserscheinung bei den Anthropomorphen. *Der Zoologische Garten,* vol. 9, 1937, p. 159-161.
32. Hegi, Vera: *Les Captifs du Zoo.* Lausanne, Spes, 1942.
33. Reed, Robert R.: *Bedlam on the Jacobean Stage.* Harvard University Press, Cambridge, 1952.
34. Koty, John: *Die Behandlung der Alten und Kranken bei den Naturvölkern.* Stuttgart, Hirschfeld, 1934.

RESUME

Des études sur les prisons, les camps d'internement, les orphelinats, etc. ont montré que certains milieux fermés exerçaient une action nocive sur l'état psychique de beaucoup de leurs hôtes. Les troubles psychopathologiques résultant d'un séjour prolongé dans les hôpitaux psychiatriques ont aussi été étudiés, mais sont plus difficiles à mettre en évidence car il est malaisé de les distinguer des symptomes de la maladie mentale proprement dite.

Une comparaison avec les troubles psychopathologiques déterminés par la captivité chez les animaux des Jardins Zoologiques pourrait aider à éclairer ce problème, si— tout en ne perdant pas de vue les différences essentielles entre l'homme et l'animal— on se réfère à certains dénominateurs communs.

Après un historique des Jardins Zoologiques, l'auteur examine quatre manifestations bien connues chez l'animal captif, pour en chercher les parallèles chez le malade d'hôpital psychiatrique:

(1) Le *choc de la captivité,* qui domine toute la psychopathologie de l'animal au Zoo. Il peut être comparé au choc de l'internement, lequel est plus fréquent et peut être plus grave qu'on ne le croit souvent.

(2) Le *processus d'adaptation,* par lequel l'animal transforme sa "prison" initiale en "territoire" (analogue au "territoire" que l'animal en liberté se délimite et défend contre les intrus). Ce processus, que l'on cherche à favoriser au Zoo, est comparable à celui de "l'enracinement" du malade à l'hôpital psychiatrique, processus à éviter chez le malade mental guérissable mais plutôt à encourager chez le malade chronique et incurable.

(3) Les phénomènes de *lutte sociale* entre animaux d'une même cage, et de frustration dues au favoritisme des gardiens et des visiteurs, tous deux producteurs de grandes souffrances pour beaucoup d'animaux captifs. Ils sont comparables aux troubles observés chez certains malades mentaux dans des services mal surveillés.

(4) Les phénomènes de *détérioration psychique* et surtout reactive, manifestés par certains symptomes tels que stéréotypies motrices, coprophagie, etc. Ils résultent de mauvaises conditions de captivité, et peuvent être comparés à la pseudo-démence de certains vieux schizophrènes.

L'auteur conclut en signalant les études récentes sur la caractère foncièrement irrationnel de l'intérêt porté par les visiteurs des Jardins Zoologiques aux animaux des diverses espèces. Les motivations inconscientes des visiteurs des Zoos commencent à être un peu mieux connues. Il faut espérer que des études analogues dans les hôpitaux psychiatriques permettront d'éclaircir les motivations inconscientes qui font que certains malades mentaux déterminent soit la sympathie, soit l'antipathie, soit encore l'indifférence ou une attitude ambivalente. De telles études permettraient peut-être d'ouvrir de nouvelles avenues pour le traitement individuel ou collectif des malades mentaux.

3. Parallels Between Animal and Human Neuroses

J. WOLPE*

In J. ZUBIN & H. F. HUNT (Eds.), *Comparative Psychopathology: Animal and Human,*
New York: Grune & Stratton, 1967, 305-13. Reprinted by permission of Grune &
Stratton, Inc. and the author.

Experimental neuroses have been a widely recognized phenomenon since they were
first produced in Pavlov's laboratories more than half a century ago. These are states
of chronic behavioral disturbance produced experimentally by behavioral means (as
opposed to direct assaults on the nervous system by chemical or physical agents). The
bizarreness of some of the neurotic behavior early encouraged the belief that experimental neuroses were the result of some kind of lesion in the central nervous system—a
view that is still widely held, despite published evidence[15] showing beyond reasonable
doubt that they are a special class of learned emotional reactions. In this paper I propose to present this evidence concisely and then to show that in all respects in which
comparisons have been made human clinical neuroses have the same attributes as those
experimentally induced.

There are two basic methods for producing experimental neuroses. The first is typi-
fied by Pavlov's celebrated circle-and-ellipse experiment. At the beginning of the
experiment, a luminous circle was projected before a dog confined by the usual harness
on the laboratory table and each time was followed by a piece of food within easy reach
of the animal, to condition an alimentary (food-approach) response to the circle. After
this, an ellipse was conditioned as an inhibitory stimulus through being consistently
not followed by food; and then, subsequently, the shape of the ellipse was made rounder
in stages. At each rounder stage the inhibitory effect of the ellipse was clearly established by interspersing its nonreinforcements with reinforced presentations of the circle.
But a point arrived at which discrimination between the two shapes was no longer
possible. The animal then became increasingly agitated, and finally a state of severe
disturbance developed. Disturbance was henceforth always manifest when the animal
was brought back to the experimental chamber. (It is now known that the autonomic
disturbance produced by strong simultaneous incompatible action tendencies is indistinguishable from that produced by noxious stimulation.[2])

The other basic method for producing experimental neuroses consists of applying to
the spatially confined animal either a large number of weak noxious stimuli (usually in
the form of electric shocks) or a small number of stronger noxious stimuli. About a
quarter of a century ago, numerous experiments employing noxious stimulation were
carried out, particularly by Liddell and his associates (e.g., Liddell;[6] Anderson and
Parmenter[1]) at Cornell and by Masserman[7] in Chicago. Misled by certain features of

---

* Temple University Medical School, Philadelphia, Pa.

their own experimental arrangements, these workers were at one in believing that these neuroses were also due to conflict. Masserman,[7] for example, ascribed the neuroses he induced in cats to a conflict between food-approach motivation and avoidance-of-shock motivation, because the high-voltage low-amperage shock was inflicted on the animals at the very moment when they were approaching food in response to a conditioned stimulus. However, I subsequently demonstrated,[14,16] in a similar experimental setting, that such neuroses could be produced by shocks administered to animals that had never been fed in the experimental cage. Recently, Smart[13] found, in a comparative study of variations on this experimental model, that there was very little difference on 16 measures of neurotic behavior between a "shock only" group of cats and two groups who were shocked either while approaching food or while eating in the experimental cage.

EXPERIMENTAL NEUROSES AS LEARNED BEHAVIOR

The fact that at least some experimental neuroses can be induced without conflict in itself removes the grounds for the supposition that they result from neural damage or "strain" and provides a presumption that learning is their basis. In that case the typical positive characteristics of learned behavior should be evident. If experimental neuroses are learned, they must have the following features in common with all other learned behavior.

1. The neurotic behavior must be closely similar to that evoked in the precipitating situation.

2. The neurotic responses must be under the control of stimuli that were present in the precipitating situation—that is, the responses must occur upon the impingement on the organism of the same or similar stimuli.

3. The neurotic responses must be at greatest intensity when the organism is exposed to stimuli most like those to which the behavior was originally conditioned and diminish in intensity as a function of diminishing resemblance, in accordance with the principle of primary stimulus generalization.

All three of these features were clearly demonstrable in the neuroses I produced in cats by administering high-voltage, low-amperage shocks in a small cage.[14,16] The shocks evoked a variety of motor and autonomic responses (e.g., pupillary dilation, erection of hairs, rapid respiration). After an animal had received between three and about a dozen shocks it would be found to be continuously disturbed in the experimental cage; and then no more shocks would be given. The disturbance in each case consisted of just such responses as had been evoked by the shocks. Muscle tension, pupillary dilation, and other reactions of the sympathetic division of the autonomic nervous system were found in all animals, and vocalizing and clawing at the netting in most. But some displayed special reactions which, invariably, had been observed previously in response to the shocks. For example, one cat who had urinated while being shocked always urinated subsequently within a few seconds of being put into the experimental cage. Another developed a symptom that it seems permissible to call hysterical. He jerked his shoulders strongly every few seconds in the experimental cage. This jerking suggested an abortive jumping movement and seemed clearly relatable to the fact that on the first occasion on which he was shocked he had jumped through a hatch in the roof of the cage that had been left open. This similarity between evoked behavior and acquired behavior satisfied the first of the stated criteria of learned behavior.

The control of the neurotic reactions by stimuli involved in the causal situation was evident in several ways. First, the reactions were always at their strongest in the experimental cage, and the animals strongly resisted being put into it. Then, the sounding of a buzzer that had preceded the shocks could invariably intensify whatever reactions were going on. Finally, in the case of animals to whom the experimenter had been visible at the time of shocking, his entry into the living cage could at once evoke these reactions in the animal previously at ease.

Primary stimulus generalization was evident on several continua. Each animal displayed neurotic reactions in the experimental room (Room A) *outside the experimental cage,* though at an intensity clearly less than within the cage. Since stimuli from this room were acting upon the animal at a distance at the time of shocking, direct conditioning to them of neurotic reactions must have occurred. Now, if the animals were placed in one of three rooms* called B, C, and D in order of their physical resemblance to Room A, neurotic reactions would be aroused in each of them, but always least strongly in Room D and most strongly in Room B, though never as strong there as in Room A. Another instance of primary stimulus generalization was on an auditory intensity continuum. Presentation at close range of the buzzer that had preceded the shocks would always disturb an animal greatly, and the farther away he was when it sounded the weaker would his reactions be.

Thus, these experimental neuroses had all three of the qualifying characteristics of learned behavior. As will be shown below, human neuroses, too, possess these characteristics and also resemble those experimentally produced in other telling respects.

HUMAN NEUROSES AS LEARNED BEHAVIOR

The commonest human neurotic response constellation is anxiety—a sympathetic-dominated pattern of autonomic responses. In those neurotic patients—a large majority—in whom a history of the onset of unadaptive anxiety reactions can be obtained, one finds their origin almost always related to an occasion or recurrent occasions of high anxiety, or to a chronic anxiety-evoking state of affairs. Symonds,[19] reviewing the onset of anxiety states in 2000 flying crew members of the Royal Air Force, found a history of anxiety evocation at the onset of 99 per cent of cases. As might have been expected, the nature and degree of stress needed to evoke significantly high degrees of anxiety varied according to pre-existent factors in the individual—as is also true of experimental animals.

Just as in the experimental neuroses, stimulus aspects of the causal situation making impact on the person at the time of causation become conditioned to human neurotic anxiety responses. For example, a lawyer's fear of public speaking was traced to an occasion in law school when he was humiliated by a lecturer when speaking before a class: and a woman's phobia for sharp objects began when she was in the hospital after an unwanted pregnancy, when, while cutting fruit with a sharp knife, she was assailed with terror at the thought that she might harm the baby with the knife. Of course, it is not to be inferred from this that *only* stimuli present at the precipitating events are triggers to neurotic reactions, for second order conditioning often occurs (see below).

---

* Rooms A and B were both situated about 30 feet above ground level, overlooking a fairly busy street, but Room A was the brighter, also having windows on its sunny side. Both rooms contained very dark laboratory furniture, the greater quantity being in Room A. Room C, about half the size of A or B, contained laboratory furniture lighter in color and less in quantity than that in B, and was out of earshot of the busy street. Room D, situated on the next floor up, was extremely bright with white-washed walls and with large windows on two sides. It contained only a light-colored kitchen sink, a concrete trough, and some large cartons.

Both primary stimulus generalization and secondary generalization are found in human neuroses. In almost all phobias of the classical kind there is primary stimulus generalization. For example, fears of heights increase monotonically with increasing height, and claustrophobia varies in inverse relation to available space and in direct relation to span of confinement. Secondary generalization also occurs, in which the stimulus situations are not physically similar but produce a common mediating response in Osgood's[10] sense) to which anxiety is a consequent. For example, in a particular patient a tight dress and irremovable nail polish, though physically disparate, were placed in the same continuum of secondary generalization because both produced a closed-in feeling.

OTHER POINTS OF CORRESPONDENCE BETWEEN ANIMAL AND HUMAN NEUROSES

Second Order Conditioning

Once neurotic anxiety responses—i.e., high intensity responses to stimuli that *objectively* spell no danger—have been conditioned, second order conditioning becomes possible in both animals and humans. The following experiment was done on each of two cats.

The animal's neurotic anxiety responses to all the visual stimuli had been deconditioned (by a technique briefly described below), but were still elicited by the buzzer. A piece of meat was dropped in a corner of the laboratory, and as the animal eagerly ran towards it, the buzzer was sounded. It recoiled, hair erect, pupils dilated, body rigid: and hesitated before again advancing, upon which the buzzer was again sounded. Repeating the procedure several times resulted in the establishment of anxiety and avoidance reactions to that corner of the room and also to the sight of food dropped on *any* floor. The spread of human neurotic reactions to new stimuli in a precisely parallel way is extremely common. For example, a patient who had developed a fear of social groups, one day sat calmly in a half-empty movie house. During the interval the place became crowded and she was surrounded by people on all sides. A high level of anxiety was aroused: and this, by contiguity, became conditioned to movie houses, even if empty.

Similarity of Precipitating Factors

I have referred to the fact that experimental neuroses are produced either by ambivalent stimulation, which evokes simultaneous high intensity incompatible responses, or noxious stimulation. At the source of human neuroses, either conflict or the presence of a stimulation that directly evokes intense anxiety is similarly found. The crucial point appears to be that both of these kinds of stimulation produce high levels of autonomic disturbance, which Fonberg[2] has demonstrated to be for all practical purposes physiologically identical.

Resistance to Extinction

An outstanding feature of human neuroses is their resistance to extinction—i.e., the neurotic response does not decrease in strength no matter how often the patient is exposed to the stimulus situations that evoke them. It is the same with the neurotic cat, who shows the same high level of anxiety when placed in the experimental cage again and again, even if for hours.

The core of this resistance is the autonomic complex of reactions that comprises anxiety. Motor response components of experimental neuroses are far less resistant to extinction. Two factors appear to account for the resistance of anxiety to extinction. First, a relatively low level of muscle action is apparently involved in autonomic responses, so that there is presumably little of the fatigue-associated process responsible for reactive inhibition (RI) upon which extinction apparently depends.[3] Second, each time an organism is removed from an anxiety-evoking situation, there is a sharp reduction of the neural state of excitation that is conveniently termed anxiety drive. The reinforcing effect that this drive-reduction has upon the anxiety response habit counteracts any tendency toward extinction.[14]

At this point, taking together the similarities noted, it is plain that both the animal and human neuroses are subsumed by the following definition (cf. Wolpe[14]):

> A neurosis is a persistent unadaptive habit acquired in one or a succession of anxiety-generating situations. Autonomic responses of an anxiety pattern are usually their preeminent constituent.

But there are further resemblances.

Simultaneous Approach and Avoidance Gradients

It is a fairly common clinical experience to find a patient who is repeatedly drawn into situations that evoke great anxiety. From afar the situation is attractive—"the brave music of a *distant* drum"—but within there is nothing but distress. A parallel phenomenon was observed in those neurotic cats who had received food-approach conditioning in the experimental cage before the neurosis was induced by noxious stimulation. These had learned, during the period of their food-approach training, to jump spontaneously into an open "carrier" cage (in which they were to be carried to the laboratory) when it was placed upon the floor of the living cage. After they had been made neurotic they continued their spontaneous jumping into this "carrier" cage, and only began to manifest anxiety on the way downstairs to the laboratory. This observation, of course, exemplifies the rule that the spatial gradient of avoidance is steeper than that of approach.[8]

Elimination of Neurotic Habits by Counterconditioning
(Reciprocal Inhibition Mechanism)

Even after 2 or 3 days' starvation, neurotic cats were inhibited from eating in the experimental cage, or in the experimental room, and usually in one or more of the rooms, B, C, and D (described above) that in varying degrees resembled the experimental room. But always there was a room in which generalization was low enough to evoke a measure of anxiety so weak that eating was not inhibited. The eating was at first delayed and constrained, but subsequent portions of food were accepted with progressively increasing alacrity, while manifestations of anxiety reciprocally diminished, eventually to zero. The animal would thereafter eat in a room more similar to the experimental room, where successive feedings likewise eliminated all signs of anxiety. The same treatment was successfully applied right up the generalization continuum to the experimental cage. Apparently each act of feeding to some extent inhibited anxiety and diminished its habit strength in the stimulus situation concerned.

Eating was long ago employed clinically in similar fashion by Jones[4] to overcome children's phobias. In the human adult, parallel effects have been achieved with more than a dozen other responses that are also inhibitory of anxiety.[18] The most widely applied have been assertive, sexual, and relaxation responses.[16] The use of relaxation in a technique called systematic desensitization corresponds particularly closely with the therapeutic animal experiments described above. The patient is trained in deep muscle relaxation, and, subsequently, when he is deeply relaxed, stimulus situations that evoke neurotic anxiety responses are presented to his imagination. At first, the weakest member of a continuum of disturbing situations is presented—for example, in an acrophobic continuum it might be looking out of a second floor window. The visualizing is terminated after a few seconds, and then, a few seconds later, repeated. With repetitions the amount of anxiety evoked by the scene diminishes; and when it has fallen to zero a "stronger" scene—e.g., looking out of a 3rd floor window is introduced and similarly treated—and so on, until the greatest relevant (asymptotic) height has been dealt with. There is almost invariably complete transfer between what can be imagined without anxiety and what can be experienced in reality without anxiety.[12,16]

These therapeutic changes in animal and human neuroses accord with a common rule—that *if a response inhibitory to anxiety can be made to occur in the presence of anxiety-evoking stimuli, it will weaken the conditioned connection between these stimuli and the anxiety responses.* Conditioned inhibition of anxiety evidently develops on the basis of reciprocal inhibition.[15]

Permanence of Therapeutic Effects

When anxiety response habits are thoroughly deconditioned in the animals, relapse and symptom substitution are never observed. The same is the case with human subjects who are treated by conditioning methods. It is important, however, to realize that *thorough* treatment always implies removing from the stimuli concerned *all* power to evoke anxiety.[9] *The stimuli must be disconnected from the responses:* This is fundamental therapy, in contrast to attempts to modify responses as such—for example, by direct suggestion—without reference to their stimulus sources. There is strong evidence that once anxiety response habits are eliminated, they do not relapse. There is *no* evidence of an "unconscious" reservoir of forces that may at any time erupt in symptomatic discharges. In a study of follow-up studies of 249 cases who had apparently recovered after nonpsychoanalytic types of therapy of various kinds, it was found that only 4 relapses had occurred after periods ranging from 2 to 15 years.[17]

CONCLUSION

The practical implication of the general parallelism between animal and human neuroses is that if the latter, like the former, can be considered to be purely a matter of habits (predominantly of the autonomic nervous system) their treatment will be most effective when designed according to laws of learning. Methods so designed have already been yielding almost 90 per cent recoveries or marked improvements in neurotic cases in an average of about 30 sessions per patient.[5,16] Recently, in a striking and beautifully controlled study at the University of Illinois, Paul[11] showed that "dynamically" oriented psychotherapists, in treating students with severe anxieties in public speaking situations, obtained significantly better results with a conditioning technique—systematic desensitization—than they did with their own brand of insight therapy.

REFERENCES

1. Anderson, O. D., and Parmenter, R. A.: Long term study of the experimental neurosis in the sheep and dog. Psychosom. Med. Monogr. 2 (No. 3 and 4): 1941.
2. Fonberg, E.: On the manifestation of conditioned defensive reactions in stress. Bull. Soc. Sci. Lettr. Lodz. Class III. Sci. Math. Natur., 7, 1, 1956.
3. Hull, C. L.: Principles of Behavior. New York, Appleton-Century-Crofts, 1943.
4. Jones, M. C.: A laboratory study of fear. The case of Peter. J. Genet. Psychol. 31:308, 1924.
5. Lazarus, A. A.: The results of behavior therapy in 126 cases of severe neuroses. Behav. Res. Ther. 1: 69, 1963.
6. Liddell, H. S.: Conditioned reflex method and experimental neurosis. *In:* Personality and the Behavior Disorders. J. McV. Hunt, Ed. New York, Ronald Press Co., 1944.
7. Masserman, J. H.: Behavior and Neurosis. Chicago, University of Chicago Press, 1943.
8. Miller, N. E.: Experimental studies of conflict. *In:* Personality and the Behavior Disorders. Hunt, J. M., Ed. New York, Ronald Press Co., 1944.
9. Napalkov, A. V., and Karas, A. Y.: Elimination of pathological conditioned reflex connections in the experimental hypertensive state. Zh. Vyssh. Nerv. Deiatel. Pavlov 7: 402, 1957.
10. Osgood, G. C.: Studies on the generality of affective meaning systems. Amer. Psychol. 17: 10, 1962.
11. Paul, G. L.: Insight Versus Desensitization. Stanford, Stanford University Press, 1966.
12. Rachman, S.: Studies in desensitization III. Speed of generalization. Behav. Res. Ther. 4: 7, 1966.
13. Smart, R. G.: Conflict and conditioned aversive stimuli in the development of experimental responses. Canad. J. Psychol. 19: 208, 1965.
14. Wolpe, J.: Experimental neuroses as learned behaviour. Brit. J. Psychol. 43: 243, 1952.
15. Wolpe, J.: The formation of negative habits: a neurophysiological view. Psychol. Rev. 59: 290, 1952.
16. Wolpe, J.: Psychotherapy by Reciprocal Inhibition. Stanford, Calif., Stanford University Press, 1958.
17. Wolpe, J.: The prognosis in unpsychoanalyzed recovery from neurosis. Amer. J. Psychiat. 116: 35, 1961.
18. Wolpe, J., and Lazarus, A. A.: Behavior Therapy Techniques. London; Pergamon Press, 1966.
19. Symonds, C. P.: The human response to flying stress. Brit. Med. J. 2: 703, 1943.

4. Experimental Psychiatry and the Humane Study of Fear

W. M. S. Russell and R. L. Burch

The Principles of Humane Experimental Technique, London: Methuen, 1959, 142-53.
Reprinted by permission.

EXPERIMENTAL PSYCHIATRY AND THE SCREENING OF TRANQUILIZERS

The recent rapid progress of neurochemistry and neuropharmacology have increased the importance for psychiatry of experimental work on animals. We are faced with a battery of new drugs acting upon the brain, and with the possibility of developing both more and better ones.

The most famous of these drugs are the so-called tranquillizers. The extremely vague specification for their common property is that of easing 'anxiety and psychomotor agitation without affecting consciousness to any extent' (Shorvon, 1957). They are extremely heterogeneous both chemically and pharmacologically, and include Chlorpromazine (Largactil) and its chemical relative Mephazine (Pacatal); Reserpine (Serpasil), an alkaloid derived from a plant; benactyzine compounds (Suavitil, Nutinal, Covatin); meprobamates (Equanil, Miltown and Mepavlon); and hydroxyzine compounds (Atarax). All have come into use in the fifites, and all except reserpine are synthetic (Shorvon, 1957). Chlorpromazine and reserpine seem to be related pharmacologically to the hallucinogenic drug lysergic acid, and all three to the substance serotonin found widely in the body and having important vasomotor properties, but it is doubtful if interactions of this kind account entirely for their central nervous effects (cf. e.g. Bianchi, 1957; Bonnycastle *et al.,* 1956; Axelrod *et al.,* 1956; Vogt, cited in Anon., *Nature,* 1956c). Some of the tranquillizers, notably chlorpromazine, have marked actions on the hypothalamus, and hence on all six adenohypophyseal hormones and their targets (Sulman and Winnik, 1956). Despite the serious effects of some of them (e.g. jaundice, Parkinsonism, and severe depressions), many of these drugs are already being used clinically on a remarkably wide scale, especially in the U.S.A.; 5-10 per cent of all prescriptions in New York City in March, 1957, were said to be for tranquillizers. It is estimated that about 35 million prescriptions for them were written in 1956 in the U.S.A. Attempts are now being made to control their use. The most popular of all, Miltown, has become the fourth most commonly prescribed drug in America, "and there is no doubt that Equanil, the same drug in England, is greatly in demand" (Shorvon, 1957; cf. Anon., *Nature,* 1957). The rapidity with which new tranquillizers are now being synthesized, in the "feverish search for a panacea for anxiety" (Shorvon), is considerable.

Whatever the demerits of the existing tranquillizers, the feverish search continues unabated. More generally, it is a search for new compounds with powerful effects on behaviour of as yet dimly envisaged kinds. The organic chemist can oblige almost *ad libitum,* and the key problem is that of devising tests, not for the existing tranquillizers, most of which can be assayed chemically, but for the screening of a host of new compounds in search of the desired properties. A good deal is known about the present drugs neurochemically and even neurophysiologically, but no successful attempt has been made to clarify exactly what effects on behaviour are involved. This urgent need is thrown into relief by the screening problem, but is no less urgent for purposes of experimental psychiatric research, which might rationalize the situation and guide the search. In both contexts, experimental animals are necessary.

We may quote some remarks of Chance (1957a) in this context.

"Now the advent of 'tranquillizers' has found us completely unprepared. The concept, although originally definable in terms of the observations made on chlorpromazine, reserpine, and benactyzine, now obscures a confusion which can only become greater without a systematic knowledge of the way behaviour is organized in laboratory mammals. The interest that the discovery of these substances has aroused in the screening of new substances for tranquillizing action arises from a keenly felt but poorly informed awareness that brain function can be modified by drugs in many more ways than has been suspected so far. Under the guise, therefore, of searching for 'tranquillizers' every kind of test of behaviour is being pressed into service, in the scramble for new drugs with possible useful actions on the brain. . . . Only when the manifestations of the integrative activity of the brain are recognizable from a *knowledge of the behaviour of each species of animal* [our italics] will it be possible to distinguish readily between drugs producing disruption of normal brain function and those possessing a smooth selective action."

The actions of these drugs must be complex and multiple, and a variety of central nervous mechanisms must be implicated. Some of these mechanisms must be specifically mammalian, and related to all those changes in neurological and behavioural organization associated with the presence of an extensive neocortex. Others, however (at the base of the brain-stem, perhaps), may be common to most or all vertebrate groups. These mechanisms may well show the remarkable chemical stability, which, as much of endocrinology testifies (cf. Medawar, 1953), we commonly find in biochemical systems designed for control functions. One thinks here of such behaviourally separable mechanisms as the flight, attack, and mating drives (fear, rage, sex), prominent in the social behaviour of almost all vertebrates—for it is primarily *social* behaviour that concerns psychiatry, experimental or clinical. It is the presence among these of the flight drive (or, as we also call it, *fear*), that lends special interest to the problem in the present context. What we require is a set of models which will discriminate and measure effects upon these drives, as well as models of higher fidelity which will indicate the response of the mammalian brain as a whole and its special structural and functional mechanisms. Notice that for the former purpose the non-mammalian vertebrates might well be possible candidates, though they could not necessarily replace the mammals when we wish, as it were, to put the pieces together again.

The concept of drive is susceptible of rigorously precise analysis (Russell *et al.,* 1954; Russell, in press, c; Russell and Russell, in press). Any given primary drive may be expressed in a great variety of *acts.* It is such fundamental central mechanisms as primary drives which the psychiatrist is concerned to influence, rather than the particular actions in which they are expressed in individuals, the extremely diverse results of specific patterns of conditioning. If this were not so, animals would be useless as models here. Attempts have often been made in the history of psychology to abandon the notion of primary drives. Such attempts originate from a dislike of, and naïvety about, physiology and pharmacology. Those who make them choose to paint the box blacker than it really is, and theorize on the assumption that the animal or human skull is full of sawdust. The repressed concept inevitably returns, as in the notion of peripheral 'tension', which of course is quite meaningless without postulating a central mechanism to rank peripheral inputs in terms of their tenseness. In all vertebrates, the acts controlled by a particular primary drive are determined partly innately and partly by conditioning. Mammals differ from lower vertebrates in a greater capacity to reverse a conditioned response; they are better at *unlearning* (Diebschlag, 1941; Russell and Russell, 1957 and in press). Man of course has developed a new mode of behavioural organization—that of unified intelligence; his *pathology*, and therefore the whole province of psychiatry, is ultimately a matter of conditioning-like processes, which impair, cripple, and distort the development of his intelligence (Russell and Russell, 1957). In this way (among other things) man loses control of the rhinencephalic mechanisms, painfully acquired in mammalian and primate evolution to control the primary drive mechanisms associated with older brain structures (cf. e.g. Chance and Mead, 1953; Rothfield and Harmon, 1954).

Rational use of animals for experimental psychiatry thus depends on an accurate knowledge of "the behaviour of each species of animal" (p. 144 above), so that we can trace the interaction of such mechanisms as primary drives in the whole pattern of behaviour of a species. We can then make use of the natural occurrence, in the lives of the animals, of the behavioural states it is desired to influence. This is an important principle for both humanity and efficiency. In fact, the emergency has thrown into prominence, as Chance points out, our extreme relative ignorance of the behaviour of the commoner laboratory mammals (p. 129). Recourse is therefore being had to a miscellany of desperate methods. Where the flight drive (fear) is concerned, a tendency is already emerging to race for the electric grid, as the most convenient Procrustean method for terrorizing rats. This is a rat-race better stopped before it starts in earnest. Nor will such methods, full of flaws due to our ignorance, contribute anything useful to the problem in hand.

The Use of Lower Vertebrates

There are only two solutions to this increasingly urgent problem. One is the intensive and systematic study of the social behaviour of the commoner laboratory mammals themselves. This is the approach suggested by Chance (1957a), and we have already seen how urgently it is needed for other purposes (Chapter VI). This course is desirable and necessary in any case. It is no part of our intention to oppose it. But it can be usefully supplemented, especially in the early stages, by a different approach, which well illustrates most of the principles we have urged in this chapter. There are in fact two natural and complementary solutions: *behavioural study of existing laboratory species, and recruitment of behaviourally well studied ones.* Our ignorance of the behaviour of common laboratory mammals is off-set by a wealth of knowledge about that of numerous lower vertebrate species. Many of these would make eminently suitable recruits to the laboratory. And this knowledge is concentrated on precisely those aspects of behaviour likely to be of service in the screening of new neurotropic drugs. As we have seen, models discriminatory for the widespread vertebrate mechanisms of flight, attack and mating are just what we require for at least a major part of the purposes of experimental psychiatry. A great variety of such models have been made available. This is due to the progress of ethologists in the analysis of *threat* and *courtship* movements and postures of both birds and fishes into the component drives which make up their central motivation (see e.g. Tinbergen, 1952a, b; 1953a, b; 1954; Tinbergen and Moynihan, 1952; Russell, 1952; Hinde, 1953; 1954; Van Iersel, 1953; Morris, 1952; 1954a, b; 1955; 1956b;[1] Moynihan and Hall, 1954; Moynihan, 1955; Baerends *et al.,* 1955; Baggerman *et al.,* 1956; Marler, 1956; Spurway, 1956; Weidmann, 1956; Wood-Gush, 1956; Andrew, 1957; Forselius, 1957; Hoogland *et al.,* 1957). This development owes its ultimate origin to a classical paper by Lorenz (1935); its vigorous promotion in the fifties stems from an inspired hypothesis of Tinbergen.

Threat can be dissected into flight and attack drives, courtship into those for flight, attack, and mating. Differences in the proportions of the two or three components can be accurately inferred from the qualitative and quantitative properties of the resulting movements and postures. These movements and postures, whether they arise innately or by conditioning, are exceptionally stable and stereotyped, on account of the signal function which has governed their evolution (cf. Morris, 1957). In this way, specific central mechanisms can be separately studied, often at the same time. (For the technical problem of behaviour measurement, cf. Russell *et al.,* 1954; Chance and Mead, 1955; Morris, 1957.) The composition and balance differ between species. Thus the role of the flight drive in courtship is less marked in the three-spined than in the ten-spined stickleback, owing to the fact that the former species, better protected by its efficient spines, is less timid in general (Morris, 1955; Hoogland *et al.,* 1957. The three-spined stickleback is a territorial animal, and since the male courts in his own territory he is almost devoid of social fear, as well as of fear of predators—cf. Tinbergen, 1953a). A strong flight component is found in many species of birds, and gives rise to a definite "individual distance" (Hediger, 1955). That is, birds of such species will not normally approach each other nearer than a certain distance, characteristic for the species concerned. This may be an unavoidable generalization of a principle salutary enough in animals which can escape their predators by taking to the air, if only they have sufficient time for take-off. At all events, birds of such species *do* have to break the rule in the breeding season, and it is this that often accentuates the flight component in their courtship. Observe here that we can thus study fear without imposing any punishment at all, and indeed merely by means of conditions which the bird necessarily encounters in the course of its normal life—specifically, when it has to approach its mate for breeding purposes.[2] It is now perhaps clear that even fear can be studied without anything we can rationally call inhumanity.

Sometimes, as in the male zebra finch, the attack drive is lowered in courtship at an earlier, separate stage. There is then left a precopulatory ceremony which is a simple composite of the flight and mating drives. Its most prominent feature in the zebra finch is the "pivot dance", in which the male approaches the female along a branch in a series of swings, which take him alternately towards and away from her (see Fig. 1). The size of the swings in a particular direction reflect the level of the drive concerned.

---

[1] A useful systematic discussion of the field.

[2] Besides threat and courtship, a third situation susceptible of similar analysis is that of reactions of animals to their young. Analysis here has barely begun (see Russell and Russell, 1957 and in press; Russell, in press, d; and cf. Tinbergen, 1953a, Chapter III).

This species breeds all the year round, and the birds "begin to nest-build and court within minutes of their release into the aviary" (Morris, 1954, also 1956). Here is an obvious potential recruit for the laboratory ranks. A number of finch species have been studied in this way. A schoolboy recently reported a series of interesting observations on British finch species, and remarked that they were suitable for his purpose 'on account of the ease with which they may be kept under conditions almost natural to them' (Hughes, cited by North, 1956).

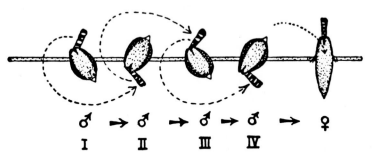

Figure 1. THE PIVOT DANCE IN THE MALE ZEBRA FINCH (From Morris, 1954, Figure 7)

This diagram shows the movements of the pivot dance in the male zebra finch, seen from above.

♂ position of male
♀ position of female

Four successive stages of the ceremony are shown—I, II, III, and IV. The broken arrows show how the male moves from one position to the next. The long bar running along the diagram is a twig on which both birds are perched.

As the figure shows, the female remains stationary, facing across the twig. The male moves towards her in a series of pivoting movements, swinging from side to side. His tail moves through an even wider arc than his body. The dance can be seen as the outcome of a conflict between *flight* and *mating* drives, the former causing the male to avoid the female, the latter to approach her. The amplitude of the swing in each direction reflects the level of the corresponding drive.

For further explanation, see text.

We can thus begin to envisage the progressive specification of a drug—it does, or does not, change the balance of the zebra finch pivot dance (by an effect on the flight drive); it does, or does not, reduce the attack component in the courtship of the three-spined stickleback; and so on. For screening purposes, every different test combination is available. Sometimes both flight and attack components are missing from a courtship which, as a result, is extremely simple. This is the case, for various reasons, in male frogs and toads of many species (Russell, 1952). The male clawed frog (*Xenopus laevis*) is, for many reasons, a sterling laboratory animal, and already in use for other purposes (Table 13). In its exceptionally pure[1] mating behaviour it yields a test for sex hormones which is of unique specificity (Russell, 1954). The flight drive may interfere with mating in other ways in this species, though not in other frogs and toads. Finally, in this group, neurological study has kept in step with the analysis of behaviour (Aronson and Noble, 1945; Russell, 1954).

This last condition is unfortunately far from met in teleosts and birds. Their status is the exact inverse of laboratory mammals. The behaviour of many bird and teleost species is already richly studied, while our knowledge of the structure of their fore-

---

[1] i.e. not contaminated with flight or attack components—the word is not used in Bunthorne's sense!

brains is surprisingly slim—just how slim may be inferred from the achievement of Erulkar (1955), who by employing modern techniques in a few simple experiments has been able to revolutionize our picture of the bird thalamus. The bird and teleost forebrains are strikingly different from those of mammals, except in the region of the hypothalamus (Herrick, 1924; Kappers *et al.,* 1935). Their high-level behavioural organization is no less profoundly different from that of mammals (Diebschlag, 1941; Russell *et al.,* 1954; Russell and Russell, in press). For two reasons, our neurological ignorance need not disqualify lower vertebrate recruits. First, there is no ground for supposing any radical differences between mammalian and non-mammalian vertebrates in the basic drive mechanisms we have discussed. Second, the entities studied by psychiatrists are behaviourally and not neurologically defined. Hence we need not hesitate to use lower vertebrate species as functional models.

Many birds present a more practical obstacle. The very timidity that issues in individual distance has an unfortunate consequence—the trauma of injection is liable to cause behavioural disturbance sufficiently prolonged to interfere with the proposed tests. But the use of aerosols would overcome this obstacle, and if birds dictated the development of this technique they would confer a benefit on experimental animals of all species (p. 139).

This sketch may show that, by judicious choice of species and due consideration of their natural behaviour, a great and urgent pure and applied research problem might be tackled successfully. We do not discount Chance's proposal to study systematically the existing laboratory mammals. This would confer a host of benefits, and is wedded to the same principle. By all means let us find out what part these same mechanisms play in the ordinary course of life in the mouse and rat. For instance, tranquillization might overcome the resistance of the rat to exploring new terrain outside its base—a resistance which appears without any previous punishment. What we wish above all to emphasize is that by such methods we can overturn the paradox and study fear without inhumanity.

All these suggestions were made at the UFAW Symposium on Humane Technique in the Laboratory, held on the 8th of May, 1957 (Russell, 1957b). Dramatically enough, it was on the very next day (9th of May) that Eckhard Hess published an important paper on experiments with mallard ducklings (Hess, 1957). In the course of these experiments, he showed conclusively that meprobamate and chlorpromazine reduce or eliminate flight reactions in this bird species. The drugs, incidentally, were given by the oral route, so the trauma difficulty mentioned above did not arise. We shall not discuss in detail Hess's profoundly interesting work, on which comment has been made elsewhere (Russell and Russell, in press). Three observations will suffice. First, Hess has provided yet another behavioural situation which could be used for the test purposes we have discussed. Second, the fear he was able to alleviate was not induced by previous punishment, but was an inevitable feature of the life of a duckling. Third, there is some ground for supposing that the most dramatic effect of meprobamate—the prevention of the very rigid conditioning process called imprinting—was due to the suppression of a latent fear not expressed in any overt action. If this interpretation is correct (it is not that of Hess) the implications for human psychopathology are prodigious. The whole situation may be of special interest as an illustration of the ideas we have put forward, and might afford a particularly humane test.

For our present purposes, fear is the most important of the mechanisms discussed. It does no harm to have many alternative suggestions ready; on the contrary, this is a natural outcome of the list-making activity we have recommended (p. 140). We shall therefore close this chapter with yet another possibility of achieving the same object— the humane study of fear (see again Russell, 1957b). Thus we may show how many degrees of freedom are available even in this most delicate of investigations. In its recruiting campaign, experimental psychiatry would be ill-advised to look the humblest gift-finch in the beak. But the animal we shall now consider is the homely pigeon, already a member of that existing non-mammalian 5 per cent (p. 142). We obtain this instance from the beautiful experimental work of Diebschlag (1941), a refiner if ever there was one.

Diebschlag was trying to train his pigeons to perform certain simple tasks. Specifically, he wished them to choose one of two platforms in front of their cage. He found that the birds could soon be trained to mount a platform in search of food, which was provided on top of the platform in a dish, invisible until the platform was mounted. His next problem was to find how to make the pigeon *avoid* a given platform. To begin with, he simply put no food on this forbidden platform. This was useless, for the pigeon would simply try the right platform first, once it had been trained to do so, and then fly to all the other 'forbidden' ones, as if to make sure there was no food there as well. It continued to repeat this procedure over many trials. So absence of food did not prevent the bird from visiting a platform repeatedly. Diebschlag now tried to scare the bird when visiting the forbidden platform, by means of a sort of scarecrow. This was a fiasco. After a few such scares, the birds would not visit any platforms at all, and stayed in their cages. Instead of resorting to new and worse scares (as, one feels, some experimenters might have done), Diebschlag now hit on a simple expedient. He placed on the forbidden platform a dish of food covered with a transparent plate. A pigeon arriving there would now make a number of fruitless pecks, and finally give up. This time it did succeed in learning not to visit the frustrating platform. Diebschlag used this punishment-free method throughout one of the most important learning studies ever performed, and the story is already instructive enough for those wishing to study learning in birds.

But an interesting by-product now emerged. In some of his experiments, Diebschlag wished to *re*-train his birds. For instance, after learning to mount the left-hand platform and avoid the right-hand one, the bird would now be expected to learn exactly the opposite. To bring this about, Diebschlag put accessible food on the right-hand, and inaccessible food on the left-hand platform. In order to get the food, the bird had now to mount the platform it had hitherto learned to avoid. This re-training proved surprisingly difficult. For the first three trials, such a bird made futile efforts on the left-hand platform, and *never* approached the one it had learned to avoid. In order to bring about re-training, Diebschlag had to bring the two platforms so close together that a hungry bird, standing on the left-hand one, could actually see the food on the right-hand one. After hesitating for minutes, such a bird hopped gingerly over to the formerly forbidden spot. It ate here with marked uneasiness, and a small sudden noise was enough to make it take to flight in a panic. After one such experience the bird would be even more hesitant in approaching the formerly forbidden platform, and would sometimes try to reach it from the "safe" one by stretching as hard as it could. In short, once the bird had been frustrated on a given platform, that platform was taboo, and a place of terror.

In the light of some other observations, Diebschlag was able to interpret this curious result. Apparently, once a bird had been frustrated in a certain place, it henceforward regarded that place as part of the territory of a rival bird. The terror it showed was therefore terror of an imaginary rival. The slightest noise seemed to threaten an immediate return of the owner, and sent the trespasser flying for the safety of his own familiar territory. The degree of fear shown becomes intelligible when we recall that birds of this family are peculiarly merciless and ferocious fighters. They have evolved no effective means of inhibiting attack, since they normally seek safety from each other on the wing (Lorenz, 1952). Diebschlag specifically noted that he had himself imposed no punishment of any kind—and indeed, if he had, he would not have made this intriguing observation.

Suppose we wish to study a drug which reduces fear, or is intended to do so. We could make use of these observations in the following way. A pigeon could be trained to avoid a platform, as a result of the very mildly distressing experience of having found inaccessible food there. We should now not even have to expose it to its own imaginary terrors, by trying to re-train it. We could simply administer the drug and see whether the bird now spontaneously and without any alarm visited the forbidden platform. We could expect it to do this if no longer afraid, in the light of the original observation that pigeons freely visit unrewarding platforms when hungry. If this very probable prediction were realized, *we should have a method of testing the fear-reducing activity of a drug without at any stage of the process inflicting any fear on the animal.* It would be hard to think of a problem which seemed at first sight so totally insoluble, yet we have now considered more than one kind of solution. It is clear, *a fortiori,* that in less exacting investigations the freedom of choice of the experimenter is often very much wider than at first appears. The full use of this freedom is the mark alike of humane and successful experimentation. "Violence is the last refuge of the incompetent" (Asimov, 1953). If we prefer not to seek that refuge, there is perhaps no limit in animal experimentation to the progress of refinement.

REFERENCES

Andrew, R. J. (1957) The Agressive and Courtship Behaviour of Certain Emberizines, *Behaviour,* **10,** 255-308.

Anon. (1956c) Hypotensive Drugs and the Control of Vascular Tone in Hypertension, *Nature,* **178,** 131-4.

Anon. (1957) Tranquillizing Drugs in the United States, *Nature,* **179,** 514-15.

Aronson, L. R. and Noble, G. K. (1945) The Sexual Behaviour of Anura. 2. Neural Mechanisms Controlling Mating in the Male Leopard Frog, *Rana pipiens. Bull. Amer. Mus. Nat. Hist.,* **86,** 89-139.

Asimov, I. (1953) Saddle and Bridle, *In: Foundation,* Asimov, 85-144; Weidenfeld & Nicolson, London.

Axelrod, J., Brady, R. O., Witkop, B. and Evarts, E. V. (1956) Metabolism of Lysergic Acid Diethylamide, *Nature,* **178,** 143-4.

Baerends, G. P., Brouwer, R. and Waterbolk, N. Tj. (1955) Ethological Studies on *Lebistes reticulatus* (Peters), I. An Analysis of the Male Courtship Pattern, *Behaviour,* **8,** 249-334.

Baggerman, B., Baerends, G. P., Heikens, H. S. and Mook, J. H. (1956) Observations on the Behaviour of the Black Tern, *Chlidonias n. niger* (L.), in the Breeding Area, *Ardea,* **44,** 1-71.

Bianchi, C. (1957) Reserpine and Serotonin in Experimental Convulsions, *Nature,* **179,** 202-3.

Bonnycastle, D. D., Paasonen, M. K. and Giarman, N. J. (1956) Diphenyl-hydantoin and Brain-Levels of 5-Hydroxytryptamine, *Nature,* **178,** 990-1.

Chance, M. R. A. (1957a) Mammalian Behaviour Studies in Medical Research, *The Lancet,* Oct. 5th, 687-90.

Chance, M. R. A. and Mead, A. P. (1953) Social Behaviour and Primate Evolution, *Symp. Soc. Exper. Biol.,* **7,** 395-439; U.P.

Chance, M. R. A. and Mead, A. P. (1955) Competition between Feeding and Investigation in the Rat, *Behaviour,* **8,** 174-82.

Diebschlag, E. (1941) Uber den Lernvorgang bei der Haustaube, *Z. Vergl. Physiol.,* **28,** 67-104.

Erulkar, S. D. (1955) Tactile and Auditory Areas in the Brain of the Pigeon. An Experimental Study by means of Evoked Potentials, *J. Comp. Neurol.,* **103,** 421-58.

Forselius, S. (1957) Studies of Anabantid Fishes. III. A Theoretical Discussion of the Differentiation, Function, Causation and Regulation of Reproductive Behaviour, *Zool. Bidrag fran Uppsala,* **32,** 379-597.

Hediger, H. (1955) *Studies of the Psychology and Behaviour of Captive Animals in Zoos and Circuses,* Butterworths, London.

Herrick, C. J. (1924) *Neurological Foundations of Animal Behavior,* Henry Holt, New York.

Hess, E. H. (1957) Effects of Meprobamate on Imprinting in Waterfowl, *Ann. N. Y. Acad. Sci.,* **67,** 724-32.

Hinde, R. A. (1953) The Conflict between Drives in the Courtship and Copulation of the Chaffinch, *Behaviour,* **5,** 1-31.

Hinde, R. A. (1954) The Courtship and Copulation of the Greenfinch (*Chloris chloris*), *Behaviour,* **7,** 207-32.

Hoogland, R., Morris, D. and Tinbergen, N. (1957) The Spines of Sticklebacks (*Gasterosteus and Pygosteus*) as means of Defence against Predators (*Perca and Esox*), *Behaviour,* **10,** 205-36.

Iersel, J. J. A. van (1953) An Analysis of the Parental Behaviour of the Male Three-spined Stickleback (*Gasterosteus aculeatus* L.), *Behaviour Supplement,* **3,** 1-159.

Kappers, C. U. Ariens, Huber, G. C. and Crosby, Elizabeth C. (1936) *The Comparative Anatomy of the Nervous Systems of Vertebrates, Including Man,* MacMillan, New York.

Lorenz, K. (1935) Der Kumpan in der Umwelt des Vogels, *J. F. Ornithol.,* **83,** 137-212; 289-413.

Lorenz, . (1952) *King Solomon's Ring,* Transl. Marjorie Kerr Wilson, Methuen, London.

Marler, P. (1956) Behaviour of the Chaffinch *Fringilla coelebs, Behaviour Suppl.,* **5,** 1-184.

Medawar, P. B. (1953) Some Immunological and Endocrinological Problems Raised by the Evolution of Viviparity in Vertebrates, *Sympos. Soc. Exper. Biol.,* **7,** 320-38, C.U.P.

Morris, D. (1952) Homosexuality in the Ten-Spined Stickleback, (*Pygosteus pungitius* L.), *Behaviour,* **4,** 233-61.

Morris, D. (1954a) The Reproductive Behaviour of the Zebra Finch (*Poephila guttata*), with special reference to Pseudofemale Behaviour and Displacement Activities, *Behaviour,* **6,** 271-322.

Morris, D. (1954b) The Reproductive Behaviour of the River Bullhead (*Cottus gobio* L.) with special reference to the Fanning Activity, *Behaviour,* **7,** 1-32.

Morris, D. (1955) Sticklebacks as Prey, *Brit. J. Animal Behav.,* **3,** 74.

Morris, D. (1956) The Function and Causation of Courtship Ceremonies, *In: L'Instinct dans le Comportement des Animaux et de l'Homme,* 261-84; Masson & Cie, Paris.

Morris, D. (1957) 'Typical Intensity' and its Relation to the Problem of Ritualisation, *Behaviour,* **11,** 1-12.

Moynihan, M. (1955) Some Aspects of Reproductive Behaviour in the Black-Headed Gull (*Larus ridibundus ridibundus* L.) and Related Species, *Behaviour Suppl.,* **4,** 1-201.

Moynihan, M. and Hall, M. Fae (1954) Hostile, Sexual and other Social Behaviour Patterns of the Spice Finch (*Lonchura punctulata*) in Captivity, *Behaviour,* **7,** 33-76.

North, F. J. (1956) Science by the Upper Form, *Nature,* **178,** 670-1.

Rothfield, L. and Harmon, P. J. (1954) On the Relation of the Hippocampal-Fornix System to the Control of Rage Responses in Cats, *J. Comp. Neurol.,* **101,** 265-82.

Russell, W. M. S. (1952) Quantitative Studies of Vertebrate Instinctive Behaviour, with Special Reference to the Influence of Hormones, *Dissert, for Degree of D.Phil., U. of Oxford,* 1-363.

Russell, W. M. S. (1954) Experimental Studies of the Reproductive Behaviour of Xenopus laevis. I. The Control Mechanisms for Clasping and Unclasping, and the Specificity of Hormone Action, *Behaviour,* **7,** 113-88.

Russell, W. M. S. (1957b) Refinement in Research. Paper at UFAW Symposium on Humane Technique in the Laboratory, May 1957; abstract in *Coll. Papers Lab. Animals Bur.,* **6,** 79-81.

Russell, W. M. S. (in press, c) *The Comparative Physiology of the Vertebrates,* Pitman & Sons, London.

Russell, W. M. S. (in press, d) The Malfunction of Parent-Young Relations in Vertebrates other than Man, *L'Evolution Psychiatrique.*

Russell, Claire and Russell, W. M. S. (1957) An Approach to Human Ethology, *Behav. Sci.,* **2,** 169-200.

Russell, Claire and Russell, W. M. S. (in press) *Human Behaviour: A New Approach,* Deutsch, London.

Russell, W. M. S., Mead, A. P. and Hayes, J. S. (1954) A Basis for the Quantitative Study of the Structure of Behaviour, *Behaviour,* **6,** 153-205.

Shorvon, H. J. (1957) (Untitled Contribution to) Discussion on the Treatment of Morbid Anxiety, *Proc. Roy. Soc. Med.,* **50,** 13-15.

Spurway, Helen (1956) (Untitled Contribution) in: *L'Instinct dans le Comportement des Animaux et de l'Homme,* 185-6; Masson & Cie, Paris.

Sulman, F. G. and Winnik, H. Z. (1956) Hormonal Depression due to Treatment with Chlorpromazine, *Nature,* **178,** 365.

Tinbergen, N. (1852a) 'Deprived' Activities; their Causation, Biological Significance, Origin and Emancipation during Evolution, *Quart. Rev. Biol.,* **27,** 1-32.

Tinbergen, N. (1952b) A Note on the Origin and Evolution of Threat Display, *Ibis,* **94,** 160-2.

Tinbergen, N. (1953a) *Social Behaviour in Animals,* Methuen, London.

Tinbergen, N. (1953b) Fighting and Threat in Animals, *New Biology,* **14,** Johnson & Abercrombie (eds.), 9-24; Penguin Books, London.

Tinbergen, N. (1954) The Origin and Evolution of Courtship and Threat Display, *In: Evolution as a Process,* Huxley, Hardy & Ford (eds.), 233-50, Allen & Unwin, London.

Tinbergen, N. and Moynihan, M. (1952) Head Flagging in the Black-Headed Gull: Its Function and Origin, *British Birds,* **45**, 19-22.

Weidmann, U. (1956) Verhaltensstudien an der Stockente (*Anas platyrhynchos* L.) I. Das Aktionssystem, *Z. f. Tierpsychol.,* **13**, 208-71.

Wood-Gush, D. G. M. (1956) The Agonistic and Courtship Behaviour of the Brown Leghorn Cock, *Brit. J. Animal Behav.,* **4**, 133-42.

Section II

ORIGINS AND SYMPTOMATOLOGY IN PSYCHOPATHOLOGY

5. Neurotic Behavior

H. S. LIDDELL

Emotional Hazards in Animals and Man, Springfield: Thomas, 1956, 51-67. Copyright
1956 by Charles C. Thomas. Reprinted by permission.

NEUROTIC BEHAVIOR

The attempt to understand emotional disorders responsible for the inability of psychoneurotic patients and experimentally neurotic animals to cope with real life situations
as they occur poses the same basic problem for psychiatrist and behaviorist. If the
behavior of an individual, patient, or animal, seems to the investigator strange and
unaccountable, he must perseveringly explore the life history of that individual until
his strange or ever irrational actions become natural and understandable.

Ernest Jones says of Freud's characteristic way of working: "His great strength,
though sometimes also his weakness, was the quite extraordinary respect he had for the
singular fact. This is surely a very rare quality. In scientific work people continually
dismiss a single observation when it does not appear to have any connection with other
data or general knowledge. Not so Freud. The single fact would fascinate him and he
could not dismiss it from his mind until he had found some explanation of it. The practical value of this mental quality depends on another one: judgment. The fact in question may really be insignificant and the explanation of it of no interest: that way lies
crankiness. But it may be a previously hidden jewel or a speck of gold that indicates a
vein of ore. Psychology cannot yet explain on what the flair or intuition depends that
guides the observer to follow up something his feelings tell him is important, not as a
thing in itself but as an example of some wide law of nature.''

A strong suspicion arises, however, that this flair or intuition is for the most part the
result of dispassionate and persevering observation; in other words, long continued
hard work.

Before turning to a discussion of the implications for mental medicine of experimental neurosis it will be useful to review some *singular facts* which have been noted
from time to time in the course of our studies of sheep and goat behavior. Each of these
singular facts would have seemed to the casual observer strange, unaccountable, even
irrational. But when reviewed in relation to the individual's known life history, they
become understandable and reasonable. They then take their proper place in the
animal's contemporary emotional organization.

On one occasion the animal attendant at the laboratory came to us to report a disturbing experience. When he went to the barn to feed the animals, one of his favorite goats
fled in alarm at his approach. It would not come to him even when offered a bucket of
oats although they had been on friendly terms since it was a kid. He feared that we
might suspect him of mistreating the animals. Actually, we had learned to trust his

practical knowledge of farm animals. Their well-being was his principal concern.

Although this attendant regularly assisted us in preparing our sheep and goats for their daily training sessions, he did not really know what we were up to. He only knew that ordinarily the animals came willingly to the laboratory and that they were not mistreated by punishment or rough handling. What he did not know was that his friend, the goat, had reached a stage in its stressful conditioning in which it had begun to carry its troubles back to the barn. Fleeing from the familiar attendant was a clear indication to us that this goat's anxious apprehension had spread from its place of origin in the laboratory to its living quarters. It was already flinching or withdrawing from its familiar environmental contacts and was entering upon a state of continuing pain and fear; namely, a chronic loss of emotional control or experimental neurosis. Thus, the singular fact of the goat's irrational fear of the friendly attendant was for us an important datum in analyzing its case history.

Another singular fact was noted by this same attendant, who regularly reported cases of sickness in the flock. In mid morning of a pleasant summer day he entered the barn through the doors which had been left open and found a solitary lamb three months of age lying on its side. The other sheep were in the pasture. He at once reported a sick lamb in the barn but when he returned, it had already joined the flock. This lamb, just before it was found lying in the barn, had been released from the laboratory at the end of its daily conditioning test. It was the same castrate male lamb, mentioned in the previous chapter, which was being subjected to our twenty darkness signal stress routine in the absence of its mother. When it was observed lying alone in the barn, it had already begun to exhibit profound lethargy and almost complete inertness upon stimulation during the experimental hour. Shortly after entering the laboratory room it lay down with head pressed to the floor. At the dimming of the lights for ten seconds it, typically, gave no observable response and rolled but slightly to the side at the shock which followed. Moreover, this was the twin lamb which, as already related, had recently given up following his mother and twin brother as she was led to the laboratory with the normal brother following. It will be remembered, also, that this was the same lamb that died at ten months while its "protected" twin attained healthy maturity. This lethargy and solitariness in a lamb so young when on its own outside the laboratory was certainly a singular fact.

Reviewing the three decades of our uninterrupted observations on conditioning and experimental neurosis in sheep and goat has brought to light a number of disturbing considerations. Perhaps the most serious handicap to the progress of our work in years gone by was a *quantitative delusion*. We were too often preoccupied with the measurement of stimuli to the neglect of the *meaning of these stimuli* for the individual animal.

If a motor nerve is stimulated electrically, its muscle contracts and the strength of the stimulus in relation to the magnitude of the contraction is precisely measurable. It will be remembered that this was not so in Robert's case. An electric current barely perceptible to us elicited a vigorous withdrawal of his foreleg. This brief and feeble electric current meant danger and, because of his previous experiences, so did the metronome clicking once a second and the sounding of the door buzzer. Fast and slow metronome rates, bell and buzzer could be called conditioned stimuli, thus suggesting the primary importance of measuring them as exactly as possible. Their significance for Robert, however, was that they were questions to which he knew the answers. When one of these signals was given, he knew what to expect and acted accordingly.

Although we do not underestimate the importance of careful graphic recording and measuring of conditioned responses, our often overly elaborate instrumentation caused us to lose sight of our animal in a thicket of levers, cables, wires, recording pens and reams of kymograph paper. We have kept as a souvenir of those days a kymograph record of a goat's conditioned reflexes. During an interval between signals the respiratory tracing shows a puzzling series of violent and rapid excursions of the recording pen. The goat was only scratching his ribs with his horn.

Another handicap to the progress of our work has been that the investigator was inclined to become laboratory-centered both in his observing and thinking. In that cloistered atmosphere with his familiar tools at hand he saw his animal subjects come and go. When they left the laboratory at the end of a session with their behavior therein duly recorded, the temptation was great to adopt the attitude of "out of sight, out of mind." The psychiatrist with a full schedule of appointments for his working hours can become similarly cloistered in his consulting room. It is a mental hazard shared, at least to some degree, by behaviorist and psychiatrist.

Now this laboratory-centered habit of thinking has perhaps in the past led us unwittingly to misrepresent the nature of the experimental neurosis. The impression was somehow conveyed to psychiatrists that the experimental neurosis in animals was a laboratory artifact or trick. Quite "artificial" behavior was produced; somewhat like teaching a horse to count. Hence, it was believed that neurotic behavior in animals could have little or no relevance for everyday emotional problems or psychoneurotic disturbances.

This misapprehension of the nature of experimental neurosis has resulted from confusing two questions. First, what are the symptoms of the animal's lack of emotional control? Then, what specific procedures were employed in the laboratory to precipitate this chronic emotional disability? It was reasoned that since the specific symptoms originated from stresses imposed upon the animal during its laboratory tests, that these symptoms must be found in the situation of their origin, namely, the laboratory. Therefore, bringing the animal to the laboratory, or seeing its trainer outside the laboratory, or anything specifically reminding it of its experiences in the laboratory will elicit the appropriate symptoms of alarm. Otherwise its behavior will be normal.

This is wrong. Our neurotic animals' chronic emotional disturbance is self-perpetuating. It lives a life of its own and reveals itself in whatever situation the animal finds itself: pasture, barn, laboratory, or lecture hall. In any of these situations the seemingly normal sheep or goat will exhibit, upon occasion, easily overlooked eccentricities of behavior indicating that all is not well in its emotional world.

For example, the animal with most experience in conditioning at the Behavior Farm Laboratory is the goat, "Brown Billy," now in his ninth year. His responses are so precise and dependable that we have used him for several years to demonstrate conditioned reflexes to psychiatrists and psychologists. His deportment in lecture hall, laboratory, or barnyard is at all times dignified and venerable. Quite by accident, however, we discovered that he was a very worried animal. A new electric fence had been installed in the barnyard. One of my colleagues glancing out of the laboratory window saw Brown Billy approach the unfamiliar strand of wire. He hesitantly touched the wire with his muzzle and instantly wheeled and dashed away. But then he suddenly stopped, wheeled to face the wire and precisely flexed his *right* foreleg.

This peculiar and, indeed, unrealistic reaction to a situation of danger would puzzle a casual observer. What purpose was served in facing the electrified wire and so precisely flexing his foreleg after the shock on the muzzle had already been experienced?

No other peculiarities of behavior had been noted which would set him apart from the other goats in our flock. As previously mentioned, when a person behaves in what seems to us a peculiar manner, his conduct often becomes familiar and reasonable when we learn more of his past and particularly of certain significant emotional problems that he has faced. This is common sense psychology and makes life happier for all of us. Our knowledge of Brown Billy's previous emotional experiences in the laboratory enables us to understand his peculiar behavior in the barnyard.

He had been trained in the laboratory for several months according to the following schedule. For an hour each day, while confined by a restraining harness and with electrodes attached to the right foreleg, a buzzer was sounded for 10 seconds, followed immediately by a mild electric shock to this limb. Forty of these buzzer signals, spaced a minute apart, were given at each session.

If the goat kept his foreleg flexed until the buzzer stopped, he received no shock. After a few days he caught on and always flexed his foreleg at the buzzer and kept it flexed until the sound ceased. Although he had not received a shock for several weeks, his prompt and precise flexion at the sound of the buzzer continued without lapse. Now, in the barnyard, the novel experience of electric shock on the muzzle promptly released the inappropriate behavior of running from the fence, wheeling, and *then* making the avoidance response.

During the past two years further observations indicate that this goat has developed a definite and chronic emotional disorder (which is all that Pavlov meant by his unhappy term, experimental neurosis). As illustrated by his bizarre behavior toward the electric fence, the pattern of Brown Billy's emergency reaction to danger has become *highly simplified and stereotyped*. We no longer apply shocks to his foreleg no matter what he does during the test period, and although the buzzer signal has now been repeated more than 2,000 times, the goat still continues to maintain flexion of his right foreleg as long as the buzzer is sounding. He will not, or cannot, take a chance. He has become a perfectionist and always does just the right thing when menaced by the buzzer. However, his perfectionism now amounts to mental illness. All sudden stimuli such as turning on bright lights, starting a movie camera, tapping his side lightly with a wooden rod instantly evoke a brisk and maintained flexion. All alarms are now channelled through his right foreleg.

What keeps this simple and stereotyped response going when there is no longer anything in Brown Billy's real situation to be avoided? Is not this fundamentally the same question which the psychiatrist faces in combating his neurotic patient's phobias? There seems to be no reason why the operation of painful or "traumatic" memories may not be inferred in both cases.

In attempting to understand these chronic emotional incapacities in our neurotic sheep and goats *originating situations* must take precedence over *resulting symptoms*.

Because of man's incredibly complicated cognitive machinery, his neurotic symptoms may exhibit a bewildering diversity. Nevertheless, our emotionally disturbed animals under careful observation show many of the same or closely similar symptoms. The physician is in a much better position, however, to explore and analyze his psychoneurotic patient's symptomology than is the behaviorist in the case of his experimentally neurotic animal. When it comes to analyzing the *originating situations,* responsible for chronic loss of emotional control, the shoe is on the other foot. The behaviorist can *create and rigorously control* the situations in which experimental neuroses originate. Moreover, these laboratory situations can be *exactly recreated* by other investigators.

For the sheep or goat its laboratory room becomes, through daily association, just a corner of the pasture. This familiar room is then a small part of the animal's total living space. The scheduled test hour, likewise, can become just as specific and familiar a portion of its daily round of activities as milking time is for the cow. When time and place for conditioning thus become an accepted part of the sheep or goat's daily experience, there is no reason for regarding the atmosphere of the laboratory as in any sense artificial. The experimental animal's behavior therein is just as "natural" as its behavior whilst loitering in the barnyard or grazing in pasture.

The essential difference, however, between its loitering in the barnyard and its deportment during the conditioning tests is this. As the animal enters the laboratory room and takes its station in the restraining harness, its habitual self-imposed restraint forces it to submit to the "rules and regulations" of the testing hour. These rules and regulations consist in the conditioning procedures which the experimenter elects to employ. The animal does not rebel against these familiar rules and regulations because, through training, it has relinquished its freedom of action and, for the hour, becomes a passive agent responding to the experimenter's signals as best it can.

Lenin was enthusiastic about Pavlov's work—so much so that he caused continued support of Pavlov's laboratories to be written into Soviet law. There is reason to believe that his enthusiasm was based upon practical considerations. Animal conditioning offered him a key to social control. It pointed the way to achieving passive acceptance of social, economic and political "rules and regulations" by the masses. Later on, we shall pursue some leads from investigations of animal behavior indicating possible ways in which such attitudes of fatalism and passive acceptance may be combated.

For the present, however, let us follow the course of a typical experimental neurosis in the sheep from the place and circumstances of its origin. In this way we shall discover how the onset of such an emotional crisis and its perseveration will distort the animal's subsequent pattern of living and will disable it in its attempts to master successfully the critical situations it may later encounter.

In our laboratory seven doors lead from the barnyard into adjoining experimental rooms, each ten feet square. For the experiment now to be described two of these rooms A and B, were provided with identical equipment for conditioning. A sheep six months old was brought daily to room A for simple conditioning to the sound of the door buzzer always followed by shock to the foreleg. With a schedule of ten buzzer signals per day irregularly spaced over the test hour, training was continued to include one hundred repetitions of the buzzer each followed by the usual brief, mild shock. As in Robert's case, this sheep's response to the sound of the buzzer shortly assumed the usual pattern of precise and unhurried flexions of the foreleg.

It has often happened in the course of our work that an attempt to demonstrate to students what we think we know about the animal's behavior has resulted in the animal teaching us. That is what transpired in the present case. The sheep under discussion had been briefly conditioned to the buzzer in preparation for a demonstration to students of what happens during the extinction of a conditioned reflex.

On the day of the demonstration our sheep was led into the unfamiliar room B, next door to A, where her preparatory training had taken place. The demonstration then proceeded as follows. The buzzer was sounded and the sheep gave her usual precise response followed by brisk withdrawal of the foreleg at the shock. After a minute the buzzer again elicited the conditioned response terminated as always by shock. Now after a pause of three minutes we were prepared to demonstrate the extinction of a conditioned reflex. The sheep meanwhile was not distracted by the students' presence since they were viewing her through a window.

Since the sounds of door bell and door buzzer are somewhat similar, experience had shown us that the sheep would doubtless respond to the bell as she did to the familiar buzzer, thus demonstrating the phenomenon of generalization of the conditioned reflex. So, in order to bring about extinction, we chose to sound the door bell for ten seconds every minute. When the sheep no longer flexed her leg at the bell, extinction would be complete. However, our demonstration proved a signal failure.

At the first sound of the bell our ewe, as we had predicted, gave the same precise conditioned response as she had to the buzzer just three minutes before. Now, as the bell continued, for 10 seconds every minute, the repeated flexions of her foreleg at this sound gradually diminished in number and amplitude with increasing sluggishness of response. So far so good. But beginning with the twentieth repetition of the door bell the frequency and vigor of these movements began increasing and by the thirtieth bell the sheep was visibly disturbed. Meanwhile, numerous small tic-like movements of her foreleg were noted during the pauses between signals. These characteristic nervous movements, as we knew from previous experience, clearly indicated that an experimental neurosis had been precipitated.

On the next day the sheep was brought again to room B and the previous schedule repeated. Her agitation was now intense, with frequent and vigorous flexion of the foreleg not only in response both to bell and buzzer but every few seconds during the pauses between signals. Our sheep was now manifesting the signs of a full-blown experimental neurosis of the agitated type. These signs included constant head and ear movements, frequent shifts of posture, sudden starts as if in response to a loud noise, frequent and seemingly involuntary movements of the trained foreleg (as just mentioned), labored breathing, rapid irregular pulse, together with frequent micturition and defecation. This agitated type of experimental neurosis is common in sheep subjected to the stress of conditioning and its signs were quite familiar to us. Moreover, in such cases the onset of the animal's uncontrolled agitation occurs with dramatic suddenness.

Our demonstration which was intended to illustrate the phenomenon of extinction but turned into a demonstration of the onset of experimental neurosis had an important outcome, largely the result of accident. It had usually been our practice to continue the conditioning of a sheep or goat in the same laboratory room from start to finish. In the present instance, however, we were fortunate in having carried through the brief preliminary conditioning of our demonstration sheep in room A while its emotional breakdown occurred soon thereafter in room B next door. What would happen if this very recently neurotic sheep were returned to room A where all had gone well?

To answer this question the following experiment was performed. With her manifest neurosis but two days old, our demonstration sheep was brought to room B, placed in the restraining harness with recording apparatus adjusted as before, but no signals or shocks were given. Her extreme agitation continued for fifteen minutes. She was then released, led into the barnyard and then at once into room A. Once more with recording apparatus adjusted, she was allowed to stand in the restraining harness without signals or shocks for another fifteen minute period. During this time her behavior was normal in every observable respect. Her pose was quiet but alert, with little or no head movement, breathing was slow and regular, and there was no fidgeting with the trained foreleg or other manifestations of nervousness. *At this stage her neurotic symp-*

toms were strictly limited to the situation of their origin in room B. In room A she resumed her status of normal sheep.

Now on each day she was allowed to stand for fifteen minutes in the restraining harness without signals or shocks, first in one room then the other. Whether she was taken first into room A or room B was left to chance. *But within three days of the beginning of this routine without signals or shocks she was as agitated in room A as in room B.* Room A was no longer a safe place. Her neurotic symptoms had now broken free from their place of origin in room B.

Our animals, in which loss of emotional control is chronic, will exhibit the characteristic signs of their experimental neurosis in any laboratory room in the building. We had never before caught the neurosis at its place of origin and timed its spread to embrace the rest of the animal's daily environment.

To trace the life course of the neurotic process further, let us imagine a *composite sheep* whose eccentricities and symptoms include all the neurotic sheep we have known.

If our composite sheep is with the flock clustered closely together in the barnyard, he will give himself away if we casually stroll toward the flock. As we approach, the flock will shortly take alarm and dash away. The neurotic sheep, on the other hand, will run in the opposite direction all by himself. When dogs get into the pasture, it is always this composite sheep which we later find dead from its injuries.

Furthermore, the neurotic sheep gives evidence of continuing in a state of anxious apprehension both by night and by day. Since sheep do not sleep as soundly as dogs, pigs, or men, it would be inappropriate to speak of the neurotic sheep as a sufferer from insomnia. If the sheep's movements are registered from a recording platform in the barnyard, the normal animal will be found to be resting quietly at night. Our composite sheep, on the other hand, is "walking the floor" all night long and continues his restless pacing during the day as well.

Another evidence of the neurotic animal's continuing alarm during the night appears if we examine its heart rate without its knowledge. This is most simply accomplished by means of a long distance stethoscope—a long thick-walled rubber tube leading from the animal's chest to a listening post outside of the barn where the flock is resting. In contrast to the normal sheep's slow, steady heart beat during the night, the disturbed animal's heart rate is rapid and variable responding by sudden acceleration to slight sounds which have no effect on the steady heart rate of the normal sheep.

As old age approaches, our composite sheep's neurosis does not abate. He is a long-life neurotic. Vacations at pasture for as long as three years bring only temporary improvement. When he returns to the laboratory and resumes his conditioning routine, the neurotic manifestations exhibited there are soon as prominent as before. Moreover, change of scene is of no benefit. He brings his neurosis with him to a new farm and a new laboratory.

Among the disturbing considerations which a review of our previous work has brought to light the most disturbing has been saved until the last. *How do we know when a sheep or goat has become experimentally neurotic?*

Our composite sheep, whose life-long neurotic disabilities we have been describing, is a synthetic product of those animals in which the experimental neurosis appeared with dramatic suddenness as uncontrollable agitation in the familiar laboratory environment. However, such clear-cut cases of severe experimental neurosis only point the way to a much more difficult field of investigation.

During the past ten years we have become convinced that all conditioning procedures which are based upon the animal's self-imposed restraint will, if long enough continued, cause that animal to become experimentally neurotic. When does the neurosis begin and by what signs may we first detect it?

Our sheep, Robert, and our goat, Brown Billy, were long considered to be highly skilled in their conditioned behavior and completely normal animals. It was only by accident that we became aware of Robert's sexual disturbance and it was by chance, also, that Brown Billy's eccentric behavior at his first contact with the new electric fence was noted.

6. Animal Behavior and Mental Illness

C. B. FERSTER

Psychological Record, 1966, *16*, 345-56. Copyright 1966 by The Psychological Record.
Reprinted by permission.

This article presents a functional analysis of clinical depression by describing the kinds of variables which may increase or decrease the frequency of an arbitrary response in animal experiments. The animal results were extended to the clinical phenomenon by noting how these same variables might operate in the natural environment. Since depression is a phenomenon of the individual's total repertoire, animal experiments are described which extend the experimental analysis of behavior from the study of simple arbitrary response in a single animal to more complex behavior in social environments.

People who experiment with animal behavior for the purpose of finding physiological bases of behavior, or new tranquilizers, frequently ask whether we can produce psychosis in animals. The answer to such a question is that animals usually do not have enough behavior to be psychotic. We identify psychosis by noting a discrepancy between the psychotic person's repertoire and the repertoire which is required by his environment. An animal could be psychotic if his repertoire and its controlling environment approached the size and complexity of man's. To find out how to use animal laboratory paradigms the first step is to define the component processes of a complex repertoire so that they can be synthesized in animal experiments.

We define clinical depression, for example, as an emotional state with retardation of psychomotor and thought process, a depressive emotional reaction, feelings of guilt, self criticism, and delusions of unworthiness. All of these qualities refer to a change in complex performances with which the individual customarily interacts with his environment. While such a definition allows us to identify a depressed person and even characterize details of his repertoire, we need to state the actual behaviors in more detail to use the experimental analysis of behavior from the animal laboratory. One of the main contributions of the animal laboratory has been an objective and technical language with which the phenomena of mental illness can be described. First, we must describe a depressed person from the point of view of an experimental analysis of his repertoire and its controlling environment.

Looking broadly at the total repertoire of the depressed person we see as our major datum a reduced frequency of many behaviors in which the person normally engages (Skinner, 1953). He sits silently for long periods, even staying in bed all day. While he may answer questions, ask for something, or even sometimes speak freely, the overall frequency of speaking is very low. Certain kinds of verbal behavior may seldom occur, like telling an amusing story, or writing a report or letter. Complaints or requests for help may be the bulk of verbal repertoire. Frequently, most of the missing performances are potentially in his repertoire. He has, in the past, dressed properly, traveled to work, completed his job, even written successful books. The essential fact is that the frequency of these performances is now depressed and their failure to occur now is causing trouble for him as well as for various other persons, such as his spouse or employer, whose behavior, in turn, depends on his behavior.

Bizarre or primitive behavior, sometimes called psychotic symptoms, may be a prominent part of a psychosis, largely because they are annoying and disruptive to those around the psychotic person. The individual may repeatedly engage in simple repetitive acts which interfere with or annoy others, and which have no functional relation to the accepted environment. He may talk excessively without regard for a listener, he may become incoherent, or he may repeat hand gestures over and over. Similar psychotic symptoms are common with schizophrenic or autistic children (Ferster, 1961). The autistic child engages in simple repetitive acts and rituals because there are no other significant behaviors in his repertoire. Whenever the child learns to deal successfully with the normal environment we find that the new repertoire pre-empts primitive behaviors.

Such bizarre behavior actually occurs with the average person, particularly when most of his repertoire cannot occur, as, for example, at a compulsory conference. Even though the conference speaker does not engage him, the listener must still remain, and appear to be, under the control of the speaker. We see one person repetitively rubbing a spot on the table: a second doodles. A third person may repeatedly scratch his back, touch his forehead and stretch, and so on. The doodler in the conference room is in parallel position to the psychotic because the bizarre behaviors are for the most part determined by the lack of any other stronger performances. While these bizarre or annoying behaviors may have a very high frequency, they should not distract us from the more important fact that they are occurring in the place of those performances which define a normal interaction with the environment.

If the major feature of clinical depression is a reduced frequency of behavior under normal control by the environment, to apply a laboratory analysis of behavior we need first to determine how the basic behavioral processes might increase or decrease the frequency of behavior. The standard operant laboratory paradigm emphasizes frequency of behavior by the use of a simple arbitrary response easily repeatable, easily recorded, and of the same form each time. An arbitrary performance, such as the pigeon's peck, has been an important device for finding many variables, of phylogenetic generality, which influence the frequency of behavior. Now we may turn to several general behavioral processes which may influence the frequency of occurrence of a performance.

The first important variable is how much behavior is required before the individual alters his environment: the schedule of reinforcement of a performance (Ferster and Skinner, 1957; Skinner, 1938). In general, when the environment requires a large amount of behavior to produce a significant change in it the frequency of a performance may be drastically reduced. After studying for an examination, for example, the student will usually pause for a period before resuming work. We are much more likely to take short rather than long walks; the salesman whose ratio of selling behavior to sales get too large soon stops trying. An animal, such as a pigeon, with a simple, easily repeatable arbitrary response is the ideal place to study the properties of intermittent reinforcement. We discover that reinforcement which requires large amounts of behavior leads to long pauses after reinforcement so that the animal might starve to death even though the physical exertion of the behavior could not itself produce fatigue. The pigeon's peck is taken as an arbitrary item in his repertoire and the same result is obtained, although not so conveniently, with other species, and with other performances in the same pigeon's repertoire. The result would be the same, for example, if the pigeon operated a pedal with its foot or pulled a chain with its beak. The component performances of writing a novel may be very complex, but the performance bears the same relationship to its reinforcement, completing the novel, as the pigeon's pecking bears to the delivery of food. For the pigeon there is a long pause after reinforcement, during which the animal engages in other activities. The novelist gathers materials, rests, sharpens pencils, travels, and waits for an idea. Lindsley (1963) observed the relationship between pause of the reinforcement and psychotic behavior in experiments with chronic schizophrenics who were reinforced every so many times they pulled a key. The bizarre behavior occurred only during the pause after reinforcement, not when they were operating the devices.

A second way to reduce the frequency of performances is by aversive stimuli, particularly the conditioned aversive stimuli preceding the aversive event. The control by the dentist's office on the waiting patients is an example. The waiting room, a set of stimuli preceding a highly aversive event, reduces the frequency of many performances. People flip pages, scarcely reading them, conversation is muted; some sit and stare. Frequently aversive control of an individual's behavior becomes internalized when his very own behavior becomes aversive as it precedes punishment or aversive stimuli. Any disposition to engage in such behavior may lead to anxiety, a general state of the organism whose most obvious effect is to reduce the frequency of and disrupt, the ongoing operant repertoire. The experimental paradigm for studying these general effects of aversive control on an animal is a sustained and predictable rate of a performance, reinforced with food (Skinner, 1938). The pigeon's peck, for example, is taken to be a representative item of its operant repertoire, analogous to say, reading in the dentist's waiting room. A buzzer followed some minutes later by an aversive event like an electric shock disrupts the bird's ongoing performance, much as the dentist's waiting room disrupts the ongoing behavior of the patient. We limit the bird's performance to a simply measured, easily repeatable response for experimental purposes, presuming that the buzzer would disrupt any other item in the bird's repertoire. To evaluate how drugs could reduce the disruption of the ongoing behavior by the aversive stimuli, we have to focus on the frequency of the ongoing performance. For example, the disruption of a performance may be more a result of its general weakness and susceptibility to disruption, than the aversive stimulus.

The third way in which behavior may be radically weakened is by a sudden change in the environment, such as the death of a close companion. Under certain conditions such a sudden change may virtually denude an individual of his repertoire. The secluded elderly spinster lady, for example, may lose her entire repertoire on the death of her close companion because each person's behavior was narrowly under the control of the other. The close interpersonal control in the case of the secluded ladies is an extreme case, but the same process may operate in a wide range of circumstances and in varying degrees. The weakening of behavior when it comes under the control of the environment is a common experience in the animal laboratory whenever we bring a pigeon's behavior differentially under the control of colors. The bird who pecks at the key when it is colored green, but not when it is red, does so because its behavior in response to the red has been weakened by nonreinforcement. It then becomes possible to separate the bird from its repertoire simply by changing the color of the key from green to red, just as the secluded spinster lost her behavior when her companion was no longer with her. In general, changes in important stimuli are a profound way to weaken behavior. The loss and reinstatement of behavior when its controlling stimulus has been suddenly removed is a technical problem, the solution to which is at least in part found in these simple animal experiments.

Adolescence represents a sudden change in the environment of a different sort. During the rapid physical and biological growth and development of adolescence we require an ever increasing complex repertoire from the youngster who in the past achieved his important effects on the environment simply and easily. The youngster now has to work for money; his social interactions require new complex skills and large amounts of behavior; the educational institutions demand larger and more sustained performances with delayed reinforcement, and sexual maturity requires an elaborate operant repertoire before any behavior may be reinforced. When the transition is successful it represents a wonderfully subtle example of successive approximation of a complex repertoire. Each increment in the child's repertoire prepares him for the next until the complex repertoire necessary to deal with the adult environment is achieved.

When the process is unsuccessful, however, the community requires behaviour more appropriate to the youngster's physical development than to his behavioral development. Slack (1960), for example, has discovered juvenile delinquents who steal in a department store, with money in their pocket, simply because they cannot sustain the longer behavior sequences needed to get a clerk to ring up the purchase. Many accidents in the environment may temporarily stop the behavioral development of a youngster so that he loses contact with the reinforcement contingencies that the community is likely to provide. Accidents parallel to those of the adolescent can be constructed in animal experiments, for example in the transition from one schedule of reinforcement to the next. If a pigeon who has been reinforced every time it pecks is suddenly reinforced only after every 150 responses, the bird would soon stop pecking altogether and even starve to death. The same bird could sustain its performance, even at larger requirements, if the number of responses required is increased a step at a time, paced with the bird's performance at smaller requirements. Many of the technical properties of schedules of reinforcement give information about how behavior can be maintained or weakened during transitional states.

The proportion of an individual's behavior maintained by negative rather than positive reinforcement will influence his susceptibility to disruption by a change in the environment. Consider, for example, a man whose behavior is disproportionately maintained by escape and avoidance rather than positive reinforcement. His job is motivated by reducing the displeasure of his employer. He empties trash at home to terminate his wife's nagging and he works for money to prevent a calamity in his old age. Sudden removal of all of the threats may expose the meagerness of his repertoire. If placed in a free work environment, like a research scientist or a free lance writer, this man might have such an impoverished repertoire in relation to positive reinforcement that he would be effectively denuded of behavior unless there was an effective transitional environment. The man who works to escape his employer's displeasure appears, at least topographically, similar to the man who works because the job accomplishment is rewarding. Yet the performances are functionally different because the reinforcers maintaining the behavior are different.

Punishment is another way to weaken behavior seriously, particularly if the punishment is by criticism, anger, fines, incarceration, or withdrawal of privileges or favors (Skinner, 1953). The common feature of all of these practices is that they are occasions on which large segments of the individual's repertoire go unreinforced. While it is not unusual for an occasional performance to go without reinforcement, the overall level of an individual's behavior may be seriously reduced if extinction occurs in enough parts of the total repertoire. To study the withdrawal of reinforcement as an aversive stimulus, functionally analogous to incarceration, fines, or anger, we first bring the animal's behavior under the control of some stimulus, such as a token, as an occasion on which an animal may be reinforced in several areas of deprivation. We may then carry out operations functionally parallel to aversive control with electric shock by simply changing the color of the light, or requiring the animal to deposit a token before the experiment can continue.

Just as the adolescent may fail to develop new behavior during the period of his physical growth, the aging person may lose behavior because physical changes no longer make it possible for him to act on the physical and social environment as he has in the past. The athlete is the extreme case of someone suddenly unable to engage in one of the most important performances in his repertoire. He must develop new repertoires, within the limits of his physical capacity, under the control of a new environment. Although aging does not produce such dramatic changes in the average person as it does in the athlete, the later years are times when new performances under the control of new reinforcers must emerge. Decreased physical activity reduces the amount of food necessary. The level of sustained activity on the job has to be reduced, especially strenuous exertion. Disease may limit the range of performance that it is possible to maintain; retirement itself may impose an even more drastic change in the older person's environment than the physical changes resulting from age itself. To continue the person's interaction with the environment during retirement a new repertoire needs to be successively approximated. The transition depends on whether the retired person has non-professional behaviors which are effective in producing reinforcers in the retirement environment.

We sometimes see a lack of behavior simply because the relevant performances have never been established in the repertoire. In this case we are more likely to speak of an educational deficit than of depression. Such a person may superficially look like a depressed person in many ways, but the repertoires have very different functional significance. In the one case we try to reinstate a previously intact repertoire; in the other case an environment is required which will make contact with the existing behavior and successively approximate the missing performances.

The preceding analysis of depression emphasizes a loss of behavior as the common denominator of depressed persons. Any of the behavioral processes discussed are means for increasing or decreasing the amount of behavior a person will emit. No one of the processes, alone, is likely to be responsible for a change in a total repertoire (Ferster, 1966). The frequency of the performances in the depressed person's repertoire is simultaneously a function of many variables. Every process studied in the animal laboratory using the frequency of a simple arbitrary response tells something new about how the environment may influence the frequency of occurrence of a performance. In any given case one process such as intermittent reinforcement may be prominent; in another case extinction may be the prominent feature. Nor are we likely to find a single cause of depression in the sense of a tumor which can be excised, a defective brain center which can be revitalized, or a psychic mechanism which can be released, even though each of these may be a potential agent for weakening behavior. Given an intact organism, the frequency of the operant repertoire is determined by its interaction with the environment. General states of the organism such as systemic effects of hormones and steroids are parameters of the behavioral process. We have the behavior of the organism reinforced, shaped, and determined by its interaction with the environment, and modified by the parameters of the physiological substate.

Discussion of thought processes and descriptions of mood, have been omitted not because these are not significant data or the proper concern of the experimental analysis of behavior—they are. There is a priority, however, for the general variables which determine the overall availability of behavior. The processes governing the frequency of response are phylogenetically general, linking man to the rest of the vertebrates.

The analysis of complex behavior using data from a simple arbitrary operant in the animal laboratory assumes that the frequency of the pigeon's peck may be taken as representative of each of the components of the complex repertoire. We assume also that any other performance in the pigeon's repertoire could have been substituted for its peck with the same result. We would guess that the disruptive effect of the buzzer which warns of impending shock would be the same were the pigeon pressing a foot pedal instead of pecking a key. Although we know many of the behavioral processes which determine the frequency of occurrence of a simple arbitrary response, it might be fairly said that depression is a phenomenon of the total repertoire and that the whole might have properties beyond the parts. In a natural-science enterprise the answer to such a question is an experimental paradigm in which an animal is engaged in a wide range of behaviors, each under the control of the experimental environment through a range of behavioral processes. With such an experimental arrangement many items of performance in a total repertoire could be measured in the context of a complex, but experimentally synthesized, environment.

Fig. 1. Overall view of the experimental space showing one chimpanzee in the work chamber while the other is exercising in the social-play area.

Over the past five years, my colleagues John Randolph, Clifford Hammer and I have been experimenting with environments which support several behavioral processes in the same animal and in which the animals live and work continuously (Ferster, 1964; Ferster and Hammer, 1966) in semi-natural conditions. Figure 1 illustrates the basic plan of the environment. In this particular experiment, designed for the long-term development and analysis of arithmetic behavior, two chimpanzees lived together continuously in the large space during a 5-year period. In order to eat, however, the animals needed to enter the small chambers where they worked for food. They went through the three chambers in turn, returning finally to the social area. The performances in the small work chamber were controlled as in any operant experiment but in the social area the chimps could interact freely, as might be expected from animals in the natural environment with few imposed requirements. Figure 2 shows the geometry

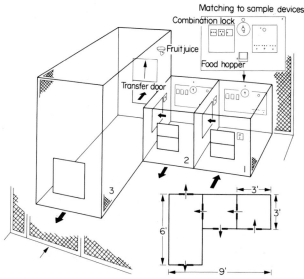

Fig. 2. Diagram of the experimental space, showing the combination locks, the intelligence panels and the directions of travel.

of the space. The combination lock and other simple relay devices allow us to program and record automatically and separately for each individual animal even though they lived together. We have used similar experimental spaces with baboons, but only the chimp experiments need to be described for the present.

The experimental environment supported a wide range of behaviors under the control of a wide range of behavioral processes.

1. First, the animals went through at least three experiments, one following the other. In the first chamber he chose a binary number that corresponded with a number of geometrical forms. In the second chamber he wrote the binary number by adjusting the pattern of three lights to correspond with the number of geometric forms, and finally the chimp "counted" by writing the binary stimuli in order, each from the preceding number. These performances were more complex than the simple arbitrary operant with which we emphasized the frequency of a response. Each response unit now was a complex performance which has two dimensions: the form of the behavior could vary, as for example, if the chimp chose a binary number "three" when there were four

triangles in the window. The frequency of occurrence can still vary continuously over a wide range so the animal's disposition to engage in the behavior can be measured.

2. During much of the experiment the chimps had to repeat each complex performance unit a certain number of times just as with schedules of intermittent reinforcement with pigeons. For example, a buzz indicated that a correct binary number had been selected but only after, say, 30 successively correct performances was food delivered. In one experiment food was delivered only after the animal had gone through three experiments in order, each consisting of many repeated instances of the performance. Thus the total repertoire was a complex sequence some 20-30 minutes long, during which the chimp carried out each of three arithmetic behaviors some three or four hundred times.

3. The movement of the animal from one compartment to the other was an orderly sequence of behavior of some complexity and delicacy, occurring daily, perhaps analogous to a man's daily routine. An animal first operated the door and combination lock system noting which lights were on and which behaviors were appropriate to them. These performances are not considered a part of the experiment any more than we pay attention to a man's dressing and performing his toilet. Yet both, as acquired repertoires, may break down in extreme circumstances. Second, there is the general activity of each animal in the large area, playing with swings, climbing, sleeping, self grooming, manipulating or chewing small objects.

Even though all of the food each animal receives comes from the experimental chambers the chimps' performances were stably and durably maintained without starving the animal as in the usual pigeon experiment. The laboratory environment, artificially created, supports a wide range of behaviors under the control of many reinforcers and behavioral processes. Both animals, by working a modest day, perhaps 4 to 6 hours and 3-5,000 responses, maintained essentially free feeding body weights and a routine sleep-wake cycle. When the two animals are in the large social area together they, of course, control much of each other's behavior. They groom each other, chase each other around the cage. One chimp beats, bites and otherwise abuses the other who in turn cowers, cringes, runs away, or placates the first. Given the opportunity they will steal each other's food. Each part of the cage is under constant examination for weak parts or susceptibility to banging or movement.

Although the goal in these experiments was to build and then analyze a complex cognitive repertoire, we occasionally made errors, as any parent might, which weakened the overall repertoire of an animal seriously. One such incident occurred about six months after the start of the experiment when we were forced to replace the female of the pair because we thought she was organically defective. When we substituted another female the result was a profound disruption of the male's behavior. He and new female spent their time together at opposite sides of the cages except when he bit her, pummelled her with fists, kicked her, or pushed her. He entered the work chambers fewer times than before and worked for shorter times whenever he did enter. For several weeks his food intake was less than 80 per cent of normal. The quality of his work, when it occurred, was not impaired. We could have described Dennis as angry and depressed, and we would not have been too far off the mark, but the experimental measurements, even short of a controlled experiment, went further than these conversational accounts. We described changes in the frequency of items in his repertoire from which one would usually infer depression. This incident was not planned to study depression, yet it comes close to an experimental paradigm for that purpose. This accidental result illustrates how critical it is to have operant behavior under the control of the experimental environment if we are to devise animal paradigms which have relevance to complex human behavior. Single animal experiments will tell us much of the component processes which influence the frequency of occurrence of a performance. To study broad effects, such as those of emotion and anxiety, we need an experimental paradigm closer to the natural environment. One possible direction is observation of animals in their natural environments. These are obvious advantages to an experimentally synthesized repertoire, however, and our present theoretical and technical skill make it possible to build behavior in the laboratory of far greater subtlety and complexity than is formed in the animal's natural state.

The use of drugs to ameliorate mental illness illustrates the importance of a functional analysis of operant behavior. The absence of a performance from a repertoire is not sufficient information to determine the potential usefulness of a drug. We can no more expect a drug to produce pecking behavior in a pigeon who has not been trained to peck a key than we can expect it to produce the ability to write a novel. Both the behavior of the novelist and the pigeon come from an educational interaction with the environment. While we might expect a drug to break down the narrow control of a person's behavior by its controlling stimuli as, for example, in the case of the recluse mentioned above, we would not expect it to reinstate behavior the recluse had never engaged in before.

Drugs do not create behavior; they only influence the existing repertoire of the organism. The effects of drugs on behavior suggest a situation much as with the effects of a drug on cell or organ physiology. A drug can make a cell do more or make it do less but it cannot make the cell do what it does not do anyway. A kidney will excrete more and less urine under the influence of drugs, but it is unlikely that a drug will make the kidney produce thyroxin. A drug is not likely to alter depression *per se* although it can alter the frequency of a response under the control of some behavioral process.

Animal experiments allow us to identify the component processes responsible for complex behavior. By studying the frequency of occurrence of an arbitrary response we have discovered many variables, of considerable generality, which influence the animal's disposition to engage in the behavior. Once we have identified these component processes it becomes possible to make a functional analysis of the complex case to determine what kinds of experiences can reduce the frequency of a performance in the complex natural environment. Animal experiments do not tell us why a man acts but they do tell us where to look for the factors of which his behavior is a function. The use of frequency as a dependent variable emphasizes the functional relation between the individual's performance and its past relation to the environment rather than its topographic or immediate appearance.

REFERENCES

Ferster, C. B. In Press. An operant reinforcement analysis of infantile autism. *Amer. J. Psychother.*

Ferster, C. B. 1964. Arithmetic behavior in chimpanzees. *Scientific American,* 210, 98-106.

Ferster, C. B. 1961. Positive reinforcement and behavioral deficits in autistic children. *Child Development,* 32 (3), 437-456.

Ferster, C. B. and Hammer, C. 1966. The synthesis of arithmetic behavior in chimpanzees. In W. K. Honig (Ed.). *Operant behavior: areas of research and application.* New York: Appleton-Century-Crofts.

Ferster, C. B. and Skinner, B. F. 1957. *Schedules of reinforcement.* New York: Appleton-Century-Crofts.

Lindsley, O. R. 1963. Direct measurement and functional definition of vocal hallucinatory symptoms. *J. nerv. ment. Dis.,* 136, 293-297.

Skinner, B. F. 1938. *The behavior of organisms.* New York: Appleton-Century-Crofts.

Skinner, B. F. 1953. *Science and human behavior.* New York: Macmillan.

Slack, C. W. 1960. Experimenter-subject psychotherapy: a new method of introducing intensive office treatment for unreachable cases. *Ment. Hyg.,* 44, 238-256.

7. Stereotyped Activities Produced by Amphetamine in Several Animal Species and Man*

A. RANDRUP and I. MUNKVAD

Psychopharmacologia, 1967, *11*, 300-10. Copyright 1967 by Springer-Verlag.
Reprinted by permission.

The word "stereotype," in the present and previous papers on amphetamine (Randrup and Munkvad, 1963, 1965, 1966; Munkvad and Randrup, 1966) is used to describe a form of behaviour with little variation. In extreme cases one single activity is performed continuously and dominates the animal's behaviour, e.g. sniffing at the cage wires. In less pronounced cases the animals repeat certain behavioural repertoires many times in a regular fashion as described in the examples below. (See also Lat and Gollova, 1964).

The term "stereotype" is also used by others as a description of abnormal behaviour after amphetamine (Lat, 1965; Hauschild, 1939; van Nueten, 1962; Lapin and Schelkunov, 1965; Quinton and Halliwell, 1963; Chance and Silverman, 1964), but this behaviour is also characterized as compulsive ("Zwangsnagen", Janssen *et al.,* 1965) or purposeless ("constant purposeless searching head movement", Emele *et al.,* 1964).

We prefer the term "stereotype" because it is exclusively descriptive. Stereotyped sniffing, licking, and biting activity produced in rats by moderate doses of amphetamine have previously been described in the publications cited above. In experiments with other species we have observed varying types of behaviour due to amphetamine; however, in every species a sufficient dose of the drug induced some kind of stereotyped hyperactivity. In the present paper the observed types of amphetamine-induced stereotyped behaviour in some species will be described and its possible relation to stereotyped behaviour observed in the psychiatric clinic will be tentatively discussed.

METHODS

The descriptions are based on a constant observation during 4 hrs or more of groups of 2 to 12 animals per experiment. Since the animals' behaviour was unchanged for long periods, it was possible to record the observations by hand-writing. The animals remained in their home cages, one or a few (up to three) individuals in each cage. D-amphetamine (Dexedrine®) was given subcutaneously. The doses were calculated as D-amphetamine sulphate.

RESULTS

Rats. A prominent feature of the behaviour after 5 mg/kg D-amphetamine s.c. is

* This investigation was supported by grants from Knud Hojgaards Fond and from the Copenhagen Hospital Administration. The authors want to thank Mrs. Reiko Okada and Mrs. Johanne Mengel for translation of Japanese and Italian literature.

continuous sniffing, licking or biting of the cage wire netting, the forepaws or very exceptionally, also its own body; these effects commence 20 to 30 min after the injection and last for 2 to 3 hrs. A detailed description has been given in earlier papers (Randrup and Munkvad, 1963, 1965, 1966; Munkvad and Randrup, 1966).

The normal activities, such as moving forwards and grooming, are clearly suppressed during the period of stereotyped activity, but are above normal in the first 15 to 20 min after the injection and again in the final phase 3 to 5 hrs later (Randrup and Munkvad, 1965a).

These behavioural effects of amphetamine are highly reproducible. In our observations on more than 200 rats given 5 mg/kg s.c. D-amphetamine, all displayed the described stereotyped activity.

All the above observations were made from acute experiments. In one chronic experiment we gave 7 rats amphetamine daily, except on Sundays, for 2 months. After every injection the behaviour became stereotyped, as described above, and the rats appeared normal the following day. Three of the rats, however, were kept together in one cage; sometimes they interrupted their stereotyped activity by fighting each other (attacks, spitting, defense postures, etc.). Fighting only appeared after one month's drug-treatment, and was never seen in acute experiments. Fighting between rats after repeated doses of amphetamine, but not after a single dose, has also been reported by Ehrich and Krumbhaar (1937).

Stereotyped sniffing, licking or biting was also produced by derivatives of amphetamine such as methamphetamine (Pervitin®, 10 mg/kg s.c.) and phenmetrazine (Preludin®, 50 mg/kg s.c.). The behaviour produced by these two drugs was in all respects very similar to that seen after amphetamine.

Mice. Young males 40 to 60 days old, weighing 28 to 38 g, (N.M.R.I. strain) were observed after doses of 7.5 or 10 mg/kg D-amphetamine s.c. Their behaviour was similar to that of the rats given 5 mg. Locomotion was, however, not as completely suppressed in the middle phase as with the rats. Some of the mice climbed the wire netting of the cage walls and performed their stereotyped sniffing, licking or biting while sitting on the upper part of the wall. As with the rats there were initial and final phases with increased locomotion on the floor of the cage, some mice running very fast, and grooming. During the end of the initial phase a characteristic simplified form of grooming appeared very frequently; the forelegs were used to wash only the snout.

Only two out of more than the 100 mice which were observed differed from this behavioural pattern. One of these showed no evidence of stereotyped behaviour. The other repeated a more complicated sequence of acts reminiscent of the behaviour of rats described by Lat (1965), see "Discussion": this mouse walked round the cage following a definite track and in addition performed grooming of snout, sniffing the air and standing up against the cage wall, each of these three acts was carried out at a definite place on its route round the cage.

When more than one mouse was placed in each cage we often observed fighting and other features of aggressive or defensive behaviour after amphetamine, in agreement with other reports in the literature (Lapin and Samsonova, 1964; Chance, 1948; Moore, 1963). This behaviour was seen mostly during the first ½ to 1 hour after the injection, but after the onset of stereotyped behaviour temporary fighting episodes ("mock fighting") also occurred. Fighting often led to exhaustion and subsequent death of the animals (see also Moore, Lapin and Samsonova, 1964); death also occurred, although very infrequently, among mice in individual cages.

Fig. 1. Guinea-pigs two hours after amphetamine (5 mg/kg s.c.).
One bites the edge of the bowl the other became immobile, "froze"
as the observer approached to take the picture.

Guinea-pigs. Observations were made on twenty-five young male guinea-pigs about 3 months old and weighing 400-500 g. after doses of 5 - 20 mg/kg amphetamine s.c. All the guinea-pigs showed stereotyped activity. Two of the animals showed continuously tossing, vertical movements of the head, and 23 bit continuously at the wire netting of the walls, the edge of their clay food bowls (see Fig. 1), straws, and the skin of other guinea-pigs. In four animals the biting was preceded or followed by continuous head movements.

Two guinea-pigs performed the stereotype activity only when the observer left the room to watch the animals through a window or the door. With the observer in the room, these animals remained completely immobile and "frozen".

With 5 mg amphetamine per kg (12 animals) the period of stereotypy started ½ to 1 hr after the injection and ended about 3 hrs later. After this the activity of the animals gradually became more varied and included locomotion and grooming, which were almost completely absent during the period of stereotypism. During the first ½ to 1 hrs after the injection locomotion and grooming were also seen in some animals while others "froze" immediately after the amphetamine injection and remained in this state until they started the stereotyped activity.

Cats. Eight cats (four male and four female) were treated with 13 mg/kg amphetamine i.p. They were all stray cats. The weights were 1.8 to 4.3 kg and ages unknown. All these cats performed head movements which became clearly stereotyped 20 min to 2 hrs after the injection (see Fig. 2) and lasted more than four hours. During this time the cats lay or sat in the cage with very little locomotion, although stereotyped movements of the body were seen in some instances. The head movements were mostly sidewards, the cats appeared to be looking round, and this stereotypy was preceded by a period in which only the eyes moved from side to side. Two cats vomited several times and died about two hours after amphetamine.

Hissing and spitting without interruption of the head movements were observed occasionally. They were very prominent in one cat during a period of one hour beginning 40 min after the injection: this cat was otherwise very tame and friendly, it had

Fig. 2. Cat 20 min after amphetamine 13 mg/kg s.c.

Fig. 3. Monkey No. 4. 75-90 min after amphetamine
(2.6 mg/kg) bending down and appearing to stare intensely.

been in the laboratory for two months and was well-known to the personnel.

Squirrel monkeys. We observed four squirrel monkeys treated with 1.7 mg/kg amphetamine i.m. All performed stereotyped activity for a prolonged period, but the form of stereotypy varied from individual to individual.

No. 1 (female, 410 g) opened and closed continuously all four paws while sitting at the edge of a shelf or on a branch.

No. 2 (female, 540 g) made continuous rapid body movements, mostly sidewards but also backwards and forwards. For a period these movements were interrupted by low bows (about 3 per minute) with ''staring'' resembling the movements described in monkey No. 4 below.

No. 3 (female, 670 g) performed rapid sidewards movements of the body and forelimbs at a rate of about 30 cycles per minute.

No. 4 (male 950 g) bent down deeply about 4 times a minute appearing to look or stare intensely (see Fig. 3). Rapid body movements were also seen part of the time.

During the first minutes after the injection of amphetamine the rate of head movements was increased, locomotion decreased and the animals crouched in a corner. The behaviour described above then appeared gradually. Monkey No. 2 appeared sedated during the first hour after the injection, being very quiet with closed eyes most of the time. The movements decribed became stereotyped ½ and 1½ hrs after the injection, and continued for 1½ to 3 hrs. During this period other activities such as locomotion, grooming and eating were almost completely absent. Except during the periods of "staring" of monkeys No. 2 and 4, the frequent head movements which these animals normally perform were retained, but increased in rate, from about 1 per sec to 1.5 to 2 per sec so that they became continuous and thus acquired a stereotyped character. Two to four hours after injection the locomotion and grooming began to reappear. Locomotion in monkeys No. 2 and 4 was stereotyped in the beginning, the animals repeatedly followed a definite route in the cage many times, about 6 hrs after the injection their locomotion became more irregular and extended. In monkey No. 3 the locomotion was irregular from the beginning.

The experiment was repeated four months later with a larger dose of amphetamine (2.6 mg/kg) on monkeys no. 3 and 4. Again each of the monkeys performed the same individual form of stereotypy as previously seen but for a longer period of time. No. 3 made a sound which resembled a combined barking and spitting: this was not heard from untreated animals, except when they were caught in order to receive an injection.

DISCUSSION

Other authors, working with similar doses of amphetamine, have described behaviour which resembles our own observations in rats (Hauschild, 1939; van Neuten, 1962; Lapin and Schelkunov, 1965; Schelkunov, 1964; Quinton and Halliwell, 1963). By courtesy of Drs. Quinton and Halliwell, England, and Drs. Lapin and Schelkunov, U.S.S.R., one of us has had the opportunity of watching amphetamine treated rats in their laboratories. In both places the behaviour of the rats was closely similar to that observed in our own laboratory. Other forms of stereotypy have been reported. Lat (1965) showed that rats under amphetamine in smaller doses when put in a new cage may follow a definite track in the cage and repeat this procedure many times; by contrast, untreated rats explored all parts of the cage, following a most irregular track. Lat also demonstrated a stereotyping effect of amphetamine on the rats' vertical movements ("standing up"). He observed sniffing and biting of cage wire netting too and suggests that the form of stereotypy become simpler with increasing doses of drug. These observations, which were all confirmed by Lapin and Schelkunov (1965) (p. 214), also conform to our experience. Antweiler (1942) describes a continuous running in circles by amphetamine-treated rats.

Examples of amphetamine-induced stereotyped responses from rats during more complicated experiments have also been described. Thus in shock-avoidance experiments Teitelbaum and Derks (1958) found that amphetamine-treated rats under various experimental conditions drank or turned a wheel steadily even for hours, while untreated rats responded only for a short period after each shock. Bättig (1963) in experiments with a T-maze found that amphetamine, in contrast to ethanol, sodium barbital, chlorpromazine, meprobamate, imipramine, and caffeine, made the rats show an increased tendency to run to the same side in repetitive trials. Carlton (1961) has reported that amphetamine decreased alternation between two levers in a reward situation. Chance and Silverman (1964), who studied social behaviour in rats, found that amphetamine rendered the exploratory behaviour stereotyped and the emotional behaviour aimless. Their observations seem to agree with ours on mice (see "Results").

Stereotyped activity of mice after amphetamine has also been reported by Lapin (1966) and by Schelkunov (1964). Lapin reports that in three strains of mice the forms of stereotypy are different, consisting in one strain of grooming and sniffing, in another of vertical movements and in a third of gnawing.

"Constant purposeless searching head movements" of cats after amphetamine have been briefly mentioned by Emele *et al.* (1961).

A behaviour which undoubtedly may be interpreted as stereotypy after amphetamine has also been described in other species. Thus in chicks there has been described continuous twitter (Key and Marley, 1962; Clymer and Seifter, 1947; Spooner and Winters, 1966; Selle, 1940): in pigeons pecking (Schelkunov, 1966): in dogs continuous rotating movements (Chistoni and Beccari, 1940; Accornero, 1947): and in chimpanzees body and head movements, as well as self-picking to the point of producing sores (Fitz-Gerald, 1967).

Clinical observations on the behavioural effects of amphetamine in humans are, of course, much more varied than those made in animal experiments. Investigating psychiatrists have been more interested in psychiatric interviews than in behavioural observations of the undisturbed patients. Nevertheless, some cases of clearly stereotyped activity are described in the literature; for example, in the monograph on methamphetamine psychosis by Tatetsu, Goto and Fujiwara (1956) there is a description of two patients' behaviour immediately after hospitalization: ". . . their incomprehensible, odd and very unnatural movements were constantly, identically and energetically repeated." The picture of one of these patients shows a man in a boxing attitude (p. 81). A more detailed description of odd movements of body, limbs and head, which are "constantly and identically repeated" is given in their case history No. 3 p. 150-151. These unusual movements were "greatly enhanced" when, two days later, an intravenous injection of 30 mg methamphetamine was given. Patient No. 5 repeated the same few sentences ". . . constantly and identically. She does not stand up or move, but keeps sitting while continuously talking." (p. 157). In a summary of the monograph in German, Tatetsu (1960) states: "Unter die katatone Symptomen sind besonders zu rechnen: Stupor, Hyperkinesie, Katalepsie, Manieren, *Stereotypien* (italics by us), Negativismus, impulsive Gewalttat und Grimassen."

Clear cases of stereotyped behaviour in amphetamine psychosis are also described in two other monographs on the subject, i.e. that of Bonhoff and Lewrenz (1954) (p. 104) and that of Connell (1957) (case 20).

Recently Rylander (1966) published a study of 150 patients, who had abused Preludine (phenmetrazine), a close analogue of amphetamine (see "Results" section on rats). He noticed a symptom called "pundning" in Swedish patient-slang. This is described as compulsive or automatic continuation for hours of one aimless activity, such as sorting objects in a handbag, manipulating the interiors of a watch, polishing fingernails to the point that sores are produced, etc. The symptom was first overlooked, since the patients seldom report it spontaneously, but when investigated, it was found in 29 out of 43 cases.

In many other case reports of amphetamine psychosis, repetitions of compulsive and purposeless acts are described, but the descriptions are so incomplete that it cannot be decided whether the behaviour satisfies our definition of stereotyped activity as given above in the introduction, Tatetsu *et al.* (1956), Sano and Nagasaka (1965), Connell (1957 and 1958), Shanson (1956), Kalus *et al.* (1942), Bonhoff and Lewrenz (1954),

Kalus (1950), Binder (1945), Daube (1942), Staehlin (1941), Martimor (1955), Norman and Shea (1945), Greving (1941), Haguenau (1947), Gericke (1945), Schneck (1948), Kalant (1966).

The doses of amphetamine which have caused psychosis are of the same order of magnitude (1-20 mg/kg) as those reported above in the animal experiments. The psychosis is usually found in addicts, but several cases caused by a single dose are on record (Connell, 1957, 1958; Beamish and Kiloh, 1960; Hampton, 1961; Shanson, 1956; Kalant, 1966), in some of the chronic cases acute psychotic effects of a single dose are reported (Tatetsu *et al.*, 1956, case 3; Connell, 1957 in Appendix B case 13, p. 93-94, case 20, p. 154-155, case 31, p. 282, case 42, p. 398; Kalus *et al.*, 1950 case 1; Staehlin, 1941). The above mentioned clinical reports on cases of amphetamine psychosis repeatedly describe phenomena closely resembling those of schizophrenia and misdiagnoses were made. The diagnoses were corrected when the intake of amphetamine was discovered and discontinuation of the drug led to remission of the psychotic symptoms. It should, however, be considered that schizophrenics may also ingest amphetamine with the result that psychotic symptoms including catatonia and stereotypy are intensified. Such cases are also described in the literature (Belart, 1942; Delay *et al.*, 1947).

It may be that studies of the amphetamine effects will lead to results of interest for basic research into the psychoses. This has been our principal idea and the observation that stereotyped behaviour has also been described in man may support this point of view.

Other authors (Utena, 1964; Karli, 1960; Belart, 1942) have also indicated that studies of the effects of amphetamine might be of interest for psychosis research. Utena (1961) compared amphetamine-induced abnormal behaviour in man and animals, but while we have studied the acute effects of a single dose, Utena has concentrated on behavioural features observed during the first weeks after discontinuation of prolonged methamphetamine intoxication.

SUMMARY

Experiments with chickens, pigeons, mice, rats, guinea-pigs, cats, dogs, squirrel-monkeys and chimpanzees show that stereotyped activity can be produced by amphetamine in doses of 1-20 mg/kg in all these species ranging from birds to primates.

In man amphetamine in similar dose, i.e. higher than the therapeutic doses, can produce a psychosis, which so closely resembles schizophrenia, that misdiagnoses have been made. All the known symptoms of schizophrenia are reported, including stereotyped activity.

REFERENCES

Accornero, F.: Intossicazione sperimentale de betafenilisopropilamina. *Lav. neuropsychiat.* **1**, 307-327 (1947).

Antweiler, H.: Beitrag zur Frage der Pervitingewöhnung im Tierexperiment. Inaug. Dissertation. Universität Köln 1942.

Beamish, P. and Kiloh, L.: Psychoses due to amphetamine consumption. *J. ment. Sci.* **106**, 337-343 (1960).

Belart, W.: Pathogenetisches und Therapeutisches aus Pervitinversuchen bei Schizophrenie, *Schweiz. med. Wschr.* **72**, 41-43 (1942).

Binder, H.: Kriminalität infolge Pervitinmißbrauchs. *Schweiz. Arch.* **55**, 243-254 (1945).

Bonhoff, G. und Lewrenz, H.: Über Weckamine (Pervitin und Benzedrin). *Monogr. Gesamtgeb. Neurol. Psychiat.* **77**, 1-144 (1954).

Bättig, K.: Differential psychopharmacological patterns of action in rats. In Z. Votava (Ed.): *Psychopharmacological methods.* London: Pergamon 1963.

Carlton, P.: Some effects of scopolamine, atropine and amphetamine in three behavioral situations. *Pharmacologist* **3**, 60 (1961).

Chance, M.: A peculiar form of social behavior induced in mice by amphetamine. *Behaviour* **1**, 64-69 (1948).

—, and A. Silverman: The structure of social behavior and drug action. In H. Steinberg, A. Reuck and J. Knight (Eds.): *Animal behaviour and drug action,* London: Churchill 1964.

Connell, P. H.: Amphetamine psychosis. Maudsley Monograph No. 5. London: Chapman & Hall 1958, and Thesis, University of London 1957.

Daube, H.: Pervitin-Psychosen, *Nervenarzt* **15**, 20-25 (1942).

Delay, J., Collet, T., Silva, E., Pichot, P. et Romanet, B.: Le choe amphetaminique dans la psychose maniacodepressive et les catatonies. *Ann. méd. psychol.* **105**, 405-417 (1947).

Ehrich, W. and Krumbhaar, E.: The effects of large doses of benzedrine sulphate on the albino rat: functional and tissue changes. *Ann. intern. Med.* **10**, 1874-1882 (1937).

Emele, J., Shanaman, J. and Warren M. Chlorphentermine hydrochloride, p-chlor-*α*-*α*-dimethylphenethylamine hydrochloride, a new anorexigenic agent. II. Central Nervous System Activity. *Fed. Proc.* **20** (Part I), 328 (1961).

Fitz-Gerald, F.: Effects of d-amphetamine upon behavior of young chimpanzees reared under different conditions. In H. Brill and J. Cole (Eds.): *Neuropsycho Pharmacology,* Vol. 5. Amsterdam: Elsevier 1967 (in press).

Gericke, O.: Suicide by ingestion of amphetamine sulfate. *J. Amer. med. ass.* **128**, 1095-1099 (1945).

Greving, H.: Psychopathologische und körperliche Vorgänge bei jahrelangem Pervitinmißbrauch. See Fall 1, p. 397. *Nervenarzt* **14**, 395-405 (1941).

Haguenau, J. and Aubrun, W.: Intoxication chronique par le sulfate de benzedrin. *Rev. neurol.* **79**, 129-131 (1947).

Hampton, W.: Observed psychiatric reactions following use of amphetamine and amphetamine-like substances. *Bull. N. Y. Acad. Med.* **37**, 167-175 (1961).

Hauschild, F.: Zur Pharmakologie des 1-phenyl-2-methylaminopropans (Pervitin). *Naunyn-Schmiedebergs Arch. exp. Path. Pharmak.* **191**, 465-481 (1939).

Janssen, P., Niemegeers, C. and Schellekens, K.: Is it possible to predict the clinical effects of neuroleptic drugs (major tranquillizers) from animal data? *Drug Res.* (Arzneim.-Forsch.) **15**, 104-117 (1965).

Kalant, O. J.: *The amphetamines: Toxicity and addiction.* Alcoholism and drug Addiction Research Foundation of Ontario. Toronto 1966.

Kalus, F.: Über die psychotischen Bilder bei chronischem Pervitinmißbrauch. *Psychiat. Neurol. med. Psychol.* (Lpz.) **2**, 138-144 (1950).

—, J. Kucher u. J. Zutt: Über Psychosen bei chronischem Pervitinmißbrauch. *Nervenarzt* **15**, 313-324 (1942).

Karli, P.: Troubles du comportement induits chez le rat par l'amphétamine et le phenidylate (*ritaline*). *Arch. int. Pharmacodyn.* **122**, 344-351 (1960).

Key, B. and Marley, F.: The effects of the sympathomimetic amines on behaviour and electrocortical activity of the chicken. *Electroenceph. clin. Neurophysiol.* **14**, 90-105 (1962).

Lapin, I.: Intoxication with amphetamine in mice and rats of different ages under conditions of grouping and isolation. In D. Kvasov (Ed.): *Problems of general and age pharmacology* (in Russian), pp. 67-79. Leningrad: Medicine 1966.

—, and M. Samsonova: *Bull. exp. Biol. Med.* **11**, 66-70 (1964) (russ.).

—, and E. Schelkunov: Amphetamine-induced changes in behaviour of small laboratory animals as simple tests for evaluation of central effects of new drugs. In M. Mikhelson and V. Longo (Eds.): *Pharmacology of conditioning learning and retention.* Proceedings of the 2nd International Pharmacological Meeting, Vol. 1, pp. 205-215. London and Praha: Pergamon 1965.

Lát, J.: The spontaneous exploratory reactions as a tool for psychopharmacological studies. In M. Mikhelson and V. Longo (Eds.): *Proceedings of the 2nd International Pharmacological Meeting,* Vol. 1, pp. 47-66, 214. London and Praha: Pergamon 1965.

—, and E. Gollova: Drug-induced increase of central nervous excitability and the emergence of spontaneous stereotyped reactions. *Activ. nerv. sup.* (Praha) **6**, 200-201 (1964).

Martimor, E., Nicholas-Charles, P. and Dereux, J.: Délires amphetaminiques. *Ann. méd psychol.* **113**, 353-368 (1955).

Moore, K.: Toxicity and catecholamine releasing actions of D- and L-amphetamine in isolated and aggregated mice. *J. Pharmacol. exp. Ther.* **142**, 6-12 (1963).

Munkvad, I. and Randrup, A.: The persistance of amphetamine stereotypies of rats in spite of strong sedation. *Acta psychiat. scand. Suppl.* 191, **42**, 178-187 (1966).

Norman, J. and Shea, J.: Acute hallucinosis as a complication of addiction to amphetamine-sulfate. *New Engl. J. Med.* **233**, 270-271 (1945).

Quinton, R. and Halliwell, G.: Effects of *α*-methyl DOPA and DOPA on the amphetamine excitatory response in reserpinized rats. *Nature (Lond.)* **200**, 178-179 (1963).

Randrup, A. and Munkvad, I.: Dopa and other naturally occurring substances as causes of stereotypy and rage in rats. *Acta psychiat. scand. Suppl.* 191, **42**, 193-199 (1966).

—— Special antagonism of amphetamine-induced abnormal behaviour. *Psychopharmacologia* (Berl.)**7**, 416-422 (1965a).

— — Pharmacological and biochemical investigations of amphetamine-induced abnormal behaviour. In

D. Bente and P. Bradley (Eds.): *Neuropsychopharmacology,* Vol. 4, pp. 301-304. Amsterdam: Elsevier 1965b.

——, and Udsen, P.: Adrenergic mechanisms and amphetamine induced abnormal behaviour. *Acta pharmacol.* (Kbh.) **20**, 145-157 (1963).

Rylander, Gösta: Preludin-narkomaner fran klinisk och medicinsk-kriminologisk synpunkt. *Svenska Läk.-Tidn.* **63**, 4973-4979 (1966).

Sano, I. und Nagasaka: Über chronische Weckaminsucht in Japan. *Fortschr. Neurol. Psychiat.* **24**, 391-394 (1965).

Schelkunov, E.: The Technique of ''Phenamine Stereotypy'' for evaluating the effect produced by remedial agents on the central adrenergic processes. *Farmakol. i Toksikol.* **27**, 628-633 (1964) (russ.).

— Personal communication (1966).

Schneck, J.: Benzedrine psychosis: report of a case. *Milit. Surg.* **102**, 60-61 (1948).

Selle, R.: An effect of benzedrine sulfate on chicks, *Science* **91**, 95 (1940).

Shanson, B.: Amphetamine poisoning. *Brit. med. J.* **1956**, 576.

Spooner, C. E. and Winters, W. D.: Neuropharmacological profile of the young chick. *Int. J. Neuropharmacol.* **5**, 217-236 (1966).

Staehlin, J.: Pervitin-Psychosen. *Z. ges. Neurol. Psychiat.* **173**, 598-620 (1941).

Tatetsu, S.: Pervitin-Psychosen. *Folia psychiat. neurol. jap. Suppl.* **6**, 25-33 (1960).

— A. Goto, and T. Fujiwara: *The methamphetamine-psychosis* (Kakuseizai cudoku): Tokoy: Igaku Shoin 1956 (In Japanese).

Teitelbaum, P. and Derks, P.: The effect of amphetamine on forced drinking in rat. *J. comp. physiol. Psychol.* **51**, 801-810 (1958).

Utena, H.: Behavior and neurochemistry. A Special type model psychosis: A. Chronic methamphetamine intoxication in man and animal. *Brain and Nerve* (Jap. in English) **13**, 687-692 (1961).

— Behavioural aberations in methamphetamine-intoxicated animals and chemical Correlates in the Brain. *Progress in Brain Research,* vol. 24B. Amsterdam 1966.

8. Animal Model of Depression, I. Review of Evidence: Implications for Research

W. T. McKINNEY AND W. E. BUNNEY

Archives of General Psychiatry, 1969, *21,* 240-8. Copyright 1969 by the American Medical Association. Reprinted by permission.

This paper has three major purposes: (1) to present the need for an experimental animal model of "depression", ie, why the creation of such a model would be useful; (2) to review pertinent evidence from a variety of fields which points to the feasibility of such a model; and (3) to discuss possible research strategies which could be used to create an experimental animal model of depression.

Depression in man is a poorly defined entity. As Lehmann[1] points out, the term may refer to a symptom, a syndrome, or a nosological entity. We are interested in the depressive syndrome which is often defined as consisting of both primary and secondary symptoms. The primary symptoms in man consist of a despairing emotional state and the depressive mood. The secondary symptoms vary and are less regularly found. They may include such things as social withdrawal, psychomotor retardation, anorexia, weight loss, and sleep disturbances. No experimental model exists at present for such depressive states in animals.

Because of the difficulties in objectively evaluating the primary emotional state of animals, "depression" is used in this paper in an operational sense to refer to observable behavioral changes occurring in animals which are behaviors commonly associated with depression in humans, ie, the "secondary" symptoms. Such behavior would vary from species to species but could include changes in the animal's responsiveness to the external environment, changes in play activity, decreased appetite and weight, decreased motor activity, huddling posture, and sleep disturbance—all progressing to death in some instances. Analogous changes in some of these parameters often occur in human depression and could be studied in animals in connection with experimental events calculated to induce depression.

NEED FOR AN ANIMAL MODEL OF DEPRESSION

There is a need for an experimental system in which the social and interactional variables thought to be important in depression can be systematically manipulated and their relationship to depression clarified. There is only limited opportunity to manipu-

Submitted for publication March 4, 1969.

From the Psychiatry Training Branch (Dr. McKinney) and the Section on Psychiatry, Laboratory of Clinical Science (Dr. Bunney), National Institute of Mental Health, Bethesda, Md.

Reprint requests to Department of Psychiatry, University of Wisconsin School of Medicine, Madison, Wis. 53706 (Dr. McKinney).

late these variables in humans in a controlled manner.

Similar considerations apply to the relationship of biological variables to depression. For example, the theories relating catecholamines and serotonin to depression are based on limited and, of necessity, indirect evidence.[2-4] This indirect evidence stems largely from the fact that drugs such as the monoamine oxidase inhibitors and the tricyclic antidepressants which are effective in the treatment of human depression are drugs which in some animals elevate the functional levels of catecholamines or serotonin or both, while drugs such as reserpine or α-methyl-dopa which are thought to induce depression and lower the functional levels of catecholamines or serotonin or both.[5-8] No model exists at present which makes it possible to study directly the relationship of biogenic amines to depression. The experimental production of depression in animals would allow the investigation of brain amines and other biological variables while the animal is depressed. Some techniques for directly studying monoamine metabolism in the central nervous system of intact animals are already available.[9]

The most prevalent experimental model of depression currently in use is a pharmacological one, the reserpine model. Reserpine has been observed to induce severe depression in a small but consistent number of humans treated for hypertension[5-7] and these drug induced depressions have been considered possible pharmacological models of the naturally occurring disorders. Also, the effects of reserpine have been extensively studied in experimental animals in *in vitro* systems. Reserpine, when given to animals, produces sedation and accompanying depletion of brain levels of norepinephrine, serotonin, and dopamine. Changes in these amines following reserpine administration in animals have been postulated to be significant in reserpine-induced depression in man as well as in other kinds of depression. There is additional indirect evidence to suggest that amine changes may, indeed, be very important in human depression, but the model system in which these changes are currently being studied represents a pharmacologically induced sedation rather than anything resembling human depression.

EVIDENCE FOR ANIMAL DEPRESSION

The currently available evidence which indicates the feasibility of an animal model of depression comes largely from separation experiments in animals and anecdotes available from a variety of sources concerning case histories of individual animals. This material is summarized in the Table.

Separation Experiments

There are a variety of separation experiments in animals which have relevance to depression. These include, among others, the separation studies of Harlow *et al.*[10-17] In one experiment[16] they separated four mother-infant pairs of rhesus monkeys for a three-week period. The mothers and infants were denied physical contact but allowed auditory, visual, and olfactory intercommunication. All mothers and all infants showed emotional disturbance in response to separation, but the infants' disturbances were more intense and more enduring than the mothers'. The initial disturbance of the infants took the form of agitation or "protest" and consisted of disoriented scampering around, high-pitched screeching, and crying. The second phase was characterized by increased viewing of the mother, including huddling against the glass separating them from their mother, decreased play activity, and decreased infant-infant interaction. When reunited, there was an immediate increase in mother-directed behavior in three

of the four infants. The fourth showed a decrease in mother-directed behavior as compared to the preseparation period. Similar results were obtained in another experiment when there was no visual contact following separation, except that the intensity
of the infants' protest was less when they were not frustrated by being able to see but
not contact the mother.[17] The same workers have also completed a number of studies
of mother-infant separation at 6 months of age. After separation, the mother is transiently, but only transiently, "depressed". The infants, however, show behavioral
changes similar to those described above for longer periods of time, including severe
appetite and sleep disturbances (according to a letter from Harry F. Harlow in December
1967).

Hinde *et al.*[18] separated four rhesus monkeys from their mothers for six-day periods
at 30 to 32 weeks of age. During this separation period, the infants sat huddled in a
corner much of the time. Upon return to the mother all but one were back to their
preseparation level of activity within one week. The observation was made that the
more they had been away from the mother before separation, the less clinging they
showed on return. Jensen and Tolman[19] studied the short-term effects of separation
of mother-infant monkey pairs for less than one hour, and found that the infants screamed
almost continuously during the separation. The mothers attacked the cages and tried
to escape. On return of the infant there was a striking increase in the intensity of the
mother-infant relationship.

The recent reports of Kaufman and Rosenblum[20,21] provide additional data relative to possible "depression" in nonhuman primates. They studied the reaction of
four group-living pigtail monkey infants to removal of the mother. All showed distress, followed in three of the four by profound behavioral changes. The syndrome
consisted of three phases: (1) a phase of "agitation" lasting 24 to 36 hours; (2) a phase
of decreased activity, lasting five to six days: and (3) spontaneous recovery in stages
alternating with "depression". In the second or "depressed" phase, each of the three
infants sat hunched over with his head often down between his legs. There was a marked
decrease of movement, and social interaction or play behavior virtually ceased. In
their discussion, the authors focused on the adaptive value of the different stages of the
syndrome. With reintroduction of the mother, there was a tremendous reassertion and
persistence of the dyadic relationship. The one infant who did not show "depressive"
behavioral changes was the offspring of a dominant female and the question was raised
about the relationship of a dominant and aggressive mother to the infant's failure to
show any depressive changes following separation.

In another paper the same workers also called attention to some dramatic differences
between species in the infant's reaction to separation from the mother.[22] In contrast
to the pigtail infants (Macaca Nemestrina) used in the above study, the bonnett macaque
(Macaca Radiata) infants responded to separation from the mother by a marked increase
in interaction with other adults. This fact seemed to prevent serious behavioral changes.
The difference in response to separation in these two groups may be related to the gre-
garious quality of group interaction in bonnetts and the readiness of all bonnett infants
to move toward and be accepted by other adult members of the group. In contrast,
the pigtail infant lacks this interactional experience and is more distinctly and profoundly attached to its own mother.

Many of the changes seen following mother-infant separation in monkeys occur in
phases similar to those described by Bowlby and Robertson as part of the separation
anxiety seen after human infants are separated from their mothers.[23-25] They also

Some Reported Cases of Behavioral Reaction to Loss in Animals

Investigator	Animal(s)	Behavioral Changes	Precipitating Incident	Course	Duration of Change
Harlow et al	Rhesus monkeys	(1) Crying ↑ (2) Play ↓ (3) Social interaction ↓ (4) Appetite ↓ (5) Sleep disturbances	Experimental mother-infant separations	Immediate reacttachment in most instances following reunion	Until reunion
Hinde et al	Rhesus monkeys	(1) Activity ↓ (2) Sitting huddled in corner	Experimental mother-infant separation	Preseparation activity level regained within one week with reunion	Separation period of six days
Jensen and Tolman	Rhesus monkeys	Infants-constant screaming	Experimental mother-infant separation	Reunion results in increased intensity of mother-infant relationship	Less than one hour
Kaufman and Rosenblum	Pigtail monkey infants (Macaca nemestrina)	(1) Agitation (2) Sitting hunched over with head down between legs (3) Activity ↓ (4) Social interaction ↓ (5) Play behavior ↓	Removal of mother from group living situation	(1) Reintroduction of mother led to greatly increased closeness of infants and mothers (2) Some spontaneous recovery in stages	Six to eight days
Dilger and Prange	African parrot (genus Agapornis)	(1) Plumage becomes rough and bare (2) Activity ↓ (3) Death	Being left out in the presence of an observable bond formation	Death frequent within six months	Indefinite
Saul	Dog (boxer) ("Bonda")	"Classically depressed"	Litter killed by car	Spontaneous remission	Three months
Lorenz	(1) Geese (2) Jackdaw birds	(1) "Acute grief" (2) Appetite ↓	Sudden separation from family	Constantly searching for lost partners	Continuous
Hebb	Chimpanzee ("Kembi")	(1) Responsiveness to environment ↓ (2) Play activity ↓ (3) Grooming activity ↓	None	Cyclic mood changes	Six to eight months at a time
Mason	Monkey (Callicebus species)	(1) Appetite ↓ (2) Weight ↓ (3) Interest in environment ↓ (4) Sitting huddled for long periods of time	Arrival in the laboratory	Unusually high mortality rate in this group	Not mentioned
Tinkelpaugh	Rhesus monkey	(1) Self-mutilation (2) Agitation (3) Anorexia (4) Social withdrawal	Separation from female partner and then subsequently seeing her again	Gradual recovery following reunion with partner	14 months
Senay	Puppies (German shepherd)	Change in object seeking and avoidance based on preseparation temperament	Experimental separation from investigator	Persisted until reunion with investigator after two months	Until reunion (two months)

remind one of the anaclitic depression described by Spitz in infants separated from their mothers during the second one half of the first year of life.[26]

There is also some evidence to suggest that "depression" can be induced by separation experiences in a very different animal, the African parrot (Agapornis) ("love birds"). For example, Dilger[27] and Prange (according to an oral communication from Arthur J. Prange, MD in November 1967) have observed that if an individual member of one of the more social species of this animal is deprived of normal social interaction in the presence of an observable bond formation, it becomes ill and dies in a short period of time. That is, if three African parrots are put in a cage and two of them form a pair, the one left out develops signs which are obvious to independent observers in that its plumage becomes progressively rougher and bare, patches appear, and it dies within six months. In this instance it seems that being left out in the presence of an observable bond formation can induce severe changes. In contrast, one love bird left alone does fine if not in the presence of an observable bond.

Collection of Case Histories

In addition to examining instances of behavioral change occurring in separation experiments, an important step in approaching the problem of an animal model of depression is the collection of case histories of "depressive-like" syndromes in animals and an attempt to sort out any common factors that may be present. Such case histories are available in the veterinary and medical literature as well as from such sources as veterinarians, keepers of kennels and pounds, zoo keepers, and from primate research centers. They can give information about the natural occurrence of a "depressive-like" syndrome in animals and the context in which it occurs. It may be important to pay particular attention to such things as the age and sex of the animal, type of animal, present illness, environmental losses or stresses preceding onset, past history including background, environment, and the clinical course of the syndrome. The case histories collected in the Table suggest that a "depressive-like" syndrome might occur in a variety of animals.

Saul[28] has presented the idea that veterinary medicine should be a rich field for psychosomatic studies and that clinical observations of animals living with us as pets could be illuminating in relation to formulating theories about human behavior. As an example, he cites the case of Bonda, his female boxer, who was "depressed" for three months after the last of her litter was killed by a car. Lorenz (according to a letter from Konrad Z. Lorenz in August 1967) described the symptoms of what he called "acute grief" in a goose who, after normal development, was suddenly separated from its family. The goose suffered from decreased appetite and constantly searched for its lost family. Lorenz has also described the searching behavior of jackdaw birds separated from their mates or other members of the flock.[29]

There are other examples of animal "depression" which suggest probable experimental models to study. For example, Hebb[30] reports the case of Kembi, a chimpanzee, who before adolescence gave the impression of being an "unstable introvert". During adolescence there was a great increase in emotional instability, including cyclic mood changes. In the postadolescent period, Kembi would show behavioral changes resembling "depression" for periods as long as six to eight months. During this time, the animal would sit unresponsive to the environment for long periods of time and never participate in grooming or play. In this case no specific experience could be related to the disturbance.

Mason (according to a letter from W. A. Mason in January 1968) describes the natural occurrence of a syndrome resembling "depression" in a species of South American monkey (Callicebus) upon arrival in the laboratory. Prominent symptoms include loss of appetite, weight loss, decreased motor activity, assumption of a characteristic huddling position ordinarily seen during sleep, and general loss of interest in the environment.

Yerkes and Yerkes[31] have attributed the high death rate of newly captured gorillas to "psychogenic" factors, citing the loss of familiar surroundings and the severance of all meaningful bonds as antecedent causes of their deaths. They also observed behavioral changes in chimpanzees and suggested separation as a probable cause.

Tinkelpaugh[32] reports the case history of "Cupid," a young rhesus monkey, who developed marked behavioral changes following separation from a female monkey with whom he had lived monogamously for three years. Behavioral changes included repeated self-mutilation, agitation, anorexia, and social withdrawal. Reunion with the female initiated a gradual process of recovery.

IMPLICATIONS FOR RESEARCH

Evaluation of Baseline Data

In creating an experimental animal model for depression, it is necessary to have careful knowledge of the baseline behavior of the species being used. This should include naturalistic observations of the animal in his native habitat, as well as in the laboratory, plus genetic and early environmental data. As Hamburg[33] has pointed out, animal behavior may be investigated in diverse settings such as laboratories, artificial colonies, and natural conditions. Data obtained in each setting has its distinctive advantages and limitations.

Induction of Depression

Separation Experiments

The experimental induction of "depression" is not without precedent, even in humans. Engel and Reichsman[34] were able to experimentally induce "depression" in the infant Monica and to study a depressive reaction which could be provoked and terminated at will by the introduction or withdrawal of a stranger. They spoke of the potential research advantages of being able to experimentally produce a depression-withdrawal reaction in order to examine some theories concerning depression. Using hypnotic techniques, Kehoe and Ironside[35,36] studied the experimental induction of the "depressive" affect in human subjects in relation to gastric acid secretion. It is apparent, however, that the opportunities to create an experimental system in humans are limited.

If one accepts the importance of separation experiences in producing depression and uses this as a central concept, one issue becomes that of deciding what is a meaningful separation experience for the animal being studied. A useful contribution in the creation of an experimental animal model of depression would be the development of a scale of meaningful species-specific separation experiences; that is, separation experiences which result in significant emotional or behavioral changes or both when the animal, either in captivity or in the field, is subjected to them. For example, most of the nonhuman primate studies have focused on the mother-infant separation. It is clear that this is indeed a meaningful separation experience for both mother and infant and can provide considerable information about the mother-infant relationship and, probably, anaclitic depression.

The question remains as to whether one can produce in nonhuman primates a syndrome comparable to the depression of adult humans. Would separation experiments utilizing peers rather than the mother and infant produce a depressive-like syndrome? If it were possible to do so with juvenile or adult primates, many developmental and nutritional dependence issues could be circumvented. The work of Miminoshvili[37] is suggestive in this regard. He studied adult male baboons isolated from their colony. The development of symptoms was more rapid if the isolated animals were restricted to cages within the colony compound and allowed to observe the group in action before them than if they were totally isolated from the group. Symptoms included stereotyped motor behavior, self-mutilation, failure to perform well on overlearned stimulus-response relationships, and somatic changes.

In addition to mother-infant separations and peer separations, the separation of an animal from its human environment may provide another means for studying behavioral reaction to object loss. For example, one possibility is to place dogs in individual homes for rearing and for the formation of close attachments and to subject them to separation experiences by removing them from the home at various stages of attachment. This kind of experiment is based on the known attachment of dogs to families and the widespread anecdotal evidence that dogs can show marked behavioral changes when a family has to leave its dog alone for a significant period of time. Senay[38] has spoken of this need for maximum gratification for the experimental animals in order for a profound behavioral change to occur in response to separation. In his work concerning an animal model of depression, Senay formed a personal relationship with each of a litter of 3-week-old German shepherd puppies over a nine-month period. During this time, he was their sole consistent human figure. Then, for a two-month separation period, the animals had no contact with him. This was followed by a one-month reunion period in which the author resumed his former relationship with the animals. Independent observers scored the animals on object seeking, object avoiding, and aggressive behavior throughout the experiment. It was found that separation was associated with increase in object seeking for animals of the approach temperament, and increase in object avoidance and aggressive behavior for animals of the avoidance temperament. Senay felt that the observations made supported the contention that animals exhibit predictable behavioral changes following object loss and indicated that experimental psychobiologic models of separation could be constructed in animals. Attention was called to the importance of temperament and the preloss levels of gratification in understanding separation phenomena.

Alteration of Dominance Patterns

Another kind of model might be based on the importance of dominance in the relationships of many nonhuman primates. As Price[39] has pointed out, macaques and baboons have particularly marked hierarchical and social systems in which virtually every interaction between two animals is affected by their relative status in the hierarchy. It is postulated that, with changes in the stability of their hierarchical arrangement, behavioral alterations occur. The evidence for particular behavior patterns occurring in association with specific changes in the hierarchy is fragmentary but suggestive. Price speculates that the behavior which occurs on going up the hierarchy may be elation; on going down, it may be ''depression''. The ''depression'' is postulated to be adaptive in nature since it prevents the descending animal from fighting back. If this is so, one could try to induce "depression" by experimentally altering the dominance hierarchy relationship in some nonhuman primates.

Sensory Deprivation or Social Isolation or Both

In the case of a given species of animal, it may also be necessary to use a variety of techniques to develop a successful way to experimentally induce "depression". For example, in addition to the above-mentioned methods, one could use social isolation or sensory deprivation or both in the laboratory as a method of inducing "depression" in animals. The work of Harlow *et al.*,[40-42] concerning the effects of total and partial social isolation in monkeys, is relevant in this regard. Their findings suggest that sufficiently severe and enduring early isolation reduces the animals to a social-emotional level in which the primary social responsiveness is fear. The age at which social isolation or sensory deprivation or both is imposed, and the duration of its imposition, may be relevant in determining the nature of the response induced. Perhaps at certain developmental stages the reaction would be "depression" rather than fear.

Neurosurgical Approaches

In a recent study, Kling[43] found that amygdalectomy resulted in a marked change in behavior which might be interpreted as "depression". The primates were withdrawn and refused to socialize or eat. They also wandered off and failed to rejoin their colony. He also noted the behavioral differences in animals who were in the field and those who were in the laboratory following amygdalectomy.

Sensitization to Depression

Selection of Genetically Susceptible Species

There are no data concerning whether it might be possible to breed for animals prone to have depressive disturbances. If experiments showed this to be possible, the use of such animals would facilitate the creation of an experimental animal model of "depression".

Behavioral Sensitization

It might be useful to use animals with a history of early separation experiences during certain critical developmental stages. Such animals might be more prone to develop a "depressive" reaction following separation later in life. It would be useful to have some animal data concerning this question.

Biochemical Sensitization

Experiments could also be done to determine whether pharmacological treatment of animals with such drugs as reserpine or α-methyl-dopa would sensitize them to later separation experiences.

Evaluation of Change

Attempts need to be made to develop behavioral rating scales which have some degree of specificity for the species being studied. Also, it is necessary to focus specifically on depression when designing animal studies and when analyzing data. Although much of the data obtained as a result of separation studies in nonhuman primates has marked relevance to depression, a systematic focus on a study of depression as an entity has not been done. The emphasis in many of the previously mentioned primate studies has been on the nature of the mother-infant relationship. Kaufman and Rosenblum, in the previously mentioned report, did focus on depression in terms of integrating their observations with the clinical reports of Spitz, Bowlby, and Engel.

Reversal of "Depression"

The creation of an experimental animal model of a "depression" could potentially provide a system in which a variety of treatment techniques could be evaluated. This could include the use of social and environmental changes, electroshock treatment, the monoamine oxidase inhibitors and tricyclic antidepressants, and precursors of norepinephrine and serotonin.

Minimal Requirement for an Animal Model of "Depression"

The initial emphasis in this field needs to be on the establishment of methodologies for producing a depressed animal which could serve as an experimental model. It is important to use animals that form social bonds because within the animal kingdom "depression" seems to occur most frequently in those animals that form bonds. The "depression" induced within a social interactional system would then be available for a variety of biochemical and behavioral studies. It would permit the exploration of the significance of object loss in relation to depression. It would be possible to study such issues as the effects of separation at varying stages of bond formation or attachment and the effects of reunion with the lost object at varying times following the separation. What is the effect of age on the response to separation? Also, is there a critical time beyond which reunion has no effect, as suggested in humans by the work of Spitz?

A model system should therefore meet at least the following minimum requirements:

1. The symptoms of the depression so induced should be reasonably analogous to those seen in human depression.

2. There should be observable behavioral changes which can be objectively evaluated.

3. Independent observers should agree on objective criteria for drawing conclusions about the subjective state.

4. The treatment modalities effective in reversing depression in humans should reverse the changes seen in animals.

5. The system should be reproducible by other investigators.

COMMENT

In addition to the practical and conceptual issues that must be dealt with in creating an animal model of depression, there are some philosophical issues. Studies of animal behavior are often accepted as interesting but thought to be of little direct relevance to the human scene. There is a certain adeptness at either disregarding animal studies or keeping them in a separate and isolated compartment when one is formulating theories about human behavior. As Levy[44] says, "We have accepted our kinship with the animal world structurally and biochemically, but we remain isolationists psychologically." It is indeed true that devices and methods used in some animal laboratories are often poor analogues to human clinical situations and that clinicians in these instances have been unaccepting of animal experimentation in reference to behavioral problems. This limitation needs to be overcome.

As stated by Zegans,[45] it would be a mistake to view ethology as either confirming or negating current psychiatric theories. The fact that there is often a lack of homology between species does not, however, negate the value of a comparative approach to the study of man. A comparative approach can identify new significant problems for research and can also provide a system for investigating and clarifying concepts by allowing them to be tested on an observational and experimental level in animals. Since depression is a clinical problem of enormous magnitude, further identification of crucial variables requiring investigation is badly needed, along with experimental investigation of some currently held concepts. An animal model would provide a beginning in both of these areas. It might, indeed, be true that we share with higher animals disorders of mood more than disorders involving the higher thought processes, and that these disturbances could profitably lend themselves to comparative studies.

SUMMARY

The purpose of this paper is to review the data relevant to the development of an animal model of "depression" and to discuss possible research strategies which could be used to create such a model. There is a need for an experimental system in which the social and biological variables thought to be important in depression can be systematically manipulated and their relationship to depression clarified.

The evidence that has been reviewed in this paper, which suggests the possibility of creating an animal model of depression, comes from two main sources: (1) animal separation experiments; (2) anecdotal case histories of animals who have developed "depressive-like" syndromes.

The implications for research are discussed under six major categories: (1) evaluation of baseline data, (2) methods for induction of depression, (3) sensitization to depression, (4) methods to evaluate change, (5) reversal of depression, and (6) minimal requirements for an animal model of depression.

The limitations of animal experimentation in reference to confirming or negating current psychiatric theories are recognized. A comparative approach might, however, identify some new significant problems for research and can provide a system for investigation of concepts by allowing them to be tested on an observational and experimental level in animals.

REFERENCES

1. Lehmann, H. E.: Psychiatric Concepts of Depression: Nomenclature and Classification, *Canad Psychiat Assoc J* **4**:1-12 (March) 1959.
2. Bunney, W. E., Jr. and Davis, J. M.: Norepinephrine in Depressive Reactions, *Arch Gen Psychiat* **13**: 483-494 (Dec) 1965.
3. Schildkraut, J. J.: The Catecholamine Hypothesis of Affective Disorders: A Review of Supporting Evidence, *Amer J Psychiat* **122**: 509-522 (Nov) 1965.
4. Schildkraut J. J. and Kety, S. S.: Biogenic Amines and Emotion, *Science* **156**: 21-37 (April) 1967.
5. Achor, R. W., Hanson, N. O. and Gifford, R. W.: Hypertension Treatment With Rauwolfia Serpentina and With Reserpine, *JAMA* **159**: 841-845 (Oct) 1955.
6. Harris, T. H.: Depression Induced by Rauwolfia Compounds, *Amer J Psychiat* **113**: 950-951 (April) 1957.
7. Muller, J. C., *et al.*: Depression and Anxiety Occurring During Rauwolfia Therapy, *JAMA* **159**: 836-840 (Oct) 1955.
8. McKinney, W. T. and Kane, F. J.: Depression With the Use of Alpha-Methyl-Dopa, *Amer J Psychiat* **124**: 80-81 (July) 1967.

Drs. David Hamburg, Douglas Bowden, Dennis L. Murphy, and Frederick K. Goodwin helped in the preparation of this manuscript. Miss Sally Dunbar provided invaluable assistance.

9. Maas, J. W. and Landis, D. H.: A Technique for Assaying the Kinetics of Norepinephrine Metabolism in the Central Nervous System in Vivo, *Psychosom Med* **28**: 247-256 (May-June) 1966.

10. Harlow, H. F.: "Development of the 2nd and 3rd Affectional Systems in Macaque Monkeys," in Tourlentes, T. T. Pollack, S. L. and Himwich, H. E.: *Research Approaches to Psychiatric Problems, a Symposium,* New York: Grune and Stratton, Inc., 1962, chap. 12, pp 209-229.

11. Harlow, H. F.: Love in Infant Monkeys, *Sci Amer* **200**: 68-75 (June) 1959.

12. Harlow, H. F.: "The Development of Affectional Pattern in Infant Monkeys," in Foss, B. M.: *Determinants of Infant Behavior,* New York: Wiley and Sons, Inc., 1961, pp. 75-88.

13. Harlow, H. F.: The Nature of Love, *Amer Psychol* **13**: 673-685 (Dec) 1958.

14. Harlow, H. F. and Harlow, M. K.: "The Affectional Systems," in Schrier, A. M., Harlow, H. F. and Stollnitz, F.: *Behavior of Nonhuman Primates,* vol 2, New York: Academic Press, Inc., 1965, pp 287-334.

15. Harlow, H. F. and Zimmermann, R. R.: Affectional Responses in the Infant Monkey, *Science* **130**: 421-432 (Aug) 1959.

16. Seay, B., Hansen, E. and Harlow, H. F.: Mother-Infant Separation in Monkeys, *J Child Psychol Psychiat* **3**: 123-132 (July-Dec) 1962.

17. Seay, B. and Harlow, H. F.: Maternal Separation in the Rhesus Monkey, *J Nerv Ment Dis* **140**: 434-441 (June) 1965.

18. Hinde, R. A., Spencer-Booth, Y. and Bruce, M.: Effects of 6-Day Maternal Deprivation on Rhesus Monkey Infants, *Nature* **210**: 1021-1023 (June) 1966.

19. Jensen, G. D. and Tolman, C. W.: Mother-Infant Relationship in the Monkey, *Macaca Nemestrina*: The Effect of Brief Separation and Mother-Infant Specificity, *J Comp Physiol Psychol* **55**: 131-136 (Feb) 1962.

20. Kaufman, I. C. and Rosenblum, L. A.: Depression in Infant Monkeys Separated From their Mothers, *Science* **155**: 1030-1031 (Feb) 1967.

21. Kaufman, I. C. and Rosenblum, L. A.: The Reaction to Separation in Infant Monkeys: Anaclitic Depression and Conservation-Withdrawal, *Psychosom Med* **29**: 648-675 (Nov-Dec) 1967.

22. Rosenblum, L. A. and Kaufman, I. C.: Variations in Infant Development and Response to Maternal Loss in Monkeys, *Amer J Orthopsychiat* **83**: 418-426 (April) 1968.

23. Bowlby, J.: Separation Anxiety, *Int J Psychoanal* **41**: 89-113 (March-June) 1960.

24. Robertson, J. and Bowlby, J.: Responses of Young Children to Separation From their Mothers. *Cours du Centre International de l'Enfance* **2**: 131-142 (March) 1952.

25. Bowlby, J.: Processes of Mourning, *Int J Psychoanal* **42**: 317-340 (July-Oct) 1961.

26. Spitz, R. A.: Anaclitic Depression: An Inquiry Into the Genesis of Psychiatric Conditions in Early Childhood, II, *Psychoanal Stud Child* **2**: 313-342, 1946.

27. Dilger, W. C.: The Comparative Ethology of the African Parrot Genus *Agapornis. Z Tierpsychol* **17**: 649-685 (June) 1960.

28. Saul, L. J.: Psychosocial Medicine and Observation of Animals, *Psychosom Med* **24**: 58-61 (Jan-Feb) 1962.

29. Lorenz, K. Z.: *King Solomon's Ring,* New York: Thomas Cornwell, Co., 1952.

30. Hebb, D. O.: Spontaneous Neurosis in Chimpanzees, *Psychosom Med* **9**: 3-16 (Jan-Feb) 1947.

31. Yerkes, R. M. and Yerkes, A. W.: *The Great Apes,* New Haven: Yale University Press, 1929.

32. Tinkelpaugh, O. L.: The Self-Mutilation of a Male Macacus Rhesus Monkey, *J Mammal* **9**: 293-300 (Nov) 1928.

33. Hamburg, D. A.: "Evolution of Emotional Responses: Evidence from Recent Research on Non-Human Primates," in Masserman, J. H. (ed.): *Science and Psychoanalysis,* vol 12, *Animal and Human,* New York: Grune and Stratton, Inc., 1968, pp 39-54.

34. Engel, G. L. and Reichsman, F.: Spontaneous and Experimentally Induced Depressions in an Infant With Gastric Fistula: A Contribution to the Problem of Depression, *J Amer Psychoanal Assoc* **4**: 428-452 (July) 1956.

35. Kehoe, M. and Ironside, W.: Studies on the Experimental Evocation of Depressive Responses Using Hypnosis: II. The Influence of Depressive Responses Upon the Secretion of Gastric Acid, *Psychosom Med* **25**: 403-419 (Sept-Oct) 1963.

36. Kehoe, M. and Ironside, W.: Studies on the Experimental Evocation of Depressive Responses Using Hypnosis: III. The Secretory Rate of Total Gastric Acid With Respect to Various Spontaneous Experiences Such as Nausea, Disgust, Crying, and Dyspnea, *Psychosom Med* **26**: 224-249 (March-June) 1964.

37. Miminoshvili, cited by Bowden, D.: Primate Behavioral Research in the USSR: The Sukhumi Medico-Biological Station, *Folia Primat* **4**: 346-360 (Sept-Oct) 1966.

38. Senay, E. C.: Toward an Animal Model of Depression: A Study of Separation Behavior in Dogs, *J Psychiat Res* **4**: 65-71, 1966.

39. Price, J.: The Dominance Hierarchy and the Evolution of Mental Illness, *Lancet* **2**: 243-246 (July) 1967.

40. Harlow, H. F., Wadsworth, R. O. and Harlow, M. K.: Total Social Isolation in Monkeys, *Proc Nat Acad Sci, USA* **54**: 90-97 (July) 1965.

41. Griffin, G. A. and Harlow, H. F.: Effects of Three Months of Total Social Deprivation in Social Adjustment and Learning in the Rhesus Monkey, *Child Develop* **37**: 533-547 (Sept) 1966.

42. Cross, H. A. and Harlow, H. F.: Prolonged and Progressive Effects of Partial Isolation on the Behavior of Macaque Monkeys, *J Exp Res Personal* **1**: 39-49 (Feb) 1965.

43. Kling, A.: "Amygdalectomy in Free Ranging Vervet," read before the Psychiatric Research Society, New Haven, Conn, Dec 4-5, 1968.

44. Levy, D. M.: "Animal Psychology in its Relation to Psychiatry," in F. Alexander (ed.): *Dynamic Psychiatry,* Chicago: University of Chicago Press, 1952, chap 15, pp 483-507.

45. Zegans, L. C.: An Appraisal of Ethological Contributions to Psychiatric Theory and Research, *Amer J Psychiat* **124**: 729-739 (Dec) 1967.

Section III

ANIMAL NEUROSES

9. Some Observations on Neurosis in Farm Animals*

P. G. CROFT

Journal of Mental Science, 1951, *97*, 584-8. Reprinted by permission.

It is important, at the outset, to define the purposes which can be served by studying the subject of neurosis in animals, and they appear to be twofold. Firstly, animals display emotions in a simplified form, because their behaviour is not influenced by social conventions, and thus one can sometimes recognize vital underlying human feelings which are masked by other less important habits. A simple example of this is seen when two animals are given identical meals in separate feeding dishes; each animal is convinced that the other has a better meal, and they will not be happy till they have changed dishes. In human relationships, the feeling that the other person has something better often plays a major part in determining behaviour, but it is frequently disguised and seldom admitted by the person concerned. The second way in which animals can help in the study of human medicine is in controlled experimental work; for instance, the relative effects of heredity and environment can be studied comparatively easily in animals, and although it is important to remember that arguments based on animal behaviour cannot be applied directly to human behaviour, much can be gained by an exchange of information between workers in the two fields.

This paper is essentially the result of observations made over a long period of time, and of information collected from people whose life has been devoted to looking after animals of many different species; such people, whether they keep animals for pleasure or profit, usually have exceptionally good powers of observation, and a knowledge of animal behaviour which the mere scientist can never achieve through laboratory experiments. Certain terms, common to veterinary and human medicine, have slightly different meanings in the two subjects; in this paper, which describes animal behaviour, the terms have been used in the veterinary sense.

There are three main points which will be considered:

(1) Forms of neurosis in animals
(2) Possible causes
(3) Treatment and future research

FORMS OF NEUROSIS

The behaviour of cows has been studied extensively, because milk yield is an important item on every dairy farm; cows vary enormously in their temperament, both from one individual to another and from one breed to another. Anxiety neurosis is commonly

---

* A paper read at the Quarterly Meeting of the Royal Medico-Psychological Association held at 11, Chandos Street, W.1, on 15 February, 1951.

seen, and can be readily recognized by the fact that the cow will refuse to "let down" her milk; a stranger in the cowshed at milking time may cause neurotic cows to give almost no milk, although he does nothing more than stand in the door of the shed. "Let down" incidentally is an example of an easily-formed conditioned reflex, and stimuli such as music, or warm water on the udder, can be used very effectively. The correlation of physiognomy with neurotic temperament is very noticeable among the different breeds—the heavy South Devon cows are typically phlegmatic, while the more finely-drawn Ayrshires are prone to neurosis. Again, among bulls, neurosis is an important factor in the mating process; the presence of a stranger will often prevent a bull from mounting, and any disturbance in the established routine may cause the bull to become quite unmanageable.

Neurosis in horses can be readily recognized by the fact that the animal breaks out in a profuse sweat and often trembles all over, with widely dilated nostrils and wild staring eyes. This behaviour is more common among the lighter breeds, but instances of it occur among draught horses also. It is a far more difficult thing to rationalize than the neurosis of the cow, because it often occurs every time a horse passes a certain spot in the road, where, so far as is known, nothing alarming has ever occurred. The horse has a phenomenally long memory, and this may sometimes be the explanation, but there are definite cases recorded in which it is known that the horse has never been to the spot before.

The effect of the temperament of the human being on the behaviour of the animal is of course obvious in almost all species, but it is shown more definitely in the association between horse and rider (or driver) than anywhere else. A neurotic rider will reduce a normally calm horse to such a state of nervous tension that one can hardly believe it is the same animal—it seems to lose all power of reason; conversely, one can see the trembling of a nervous horse cease as a confident rider mounts.

Neurosis in goats may occur as an exaggerated sequel to a slight fright, or, very commonly, as a sequel to anger and frustration of will. A goat which had had a simple intra-muscular injection fell down and seemed paralysed on seeing the veterinary surgeon enter the stable some days later. Similarly, certain goats when led in the direction in which they do not want to go will fall down as if in an epileptic fit, but will recover at once if allowed to have their own way.

It is of some interest, from the point of view of human medicine, that abortion has profound psychological effects on a goat. The animal will bleat continuously for weeks after an abortion, in what can only be described as a hysterical manner, and nothing will comfort her (although in one case a kitten was given to the goat in place of its kid, with remarkably good results).

Hysteria in dogs is a well-recognized condition, and is becoming increasingly common, both among farm and pet dogs. The dog is usually stimulated by some unknown "trigger" and thereupon loses all reason, recognizing no one and running off howling wildly. Sometimes it runs in circles, but more commonly in a straight line, until exhausted; it then lies down still dazed, and gradually, in anything from 5-15 minutes, emerges from its stupor. As soon as it is fully conscious it is quite normal and there are no signs of hysteria until the next attack. Dogs are also subject to fits, similar to human epileptic fits, and to meningitis and rabies, but these conditions are quite distinct from the neurotic hysteria.

POSSIBLE CAUSES

These can be considered under three main headings—heredity, environment and feeding. No doubt each of these factors can play a part, but there is strong evidence to suggest that heredity is the most important factor. This evidence consists of general observations, and of a particular experiment.

During the past 50 years in-breeding has been practised to an alarming extent in the dog-breeding world, and to a lesser extent among dairy cows and racehorses. The increase in hysteria and in a generally unstable temperament is obvious to anyone who has seen much of pedigree dogs during this period, but no similar increase is apparent among mongrels. It is significant that the society responsible for training dogs to lead blind people have had to reject 80 per cent of the pure-bred Alsatians which they used to use for this work, and are now using first crosses from Labradors and Alsatians. They need dogs which can be relied upon not to become neurotic under the most trying circumstances, and find that the cross-bred animal is definitely more satisfactory.

Eight dogs have lived under identical conditions in my own home, and have been carefully observed throughout their lifetime; the mongrels alone showed no neurotic symptoms. Whether neurosis appears when "hybrid vigour" is lost, or whether it is due to a recessive gene brought into action by in-breeding, is a question which only long-term genetical experiments can answer.

The experimental work on the relative effects of heredity and environment was carried out in a herd of dairy goats; the environment and husbandry of the goats was identical in every case, and in the majority of the matings the male was the same animal. The kids did not suckle their dams, and during the day were in a separate "play-pen," but they did spend the nights with their dams when young.

The herd consisted initially of three goats of widely differing temperaments. No. 1 was a highly intelligent goat, easily upset and liable to attacks of extreme hysteria on the least provocation; she was the natural leader of the herd. No. 2 was a calmer goat and with less intelligence than No. 1, fond of human beings and greedy; she seldom showed hysterical symptoms except when frustrated, and then she would become rigid. No. 3 was a very peaceful animal, anxious to cause no one any trouble. The children and grandchildren of these three goats have now been reared. The offspring of No. 1 showed all her intelligence and all her neurosis; her daughter screamed for weeks after an abortion, and her granddaughter shivered and shook during the whole of a 20-mile car journey when every other kid had settled down and started to eat hay after a few miles. The children of No. 2 have inherited her need for human companionship, her greed and her hysterical rigidity when their will is frustrated—her daughter shows this is an exaggerated form, falling down as if in a fit. Finally the children of No. 3 are placid animals, undisturbed by changes in routine and showing no neurosis.

Environment, no doubt, plays some part in the production of neurosis, but it seems to be a minor one superimposed on the basic hereditary make-up of the animal. The interplay between the human being's temperament and the animal must have some bearing on the appearance of neurosis. Pavlov's classical experiments on the production of neurosis in dogs by the presentation of increasingly difficult problems have been confirmed in the field on one or two occasions. A pack of hounds which was watched over a period of years occasionally had widespread outbreaks of hysteria; these attacks always occurred at a check, when scent was poor, and the brains of the hounds presumably were severely taxed.

The feeding experiments of Mellanby and others do indicate that both fits and hysteria can be produced by toxic factors in agenized flour, but it is doubtful if this factor operates in practice, because there are so many instances of only one animal showing neurosis in a group having an identical diet. The vitamin B complex has been considered important by some workers, but again it appears to have little therapeutic value in established cases of neurosis. One case of canine hysteria responded well to parathyroid extract, but this was an isolated case and numerous other dogs have failed to respond.

Some years ago a thesis was written showing that dogs contract hysteria from sniffing the urine of dogs which are hysterical. This theory was subsequently ridiculed, but recently we have realized that Leptospira canicola is contracted in just this way, and since one of the symptoms of leptospirosis is meningitis, the original thesis contained some element of truth.

In every species it is the animals with the highest intelligence that most often show neurosis, and this fact would seem to fit in with Pavlov's experiments in showing that neurosis occurs when the intelligence of the animal is strained.

TREATMENT AND FUTURE RESEARCH

As in-breeding appears to be one of the main factors causing neurosis in animals, it should be possible to produce animals with stable temperaments by cross-breeding, or, if necessary for other reasons, at least only line-breeding. Since temperament is inherited, any animal known to be neurotic should not be allowed to breed. In practice this policy can never be followed strictly, because if the animal is, for example, a high milk yielder, the farmer will wish to breed from her regardless of her temperament.

The problem, then, becomes one of cure rather than of prevention; much can be done by the human beings in contact with the animal, but it is doubtful if this ever constitutes a permanent cure: the neurosis will not be apparent while the animal is with that particular person, but the unstable temperament remains, and if the environment changes for the worse, the neurosis will reappear.

Finally, it is interesting to speculate on the possible future developments of research in animal behaviour. There are many strange stories connected with animals; one which is a first-hand experience of the author is of a saloon car in which a dog had suddenly become hysterical; the windows of the car were shut and nothing unusual could be heard from outside. The car passed by a pack of hounds waiting at a meet, and within a few seconds more than half the hounds were having an attack of hysteria. There are numerous accounts of animals being conscious of events occurring hundreds of miles away; no doubt some of these can be put down to coincidence, or imagination, but they cannot all be explained, any more than the homing instinct of animals can be explained.

It seems that we must acknowledge that animals have sensory receptors that we do not understand, and cannot, as yet, locate, and it may well be that these receptors receive the trigger stimuli responsible for hysteria in dogs, and in other animals. Professor Rhine, in America, and Dr. Thouless, in this country, have done pioneer work on extra-sensory perception (E.S.P.), and we can no longer deny that E.S.P. does exist in man; perhaps we can learn more about it from studying the behaviour of animals.

SUMMARY

The forms which neurosis takes in various farm animals are described, and the relative importance of heredity, environment and diet as contributory causes is discussed. Possible methods of treatment are considered.

REFERENCES

Bechterew, W., *J. Parapsychol.*, 1949, **13**, 166.

Rhine, J. B. and Rhine, L. E., *J. abnorm. soc. Psychol.*, 1929, **23**, 449.

Idem, Proc. Roy. Soc. Med., 1950, **43**, 11, 804.

Idem, The Reach of the Mind, 1948, London.

10. Spontaneous Neurosis in Chimpanzees: Theoretical Relations with Clinical and Experimental Phenomena[1]

D. O. Hebb

Psychosomatic Medicine, 1947, *9*, 3-16. Reprinted by permission.

It may be taken for granted that the concept of neurosis is derived from human behavior, and that it is anthropomorphic as applied to animals. Such anthropomorphism may be good as well as bad. If human and animal behavior is the same in some respect, it is not only proper but scientifically necessary to recognize that this is so, not to use one name for some feature of animal behavior and another for the same thing in man. Anthropomorphism is bad only when it implies that animals have human attributes (real or mythical) which, in fact, they have not. Thus in any particular instance of anthropomorphism one must decide whether the implied analogy between animal and human behavior is sound. The essential question would be whether the processes referred to—not the external behavior, but the mechanisms controlling it—are the same or not. As far as neurosis is concerned, or perhaps any other specific concept, omitting such generalized concepts as those of learning, intelligence and so on, a final answer evidently cannot be given at present since we know so little of the mechanisms of cerebral action; but we can ask whether in the light of what we do know the identification is plausible and likely to add to scientific understanding.

This report, first, describes two cases of apparent neurosis (or psychosis[2]) in the chimpanzee. These raise the question of the cues or symptoms by which neurosis is to be identified in animals; I propose, therefore, in the second place, to make an analysis of the recognition of neurosis in man in order to find criteria of neurotic as contrasted with other disturbances of behavior. In the third place, these criteria are applied to a critique of the so-called experimental neurosis. Finally, I shall ask further what our present knowledge justifies in the way of hypothesis about the underlying processes of neurosis. In doing so I shall draw on the results of two recent studies of emotion in chimpanzees. One, on the recognition of emotion (10), bears on the question of how neurosis in animals is to be identified. The other (11), in which a hypothesis of the nature of fear is developed, suggests a theoretical approach to neurosis which appears

---

[1] This paper was prepared for presentation at the conference of the Committee on Physiological Mechanisms and Animal Experimentation, American Society for Research in Psychosomatic Problems, New York, December 14, 1945. Because of time limitations the paper was not read in full.

[2] No attempt is made here to distinguish carefully between neurosis, and psychosis without intellectual deterioration; at best the distinction is hard to make except as a matter of degree, and for the purposes of this discussion it would certainly be oversubtle.

to put the causal factors of experience and innate or constitutional defects in better perspective relative to each other, and thus may aid in the orientation of experiment.

TWO CHIMPANZEE HISTORIES

Alpha, now 15 years old (she was born in 1930), is an adult chimpanzee who was born in captivity, taken from her mother without delay and reared without sight of other chimpanzees until the age of one year (13). Thereafter she lived frequently as one of a group of four females, Alpha, Kambi, Bula, and Bimba, being handled often by the staff. The menarche was at age 8, there was nothing unusual about her sexual behavior with male chimpanzees, and she has had five infants. At maturity she was regarded by the staff as having a strong liking for human company, not getting on well with other female chimpanzees, obstinate, not overly bright, and, with apparently trivial exceptions, well adjusted emotionally.

The exceptions were Freudian: a definite avoidance of any carrot that was forked or doublerooted, and of long, narrow cylindrical pieces of food such as okra; and a marked tendency to masturbate against the water faucet projecting from the wall of her cage, whenever human beings came in sight. It is interesting to think what could be done with the interpretation of such symbols, any one of which has an unmistakably Freudian meaning; and I give you my word that the facts have not been selected or distorted to make a better story of it. The only other peculiarity was in Alpha's childhood, and also apparently minor. She showed an unusually persistent disturbance at the sound of a hissing steam radiator in the Yale Laboratories, Northern division, and a marked fear of certain coils of rope (fear of rope has occurred in other animals of the colony). No great weight was given to any of these things until the sudden appearance at the age of 12, of a gross behavioral disturbance.

At the night feeding of November 6, 1942, with no earlier signs of abnormality, Alpha refused all solid foods. There was no other sign of illness, and she was clearly hungry next day, in spite of the pieces of food lying untouched in her cage. She accepted milk eagerly, and it was then found that she would accept any of her untouched food if it was cut up into small pieces before being given to her. Exhaustive tests made then and on subsequent occasions showed conclusively that she was afraid of any large piece of food. No coaxing could persuade her to touch the food with her hands; ordinarily Alpha would pick up and give an observer any object he "begged" for, but she was not willing even to approach a large piece of food, let alone touch it, and would make a wide circle around one that she had to pass in moving about the cage. Four weeks later her behavior was somewhat more normal, and in the subsequent months there was marked improvement although with occasional minor relapses. In this later period a moderately large piece of food thrust through the wire of the cage was permitted first to fall on the floor and lie there for a minute or so. Alpha would then approach cautiously, pick up the food with only her long fingernails touching, and take her time about eating. Often at the moment of touching the food she would leap back as if it were hot.

It may be fantastic to infer that Alpha suffered from hallucinations; but it is not going beyond the facts to say that her behavior in every respect was consistent with that idea.

Four months after the onset of the illness, when the avoidance of food though still definite was much less marked, Alpha showed a sudden and marked avoidance of the attendant who had been feeding her daily (at noon only) but no fear of food. The attendant was myself, there had definitely been no injury to her while I was present or in the neighborhood, and she showed no avoidance whatever of other persons. This lasted seven days. On the eighth, there was again fear of food and none of me. Shortly afterward fear of me returned, fear of food once again disappearing; and when I persisted in trying to touch her she became viciously aggressive. It is known with some certainty that this is the first time in her life when she deliberately tried to injure a human being. Later I punished her, by soaking her with water from a hose, for trying to attack me. She then became completely friendly, although her fear of food persisted. The food-taking disturbance seemed to have cleared up after fluctuating in severity for some twenty to twenty-four months, and then, at thirty-six months, while this was being written, an acute and severe disturbance again appeared, practically identical with that three years before, but clearing up much more quickly.[1]

From a number of considerations, which I shall try to summarize here, it appears that the main cause of Alpha's fears could not have been an association of food with some frightening event or injury. First, the frightening event would have to be in the food itself; loud noise, or an injury from an attendant at the moment of feeding would, from everything we know about the adult chimpanzee's intelligence, result not in fear of food but of the separate source of noise or injury. That is, the food itself would have to appear to the chimpanzee to be a source of injury in order to explain fear of food, and this could only be due to some sharp object in the food or a stinging insect. Second, if a thorn or wasp in the food injured Alpha, it would have to be at the moment of swallowing; a prick or sting on a finger could hardly occur without Alpha's seeing the wasp or finding the thorn—the chimpanzee is incredibly acute and interested in finding and removing minute thorns, and a wasp in Alpha's cabbage would have no more chance of stinging her, without being seen, than of stinging a man. But if the injury occurred at the moment of swallowing, how can we account for Alpha's not being willing even to have the food come within a couple of feet of her body; for her fear of all foods, not only the food that hurt her; for the multiple recurrences of the fear, after remission for months at a time; and for the sudden transfer of the fear to an attendant? It is at least unlikely that a wasp or thorn could escape the acute vision of the chimpanzee and be swallowed in the food, but it is to the highest degree unlikely that it should happen a number of times to one chimpanzee and to that one only. Alpha's emotional disturbance may have been precipitated by some injury, but in all probability was not caused by it.

There is no connection discoverable between Alpha's menstrual cycle or pregnancies and the fluctuations of her fear of food. Since there are suggestions that the diet of the captive chimpanzee may sometimes be deficient in thiamin, we gave thiamin, without discoverable effect. Apart from this no therapy has been attempted, partly because we have been very interested to observe the natural course of the illness.

This is not a wholly unique history, although it is the most spectacular. A sudden

---

[1] In correcting proof, I take the opportunity of filling in some facts omitted in my original account of Alpha's illness, in view of Dr. Mowrer's diagnosis in his comments following this paper. The self-imposed repression in a chimpanzee required by the Freudian analysis is at first a somewhat surprising idea, but perhaps not impossible. Although Alpha shows no slightest inhibition, sexual or otherwise, in dealing with other chimpanzees, it is conceivable that her innate delicacy, and repugnance to an extra-species eroticism, has developed her Superego in this zone of behavior.

I must, however, disclaim the romantic role, flattering as it is, in which Dr. Mowrer has cast me. Alpha saw me at noon only, and was mainly fed and handled by others; I was not present at the night feeding when the phobia first appeared; the genital *inspection* (not a pelvic manipulation) was at that time always made by one of two persons to whom Alpha showed no special responsiveness, either sexual or aggressive. If anyone had captured her girlish fancies, it was a member of the staff whom she saw only at irregular intervals, and who neither fed nor examined her. It is too bad to pour cold water on such a charming hypothesis, but the fact is that no relationship could be discovered between Alpha's phobia and her love-life.

unprovoked fear of a familiar attendant, lasting a week or more, has been recorded by Elder (diary of the chimpanzee Mimi, Yerkes Laboratories).

Next, a second history:

Kambi, now 16 years old, is an adult female captured at the estimated age of nine months and reared in the constant company of other chimpanzees her own age. From the age of eighteen months she lived as one of a group of four, including Alpha (as noted above), and was handled frequently by attendants until she reached maturity. Morphine addiction was briefly established at age 8. Menarche was at 9 years. Sex activity before and after was almost nonexistent, and she was spayed at the age of 12. Her behavior at maturity is regarded by the staff as unpredictable; she is emotionally unstable, very desirous of human attention, easily frustrated. Before adolescence, Dr. Henry Nissen reports, she gave the impression of being a rather unstable introvert as far as her *behavior* corresponded to that of man; with adolescence there was a very great increase in emotional instability. This refers to a period of about three years, ages 9 to 12. The post-adolescent picture shows less frequent fluctuations of mood, but, just as in the adolescent period, the troughs of depression are deeper, the crests of euphoria less high than before adolescence. She may appear to be fairly well adjusted and not unhappy for several months at a time, and then to be in a profound depression without intermission for periods as long as six or eight months. The condition is not due to the removal of the ovaries. No apparent effect was observed after operation, she was as "crazy" before as after operation, in the words of the caretaking staff, and other spayed females have shown no such symptoms. Also her lack of sexual responsiveness was complete long before spaying. She was chosen for the experimental operation for this reason since she was useless as a breeder.

You may quite properly object to the anthropomorphism of such a description. I have used it as the most efficient means of communicating a description of behavior, and what I mean by it is that the behavior at times is, so far as I and others of the staff of the Yerkes Laboratories can see, identical with that of some human patients with depression. My theoretical justification for such identifications will appear shortly (10). Let me say here that the extent to which human temperamental patterns are duplicated in the chimpanzee is little short of extraordinary. We think of the anthropoid apes as approaching man in intelligence, but the intellectual gap is enormous compared to the almost negligible separation of the species in their temperamental and emotional patterns. Yerkes (28) has tried to convey this fact by describing various individuals but I have come to the conclusion that there is really no adequate way of doing this in words, and that only prolonged exposure to a number of adult animals can possibly permit one to see the very real facts to which Dr. Yerkes was referring. If my analysis of emotional recognition (10) is correct, recognition of the identity of an emotional pattern may require months or years of exposure to the subject. Criticism of the conclusion that mental depression can be recognized in an ape is therefore not sound, if it is based merely on an observer's failure to recognize anything of the sort in a week or two of observation.

The actual behavioral evidence of Kambi's depression is roughly as follows (discovering the real cues on which ones's judgment is based, in such cases, is apt to be very difficult): (1) long-term inconstancy of behavioral baseline, (2) periods of extreme lack of spontaneous activity or responsiveness, and (3) an exceptional emotional instability and ease of frustration at such times as she is responsive and not obviously depressed. To this, as an additional symptom, which, however, would not be diagnostic in itself, we can add (4) her marked sexual abnormality. These can be considered one by one.

(1) The baseline inconstancy is something different from characteristic female changes with the menstrual cycle, or the unreliability of many females' behavior from one moment to another (I am referring now to chimpanzees only). On the whole the chimpanzee's behavior is predictable—not as regards a single act, but in the frequency with which an animal will attempt to reach certain objectives, over a period of time such as a week or month. Also, the probability with some acts may be so high or so low in the individual case that one can almost predict the individual act, if this is defined with fairly broad limits. (Pan will attempt to frighten strangers by a ferocious attack on the intervening wire, first working himself up to the necessary pitch; Pati will almost never invite petting, rarely becomes excited; Bula in heat will always court attention from human beings, almost always from the one in a group whom she knows least well; and so on.) Kambi may show consistency for a time, but the consistent behavior of one six months' period may be very different from that of another.

(2) A prominent, recurring feature of Kambi's behavioral instability is a period of months' duration in which she is extremely unresponsive to environmental events and shows an extreme lack of spontaneous activity. She sits for hours with her back to the wall, hunched over and staring at the floor of the cage, not looking up when attendants pass or even when they speak to her, although ordinarily human beings are her main interest in life. That is, they are the most reliable excitant. During these periods Kambi is never seen taking part in grooming or play, and is so little responsive at feeding times that unless she is caged alone she tends not to get enough food. Kambi's last attack began with an intestinal disturbance, but this disappeared long before the behavioral disturbance, and we have not been able to ascribe her "depression" to any specific physiological origin.

(3) During her better periods her frustration tolerance is low—even for a chimpanzee. She gives up the effort to reach a desired object very readily, and may have a temper tantrum over not getting food after having made no real effort to get it. During such periods she is very fond of petting and attention, but frequently spits at a person who is not at the moment paying attention to her—though he may have done so a moment before—and this habit of course gets her still less attention. Most of the staff dislike her.

(4) Kambi has copulated only once, shortly after the menarche. There was nothing unusual about the mating, and she had already shown a definite lack of sexual responsiveness *before* that one copulation. We have then no basis for explaining her frigidity by postulating some traumatic sexual experience. (Her record in this respect is not unique; one other female (Nira) of the Yerkes colony is known to have copulated only once, with a younger, immature male, and otherwise has demonstrated a masculine aggressiveness rather than feminine receptivity when in oestrus.)

In commenting on these two cases of apparent neurotic or psychotic conditions, I should like to make three points. (A) One is that Kambi's disturbance began during development and so gradually that, in spite of the detailed notes of her diary history, one can find no point at which to say,—here her behavior began to deviate from the norm; while Alpha's behavioral upset was on the whole sudden and acute, and delayed until well after the period of development had concluded.

(B) The second point is that in neither case can one plausibly attribute the disturbance to any *specific* experiences. I certainly have no proof that either disturbance was not due to conflict or some other consequence of experience; but I would like to point out that the details of the whole life of the captive chimpanzee can be known to an extent that is infinitely greater than with human subjects, and no suggestion of an experiential cause for the differences of behavior between (let us say) Kambi and Bimba, or Alpha and Bula, can be found in any of the four histories. In man, neurosis or psychosis again and again occurs without apparent cause in experience. It is common to assume that if we only knew enough about the subject's past we should find such a cause. In recent years, however, there has been repeated demonstration that the kind of mental disturbance that occurs in neurosis can be precipitated by metabolic factors alone (2, 4, 9, 16, 22, 25, 26, 27), although it is usually clear that experience and constitutional factors have both contributed to the disturbance (12) and the effectiveness of a specific metabolic condition, such as anemic disorder, must not be over-rated (5). Only dogma, unsupported and even contradicted by fact, can assert that neurotic behavior in man results always from psychological strain alone. There is even less justification for assuming that Alpha's and Kambi's "neuroses" were due to some experience unknown to their attendants.

(C) The third point is that, despite a number of things about chimpanzee behavior which *remind* one of the neurotic, I know of no other instances in which clear identification is possible. This part of my paper might be expanded to treat other phenomena which can be called aberrant or neurotic but I have the trouble that the chimpanzee is altogether too human in the demonstration of behavior which may or may not be pathological. I find myself lost when it comes to the interpretation which is involved. There is a great deal of chimpanzee behavior which, from one point of view or another, is aberrant; but where is a line to be drawn between aberrant behavior which is relevant to the problem of neurosis and aberrant behavior which is not?

Consider, for example, such biologically unsatisfactory behavior as the following: the masculine behavior by the chimpanzee Nira when in oestrus, and refusal to copulate; the frequent fear by the captive primiparous chimpanzee of her first-born, at the moment of birth and for hours thereafter; May's first acceptance of her baby and later deliberate injury and lack of care; Bimba's overprotectiveness of her infant; Cuba's underprotectiveness of hers; or Wendy's anus-picking, to the point of gross self-injury, when deprived of the company of her preferred cage-mate, Josie. Again, Fifi has long shown what have been called tics: she sits for hours banging her shoulders against a door, and when visitors approach will almost invariably pluck hair from herself, slap them with her hand and bite off their roots, in a highly stereotyped form of behavior. In one sense or another all these things are aberrant. Or take the almost general feces-eating and smearing of the colony. This is certainly suggestive of human psychotic behavior. Is it to be interpreted so? I don't know. It may have been due originally to a dietary lack, and now simply be a habit; or it may be due only to boredom. The amount of time spent by the chimpanzee in manipulating feces with his mouth and in spreading it on the walls and wire of his cage suggests the latter interpretation.

Also, there are the phenomena of "tension-reducing" habits in the chimpanzee, which Yerkes (28) has discussed. These also are suggestive of certain theories of neurosis. While I agree with Yerkes' identification of such behavior with behavior which is called tension reducing in man, I do not think that the behavior is any more clearly neurotic than is doodling while waiting for a telephone call to go through, or drumming on the table by a bridge-player who cannot make up his mind what card to lead.

In short, the two cases I have presented of apparent chimpanzee neurosis offer the only instances of behavior in the Yerkes colony which seem to me to justify the analogy with human neurotic behavior. The position adopted here will, I think, be clearer after discussing the recognition of neurosis.

DIAGNOSIS OF HUMAN NEUROSIS

The behavior of Alpha and Kambi serves in the first place to show that behavioral disturbance in animals can parallel human neurosis or psychosis to a surprising degree, in spite of the lack of verbal communication. The first simulates a pathological phobia in every detail, the second suggests in many ways the objective picture of human depression. Contrasted with Pavlovian neurosis in the dog or cat, the chimpanzee behavior then emphasizes, in the second place, the very limited similarity to human neurosis in the behavior of the carnivora. In itself this does not show that Pavlovian and clinical neurosis should not be identified; but the chimpanzee data do show that it is not merely a verbal report from the dog or cat which is missing when one tries to find an identity between the experimental and the clinical condition; for we have no verbal report from Alpha or Kambi and still have a much more convincing picture of clinical phenomena.

The question is thus raised as to the kind and degree of disturbance in animals that is to be called neurotic. This question is not at all an academic hair-splitting but is directly important for theory, as the recent literature on rat convulsions will testify. It is always of fundamental importance for research to know what aspects of animal behavior can be identified, at least provisionally, with any form of human behavior in which we are interested, if the mechanisms of the human brain are to be understood from animal experiment. It can be shown, I believe, that failure to ask this question, or a wrong answer, has repeatedly produced a waste and confusion of effort in psychological research.

Neurosis is anthropomorphic. Let us now ask, therefore, what the identifying marks of the condition are in man, the species in which neurosis was first identified. We can then see what conditions in other animals may be regarded as having the same properties.

In trying to answer the question, we shall do well to keep the following guiding principles in mind (these are justified elsewhere (10)):

(1) One must distinguish sharply between the behavior which is thought of as arising from a central event or state, and the central state itself. The distinction between neurosis and neurotic behavior must constantly be kept clear if confusion of thought is to be avoided.

(2) The central state is a construct or postulate, not an empirical fact; neurosis is a hypothetical entity which "explains" certain kinds of behavior (the actual function of such postulates seems to be, first, that they set up a classification of behavior; and second, that they may eventually guide research at the physiological level).

(3) The "recognition" of the central state is thus an inference that the postulated state exists in the subject observed—neurosis is *inferred* from behavior, including of course verbal behavior.

(4) The inference may be made (a) from behavior which is intrinsically characteristic, or always recognized as due to neurosis; or (b) from "associated signs": behavior which would not in itself be so classified, but which in a particular species, group or individual has been observed to accompany neurosis and has thus become diagnostic.

It should be said at once that no single act can be intrinsically diagnostic, and that the pattern of behavior which would of itself be classified as due to neurosis would have to extend over a period of not less than weeks and perhaps years. This can be seen from the diagnostic importance given to the patient's history. It does not of course mean that the diagnostician himself must have observed the patient for years, nor that the illness must be of long duration. The disturbance of behavior may be brief, but classifying it as due to neurosis or psychosis involves a knowledge of its history. With associated signs, the matter may be somewhat different, and a single act or remark might give some certainty of diagnosis when it can be assumed that the patient is from a particular culture and has not had any very unusual experiences. Even here, however, the history is presumptively known.

With this in mind, one can see better the meaning of the recognition of neurosis after brief observation. The patient's history may serve, first, to present an intrinsically recognizable long-term disturbance of behavior—the sort of disturbance that is the ultimate reference of the term "neurosis". If so, what the history really does is to extend the period of clinical observation over the patient's life-time. Secondly, the history may provide only the background against which a disturbance of short duration can be evaluated. It may lead the diagnostician to expect other symptoms, in view of the way in which symptoms, in themselves not necessarily neurotic, have already appeared. Such recognition by associated signs essentially involves prediction, and is subject to error; and the signs from which prediction is made are not essentially what is meant by the terms neurotic or psychotic.

To illustrate: suppose that a white woman feels contaminated by a chance contact with the hand of a Negro. The prognostic significance of such an attitude depends on the subject's background. If she is from the southern United States, the probability is low that this is a sign of the kind—or degree—of disturbance that takes people to mental hospitals. In a patient from another part of the country the same limited disturbance might have a very different meaning. Again, a man complains that his bed is electrified at night and gas is being pumped into his room: a symptom so specific that one might tend to think of it as *per se* psychosis. It might justify detention in a mental hospital. But if we ask why it can do so, we see at once that this is only a sign of something else. Locking the patient up on the basis of his verbal statement alone is in effect predicting (having in mind the circumstances in which the behavior appeared) that a more serious disturbance will follow. Otherwise there is no reason for the detention.

Thus a small segment of behavior may be an almost infallible sign of a psychopathological condition, and one may think of it as essentially neurotic. Yet it will be found in all such instances that it is the circumstances in which the behavior appeared that make it diagnostic, and precisely the same behavior in other circumstances can have a very different meaning. Consequently, such associated signs of neurosis do not tell us what the real nature of the neurotic disturbance is.

Also, we must eschew analysis of conditions which are called neurotic only because they fit some theory or other. Theory is of course fundamentally important, and in a later part of this paper I shall discuss a possible theoretical approach to the problem. But we must recognize that there is no sure way at present of choosing from among the dozens of theories (including my own) as to the nature of neurosis. The present discussion is really an attempt to separate the facts in this field from theory, so as to find a secure foundation on which theory can rest. It will be hard for any psychologist or psychiatrist to accept the limited aim of this part of my discussion, or to remember that it is *not* asking whether some theory is good or bad—but only what the conditions are that affect the recognition of human neurosis, to see if we can find criteria by which to test whether a given disturbance of animal behavior should be called neurotic.

The first step in this undertaking was to list the apparent properties of neurosis, and eliminate from it the trivial and redundant items. The next step was to see whether there are conditions which are frequently recognized as neurotic but which did not have some of the characteristics which were listed; and finally, to make a list of conditions which are not in practice called neurotic although they have a number of these characteristics.

Six criteria, (A) to (F) as listed below, were found to be consistent features in recognizing human neurosis. All of these must be retained in a definition of neurosis as it is in practice identified by sophisticated persons; if any one is omitted, it will be found that the definition would include other conditions which are by common agreement not neurosis (apart from theoretical preconceptions). After each of the six criteria I have listed two or more conditions which, in practice, are not regarded as needing a psychiatrist's attention but which would have to be, if that particular criterion were omitted from the empirical definition. (A) must be retained, or else the humanitarian would be treated as a neurotic; (B) must enter the definition, or plain laziness is neurosis; and so on. It is quite possible that any of these characteristics and neurosis will eventually be shown to have the same mechanisms; I am not analyzing theory here, however, but the things which, in practice, can be seen to affect the distinction between what is neurosis and what is not. Freud may be quite right in holding that social taboos and therefore the prudishness of this Western civilization are neurotic in origin, but we still do not understand the mechanisms of behavior well enough to treat this as a fact and not as theory, and in practice the person with even a marked degree of prudery is not thought to need medical attention. What we want to do is to find out what the marks are of the condition which is recognized as neurotic before any theorizing is begun.

Putting into one group the conditions which, in practice, are usually called neurosis, and into another group conditions which are usually not called neurosis, the neurotic conditions are distinguished by satisfying all six of the following criteria (A to F). *Empirically, human neurosis is a state which is:*

(A) *Evaluationally abnormal* (or *undesirable*—one facet of the word 'abnormal': what people tend to avoid in themselves, or to change in others).

This criterion must be retained in the definition else chronic high spirits; exceptional love of sports, or pride in one's work; persistent, marked concern for human welfare; would be neurotic; such things satisfy the other criteria, and seem not to be called neurotic because they are regarded as "good", "desirable" or "healthy". Psychopathology is a science which essentially involves normative procedures. It deals with behavior which may represent only the extreme of a curve of normal distribution, and the line of abnormality is drawn on the basis of a social evaluation.

(B) *Emotional* (involves emotional activity or like an hysterical paralysis derives from it).

This must be an essential feature of neurosis and not adventitious. It excludes: unusual laziness; a low level of emotional activity, such as lack of sexual motivation; endogenous mental deficiency: as *per se* neurotic. When such things, which satisfy other criteria, are thought of as not arising from emotional conflict or disturbance, they are not called neurotic.

(C) *Generalized* (tending to be manifested in a number of ways, not a response to a specific excitant).

This criterion excludes: an unusual prejudice, dislike of cats; prolonged anxiety in a person with reason to anticipate a real and injurious event; anger or fear responses to a conditioned stimulus, adequately reinforced in the past: as not neurotic.

    (D) *Persistent or chronic* in some degree.

This excludes transient unexplained conditions of irritability and depression which seem not to be called neurosis, although in every respect except duration they appear to be the same as neurotic conditions.

    (E) *Statistically abnormal (relatively infrequent*—the alternative meaning of ''abnormal'').

This criterion must be included in a definition, or else all persons would be called neurotic who show: fear, suspicion or aggression toward out-groups; prudery—excessive avoidance of bodily exposure, for example, with emotional components; or fear of some forms of contamination well beyond what bacteriological knowledge justifies.

    (F) *Not due to a specific, gross neural lesion.*

This excludes pathological laughing and crying; emotional changes with aphasia; and conditions arising from a cerebral tumor which may be ''mistaken'' for neurosis or psychosis, and which would in other respects fit a definition of neurosis.

    Next, consider three criteria which seem not to be valid but which evidently have had some influence in determining what is called neurosis:

    (G) (*not essentially true*) neurosis has no known physiological basis;

    (H) (*not essentially true*) it produces a marked change of behavior from an earlier baseline;

    (I) (*not essentially true*) it follows some theoretically ''traumatic'' experience, such as conflict or frustration.

Criteria (G), (H) and (I), which have been called ''not essentially true,'' are worth consideration in some detail, for these have been the source of theoretical confusion. Each proposition may be frequently true, but is not necessarily or essentially so.

    First, (G): neurosis has no known physiological etiology. The terms psychopathic and psychasthenic remind us of an earlier day in which it was possible to think of a disorder of the mind as distinct from any bodily etiology. It seems certain that the classification of clinical conditions, which I am loosely referring to here as neurotic, was determined in part by the lack of any known constitutional source. Moreover, the effect of such ideas still exists: when a physical cause of psychosis, for example, is discovered, such as nicotinic acid deficiency, the tendency is at once to set the psychosis aside in a special class and distinguish it from ''true'' psychosis; when it is discovered that a chloride deficiency is the cause of anxiety, the syndrome is described as a chloride deficiency *simulating* neurosis (26), or when hypoglycemia has the same effect, the physician speaks of hypoglycemia being ''mistaken'' for neurosis (25). Unless the idea is entertained that neurosis cannot be due to a known physiological state, would it not be truer, and medically more valuable, to speak of chloride deficiency, or hypoglycemia, as one cause of neurosis? It is often true that neurosis appears to have no metabolic etiology, but it is still neurosis if such an etiology *is* discovered. Otherwise neurosis must be, in the old sense, a disease of the mind and not of the body.

    The tendency to think of neurosis as without physiological basis also has an undesirable manifestation in medical practice. The psychiatrist is bound to welcome recognition by the general practitioner of the importance of psychological factors in illness. But the pendulum may have swung too far, and the diagnosis of ''neurasthenia'' is sometimes made simply because the physician is not able to make any other diagnosis. Such a group as this Society should, it seems to me, be especially vigilant on this point;

for to some persons the "psychosomatic" concept seems to mean only an influence of mind on body, with little interest in the influence of body on mind—more precisely, little interest in the physiological mechanisms controlling behavior. Without this interest, the psychosomatic concept implies a dualism, and becomes a shield behind which animistic thought can flourish.

(H) The concept of neurosis as a breakdown, or deviation from an earlier baseline of behavior, evidently has affected research to too great an extent. The history of the chimpanzee Kambi is a reminder that many human patients were "screwballs" from the earliest age at which they were big enough to manifest this well-known clinical condition. True, human neurosis is often an acute breakdown, as the chimpanzee Alpha's was, and a sudden deviation of this kind is certainly an aid to recognition. A sudden change of behavior suggests the abnormal. But other abnormal behavior is equally important for theory, and worth study. No one, as far as I know, has regarded as neurosis and attempted to analyze the congenital abnormalities of timidity and maladaptivity in the dog described by James (15), or by Anderson and Parmenter (1), before any experiment by these writers was begun. Yet it seems that the behavior these workers have described is a far better approximation to clinical neurosis than that which results from laboratory procedures alone. Analysis of the congenital abnormality would have been therefore at least as important as analysis of the experimentally induced changes of behavior in other animals. The search for acute breakdown has greatly influenced research on the problem, but it must be concluded that this is not an essential and that in experimental work more attention might be given to spontaneous abnormalities.

(I) The idea, finally, that neurosis is what follows some theoretically defined cause is evidently common: it is, for example, all that can account for Maier's (18) identification of convulsive fits with neurosis. Clearly, human neurosis can be precipitated by psychological strain, by a particular experience; but clearly, also, it can be the result of nutritional or metabolic processes, without any unusual psychological shock or strain. This point was documented earlier, in discussing the origins of behavioral disorder in the chimpanzees Alpha and Kambi.

These are my reasons for denying that (G), (H) and (I) are necesarily true propositions concerning neurosis. Now let us return and examine those criteria which have been retained as essentially involved in the recognition of neurosis.

Criterion (E), that neurosis occurs in a minority of the population, is evidently accidental or adventitious and has no reference to any intrinsic characteristics of the neurotic process. Criterion (F), that neurosis is not due to a gross neural lesion, is open to an objection that has been advanced against (G), and is not logically defensible. It is quite clear, however, that both (E) and (F) have played a consistent part in the clinical identification of neurosis and cannot be left out of an empirical definition. One can find many instances of human neurosis, identified as such in practice, which show that (G), (H) and (I) do not consistently affect the diagnosis; but none to show that (E) and (F) do not consistently affect it. We can recognize, however, that (E) and (F) are doubtful theoretical elements in a definition. If at some future time the "normal" prudishness of this culture should be definitely shown to have the same mechanism as what we now call neurosis, the definition would at once be changed. We could say then that neurosis might occur in a majority of the population. Or if it should be found that the physiological disturbance which is set up by a brain tumor, and which may produce the classical frontal lobe signs, is identical with the physiological disturbance of neurosis, it could then be said that tumor is one cause of neurosis. Gillespie's (8) discussion of the problem of differentiating psychological and constitutional reaction to head injury shows again that it is very unsafe, for theoretical purposes, to give weight to a distinction between abnormal behavior with and without organic basis.

This leaves us with four criteria, (A) to (D), as apparently necessary and inescapable in a definition. Even here, however, there are still difficulties. I can find no way of escaping criterion (A), that neurosis is an undesirable state; yet it seems not to belong at all to the same universe of discourse as the others (B to D). The illogic of putting (A) on the same footing as (B), (C) or (D) may perhaps mean that the concept of neurosis itself is not wholly impersonal and unconfused.

A definition of neurosis, from an empirical approach. Adding up the criteria, we arrive at the following definition of neurosis, as a summary statement of the factors which have been found empirically to affect identification of the condition: *Neurosis is in practice an undesirable emotional condition which is generalized and persistent; it occurs in a minority of the population and has no origin in a gross neural lesion.* It may or may not have a known physiological etiology, may or may not occur as a deviation from an earlier, more normal condition, or follow some unusual psychological shock or strain. In this definition, as we have seen, there may be logically or scientifically unsatisfactory elements, but it appears to reflect accurately what is really involved in the identification of neurosis.

Although the definition undoubtedly has defects, this is the only attempt I know of to proceed at a factual level and at the same time to avoid begging the question implicitly, in saying what is meant by the term "neurosis". That neurosis is disturbed behavior, for example, may be a factual statement; but as a sufficient definition it begs the question—what is disturbed behavior and what is not? Defining neurosis as the result of conflict is a theoretical definition which seems to beg the question (what is conflict?) or to be false (6). Such as it is, let us use the definition that has been arrived at here, and ask what animal behavior approximates to it.

THE DIAGNOSIS OF NEUROSIS IN ANIMALS

If the behavioral disturbances in the chimpanzees Alpha and Kambi are now recalled, I think it will be evident that the conditions described in these animals adequately meet the requirements for identifying neurosis, as far as this can ever be possible in the absence of a verbal examination of the patient. I have shown elsewhere (10) that the recognition of an emotional state in an animal can be valid; and it should be recalled that the clinician does not always, or necessarily, depend on verbal evidence in diagnosis with an uncommunicative human patient.

I believe also that the innately established maladaptation sometimes seen in the dog may satisfy the definition, if the condition referred to by Pavlov (24), James (15) and Anderson and Parmenter (1) corresponds, as it seems to, with what I have observed in a laboratory-reared inbred Irish terrier bitch, "Lizzie". This dog was not merely very timid. She was allowed the run of the laboratory during the day, without exception, and allowed to run outdoors for an hour or two also. She was a breeding female, and no experimental work was done with her to produce behavioral disturbance. Yet when she was admitted to the laboratory suite, she invariably went directly to the same dark corner and lay there without moving for hour after hour and would eventually urinate there if she was not taken outdoors. I succeeded in training her to the leash, but when she escaped from the leash outdoors she either appeared to be lost or else always ran directly to the same group of buildings not far from the laboratory. There she would run round and round the block of buildings, in the middle of Queen's University campus. Once on this beat she would run steadily and would not come to a call, even when it was feeding time, and would only run faster if one tried to catch her from behind. If one turned, however, and went the other way, to *meet* Lizzie on her treadmill, she would stop, and could be caught with no trouble whatever and taken back to the laboratory. Such behavior, it seems, could plausibly be called neurotic, and a good case might be made out for the scientific value of such a diagnosis.

With the so-called experimental neurosis, however, it seems that the matter is not so clear. Pavlov's (24) original description does not show clearly that the behavioral disturbance produced by conditioning procedures was both chronic and generalized beyond the training situation (see criteria C and D). Dr. Gantt may be able to correct me here; Pavlov did not give this point special consideration in his written reports, and he may have had evidence which he did not publish. A lasting disturbance of behavior in the special situation which produced it, *or* a transient generalized disturbance, is not called neurotic in man: the human condition is *simultaneously* generalized and persistent after cessation of the exciting cause. To clarify this, take as a parallel to Pavlov's observation the following: a schoolboy attends school regularly, likes kindergarten and the first grade, but later finds the work of increasing difficulty. One day, following failure at school, he shows emotional disturbance at home; refuses to return to school except under pressure. When he is obliged to attend, he does even worse work than before his "breakdown". Would this be equated with neurosis? Actually, it happens every day, and when the symptoms are so limited to a particular situation it is certainly not called neurosis. Although the symptoms may be generalized—that is, they occur outside of school—they are generalized only while the boy is still made to go to school daily; and although lasting, they arise from a single, repeatedly arising situation and are not meaningfully called chronic, since the exciting stimulus continues to be presented.

We must therefore begin with some skepticism about the experimental neurosis, so called.

I shall make my general position clear later on, but even at this point it is desirable to say that Pavlov's observations and the later ones of Dr. Liddell, Dr. Gantt and Dr. Masserman, evidently have a considerable value and deal with important phenomena. What I am asking is the question which in one sense has already been asked by Dr. Gantt (7) and Dr. Liddell (17): whether it is of value to identify the animal phenomena with a specific clinical condition, "neurosis". But although Gantt and Liddell have doubted the value of this *terminology*, they do seem to assume that in the Pavlovian procedure there occurs a state which is psychopathological: that there has been some breakdown of the emotional mechanism. If there is such a breakdown, it is not too important what name is given to it. My question goes further. What evidence is there to justify the assumption that the experimental animal does anything more than respond in a particular way to a particular situation?

The behavior cited by Pavlov (24), Dworkin (3), Gantt (7), Liddell (17), and Masserman (19, 20) as evidence of an abnormal state in their animals includes: (a) unusual behavior in the test situation: catalepsy, somnolence and refusal to eat; (b) attack on apparatus, sudden refusal to enter the experimental room, disturbance of sexual motivation there, and change of behavior toward experimenter; (c) failure to eat *outside* the apparatus, after feeding has been associated with a disruptive stimulus; (d) failure of discrimination in the test situation; and (e) outside the test situation, change of behavior toward cagemates, lowered limen for startle, general hyperactivity, and disturbance of pulse and respiration.

Most of this evidence I believe is irrelevant to the question. The phenomena (a) of catalepsy and somnolence, and of failure to eat when no injury has been done the animal, are extremely interesting, but in my experience with the Pavlovian procedure in Professor Babkin's laboratory, and according to my understanding of the literature, the phenomena are not unusual but can be seen in almost all dogs as the conditioning procedure goes on, and with no suggestion of any change of behavior outside the experimental room. In the feeding: salivary-secretion method, the gradual diminution of spontaneous activity and increase of unresponsiveness are foreseen from the first, not as a peculiarity of a few dogs but as an inevitable development in almost all. As far as I could learn from Dr. Babkin and Dr. L. A. Andreyev, Pavlov considered that significant salivary records can be obtained from the dog only after interim salivary secretion has stopped. But this stage coincides with the appearance of the characteristic (and most interesting) immobility of the dog between stimulations. Therefore Pavlov's aim from the first was (1) to induce a certain degree of catalepsy as quickly as possible, and then (2) to delay its further extension as long as possible. Sooner or later, it was recognized, the degree of catalepsy which permits consistent salivary records will develop into the hypnotic state or sleep. Conflict does not contribute to the development of this catalepsy, but delays it, as Pavlov (23) has pointed out: a standard feature of his method is to introduce inhibitory stimuli early, to delay catalepsy; and to break up the unresponsiveness when it does appear by the "extinction" of a conditioned reflex—a conflictful procedure, since the formerly positive is now made a negative stimulus. To use positive conditioned stimuli only is the very opposite of conflict in the feeding method (not of course when a noxious unconditioned stimulus is used), and this lack of conflict is what most facilitates catalepsy and somnolence. Thus there is no basis at all for regarding such phenomena as evidence of neurosis. Pavlov himself treated this unresponsiveness as a form of hypnosis; and I see no ground either for rejecting his conclusion or for calling hypnosis neurotic.

Phenomena (b) and (c), excitement in the apparatus, change of behavior in the experimental room or toward the experimenter outside it, and the refusal of Dr. Masserman's cats to feed after feeding had been associated with a frightening airblast, are too specific to a particular situation to be identified with neurosis (see Criterion C). When the avoidance follows stimulation with electric shock, burning the skin, or the air-blast, it seems to me no more neurotic than a child's avoidance of a hot stove. The refusal of Dr. Masserman's cats to eat is in the same class; or at least, there is no evidence that it is not. The cat may have made the association between *eating* (no matter where) and the terrifying air-blast. Similar data are reported by Pavlov (24, pp. 228-229): if a noxious stimulus comes first, then food, the pain is a signal to eat; but if the order is reversed, eating (or the sight of food) is a signal that the pain will follow, and the animal refuses to eat. Masserman and Siever (21) have argued that the behavior of the cats is not a clear-cut avoidance but involves vacillation, and therefore that it must be neurosis. This of course does not follow. Undoubtedly a conflict of motivations was set up, and the analogy with human anxiety is justifiable; but indecision and anxiety, as such, are not synonymous with neurosis. Gantt's observation that copulation was disturbed in the experimental room, although there had been no painful stimulation, certainly indicates that the disturbance is generalized in the sense that more than one kind of activity is involved; but with respect to the exciting cause, the disturbance is still specific to the one situation, the experimental room.

In phenomenon (d), the decreased accuracy in discrimination following a series of failures even when no pain stimulus was used to produce disturbance, it is evident that we have behavior well worth investigation. Pavlov's original observation was of both practical and theoretical interest. The practical importance of the observation is with respect to education, and it deserves more stress in applied psychology than it has received. But the analogy that I have already given, with the schoolboy who hates school following experience with problems that are too difficult for his understanding, shows that (d) is in itself not enough to justify a diagnosis of neurotic behavior.

In phenomena (e), it appears, is the only real evidence of something that might be neurosis. Under this heading are the disturbances which take place outside of the experimental situation; and even here the evidence does not appear to be complete. It can be granted at once that the symptoms described support the parallel with human anxiety states, but anxiety[1] which arises when there is good cause to anticipate recurring injury (see Criterion D) is not diagnosed as neurotic in man. We may distinguish, perhaps, between "exogenous" and "endogenous" anxiety. The exogenous is anxiety aroused in anticipation of a recurrent noxious stimulus, and cannot be called neurotic. Endogenous anxiety would include both the anxiety which occurs spontaneously, and that which, although originally exogenous, continues long after termination of the precipitating noxious events. This is neurotic. The question then is whether there is endogenous anxiety in the experimental animal. Did the sexual disturbances of Dr. Gantt's dog, the hyperactivity and vascular abnormality of Dr. Liddell's sheep, or the agressiveness of Dr. Masserman's cats and the restlessness and fearfulness of his two dogs continue long after termination of the daily experiments? Longer, that is, than would be accounted for by normal emotional conditioning? Anxiety at night is not evidence of abnormal emotional functioning when the animal is exposed every morning to noxious stimuli. Also, we must ask whether the apparatus which Dr. Liddell attached to his sheep, to make the nocturnal observations of heart rate and breathing, was not itself a conditioned stimulus for pain reactions? In the descriptions of experimental neurosis I have not found a detailed treatment of such points, and I may be wrong in thinking that satisfactory evidence of abnormal emotionality is lacking. It is certain, however, that these points must be considered explicitly before the diagnosis of neurotic behavior, experimentally induced, is justified.

In this report no attempt is made to deal systematically with the literature. Also, the purported studies of neurosis in rats can be disregarded. If, as it seems, there may be some doubt whether the experimental disturbances in carnivores and ungulates have the properties of human neurosis, rat behavior is still farther removed from man's, and I have seen nothing in the literature which remotely justifies calling rat behavior neurotic. Finally, while I am touching on phylogenetic differences, I should mention references to experimental neurosis in the chimpanzee by Jacobsen, Wolfe and Jackson (14) and Yerkes (28) which most succinctly illustrate the point of this discussion. They describe temper tantrums, refusal by the chimpanzee to enter the experimental apparatus or lack of motivation, after failures in problem solving. Such behavior would never be called *per se* evidence of psychopathology in man—it is much too normal. The point is clear when we contrast the behavior which I described earlier in Alpha and Kambi, which does seem to correspond to neurosis. Dislike of a particular thing or place is not neurosis; nor yet temper tantrums, nor avoidance of persons or things associated with unpleasant events.

---

[1] "Anxiety" is used in its common meaning, not in the sense sometimes given to it in the psychiatric literature of anxiety without environmental cause.

A THEORETICAL APPROACH TO NEUROSIS

The conclusion of the preceding discussion is that there must be, at the present time, still some doubt about the value of the analogy drawn between human neurosis and the experimentally induced changes in the dog, cat or sheep. This is doubt only, and quite possibly evidence can be presented to banish it. Furthermore, the doubt does not diminish, though it may change, the significance of the observations in question.

A different approach to the problem has been found in an analysis of fear in man and chimpanzee (11). It appears that fear, like neurosis, may occur in circumstances which suggest that a conflict of some sort causes it; but, again like neurosis, may occur when no plausible reference to conflict is possible. To account for the fear-producing effect of a conflict (or incompatibility) between two perceptions, neither of which alone has any emotional value, an hypothesis was developed which unexpectedly generalized itself to provide for other phenomena: showing how fears not due to conflict but to sensory deficit or metabolic disturbance would fit into the same hypothesis, why the manifestations of fear should be so variable, and how fear might be related theoretically to such things as rage, fawning and mental depression.

The key assumption, for which some independent evidence can be found, is that the integration of ordinary unemotional behavior depends fully on a precise timing of cellular firing in the cortico-diencephalic system, and that coordination in the firing of independent cells is to a great extent determined by experience—that is, by the pattern and timing of sensory excitations in the past. Disruption of functional organization involving the cortext might then result from (1) "conflict"—the simultaneous occurrence of processes which do not reinforce each other's effects; (2) sensory deficit—the absence of afferent excitations which are essential to the maintenance of the precise timing of neuronal activities; and (3) metabolic disturbance which changes the rate of firing of individual cells and thus changes their relationship to other cells. The hypothesis then proposes that fear or mental depression is directly related to such a disruption of functional organization, and that each of these emotional conditions is distinctive, in part at least, by the nature of the processes which tend to reestablish the normal organization. In the case of fear, these processes include activation of the avoidance mechanisms, liminally or subliminally; but in mental depression the distinctive feature would actually be a persistent failure of such redintegrative processes. The main defect of the hypothesis is that it offers no prediction as to the extent of the physiological disruption that produces emotional behavior, as contrasted with the disruptions which, obviously, must frequently occur without definitely emotional effect; and it offers no prediction as to the differences of pattern in the disruption which determine whether avoidance, aggression or other overt activity will emerge from the primary incoordination of the effectors. The hypothesis is thus vague on crucial points, but it has some of the characteristics of good theorizing in that it introduces conceptual order into a number of formerly unrelated facts, and further advances in neurophysiology may make it possible to state the hypothesis in a form specific enough to have definite explanatory value and be susceptible to experimental test.

For the present problem the hypothesis has at least one specific value. A major difficulty in understanding the nature of neurosis has been the fact that it may arise from such different causes as (1) a conflict of fear and loyalty, and (2) failure to eat good food. The hypothesis meets this difficulty by treating such things as remote, not immediate causes and (just as with the diverse sources of fear) shows how conflict and malnutrition might have the same effect on behavior. A way is thus suggested in which experience and constitution may be related in the production of neurosis, which may aid in keeping clear the true nature of the problem. I have found in myself a persistent tendency to oppose these two sources of mental illness; and the literature is infested with discussions which treat them as mutually incompatible explanations. As a result such discussions are more than a waste of paper; they are positive contributions to confusion and incite the student to a waste of effort in his research. Even if a statement of an interaction between the experiential and the constitutional in mental illness were no more than a verbal solution, it would be of value if it helped to keep in mind the fact, obvious enough in an unbiased reading of the evidence, that mental illness is usually the joint product of experience and the constitution on which experience acts. There are two factors in mental illness: It seems certain that prolonged exposure to Gestapo methods in a concentration camp might produce a breakdown of behavior in *any* person, whatever his constitution; and on the other hand, evidence has been cited earlier in this paper to show that nutritional deficiency causes neurosis and psychosis with no traumatic experience. On the existing evidence, we can thus assume at one extreme that experience alone can cause psychopathology; at the other that constitutional disturbance alone can do so; but that in most instances both factors operate together.

Finally, the hypothesis has the implication that "experimental neurosis" and the clinical condition are intimately related, if for no other reason than that an environmentally induced anxiety in man (the apparent analogue of the experimental neurosis) is capable of leading to a pathological breakdown—given the susceptible constitution. It is certainly to be hoped that workers on the experimental neurosis, by whatever name it may be called, can continue to elucidate the nature of the changes which occur in the experimental animal; for if we could once understand the mechanism of the (at present) inexplicable change of motivation which Pavlov and Gantt describe, or the factors which control the presence or absence of the anxieties induced in their experimental animals by Liddell and Masserman, it might be a short step to an understanding of clinical neurosis. The problems investigated by these workers are fundamental, and the phenomena they have demonstrated must be considered and dealt with not only in the discussion of psychopathology but in any theory of behavior.

BIBLIOGRAPHY

1. Anderson, O. D., and Parmenter, R.: A Long-Term Study of the Experimental Neurosis in the Sheep and Dog. Psychosom. Med. Monog., Nos. 3 and 4, 1941.
2. Bowman, K. M.: Psychoses with pernicious anemia. Amer. J. Psychiat., **92**: 371, 1935.
3. Dworkin, S.: Conditioning neuroses in dog and cat. Psychosom. Med., **1**: 389, 1939.
4. Egana, E., Johnson, R. E., Bloomfield, R., Brouha, L., Meiklejohn, A. P., Whittenberger, J., Darling, R. C., Heath, C., Graybiel, A., and Consolazio, F.: The effects of a diet deficient in the vitamin B complex on sedentary men. Amer. J. Physiol., **137**: 731, 1942.
5. Ferraro, A., Arieti, S., and English, W. H.: Cerebral changes in the course of pernicious anemia and their relationship to psychic symptoms. J. Neuropathol. Exp. Neurol., **4**: 217, 1945.
6. Finger, F. W.: Abnormal animal behavior and conflict. Psychol. Rev., **52**: 230, 1945.
7. Gantt, W. H.: Experimental Basis for Neurotic Behavior: Origin and Development of Artificially Produced Disturbances of Behavior in Dogs. Psychosom. Med. Monog., Nos. 3 and 4, 1944.
8. Gillespie, W. H.: The psychoneuroses. J. Ment. Sci., **90**: 287, 1944.
9. Harris, H. J.: Brucellosis: a case report illustrating a psychosomatic problem. Psychosom. Med., **6**: 334, 1944.
10. Hebb, D. O.: Emotion in man and animal: an analysis of the intuitive processes of recognition. Psychol. Rev., **53**: 88, 1946.
11. —: On the nature of fear. Psychol. Rev., **53**: 259, 1946.
12. Hobbs, G. E.: Mental disorder in one of a pair of identical twins. Amer. J. Psychiat., **98**: 447, 1941.
13. Jacobsen, C. F., Jacobsen, M. M., and Yoshioka, J. G.: Development of an Infant Chimpanzee during her First Year. Comp. Psychol. Monogr., 9, 1, 1932.

14. Jacobsen, C. F., Wolfe, J. B., and Jackson, T. A.: An experimental analysis of the functions of the frontal association areas in primates. J. Nerv. Ment. Dis., **82**: 1, 1935.

15. James, W. T.: Morphological form and its relation to behavior. In Stockard, C. R.: The Genetic and Endocrine Basis for Differences in Form and Behavior. Philadelphia, Wistar Inst., 1941.

16. Joliffe, N.: The neuropsychiatric manifestations of vitamin deficiencies. J. Mt. Sinai Hosp., **8**: 658, 1942.

17. Liddell, H. S.: Conditioned reflex method and experimental neurosis. In: Personality and the Behavior Disorders. Vol. I. Ed. by J. McV. Hunt. New York, Ronald, 1944.

18. Maier, N. R. F.: Studies of Abnormal Behavior in the Rat; the Neurotic Pattern and an Analysis of the Situation which Produces It. New York, Harper, 1939.

19. Masserman, J. H.: Psychobiologic dynamisms in behavior: an experimental study of neuroses and therapy. Psychiatr., **5**: 341, 1942.

20. —: Behavior and Neurosis. An Experimental Psychoanalytic Approach to Psychobiologic principles. Chicago, Univ. Chicago Press, 1943.

21. —and Siever, P. W.: Dominance, neurosis and aggression: an experimental study. Psychosom. Med., **6**: 7, 1944.

22. Matthews, R. S.: Pellagra and nicotinic acid. J. Amer. Med. Assoc., **111**: 1148, 1938.

23. Pavlov, I. P.: Conditioned Reflexes. Oxford, Humphrey Milford, 1927.

24. —:Lectures on Conditioned Reflexes. New York, International, 1928.

25. Romano, J., and Coon, G. P.: Physiologic and psychologic studies in spontaneous hypoglycemia. Psychosom. Med., **4**: 283, 1942.

26. Saphir, W.: Chronic hypochloremia simulating psychoneurosis. J. Amer. Med. Assoc., **129**: 510, 1945.

27. Spies, T. D., Aring, C. D., Gelperin, J., and Bean, W. B.: The mental symptoms of pellagra. Their relief with nicotinic acid. Amer. J. Med. Sci., **196**: 461, 1938.

28. Yerkes, R. M.: Chimpanzees: A Laboratory Colony. New Haven, Yale Univ. Press, 1943.

11. Conflict and Conditioned Aversive Stimuli in the Development of Experimental Neurosis

Canadian Journal of Psychology, 1965, *19*, 208-23. Reprinted by permission.

ABSTRACT

The purposes of this experiment were to repeat certain features of Masserman's and Yum's study of experimental neuroses and to determine some of the necessary conditions for the development of experimental neuroses. It was hypothesized that experimental neuroses are dependent upon the conditioned aversive stimuli created. The necessity of a conflict situation was also investigated. Cats were trained in an apparatus similar to Masserman's and Yum's and then exposed to various shock conditions creating different conditioned aversive stimuli and conflict conditions. It was found that neurotic behaviour depends partially upon the conditioned aversive stimuli created and that conflict is not necessary for their creation.

Masserman and his associates (1943, 1946) have frequently investigated the effects of "motivational conflicts" on the production of behaviours termed "experimental neuroses." In these studies cats were trained to open a food box to secure pellets of food and were later given shock or airblasts to the head so that a "conflict" developed between response tendencies based on hunger and fear. Cats then "developed feeding inhibitions [i.e., cessation of switch pressing, food box openings, and eating responses], startle and phobic responses to sound and light stimuli, loss of group dominance, aversive behaviour to various configurative elements [e.g., signals, food, experimenter] previously associated with the conflictual situation and other 'neurotic' behaviours" (Masserman and Yum, 1946, p. 36).

These "neurotic behaviours" were based upon observations made on 4- and 6-point scales most completely reported by Masserman and Yum (1946). Unfortunately, the latter study has a number of methodological weaknesses which require clarification in further studies of Masserman's "experimental neuroses." For example, the actual behaviours observed and the sequence in which they were made is unclear. Further, the timing of shocks, their spacing throughout the trials, and the method of determining the number of shocks for a particular cat have not been made clear.

Masserman's studies of "neurosis" are important because they are possibly analogous to human neurosis. For example, Fenichel (1954, p. 19) has stated that:

Psychoneurosis is represented by the artificial neuroses that have been inflicted

---

[1] This paper is based upon a Ph.D. dissertation submitted to the University of Toronto. The author wishes to thank his thesis advisors, Professors H. E. Bishop, R. J. Gibbins and A. Amsel for their advice and encouragement.

upon animals by experimental psychologists (Masserman, 1943, mentioned). Some stimulus . . . which had served as a signal that some action would now procure gratification is suddenly connected by the experimenter with frustrating or threatening experiences . . . the animal then gets into a state of irritation which is very similar to that of a traumatic neurosis.

The actual behaviours observed by Masserman and Yum are not similar to human neurotic behaviour but the conflict conditions are.

The necessity of a conflict between eating and shock avoidance for creating the "neurotic" behaviours found by Masserman have never been clarified. Masserman has stated that a "motivational conflict" is necessary and that giving shock in the same apparatus but not contingent upon eating fails to produce "neurotic" behaviour (Masserman, 1943). Similar contentions have been made by Jacobsen and Skaarup (1955) but supporting empirical evidence is lacking. There is a suggestion in Watson's study of experimental "neuroses" (1954) that shock not paired with eating behaviour (non-conflict) does not produce the same degree of disturbance as does shock contingent on eating (conflict). Unfortunately, the experimental methods used and the quantitative data obtained have not been reported.

Wolpe's experiment (1952) indicated that shock connected with eating may *not* be a necessary pre-condition for "neurotic" behaviour. Wolpe repeated Masserman's studies of experimental "neurosis" with similar procedures but with the addition of a non-conflict group. The conflict group was trained to open a box for food in an apparatus similar to Masserman's. Subsequently, subjects were given 2 or 3 brief shocks during feeding trials so that a conflict was created between eating and shock avoidance behaviour. Each subject in the control group received two series of 5 to 10 shocks while in the experimental cage, but these shocks were not given for food approach and were presented while the subjects explored the cage. Wolpe found that the two groups displayed similar "neurotic" symptoms (defined as unadaptive responses characterized by anxiety and persistence) such as phobic and escape behaviours, resistance to being placed in the cage, mydriasis, muscular tension, and feeding inhibitions. Wolpe concluded that conflict is not necessary for the development of "neurotic" behaviour. However, his non-conflict group got three times as many shocks as did his conflict group, and Masserman and Yum (1946) found a significant positive correlation between the number of shocks received and the extent of "neurotic" behaviour developed. Further difficulties relate to the small number of cats used (N = 4 and 6), the vague observations made, and the lack of quantitative data reported. One purpose of the present experiment is to determine whether a conflict between eating and shock avoidance is a necessary condition for these "neurotic" behaviours where the shocks for conflict and non-conflict groups are identical, and where the observations made and quantitative data are clearly outlined.

The present study also examined the possibility that experimentally created "neurotic" behaviours depend upon the conditioned aversive stimuli developed. In Masserman's and Yum's experiment, shock was given "at the moment of conditioned food taking" (1946, p. 43). No further specification of shock timing is available and it is uncertain whether shock was contiguous with approach to food (pre-consummatory behaviour) or with eating (consummatory behaviour). Numerous experiments have shown that when initially neutral stimuli are paired with shock then the later presentation of these stimuli results in (*a*) the instrumental behaviours made to noxious stimuli such as escape and avoidance behaviours (Miller, 1948), and (*b*) autonomic respondents (Hunt and

Brady, 1951). If shock is contingent upon consummatory or pre-consummatory behaviour, or upon neither of these, then it will be paired with different visual, proprioceptive, and tactual stimuli and hence different stimuli may become aversive. These aversive stimuli should have an important bearing on the type and number of "neurotic" behaviours developed, since most of them are escape, avoidance, or autonomic responses to aversive stimuli.

The importance of pairing shock with different stimuli has been indicated in a study by Lichtenstein (1950). He trained groups of dogs to eat food from a feeder while they were restrained in a conditioning harness, and, subsequently, one group received shock with the presentation of food (pre-consummatory) and the other with eating behaviour (consummatory). The Consummatory group required fewer shocks to inhibit eating than did the Pre-Consummatory group and it also had more food aversions outside the experimental situation. These results support the hypothesis that "neurotic" behaviours are due to the development of apparatus and experimenter cues as conditioned aversive stimuli. They also suggest that the number and type of such behaviours might depend upon the stimuli contiguous with shock. The "neurotic" behaviours observed, then, should be different if shock was paired with pre-consummatory or consummatory behaviours or with neither of them.

Three stimulus groups were formed to study the effects of pairing shock with different stimuli in the Masserman and Yum situation. Cats in the Pre-Consummatory group received shock when they touched the food box, those in the Consummatory group when they ate the food, and those in the Shock Alone group received shock not contiguous with pre-consummatory or consummatory behaviour.

The "neurotic" behaviours observed in the Masserman and Yum experiment were divided into sub-classes according to the conditioned aversive stimuli involved. Behaviours such as attraction to apparatus (A), escape behaviour (B), reaction to experimenter (E), initial interanimal conflict (F), neurotic hypersensitivity (I), situational retreat (K), fear of constriction (L), and substitutive behaviour (O) appear to involve escape and avoidance reactions to apparatus and experimenter cues which have become conditioned aversive stimuli. Neurotic motor disturbance (M) and autonomic responses (N) appear to involve autonomic respondents and involuntary skeletal muscle movements elicited by stimuli in the total situation. Since the three groups receive the same number and intensities of shock, the groups were assumed not to differ on behaviours A, B, E, F, I, K, L, M, N, O.

However, the groups differ in the opportunities for stimuli associated with pre-consummatory and consummatory behaviour to become aversive. The Consummatory group had shock paired with salivating, and with chewing and swallowing of food, hence, proprioceptive and tactual stimuli arising from these activities could become aversive. This group should show more neurotic food avoidance (G), loss of attraction to caged mice (D), and loss of intercat dominance (P) in food-getting competition than those for which shock is not associated with consummatary behaviour. The Consummatory group should show fewer eating responses than the other two groups. The assumption here is that caged mice and food evoke salivating responses which, because of an earlier association with shock, should elicit avoidance behaviour. Lichtenstein's results (1950) suggest that giving shock during eating behaviour develops eating inhibitions and food aversions more rapidly than shock paired with pre-consummatory behaviour.

Since the Pre-Consummatory group had shock paired with food-box approach, it was expected that stimuli aroused by this activity would become aversive. The Pre-Consummatory group should show more neurotic reactions to food box (C), more neurotic switch avoidance (H), and more neurotic reaction to signal (J) than the Shock Alone group. The Pre-Consummatory group should show fewer switch presses and fewer food-box openings than the Shock Alone group. Since shock for both the Pre-Consummatory and Consummatory groups was given after food-box approach differences between these groups in terms of pre-consummatory responses are difficult to predict.

In this experiment, the Pre-Consummatory and Consummatory groups entail conflict, that is opposition between incompatible responses based on eating behaviour and shock avoidance. The Shock Alone group does not involve a conflict between eating and shock avoidance, hence Wolpe's assertion that such a conflict is not essential for "neurotic" behaviour can be studied.

METHOD

Subjects and Apparatus

The Ss were 30 male and female cats over one year of age and were unselected as to breed and strain. The experiment was performed as a series of 10 replications with each replication containing one cat in each of the three stimulus groups, Pre-Consummatory, Consummatory, and Shock Alone. Cats were randomly assigned to replications.

The apparatus was similar in size, construction, and operation to Masserman's and Yum's (1946). The task was to learn to press a switch which activated a feeder and then to lift a lid and obtain food.

The experimental cage was a metal box 40 × 20 in., with plastic sliding doors and a roof of welded wire fence cloth. The floor was made of ⅜-in. brass tubes placed ¾ in. apart. It was electrifiable and was balanced on springs and microswitches so that activity measures could be obtained. A squeeze partition could be moved the length of the cage and positioned at various points across its width. The use of this partition in determining the cat's responses to constriction is described in the Appendix.

The food box (4½ in. × 6½ in.) was located in one end wall of the cage and was covered by a clear plastic lid. The cats' switch was adjacent to this food box and it consisted of an oval piece of plywood (4½ in. × 6½ in.) positioned close to the floor. Slight pressure on it closed a microswitch and activated the feeding mechanism and the signal. The feeding mechanism was a large bicycle wheel with 50 cups (each containing 2 gm. of food) attached to the outside rim. The wheel was placed horizontally and a hole was cut in the end wall so that the food cups could enter the food box. A switch press moved the wheel so that one full cup was available in the food box.

The signals were sound and light stimuli similar to those used by Masserman and Yum (1946). The light stimulus was provided by four 100-watt bulbs above the cage and the sound by a 800 c.p.s. tone. The clicking stimulus used in neurotic hypersensitivity (below) was 16 c.p.s. Sound and light stimuli were activated simultaneously by the cats' switch but went off automatically after two sec.

The shocks were 3.5-ma. A.C. and about one sec. in duration. They were administered from the control panel by the E.

Procedure

Preliminary Training

Prior to training all Ss were placed on a 24-hr. food deprivation schedule and reduced to 80 ± 2% of their normal body weight. Training was then given once per day by the method of successive approximation (Skinner, 1951, 1953). Each S was trained to approach the food box, lift the lid, and eat the food on signal (signal response criterion) until it performed five consecutive eating responses with less than a 20-sec. latency. Ss were then trained to press the switch which turned on the signal and turned the food wheel (switch response criterion) until they made three such responses in the first three min. after being placed in the cage. As in Masserman's and Yum's experiment (1946) each S was given food only during experimental sessions but water was freely available in the home cages.

Dominance Trials

On the day after each S had reached the criterion for the signal response, dominance trials were begun. These trials were given once a day for the duration of the experiment in a session which began 25 min. before the major experimental session. Two cats were placed in the cage, with the switch off, and the signal was presented (followed by food) on five occasions. For these trials each experimental S was placed with a cat which was submissive to it (i.e., one which failed to eat before the experimental S on 4 of the 5 trials on two previous days). The same two cats were paired on the training days, and each of the shock days. In some instances it was necessary to try several cats until one was found to be submissive to each experimental cat.

Shock Sessions

Shock sessions were begun on the day after the S had reached the criterion for switch pressing and they continued for four days. The Pre-Consummatory S in each replication was run first and the Consummatory and Shock Alone Ss received the same number of shocks as did the Pre-Consummatory S in their own replication. During each shock session eight shocks were randomly interspersed throughout the 40 trials. The trials on which shock was given differed for each day, but cats in the sample replication received shock on the same trials. The number of shocks ranged from 3 to 7 with an average of 5.2. Shock sessions were limited to a period twice as long as that required to complete 40 trials on the last non-shock day.

The Pre-Consummatory Ss received shock after pressing the switch, while the lid was being lifted but before eating. Consummatory Ss received shock one sec. after food had been taken into the mouth. Shocks for the Shock Alone group were given at least 30 sec. after any pre-consummatory or consummatory behaviour, and they were given preceding the same trials on which the Pre-Consummatory and Consummatory cats were shocked. The amount of food each S received in the shock sessions was estimated and two hr. after more food to a total of 80 gm. was given. Ss were then on a 22-hr. deprivation schedule.

Observation of Neurotic Behaviours

The "neurotic" behaviours observed by Masserman and Yum and the sequence in which they were observed is not clear in some instances; many could be reliably rated (e.g., behaviours C, G, and H) with little change but some were revised and clarified (e.g., behaviours A, E, and D). Observations of "neurotic" behaviour and the numbers of switch presses, and food-box opening and eating responses (pre-consummatory and consummatory responses) were made for each S on the last non-shock day and on the second, third, and fourth shock days.[1] A summary of the observations of "neurotic" behaviour is shown in the Appendix.[2] It can be seen that behaviours F and P were observed during the dominance trials, behaviour E was observed as the cat was taken from the home cage, and all others were observed during the major experimental session.

RESULTS

Method of Establishing the Presence or Absence of Neurotic Behaviours

Most of the primary data for this experiment consisted of ratings of neurotic behaviours. The numerical ratings which Masserman and Yum assigned to these behaviours could not be used in statistical analyses because they lack ratio or interval scale properties. Consequently, the scale for each behaviour was dichotomized into "present" and "absent." The dichotomization points were determined for each neurotic behaviour separately and the same point was used for each cat. The points put all cats, regardless of their stimulus group, in the absent category on the last non-shock day. Behaviour prior to shock was defined as "non-neurotic" and behaviour after shock was compared to it to see how many cats deviated from this base line. Cats whose behaviour did not fall into the absent category were scored "present" on the shock days. The number of cats scored present and absent after shock was used to establish the effects of conflict and conditioned aversive stimuli on "neurotic" behaviour. Since some gradual development of "neurotic" behaviour occurred the data for the fourth shock day seemed to represent the maximal effects of shock and hence only the data for this day were analysed.

Behaviour before shock was defined as "non-neurotic" but after shock many subjects changed markedly and most were scored present for neurotic behaviours on the fourth shock day. Chi-square analyses for the significance of changes were made to determine whether the differences between the last non-shock day and the fourth shock day were significant. Table I shows the results of these analyses and for all behaviours except initial inter-animal conflict (F) a significant number of cats changed from absent to present from the last non-shock day to the fourth shock day. The conclusion is that "neurotic" behaviour was produced by the shock contingencies used.

Conditioned Aversive Stimuli and Neurotic Behaviour

The significance of the differences among the stimulus groups in the number of cats for which a behaviour was present was tested for each behaviour individually. Table II shows the results of the chi-square tests for each "neurotic" behaviour. In accordance with the first hypothesis there were no significant differences for behaviours, A, B, E, F, I, K, L, M, N, and O in the number of cats scored present on the fourth shock day.

The second hypothesis predicted that more cats in the Consummatory group than in the other groups would be scored present for loss of attraction to caged mice (D), neurotic food avoidance (G), and loss of intercat dominance (P). Table I shows that only the chi-square for loss of attraction to caged mice (D) was significant ($x^2 = 11.111$,

---

[1] The reliability of the Masserman and Yum scale of neurotic behaviours has never been determined. In this experiment an independent rater observed 6 Ss on 18 occasions and on all neurotic behaviours there were 15 or more complete agreements on the ratings assigned (4- or 6-point scales).

[2] The exact procedures involved in these observations are described in a mimeographed document available from the author.

Table I. Number of Cats which Changed from Absent to Present and from Present to Absent from the Last Non-shock Day to the Fourth Shock Day (The results of the chi-square analyses for the significance of changes are also shown.)

Neurotic behaviour		Number which changed from		Chi square	Probability of the observed increase in neurotic behaviour
		Present to absent	Absent to present		
Attraction to apparatus	(A)	0	22	20.045	
Escape behaviour	(B)	0	20	18.050	
Reaction to food box	(C)	0	25	23.040	< .001
Attraction to caged mice	(D)	0	20	18.050	
Reaction to experimenter	(E)	0	14	12.071	
Initial interanimal conflict	(F)	0	0	0	
Neurotic food avoidance	(G)	0	28	26.036	
Neurotic switch avoidance	(H)	0	28	26.036	
Neurotic hypersensitivity	(I)	0	21	19.048	
Neurotic reaction to signal	(J)	0	17	18.050	< .001
Situational retreat	(K)	0	23	19.048	
Fear of constriction	(L)	0	24	22.043	
Neurotic motor disturbance	(M)	0	27	25.037	
Autonomic changes	(N)	0	21	19.048	
Substitutive behaviour	(O)	0	7	5.143	< .05
Loss of intercat dominance	(P)	0	30	28.033	< .001

Table II. The Chi-square Analyses of the Significance of the Differences between Stimulus Groups in the Number of Cats Scored Present and Absent on Each Neurotic Behaviour (The clusters indicated group behaviours about which different predictions were made.)

Neurotic behaviour		Chi square	Probability
Attraction	(A)	1.362	.50
Escape behaviour	(B)	1.200	.70
Reaction to experimenter	(E)	1.874	.50
Initial interanimal conflict	(F)	a	—
Neurotic hypersensitivity	(I)	2.856	.30
Situational retreat	(K)	14.92	.50
Fear of constriction	(L)	1.250	.70
Neurotic motor disturbance	(M)	2.856	.30
Autonomic changes	(N)	2.384	.50
Substitutive behaviour	(O)	.362	.90
Attraction to caged mice	(D)	11.111	.01
Neurotic food avoidance	(G)	1.066	,70
Loss of intercat dominance	(P)	a	—
Reactions to food box	(C)	3.339	.20
Neurotic reaction to signal	(J)	13.306	.01
Neurotic switch avoidance	(H)	1.066	.70

[a]A chi-square was not performed because the frequencies are identical and hence the chi-square must be zero and nonsignificant.

$p < .01$). Further analyses were performed on the data for behaviour D to determine which of the differences between the stimulus groups was significant. The Fisher Exact Probability Test was applied to the following combinations: Pre-Consummatory-Consummatory, Consummatory-Shock Alone, and Pre-Consummatory-Shock Alone.

Only the difference between the Consummatory and Shock Alone groups was significant ($p < .01$). One significant difference (behaviour D) with $p < .01$ out of three actually tested would occur by chance fewer than once in a hundred times, so a significant stimulus group difference exists for these three behaviours as a cluster.

The second hypothesis also predicted that the Consummatory group would show fewer eating responses than would the other stimulus groups. A simple analysis of variance was performed on these data. There were no significant differences among the stimulus groups ($F = .80$). It is concluded that the groups did not differ in the number of eating responses for the fourth shock day.

Hypothesis 3 predicted that more cats in the Pre-Consummatory group than in the Shock Alone group would be scored present for reaction to food box (C), neurotic reaction to signal (J), and neurotic switch avoidance (II), and that the Pre-Consummatory group would show fewer switch presses and food-box openings than the Shock Alone group. Table I shows that the chi squares were non-significant for behaviours C and H but highly significant for behaviour J ($x^2 = 13.306$, $p < .01$). Again, the Fisher Exact Probability Test was applied to the 2×2 combinations and it was found that the Pre-Consummatory group contained significantly more cats scored present than did the other two groups ($p < .01$ for both comparisons). One significant difference out of three tests would occur less than once in a hundred times by chance. The analyses of variance outcomes for the numbers of switch presses and food-box openings showed no significant differences ($F = 1.28$ and .85 respectively).

The Importance of Conflict in Establishing Neurotic Behaviour

The lack of significant stimulus group differences in neurotic behaviour (Table II) indicates that there is very little difference between the conflict (Pre-Consummatory and Consummatory) groups and the non-conflict group—except for behaviours D and J. Further support for this contention was found in the comparison of the total number of neurotic behaviours in the various stimulus groups. An analysis of variance showed no significant stimulus group difference in the total numbers of behaviours scored present ($F = 1.94$). These analyses failed to demonstrate a difference between conflict and non-conflict conditions in the extent of "neurotic" behaviour developed.

As mentioned, stimulus group comparisons were also made for the numbers of switch-pressing, food-box-opening, and eating responses. The analyses of variance outcomes were all non-significant and hence there is no conflict—non-conflict difference in pre-consummatory and consummatory responses.

DISCUSSION

This experiment was designed to improve and extend Masserman's and Yum's study (1946) by repeating their experiment with some methodological changes and by determining variables relevant to the production of experimental neuroses. In particular, the effects of different conditioned aversive stimuli and of various conflict situations were investigated.

There were some similarities and some differences between this experiment and Masserman's and Yum's. The apparatus, the nature and length of training periods, and the number and distribution of shocks were similar, but the scales of "neurotic" behaviours used differed. Items in the revised scale were clearly defined and a specific sequence was followed in making the observations, and also, their interrater reliabilities were determined and found to be high. A further difference concerned the dichotomization of the scales for individual behaviours into present and absent, rather than using the numbers arbitrarily assigned to them by Masserman and Yum. Since this experiment found a significant change in "neurotic" behaviour after the introduction of shock it strengthens the empirical evidence for the effects of shock contingencies Masserman and Yum used.

An important question concerns the similarities between the defining conditions for human neurotic behaviour and those in this experiment. Fenichel (1954) has assumed that a close analogy exists between the two. However, Eysenck holds a completely opposed view and has stated (1959) that: "Fenichel is completely wrong in claiming that 'experimental neurosis' is in any way analogous to the Freudian model of human neurosis. It appears, therefore, that in so far as these studies [Masserman's] are relevant at all they can be regarded as demonstrating nothing but simple conditioned fear responses." These statements were made partly because Masserman's neurotic behaviours do not meet Hebb's criteria (Hebb, 1947) for states in animals analogous to human neuroses. These criteria require that the experimental neurosis be "an undesirable emotional condition which is generalized and persistent; it occurs in a minority of the population and has no origin in a gross neural lesion" (Hebb, 1947, p. 11). Of course, Masserman's and Yum's "neurotic" behaviours do not fit these criteria, except that they are "emotional" and probably not due to a "gross neural lesion." Fenichel's point seems to be, however, that the essential *conditions* of conflict are similar for human and experimental neuroses. On this point, Eysenck has quoted Wolpe's experiment (1952) as showing that Masserman's and Yum's conflict is in no way analogous to the conditions for human neurosis. The results of this experiment support Wolpe's findings, in that they show that a conflict between eating and shock avoidance is not a necessary condition for the neurotic behaviours found by Masserman and Yum. Because the experimental conditions employed approximately those believed by psychoanalysts to be crucial in human neuroses they provide a useful laboratory analogue, although it is realized that human neuroses may differ from them in numerous ways.

Although a conflict between eating and shock avoidance has been assumed to be necessary in creating "neurotic" behaviour of the type studied, this experiment failed to show any differences between the conflict groups. In addition, the numbers of switch-pressing, food-box-opening, and eating responses were the same in the various conflict groups. This finding is similar to that reported by Wolpe (1952), but his was based on an experiment which could not give sufficient warrant for this conclusion.

Even if Wolpe's conclusions are taken at face value they do not indicate whether conflict facilitates the production of experimental neuroses when shock is used. The present study clearly indicates that conflict does not facilitate their production. An important aspect of Wolpe's experiment has not been investigated here—that is, demonstration that the neurotic behaviours are persistent and generalized.

The results indicate that a conflict between eating and shock avoidance is not necessary for the creation of this type of neurotic behaviour. This finding runs counter to Masserman's assertions about the necessity of such conflict (Masserman, 1943) and counter to the more general suggestions of Dollard and Miller (1950) and Fenichel (1954). The results tend to support theories which attribute these types of behaviour to the creation of conditioned responses (Eysenck, 1959; Skinner, 1953).

The failure to confirm all predictions for the Consummatory and Pre-Consummatory groups is difficult to explain. Perhaps shock for the Shock Alone group was paired with proprioceptive and tactual stimuli associated with movement in general or with imperceptible movements toward the switch or food box—movements which would be punished and hence decrease in frequency. Shock might have been paired with food approach behaviour in the Consummatory and Pre-Consummatory groups and hence similar conditioned aversive stimuli developed. However, significant differences were found for behaviours D and J. Also, the Shock Alone group did not differ from the other groups in behaviours, G, P, C, and H, or in the number of pre-consummatory and consummatory behaviours, even though its shock was 30 seconds after the last switch press—an unfavourable interval for conditioning (Davitz, Mason, Mowrer and Viek, 1957). These arguments suggest that different conditioned aversive stimuli should have been developed, although they were not sufficiently important to result in all of the predicted changes.

The finding that all stimulus groups developed most of the "neurotic" behaviours and inhibitions of consummatory and pre-consummatory responses are not explicable solely with reference to group differences in conditioned aversive stimuli. These findings are, however, in line with Amsel's finding (1950) that administering shock in an apparatus where previous drinking had occurred resulted in a decrease in drinking and autonomic responses even if shock were not paired with consummatory behaviour. This decrease in drinking developed because responses incompatible with drinking (defecation, freezing, crouching, etc.) were conditioned to apparatus cues. A similar situation existed in this experiment where immobility, autonomic responses, and escape attempts could have competed with eating. Further support for this "response competition" explanation would occur if successive exposures to the conditioned aversive stimuli (in the absence of shock) resulted in a decrease in competing responses and an increase in consummatory behaviour.

RÉSUMÉ

L'expérience consiste à reproduire certaines caractéristiques de l'étude faite par Masserman et Yum sur les névroses expérimentales et cherche à préciser certaines des conditions nécessaires à l'établissement de ces névroses. L'hypothèse à vérifier suppose que la névrose expérimentale résulte de la création de stimuli conditionnés de nature aversive. Le problème se pose également de savoir s'il faut faire intervenir une situation de conflit. Une fois entraînés dans un appareil analogue à celui qu'employaient Masserman et Yum, des chats sont soumis à des conditions variées de choc électrique produisant des conditions de conflit ainsi que des stimuli conditionnés de nature aversive. On observe que le comportement névrotique dépend en partie de la production de stimuli conditionnés de nature aversive et que cette production n'exige pas nécessairement une situation de conflit.

APPENDIX

The Revised Schedule for Neurotic Behaviours as Used in the Present Experiment

A: Attraction to apparatus (observed during first 3 min. of experimental session)

  0 Violently resists entry to cage (struggles to avoid entry or balks at entry)

  1 Agitated (pacing and hyperaesthetic (tremors) in cage)

  2 Restless, paces or seeks release (when inside cage)

  3 Immobile: crouches in corner (for 3-min. period)

4 Indifferent to entry or confinement (no attempts to enter cage or to escape)
5 Readily seeks to enter and remain (struggles to get free and enter cage)

B: Escape behaviour (observed during 3 door openings in first 3 min. of experimental session)
0 Energetically tries to force escape (scratching at doors or roof of cage)
1 Invariably leaves cage when permitted (on all 3 openings)
2 May leave or remain when door open (on 1 or 2 door openings)
3 Indifferent to escape (no escape on any door opening)
4 Remains despite inducement to leave (food inducement)
5 Actively resists removal from cage (struggle or retreat when picked up)

C: Reactions to food box (observed on every trial or on one guided trial at end of session if no switch pressing occurred)
0 Violently resists approach to box (on guided trial)
1 Crouches in far corner (no food-box opening at all)
2 Avoids immediate vicinity of the box (opens box on fewer than 20 per cent of the trials)
3 Desultory in signal response (opens box on fewer than 79 per cent of trials)
4 Opens box 4/5 signals (80-89 per cent of trials)
5 Avidly opens and explores box on signal (90-100 per cent of trials)

D: Attraction to caged mice (observed on presentation of mouse after all switch pressing was completed during experimental session)
0 Avoids or phobic to mice (cat retreats, or moves away from mouse)
1 Indifferent to mice (no observations or approach but no retreat)
2 Occasional desultory observation (only a few glances at mouse but no approach)
3 Interested but readily distracted (approach to mouse but observation sporadic)
4 Watches intently (complete attention given to mouse but no attempts to capture)
5 Active attempts to capture (i.e., claw or bite)

E: Reaction to experimenter (observed in S's home cage just prior to experimental session)
0 Active resistance to handling (struggle to get free, hissing, clawing, or arching back)
1 Selective hostilities (no resistance to removal from cage, but resistance when being carried)
2 Indifferent: avoids handling
3 No resistance to handling but not seeking petting
5 Actively seeks petting and handling

F: Initial inter-animal conflict (observed during five dominance trials)
0 None: peaceful relationships (no fighting or shouldering)
1 Occasional shouldering for food (one trial only)
2 Persistent competition for food (more than one trial)
3 Snarling, arching, threats (on any trial)
4 Occasional overt fighting (i.e., striking with paws, scratching, or biting on any trial)
5 Persistent vicious combat (overt fighting on more than one trial)

G: Neurotic food avoidance (observed during entire experimental session)
0 Feeds freely on pellets (80 per cent or more of the eating responses on last non-shock day)

   1 Eats erratically (fewer than 80 per cent)
   2 From box only when guided
   3 Hand feeding only
   4 Special food only (milk)
   5 Rejects all food

H: Neurotic switch avoidance (observed during first 3 min. (criterion) and during entire experimental session)
   0 Works switch spontaneously (criterion rate and 80 per cent or more of the trials on the last non-shock day)
   1 Works switch with guidance (50-79 per cent of the trials on the last non-shock day, after one guided trial)
   2 Use irregular or sporadic (less than 50 per cent of those on the last non-shock day)
   3 Hesitant and incomplete switch presses (in addition to irregular use)
   4 Will not use switch (no switch press)
   5 Shows active avoidance (no switch press plus immobility)

I: Neurotic hypersensitivity (observed on one trial chosen at random during experimental session when 16 c.p.s. click sounded)
   0 Response focused on feeding situation (animal continues approach)
   1 Alert but not distractable (i.e., not turning head)
   2 Over-alert, distractable (turning away from food box)
   3 Occasional generalized startle (tremors or horripilation)
   5 Marked phobias; crouching, panic (i.e., retreat to rear of cage)

J: Neurotic reaction to signal (oberved on every trial)
   0 No fear of signal (i.e., no startle or fear responses)
   1 Slight startle (mild tremors or horripilation)
   2 Occasional fear (crouching and startle on 20 per cent or fewer trials)
   3 Occasional fear, maximal (21-50 per cent of trials)
   4 Consistent fear, submaximal (51-80 per cent of trials)
   5 Consistent fear, maximal (81-100 per cent of trials)

K: Situational retreat (observed during second 3-min. period of experimental session when S is confined behind barrier on the side opposite the switch)
   0 Passes barrier and presses switch
   1 No preferred position in cage (passes barrier but no switch press)
   2 Prefers rear; emerges for signal (but no resistance when guided past barrier)
   3 Remains in rear unless guided (no resistance when guided)
   4 Resists guidance around barrier (struggle and escape attempts when guided)
   5 Persistent attempts to escape (scratching at doors, barrier, or roof of cage)

L: Fear of constriction (observed on first trial after situational retreat (K) when S is confined by barrier on the side nearest the switch)
   0 None, feeds on signal
   1 Slight restlessness but feeds (pacing)
   2 Leaves food at barrier movements
   3 Ignores signal when constricted (no movement towards food)·
   4 Phobic reactions under increased constriction (crouching, immobility)
   5 Panic reaction when constricted (struggle, escape attempts)

M: Neurotic motor disturbance (based on activity measures obtained throughout the entire experimental session)
  0 No motor disturbance (activity measure ± 25 per cent that on last non-shock day)
  1 Hyperactive (activity measure more than 25 per cent above that on last non-shock day)
  1 Hypoactive (activity measure more than 25 per cent below that on last non-shock day)
  3 Immobility (no movement for over half the session)
  5 Convulsions (involuntary muscle contractions)
  5 Catalepsy (waxy rigidity of limbs)

N: Autonomic changes (observed as they appeared during the entire experimental session)
  0 None grossly observed
  1 Horripilation (standing up of fur), mydriasis (dilation of pupils)
  3 Trembling, irregular breathing, excessive salivation, retching
  5 Vomiting, urination, defecation

O: Substitutive behaviour (observed as behaviours appeared during entire experimental session)
  0 None
  1 Preening, playing, rubbing
  3 Deviant responses (prolonged switch pressing, excessive clawing, pacing)
  5 Persistent bizarre responses (e.g., continuous loud vocalizing)

P: Loss of intercat dominance (observed during five dominance trials)
  0 Maintained dominance (all 5 trials)
  1 Occasional surrender of food (one trial only)
  2 Frequent surrender of food (on more than one trial)
  3 Mild phobic responses; fighting (any trial)
  4 Avoidance of subdominant partner (any trial)
  5 Signal phobia, immobility, catalepsy (all trials)

REFERENCES

Amsel, A. The effect upon level of consummatory response of the addition of anxiety to a motivational complex. *J. exp. Psychol.,* 1950, **40**, 709-15.

Davitz, J. R., Mason, D. J., Mowrer, O. H., & Viek, P. Conditioning of fear: a function of the delay of reinforcement. *Amer. J. Psychol.,* 1957, **70**, 69-74.

Dollard, J., & Miller, N. E. *Personality and psychotherapy.* New York: McGraw-Hill, 1950.

Eysenck, H. J. Learning theory and behaviour therapy. *J. ment. Sci.,* 1959, **105**, 61-75.

Fenichel, O. *The psychoanalytic theory of neurosis.* New York: Norton, 1954.

Hebb, D. O. Spontaneous neurosis in chimpanzees: theoretical relations with clinical and experimental phenomena. *Psychosom. Med.,* 1947, **9**, 3-16.

Hunt, H. F., & Brady, J. Some effects of electro-convulsive shock on a conditioned emotional response. *J. comp. physiol. Psycho.,* 1951, **44**, 88-98.

Jacobsen, E., & Skaarup, Y. Experimental induction of conflict behaviour in cats: its use in pharmacological investigations. *Acta Pharmacol. Toxicol.,* 1955, **11**, 117-24.

Lichenstein, P. E. Studies of anxiety. I. The production of a feeding inhibition in dogs. *J. comp. physiol. Psychol.,* 1950, **43**, 16-29.

Masserman, J. H. *Behaviour and neurosis: an experimental psychoanalytic approach to psychobiologic principles.* Chicago: University of Chicago Press, 1943.

Masserman, J. H., & Yum, K. S. Analysis of the influence of alcohol on experimental neuroses in cats. *Psychosom. Med.,* 1946, **101**, 36-52.

Miller, N. E. Studies of fear as an acquirable drive: I. Fear as motivation and fear reduction as reinforcement in the learning of new responses. *J. exp. Psychol.,* 1948, **38**, 89-101.

Skinner, B. F. How to teach animals. *Scientific American,* 1951, **185**, 26-9.
—*Science and human behavior.* New York: Macmillan, 1953.
Watson, R. E. Experimentally induced conflict in cats. *Psychosom. Med.,* 1954, **16**, 340-7.
Wolpe, J. Experimental neurosis as learned behaviour. *Brit. J. Psychol.,* 1952, **43**, 243-68.

12. Experimental Neurosis in Monkeys*

D. I. MIMINOSHVILI

In I. A. UTKIN (Ed.), *Theoretical and Practical Problems of Medicine and Biology*
Experiments on Monkeys, Oxford: Pergamon Press, 1960, 53-67. Copyright 1960 by
Pergamon Press. Reprinted by permission.

The experimental pathology of higher nervous activity is one of the most important
parts of I. P. Pavlov's teachings. The importance which he attached to this question is
expressed in the following quotation from his writings: 'The experimental study of
pathological changes of fundamental processes of the nervous activity of animals will
enable us to understand the physiological mechanism of a number of neurotic and
psychological symptoms, whether they exist independently or as part of certain forms
of disease.'

I. P. Pavlov's pupils, M. K. Petrova, A. G. Ivanov-Smolenskii, M. A. Usievich,
P. S. Kupalov *et al.* have considerably widened the field of experimental pathology of
higher nervous activity.

Knowledge of the laws governing the development of the neurotic state has helped to
get experimental models of the so-called psychological illnesses, the neurogenous disturbances of a number of organs and systems.

P. S. Kupalov, studying experimental neuroses in animals, has recently obtained
some new data. The first experimental neuroses in monkeys were obtained by C. D.
Kaminskii, L. A. Bam and B. Ia. Kriazhev.

The development of the study of experimental pathology and of higher nervous activity was accompanied by the development of experimental therapy of neurotic conditions.

"Before our eyes", said I. P. Pavlov, "the physiology of the cerebral hemispheres
has gone over to their pathology and therapy".

At the moment the study of aetiology, pathogenesis and experimental therapy of
some psychogenous diseases of man cannot be studied without first producing a model
of these pathological conditions in animals.

In order to obtain a model of hypertension and of cardio-vascular disorders we used
monkeys, as they are biologically closest to man. We set ourselves the task of working
out the most suitable form of overstraining their higher nervous activity and of achieving extreme disturbances in order to study the neuroses we had thus produced.

While studying the higher nervous activity, we also investigated certain vegetative
functions of our experimental animals (the functions of separate internal organs). We
followed the dynamics of the disturbance of these functions resulting from disturbance

---

* Presented to the widened meeting of the Department of Medico-Biological Sciences. Academy of
Medical Sciences of the USSR, 18th April, 1953, in Sukhumi.

of higher nervous activity. That section of our work is presented in a separate communication in this book (Miminoshvili, Magakian and Kokaia).

I. P. Pavlov divided all the disease-producing influences which act on the higher nervous activity and lead to neuroses into three categories: (1) overstraining of the excitatory process; (2) overstraining of the inhibitory process; and (3) the overstraining of the mobility of nervous processes.

'This is to be called the collision of the excitatory and inhibitory processes', said I. P. Pavlov.

All experiments in which attempts were made to produce neuroses have usually employed these three measures on the basis of food conditioned stimuli. We tried to obtain a functional disturbance of the higher nervous activity by the clash of excitatory processes in the cerebral cortex.

In speaking of the collision of excitatory processes in the cerebral cortex as one of the experimental methods for obtaining a neurosis, we do not add another to the three categories described by I. P. Pavlov. On the contrary, closer examination of the physiological mechanism of this procedure reveals that it is fully covered by the third category of procedure, i.e. by the overstraining of mobility. Instead of the collision of the two opposite nervous processes of excitation and inhibition, the two cortical processes involved induce each other negatively. In this kind of collision, the inhibitory process which acts reciprocally with the excitatory process, has arisen as the result of negative induction.

During I. P. Pavlov's lifetime and at his instigation, G. P. Konradi and B. P. Rikman undertook a special study of the reciprocal action of excitatory processes and of their relationship to various cortical and subcortical centres. They revealed that the clash of that kind of excitations leads to a breakdown of higher nervous activity. The resultant disturbance of cortical activity is considerably greater than that following a collision between positive and inhibitory stimulation.* It was shown that this form of collision is more effective than the usual one, as it even led to disruption of the higher nervous activity of a strong, balanced dog.

The choice of this particular form of overstraining of higher nervous activity for the purpose of producing a neurosis in monkeys was determined by the following considerations:

(1) The work of C. D. Kaminskii, Ia. Kriazhev *et al.*, as well as our own investigations, have definitely shown that overstraining of the higher nervous activity of monkeys on the basis of food conditioned reflexes leads only to weak and temporary disturbances. Consequently, stronger measures based on other conditioned and unconditioned reflexes which would involve great strain on cortical activity had to be used.

(2) The collision of excitatory processes, directed against various cortical and subcortical centres, is most common in the circumstances of everyday life where it leads to neurosis and somatic illness. For this reason, this form of nervous strain seemed most adequate and closest to the harmful factors of real life which cause breakdowns of higher nervous activity.

(3) All cases of hypertension and of coronary insufficiency which occurred amongst the monkeys kept by us were regarded as the result of the breakdown of their higher nervous activity, and we therefore examined the animals in question. These breakdowns were frequently caused by conflicting situations which had arisen under the

---

* Pavlovskie sredy, 1, 169, 172, 180 (1949).

particular conditions under which they were kept, i.e. the collision of excitations which exerted reciprocal negative induction, e.g. defence, feeding, sexual, etc. We had to reproduce these influences on the nervous system experimentally in order to prove our theory and also to explain the mechanism of certain harmful influences acting on the monkeys in their environment. For this purpose a normal, healthy monkey had to be kept under deliberately unfavourable conditions, ensuring that he would be subject to constant conflicting situations in which natural and incompatible excitatory influences would clash. It then remained to show that this actually leads to neuroses and eventually to vegetative somatic disturbances.

Five monkeys were used for the experiment: 2 rhesus macaques and 3 sacred baboons. Four of these already possessed positive and negative motor food conditioned reflexes in response to sound and light signals. With the aid of these established reflexes the type of nervous activity of each monkey had been determined. The dynamics of their higher nervous activity was investigated throughout the whole of the experimental period.

Two of the monkeys under investigation were fixed in a special stand during experiments, the remainder were allowed to move freely in the dwelling cage. With 2 of the monkeys the overstraining of the higher nervous activity was achieved by natural conditioned stimuli.

As the form of experimentation and the form in which the neurosis manifested itself in different monkeys varied somewhat, it is most convenient to describe each animal separately.

The monkey Karabas, a male rhesus macaque, born in 1948, was subjected to experiments starting in April 1951. A positive motor food conditioned reflex in response to Sd_1 and differentiation in response to Sd_2 were established whilst Karabas (Fig. 1) was

Fig. 1. The monkey Karabas, fixed in a stand by means of an apron. Electrodes for stimulation are applied to the left hind-leg by means of a sock, enclosed by a box. In response to the signal the monkey presses the lever, after which he obtains food from the food-container.

fixed in a stand (Sd_1 and Sd_2 differed from each other in timbre). The monkey had difficulty in getting used to the experimental situation, and this process took one month. Both positive and negative food conditioned reflexes were formed with difficulty. Special investigations gave us grounds for regarding Karabas as belonging to the type with weak nervous activity. His positive conditioned reflexes were easily fatigued and were unstable, indicating the weakness of his excitatory process. Differentiation after prolongation (up to 2 min.) and sometimes even without prolongation was often broken, indicating the weakness of the inhibitory process. The monkey frequently lapsed into a state of drowsiness during experiments even though the experiment rarely lasted more than 8-10 min. and the intervals between the stimuli never exceeded 50 sec.

Following the stabilization of positive and negative food reflexes, two light-signals were introduced; a red light which was reinforced by electrical stimulation of the skin above threshold strength and a green light which was the differential stimulus to it.

After the conditioned reflexes to the new signals had been stabilized, we proceeded to change the meaning of the light stimuli with the aim of causing a breakdown of the higher nervous activity. For the same reason the length of the defence signal was occasionally extended to 1-2 min., leading to overstraining of the excitatory process.

Soon the monkey began to show signs of neurotic state; he ceased taking the food, persistent motor excitability appeared, and he responded to both positive and negative feeding signals with prolonged pressure on the lever or with general motor excitability. The change in the form of his motor responses (from short quick ones to prolonged inert ones) indicated the gradual formation of a dominant focus in the cortex. The differentiation became disinhibited (Fig. 2). From then onwards occasional general torpor was noticeable. The animal reminded one of an automaton. He responded to the positive food signal with pressure on the lever, but not only did he fail to eat the food, he

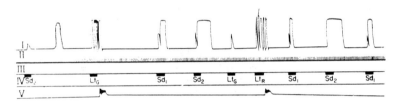

Fig. 2. Kymogram of monkey Karabas. Breakdown of differentiation. 1—Motor food reaction of the animal (pressure on the lever); II—Time in seconds, III—Action of conditioned stimulus; IV—Reinforcement with electric shock; V—Defence motor reaction (lifting of leg).

did not even look into the food-container whilst staring fixedly at the lamp—the source of the defence signal. This was characteristically accompanied by strong tachypnoea. The number of respiratory movements went up to 75 per min. (the normal number is 28). Frequently, in response to the conditioned defence signal, the monkey thrust unusually large quantities of food into his mouth and masticated it without swallowing.

For the further deepening of the neurotic state experimental collision between the food conditioned reflex and the defence reflex was used. The defence signal was given either immediately following the positive food conditioned stimulus or together with it. The reaction to such a collision was usually extremely violent. General motor excitability was observed and less frequently a cataleptic state, general torpor and drowsiness.

This monkey was maintained in his neurotic state for 1½ years. Whilst refusing all food, the animal occasionally reacted to a positive food signal with prolonged pressure on the lever (Fig. 3). It was also characteristic of this monkey to assume a definite pose in response to the defence conditioned stimulus and to remain in it for a considerable period—up to 30 minutes (Fig. 4). It is interesting to note that while the monkey

Table 1. Monkey Karabas Record of Experiment No. 52, 11 Sept., 1951

Time a.m.	Stimulus	No. of stimulus	Duration of isolated action in sec.	Latent period in sec.	Conditioned reflex	Food reinforcement	Remarks
9.45	Sd_1	514	5	1	+	+	Sd_1 + positive food signal
9.46	Sd_2	180	10	–	–	–	Sd_2 – differential signal
9.47	Sd_1	515	5	1	+	+	
9.48	Sd_2	181	10	2	+	–	
9.49	Sd_1	516	5	2	+	+	
9.50	Sd_2	182	10	1	+	–	
9.51	Sd_1	517	5	–	–	–	
9.52	Sd_2	183	10	–	–	–	
9.53	Sd_1	518	5	–	–	–	
9.54	Sd_2	184	10	1	+	–	
9.55	Sd_1	519	5	–	–	–	Drowsing
9.56	Sd_2	185	10	–	–	–	
9.57	Sd_1	520	10	–	–	–	
9.58	Sd_2	186	10	–	–	–	
9.59	Sd_1	521	10	–	–	–	

was in this state, any further conditioned stimuli (either food or repeated defence stimuli) failed to elicit the usual feeding or defensive responses, but instead led to a prolongation of the cataleptic state of the animal.

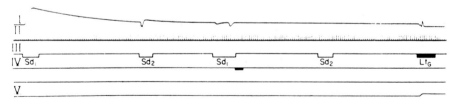

Fig. 3. Kymogram, illustrating the neurotic state of the monkey Karabas. Symbols as in Fig. 2.

Fig. 4. The monkey Karabas in a characteristic pose during catalepsy.

Karabas's general behaviour showed the following characteristic peculiarity: he assumed a particular sitting posture while in his dwelling cage and remained thus for hours; his head was pushed down between his legs which he clasped with his hands. This differed from the fixed position which we observed in the experimental chamber in that the animal quickly emerged from his torpor as the result of incidental noise, shouts or sounds of tribal significance, etc.

The whole of this complex of symptoms, the failure of the conditioned reflex to become extinguished in response to a positive food signal (Sd_1), the appearance of prolonged motor reactions, the cataleptic state, the relative reluctance of the excitatory process to yield to the inhibitory process—all this leads us to conclude that the monkey Karabas had developed a pathological inertness of the excitatory process, and that a pathological dominant had appeared at an isolated point of his cerebral cortex.

The animal was given a rest for two months. During that time his weight increased. The patches of skin which had become bald during the neurosis became covered with dense, glossy fur.

The resumption of experiments on his food conditioned reflexes in the previous experimental surroundings quickly led to renewed loss of hair on the hindquarters. The monkey stubbornly refused the food offered during experiments from the first day, although he responded to the positive signal by pressing the lever. The pressure took the normal form and was not prolonged as had been characteristic of Karabas during his neurotic state.

Although the defence signals were never used after the rest-period and the lamp from which the defence light-signal had emanated had actually been removed from the experimental chamber, we observed a persistent reaction by the animal to the place where the lamp had hung before. In order to stop this tiresome behaviour we placed the lamp on the opposite (right) side but, as before, we did not use it as a source of stimulation. Rarely and only for short periods of time did the monkey glance at the actual lamp while continuing to look stubbornly at the imaginary lamp on the left side, turning his whole body in that direction. Repeated observations (30 experiments) convinced us that this reaction to the non-existent lamp was too strong to be changed by passive measures. It was decided to embark on an active alteration of the reaction to the left side. For this purpose the previous defence light-signal was given from the other (the right) side, and this was reinforced as before with electric shock to the skin of the left hindleg. We succeeded, but with great difficulty and after a long period in getting the new reaction to equal that to the imaginary lamp. The stability of the old reaction to a non-existing stimulus was quite astonishing. Notwithstanding the length of the experiment (three months), we did not succeed in completely extinguishing this persistent reaction.

It is interesting that the use of the defence light signal from the right (i.e. from a new side) resulted in a fundamental improvement in the monkey's conditioned reflex activity. This first became apparent when, after a long period (over a year) of stubborn rejection of food during experiments, the monkey started to accept the food offered. The positive conditioned reflex motor reaction became stable and complete.

The fact that the change of the side from which the stimulation was given had such a favourable effect on the cortical activity calls for further careful investigation.

The second monkey, the sacred baboon Volshebnik, belonged to the strong, excitable, impetuous type. Positive food reflexes were established in response to a bell (Sd_1) and to green light while the monkey was fixed in a stand. The light signal was the weaker of the two stimuli, as could be seen from various signs. In addition, two differentiations were established with difficulty; one in response to a bell of a different timbre (Sd_2), the other to a red light. After stabilization of these reflexes, the differential stimulus was extended from 10 sec. to 2 min., which resulted in a short disturbance of the conditioned reflex activity which took the form of disinhibition of differentiations and increased intersignal pressures on the lever. A number of repeated collisions were also used, and the usual stereotyped pattern of the stimuli was changed. The monkey managed, however, to cope with this task without significant disruption of his nervous activity.

Later a defence conditioned reflex in response to a white light was established, reinforced by electrical stimulation of the skin. We then proceeded in the following manner: immediately after the action of the positive food signal we used the conditioned defence signal, i.e. the white light, or we reinforced the influence of the positive food signal with electric shock instead of food. As a result a very pronounced disturbance of the animal's higher nervous activity appeared. First of all, the animal's behaviour became drastically altered. Refusal to eat was characteristic, although the animal responded to the conditioned food stimulus with the motor reaction of pressing the lever. Paradoxical and ultraparadoxical phases appeared in his conditioned reflex behaviour. In response to a weak signal, the green light, the motor reaction was more intensive than in response to the strong signal (Sd_1). The ultraparadoxical phase consisted in the absence of response to a positive signal whilst a full response was given to the negative signal. Superfluous pressures between signals were considerably more intense than pressure in response to signals (Fig. 5).

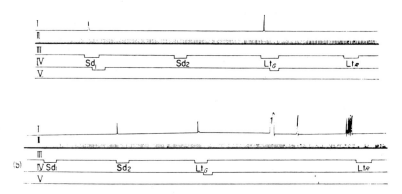

Fig. 5. Kymograms illustrating the paradoxical (a) and ultraparadoxical (b) phases in the conditioned reflex activity of the monkey Volshebnik. Meaning of symbols as in Fig. 2.

We can speak of the existence of pathological lability of the excitatory process in Volshebnik, i.e. excitatory weakness or explosiveness. In response to the conditioned stimulus a violent motor reaction set in, consisting of repeated pressures on the lever accompanied by screaming. This motor activity soon decreased or disappeared however, and the monkey refused the food. Intensive motor activity also appeared during the intervals; besides the repeated pressing of the lever and shaking of the stand, accompanied by screaming, this abnormal activity expressed itself in a peculiar relationship to surrounding objects. The monkey gnawed at everything that was available, particularly at the wooden stand, which had to be replaced. It was characteristic that this motor activity during intervals arose in response to any incidental stimulus: decreased lighting in the chamber, caused by a fall in electric power or any accidental sound, even a slight rustle. Always starting with maximal force, the motor activity subsequently diminished sharply, indicating the quick exhaustion of the excitatory process.

Because the use of harmful influences in the same chamber where the conditioned reflex activity of the animal had been studied could obscure the actual state of cortical activity, we decided to carry out any drastic interference outside the experimental chamber. A special cage was erected where the animal was stimulated by electric shock, accompanied by an electric bell. This procedure was repeated many times during the course of the day and particularly before or during feeding time. By this means the collision between defence and food excitation was brought about.

Later a period of marked weakening of the monkey's cortical activity set in. The animal failed to respond to any conditioned stimuli whatever and hung in the stand with lowered head comletely apathetic to everything (Fig. 6).

Fig. 6. Kymogram of the monkey Volshebnik. Inhibitory phase.

In this way Volshebnik's neurosis first appeared in the form of excitatory weakness, explosiveness, which then gave way to an extremely inhibited state, indicating a functional weakening of the cerebral cortex.

The next monkey, Gvidon, a sacred baboon, belonged to the strong type with predominance of the excitatory process. In his case the conditioned reflexes were established and studied in a special chamber in which free movement was possible. Both positive and negative conditioned reflexes became established fairly quickly; the positive reflexes appeared in response to the bell (Sd_1) and to a metronome 120 (M_{120}) and the differentiations in response to Sd_2 and M_{60}.

After unsuccessful attempts to evoke a lasting breakdown of the higher nervous activity in Gvidon on the basis of food conditioned stimuli, we carried out experiments in the previously described special cage. In these experiments defence and food excitability were made to clash repeatedly during the course of the day. The picture of Gvidon's neurotic state was in general a repetition of that observed in the previous monkey. It must be noted that even though the conditions of experimentation were different (immobilization in the first case, free movement in the second) the neurotic state took about the same time to develop following the harmful influences on their higher nervous activity. In Gvidon the ultraparadoxical phase further expressed itself in that he ran away when the food container was offered to him, but reached after it once it had been removed and scratched the wall around the opening through which it had been withdrawn. Gvidon's general behaviour changed even more considerably than Volshebnik's. His conditioned reflex activity became chaotic. The correct and adequate reactions in response to conditioned stimuli changed; in response to the signal, either an unusually strong or an unusually weak reaction appeared.

In the remaining two monkeys (Tigr and Zevs) the overstraining of their higher nervous activity was achieved by natural rather than artificial conditioned stimuli. Such natural conditioned stimuli were connected with defence, food, sex and other tribal factors. The monkeys were subjected to the action of these stimuli quite naturally without the constant presence of the experimenter.

Both monkeys, the sexually mature rhesus macaque Tigr and the sacred baboon Zevs were in dwelling cages in the vicinity of monkeys of both sexes. Both these monkeys belonged to the strong, excitable type. Zevs, after he had been together with the females for 1-2 weeks, was placed in a solitary dwelling cage neighbouring on a group of female monkeys headed by a male 'rival' (Fig. 7). In order to arouse his food excitability, Zevs was the last monkey to be fed. The monkey's behaviour as well as all the influences acting on him during the course of the day were recorded.

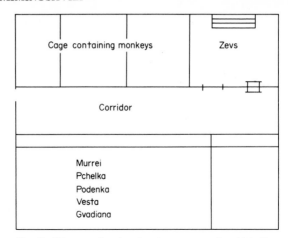

Fig. 7. Diagram showing the circumstances in which Zevs was kept.

EXTRACT FROM RECORDS OF ZEVS' BEHAVIOUR
20 AUGUST, 1952

8 a.m.-8.30 a.m.

Sits, pressing against the wire-netting. Picks at his toes. Looks at the neighbouring cage. Gets up and runs back and forth on two legs. Runs in circles. Sits. Presses against the wire net. Stares at females. 'Chatters'. Scratches, masturbates. Gets up and runs in circles. Walks back and forth on hind legs. Shakes net. Yawns frequently. Climbs up on the wall and shakes it for a long time. Sits on the ground. Shakes net for 3 min. Gets down. Walks on two legs, yawns, growls, watches as one monkey mounts another. 'Howls', growls. Beats the net with his hands. Grinds his teeth, yawns, growls. Does not calm down for a long time. Yawns, Walks back and forth on two legs for 4 min. Runs in circles. Grinds his teeth at the sight of the male.

9 a.m.-9.30 a.m. (food is being distributed)

Watches the attendant. Runs back and forth in agitation. Looks at the neighbouring cage continuously. Sits down. One monkey of Murrei's group mounts another. Is angry, yawns. Runs in circles; sits down. Runs back and forth in cage. Food is carried past him. Runs faster. Stares fixedly at the others being fed. Yawns. Sits down. Bites his fingers. Scratches. Walks back and forth. Sits down, scratches. Sucks his tongue. Sees female—erection. Runs on hind legs with head thrown back. Growls. Runs in circles, back and forth, again in circles. Sits at the door and tries to push it open with his hands. Gets up. Goes back and forth. Looks at monkeys. Sits down. Scratches. Looks at chink. Receives food. Eats greedily.

1.30 p.m.

Sits, eats. Female approaches (Pchelka). Crosses legs, scratches; gathers nuts to himself; scratches. Gets up. Walks back and forth. Walks in circles around the cage. Rises on hind legs and looks at Pchelka. Erection. Climbs up on wall. Roars, looking at the male in the adjoining cage. Gvadiana approaches in response to the shout. Sits.

Gvadiana shouts, he grinds his teeth at the male in the neighbouring cage (uninterrupted erection; spermorrhoea). Simultaneously continues his eating. 'Chatters' to Gvadiana. Walks back and forth. Sits down. Gvadiana goes away. He roars. Gvadiana returns. He 'grunts'. Gvadiana goes away. Strong excitement, shouts. Walks on hind legs with head thrown right back. Tosses nuts about.

In this way, by deliberately creating unfavourable conditions, the strongest natural conditioned stimuli were acting on various subcortical and cortical points and colliding repeatedly during the course of the day, thereby producing overstraining of the cortical cells and disruption of the monkey's higher nervous activity.

How the higher nervous activity of monkeys can be disturbed by this form of influence can be seen from the parallel investigation of the monkey Tigr, which was carried out by our co-worker, Z. I. Daneliia.

Tigr had formed a positive food conditioned reflex in response to a red light and to the metronome (M_{120}) and differentiation to M_{60}. During the course of the development of his neurosis, the differentiation became disinhibited and a large number of intersignal reflexes appeared. The conditioned reflexes acquired a chaotic, unstable character and reflexes were frequently omitted until finally all established reflexes disappeared. Food was refused. The use of fasting for 24 hr. in order to increase the excitability of the feeding centre did not restore the conditioned reflex activity.

The impression is gained that the overstraining of higher nervous activity brought about by natural conditioned stimuli leads more readily to the disruption of the working of the cerebral cortical cells than the same interference brought about by artificial conditioned stimuli. This is quite understandable in view of the fact that natural conditioned stimulation evokes much more forceful nervous processes than artificial stimulation.

On the basis of the parallel investigation of the dynamics of higher nervous activity in the process of the development of neurosis, we got the definite impression that in monkeys a certain resistance to harmful influences develops, as was previously observed by Kaminskii, Bam, Kriazhev. This resistance appears with any method used for the disruption of their higher nervous activity. It is characteristic of monkeys that their disturbed conditioned reflex activity returns to normal quite rapidly after a short period of rest (2-3 weeks) unless the neurotic state has gone too far or the monkey has a weak type of nervous activity, as was the case with Karabas.

Speaking of the difficulty of causing neuroses in monkeys as compared with dogs, one circumstance must receive special mention. Both we and our predecessors have tried to produce neuroses in monkeys using food conditioned stimuli. If the ecology of monkeys is taken into consideration, one should not expect them to develop a neurotic state on the basis of food conditioned reflexes as readily and easily as dogs. Certainly food conditioned stimuli have not got the same biological meaning for them as for dogs, who belong to the predatory mammals. The means by which the food is obtained is of definite significance. For the predator (dog) the loss of the food he has obtained (collision) with difficulty by tracking, catching, etc., represents a biologically much more important event than it does to the omnivorous or herbivorous monkey. Having lost his prey, the predator may remain hungry for a long time. For the fruit and vegetable eater, the loss of food can always be made up. Clearly, the corresponding cortical processes arising from food stimulation are of different strengths in monkeys and in dogs. It must be for this reason that one can get a profound disturbance of the higher nervous activity of a dog relatively easily on the basis of food conditioned reflexes, often after only one experiment. In monkeys many repeated collisions caused by food stimuli may fail to produce a disturbance for a long time. When they do, the neurotic state produced is shallow, brief and easily reversible. It is a different matter if the clash is caused by defence reflexes. With these it appears that the cortical nervous processes are very intense, particularly in monkeys, and therefore clashes between them or their over-straining, leads more readily to a serious disturbance of cortical activity.

CONCLUSIONS

(1) The method of collision between excitatory processes directed at various sub-cortical and cortical points is fundamentally a clash between the processes of excitation and inhibition in the cerebral cortex. The simultaneous appearance of competing foci of excitation in the cortical representation of unconditioned reflexes leads more readily to the disruption of higher nervous activity than the clash of food conditioned excitation and inhibition.

(2) Depending on the original type of nervous activity, the neurosis takes the form either of pathological inertness of excitation or of excitatory weakness and consequent weakening of cortical activity.

(3) Taking into consideration the ecology of monkeys, the most adequate methodology both for the study of their normal higher nervous activity and for experimental inter-ference with it is the use of conditioned reflexes based on ecologically adequate stimuli (defence, sex, orientative-investigatory). Food conditioned reflexes in monkeys, as opposed to dogs (representing the predators), do not seem to exert as much of a strain on cortical processes.

REFERENCES

Bam, L. A. *Fiz. zh.* **27**: 1, 1939.
Bam, L. A. and Kaminskii, C. D. *Biull. cksp. biol. med.* **14**: 3, 1942.
Bam, L. A. and Kaminskii, C. D. *Biull. V.I.E.M.,* 11-12, 1935.
Kaminskii, C. D. *Biull. V.I.E.M.,* 9-10, 1935.
Kaminskii, C. D. *Biull. V.I.E.M.,* 11-12, 1935.
Pavlov, I. P. *Collected Works.* II, Moscow, 1951.
Pavlov, I. P. *Collected Works,* III, Moscow, 1951.

Section IV

PSYCHOSES IN ANIMALS

13. The History of a Catatonic Dog

J. E. O. NEWTON and W. H. GANTT

Conditional Reflex, 1968, *3*, 45-61. Copyright 1968 by J. B. Lippincott Co.
Reprinted by permission.

Abstract—This article is a condensed life-history of a dog ("V3") born and reared in the Pavlovian Laboratory and studied until his death in 1961. A detailed study was made of his pathologic development, his relations to people, and the effects of drugs. Measurements recorded were heart rate, blood pressure, respiration, 24-hour activity, sexual reflexes, general behavior. Although early experiments were done chiefly for recording and were not considered noxious or traumatic, this dog's general development and symptoms seem to have been "constitutionally" rather than environmentally determined. His external behavior was strikingly similar to that of a catatonic patient—flexibilitas cerea, general immobility. Of particular interest was the "Effect of Person": in the presence of all humans who confronted him he showed catatonic postures, cardiovascular disorders (tachycardia up to 200 beats/min., bradycardia to 12 beats/min., drop of blood pressure from 150 to 75 mm Hg, arrest of heart-beat for as long as 8 seconds), moribund poses. His response to drugs illustrated the specificity to a definite "constitutional type": sexual activity markedly increased by alcohol and rarely present except after administration of alcohol; no improvement after administration of tranquilizers, except alcohol and meprobamate, which made him act like a normal dog in behavior and in relations to people. His symptoms and reactions to both people and drugs were generally opposite to those of another dog, "Nick", studied over his life span: Nick showed excessive activity in physiologic systems; hyperactivity (running); generally, improvement through "Effect of Person"; sexual inhibition with alcohol. Observations of the two dogs suggest that symptoms as well as reactions to drugs are the result of the "type" rather than the procedure used, that perhaps psychopathologic symptoms are due more to inborn constitution than to "conflict" ("collision") between excitation and inhibition, and that neurotic or psychotic symptoms may not interfere with longevity—Nick lived to be 14 years old and died fighting; V3, who also spent most of his life in the laboratory, died at the age of 14.

This paper presents the life history of a male French poodle named V3, born in the Pavlovian Laboratory in the summer of 1947, observed and experimented on from the time he was a puppy until his death in 1961 at the age of 14. He was born of siblings,

This work was supported in part by grants from the American Heart Association to W. H. Gantt, and was done while J. E. O. Newton had a postdoctoral fellowship from the National Institute of Mental Health of the U.S. Public Health Service.

and was raised mostly in isolation from other dogs. During the early experimental years of his life he was without special attention from the human beings around him.

The special interest of this dog derives from his very marked catatonic-like behavior, which developed early and continued throughout the remainder of his long life. This behavior was almost irreversible and the dog showed greatly exaggerated autonomic responses (heart rate and blood pressure), respiratory abnormalities, and abnormal sexual behavior. V3 impressed many psychiatrists as a catatonic animal. He exhibited in a very pronounced way the Effect of Person—in fact, the presence of people evoked dramatic changes in V3's heart rate, as well as the catatonic posturing.

The dog apparently had a biochemical defect and exhibited homosexual behavior. Alcohol and meprobamate, in moderate doses, made him appear almost normal. V3's remarkable inhibitory-type behavior contrasted strongly with the excitatory behavior exhibited by Nick, whose long life and many symptoms are described elsewhere (Gantt, 1944).

Observation, Vagal Stimulation, Orienting to Tones

From an early age, before any experimental work, V3 was very timid, easily frightened, and always running away from people. He was housed in a kennel with other dogs, by many of which he was easily intimidated.

Later during his second year the dog became a subject for vagal stimulation experiments. After a few experiments using both mechanical and faradic stimulation of the subcutaneously placed vagus nerve, which caused slowing of the heart, the effect on the heart disappeared and the dog was no longer used for these experiments.

He was then studied by a medical student, Arthur Humphries (now a surgeon in Augusta, Ga.), who worked with him from February until July, 1950. The careful notes of Humphries show that V3 was already an abnormal dog: "Extremely resistant to collar around neck—crouched. Did not walk *at all* on the way from the kennel. Carried up steps. Eyes looked dull. Would not look around. When I pulled on the leash, he would hold one position regardless of which way I tugged; that is, he would be pulled over backwards rather than maneuver into a position in which he could better resist my tugging. When we came into the lab, he made a few bursts of energy but then went back into unresponsive lethargic state. Five minutes later—went through violent 30-second series of motions when I came back to take leash. Would not more than sniff milk. But when I left him again, he lapped milk. Panted more normally now. Looked around more when I was not holding him. A dog in a cage whining seemed to 'bother' him, as he would look in direction of dog with each whine of the dog. Tail tucked between legs always. When I approached, he hid under the table. Vomited." (9 Feb. 1950—Humphries' first note.)

Similar notes were made almost daily, showing some stereotypy already. The laboratory procedures used were generally innocuous, as measured in their effects on other dogs. For example, on 26 Mar. 1950, tests of the orienting reflex were begun, using a bell sounded for 10 sec. as the orienting stimulus. V3 gave strong orienting reflexes with a short latent period and median duration of the orienting reflex of approximately 10 seconds. He tended to jerk around during the bell. After four more experimental sessions of testing with the bell, the orienting reflex had practically extinguished (6 Apr. 1950).

His behavior on 16 Apr. 1950 was quite abnormal, as described by Humphries: "He went into a tantrum in the camera. Bit at nails and chain until mouth bled.'' On 6 May, he noted that V3 went berserk in the camera.

Convulsion and First Catatonic Episode

On 13 May 1950, although no experiments had been done for a week, there was a very marked episode of neurotic behavior. On this day he had a striking convulsion in the stand, showing flexibilitas cerea. Humphries' notes for that day are as follows: ''When I appeared at the door of the kennel V3 barked at the large bully dog of the kennel and was promptly chased into the corner by latter as usual. He came easily from the kennel to the laboratory. He went into camera readily but was lifted into harness as usual. At no time did I leave him, but sat in a chair petting him on the head (he was tied loosely to top of harness by neck leash). He never responded to petting, keeping his head lowered and not looking me in the face. He did not stand in the harness nor sit on haunches gracefully but rather stiffly, awkwardly, inefficiently; he stood when I hoisted him by his abdomen. Miss Otterback came in to place the electrodes to record EKG for the first time and placed the respiratory pneumograph apparatus around his chest. The dog was making no noise, was still slumped almost to the point of choking on the leash. Suddenly, without visible motion, queer grating noises were emitted from his throat. And then suddenly he collapsed, his hind legs giving first, then his forelegs, and he was suspended only by the taut leash. About five seconds later he voided forcefully about 40 cc and his penis was limp, whereas at least 4 minutes prior to collapse it was on strong erection (first time erection ever noted). His eyes were open, but did not blink. Rate of respiration was not noted until 2 minutes after collapse, at which time, and until he got up 5 minutes later, it was rapid, short and abdominal. Five seconds after collapse the leash was released but his head sank only halfway to the floor—he was stiff and catatonic (according to Dr. Gantt) and his limbs were stiff as well. No orienting reflex was detected upon loud noise or threatening passes at head. Gradually (between 4th and 7th minute) blinking returned. His limbs showed waxy flexibility upon being raised passively. No knee jerks. When forepaw was extended, ipsilateral hind leg extended. For 4 or 5 minutes the head and thorax were held at the same angle. When his head was pushed forcefully in the direction of the floor, more resistance was encountered than when pushed toward ceiling. Mouth was tightly closed. When Miss Otterback moved to go out of camera, the dog looked toward door—but when she returned with biscuit he went back into pose. Then all of us went out and looked through the one-way window and he got up immediately. When the door of the camera was opened, he peered out, and when I called and clapped my hands, he ran out quickly to the far end of the lab. Then when I approached him (he was cornered from the other exit by Dr. Gantt), he permitted me to pet him. When I took him back to the kennel, he came more easily than ever before.''

From this time onward V3's typical behavior in the presence of people was that of a cataleptic patient, except under certain drugs, as will be described later. As we will also cover in more detail in another section of this report, the person had many other interesting and important effects on V3. Whenever V3 was alone in the experimental room, being observed through a one-way window, he tended to be hyperactive, struggling, jumping around, attempting to free himself from the leash. When observed in his paddock on many occasions, the person approaching the paddock very quietly and standing motionless, V3 was noted to be more like a normal dog, walking around, lying down, eating or drinking water occasionally.

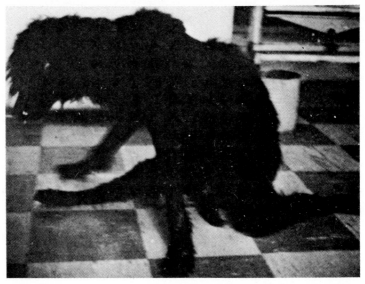

Fig. 1. Bizarre position typical of that in which V3 could be placed. He remained in this pose for ten minutes, sinking gradually to the floor.

Fig. 2. A typical pose of V3 when in the presence of a person.

Typical Catatonic Behavior

The behavior which we have characterized as "catatonic" or "cataleptic" was as follows: the dog would stand in a rigid posture, essentially immobile, for 5 to 30 minutes in the presence of persons, during which time his limbs could be flexed, extended, or put into all manner of rather bizarre positions in which they would remain for periods of time as long as 30 minutes. Figures 1 and 2 illustrate some of his unusual postures. In addition to the catalepsy, from 13 May 1950, onward throughout practically all his life, V3 exhibited other stereotyped responses in the presence of a person, depending on what the person was doing. This included such behavior as dashing out of the just-opened paddock door into the corridor, running to a smaller room in which he was usually observed. On many occasions, when a person was standing outside the closed paddock door, he would run continuously in circles in a stereotyped manner. In the presence of a person V3 rarely gave orienting reflexes either to loud sounds made by the person or to extraneous noises. There was little reaction to painful stimuli such as a pin prick, though a slight noise such as scratching on the wall would cause orienting and some excitement (this is reminiscent of Pavlov's observation of the marked effect of weak stimuli in neurotic animals—"paradoxical phases").*

Impressions of Onlookers

The following notes are descriptions of V3 by a prominent writer and two psychiatrists. John Dos Passos, who saw V3 on 28 May 1952, said:

"The dog had the drooped dejected look of a dog that has just been given a beating. Showed no sign of pleasure at being spoken to. When the door was opened he ran apprehensively out of his cage into the hall, and then ran up and down, nose down, tail limp as if trying to run away. The dog made no effort to escape up the steps into the corridor from which we had come, as a normal dog probably would, trying to escape. When the door to the little closet where the experiments had been conducted was opened the dog dashed in. We found him motionless standing under a shelf in the back of the closet with his head a little to one side. When Dr. Gantt lifted the paw of one leg, the leg remained in the position he put it in, with the paw twisted up. The dog showed no reaction to pricks with a hypodermic needle or to loud clapping of the hands, though he seemed to notice a slight scratching on the woodwork.

"I don't quite remember how the dog came to leave his frozen position. Once out in the hall he resumed his aimless, anxious running up and down."

Dr. George Sutherland, from the Mental Health Branch of the Maryland Department of Health, who saw V3 on 24 May 1952, wrote this comment:

"Dog came out of room or cage readily enough but hesitated to pass by me (there were also 2 strange cats in the room with me)—finally with a shove he ran by into the laboratory—where I followed along with Dr. Gantt. He had assumed an awkward, semi-crouching position and appeared to be staring vacantly. He remained in this position roughly 5 minutes, during which time Dr. Gantt changed the position of his right front and back leg. He made no visible effort to resist the passive molding of the limbs. Very slight response to loud clapping of hands; or being pricked with a hypo needle. He would half-orient to mild scratching sounds but not to Dr. Gantt's voice or to mine.

"When Dr. Gantt left the room, I prevented the dog from leaving also, which he made a rather feeble effort to do. In the room with me at first he was restless but after about 1 minute became almost immobile. I could hear Dr. Gantt moving outside the door from time to time. The animal oriented himself toward the source of this sound, giving a start at each new sound. After 2 minutes he began to 'heave' and finally vomited his food, and became passive once more. After 3 minutes I opened the door and he dashed out and appeared to make for Dr. Gantt."

Between 1952 and 1958, V3 was seen by many people, among them several psychia-

---

* Pavlov compared this to some human psychoses (WHG).

trists from other countries. One of these, Dr. Ferguson Rodger, from the University of Glasgow, Scotland, wrote the following description on 17 May 1956:

"I saw V3 this afternoon.   When we approached his cage he became excited, making continuous circling movements. When the door of his cage was opened he ran out, then checked his advance as if afraid, and turned to seek the shelter of a corner. When the door to the corridor was opened he ran down the corridor and into the experimental room. Then he stood in a trance-like state. Movement of a limb was held, exactly as in the well-known psychotic phenomenon of flexibilitas cerea. He retained the odd position he was put into for several minutes and Dr. Gantt informed me that he would have sunk to the floor. He was unresponsive to pin-prick and was aroused only with difficulty. When we left the room, he immediately ran out with us and went ahead of us back to his cage.

"As we would define schizophrenia in terms of disturbance of motility, sensation and overt behavior, this is a schizophrenic dog showing stereotypy and ambivalence. The conclusion that the disorder from which this dog is suffering is akin to the human disease seems to my mind inescapable. If ever there was a schizophrenic dog, this is one."

Sexual Reflexes

In October 1950, the study of V3's sexual reflexes was undertaken by Y. Mawardi and WHG. The method used for this investigation consisted of genital stimulation for one minute, as more fully described elsewhere (Gantt, 1952). In normal dogs, this procedure produced erection and copulatory movements with ejaculation. However, V3 showed only very slight erection on one occasion and no copulatory movements or ejaculation the first three times that sexual reflexes were tested. The first administration of alcohol by stomach tube led to spontaneous strong erection, which subsided when a person approached. Later that same day, genital stimulation evoked strong, sustained erection, without copulatory movements or ejaculation. When next tested, without alcohol, V3 showed no sexual reflexes of any degree to genital stimulation. After administration of alcohol, later the same day, the stimulation again produced strong sustained erection. This effect of alcohol to produce strong erections was demonstrated on three occasions during this time, when the stimulation in the absence of alcohol evoked only very slight, short-lived erections on two occasions and no erection at all on three other occasions. Then alcohol experiments were discontinued and the dog was given several injections of testosterone. Strong, sustained erections, sometimes accompanied by copulatory movements, and occasionally even by ejaculation, began to occur during genital stimulation. It is significant that, for a month after the testosterone injections were discontinued, genital stimulation continued to evoke strong erections, often with copulatory movements and ejaculation. This tendency of the sexual reflexes to persist, once having been disinhibited by the testosterone, seems to be an example of positive autokinesis. Autokinesis, as we have previously noted (Gantt, 1953), is the tendency of a process, once initiated in the nervous system of the organism, to continue and to become elaborated in complex ways by the organism, either to the advantage (positive autokinesis) or to the detriment (negative autokinesis) of the animal. This tendency of improvement in the sexual reflexes, however, dissipated after a month, so that on several occasions, genital stimulation evoked little sexual response. Then a single dose of alcohol restored the sexual reflexes, so that even without the alcohol, on four occasions, strong erections occurred, two of them with ejaculation. It is likely that conditioning played some part in the greater development of strong sexual reflexes after the alcohol and the testosterone, since there were many instances of spontaneous erection and even, on one occasion several days after alcohol, movements of the experimenter toward the genitalia of the dog evoked ejaculation.

The experiments on sexual reflexes were discontinued for a year, until early 1952. Genital stimulation at this time produced only very slight, transient erection, with no copulatory movements or ejaculation.

Behavior with Other Dogs, Apparent Homosexuality

V3 was observed on a number of occasions in the presence of other dogs, both male and female. He was much more like a normal dog in the presence of other dogs. He seemed less affected by the presence of people (unless they came too close, or interrupted his interaction with the other dog), would play with the other dog, exhibited what appeared to be sexual activity, showed little of the cataleptic behavior. An example of this behavior with two female dogs is given in the notes of WHG for Nov. 1954:

"When Skipper, female dog, is brought into paddock, V3 is very alert, sniffs Skipper's genitalia, runs out with Skipper, pays no attention to me until I drive him back. V3 shows same behavior with Taffyfoot (another female dog), sniffs genitalia, urinates lifting leg (have never seen him lift leg before). Makes copulatory movements without mounting when left with Taffyfoot. Taffyfoot plays with V3 and shows interest."

On 19 Sept. 1956, V3's behavior toward a male dog, Pedro, who lived in the room-cage next to V3, was noted by JN:

"I let V3 out into the passageway connecting the 3 cages. His activity at first was as usual, running in circles, then dashing out into the passageway, then the catatonic-like stances, the crouching when touched, and the urinating without lifting his leg. A sort of behavior which I have never before observed in V3 occurred after about 10 minutes. V3 had backed into the corner near Pedro's cage and Pedro (male dog) pushed his head out through the hole in the screen of the door. He began whining and fondling V3 with his nose and mouth over various parts of V3's body. Pedro was obviously quite excited and V3 also became excited, as manifested by panting, opening and closing his mouth many times, nuzzling Pedro occasionally, trembling all over. Pedro often stuck his forepaws through the screen to touch V3, then stuck his head back out through the screen frantically trying to reach V3. I let V3 back into his paddock, by opening the door, then standing a little out of the way. He dashed into the cage and when I closed the door he ran to the back corner next to Pedro's cage and began whining. Pedro did likewise, and it appeared that the 2 dogs were communicating through the wall, whining and sniffing at each other. When I again opened V3's door, he dashed out to the opposite corner of the passageway. When I left the passageway, he immediately went to Pedro's side again, urinated without lifting his leg, and the nuzzling behavior between the two dogs began again. Then V3 sat down in the corner, began panting, whining and trembling. He even wagged his tail several times at Pedro, would sit and wag his tail, then stand and nuzzle Pedro, then sit again. V3 had a partial erection, as did Pedro. It seemed that this was a type of mating behavior, both dogs whining, nuzzling, wagging tails and moving away from each other intermittently. When I came into the passageway again V3 suddenly 'went stiff,' stopped all this new behavior and stared apprehensively at me. When I left the passageway, he began to wander around sniffing here and there. Then he went back to Pedro, and the 'mating behavior' occurred again, both dogs with erections. After V3 was put back into his cage, I allowed Pedro out into the passageway. He ran up and down excitedly, stopping in front of V3's door many times, howling, whining, lifting his ears and head. V3 also ran around his cage excitedly, whining. His running was not in circles, as he does when a person comes near his cage. When Pedro was put back into his cage, both dogs ran to the common back corner, whined at each other. Pedro began to howl."

Again, 10 Oct. 1956, similar behavior was noted (JN):

"V3 was allowed out in the passage common to the 3 cages. I left the passage and stood behind the door to watch. He ran around the passage sniffing and urinating 2 or 3 times with his leg raised. He finally came to Pedro's end of the passageway and began to nuzzle Pedro, he and Pedro again exhibiting the peculiar mating-like behavior noted on 19 Sept. Both dogs whined, V3 brushed back and forth in front of Pedro, sticking his head through the hole in the screen into Pedro's cage several times, and Pedro reaching his head out to pull V3 to him by the hair. Pedro reached his front paws out several times to touch V3. V3 then sat down in front of Pedro's cage, whined, and moved alternately closer and farther away from Pedro, trembling and pawing on the floor. When I came back into the passage, V3 stiffened up, discontinued this behavior and watched me closely. When the door to his cage was opened, he dashed out to the back corner common to his and Pedro's cages and whined a little."

Attempts were made in 1960 to get V3 to mate with an abnormal female dog which was in estrus. After a dose of alcohol, V3 was placed in the room with the female and attained erection. He was obviously excited and interested in the bitch, playing and sniffing around her, but seemed not to know how to mount. The female was rather aggressive, often snarling at him, which seemed to inhibit V3. Then attempts were made by the experimenters (JN and CA, who had previously watched from the next room) to aid the dogs in "getting together." However, this proved to be futile. When the female was transferred to another male dog's room, this male almost immediately mounted her.

Effect of Person

In the spring of 1956 we began daily experiments on the Effect of Person on V3, which were continued intermittently throughout the rest of his life, involving many different people. The main aims of the experiments were the determination of the effect of the person on heart rate (HR) and a comparison between the effects in this dog and the effects in normal dogs (Gantt et al., 1966). The general procedure was as follows: the dog was placed in the experimental camera with apparatus attached for recording HR and respiration. After a period of several minutes of recording HR and respiration while the dog was alone, a person would enter the camera, stand near the door for 15 seconds; approach closely to the dog and stand for 15 seconds, then pet the dog for 20 seconds; after petting, continue to stand near the dog for 20 seconds, then exit from the room. Usually five to ten trials of this procedure would occur per daily session. With the many different people who tried this procedure on V3 the results were essentially the same, and the effects did not vary remarkably over the years. Figure 3 illustrates the striking effect of the person on the HR of this dog. When alone, V3's HR was quite rapid, varying from 120-160 beats per minute. Immediately after the person entered the room the HR would decrease 20-30 beats per minute, and with approach of the person the HR would fall even more. During petting the HR fell to the lowest value during the session which was, in many experiments, in the neighborhood of 40 to 50 beats per minute.

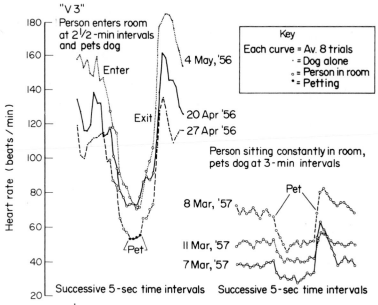

Fig. 3. Effect of Person on V3's heart rate: two different procedures, average curves on three days for each procedure. Five people were involved (one each day): JN—20 Apr. and 4 May, '56; TT—27 Apr., '56; RS—7 Mar., '57; LOG—8 Mar., '57; GLB—11 Mar., '57.

Another procedure used at times involved the person's entering the room and sitting next to the dog throughout the rest of the session. Then the person would pet the dog at 2- to 3-minute intervals for 60 seconds each trial, 5 to 10 trials per session. On these occasions V3's HR was always remarkably lower and less variable while the person was in the camera than when the dog was alone, and during petting the HR would go as low as 20 to 30 beats per minute. In addition, on several occasions the HR slowed to the extent that there was sinus arrest, that is, the heart would pause for 6 to 8 seconds, as illustrated in Figure 4. On several occasions, when BP was measured, it fell from 140 mm Hg systolic while the dog was alone to around 75 mm Hg systolic during petting.

The external behavior of the dog somewhat paralleled the cardiovascular effects. While alone, V3 was often somewhat hyperactive, biting at the air, jumping around and generally slightly restless, though sometimes he was quiet. He would stand quite still when a person was present. Regardless of what the person was doing, V3 would stand rigid, sometimes in bizarre postures, usually making no sign toward the person. Occasionally he would look cautiously at the person out of the corner of his eye. When petted by rubbing the top of his head, he would tend to crouch or even pull away from the experimenter. This behavior is very odd in the dog. The normal dog attends to every movement of the person, wags its tail, pants, moves around excitedly, usually

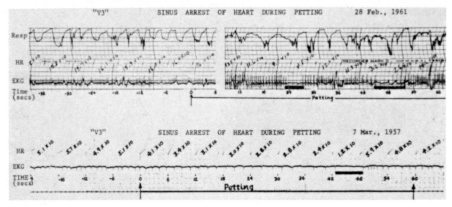

Fig. 4. Periods of sinus arrest of V3's heart during petting on two different days. Sinus arrest denoted by heavy black line under EKG record.

looks directly at the person. He will lick and/or sniff toward the person, move close to the person, becoming quiet during the petting, but never rigid (Gantt *et al.,* 1966).

With the exception of one incident, there seemed to be no difference in the effects of different people on V3's external behavior or his heart rate. This incident, on 16 Feb. 1961, occurred when several people were in the experimental room observing the dog and attempting to obtain proper placement of the cuff on V3's tail for measurement of blood pressure. The dog gradually sank to the floor of the experimental stand and began to have difficulty breathing (raucous breathing, apparently from the leash around his neck, which had become taut). Though the leash was removed, *he became flaccid and appeared moribund.* A technician summoned WHG, who came within 10 seconds. *As soon as WHG entered the experimental room,* V3 immediately stood up and perked up completely and looked around, as if nothing had happened. For the remaining 20 minutes the dog stood in the experimental room normally!

Effect of Drugs

After administration of alcohol (1, 2, 9 Nov. 1950 and 17 Jan. 1951) V3 approached people, allowed them to pet him and showed spontaneous erections as well as erection with ejaculation when his external genitalia were stimulated.

Meprobamate was administered several times in two dosages to V3. In May, June and August, 1957, he received 800 mg (50 mg/kg) orally on each of four days. Three to four hours after each administration V3 changed from his usual catatonic-like state to a friendly dog, wagging his tail, approaching people, sniffing their hands and even eating dog-food from their hands, none of which he ever did without drugs. He showed almost no catatonic-like rigidity and no dashing around when released. In contrast to his usual state, orienting reflexes to loud sounds were fairly strong and his reaction to needle prick (flinching) was much stronger than usual. These effects, especially the more friendly attitude to people and eating out of a person's hand, were markedly diminished but still present 24 hours after the meprobamate was given. During October and November, 1959, 1200 mg on three days made him like a normal dog.

The effect of phenobarbital was also tested on V3 in Sept. 1957, 30 mg of the drug being given intraperitoneally. One hour later the dog was somewhat ataxic but still ran in cage when the cage was approached. He seemed frightened, wide-eyed, withdrawing to the back of the cage when a person entered, then dashed out into the corridor as usual. There was the usual catatonic-like posture, no wagging of the tail as seen under meprobamate, though he did eventually eat meat from the hand of the person after cautious sniffing for several minutes. Three and a half hours after injection of the drug the dog was still ataxic, bumping into objects more than usual. Again there was no great change in behavior, the dog still showing catatonic-like postures and the usual symptoms on approach of the person.

In March 1954, reserpine, 0.1 mg/day, was administered to V3 for more than a week. His catatonic posturing continued, though it was less prolonged. However, he became responsive to loud sounds, showing startle responses in the presence of people. The most striking change in his behavior was in the direction of aggressiveness—he attempted to bite people on several occasions when moved, pulled, or pushed, which he had never done before. He also snapped at the leash, at cardboard boxes and other objects. Nevertheless, as usual, he did not respond to pin pricks.

V3 was given 1 cc of LSD orally through a stomach tube on 10 June 1954. This drug made the dog more agitated in running out of paddock and more resistant to being returned to the paddock. Otherwise, his behavior was as usual, showing prolonged catatonic poses, crouching, etc.

LATER EXPERIMENTS

Orienting and Food Conditioning

In May 1957, another series of experiments was carried out to test the orienting reflex. Tones of 256 and 512 cps were administered. The orienting reflexes were normal, i.e., the dog would turn his head and look up at the loudspeaker within ½ to 1 second after the stimulus onset. Heart rate changes were quite variable: sometimes an increase, sometimes a decrease or no change. Meprobamate, 800 mg given orally on five occasions, caused no change in the orienting reflexes, either motor or cardiac. During these meprobamate sessions V3's behavior in the presence of people was remarkably altered and the catatonia was abolished almost completely.

In late 1960, V3 was given another series of orienting trials, with tones of 1050 and 2100 cps. These usually produced an increase in heart rate and definite motor orienting reflexes (looking up at the loudspeaker). During about 8 per cent of the 76 trials of each tone, the heart rate decreased instead. Conditioning with food as reinforcement was then attempted, using liquefied food injected into a locked container placed in front of the dog. At the end of each 1050 cps tone (6-second duration) food was injected into the container, which was immediately unlocked. V3 never learned to open the food container at the appropriate time, showing a delayed response on a few trials but no response at all on most trials.

Apparent Biochemical Defect

In 1961, Dr. Clara Williams undertook an investigation of the urinary metabolites of dogs. Among 19 dogs studied were V3 and another abnormal dog, which exhibited marked inhibitory features in the shock-conditioning situation. The paper chromatographic analyses of the urine of V3 and the other abnormal dog indicated high urinary contents of histidine, which was present in only minute amounts in any of the normal dogs (Williams and Livingston, 1963). This high urinary histidine was present in ten out of ten specimens in V3. The urine samples of V3 and a dog with an experimental portacaval shunt consistently produced on the chromatogram another spot, unidentified, which was not present in any of the other dogs. These findings suggest that some biochemical abnormality existed in V3, which possibly could have accounted for his abnormal behavior. Unfortunately, a thorough biochemical workup of V3 was precluded by his death in late 1961.

Comparison with Other Neurotic Dogs

A comparison of V3 with the previously-reported neurotic dog Nick (Gantt, 1944) is of interest. Both dogs were raised in the Pavlovian Laboratory, spent their lives there, and were studied during most of their lives. The neurotic symptoms in Nick, like those in V3, began during early experiments. The first symptoms noted in Nick were related to a definite experimental procedure (difficult differentiation during food-conditioning), whereas V3 showed odd behavior from the very beginning of observation. It is difficult to ascribe V3's overwhelming breakdown to any clearcut precipitating factor. The mild restraint necessary during orienting training in the Pavlovian situation may have been enough to disorganize this sensitive animal. Liddell (1949) has pointed out the importance of restraint as a factor in animal neuroses.

The importance of what the individual himself brings to the situation (innate "constitution" plus prior experience) in determining his reactions to it is demonstrated by the contrast between Nick's development and that of the two other dogs ("Fritz" and "Peter") which underwent the difficult differentiation procedure at the same time: Nick went on to become extremely agitated and neurotic for the rest of his life, like V3, whereas Fritz and Peter developed mild agitation lasting only a short time (Gantt, 1944).

Both Nick and V3 exhibited remarkable reactions to people. Nick showed very varied reactions to different people: some people had a tranquilizing effect, dissipating or delaying his neurotic symptoms and reducing his tachycardia; while other persons elicited extreme "anxiety"—increased heart rate, pollakiuria, sexual erections, asthmatic-like breathing. But his reaction to a given person was more or less constant over a number of years. Nick improved by close association with certain persons. In contrast, the symptoms of V3 in the presence of a person seemed to vary very little from one person to another, and the effect was almost uniform and stereotyped. V3 gave typical catatonic reactions, retreating into a corner, becoming rigid, with flexibilitas cerea and motor insensitivity to needle-pricks. Although Nick's raucous respirations and tachycardia were somewhat improved by a person's petting him, in V3 the person not only decreased the tachycardia, but caused a pathologic decrease to a bradycardia of 20 beats/min. or less and markedly reduced blood pressure.

Murphree, Peters and Dykman (1967) found that their group of markedly psychotic-like dogs showed absolutely no change in heart rate as an "Effect of Person", either to the presence of the person or petting by the person. Their normal dogs of the same breed, run as controls, showed the usual heart-rate decrease to petting. Comparing these various effects of the same stimulus in Nick, in V3 and in Murphree et al.'s pointer dogs, we see the wide variation in different "types" and the importance of a detailed study of the individual or a control of heredity.

V3, like Nick, exhibited abnormalities of sexual arousal. V3 exhibited homosexual behavior much more prominently than heterosexual behavior, whereas Nick showed the reverse. In V3, genital stimulation normally produced no sexual erection, but under the influence of alcohol erection with ejaculation occurred after artificial genital stimulation. On the other hand, Nick responded to genital stimulation with erection and ejaculation, which were delayed or completely inhibited by alcohol, as in normal dogs. Nick's sexual abnormalities consisted of erections and ejaculation in the environment of conflict or to elements of this environment *without any stimulation of the genitalia.*

Both V3 and Nick became progressively worse in the laboratory, developing new symptoms after the initial period of experimentation. This development of new symptoms, namely *increasing pathology,* is what we call *autokinesis.* Apparently, once started, a "disorganizing" process continues, becomes worse, and spreads to include other functions without repetition of any recognizable injurious environmental factors. In the case of Nick this process manifested itself generally in an "excitatory" fashion, whereas V3 became more and more "inhibitory" as the years went along. Despite the pervasiveness of abnormalities in these two dogs, they both lived to the ripe old age of 14.

AUTOKINESIS

The above are examples of one kind of autokinesis, namely, negative autokinesis. There is another kind of autokinesis, positive autokinesis, which refers to developing processes leading to improvement of function. Positive autokinesis is seen sometimes after a single dose of a drug, or after one episode such as a single experience with another person or one conference with a therapist. It is not yet clear what the factors which produce positive autokinesis are, and what those are that produce negative autokinesis.

REFERENCES

Gantt, W. H.: *Experimental Basis for Neurotic Behavior.* Paul B. Hoeber, Inc., New York, 1944.

Gantt, W. H.: Effect of alcohol on the sexual reflexes of normal and neurotic male dogs. *Psychosom. Med.,* **14**: 174-181, 1952.

Gantt, W. H.: Principles of nervous breakdown—schizokinesis and autokinesis. *Ann. N.Y. Acad. Sci.,* **56**: 143-163, 1953.

Gantt, W. H., Newton, J. E. O., Royer, F. L., and Stephens. J. H.: Effect of Person. *Cond. Reflex, 1*: 18-35, 1966.

Liddell, H. S.: Some specific factors that modify tolerance for environmental stress. *Proc. Assoc. Res. Nerv. Ment. Dis.,* **29**: 155-171, 1949.

Murphree, O. D., Peters, J. E., and Dykman, R. A.: Effect of Person on nervous, stable and crossbred pointer dogs. *Cond. Reflex,* **2**: 273-276, 1967.

Williams, C. H., and Livingston, A.: Increased excretion of histidine found in paper chromatographic survey of dog urines. *J. Nerv. Ment. Dis.,* **137**: 395-399, 1963.

14. Behavioral Analysis of Chronic Amphetamine Intoxication

E. H. ELLINWOOD*, A. SUDILOVSKY* and L. NELSON*

Biological Psychiatry, 1972, *4*, 215-30. Reprinted by permission.

The assessment of models of psychoses requires a detailed and precise description and quantification of behavioral changes over time. This paper reports some of our methods and results in chronic methamphetamine-intoxicated cats used as their own control. Phenomenological descriptions and recordings on video tape of the ongoing behavior were used in the analysis and construction of indexes of ataxia, dystonic posture, transient and patterned movements, and a multivariate behavioral rating chart. Attention was focused on the dyssynchrony of posture and motility throughout the intoxication period.

INTRODUCTION

Of the various pharmacologically induced "psychoses," the amphetamine psychosis is the most approximate model. Often the amphetamine psychosis so closely mimics paranoid schizophrenia that it must be considered in a differential diagnosis of any patient presenting with this picture. Catatonic like and hypomanic, emotionally labile states have also been noticed following chronic amphetamine intoxication (Tatetsu, 1963). Randrup and Munkvad (1967), Ellinwood (1967), Ellinwood and Escalante (1970a,b), Kety (1960), and Griffith *et al.* (1970) have commented on amphetamine intoxication as a heuristic model of functional psychosis and on the applicability of studying these phenomena in experimental animals as well as in selected human subjects. In a clinical setting, the amphetamine psychosis develops over a period of time and is secondary to the user gradually increasing his intake of amphetamine usually to more than 150 mg and at times up to 600 to 2000 mg per day. Although acute toxic paranoid panic can be produced by a single large dose (Connell, 1958), it is well to keep in mind that with chronic abuse the paranoid psychotic state gradually evolves. There is an organization of behavior, thought, and feeling about the many acute experiences. For example, delusions of parasitosis which are not uncommon in the amphetamine psychosis appear to develop out of sequences of skin sensations and repetitive "grooming" responses and to develop over a long period of time. In our observations of man as well as of monkeys, we have noticed sequences of behavior like the grooming response take on an autonomy and centrality of their own. Thus, the differentiating factor between drug-induced hallucinatory episodes and that of psychosis is *time*. Not only is there an organization of psychological and behavioral responses to the chronic intoxica-

This work supported by National Institute of Mental Health Grants MH-15907, MH-18904, and MH-07073.

* Department of Psychiatry, Duke Medical Center, Durham, North Carolina.

tion state, but there are also physical changes that complicate the picture. There is a gradual depletion of catecholamines and subsequent neuronal chromatolysis (Escalante and Ellinwood, 1970) as well as the development of abnormal EEG patterns (Ellinwood and Escalante, 1970a,b).

To a certain extent, the study of animal models of psychosis depends on an accurate description of behavior in the human conditions with which to correlate behavior noted in the animal paradigm. Thus, there is a need to describe not only the gross measurements of behavior in humans and in animals, but also an accurate description and quantification of exact type of motor and postural behavior associated with these psychotic states as well as observations that reflect the changing neurological state during any assessment of chronic amphetamine intoxication. Itil (1969) for example, has demonstrated that paranoid schizophrenics spend approximately 88% of the time in a motor pattern described as eye-scan, whereas catatonic schizophrenics spend only approximately 17% of the time in eye-scan. Furthermore, the eye-scan decreases in time as the paranoid patients respond to pharmacotherapy. In contrast, catatonics spend an inordinate amount of time, 67%, involved in bizarre motor behavior. It is well known that there are marked postural-attitudinal changes with catatonic states, and more often that there is a vacillation between frozen postural states and hyperactive agitation. With the advent of quantifiable motor patterns in human psychotic states, these behavioral changes can be related to similar phenomena in lower animals. This report describes some of the methods and results we have obtained from various behavioral analyses of experimental animals subjected to chronic amphetamine intoxication.

METHOD

A total of 46 cats weighing between 2½ and 4 kg were chronically administered methamphetamine over a period of 11 days. The animals were housed in individual cages throughout the experiment. Starting with 15 mg/kg per day, the dosage was gradually increased to 35 mg/kg per day. The daily dosage of methamphetamine was divided and injected in two ip doses at 8 am and 4 pm, allowing 16 hr between days for recovery and sleep. Cats were not given methamphetamine on the sixth and seventh days. The injection schedule used was an attempt to reflect the "speed" runs noted in human "speed" addicts as well as an attempt to cut down the high mortality noted when cats are continuously intoxicated. Sixteen cats were stereotaxically implanted with teflon-coated stainless steel electrodes for electrophysiological recordings. Electrodes were positioned in the olfactory bulbs, the anterior amygdala, anterior septum, the olfactory tubercle and accumbens, and in various other parts of the anterior olfactory system, the extrapyramidal system and the mesencephalic reticular formation. In the implanted cats, behavioral observation and electrophysiological recordings were combined for simultaneous analysis by means of split-screen television. One TV camera was focused on the cat, the other on the EEG oscillographs. The split-screen image was recorded on an Ampex 660-P, two-inch video tape recorder for later analysis. The split-screen allowed absolute correlation of specific behavioral sequences and electro-physiological activity.

Prior to the TV taping of the chronic intoxication cycles, 30 animals had been intoxicated through the same cycle. They had been observed in a similar regime and phenomenological description of the ongoing behavior had been dictated. Following perusal of these descriptions, it was decided that most of the repertoire and its various qualities

could best be categorized according to: (i) physical location (place and orientation); (ii) relation with the environment (attitude); (iii) level of activity (activity scale); (iv) positions and movements (body changes); (v) looking activity; (vi) sniffing involvement; (vii) grooming activity; (viii) autonomic responses; and (ix) miscellaneous (including infrequent and often complex behaviors).

One-hundred-and-sixty-five items related to the animal behavior and units of behavior that were repeated frequently and which could be operationally defined by the observers were distributed into the above-mentioned categories and formed the base for our rating chart.

Some of the categories deserve more detailed consideration and definition:

Attitude is defined as body-posture and activity in relation to the environment (surroundings + own body). This category includes the following divisions: *Unaware,* completely nonreactive and unaware of environment; *Indifferent,* not interested in any element of environment; *Interested normal,* interested in environment in general; *Interested abnormal,* restricted interest with a nervous, tense, or apprehensive quality; *Investigative normal,* actively reaching out to or approaching several elements of the environment; *Investigative abnormal,* actively reaching out to or approaching with compulsive character restricted elements of the environment; *Reactive,* suddenly reacting disproportionately to restricted stimuli with a jumpy, nervous, jittery quality while maintaining general body posture; *Focused normal,* relaxed observing or reaching for one specific element of environment; *Focused abnormal,* "hooked" on one aspect of environment with a tense and apprehensive quality.

Activity scale refers not just to the amount of activity but to the characteristics of flow and speed: *Stage 0,* asleep; *Stage I,* somnolent drowsy; *Stage 2,* normal speed; *Stage 3,* fast speed and dyskinetic movements; *Stage 4,* hyperactive and dystonic; *Stage 5,* very hyperactive.

Body changes, two main features were clearly distinguishable: positions and movements. Direct observation shows that in the execution of actions, some segments of the body move most frequently in a united fashion and in coordination and synchrony with other coincidently moving or posturing segments. Therefore, in order to characterize association, disjunction, and dyssynchrony at each level, we rated separately the following body regions or ensembles: head-neck, shoulder-foreleg, hip-hind leg, trunk, and tail. Movements presented themselves in the form of transient units and patterned sequences, and each kind was used in the construction of a Transient Behavior Index and a Patterned Behavior Index. Normally flowing sporadic movements, short fast reactive movements, and broken down components of patterned sequences were considered as transient units. The patterned sequences occurring in the head-neck ensemble were isolated and identified as to specific sequences or character: Balinese (jerky circling, or lilting swing), smooth circling, up and down (smooth or jerky), minutia search (pecking-like "sniffing" movements of the head), side-to-side, and dipping (fast lowering of the head and bringing it back to the previous position). These patterned sequences of behavior happened sometimes in a pure form but at other times were contaminated with transient units of behavior or interrupted by a pause or displacement of the animal in the cage.

Sniffing involvement was rated according to its discrete or continuous occurrence on each observational interval.

Looking activity was defined by two characters: location and character. The latter was classified as: *Light gazing,* not looking at any specific object; *Casual,* glancing around;

Observant, looking at one or few specific objects; *staring,* intense looking with a noticeable duration; *Vacant staring,* intense looking but with no object; *Apprehensive,* questioning quality (what is it?); *Insistent staring,* "hooked" on a single spot for a prolonged period of time without any head movement (object?).

In order to characterize quality of posture in general as well as ataxia, specific and exclusive abnormal elements related to posture and movement were taken from the rating chart to form the corresponding indexes:

Ataxia index: stagger, sway, and wide-based legs (indications of incoordination during displacement).

Dystonic Posture Index: disjunctive positions and movement. Oestrous crouch (position of the hip-hind leg ensemble), camel (position of the trunk), rabbit (position of the legs, supporting on planch and first segment), and push-up position of the shoulder-foreleg ensemble.

TV recordings were made on days 1, 3, 11, and 12 of the chronic methamphetamine intoxication cycle. (This cycle includes days before and after intoxication since the last injection was the morning of day 11. Thus, the injection on day 12 would be 24 hr after the last dose of methamphetamine on day 11.) The chronic intoxication cycle includes days 6 and 7 with no methamphetamine injections. Each day except day 12 was divided into five 3-min recording sessions, one session taken prior to injection and the others at 10, 20, 30, and 90 min after the first injection of the day. The preinjection period of day 1 represents the pre-drug control. In rating the behavior, each 3-min observational period was divided up into 18 ten-second observational intervals. Individual items were scored within these intervals on the basis of their occurrence. For example, when a cat was in a minutia search-sniffing stereotype lasting for the 3-min period, there would be a code representing minutia search in each of the 18 ten-second observational intervals.

An additional behavioral rating chart has been devised for rhesus monkeys which were intoxicated over a six- to eight-month period beginning with a daily dose of 1 mg/kg and increasing this over the eight month period to 20 mg/kg per day. Simple behavioral rating charts have also been established for rats which have been carried through a two-week methamphetamine intoxication cycle.

RESULTS

In previous experiments on lower dose schedules and under experimental paradigms in which the cats were not manipulated for various recording sessions, we have noted a strong tendency for the evolution of a single stereotyped pattern into a successively more constricted pattern over the first weeks of intoxication. Thus, a pattern once representing a given grooming response might evolve into only a remnant of the former behavior, such as simply raising a leg. Similarly, a sniffing stereotype often would end up on day 11 as a stereotype involving only a head movement derivation which would only retain a few parts of the former complex act. In this current study involving higher doses of methamphetamine, we have primarily found and have focused our attention on the dystonic, the disjunctive, and the dyssynchronous aspects of amphetamine intoxication. Table 1 is a summary of the statistical significance of the trends we have observed in these and other aspects of intoxication. During and after day 3 when a given stereotype reaches its peak (and is only successively redefined after this point) various disjunctive behaviors still continue to increase in severity and frequency and become mixed with various dyskinetic or abnormal neurological elements. For example, dyssynchrony

Table 1. Probability Values of the Differences Observed in the Total Population
on Various Indexes and Measures of Behavior[a]

| Measure | Injection effect | | | Day effect | |
	Within day 1	Within day 3	Within day 11	Preinjection across days	Immediately postinjection across days
Ataxia	< 0.01	< 0.01	< 0.01	< 0.05	< 0.01
Dystonic posture	< 0.01	< 0.01	< 0.01	< 0.01	< 0.01
Patterned behavior	< 0.01	< 0.01	< 0.01	< 0.01	< 0.05
Transient behavior	< 0.01	< 0.01	NS	< 0.01	< 0.01
Interested abnormal	< 0.01	< 0.01	< 0.01	< 0.01	< 0.01
Investigative abnormal	< 0.01	< 0.01	< 0.01	NS	< 0.05
Reactive	NS	NS	< 0.01	< 0.01	< 0.005

[a]Analysis of variance was applied to the five observation periods within each day to show the immediate effect of each injection (Injection effect). The same test was performed between the preinjection observation periods for each of the three days (preinjection across days), and between the combined 10-min, 20-min, and 30-min observation periods of each day (immediately postinjection across days), in order to demonstrate the effect of chronic intoxication and increasing dosage (Day effect) on pre- and postinjection behavior.

was an often noted phenomenon, i.e., one body part or body segment moving without proper relation to other body parts to make a flowing vector of behavior. Similarly, as a posture, one body segment out of proper relationship with others was often noted and called disjunctive posture. Ataxia was especially frequent during the latter stages of intoxication, and appeared to be an admixture of loss of equilibrium and some degree of weakness.

Dyssynchrony, as we have defined it in our observations, represents a given body ensemble taking on an autonomous movement which did not seem to have purpose or

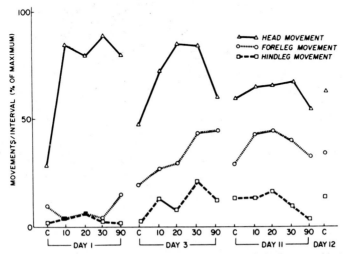

Fig. 1. Average number of individual movements in head, forelegs, and hind legs of all subjects. Ordinate: percent of maximum possible movements. Abscissa: observation periods (C = preinjection, 10 = 10 min postinjection, 20 = 20 min postinjection, etc.).

relatedness to other body segments. For example, repetitious repositioning or raising movements of the hind legs on many occasions had little or no relation to the sniffing pattern that was taking place at the head and neck ensemble. The three major body ensembles; head-neck, shoulder-foreleg, and hip-hind leg were also relatively more independently active at different parts of the drug cycle (*see* Fig. 1). On day 1 the head-neck ensemble is obviously much more active but recedes over the ensuing days, whereas the shoulder-foreleg ensemble increases dramatically over the latter days of intoxication. The hip-hind leg activity makes its appearance primarily during the third day of intoxication but never really becomes active in the same way as the foreleg and head regions. More often the hind leg was noted to be in a frozen hyperextended postural position. This particular behavioral configuration, active forelegs and frozen hind legs, often resulted, in the standing animal, in one of the abnormal movements of the trunk, i.e., hunching, and a disjunctive posture called camel, since the active forelegs at times would back up against the relatively resistant hind legs to produce the hunch or camel-back phenomenon. At other times it appears as if the cat has forgotten where a leg is positioned; thus, for example, a leg would remain in an awkward disjunctive position while the cat goes about other activities (*see* Fig. 2a). Other disjunctive postures include normally twisted uncomfortable sitting and lying positions. These are very much like those noted in human catatonics, and we have made similar observations in monkeys and rats chronically intoxicated.

Fig. 2. Disjunctive posture: a. Chronic methamphetamine intoxication. b. Chronic methamphetamine intoxication plus antabuse.

Obstinate progression was noted in three cats on days 10 and 11. When placed facing the wall, these particular cats would continue treading against it rather than turning to one side. One of these cats also demonstrated emprosthotonus and a plastic rigidity which cleared when it was raised to the standing position. Other cats demonstrated what could be called obstinate retrogression. First they would alternate a few steps forward then a few steps backwards, finally ending with the rear end against a wall pushing backwards with much effort of the forelegs. Four other cats were noted to lean against the wall of the cage gradually allowing their legs to slide out from under them, almost as if they were not aware that it was happening to them. The eventual fall did not appear to be the result of weakness in that they quickly righted themselves after the fall. From these observations as well as the general nature of stereotypies and the frozen attitudes to be described later, we have operationally classified such behaviors not on a basis of weakness or ataxia, but on a basis of loss of initiative in changing attitudes or postural-movement sets.

Development of stereotype behaviors as well as persistent attitudes are directly correlated with a marked degree of muscular tension and activity. In many previous amphetamine studies, activity has been rated more on a basis of locomotor or place-to-place movement than intensity or number of movements. Our activity scale is based on movement speed and intensity (*see* Fig. 3). Often following amphetamine intoxication, animals, including rats, demonstrate a remarkably rapid rate of movement even though frozen in the same attitude and cage location. The relation between activity level and attitude is demonstrated in Fig. 4 ($p < 0.001$). The figure demonstrates that the more

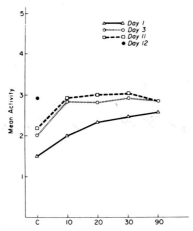

Fig. 3. Mean activity level of all subjects on the first, third, and eleventh day of intoxication. Ordinate: activity level. Abscissa: observation periods (C = pre-injection, 10 = 10 min postinjection, 20 = 20 min postinjection, etc.).

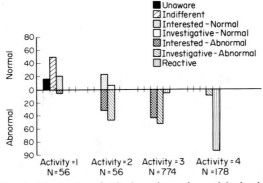

Fig. 4. Distribution of attitudes at increasing activity levels under all experimental conditions. Ordinate: percent of cases within the specified activity level. Normal attitudes shown above the line, abnormal attitudes below.

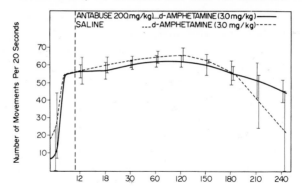

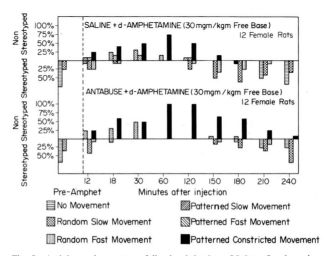

Fig. 5. Activity and stereotype following injection of 3.0 mg/kg *d*-amphetamine preceded by either saline or antabuse pretreatment 6-hr previously. Note: the solid black bar represents most constricted stereotype.

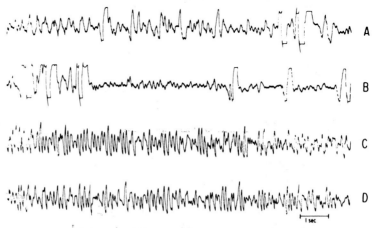

Fig. 6. Voltage output of "Animex" motometer following 5 mg/kg methamphetamine in a rat. AB = beginning constrictiveness of behavior. CD = full sniffing stereotype.

intense the activity, the more bizarre the attitude. The level of activity described as stage 4 consists primarily of intense, small rapid movements. Similar results were found in rats shown in Fig. 5. The motor activity represented as the peak is a 2.5 to 3.0 per sec rhythm which was counted from TV recordings or movies. Additionally, it can be noted that antabuse, a dopamine beta-hydroxylase inhibitor (which blocks norepinephrine synthesis) actually prolongs both the activity and the stereotypies. (This is in contradistinction to studies demonstrating that hyperactivity is related to norepinephrine effects when more gross locomotor movements are measured.) We have also recorded a 10-12 cycle/sec rhythm that represents the most intense state of sniffing stereotypies. Figure 6 demonstrates the coherence of these fast movements representing the repetitious sniffing, as measured by a tuned oscillator system with amplified voltage output. These small fast movements can only be reported quantatively as intense activity represented by stage 4 of activity level in our observation studies, since they are uncountable in real time.

In general stereotypies are most intense on days 1 and 3, and by day 11 they are often not an increasing sustained response. The stereotype pattern response falls off by 30-90 min as can be seen in Figs. 7 and 8. That this accelerated fall-off represents an

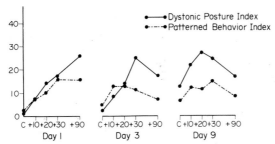

Fig. 7. Average Dystonic Posture Index and Patterned Behavior Index of all subjects. Ordinate: percent of maximum possible score. Abscissa: observation periods (C = preinjection, 10 = 10 min postinjection, 20 = 20 min postinjection, etc.). Note fall-off of both indexes between 30 and 90 min on days 3 and 11 ($p < 0.01$) with corresponding increase in Dystonic Posture Index ($p < 0.05$), and no change in Patterned Behavior Index (p = NS) during this same interval on day 1.

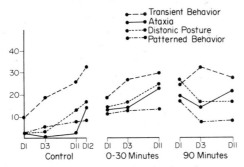

Fig. 8. Mean index values of ataxia, dystonic posture, transient behavior, and patterned behavior in all subjects. Ordinate: index value (percent of maximum possible score). Abscissa: observation periods (Control = preinjection, D1 = Day 1, D3 = Day 3, etc.).

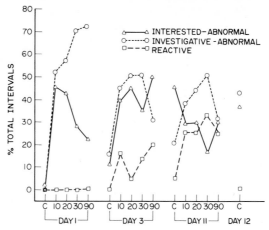

Fig. 9. Mean occurrence of abnormal attitudes in all subjects. Ordinate: percent of intervals in which attitude was observed. Abscissa: observation periods (C = preinjection, 10 = 10 min postinjection, 20 = 20 min postinjection, etc.).

inability of dopamine synthesis to sustain the amphetamine-induced response is certainly a possible hypothesis. As we have expressed previously, we strongly suspect that the dopamine action in the relative absence of norepinephrine is responsible for the more intense stereotypies as well as the bizarre dystonic postures (Ellinwood and Escalante, 1970a,b). Rats or cats pretreated with antabuse prior to amphetamine develop more intense stereotypies, as shown in Fig. 5, and also develop dramatically bizarre catatonic postures (see Fig. 2b). Figures 7 and 8 also demonstrate that both stereotype patterns and dystonic posture fall off at 90 min on days 3 and 11. This fall-off may represent a relative absence of both norepinephrine and dopamine on these days, which would be in keeping with Gunne and Lewander's (1967) biochemical assays demonstrating norepinephrine and dopamine depletion following chronic amphetamine intoxication. The dystonic posture fall-off at 90 min is in contrast to the ataxia and transient behavior indexes, both of which represent more disorganized breakdown of behavior and increase remarkably over the 11 days.

Attitudinal scales, more dramatically than either posture or stereotype, demonstrate the perseverance of a single mode of relating to the environment (see Fig. 9). The investigative abnormal attitudinal scale reflects the persistent "compulsive" searching-out of restricted "stimuli", often even when the animal may have broken from a patterned motor stereotype. Reactive attitude correlated best with the ataxia and the quick transient behavior noted most often on day 11. It was a state not unlike the hyperactive state produced when a reserpinized animal has been given amphetamine. However, even the reactive attitude was a fixed one in that the animal would react only to certain stimuli with certain quick jerking movements, but other loud and at times noxious stimuli might go totally unnoticed; thus, even in this case, there was a rather marked constricted attending to the environment.

DISCUSSION

One of the major premises of this study is that amphetamine-induced behavior can be clearly separated into three categories: movement, posture, and attitude. It has been described that each of these features has a somewhat different time-course during a period of acute or chronic amphetamine intoxication. For example, the specific posture and attitude involved in an acute amphetamine-induced stereotype may persist even after the specific movement pattern sequence has broken. Over the chronic course of intoxication one notes the breakdown of motor patterns into more constricted elements or components of movement, or into their more primary elements. Not only is there a distinction between specific patterned sequences and their elements or components, but there is also a sharp distinction between frequencies of movements. For example, following a given injection, movements gradually become less random with a predominance of slow-wave components, but this shifts at the height of the amphetamine-effect to a high frequency 10-12 cycle/sec rhythm. The fast components of movement are a relatively neglected area of research both in experimental animals and in humans. These fast components of behavior may prove to have a strong correlation with psychotic states. Condon and Brosin (1969) have noted a fairly marked microstrabismus associated with certain schizophrenics.

One interesting finding was the absolute increase in several indexes during control periods across days. This increase is pronounced in the transient behavior and the dystonic posture indexes. At first glance one would attribute this activity during the control period to residual drug-effect alone. There is a discrepancy in this reasoning, however, since the control period on day 12 which was 24 hr after the last dose of amphetamine was significantly higher than on day 11 for which there had been only 16 hr since the last injection. The explanation for this discrepancy perhaps is more on the basis of a speeded up metabolism and synthesis of catecholamines rather than strictly a residual drug-effect.

The most striking findings in our study were the dyssynchrony of movement and the postural disjunction of body segments. Normally behavior is a symphony of changes and sequences of motivative behavior, all with their proper lability of attitude and spontaneous initiative for subsequent changes. There are proper relationships and smooth flow of control and autonomy not only in a spacial sense but also in a temporal sense. Following chronic amphetamine intoxication, components of behavior became relatively fixed over time and showed a loss of cohesive flow among different initiatives with their relative priorities. In addition, there was a segmentary autonomy manifested in the dyssynchrony of movements of separate body parts. In other words, there appeared to be islands of separate organization, each establishing its own autonomy or anarchy without integration into the larger behavioral symphony. This is not unlike Janet's (1920) concept of independent "complexes". If we are to understand the discoordination between behavioral systems, it will be important to understand the natural control and coordination of these systems.

Hinde (1954) expressed the principle that "behavior is mediated by the nervous system and every particular pattern of behaviors is mediated by a particular nervous system mechanism or pattern of nervous activity." We have modified this statement to the operating principle that there are intrinsic postural-attitudinal sets which underlie and are the scaffolding upon which all behavior is organized. These are, of course, modified by experience, including both external and internal environments (including drug-induced states). As we have discussed previously, postural mechanisms are the substrate of attention and help to organize and direct the flow of behavior (Ellinwood, 1968; 1969). In schizophrenia as well as in amphetamine psychosis, one notes distortion of postural mechanisms, and this may indeed relate to the lack of coordinated control and the tendency to have behavior and attention split off into autonomous units. Schizophrenic children frequently show lack of integration or repression of the tonic neck reflex. Visual postural reflexes are severely disturbed in many schizophrenics as has been demonstrated by Lowenbach (1936) and Fitzgerald and Stengel (1945). Schizophrenics are frequently noted to have spontaneous turning around the longitudinal axis (Hoff and Schilder, 1924) and difficulty aligning a rod to the vertical while seated in a tilted chair (Teuber *et al.*, 1960). Ellinwood and Escalante (1970*a,b*) also reported righting reflexes to be severely disturbed in chronic amphetamine-intoxicated cats. Catatonic schizophrenics are well known for their schism of posture, affect, and attention. In a similar vein, Tatetsu (1963) has reported that amphetamine addicts often manifest catatonic syndromes. We have previously (Ellinwood and Escalante, 1970*a,b*) reported that chronic amphetamine-induced symptoms were secondary to stimulation as well as to depletion of catecholamines especially in those systems mediating postural and visuo-postural mechanisms such as the mesencephalic reticular system, especially in and about the vestibular nuclei and the medial longitudinal fasciculus. Depletion and stimulation in these systems as well as their projections to the extrapyramidal and limbic systems are an explanation for the rather marked postural changes with chronic amphetamine intoxication. The results of our studies indicate that not only is there depletion of norepinephrine in these systems but that subsequent amphetamine stimulates the dopamine systems in the relative absence of norepinephrine, for example, by the experiments showing that antabuse pretreatment potentiates the amphetamine-induced dystonic posture, disjunctive behavior, and constrictedness of stereotypies. In addition, Ellinwood and Escalante (1970*a,b*) using histochemical techniques found marked depletion of norepinephrine in all segments of the reticular-activating system, a system that is known to coordinate activation as well as various modes of sensory and motor inhibition. Our working hypothesis at this time is that amphetamine stimulation of various dopamine systems, without the coordinating and inhibiting effects of the norepinephrine systems, tends to allow individual lower level organizational substrates to become relatively autonomous. These same mechanisms, although induced by other means, may also be responsible for certain schizophrenic syndromes.

REFERENCES

Condon, W. S., and Brosin, H. W. (1969) Micro-linguistic-kinesic events in schizophrenic behavior, in *Schizophrenia: Current Concepts in Research.* Sankar, D. V. Siva (ed.), PJD Publications, Ltd., Hicksville, New York, pp. 812-837.

Connell, P. H. (1958). *Amphetamine Psychosis.* Chapman and Hall, London.

Ellinwood, E. H., Jr. (1967). Amphetamine psychosis I: description of the individuals and process. *J. Nervous Mental Disease* **44**: 273.

Ellinwood, E. H., Jr. (1968). Amphetamine psychosis II: theoretical implications. *Intern. J. Neuropsychiat.* **4**: 45.

Ellinwood, E. H., Jr. (1969). Amphetamine psychosis: A multi-dimensional process. *Sem. Psychiat.* **1**: 208.

Ellinwood, E. H. Jr. and Escalante, O. D. (1970*a*). Behavioral and histopathological findings during chronic methedrine intoxication. *Biol. Psychiat.* **2**: 27.

Ellinwood, E. H., Jr., and Escalante, O. D. (1970*b*). Chronic amphetamine effect on the olfactory forebrain. *Biol. Psychiat.* **2**: 189.

Escalante, O. D., and Ellinwood, E. H., Jr. (1970). CNS cytopathological changes in cats with chronic methedrine intoxication. *Brain Res.* **21**: 555.

Fitzgerald, G., and Stengel, E. (1945). Vestibular reactivity to caloric stimulation in schizophrenics. *J. Mental. Sci.* **91**: 93.

Griffith, J. D., Fann, W. E., and Oates, J. A. (1970). The amphetamine psychosis: comparison of clinical and experimental manifestations. Proceedings of Symposium on Current Concepts of Amphetamine Abuse (in press).

Gunne, L. M., and Lewander, T. (1967). Long-term effects of some dependence-producing drugs on the brain monoamines, in *Molecular Basis of Some Aspects of Mental Activity,* Wahaas, O. (ed.), Academic Press, New York, pp. 75-78.

Hinde, R. A. (1954). Changes in responsiveness to a constant stimulus. *Brit. J. Anim. Behav.* **2**: 41.

Hoff, H., and Schilder, P. (1924). *Die Lagereflexe des Menschen,* Springer, Berlin.

Itil, F. M. (1969). Quantitative analysis of "motor pattern" in schizophrenia, in *Schizophrenia Current Concepts and Research,* Sankar, D. V. Siva, (ed.), PJD Publications, Ltd., Hicksville, New York, pp. 210-219.

Janet. P. (1920). *Major Symptoms of Hysteria.* Hafner Publishing Company, New York and London.

Kety, S. S. (1960). Recent biochemical theories of schizophrenia, in *The Etiology of Schizophrenia,* Jackson, D. D. (ed.), Basic Books, New York, pp. 137-138.

Lowenbach, H. (1936). Menssende untersuchungen uber die erregbarkeit des zentialneven-systems von geistestranken, vor allem von teriodisch katatonen, mit hilfe quantitativer vestibularisreizung. *Arch. Psychiat.* **105**: 313.

Randrup, A., and Munkvad, I. (1967). Stereotype activities produced by amphetamine in several animal species and man. *Psychopharmacologia* **11**: 300.

Tatetsu, S. (1963). Methamphetamine psychosis. *Filia Psychiat. Neurol. Jap.* 377.

Teuber, H. L., Battersby, W. S., and Bender, M. B. (1960). *Visual Field Effects After Penetrating Missile Wounds of the Brain,* Harvard Univ. Press, Cambridge, p. 143.

15. Tonic Immobility in the Rhesus Monkey (*Macaca mulatta*) Induced by Manipulation, Immobilization, and Experimental Inversion of the Visual Field[1,2]

J. P. FOLEY

Journal of Comparative Psychology, 1938, *26*, 515-26. Copyright 1938 by the American Psychological Association. Reprinted by permission.

"Tonic immobility" refers to negative or quiescent behavior, even in the presence of disturbing stimulation. Such behavior has been observed in a variety of animal forms, from planarians to man, and has been variously (erroneously) described as "animal hypnosis," "catalepsy," and "death feigning" or "simulation." The term "tonic immobility," first suggested by Crozier (6, 7, 8, 9, 10) and later employed by Hoagland (10, 14, 15, 16), is most desirable, since it defines the phenomenon in terms of its concrete, observable manifestations, and avoids the pitfalls of anthropomorphic analogy to which certain comparative psychologists have fallen prey. In all organisms, regardless of phyletic status, the condition is marked by a lack of overt reactivity to external stimulation and by a high degree of plastic tonus of the skeletal musculature.

Presumably because of the analogy to human catalepsy, tonic immobility has frequently been termed "animal hypnosis," and this confusion has been strengthened by Pavlov's repeated observations (23, 24) of canine catalepsy[3] under the same experimental conditions which usually resulted in sleep, the unresponsiveness of the dogs in this state being "analogous" to that of hypnotic subjects towards persons with whom they are not in *rapport*.[4] Such an implication is entirely erroneous, as several investigators have pointed out (cf. Hull, 17).

The first experiments of this kind are usually attributed to the Jesuit Kircher,[5] who in 1646 observed that a cataleptoid state could be artificially induced in hens. According to Preyer, the experiment had been performed several years earlier by Schwenter. Czermak repeated the experiment on different animals, and announced in 1872 that a hypnotic state could be induced in other animals besides the hen. Experiments have subsequently been conducted on a wide variety of animal forms by numerous investigators, including Andova, Claparède, Cobb, Crozier, Danilewsky, Eckstein, Grasse,

---

[1] Read in part at the annual meeting of the Eastern Branch of the American Psychological Association, New York University, April 1-2, 1938.

[2] The writer is indebted to Professor C. J. Warden of the Laboratory of Comparative Psychology, Columbia University, who made available the facilities of the laboratory for the present study.

[3] Some of the conditions of sleep in dogs have been pointed out by McDougall (21).

[4] The passage of inhibition into sleep in Pavlov's dog experiments (23, 24) was not duplicated in Wendt's experiments (31) on the inhibition of food-taking reactions in monkeys. Wendt has interpreted both results in terms of competition between reaction systems.

[5] The so-called *experimentum mirabile Kircheri*.

Heubel, Hoagland, Holmes, Kieser, Löhner, Magnus, Mangold, Parker, Pavlov, Piéron, Polimanti, Preyer, Rabaud, Richet, Rieger, the Severins, Steiniger, Szymanski, Tolman, Upton, Verlaine, Verworn, Waugh, Wendt, Wilson, Wundt, Yerkes, and others. Reviews of portions of the literature will be found in Andova (1), Bramwell (4), Claparède (5), Crozier (6, 7, 8, 9, 10), Hoagland (10, 14, 15, 16), Hull (17), Mangold (18, 19, 20), Moll (22), Preyer (27), Rabaud (28), and Warden, Jenkins and Warner (30).

Tonic immobility has been produced in a variety of ways, most of which, as Warden, Jenkins and Warner (30) point out, involve a sudden displacement of the animal. The *methods* by which the phenomenon has been previously produced in vertebrates may be classified as follows:

1. (*a*) Absence of varied stimulation, and (*b*) repetitive and monotonous stimulation, such as gentle stroking, repeated handling and manipulation (especially in the eye region), and movement in and out of the visual field.
2. Gross bodily restraint.
3. Pressure on certain regions, such as the thorax.[1]
4. Sudden inversion, i.e., turning the organism into a dorsal position.

TONIC IMMOBILITY IN PRIMATES

Relatively little work has been done on tonic immobility in the Primates. This fact has led Warden, Jenkins and Warner (30, p. 387) to conclude that " 'hypnotic' states and death-feigning have not yet been studied in this group." In their comprehensive review of anthropoid behavior, Yerkes and Yerkes (32) present no evidence on the phenomenon in gibbon, orang-outan, chimpanzee or gorilla. The most relevant observation reported by these investigators (32, p. 98) is that attributed to Boutan (2; 3, pp. 60-64), who observed that extreme fatigue and sleep were induced in the gibbon by work on complicated problems requiring sustained attention. A few scattered instances in the monkey, however, have been reported by Claparède, Kieser, Mangold, and Wendt.

Claparède (5; cf. Mangold, 19) was able, by repeated stroking and by firm bodily restraint, to place a monkey in a state of "catalepsy," in which he was able to bend and stretch the animal's leg as he pleased. The animal, otherwise intractable, would retain the same bodily position as long as the stroking or restraint continued.

Kieser (cf. Preyer, 27; Claparède, 5; Mangold, 19) had already, in the time of Mesmerism, induced such a condition of immobility in various monkeys. The animal was placed in a recumbent position on the table, and Kieser "placed his thumb in the stomach region or on the head."

Thus with one monkey (*Callitrice sabaea*), not full grown, 15 minutes of handling brought only negligible symptoms of fatigue. On the second day, after 20 minutes of handling, the animal closed its eyes intermittently, and made rapid, jerky movements of the arms. In the evening, the subject became immobile after 10 minutes of such stimulation, and remained in this condition for 5 minutes. As the handling was continued for several days, the subject, a vivacious animal who during the day never remained still a moment, could be brought to close its eyes immediately during any time of the day and be put into a quiet "sleep" when a hand was placed upon its head

---

[1] May be a conditioned response, originally elicited by gross restraint as in Method 2.

or the thumb moved (*shaken*) in front of its eyes. Almost the same phenomena were observed with the monkey (*Cebus capucinus*).

Mangold (19) reports induction of a state of complete immobility in a small macaque (*Macacus cynomolgus*) by grasping the animal by the legs and suddenly turning it over on its back, "whereupon it emitted a short cry, but then remained with its legs projecting in the air, without correcting its uncomfortable position."

More recently Wendt (31) has reported instances of tonic immobility in monkeys as a result of immobilization, these observations being made in connection with experiments on habituation to rotation and on visually elicited eye-movements. For purposes of recording eye-movements the animal's body was placed in a box restricting its movements, and the head was immobilized by pressing the teeth into dental impression compound and binding the head with gauze bandage. In the rhesus monkey (*Macaca mulatta*), "the animal becomes still almost immediately it is confined, and within a short time goes into a state having some resemblances to sleep. The spiders (*Atelca ater*) and green monkeys (*Cercopithecus aethiops sabaeus*) show the same behavior, but to a somewhat lesser extent" (p. 274). Wendt (p. 275) describes the immobile condition as follows:

"The chief external signs of the condition in the rhesus monkey are absence of struggling or movement of the limbs, uniform respiration, partial or complete closure of the eye-lids, elevation and wandering of the eyes and absence of fixational eye-movements. During this condition response to stimulation is difficult to elicit. When the animal does respond to a stimulus, the response is associated with the temporary abolition of the sleep-like condition. Vestibular and visually induced nystagmus are difficult to elicit and of brief duration. The animal will endure a variety of insults without apparent reaction, insults which, in the normal alert animal, would call forth vigorous defence reactions. By increasing the intensity of stimulation, response can usually be elicited. However, the intensity of stimulation is not the only factor determining its effectiveness. The repetition of even very intense noises, etc., soon fails to elicit any perceptible response. But, under these conditions some new stimulus, even though very faint—such as a slight scratching sound, whistling, the sound of footsteps from the floor above, the slight noises of the camera motor, motion in the visual field, darkening of the room, increase in the illumination of the room, blowing against the side of the head, the smell of a banana held to the nose, and other faint stimuli—often restore the alert state. A certain method of bringing the animal back to alertness is to place the finger tips over the nostrils for a few seconds so as to shut off the air supply. When the animal is alert, the recommencement of the experimental stimulation (let us say, movement of the visual field) will often reinstate the sleep-like condition. This connection between stimulation and the onset of the sleep-like state shows that it is not solely conditioned by the procedure of immobilization."

THE PRESENT EXPERIMENT[1]

The *subject* in the present investigation was an adult female rhesus monkey (*Macaca mulatta*), a member of the primate colony at the Columbia Laboratory of Comparative Psychology in New York City. The animal was purchased from a New York animal

---

[1] Certain of the observations reported herein were obtained in the course of an experimental study of the effect of prolonged inversion of the visual field in the rhesus monkey (*Macaca mulatta*). A report of the latter study is now in preparation and will appear in *The Journal of Experimental Psychology*.

dealer and arrived at the Laboratories in December, 1930. At the time of purchase she was immature (preadolescent), her age being estimated at almost 4 years. Since most of the data in the present experiment were obtained during June, 1936, the subject was approximately 9 years old at that time. The animal was housed throughout the year in the primate quarters of the Laboratory, fed according to the standardized Columbia Dietary and Feeding Schedule for Monkeys (cf. 11, p. 53), and exercised daily in the runway, receiving a period of Sunlamp stimulation each morning. She remained vigorous and healthy throughout.

When first obtained in 1930, the animal showed no signs of former handling. She was subjected to the standardized adaptation routine in use at the Laboratory, and subsequently served as a subject in experiments on the Jenkins problem box, delayed reaction, motivation (by means of the Columbia obstruction method), imitation, brightness discrimination, and brightness constancy—the latter two experiments using a modification of the Yerkes-Watson discrimination apparatus. The subject was thus exceedingly docile and tractable.

1. Tonic Immobility Induced by Rhythmic Stroking and Manipulation

On repeated occasions during the subject's stay in the laboratory, a completely inactive response could be elicited by gentle handling and repeated stroking of certain body areas, particularly the eyes and thorax. The animal would become entirely passive and immobile, with muscles in a state of tonic contraction, and would remain in the same position until the handling or stroking was discontinued. During such a time, overt response to stimulation was difficult to elicit; in order to evoke such a response it was necessary to increase considerably the intensity of the stimulus.

The general characteristics of the subject's behavior on such occasions were the same as when tonic immobility was induced in other ways, and will be discussed in the following section.

2. Tonic Immobility Induced by Gross Bodily Restraint

The first observations of tonic immobility induced by bodily restraint were made in November, 1934, when the subject was first placed in the new type of restraining apparatus which had been especially devised for an experiment on the effect of prolonged inversion of the visual field. This apparatus, which has been described in detail elsewhere (12), was designed to retain the monkey in as near normal or "sitting" position as possible, and consisted of two essential parts: (1) a chair, with restraining devices for the body and lower extremities; and (2) a head holder, designed to keep the head rigid and motionless. This particular type of restraining apparatus was the most efficient of a series of different varieties, the remainder of which had proved ineffective.

When first placed in this apparatus on November 14, 1934, the subject was at once completely passive, submissive, and rigid for the entire 30 minutes during which she remained in the restraining device. These periods of molar inactivity were occasionally interspersed by sudden writhings of the body and extremities, these writhings being immediately followed by another inactive period of similar duration. There was an absence of struggling and movement of the limbs, and a persistent tonic contracture of the gross bodily musculature. Breathing was uniform, but shallow. There was an absence of fixational eye-movements. The subject showed a marked thigmotropism— a tendency to push against the restraining chair with the trunk or extremities, and a tendency to grasp something with the hands or feet, such as parts of the restraining chair or holder or the hands and arms of the experimenter. When in such a state of tonic immobility, the animal would allow food to be placed between her lips, but would make no effort to chew or swallow. Her jaws were firmly closed, and bits of even the preferred foods, such as raisin, apple, peanuts, and banana, would thus remain protruding from her mouth for long periods of time, eventually falling to the floor of their own weight when the more or less periodic wriggling movements occurred. Nor could the subject be induced in any way to reach for food.

This tonic, immobile condition persisted for several days, although every attempt was made to eliminate it, since it precluded the subject's participation in any experimental procedure. Final resort was made to the hunger drive, and motivation was increased considerably by withholding the animal's regular food and offering it only during these experimental sessions. In this way the condition was gradually eliminated, although on December 1st, 17 days after the initial appearance of the phenomenon, the subject became somewhat tense and lethargic at times, and on such an occasion would refuse to accept food of any sort. Repeated daily sessions, however, under strong hunger motivation, eventually served to minimize if not eliminate all traces of tonic immobility.

3. Tonic Immobility Induced by Experimental Inversion of the Visual Field

As previously stated, certain of these observations on tonic immobility were obtained in the course of an experimental investigation of the effect of prolonged inversion of the visual field upon spatially coordinated behavior in the rhesus monkey. During the course of the experiment proper, another factor was found to elicit such tonic, immobile behavior, viz., experimental inversion of the visual field.

The optical system used to achieve inversion has been described in detail elsewhere (13). It consisted essentially of binocular astronomical telescopes with detachable lenses mounted in aluminum tubes, the latter threaded securely into the brass bushings of a form-fitting aluminum mask. The mask was held in place by a leather headgear fastened with straps and surgical adhesive, so that no light could reach the eyes except through the lenses. The interpupillary distance was correctly observed, and the lenses were chromatically and aplanatically corrected so as to furnish a clear, well-defined and maximal field of view at an established fixation distance of 16 inches.[1] The entire apparatus, including the headgear, weighed 130 grams.

The reversing lenses were first placed on the subject at 2:30 P.M. on June 23, 1936, and were worn continuously for a period of exactly 7 days (cf. 13). The immediate effect of such an inversion of the visual field was to elicit a condition of tonic immobility in the subject. She became purely passive, assuming a bent-over posture, with head drooped forward. At intervals of approximately 3-4 minutes, she would squirm about, raise her head, and look around. She refused to reach for food or to transfer it to her mouth when it was placed in her hand, nor would she chew or swallow food even when it was forced into the mouth cavity. This condition of immobility was instituted by the

---

[1] The computed monocular field was slightly in excess of 30°, and after assembly the observed field for the human eye was found to be approximately 11 inches in a plane at 16 inches distance; binocularly this would give a field somewhat larger. For further description of the lens system employed, cf. 13.

lenses alone, independently of the restraining chair and headholder, and it persisted both with and without such imposed restraint.[1]

This general phenomenon was observed periodically throughout the 7 days of visual inversion, the subject frequently becoming very inactive, and assuming the characteristic bent-over posture, even when not restrained. At such times, the displayed thigmotropism was stronger than usual, the subject increasing the area of bodily contact with the substratum (floor, chair, etc.) and grasping a cord or any other object within reach with her feet, or—if nothing was available—grasping one foot with the other.

As the monkey became more and more active on successive days, making increased use of her new system of sensori-motor cues (cf. 13), these periods of extreme tonic immobility were repeatedly observed to follow immediately periods of heightened activity and visual (?) strain, the animal rising up on her hind feet, twisting her body, reaching out with her arms and moving her head around as if looking in all directions, and then suddenly resuming her typical crouched, immobile position. It is quite possible that this behavior illustrates the visual mechanism involved in such a phenomenon, i.e., tonic immobility resulting, in such cases, from a period of direct perceptual gaze and visual exploration, in so far as it is visually conditioned at all. Such a mechanism would give rise to the frequently observed periods of general activity interspersed with the relatively sudden onset of a short period of tonic immobility. These observations were repeatedly confirmed throughout the 7-day period of inversion of the visual field, and disappeared completely upon removal of the lenses.

The relationship of these results to certain findings reported in the literature might be mentioned at this point. As stated above, one of the traditional ways of producing tonic immobility in infrahuman organisms has been that of suddenly inverting the animal, i.e., placing it upon its back. Thus sudden inversion would, of course, involve stimulation through a number of sensory modalities, including in particular visual reception and stato-reception. It is interesting to note that the present observations illustrate the experimental production of the phenomenon through visual stimulation alone, no change being made in the gravity relationship between organism and environmental substratum.

4. Conditioned Tonic Immobility

One other observation of interest was made at various times during the course of the experiment. It was frequently observed, both during the preliminary sessions in 1934-1936 devoted to adaptation to the restraining chair and head-holder apparatus, and during the experiment proper in June, 1936, that the reaction of tonic immobility became conditioned to the visual or tactual stimulus of the restraining chair. Thus the sight of the chair or the mere tactual stimulation derived from being seated therein, with no restraint of any kind being imposed, would often elicit the typical symptoms of complete immobility.

Moreover, the subject's arms and feet, necessarily restrained for a while during the early days of the experimental inversion of the visual field, became conditioned so that they seldom attempted to reach up and pull at the lenses, even when left entirely free.

[1]That the phenomenon could in no way be attributed to the mere presence of the mask and supporting headgear was indicated by a subsequent control experiment in which the lenses were removed and empty aluminum tubes substituted in their place. These tubes, comparable in length and aperture to those previously used with the lenses, gave a visual field identical in size with that obtaining under conditions of inversion. The control observations also indicated that such tonic immobility could not be attributed to the slight difference in weight occasioned by the lenses.

REFERENCES

(1) Andova, A. Thantose des grossen Rosskäfers *Geotrupes stercorarius l.* Zsch. f. Morphol. u. Oekol., 1929, **13**, 722-744.

(2) Boutan, L. Le pseudo-langage. Observations effectuées sur un anthro poïde; le gibbon·(*Hylobates Leucogenys* Ogilby). Act. Soc. linn. Bordeaux, 1913, **67**, 5-80.

(3) Boutan, L. Les deux méthodes de l'enfant. Act. Soc. linn. Bordeaux, 1914, **68**, 3-141.

(4) Bramwell, J. M. Hypnotism, its history, practice and theory. London: Rider & Son, 1921. Pp. 480.

(5) Claparède, E. Verhandlungen der internationalen Gesellschraft f. med. Psychol. und Psychotherapie, 1910. J. f. Psychol. u. Neurol., 1910, **17**, 11.

(6) Crozier, W. J. Reflex immobility and the central nervous system. Proc. Soc. Exper. Biol. and Med., 1923, **21**, 55-57.

(7) Crozier, W. J. Biological researches relating to the nervous system. Carnegie Instit. Yrbk., 1924, No. 23, 227-229.

(8) Crozier, W. J. On the possibility of identifying chemical processes in living matter. Proc. Nat. Acad. Sci., 1924, **10**, 461-464.

(9) Crozier, W. J., and Federighi, H. On the character of central nervous processes. Proc. Soc. Exper. Biol. and Med., 1923, **21**, 57-58.

(10) Crozier, W. J., and Hoagland, H. The study of living organisms. In Murchison, C., ed., Handbook of general experimental psychology. Worcester: Clark Univ. Press, 1934, 3-108.

(11) Foley, J. P., Jr. First year development of a rhesus monkey (*Macaca mulatta*) reared in isolation. J. Genet. Psychol., 1934, **45**, 39-105.

(12) Foley, J. P., Jr. An apparatus for restraining monkeys and other lesser primates. Amer. J. Psychol., 1935, **47**, 312-315.

(13) Foley, J. P., Jr. An experimental investigation of the effect of prolonged inversion of the visual field in the rhesus monkey (*Macaca mulatta*). In press, J. Exper. Psychol.

(14) Hoagland, H. Quantitative aspects of tonic immobility in vertebrates. Proc. Nat. Acad. Sci., 1927, **13**, 838-843.

(15) Hoagland, H. On the mechanism of tonic immobility in vertebrates. J. Gen. Physiol., 1928, **11**, 715-741.

(16) Hoagland, H. The mechanism of tonic immobility ("animal hypnosis"). J. Gen. Psychol., 1928, **1**, 426-447.

(17) Hull, C. L. Hypnosis and suggestibility: an experimental approach. N.Y.: Appleton-Century, 1933, Pp. 416.

(18) Mangold, E. Die tierisch Hypnose. Ergebn. d. Physiol., 1920, **18**, 79-117.

(19) Mangold, E. Hypnose und Katalepsie bei Tieren (im vergleich zur menschlichen Hypnose). Jena: Fischer, 1914, Pp. 82.

(20) Mangold, E. Methodik der Versuche über tierische Hypnose. Handb. biol. ArbMeth., Abt. 6, Teil C, 1925, **1**, 319-368.

(21) McDougall, W. The bearing of Professor Pavlov's work on the problem of inhibition. J. Gen. Psychol., 1929, **2**, 231-262.

(22) Moll, A. Hypnotism. N.Y.: Scribner & Welford, 1890, Pp. 408.

(23) Pavlov, I. P. The identity of inhibition with sleep and hypnosis. Sci. Mo., 1923, **17**, 603-608.

(24) Pavlov, I. P. Conditioned reflexes: an investigation of the physiological activity of the cerebral cortex. (Trans. by G. V. Anrep.) London: Oxford Univ. Press, 1927, Pp. 430.

(25) Piéron, H. Le problème physiologique du sommeil. Paris: Masson, 1913, Pp. 520.

(26) Piéron, H. Thought and the brain. N.Y.: Harcourt Brace, 1926, Pp. 255.

(27) Preyer, W. Die Kataplexie und er tierische Hypnotismus. Jena, 1878.

(28) Rabaud, E. L'immobilisation réflexe et l'activité normal des arthropodes. Bull. biol. de France et Belge, 1919, **53**, 1-149.

(29) Szymanski, J. S. Über kunstliche Modifikationen des sogenannten hypnotischen Zustandes bei Tieren. Pflüger's Arch., 1912, **148**, 111-140.

(30) Warden, C. J., Jenkins, T. N., and Warner, L. H. Comparative psychology: vertebrates. N.Y.: Ronald Press, 1936, Pp. 560.

(31) Wendt, G. R. An interpretation of inhibition of conditioned reflexes in competition between reaction systems. Psychol. Rev., 1936, **43**, 258-281.

(32) Yerkes, R. M., and Yerkes, A. W. The great apes: a study of anthropoid life. New Haven: Yale Univ. Press, 1929, Pp. 652.

Section V

ANIMAL ADDICTIONS

16. Addiction in Animals

H. STAINTON

British Journal of Inebriety, 1941, *41*, 24-31. Reprinted by permission.

Just as treatment of some diseases in the human subject has pointed the way to control of animal diseases, so has the reverse process been of value. It is true to say that countless experiments have been effected upon animals to the advantage of man without any obvious benefit to their own species. One can quote the various artificial fistulae as devised by Eck and Pawlow, such sera as Pasteur's anti-rabic and Behring's anti-diphtheritic sera and other instances of research, which led to the elimination of glanders and the control of tetanus and tuberculosis.

Animals have subscribed much to the health of mankind, but the anti-vivisectionists still ask for total prohibition of experiments on the living animal, irrespective of the fact that the most minor surgical interference is performed under complete anaesthesia and under most severe restrictions. The horrors of true vivisection have long been relegated to a past age of enthusiastic ignorance and cold-bloodedness. Whether by a few painless innoculations on a dog you discover the control of distemper and so save thousands of other dogs or whether by feeding an animal contrary to precept you solve some dietetic problem, you are still a vivisectionist according to those whose chief argument is that the practical value of such experiments is rendered null and void by the fundamental difference from a pathological and physiological point of view between the bodies of men and the lower animals. That is, however, by the way. We often hear the expression that "animals can't tell you"—but in the majority of cases this necessary objectivity has its advantage over the subjective approach which applies in human medicine.

The veterinary surgeon has to rely on his own powers of observation and diagnosis and is not hampered by the often misleading statements of the subject.

As this Society is interested in abnormal appetites and craving for deleterious substances, it should be of value to consider these as they occur in the lower animal.

We all know of unnatural craving for nauseous substances in human beings—especially in pregnant women and neuropaths. Children also come under this category with their paint sucking and plasticine eating.

In the lower order of life the habit may be naturally advantageous, as it is not always true to say that it is contrary to the needs of the animal. One can understand to some extent earth swallowing, plasticine eating and limewash licking in this connection. Hair licking is more or less normal in the lower animal and only produces obstruction in cases when there has been breeding for length of hair.

Human hair eating may be considered as atavistic in origin.

ALCOHOLISM IN ANIMALS

Nearly all animals will acquire the taste for alcohol, and here is the story of a pony who liked beer. My father, who was a veterinary surgeon in the old horse-and-trap days, owned a pony called Moses, and this pony was generally driven by the assistant on his rounds. Apparently this assistant had been in the habit of calling at a wayside pub, which meant driving into the usual adjacent parking enclosure, and as he was not a lonely drinker he always brought out a pint of beer for the pony. One day my father had occasion to use this pony himself and, driving with a loose rein, suddenly found himself within the precincts of this hostelry, where Moses had arrived for his drink. Explanations followed, but it was a puzzled and disappointed pony that was coaxed back to the straight and narrow road.

Those who have read "San Michele" will recall the story of Billy the baboon who was taught to drink whisky by his drunken master. On the death of the latter, Munthe took Billy to his home at Capri, and in course of time thought he had cured the dipsomania. But one day, in Munthe's absence, Billy found the wine cellar and indulged in a real Bacchanalian burst of mischief and destruction. In contrast to this otherwise harmless and amusing sinner, I once knew a monkey who was a confirmed addict and dangerous when "under the influence." This, again, is another instance of human corruption, for the owner, a drunkard, found amusement in enticing the animal to find a concealed bottle of liquor and knock off the neck on a door handle in order to drink himself silly or fighting mad as the case may be. Finally, this poor victim of human depravity became savage and had to be destroyed. Not all monkeys become obstreperous, as is shown by the case of one who was a gentleman "in his cups." He had been prescribed a little brandy medicinally, but the attendant was so intrigued by the results that she overdid it to the point of inebriation. All he did was to catch imaginary flies to his own satisfaction and without offence to anybody else. By and large, I think monkeys and all animals of the so-called higher grade of intelligence become easy addicts and might get out of hand if given the liberty and opportunity.

Parrots appreciate the *taste* of sweet wine and may eventually acquire a liking for anything alcoholic. Incidentally, parrots have been known to display a fancy for tobacco, which they will absorb in quantity; if allowed, either orally or by inhalation.

Apart from accidental access to alcoholic substances, such as fermenting fruits and roots, animals are, for the most part, introduced to alcohol by therapeutic exigencies— and they react individually. Some dogs, for instance, will persistently reject such treatment, while others seem to appreciate the soothing effect of the stuff and will lap it up voluntarily with gusto. Association with the circus brings one in contact with the larger animals, such as elephants, and these are subject to pneumonic trouble on occasion. Any medicament, apart from hypodermic injection, must be given through some palatable medium such as an orange. The circus people have great faith in whisky, and I have watched, with amazement, an elephant seize a suitably doctored bottle of this in his trunk and suck in the contents, in spite of the fact that he had no interest in any other sort of nourishment. I have also seen an elephant, at the first taste, dash the bottle to the ground with angry trumpeting.

These few examples rather go to prove that alcoholism does not give much anxiety to the animal doctor nor to the patient. They may serve some purpose as an introduction to the condition known as "pica"—which is the term used to denote depraved appetite or vitiated taste in animals.

ABNORMAL APPETITES—PICA

It is characterized by an irresistible desire to lick or gnaw anything within reach—

such as walls, floors, trees, posts, earth, sand, lime, etc., and to eat all kinds of disgusting material. The following are a few specific examples of morbid appetite:

1. Licking disease in cattle.
2. Wool eating in sheep.
3. Sand eating in horses.
4. Plucking of own feathers by birds.
5. The aberration of the pregnant animal, which shows inordinate desire for material (food or otherwise) which would ordinarily be avoided (*cf.* human). Incidentally, some quote, quite wrongly, the eating of the placenta. This is a natural and proper functional instinct.
6. The eating of cinders, coal, wood and horse manure by *young* dogs.
7. The sudden preference for filth, dirty water and human excreta above good food by the *old* dog.
8. The dog suffering from rabies who, during the premonitory stage, will avoid favourite food and begin to bite and gnaw anything within reach and swallow foreign bodies such as earth, straw, glass, rags, and even its own faeces and urine (*cf.* the insane human).

So far, pica has no uniform etiological basis beyond the fact that modern concepts invariably point to one or both of two failures in the general animal mechanism. These are mineral deficiencies (including trace elements) and avitaminosis.

"HYSTERIA" IN ANIMALS

Before attempting any general survey, I think we should consider nervous diseases in animals under abnormal conditions of food and environment.

This hysteria in dogs may be defined as a nervous condition characterized by sudden extreme fright, uncontrolled barking and a tendency to hide or more often to stampede as if trying to escape from something. Others, between the paroxysms of yelping, will stare at some fixed point as if "seeing things" (*cf.* Korsakov cases). Apart from observing such cases myself in houses, I can quote two authentic examples of this curious behaviour in the open. One was a shooting dog who invariably became hysterical on passing a small copse, and the other was a pony who would never pass a certain crossroad without every evidence of extreme fear, including profuse sweating.

Although not recognized as infectious, hysteria can be transmitted throughout a kennel by mimicry or contagious panic, and on occasion it has been necessary to abandon a greyhound racing meeting because of such a mass "brain storm."

In America it was originally known as "fright disease" and one German authority has used the expression "anxiety psychosis," and this was one reason which prompted me in this attempt to draw some parallel between animal and man.

Distribution is more or less world-wide, but its incidence and mode of treatment in the Arctic regions rather tend to support our modern ideas of its etiology as a deprivation of certain essential natural substances which can produce disorganization of stomach and brain in close relationship. Hysteria of sledge dogs, "piblokto" of Eskimos (running amok), gnawing tendency of Manchurian ponies and the symptoms of scurvy in Polar travellers all point to deficiency aggravated by exposure and general malnutrition. Amundsen considered that scurvy and madness went together. He relates of his sledge dogs that he discovered, too late, that their deaths were due to *lack of fat* in their food. He was able eventually to improve the health of his party, both human and animal, by giving them seal meat, fresh blood of ice bear, fat and blubber, maize meal and margarine.

Some early investigators based their theories on elemental deficiencies appertaining to the various salts, the poor food of certain regional areas, unhygienic conditions and the dyspepsia of parasitic origin. Others were, perhaps, nearer the mark in tracing the trouble to nervous irritability, because we have come to believe that the nervous system is largely implicated. Modern knowledge allows for a more complicated machinery involving many interrelated and delicate mechanisms.

A study of the reactions of cell and tissue oxidization in association with vitamins, hormones, enzymes and the general controlling influence of the endocrine glands convinces one how easy it is to destroy the natural balance. Of the vitamins which play a part in biological oxidation, B_1 (aneurin), B_2 (lactoflavine) and C (ascorbutic acid) are among the most important for our present consideration, and the absence of one or more of these will lead to impairment of function with the result of clinical syndrome.

PHYSIOLOGICAL CRAVING

I have mentioned morbid appetite for excreta in dogs which would seem to be necessarily deleterious. But an accidental discovery during some dietetic research on rats goes to show that some benefit can on occasions be derived from this habit. An experiment involved two series of rats in two separate cages, and it was noted that in one cage the rats flourished whereas in the other they failed. Eventually, after much headache, it was discovered that in the first cage the wire mesh grid over the tray was lower and so gave access to the faecal matter, which the rats were absorbing to their advantage. In this case there was a B_1 deficiency in the diet which the rats were making good from the B_1 produced by the yeast growing in their droppings. It may be significant to note that faeces contain, apart from this adventitious B_1, inorganic salts, fatty acids, neutral fat and *cholic acid,* the compounds of which are of proved physiological value. It is known, for instance, that acetyl-choline plays an important part in its action on the sympathetic and parasympathetic systems and, further, that it can be hydrolyzed by the ferment esterase into choline, etc. There is some evidence to show that vitamin B_1 exerts an action antagonistic to choline.[1]

As regards fat, the theory has been advanced that it is more essential than carbohydrate for the maximum utilization of the protein in the diet. In some experiments of rats and dogs a diet comprising protein and fats was compared with a diet of protein and carbohydrates. Both diets were balanced by the addition of salts and vitamin concentrates. The results were in favour of the fat-rich combination. These experiments were extended in order to demonstrate the toxic action of a diet composed of protein alone and, in some cases, depending upon the nature of the protein, there was much disturbance of the central nervous system even to the point of coma and death. Such toxic effects were considerably reduced by the addition of fats.[2]

SOME NOTES ON THE TREATMENT OF PICA AND HYSTERIA

This has not yet been established satisfactorily. Tscheulin and Spinola regarded pica as a nervous disease affecting the sensory nerves of the stomach and taste organs through the derangement of the pneumogastric nerves. They are supported by Siedamgrotzky in his diagnosis of nervous irritation. It certainly falls in line with my own recent clinical experience. In the larger animal, change of pasture is essential, and this will correspond with the change of conditions and associations recommended for the human subject.

Apomorphine, which has proved an important remedy in man (a vomiting subject), has been used with equal success in the larger animals, who do not easily vomit except in extreme circumstances. The treatment does not depend upon vomition, and this appears to carry interest in a comparative study. The experimental use of hydrochlorate of apomorphine by Feser, Hackl and Reindl encouraged Lemke to employ this drug on a large scale. He reports that 226 cows, 21 oxen and 141 calves all recovered in a few days and regained their normal appetite within fourteen days. His dosage was 3 grains both for cow and calf, and he claimed that, with the elimination of any obvious exciting cause, the cure was permanent. Otherwise the effects of apomorphine would last only from three to five months. For cattle which had been suffering for some time he gave 1 ½ grains subcutaneously for three consecutive days and double that amount for those that had recently contracted the pica. Further to this, Lemke cured 800 cases of bovine malophagia (sheep-wool eaters) by subcutaneous apomorphine (1 ½ to 3 grains). We need not recapitulate the obvious steps in adjustment in regard to food imbalance, the B complex and the rest, but it should be important to link up past somewhat empirical methods with modern specific treatment such as that by apomorphine.[3]

The comparative section of medicine has justified its inception by the study of diseases intercommunicable between animals and man, of which there are many. Psychoses may or may not occur in the animal, but I believe that they do, and I am supported in some measure by the findings of Dexler and others. To quote a few examples: Pierquin cites the case of a talkative parrot who crept into a hiding-place during prolonged gunfire, and, when rescued later, had lost his vocabulary except for an attempt to imitate the noise of guns. White and Plaskett describe in a herd of North American goats a condition which they called "startled or fainting goats," where the animals collapsed from quite trifling external influences and were seized with tonic spasms, sometimes terminating fatally. On this evidence it might appear that being "frightened to death" is not necessarily a mere term. Dexler thought that these cases were due to hereditary degenerative peculiarities similar to the sensory disturbances of dancing mice and albinotic deaf animals.

In a case observed by Pierquin, a healthy and lively young cat was attacked by something like an "anxiety psychosis" after being frightened by a dog. The animal remained motionless and stupid for several hours after the dog had been removed. Melancholia, marasmus and death have been recorded frequently in dogs after the death of their masters, and this is held by some to represent one of the affective psychoses. With "mass panic," previously mentioned under hysteria in the dog, can be coupled the mad stampede of herds of cattle, during which the animals will run blindly against obstacles or precipitate themselves into fire or water. The impetus for this unreasoning flight can be traced, usually, to abnormal excitement of one or several individuals only.

Massive doses of B_1 are found to be of extreme benefit in these hysterias. (I have had four cases of hysteria in highly bred bull terriers being promptly controlled and permanently cured after one or a few injections of apomorphine, one-twentieth of a grain. Of course their diet was also attended to, but for prompt effects apomorphine was essential.—EDITOR.)[4]

In conclusion I will quote J. B. Jesson, who states that he knows of no department of psychology which promises such rich reward as that relating to the physiology and pathology of the mind in the lower animals.

REFERENCES

1. Blount, W. P., F.R.C.V.S.: "Acetyl-choline $v.$ B_1." Paper on advances in veterinary physiology presented to the Central Division N.V.M.A., May, 1938.
2. Maignon, F.: "Rôle of Fats," *Rec. Med. Vet.,* **114**, 10, 641, 1938.
3. Friedberger and Fröhner: "Use of Apomorphine," Vol. I., 42 *et seq.,* 1908.
4. Hutyra and Marek: "Animal Psychoses," Vol. II., 800 *et seq.,* 1913.

NOTES

(i.) Apomorphine is just as effective if pushed up the nose of the animal or man as if injected hypodermically in nearly the same dose.

(ii.) Does apomorphine benefit picas and "hysterias" which are due to vitamin deficiencies by enabling the patient to carry on with a smaller dose of vitamin?—Editor.

17. Tobacco Smoking in Monkeys

M. E. JARVIK

Annals of the New York Academy of Sciences, 1967, **142**, 280-94. Copyright 1967 by The New York Academy of Sciences. Reprinted by permission.

INTRODUCTION

Although cigarette, cigar, and pipe smoking has been practiced by untold millions of people throughout the world for hundreds of years, there have been few experiments in humans and practically none in animals that have examined this peculiar form of behavior. There are anecdotal reports of smoking by chimpanzees, dogs, and horses but never an attempt to quantify the behavior. It is not surprising that smoking does not occur in the natural repertoire of subhuman animals, since it requires the use of fire, a skill which has been considered characteristically human. In fact, we intend to demonstrate that smoking does not require fire and that puffing behavior resembling that seen in human smokers may be elicited in monkeys. In the studies to be described, we were interested to determine whether monkeys could be induced to puff on cigarettes or on the products from heated tobacco, and whether they would discriminate such particles and vapors from other substances.

There is no apparent physiological need for an organism to inhale substances other than oxygen. On the other hand, introduction of drugs into the pulmonary circulation is a most convenient method of getting them to the brain rapidly and also of bypassing the portal circulation, thereby escaping hepatic degradation. The efficiency of the pulmonary route of administration probably explains why substances such as marijuana, opium, and glue have been self-administered by smoking or sniffing. In the following experiments our reasoning was that if the products from tobacco smoke, including nicotine were pleasure-producing, animals would learn to inhale these substances with no other incentive. To put it another way, if an animal would go out of its way to inhale the products of tobacco for no other reason, we could say that these products had an intrinsic incentive value.

METHODS

Two main approaches were used in this research. The first involves the use of burning cigarettes and the second the distillation of tobacco and other products in specially designed machines. In Fig. 1 can be seen the most primitive device we used for studying smoking in monkeys. It consists of a cigarette holder mounted at the end of the metal tube. Our attempts to allow monkeys to handle cigarettes directly have largely failed because of their strong oral tendencies. Monkeys will almost invariably insert the entire cigarette, burning or not, into their mouths. In Fig. 2 can be seen a device in which cigarette holders were mounted on a sheet of plastic which was then placed on the front wall of the cage. With this arrangement the animal could not reach the

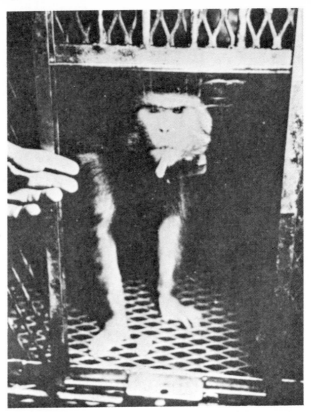

Fig. 1. Monkey smoking a cigarette. Cigarette is in a holder mounted on a plexiglass plate.

Fig. 2. Sensing device for cigarettes. Contact on either mouthpiece activates a corresponding relay.

cigarette itself with its mouth but could inhale the smoke. Each mouthpiece was wired
to a transistorized detection device so that whenever the animal made contact with one
or the other it could activate a counter. This apparatus was subject to a minimum of
mechanical breakdown, but it had the disadvantage that cigarettes had to be set in place
and lit by an experimenter.

For a variety of reasons we felt it would be desirable to have an arrangement where
smoke or a reasonable facsimile could be made accessible to the animals at predeter-
mined times even if an experimenter was not present. First of all we devised the apparatus shown in Fig. 3. Tobacco was put into the stainless steel pot which was then inserted
into a receptacle which was airtight except for an inlet and outlet tube. At the bottom

Fig. 3. Tobacco distilling apparatus. The stainless steel pot fits into the larger device. Temperature
is controlled by turning the black knob at the bottom.

was a heating compartment controlled by a bimetallic thermostat to keep the temperature at 100 to 110°C. The animal could draw air through the chamber which was satur-
ated with vapor and subsequently into his mouth. The usual procedure was to fill the
pot once a day and then allow relay circuitry and timers to determine the sequence of
availability of the vapors.

In time we found that the bimetallic thermostat was not very compatible with monkey
behavior. Monkeys will shake their cages quite vigorously, and if they can possibly
break an apparatus they will do so. Despite all kinds of locking devices, we found it
continually necessary to adjust the machines. Therefore we devised a newer version
in which a thermistor controlled a heating mantle. The device resembles an oriental
water pipe, the hookah or nargileh (see Fig. 4).

Since we were interested in puffing behavior, we utilized a sensing device in which a
needle within a glass or plastic tube was held in contact with the water in a small container. Whenever the animal puffed, it would draw a bubble of air through the tube,

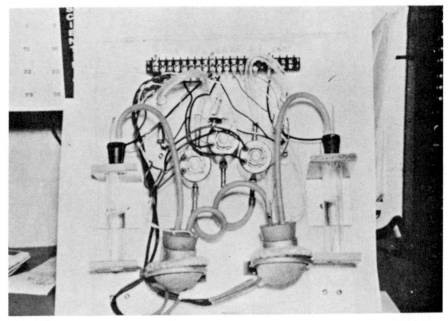

Fig. 4. Distilling apparatus for paired comparisons. Each heating mantle contacts an aluminum pot in which substances may be volatilized. The animal draws air through the test tubes into the heating and volatilizing chamber and then through a mouthpiece into his mouth. Three solenoid valves are shown because the center one is used to deliver water, if desired. Temperature is controlled with a thermistor and a safety heat fuse is also placed in the heating chamber.

thereby breaking the contact and thus activating a relay. The apparatus does not measure the depth of inspired breath or the amount of air displaced but only the number of puffs started or stopped. Therefore it is not possible to determine with this apparatus how deeply the animal inhales.

RESULTS

When the touch-sensitive cigarette holders were used, on alternate days a cigarette was put into the left and the right side and the other holder remained empty. The object was to determine the relative preference for each side. Each animal was given two ten minute trials per day. Under these conditions every animal preferred the side with the cigarette (247 puffs on the cigarette side and 101 puffs on the air side). However, the empty side was touched almost half as frequently as the side with the cigarette. One of the problems with this method was that the apparatus would respond to the touch of a hand or a foot just as well as to that of the mouth so that the figures do not represent actual sucking responses. Nevertheless it was clear that the animals were much more interested in the cigarette than in plain air, and this was true regardless of whether it was placed on the left or the right side.

In the next experiment six animals were observed directly by Dr. Bette van Laer. Two brass tubes were inserted through the front of each monkey's cage, one on the left and the other on the right. Cigarette holders were placed on the portion of the tube protruding outside the cage. The results in Table 1 are based upon observations made on two successive days, one on which the animals were given a cigarette on the right side and air on the left side and the other in which the converse arrangement was used.

Table 1. Mean Number of Smoking Periods per
Animal per Day

Animal	Lighted	Unlighted
1	44	6
2	52	26
3	62	27
4	49	31
5	53	31
6	61	11
Mean	54	22

On each day the cigarettes were presented to each animal for ten minutes and smoking behavior was scored using a time sample procedure. It was noted that the animal puffed on either cigarette during each of the 120 5-second periods throughout the ten minutes. The table shows the number of 5-second periods during which the monkey puffed at the cigarette, with each figure representing the mean of the two days. It can be seen that the animals show a strong preference for the tube from which they can obtain tobacco smoke.

During the next series of experiments the animals were tested automatically with the distillation apparatuses. In Tables 2 to 6 can be seen the relative preferences shown by monkeys for volatilized products from cigarettes compared with those from other substances. Each animal was tested for 20 minutes per day and the results shown were the average of at least five days of smoking. In Table 2 it can be seen that the animals puffed on the cigarette side 73% of the time and on the hot air side 27% of the time. I think it should be noted that the negative side was really somewhat positive since they did not avoid it. There were considerable differences between monkeys, and it can be seen that one animal, Claude, actually puffed more on the air side than on the tobacco side.

Table 2. Relative Preference of Hot Standard
Cigarette versus Hot Air at 110° C*

Monkey	Standard cigarette	Hot air
Randi	2723	723
Claude	531	870
Clyde	1919	526
Freida	555	148
Phoebe	1174	338
Emil	2030	645
Totals	8932 = 73%	3250 = 27%

*Each figure is based on 5 days of smoking.

In Table 3 one can see the relative preferences for tobacco taken from a cigarette compared with that taken from a cigar. Note that the animals do not discriminate at all between the volatilized products for these two types of tobacco. The aroma was dis-

Table 3. Relative Preference of Hot Standard
Cigarette versus Hot Cigar at 110° C*

Monkey	Standard cigarette	Hot cigar
Randi	1059	1186
Claude	934	579
Clyde	200	227
Freida	1027	1091
Phoebe	1512	1597
Emil	1100	1138
Totals	5832 = 50%	5818 = 50%

*Each figure is based on 5 days of smoking.

tinctly different to the experimenter. The animals divided their puffs almost exactly
50% of the time between the two types of smoking products. Next we were interested
to determine whether the animals could discriminate the effects of low versus high nicotine. The actual nicotine content of the tobacco was not determined, but standard
brands of cigarettes were used. It can be seen in Table 4 that there was no real difference in preference for one type of tobacco over the other.

Table 4. Relative Preference of Hot Standard Cigarette
versus Hot Low-nicotine Cigarette at 110° C*

Monkey	Standard cigarette	Low nicotine cigarette
Randi	603	635
Claude	752	937
Clyde	258	355
Freida	384	578
Phoebe	938	812
Emil	1021	1075
Totals	3956 = 48%	4392 = 52%

*Each figure is based on 5 days of smoking.

The next results shown in Table 5 come from a comparison of a very fragrant pipe
tobacco with the same standard cigarette. Here it can be seen that a marked preference
was shown for the pipe tobacco and even Claude showed a preference. Table 6 shows
the results of a rerun of the original experiment to see whether the two best discriminated
substances would still be discriminated and they were. Again hot tobacco was preferred
70% of the time to hot air, and hot pipe tobacco was preferred even more when compared to hot air than it was when compared to a standard cigarette. It must be noted,
however, that even under these circumstances the animals puffed on the air side a considerable percent of the time.

Subsequently, we attempted to determine whether animals would continue to puff
on the nontobacco side if it was unheated and they received cold air instead of warm air.
The results shown in Table 7 are the average of five 20-minute periods. It can be
seen that even with cold air an animal like Phoebe or Emil puffed a considerable por-

Table 5. Relative Preference of Hot Standard Cigarette
versus Hot Pipe Tobacco at 110° C*

Monkey	Standard cigarette	Hot pipe tobacco
Randi	977	3421
Claude	655	788
Clyde	148	809
Freida	427	1787
Phoebe	1050	2595
Emil	502	2285
Totals	3759 = 25%	11685 = 75%

*Each figure is based on 5 days of smoking.

Table 6. Relative Preference of Hot Tobacco versus Hot Air by Rhesus Monkeys*

Monkey name	Puffs of hot cigarette tobacco	Puffs of hot air	Puffs of hot pipe tobacco	Puffs of hot air
Randi	3462	1291	4728	1241
Claude	719	931	1920	908
Clyde	1922	536	1458	133
Freida	647	223	3798	290
Phoebe	1174	338	2444	397
Emil	2213	1072	3274	821
Totals	10137 = 70%	4391 = 30%	17622 = 82%	3790 = 18%

*Each figure is based on 8 days of smoking.

Table 7. Average Puffing Rate of
Monkeys for Tobacco and Cold Air*

Monkey	Cold air	Warm tobacco
Randi	55	580
Emil	100	250
Phoebe	196	230
Freida	35	712
Dorothy	103	300
Totals	489	2072

*Puffs per 20 minutes.

tion of the time on the negative side, showing us that generalization or lack of discrimination was occurring.

It was of some interest to us to determine what the pattern of smoking might be during the day if the animals were allowed 20-minute periods of access to warm tobacco. It must be pointed out that the nozzles were always present in the cage but that the tobacco was only heated during specified intervals during the day. Fig. 5 shows that

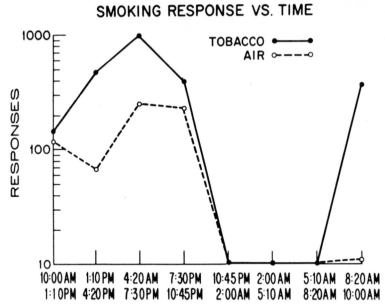

Fig. 5. Smoking response as a function of a time of day. Note that animals make no response during the night as they do, for example, with morphine.

smoking begins sometime between 5:00 and 8:00 a.m. which probably corresponded to sunrise and continued during the light part of the day (this was the wintertime) and then finally disappeared completely at night when the animals were probably asleep.

In the next experiment we attempted to determine whether animals would prefer tobacco smoke to tobacco vapor. Both kinds of apparatus were used at the same time for a given animal so that it could make any of four possible choices: it could puff on a cigarette which was burning or on the corresponding air side; or it could puff on the vapors from a cigarette or on the corresponding air side. The smoke from the actual cigarette was connected to a solenoid valve which would open for one second whenever the animal touched the mouthpiece. Frequently, the animal could take several puffs during this period of time, but it was long enough for at least one. The animals puffed on the actual cigarette a total of 968 times and on the corresponding air side 549 times, whereas they puffed only 414 times on the smoking machines delivering tobacco vapor and 258 times on the corresponding air side. This would indicate that the animals preferred actual cigarette smoke to tobacco vapor. For each of the five animals tested, the totals were greater for the real cigarette than for the smoking machine.

We noticed that with continual daily 20-minute exposures to the smoking machine, some animals would tend to lose interest with the passage of days or weeks and finally smoked relatively little. We wondered whether an intermittent schedule spread over days would tend to increase smoking behavior. In Fig. 6 it can be seen that turning the machine off for 16 days gradually eliminated responding from the animal. When the machine was turned on again, the animal smoked with apparently renewed vigor. A similar picture was seen using another monkey (Fig. 7). A third monkey, however, never stopped smoking, even though it was getting only cold air during this time interval (Fig. 8). The discrimination seemed to be somewhat better after the interval was over.

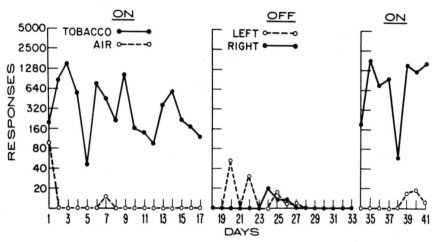

Fig. 6. Effect of a 16-day pause in smoking. This animal shows marked recovery on the first day smoking is resumed.

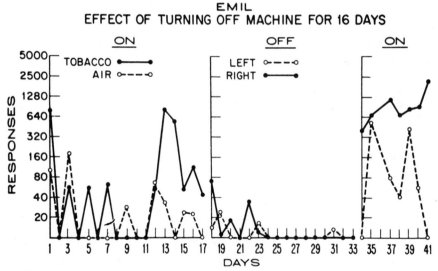

Fig. 7. Effect of a 16-day pause in smoking. This animal showed an effect similar to the first.

As an extension of this experiment, animals were given four 20-minute trials per day with tobacco on three successive days followed by three successive days without tobacco, and the cycle was then repeated (Table 8). On the tobacco days, puffing started out at a fairly high rate but the third day was always somewhat lower than the first. Similarly, on the air day the animal continued to puff on the same side where the tobacco had been, but again there was a decline from the first to the third day. A similar result was found when tobacco was shifted to the right side, but as might be expected, there

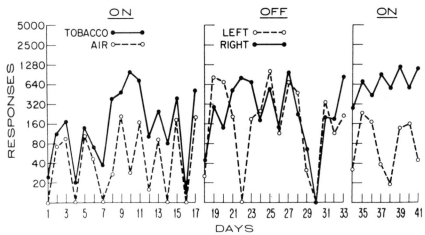

Fig. 8. Effect of a 16-day pause in smoking. This animal never stopped smoking but showed no side preference during the interval when the machine was turned off.

Table 8. Effects of a Three-day Pause on Smoking*

	Days	Left	Right		Days	Left	Right
HT-L†	1	1626	119	HT-L	13	1610	340
	2	755	21				
	3	1103	30	HT-R‡	14	605	330
					15	399	288
HA-B	4	409	14		16	322	456
	5	181	7				
	6	193	30	HA-B§	17	195	62
					18	123	245
HT-L	7	656	40		19	104	159
	8	676	29				
	9	507	14	HT-R	20	163	245
HA-B	10	102	3				
	11	255	38				
	12	81	65				

*Average number of puffs per 20 minutes (five minutes)
†HT-L = Hot Tobacco left, hot air right
‡HT-R = Hot Tobacco right, hot air left
§HA-B = Hot Air, both sides

was a continued persistence of puffing on the left side during the air days.

It was of some interest to determine whether a day-to-day preference could be determined by giving the animal only a go or no-go choice during a single day. In other words, the animal was presented with only a single choice and could either puff or not puff. The results shown in Table 9 are based upon three one-half hour intervals for each day per monkey. It can be seen that the most preferred substance given in pairs of successive days was heated tobacco. The least preferred was formaldehyde (formalin), but even on the second day of this substance there was an appreciable number of

Table 9. Preferences for Different
Substances Inhaled by Five Monkeys
on Paired Days

Substance	Day 1	Day 2
Hot tobacco	930	1050
Cold tobacco	314	284
Heated air	340	210
Cold air	93	88
Ammonium carbonate	231	83
Glacial acetic acid	512	1061
Iso-butyric acid	277	349
Formaldehyde	208	48

Table 10. Comparison of Forced versus Free
Smoking (Average Daily Number of Puffs)

	Tobacco left	Air right	Air left	Tobacco right
Puffing dependent water reward	2031	1497	692	2211
Puffing without water reward	171	17	18	94

responses. It can be seen that, even when 10% formalin was given to animals, there was an appreciable amount of puffing with more than 200 puffs on the first day and almost 50 puffs on the second day.

Table 10 gives a comparison of forced versus free smoking. The results shown are the average of five monkeys for 15 days. It can be seen that free puffing for no incentive other than the tobacco was far less effective than the condition in which a thirsty animal had to puff in order to receive a water reward. It must be pointed out that under these conditions the animal did have the dual choice of puffing on either the tobacco side or the air side, and it can be seen that the tobacco side was preferred in either case. By forcing animals to inhale tobacco vapors by this method we hope to be able to produce a physiological dependence. The method is similar to the priming method used with nicotine by Deneau and Inoki (1966).

DISCUSSION

These experiments indicate that under appropriate conditions monkeys will smoke cigarettes or suck on the vapors distilled from tobacco. There is an obvious similarity between this behavior and that seen in humans, but many questions of comparison still await answers. The habit that is developed in our monkeys does not seem to be as insistent as it is in humans, though it must be admitted that the strength of the smoking habit varies tremendously between humans. Similarly marked individual differences could be seen in the few animals that were used in our experiments.

A word should be said about the genesis of this habit for it is much more difficult to study directly the initiation of smoking behavior in humans than it is in animals. It is obvious that our experiments were not designed to answer this particular question but were rather aimed at a study of relative preferences once a firm degree of smoking behavior was achieved. At the very start of these experiments, we induced adult animals to smoke by first shaping them to suck water through a tube and then intermittently substituting a burning cigarette instead of water at the distal end of the tube. It was possible to teach less than 50% of the animals to suck water in the first place. Later we were able to obtain some young monkeys from Dr. Robert Zimmermann who had raised them under conditions of semi-isolation and parental deprivation. These animals exhibited a high incidence of thumb sucking and toe sucking and he gave us six animals which displayed this behavior (see Harlow and Zimmermann, 1958). For such animals it was not necessary to shape them to smoke cigarettes since they had a strong tendency to suck on objects. We found that they all took to the cigarettes placed in holders without difficulty, and they were then used in the experiments which were described.

In human smoking, air is drawn into the mouth either by using the muscles of respiration as in deep inhalation or by using the facial muscles and those of the tongue. The latter mechanism is used for sucking liquid into the mouth as, for example, through a straw. We have noted that all of our monkeys when they puff on cigarettes expel some of the smoke through their nose and the rest through the mouth, suggesting that inhalation is taking place. It would require very sensitive gas flow meters to determine whether the animals were actually inhaling.

Darwin, in Chapter 1 of the *Descent of Man* wrote, "many kinds of monkeys . . . will . . . as I have myself seen, smoke tobacco with pleasure." If one can assume that any behavior which is maintained by a given incentive is pleasurable, then our monkeys also were smoking for pleasure. In any case, there is smoking in the absence of any other obvious incentives. This means either that the chemical products which are sought in the act of smoking must serve as an incentive, or else the stimuli which are produced either by the sight or feel of the smoking product may serve as an incentive. Stimuli which are associated with a positive incentive tend to become secondary reinforcers themselves and add to the process of generalization. It is very likely that nicotine plays a key role in the tobacco habit, but it is difficult for animals to make a simultaneous discrimination between nicotine- and nonnicotine-containing substances because the drug has a prolonged effect which overlaps behavior associated with and without the actual administration of the drug. The experiments conducted by Denau and Inoki (1966) should throw some light on this subject.

Most of the work in animals on incentive value of substances has been done with eating or drinking behavior. In the commonly used preference testing method, an animal is allowed free access to a number of different substances which are available with approximately the same expenditure of effort, and the relative consumption of each item is measured. In the past, cafeteria types of experiments were conducted on animals in order to determine whether they would be capable of selecting a diet which would meet their needs. Such experiments were done by Evvard (1916) in the swine, by Pearl and Fairchild (1921) in hens, by Nevins (1927) in cattle, by Davis (1928) in human infants, and the results generally have indicated that subjects given free selection are capable of choosing a nutritious diet. On the other hand, Young (1928, 1932, 1933a, 1933b) has indicated that there are marked individual differences in appetitional responses in white rats. He found not only that individual differences and preferences were marked but that patterns of preference within a single animal might change with time. We have found the same type of variability in our animals without any apparent external cause.

There are undoubtedly complex social factors responsible for the initiation and maintenance of the smoking habit in man. According to Kensler (1955), "It is generally agreed that the use of tobacco involves primarily psychologic or emotional dependence, rather than physical dependence." It has been suggested that the aesthetic satisfaction derived from the aroma from the smoke, the visual stimulation of the gracious twirling of the smoke, and the pleasure from oral manipulation all play a part in the habit. Nevertheless, the evidence is strong that nicotine plays a vital role in smoking. Johnston (1942) reported that hypodermic injections of nicotine gave pleasant sensation to smokers in contrast to nonsmokers. In a self-experiment he found that he could derive more pleasure from nicotine injections than from smoking. It would seem that both psychological and pharmacological factors play a role and interact. It is unlikely that in monkeys living in isolated cages cigarette advertising or social pleasure from their peers plays much of a role in maintaining smoking behavior. One would have to assume that their behavior is maintained by a combination of sensory and pharmacological effects.

SUMMARY

It was found that a small group of monkeys could be induced to smoke cigarettes. Smoking behavior could be maintained simply by cigarettes alone and such behavior generalized for a wide variety of substances. Pipe tobacco was clearly preferred to cigarette tobacco, but the amount of nicotine in standard cigarette tobacco did not seem to have an influence nor were there any differences in preference for cigar or cigarette tobacco. When smoking was forced by the use of a stronger incentive (water for thirsty monkeys), the preference for tobacco over air persisted and the amount of tobacco vapor inhaled was increased greatly. We conclude that it is possible to elicit and maintain smoking behavior in monkeys with no other incentive and on a free choice basis, but it is relatively weak compared to other ingestive behavior, such as drinking which satisfies an obvious physiological need.

ACKNOWLEDGEMENT

I thank Drs. Bette van Laer and George Wertheim and Messrs. Jay Carley, Perry Downs, James Guyer and Robin Goldenberg for their help and advice in the conduct of these studies.

REFERENCES

Davis, C. M. 1928, Self-selection of diet by newly weaned infants, *Amer. J. Dis. Child* **36**: 661-679.

Deneau, G. A. & R. Inoki, 1967, Nicotine self-administration in monkeys, (This Annal).

Evvard, J. M., 1916, Is the appetite of swine a reliable indication of physiological needs? *Proc. Iowa. Acad. Sci.* **22**: 375-414.

Harlow, H. F. & R. R. Zimmermann, 1958, The development of affectional responses in infant monkeys, *Proc. Amer. Phil. Soc.* **102**: 501-509.

Johnston, L. M., 1942, Tobacco smoking and nicotine, *Lancet* (London) Oct-Dec: 742.

Kensler, C. J., 1955, *In The Biologic Effects of Tobacco*, F. Wynder (Ed.), Little, Brown & Co., Boston, Mass.

Nevins, W. B., 1927, Experiments in the self-feeding of dairy cows, Univ. of Ill. Agriculture Experiments Station, Bulletin **289**.

Pearl, R. & P. E. Fairchild, 1921, Studies in the physiology of reproduction in the domestic fowl, XIX: On the influence of free choice of food materials on winter egg production and body weight, *Amer. J. Hyg.* **1**: 253-277.

Young, P. T., 1928, Preferential discrimination of the white rat for different kinds of grain, *Amer. J. Psychol.* **40**: 372-394.

Young, P. T., 1932, Relative food preferences of the white rat, *J. comp. Psychol.* **14**: 297-319.

Young, P. T., 1933, Relative food preferences of the white rat, II. *J. comp. Psychol.* **14**: 149-165.

Young, P. T., Food preferences in the regulation of eating, *J. comp. Psychol.* **15**: 167-176.

18. Behavioral Maintenance of High Concentrations of Blood Ethanol and Physical Dependence in the Rat

J. L. Falk, H. H. Samson and G. Winger

Science, 1972, **177**, 811-13. Copyright 1972 by the American Association for the Advancement of Science. Reprinted by permission.

Abstract. Rats maintained on an intermittent food schedule with an available ethanol solution drink to excess (13.1 grams of ethanol per kilogram of body weight, daily). Removal of ethanol produces symptoms of physical dependence including death from tonic-clonic seizures. Overindulgence in oral self-administration of an aqueous ethanol solution, resulting in unequivocal physical dependence, approximates a model of human alcoholism.

The study of alcoholism would be facilitated if an animal model, possessing the major behavioral and physiological features of the human alcoholic, was developed. Recent reviews indicate (*1*) that presently available experimental arrangements fall short of providing such a model. One problem has been that the salient behavioral requirements of the model are quite demanding: (i) animals should orally ingest ethanol solutions excessively and chronically in a pattern that increases the concentration of blood ethanol analogous to that in the alcoholic; (ii) unequivocal physical dependence on ethanol must be demonstrated; (iii) food and ethanol should be available from sources physically separate so that the factors determining ethanol intake are not inextricably bound to those primarily concerned with meeting nutritional requirements; (iv) the experimental arrangement should retain an elective aspect to the ethanol ingestion by not programming extrinsic reinforcing events (for example, shock avoidance, food pellet delivery) contingent upon drinking ethanol. The technique we now describe satisfies all the above criteria.

Previously, one of us (*2*) found that volumes of water three to four times the normal 24-hour amounts were ingested when small food pellets were delivered intermittently to rats on a limited-food regimen. Because there is no increased fluid requirement in this method, polydipsia induced by a food schedule has been the subject of further research and theoretical speculation (see *3*).

Using the schedule-induced polydipsia technique, several investigators (*4*) have presented an ethanol solution as the available fluid instead of water. This research yielded no evidence of physical dependence on ethanol, perhaps because only single daily sessions, usually between 1 and 3 hours in length, were administered. Two studies, however, utilized longer sessions. Lester (*5*) maintained a rat on an excessive level of ethanol ingestion for a single 65-hour period. Ogata *et al.* (*6*) maintained mice on schedule-induced polydipsia for ethanol solutions during a 1- to 2-week period, but found no indications of physical dependence upon withdrawal of ethanol.

Eight male Holtzman rats, with a mean free-feeding body weight of 315.9 g, were reduced to 80 percent of their weights by limiting food rations (Purina Laboratory Chow, pelleted). They were housed in individual chambers under constant illumination. Each chamber provided a source of fluid, accessible from a stainless steel drinking tube. A Noyes (7) animal food pellet (45 mg) was delivered automatically every 2 minutes during 1-hour feeding periods that were separated by 3-hour intervals. Thus, there were six feeding periods in each 24-hour cycle, delivering a total of 180 pellets.

In the first phase of the experiment, water was the available fluid. Each day, at 10:30 a.m., the fluid intakes were recorded, and the animals were weighed, and given any additional food necessary to maintain their weights at the 80 percent level. After the establishment of schedule-induced polydipsia, increasing concentrations of ethanol were substituted for water. Starting with ethanol 1 percent (by volume), the concentration was increased in 1 percent increments every 6 to 8 days until the drinking fluid was 6 percent ethanol. One animal (No. 4) was given a maximum concentration of only 5 percent ethanol.

The mean daily water intake at the end of the initial phase of the experiment was 64.0 ml (standard error of the mean, ± 12.3 ml). Figure 1 shows the results of the

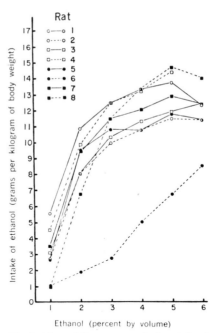

Fig. 1. Mean daily amounts of ethanol drunk by individual rats as a function of the available ethanol concentration.

incremental-alcohol phase in terms of the mean daily self-administered dose of ethanol. One animal (No. 6) failed to develop polydipsia as strongly as the others whose daily intakes at 6 percent ethanol were between 11 and 15 g of ethanol per kilogram of body weight. Because the intake of ethanol (in grams) did not increase when the concentration was changed from 5 to 6 percent, the fluid concentration was returned to 5 percent for the next 3 months, after which time the experiment was terminated. When the animals began drinking alcohol, additional food supplements were omitted for the remainder of the experiment as the animal weights were increasing.

During the early phases of ethanol drinking, the animals appeared to be intoxicated when handled at 10:30 a.m.: they were docile and somewhat ataxic. Later, presumably as tolerance developed, gross observation failed to reveal these or other signs of unusual behavior.

During their second month on 5 percent ethanol, the concentrations of ethanol in the blood of all rats was measured (8). Blood samples (50 μl) from the tail were taken 1 hour before and 1 hour after each of the 1-hour feeding periods. Serial samples were taken first between 8 a.m. and 7 p.m.; 2 weeks later, the samples between 8 p.m. and 7 a.m. were gathered. Figure 2 shows that for most animals, the concentration of

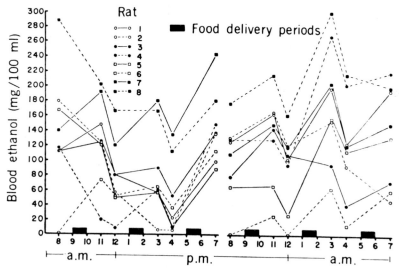

Fig. 2. Concentrations of ethanol in the blood of rats drinking 5 percent ethanol (by volume). During the indicated 1-hour feeding periods, a food pellet (45 mg) was delivered every 2 minutes.

ethanol in the blood fell below 100 mg/100 ml only in the late morning and afternoon. From 6 p.m. through 11 a.m., the concentration was greater than 100 mg/100 ml for most of the animals, and was often between 150 and 300 mg/100 ml.

Daily intake of ethanol remained quite constant during the 3-month period on 5 percent ethanol. For the last 10 days of the experiment, the mean daily intake for the eight animals was 13.1 g of ethanol per kilogram of body weight, with a standard deviation of 1.29. The percentage of the total caloric intake which was ingested as ethanol was 44.8 percent. The mean body weight of the group was 308.2 g, which was not significantly different from the free-feeding starting weight of 315.9 g.

Three to four weeks from the end of the experiment, we selected four animals for observation during alcohol withdrawal. They were removed from the experimental cages at 7 a.m., and were placed in individual observation cages with water, but no alcohol, available. Food rations, in amounts equivalent to those defined by the experiment, were given at the appropriate times. Within 3 to 4 hours after the last feeding period (5 to 6 a.m.), when most of their last draughts of ethanol presumably occurred, the animals became hyperactive. A shaking of keys near the top of the cage for 1 to 2 seconds resulted in a tonic-clonic convulsion in rat No. 8. For the next hour, tremors, spasticity, and clonic head movements occurred, and finally, a second seizure ended in death. When keys were shaken (2 to 5 seconds) for the first time after 9½ hours of withdrawal, a clonic running episode was produced in rat No. 2, followed shortly by death from a tonic-clonic seizure. Rat No. 7 showed all the preconvulsive symptoms, but keys shaken (up to 20 seconds) after 15 hours of withdrawal had no effect. Rat No. 1 was similar, but no attempt was made to trigger a convulsion by shaking keys. Attempts to produce convulsions in normal Holtzman rats by prolonged key shaking were unsuccessful, and no preconvulsive, hyperactive behavior was observed.

We are unaware of any previous report demonstrating physical dependence on ethanol in the rat as indicated by withdrawal convulsions, although this has been obtained in other species, as well as in man (9). We could also find no previous report of the development of physical dependence by self-administration in animals other than man when ethanol in water was available as the sole drinking solution.

Other methods for the production of ethanol dependence in animals have involved administration by intravenous and intragastric routes by liquid diets, and by inhalation (9.10). While useful, these methods have certain disadvantages; they are more removed from a model of alcoholism involving oral self-administration of an aqueous ethanol solution than is the method reported here. In animals consuming liquid diets in which 35 to 36 percent of the calories are derived from alcohol, the concentrations of ethanol in the blood appear to be rather low (10) unless the animals suffer considerable concomitant weight loss with presumed changes in their capacity to metabolize ethanol (6). The present method maintains high concentrations in the blood without significant body weight loss.

The percentage of total caloric intake derived from ethanol is low in most experiments utilizing ethanol in the drinking water. One study reports a caloric intake from ethanol as high as 30 percent (11). Attempts to incorporate 45 percent of the calories as ethanol into a liquid diet resulted in death of the animals (12). The 44.8 percent caloric intake in the present experiment compares favorably with this picture, and with the amount selected by human alcoholics (13).

REFERENCES AND NOTES

1. N. K. Mello, in *Psychopharmacology. A Review of Progress 1957-1967.* D. H. Efron, Ed., Publ. 1836 (Government Printing Office, Washington, D.C., 1968), p. 787; R. D. Myers and W. L. Veale, in *The Biology of Alcoholism*, H. Begleiter and B. Kissin, Eds. (Plenum, New York, 1971), vol. 2, p. 131.
2. J. L. Falk, *Science* **133**, 195 (1961).
3. ____, *Physiol. Behav.* **6**, 577 (1971).
4. R. B. Holman and R. D. Myers, *ibid.* **3**, 369 (1968); R. A. Meisch and T. Thompson, *Psychopharmacologia* **22**, 72 (1971); N. K. Mello and J. H. Mendelson, *Physiol. Behav.* **7**, 827 (1971); R. J. Senter and J. D. Sinclair, *Psychon. Sci.* **9**, 291 (1967).
5. D. Lester, *Quart. J. Stud. Alc.* **22**, 223 (1961).
6. H. Ogata, F. Ogata, J. H. Mendelson, N. K. Mello, *J. Pharmacol. Exp. Ther.* **180**, 216 (1972).
7. Composition according to P. J. Noyes Co. is: moisture, 5.0 percent; ash, 6.3 percent; ether extract, 4.9 percent; protein, 25.2 percent; fiber, 3.3 percent; carbohydrates, 55.3 percent; 4.3 kilocalories per gram.
8. N. G. Brink, R. Bonnichsen, H. Theorell, *Acta Pharmacol. Toxicol.* **10**, 223 (1954).
9. G. Freund, *Arch. Neurol.* **21**, 315 (1969); C. F. Essig and R. C. Lam, *ibid.* **18**, 626 (1968); F. W. Ellis and J. R. Pick, *J. Pharmacol. Exp. Ther.* **175**, 88 (1970); G. Deneau, T. Yanagita, M. H. Seevers, *Psychopharmacologia* **16**, 30 (1969); D. B. Goldstein and N. Pal, *Science* **172**, 288 (1971).
10. C. S. Lieber, D. P. Jones, L. M. DeCarli, *J. Clin. Invest.* **44**, 1009 (1965).
11. R. Scheig, N. M. Alexander, G. Klatskin, *J. Lipid Res.* **7**, 188 (1966).
12. G. Freund, *J. Nutr.* **100**, 30 (1970).

13. J. H. Mendelson and J. LaDou, *Quart. J. Stud. Alc.* Suppl. 2, 14 (1964).
14. Supported by NIMH grant MH 18409 from the National Institute of Alcohol Abuse and Alcoholism, and NIH grant AM 14180.

19. Evidence from Rats that Morphine Tolerance is a Learned Response

S. SIEGEL

Journal of Comparative and Physiological Psychology, 1975, **89**, 498-506. Copyright 1975 by The American Psychological Association. Reprinted by permission.

It is proposed that the direct analgesic effect of morphine becomes attenuated over the course of successive administrations of the narcotic by a conditioned, compensatory, hyperalgesic response elicited by the administration procedure, the net result being analgesic tolerance. Using the "hot plate" analgesia assessment situation with rats, this conditioning view of tolerance is supported by several findings: (a) It is necessary to have reliable environmental cues predicting the systemic effects of morphine if tolerance is to be observed, (b) a hyperalgesic conditioned response may be observed in morphine tolerant subjects when drug administration cues are followed by a placebo, and (c) merely by repeatedly presenting environmental cues previously associated with morphine (but now presented with a placebo), morphine tolerance can be extinguished.

Tolerance is said to have developed when, after repeated administrations, the effect of a given dose of a drug is less than it was originally. Tolerance to many of the effects of narcotics (especially opiates), such as analgesia, develops rapidly and reliably, and numerous hypotheses have been presented to account for the phenomenon. In summary, (a) the relevant effect of early experience with the drug may be to alter the organism's metabolism such that the drug is subsequently more efficiently metabolized (Mulé and Woods, 1969); (b) after the drug molecules exert their action on central receptor sites, they may continue to occupy these sites thereby decreasing the population of receptor sites that can be stimulated by the same drug on a later occasion (Schmidt and Livingston, 1933); (c) the initial drug administrations may induce the formation of "silent receptors," which functionally reduce the effects of later drug administrations by serving as "dead spot" receptors for drug molecules that would otherwise stimulate active "pharmacological receptors" (Collier, 1965); or (d) narcotics may be conceived of as antigens, with tolerance reflecting an immunity like process (Cochin and Kornetsky, 1968). All these theories of tolerance, hereinafter grouped together as *physiological theories* (for a review, see Cochin, 1970), postulate some systemic change within the organism as a result of the initial drug experience that decreases receptor sensitivity

This research was supported by Grant MT-3577 from the Medical Research Council of Canada. The assistance of Doreen Mitchell is gratefully acknowledged. The morphine sulfate used in these experiments was supplied by Health and Welfare Canada (Scientific Services, Health Protection Branch).

Requests for reprints should be sent to Shepard Siegel, Department of Psychology, McMaster University, Hamilton, Ontario, L8S 4K1, Canada.

to the drug, allows the drug to be metabolized more quickly, or serves to bind the drug before it can exert its action.

An alternative approach, proposed here, might be termed a *conditioning theory* of tolerance. According to this view, narcotic tolerance is the result of the learning of an association between the systemic effects of the drug and those environmental cues that reliably precede these systemic effects. Pavlov (1927, pp. 35ff) suggested that the administration of a drug could be viewed as a conditioning trial, with the actual pharmacological assault constituting the unconditioned stimulus (UCS) and the immediately antecedent environmental cues serving as the conditioned stimulus (CS). The development of the association between these stimuli may be revealed if the subject, after a history of administration of the drug, is presented with the drug administration procedure *not* followed by the systemic effects of the drug—rather, for such a conditioned response (CR) test session, a placebo is administered.

There has been a considerable amount of interest in the theoretical and practical importance of conditioned pharmacological responses (Gantt, 1957; Loucks, 1937; Siegel and Nettleton, 1970). Although many forms of drug CRs can be conceptualized and have been reported, conditioned drug responses are commonly opposite in direction to the unconditioned effects of the drug. Thus, it has been reported that in animals with a history of administration of an anticholinergic drug, such as atropine or Ditran, which induces antisialosis, the administration procedure without the drug leads to excessive salivation (Lang, Brown, Gershon and Korol, 1966; Wikler, 1948); in animals in which tachycardia has been repeatedly induced by injections of epinephrine, the injection procedure alone causes a decrease in heart rate (Subkov and Zilov, 1937); subjects repeatedly made to evidence allergic reactions by allergen injections evidence immune reactions when confronted with the injection procedure (for a review, see Hull, 1934, pp. 413-416); in animals with a history of administration of a hyperglycemic agent, such as glucose or epinephrine, the administration procedure alone leads to a decrease in blood sugar (Deutsch, 1974; Mityushov, 1954; Russek and Pina, 1962); in organisms repeatedly experiencing the hypoglycemic effects of injected insulin, the injection procedure alone leads to an elevation in blood sugar (Lichko, 1959; Siegel, 1972, 1975).[1] These anticipatory responses, being compensatory in nature, should serve to attenuate the drug-induced unconditioned response (UCR), therefore the net effect of the drug should decrease over successive drug administrations. Such a decreased response to a drug as a function of successive experiences with the drug defines tolerance.

According to the present conditioning theory, tolerance to the analgesic effects of morphine results because environmental cues regularly paired with the administration of the drug come to elicit a compensatory CR, hyperalgesia, which algebraically summates with the stable, unconditioned analgesic effects of the narcotic. Thus, environmental cues consistently predicting the systemic effects of the drug should be crucial to the development of tolerance since they enable the subject to make timely compensatory CRs in anticipation of the analgesic UCR. Several experiments by Mitchell and his colleagues (Adams, Yeh, Woods and Mitchell, 1969; Kayan, Woods and Mitchell, 1969) indicate that the rate of development of analgesic tolerance to morphine is highly dependent upon the availability of environmental cues uniquely present at the time of drug administration. Using the standard "hot plate" assessment situation

---

[1] Although the CR to physiological doses of insulin appears to be a compensatory hyperglycemic response, conflicting findings have been reported when the UCS consists of very large doses of the hormone (see Siegel, 1975).

(Jóhannesson and Woods, 1964), in which pain sensitivity in the rat is assessed by observing its latency to lick a paw when placed on a warm surface, these investigators reported that analgesic tolerance to morphine developed much more rapidly when subjects were confronted with the distinctive analgesia assessment environment on each of the five occasions that the drug was administered (even if the nociceptive stimulation was not applied until the fifth occasion) than if they were introduced into this environment for the first time on the fifth occasion that the drug was administered. Experiments 1A and 1B were designed to assess the reliability of these reports of the importance of drug associated environmental cues in the acquisition of tolerance.

EXPERIMENT 1A

Method

Subjects and apparatus. The subjects, 29 experimentally naive, male, 90-110 day old, Wistar derived rats (obtained from Quebec Breeding Farms, St. Constant, Quebec, Canada), were housed in individual cages with food and water freely available. Responsivity to pain was assessed using recent modifications of the hot plate technique (Eddy and Leimbach, 1953). Briefly, a 1,200 ml mixture consisting of equal parts by volume of acetone and ethyl formate was boiled in a rectangular copper container (19 × 19 × 15 cm). The container was completely enclosed with the exception of provision for a condenser coil to liquify the vapor and return it to the vessel. The temperature of the vapor and the top surface of the vessel were constantly monitored and remained at 54.2° C (±2° C). Pain sensitivity was assessed by placing the rat on the surface of the container for 1 min and noting the number of seconds that elapsed until it first licked a paw (hereinafter referred to as the paw-lick latency). Thus, analgesic responses are indicated by relatively long paw-lick latencies and hyperalgesic responses by relatively short paw-lick latencies.

Procedure. Three groups of rats received equivalent morphine injections on four occasions, the interval between injections being 48 hr. The fourth occasion was the test session, during which the pain sensitivity of all the rats was assessed on the hot plate in the test environment subsequent to the drug injection. The groups differed only with respect to the cues associated with the morphine administrations on the three prior sessions.

One morphine group was used to demonstrate the initial analgesic UCR of the drug and the development of tolerance over the successive drug administrations. This group was treated identically on Sessions 1-3 and Session 4, i.e., morphine-induced analgesia was assessed on the hot plate apparatus in the test environment each time the drug was administered (Group M-HP, i.e., morphine hot plate; $n = 8$). For each session, rats in this group were transported in their home cages from the colony room to a different room, which contained the hot plate apparatus, subcutaneously injected with a 5 mg kg dose (of a 5 mg/cc solution) of morphine sulfate, and .5 hr later, placed on the hot plate apparatus.

A second morphine group was included to assess whether any apparent drug tolerance observed in Group M-HP, as revealed by decreasing paw-lick latencies across sessions, may be attributable to merely increasing practice in making the possibly pain-ameliorating, paw-licking response while drugged rather than to any functional decrease in the narcotic's analgesic properties. This group was treated like Group M-HP except that the hot plate apparatus was not turned on until the fourth test session; for

Sessions 1-3, these rats were placed on the surface of the vessel when it was at room temperature (21.2°-22.2°C). For this second morphine group (Group M-CP, i.e., morphine-cold plate; $n = 7$), the environmental cues preceding the morphine effects and analgesia assessment were the same on Sessions 1-3 as on Session 4. However, these rats never practiced the paw-licking response on the hot surface until the test session; thus, relatively rapid reactions on Session 4 by Group M-CP rats would be attributable to drug tolerance rather than to acquired proficiency in paw licking while narcotized.

A third group of rats suffered the same systemic effects of the morphine equally as often and at the same intervals as rats in Groups M-HP and M-CP except that a different set of cues was associated with the systemic effects of the drug on the first three sessions than on the fourth, hot plate session. For this group, for Sessions 1-3, the morphine was administered in the colony room simply by removing the rat from its cage, injecting the drug, and returning the rat to its cage. Thus, this group (Group M-CAGE; $n = 8$), like Group M-CP, had its first morphine-induced analgesia assessment on Session 4, and differed from Group M-CP only because the environmental cues surrounding the morphine administration were different on the three prior occasions that the drug was administered.

Finally, a fourth group also received four hot plate analgesia-assessment sessions in the test environment, but all the injections were physiological saline rather than morphine. This group (Group S, i.e., saline; $n = 6$) provided an undrugged baseline, indicating the effects of the repeated injections and hot plate experiences *per se*.

Results and Discussion

The mean paw-lick latency for each group on each session is shown in Figure 1 (for Groups M-CP and M-CAGE, of course, the response was assessed only on the last session). As indicated in Figure 1, the characteristic analgesic effect of morphine was observed on the first session—rats receiving the narcotic for the first time (Group M-HP) had significantly longer paw-lick latencies than rats receiving saline ($U = 7.5$, $p < .02$). As was also expected; the analgesic effects of morphine became less and less pronounced on the successive sessions in which the drug was administered; a Wilcoxon matched-pairs signed-rank test indicated that Group M-HP rats had significantly shorter paw-lick latencies on Session 4 than Session 1 ($T = 0$, $p = .01$). As is also apparent in Figure 1, on Session 4 Group M-CP rats responded to the hot plate as did Group M-HP rats, the small difference between the two groups not approaching statistical significance, that is, Group M-CP rats evidenced the short-latency paw-licking response indicative of morphine tolerance on the fourth occasion that they received the drug despite the fact that they never experienced the heat stimulation and did not practice the response on Sessions 1-3, indicating that such practice (cf. Kayan et al., 1969) or repeated experience with the morphine while nociceptively stressed (cf. Adams et al., 1969) is irrelevant to the demonstration of analgesia tolerance in this test situation.

Both groups of morphine-tolerant rats, M-HP and M-CP, evidenced Session 4 paw-lick latencies not significantly different from that of Group S rats, despite the fact that Groups M-HP and M-CP were receiving morphine and Group S physiological saline prior to analgesia assessment.

As is obvious in Figure 1, Group M-CAGE, in marked contrast to Groups M-HP and M-CP, was not tolerant to the analgesic effects of morphine. The differences between Group M-CAGE and each of Groups M-HP and M-CP were statistically

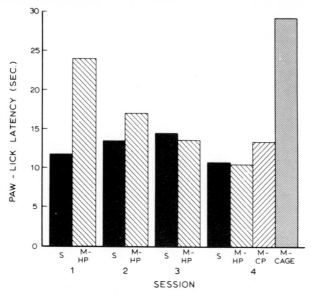

Figure 1. Mean paw-lick latency on hot plate for four sessions for groups in Experiment 1A. (Abbreviations used in group names: S = saline; M = morphine; HP = hot plate; CP = cold plate.)

significant ($U = 5.5$, $p < .002$ and $U = 12$, $p < .04$, respectively). Indeed, the Session 4 response latency of Group M-CAGE was not significantly different from that which would be expected the very first time rats receive the drug and analgesia assessment (i.e., the Session 1 value for M-HP rats). Thus, these results confirm the earlier reports of the importance of drug-associated environmental cues in the development of tolerance (Adams *et al.*, 1969; Kayan *et al.*, 1969).

Prior to the test session, all three morphine groups suffered the same morphine-induced systemic effects equally as often and at the same intervals. The rats in these groups should have been subjected to the same metabolic, cellular, or immunifacient modifications presumed to be responsible for tolerance (see Cochin, 1970). It would be expected, according to any of the physiological theories of tolerance, that the three groups should be equally tolerant to the analgesic effects of the narcotic. That Group M-CAGE, the group that received the drug in a distinctly different environment for the pretest sessions, does not evidence any indication of tolerance to morphine on the test session suggests that reliable cues associated with the drug administration are important in affecting the development of tolerance.

EXPERIMENT 1B

Method

Subsequent to the test session, Group M-CAGE rats continued to be injected with morphine at the same 5 mg/kg dose and pain sensitivity was assessed for three additional sessions (the interval between sessions remaining at 48 hr) so that the course of the development of tolerance over four drug administrations in these animals could be compared with that previously displayed by Group M-HP rats.

Results and Discussion

The mean paw-lick latencies for the four sessions for Group M-CAGE rats (subsequent to the three sessions in which they received the narcotic in their home cages) and the mean latencies previously demonstrated by Group M-HP rats on four sessions are shown in Figure 2. As is clear in Figure 2, the development of tolerance in M-CAGE rats was not at all facilitated by their earlier experiences with morphine in their home

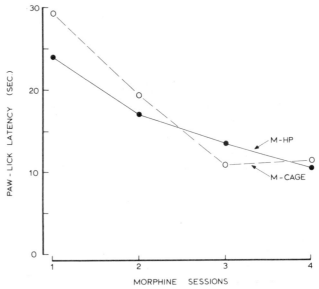

Figure 2. Comparison of the acquisition of morphine analgesia tolerance (decrease in mean paw-lick latency after successive administrations of the drug) for Groups M-HP and M-CAGE of Experiment 1B. (Abbreviations: M = morphine; HP = hot plate.)

cages, i.e., the previous experience with the drug did not lead to any "savings" in the acquisition of tolerance. Tolerance acquisition appears to depend upon a number of pairings of a distinct drug administration/assessment ritual with the direct effects of that drug rather than upon merely the frequency of drug insults. Such pairings, according to a conditioning theory of drug tolerance, are necessary for the organism to associate predrug cues with the physiological effects of the drug and to make the compensatory CR that functionally attenuates the drug UCR.

EXPERIMENT 2A

As can be seen in Figure 1, by comparing the Groups M-HP and S reaction times over the four sessions, morphine-injected rats tend to respond increasingly like saline injected control rats as they have more and more experience with the drug. Indeed, Group M-HP rats rapidly became so tolerant to the analgesic effects of the drug that they responded on the hot plate as rapidly as saline-injected animals. According to a conditioning theory of morphine tolerance, the morphine-tolerant, short-latency response of Group M-HP rats results from a preparatory hyperalgesic CR summating with the narcotic's analgesic UCR, and it should be possible to observe this conditioned increased pain sensitivity in response to those cues that have been predictors of systemic morphine. Experiment 2A was designed to demonstrate this hyperalgesic CR directly.

Method

Following the usual 48-hr intersession interval, the morphine tolerant Group M-HP rats of Experiment 1A received a fifth session which was conducted like the previous four sessions except the substance injected was physiological saline rather than morphine.

The Group M-HP placebo-elicited hot plate response was compared with the placebo-elicited responses of two control groups. One was provided by Group S, which simply received a further placebo session. Thus, on Session 5, Group S rats had the same amount of experience with the injection procedure and assessment situation as Group M-HP rats, but never received morphine. A second control group was included to assess whether any unusual placebo-elicited hot plate sensitivity of Group M-HP could be attributed to residual systemic effects of previously injected morphine or to withdrawal from dependence upon the drug (see Tilson, Rech and Stolman, 1973). This group received four morphine injections prior to the placebo test, of the same dose and at the same time as Group M-HP, but always in the colony room. Thus, this second control group, hereinafter called Group M-CAGE:4 (n = 8), was treated in the same manner as Group M-CAGE of the earlier experiment, but received four, rather than three morphine injections in the colony room. Group M-CAGE:4 received its first experience with the hot plate environment and analgesia-assessment situation when it received a placebo on Session 5.

Results and Discussion

The mean Session 5 paw-lick latencies, after the placebo, for Groups S, M-CAGE:4, and M-HP were, respectively, 10.3 sec, 9.1 sec, and 4.4 sec. The reaction latency was significantly shorter for Group M-HP than for Groups S or M-CAGE:4 (both Us = 2.5, both ps < .002), and these latter two control groups did not differ significantly from each other. Thus, in response to a ritual that had been associated with morphine administration but now not followed by the central effects of the drug, morphine-tolerant Group M-HP rats displayed hyperalgesia. Rats with equivalent experience with the ritual without association with the narcotic (Group S) or with the narcotic without association with the ritual (Group M-CAGE:4) did not evidence such hypersensitivity to pain.

EXPERIMENT 2B

A further experiment was conducted in an attempt to demonstrate in a within-subject rather than between subject design that hyperalgesia follows morphine administration cues in morphine-tolerant rats.

Method

A hot plate response-latency baseline was established for each of the six Group S rats by calculating their mean response latency for a total of seven consecutive sessions in which they received physiological saline prior to pain sensitivity assessment. Longer than baseline response latencies would be evidence of analgesia, and shorter-than-baseline latencies evidence of hyperalgesia. For the four sessions following baseline determination, these rats were injected with morphine (5 mg/kg) rather than saline prior to each hot plate placement. By comparing the rats' paw-lick latencies following each morphine injection with their baseline, the initial analgesic response and the development of tolerance could be evaluated. These now morphine-tolerant rats were left undisturbed in their home cages for 2 wk, when they again received four physiological saline hot plate sessions. With the exception of this 2-wk delay between the last morphine session and the first placebo test session, the intersession interval was 18 hr.

Results and Discussion

As would be expected from earlier work (e.g., Cochin and Kornetsky, 1964), the paw-lick latency did not vary much over the course of the inital baseline sessions (when subjects all received physiological saline prior to analgesia assessment). The overall mean baseline paw-lick latency was 12.9 sec; it was 11.7 sec on the first baseline session and 14.5 sec on the last baseline session, there being no significant trend across baseline sessions.

Figure 3 presents the mean percent change in paw-lick latency from baseline levels following each of the four morphine injections and, two wk later, four physiological saline injections. As can be seen in Figure 3, the analgesic effect of the initial injection

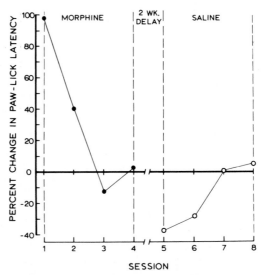

Figure 3. Percent change from baseline paw-lick latency after each of four morphine injections and, 2 wk later, after four physiological saline injections (Experiment 2B).

of morphine is clear; paw-lick latency almost doubled from baseline levels, i.e., increased by 100%. Reaction time decreased following subsequent morphine injections until by the fourth injection of the narcotic these rats were responding on the hot plate with about the same latency as their predrug baseline levels. When tested on the hot plate 2 wk later (after any residual systemic effects of the drug had dissipated; Tilson et al., 1973) after a placebo, these morphine-tolerant animals were clearly hypersensitive to the heat. Their reaction times were almost 40% below their baseline levels, a significantly shorter response latency (Wilcox on matched-pairs signed-rank test, $T = 1.0$, $p < .025$).

As is also clear in Figure 3, as these subjects were successively presented with the placebo test sessions the magnitude of the hyperalgesic response tended to decrease, i.e., their response latency returned to baseline levels. It appears that as the drug administration procedure is successively presented *without* the systemic effects of the drug, the hyperalgesic response in morphine tolerant rats is subject to extinction, suggesting that it is indeed a CR. Inasmuch as it is proposed that it is this hyperalgesic CR that is responsible for observed analgesia tolerance, extinction should be an effective procedure for eliminating tolerance.

EXPERIMENT 3

If in the morphine-tolerant animal those environmental procedures associated with the central effects of the drug elicit a compensatory CR, presenting these environmental procedures unaccompanied by the central effects of the narcotic should serve to extinguish these learned responses and morphine tolerance. In other words, placebo test sessions should constitute an effective procedure for attenuating established tolerance. This prediction of a conditioning theory of tolerance was assessed in this experiment.

Method

Two groups, each containing six experimentally naive rats of the same sex, strain, and age as those used in the previous experiments, were each given a total of six morphine analgesia assessment sessions, using the same procedures as described earlier. The interval between sessions was 24-hr with the exception of the protracted interval between Sessions 3 and 4, which was 9 days. The two groups differed only with respect to their treatment between these third and fourth sessions. One group was simply left undisturbed in its home cage (Group M-REST-M). The second group received daily placebo test sessions, i.e., they were treated in the same manner as on morphine sessions except the substance injected was physiological saline rather than morphine (Group M-P-M).

Results and Discussion

The mean paw-lick latencies of both groups on each occasion that they received morphine are shown in Figure 4. Both groups evidenced tolerance to the analgesic effects of morphine over the course of the three initial administrations of the drug. Group M-REST-M continued to evidence morphine-tolerant, short-latency responses when again tested with the narcotic after the delay interval, as would be expected from previous work demonstrating that morphine tolerance dissipates little simply with the passage of time (Cochin and Kornetsky, 1964). However, when tested with morphine after the same delay interval, Group M-P-M evidenced a nontolerant, long-latency response. There was no overlap in the Session 4 paw-lick latencies of Groups M-REST-M and M-P-M ($U = 0$, $p = .001$). As can be seen in Figure 4, Group M-P-M rats had to be "retolerated" to morphine, despite the fact that they had suffered the systemic effects of the narcotic equally as often as Group M-REST-M rats.

The finding that mere repeated presentations of a drug administration procedure unaccompanied by the central effects of the drug effectively obliterated morphine-analgesia tolerance is a unique prediction of a conditioning theory of tolerance, and is not explicable by theories of tolerance that do not emphasize the role of drug-associated environmental cues in the development of tolerance.

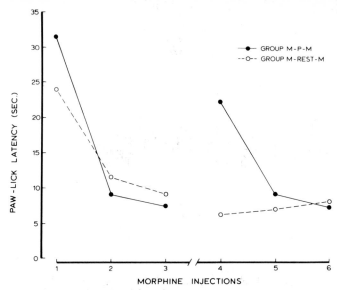

Figure 4. Mean paw-lick latencies after each of six daily morphine injections for groups receiving either nine placebo sessions (Group M-P-M) or a 9-day rest interval (Group M-REST-M) interpolated between morphine Sessions 3 and 4 (Experiment 3).

GENERAL DISCUSSION

It has been previously suggested that learning can influence responsivity to drugs (see Thompson and Pickins, 1971) and that ". . . a drug-test interaction occurs with morphine and can play a role in the development of tolerance to the analgesic effect of this drug" (Adams *et al.,* 1969, p. 251). The present experiments were designed to assess a specific Pavlovian conditioning interpretation of the phenomenon of morphine tolerance. Based on earlier reports that the CR to a variety of pharmacological agents is compensatory in nature, it seems reasonable that the direct, unconditioned analgesic effect of morphine is normally modulated by a morphine-anticipatory hyperalgesic CR, the net result being reflected by the development of morphine tolerance. This conditioning analysis of morphine tolerance is supported by several findings: (a) It is necessary to have a consistent set of environmental cues reliably predicting the systemic effects of morphine if rapid tolerance is to be observed (Adams *et al.,* 1969; Kayan *et al.,* 1969; Experiment 1A of the present report); (b) experience with morphine in one environment does not facilitate the acquisition of morphine tolerance in another environment (Experiment 1B); (c) the compensatory hyperalgesic CR may be directly observed in morphine-tolerant animals when they are confronted by the drug administration ritual not followed by the central effects of the drug (Experiments 2A and 2B), this hyperalgesic CR being subject to experimental extinction (Experiment 2B); and (d) mere presentation of those environmental cues previously associated with the narcotic, when presented in conjunction with a placebo, is an effective procedure for extinguishing established morphine tolerance (Experiment 3). The conclusions concerning the mechanism of morphine tolerance in the rat are, of course, limited to the relatively small dose of the drug (5 mg/kg) and to the analgesia-evaluation situation used in these experiments (although the hot plate procedure is perhaps the most commonly used of the simple assessment techniques for pharmacologically induced analgesia; see Evans, 1964).

The present findings concerning the importance of the interaction between conditioned and unconditioned responses in contributing to the observed effect of a drug parallel Pavlov's (1910) discussion of the significance of his original "psychic secretion" observations, i.e., that digestive responses in anticipation of feeding make a significant contribution to normally observed patterns of digestive functioning. Subsequent research has demonstrated the importance of conditional responses in the normal and pathological functioning of a variety of physiological systems in many species including humans (e.g., Adam, 1967; Bykov, 1959). This work on the interaction of learning and physiological processes, conducted mostly by Eastern European and Soviet physiologists, is the foundation of a "synthetic physiology", ". . . a science of the course of vital processes in an integral organism *during its various natural relations with the surrounding medium*" (Bykov, 1960, p. 25; emphasis added). It would appear that inasmuch as drug administration is almost invariably predicted by a set of cues (the administration procedure, or ritual), the response of an "integral organism" to a drug can be best understood as a combination of the direct reflexive effects of the drug as it acts on central receptor sites and the effects conditioned to the drug administration procedure.

REFERENCES

Adám, G. *Interoception and behaviour*. Budapest: Publishing House of the Hungarian Academy of Sciences, 1967.

Adams, W. H., Yeh, S. Y., Woods, L. A. & Mitchell, C. L. Drug-test interaction as a factor in the development of tolerance to the analgesic effect of morphine. *Journal of Pharmacology and Experimental Therapeutics,* 1969, *168*, 251-257.

Bykov, K. M. *The cerebral cortex and the internal organs*. Moscow: Foreign Languages Publishing House, 1959.

Bykov, K. M. (Ed.), *Text-book of physiology*. Moscow: Foreign Languages Publishing House, 1960.

Cochin, J. Possible mechanisms in development of tolerance. *Federation Proceedings,* 1970, *29*, 19-27.

Cochin, J., & Kornetsky, C. Development and loss of tolerance to morphine in the rat after single and multiple injections. *Journal of Pharmacology and Experimental Therapeutics,* 1964, *145*, 1-10.

Cochin, J., & Kornetsky, C. Factors in blood of morphine-tolerant animals that attenuate or enhance effects of morphine in nontolerant animals. *Proceedings of the Association for Research in Nervous and Mental Disease,* 1968, *46*, 268-279.

Collier, H. O. J. A general theory of the genesis of drug dependence by induction of receptors. *Nature,* 1965, *205*, 181-182.

Deutsch, R. Conditioned hypoglycemia: A mechanism for saccharin-induced sensitivity to insulin in the rat. *Journal of Comparative and Physiological Psychology,* 1974, *86*, 350-358.

Eddy, N. B., & Leimbach, D. Synthetic analgesics: II. dithienylbutenyl-and dithienylbutylamines. *Journal of Pharmacology and Experimental Therapeutics,* 1953, *107*, 385-393.

Evans, W. O. A critical review of some new methods in animal analgesiometry. *Journal of Clinical Pharmacology and New Drugs,* 1964, *4*, 179-187.

Gantt, W. H. Pharmacological agents in study of higher nervous activity. *Diseases of the Nervous System,* 1957, *18*, 339-341.

Hull, C. L. Learning: II. The factor of the conditioned reflex. In C. Murchinson, (Ed.), *A handbook of general experimental psychology*. Worcester, Mass.: Clark University Press, 1934.

Jóhannesson, T., & Woods, L. A. Analgesic action and brain and plasma levels of morphine and codeine in morphine tolerant, codeine tolerant and non-tolerant rats. *Acta Pharmacologica et Toxicologica,* 1964, *21*, 381-396.

Kayan, S., Woods, L. A. & Mitchell, C. L. Experience as a factor in the development of tolerance to the analgesic effect of morphine. *European Journal of Pharmacology,* 1969, *6*, 333-339.

Lang, W. J., Brown, M. L., Gershon, S., & Korol, B. Classical and physiologic adaptive conditioned responses to anticholinergic drugs in conscious dogs. *International Journal of Neuro-pharmacology,* 1966, *5*, 311-315.

Lichko, A. E. Conditioned reflex hypoglycaemia in man. *Pavlov Journal of Higher Nervous Activity,* 1959, *9*, 731-737.

Loucks, R. B. Humoral conditioning in mammals. *Journal of Psychology,* 1937, *4*, 295-307.

Mityushov, M. I. Uslovnorleflektornaya inkret siya insulina (The conditional-reflex incretion of insulin). *Zhurnal Vysshei Nervnoi Deiatel (Journal of Higher Nervous Activity)*, 1954, *4*, 206-212. (Read in translation prepared by L. J. Shein, Department of Russian, McMaster Univ.)

Mulé, S. J., & Woods, L. A. Distribution of N-C [14]-methyl labeled morphine: I. In central nervous system of nontolerant and tolerant dogs. *Journal of Pharmacology and Experimental Therapeutics,* 1969, *168,* 251-257.

Pavlov, I. P. *The work of the digestive glands* (W. H. Thompson, trans.). Charles Griffin and Company, London, 1910.

Pavlov, I. P. *Conditioned reflexes* (G. V. Anrep, trans.). London: Oxford University Press, 1927.

Russek, M., & Pina, S. Conditioning of adrenalin anorexia. *Nature,* 1962, *193,* 1296-1297.

Schmidt, C. F., & Livingston, A. E. The relation of dosage to the development of tolerance to morphine in dogs. *Journal of Pharmacology and Experimental Therapeutics,* 1933, *47,* 443-471.

Siegel, S. Conditioning of insulin-induced glycemia. *Journal of Comparative and Physiological Psychology,* 1972, *78,* 233-241.

Siegel, S. Conditioning insulin effects. *Journal of Comparative and Physiological Psychology,* 1975, *89,* 189-199.

Siegel, S., & Nettleton, N. Conditioning of insulin-induced hyperphagia. *Journal of Comparative and Physiological Psychology,* 1970, *72,* 390-393.

Subkov, A. A., & Zilov, G. N. The role of conditioned reflex adaptation in the origin of hyperergic reactions. *Bulletin de Biologie et de Médecine Expérimentale,* 1937, *4,* 294-296.

Thompson, T., & Pickens, R. (Eds.). *Stimulus properties of drugs.* New York: Appleton-Century-Crofts, 1971.

Tilson, H. A., Rech, R. H., & Stolman, S. Hyperalgesia during withdrawal as a means of measuring the degree of dependence in morphine dependent rats. *Psychopharmacologia,* 1973, *28,* 287-300.

Wikler, A. Recent progress in research on the neurophysiologic basis of morphine addiction. *American Journal of Psychiatry,* 1948, *105,* 329-338.

Section VI

ANIMAL DISORDERS OF "PERSONALITY"

20. "Hypersexuality" in Male Cats without Brain Damage

Science, 1961, *134*, 553-4. Copyright 1961 by the American Association for the Advancement of Science. Reprinted by permission.

Abstract. During 5 years of observation in a cat colony where mating tests are routinely conducted, the spontaneous occurrence of distortions of sexual activity in male cats has been recorded. Many of the behavioral patterns encountered have previously been described only in brain-damaged animals when they have been used as an index of "hypersexuality." Identical behavior occurs in normal males as a simple training effect.

The possible role of the temporal lobe in the normal regulation of sexual activity has remained a question of considerable interest since Kluver and Bucy described striking alterations in the sexual behavior of mature rhesus monkeys in the weeks after bilateral temporal lobectomy.

There is no doubt whatever that sexual manifestations in primates of both sexes increase, both in range and frequency, after such surgical interventions (*1, 2*). Observations of a similar type have been extended, on rather less secure grounds, to several infraprimate species, and attention has been given in particular to the sexual activity shown by male cats toward (i) anoestrous, nonreceptive female cats, (ii) other male cats, (iii) kittens, (iv) inanimate objects such as a child's woolly toy, and (v) alien species such as dogs, chickens, and rabbits (*2.3*). Aberrant behavior of this kind has been widely used as a criterion of abnormal hypersexuality. The observation of the occurrence of such patterns of behavior after destruction of, or lesions in, the amygdala and pyriform cortex has implicated these structures, and the temporal lobe generally, in the regulation of the sexual behavior of the male cat (*4*).

Some of the reports describing the distortions of sexual activity, which result either from altering the hormone balance or from physical interference with the brain, indicate a lack of familiarity with the range of behavior normally shown by the cat and with the shifts from the normal which can be produced by simple manipulation of the environmental situation. I have conducted several thousand mating tests with the cat during the past 5 years and, therefore, my experience may be of interest to others in this field (*5*).

If a mature male cat is trained to carry out mating tests with receptive females and is "in territory" within its home cage or test pen and is then presented with another mature male, the latter will invariably be mounted. The mounted male in most instances passively tolerates the neck grip and copulatory thrusts of the mounting male. The sequence of mounting does not depend upon the relative sizes of the animals, but upon the influence of territory; the animal in familiar surroundings in its home cage is dominant. If on a subsequent occasion, the mounted male is established in its own territory (where it has previously mated with receptive females), it will then mount the male by which it had previously been mounted. "Tandem" and multiple mounting occur readily in the laboratory when trained animals are used, and the sequence can be changed indiscriminately by changing the order in which animals are presented. Homosexual behavior in the test situation (in the sense that the sexual object is another male), as well as mounting activity between males housed in pairs, is thus a common observation (6). In contrast to the foregoing, if two stud males, both of which have frequently mated in a test room and established territory rights there, are liberated in it simultaneously, serious fighting may ensue. It can be seen, then, that totally different behavioral patterns (passive acceptance of mounting or active fighting) can be evoked merely by a rearrangement of the test situation. Inexperienced males can be trained to show intense sexual interest in inanimate objects by alternately presenting a receptive female and some object such as a toy teddy-bear. A male so trained will then mount, secure a neck bite, and attempt copulation with any suitable soft object, including the sleeve and arm of the attendant's coat. Masturbatory activity of various kinds is readily observed in young, isolated males, as well as in males housed in pairs, but only when the animals are well adapted to, and familiar with, the environment and not when newly arrived from a dealer.

Of even more interest than the sexual deviations which result from training and conditioning procedures within the laboratory is the occurrence of such phenomena spontaneously in domestic animals. Several reports of sexual activity with inanimate objects have reached me from owners of pet cats. One report, supported by a motion-picture film taken in a private home, describes a mature, intact male (Fig. 1). Although

Fig. 1. Mounting activity and ejaculation shown by a normal male cat with a child's toy rabbit (frame from a motion-picture film taken in a private home).

allowed complete freedom and the sire of many litters in the neighborhood, this cat, if left undisturbed, regularly mounted, and attempted copulation with, a child's toy rabbit from which sperm could be recovered. This type of masturbatory activity with an object which appears to stand for the true sexual object may be analogous to fetishism in the human. Careful histological examination of the temporal lobes of three such animals has failed to reveal the slightest evidence of either Ammon's horn sclerosis or any more obvious pathology. Although aberrant behavior is infrequently reported because of the distaste it arouses in animal owners who, as a consequence, have their pets castrated, it is probably more common than we are accustomed to believe (7). In all this the male cat does not appear to differ from other species of domesticated animals which can be trained to mate with artificial vaginae for sperm collection.

Every variety of abnormal behavior which has been used as a criterion of hypersexuality in male cats has been encountered, with one exception, during the past 5 years of observation of animals without brain damage. The exception is mounting activity toward alien species which I have not observed. Upon this I cannot comment except to observe that such activity may be less specifically related to the sex drive than the visual agnosia which forms part of the temporal lobe syndrome. The patterns of spontaneously occurring abnormal behavior include (i) the tenacious clinging to female partners by males during copulation when attempts at separation are made—so that both animals can be suspended in mid-air, (ii) indiscriminate mounting by males of other males, (iii) tandem and multiple mounting behavior, (iv) neck grips, mounting, and attempts at copulation with kittens of under 900 grams, and (v) masturbatory activity, mounting, and ejaculation upon inanimate objects. This latter phenomenon occurs spontaneously in freely running animals as well as in those subjected to training procedures within the laboratory. Although such phenomena as multiple mounting behavior seem at first to be very bizarre, the expression of identical patterns of behavior in animals which have not been subjected to operative interference suggests the need for caution in the interpretation of results. The observations that are presented here show clearly that many of the manifestations of so-called "hypersexuality" can either occur spontaneously or be produced as a conditioning effect by simple manipulation of the environmental situation.

It would be wrong to infer from the foregoing that the rhinencephalon is not of great importance in the regulation of sexual behavior in the cat and other species; the evidence in the rhesus monkey is overwhelmingly against this. But the spontaneous occurrence of such behavior in male cats without brain damage implies a need for quantitative studies combined with control procedures aimed at excluding the possible effects of training. Only such measurements will enable the precise role of the temporal lobe in the sexual activity of this species to be evaluated (8).

REFERENCES AND NOTES

1. H. Kluver and P. C. Bucy, *Am. J. Physiol.* **119**, 352 (1937): *J. Psychol.* **5**, 33 (1938): *A.M.A. Arch. Neurol. Psychiat.* **42**, 979 (1939).
2. J. H. Masserman *et al., Am. J. Psychiat.* **115**, 14 (1958).
3. L. Schreiner and A. Kling, *J. Neurophysiol.* **16**, 643 (1953): *A.M.A. Arch. Neurol. Psychiat.* **72**, 180 (1954).
4. _____, *Am. J. Physiol.* **185**, 486 (1956): C. D. Clemente, *Clin. Research* 7, (1959): J. D. Green, C. D. Clemente, J. de Groot, *J. Comp. Neurol.* **108**, 505 (1957).
5. R. P. Michael, *Behaviour,* in press.
6. R. E. Whalen, personal communication.
7. L. R. Aronson, *J. Comp. and Physiol. Psychol.* **42**, 226 (1949).
8. Investigation carried out during tenure of M.R.C. fellowship in clinical research.

21. The Self-mutilation of a Male *Macacus rhesus* Monkey[1]

O. L. TINKELPAUGH

Journal of Mammalogy, 1928, *9*, 293-300. Reprinted by permission.

This account deals with the self-mutilation of a male monkey after he had formed what was evidently a monogamous attachment for a female of different species and then had another female of his species introduced into the situation. I attempt no interpretation of the monkey's behavior, but try to present sufficient details so that the reader can formulate his own conclusions.

The monkey concerned is a male *Macacus rhesus* named Cupid, which the writer procured from an animal dealer in San Francisco, on January 5, 1924. He was taken to the Psychology Laboratory of the University of California, at Berkeley, where he was kept until the fall of 1927. At that time he and three other monkeys were brought to the Primate Laboratory of the Institute of Psychology, at Yale University.

When Cupid was first secured he was less than half-grown and was awkward and poorly coordinated. His testes were small and but partially descended. These facts suggest that he was between two and three years old at that time. He showed no signs of previous taming. When he arrived he was placed in a room with a female *Macacus cynomologus,* named Psyche. She was close to four years old, had already been kept at the laboratory for over fifteen months and was more gentle, affectionate, and obedient than is typical of monkeys. Her first menstruation had occurred about a year before the male was secured, and though not fully grown she was considered mature. When the two monkeys were first brought together, Cupid, though of a large species, was both smaller in stature and lighter in weight than Psyche.

When the male was first introduced into the room with the female she rushed to him, put her arms about him and her lips to his. Then she held him close to her, ''cuddling'' him and at the same time smacked her lips and made low guttural grunts. In the beginning she dominated over him, dragging him here and there as she wished, and biting him lightly about the head and neck when he resisted.

The monkeys spent most of the first afternoon before an electric heater bulb which was attached to their cage to provide heat and light. Psyche devoted much time to picking through Cupid's fur, during which process she came upon his penis. She examined it visually and manually, and then leaned over with her shoulders away from him and lowered, and with her tail elevated so that her genitals were exposed before him. During this procedure she kept hold of his fur with one hand and attempted to draw him toward her. Cupid resisted her tugging and sat staring at the light. Psyche

[1]Acknowledgment is made to the Committee for Research in Problems of Sex, National Research Council, for cooperative support of the work to which the observations of this report are incidental.

leaned back to him and bit his face and ear lightly. She then assumed the same position a second and later a third time. Cupid made no response. Psyche then returned to him, renewed her examination of his scrotum and penis, and from this turned to picking through his fur again. During the succeeding two days similar behavior was observed, and on each occasion Cupid seemed entirely unaffected by Psyche's attentions.

Two weeks after Cupid arrived he and Psyche were removed to a cage outside the laboratory building. The inclosure was approximately eight feet square and seven feet high and so situated that its occupants were concealed from passers-by by bushes. A few days later he was several times seen to mount awkwardly upon Psyche's shanks, clasp her sides with his hands and make several pelvic thrusts. This was with erection but without penetration. On these occasions Psyche took the characteristic copulatory position with her head down and hips erect. Once while this behavior was in progress, she waited for a few seconds and then bent her head back nearly under her own legs so that her weight rested on her shoulders, and in this position pulled Cupid toward her with one hand while with the other hand she drew his penis into contact with her genitals. Cupid persisted for a few seconds longer and then dismounted. He then raised Psyche's tail with one hand and examined her genitals with the other. Almost identical behavior was observed five days later.

During the next twelve months Cupid showed marked physical development. His skeletal length increased greatly and he filled out. During the latter part of the year his milk teeth loosened and were replaced by permanent ones. His testes increased in size, but still had not reached the proportions they were to attain eventually. His attempts at copulation with Psyche became more frequent and the movements involved in them showed much better coordination. Throughout this period, however, his attempts did not result in penetration. Though Psyche also grew considerably during this period, she was now smaller than the male. In spite of this disparity in size Cupid seemed to be quite dependent upon her and would rush to her or attempt to hide behind her when frightened by a strange object or sound. In contrast to Psyche's early aggressiveness toward the male, she now often avoided his unsuccessful and frequently desultory attempts to copulate.

While Cupid was still in this immature stage, he formed a habit which it is well to mention here because of its later significance. As is common with monkeys he quite obviously liked to "show off" before onlookers. I taught him to somersault by putting him through the act, that is, by forcing his head down and then pushing his body forward over it. He took his training in good part, seeming to enjoy the process, and after but few trials would perform at command. During this training process, his face was brought down in close proximity to his hind feet. At this time he first seemed to discover these members, and frequently thereafter he could be seen sitting in the cage playing with his feet. From this behavior he developed the playful, or perhaps exhibitionistic, habit of seizing one of his feet or his tail in his mouth and then whirling rapidly around or somersaulting.

Early in 1925 Cupid was first observed to secure intromission. At times he would merely mount the female, make two or three pelvic thrusts and then dismount. Occasionally the copulatory act would last as long as two minutes, ending with the quick rhythmic strokes that accompany ejaculation. Following this development the frequency of sexual congress between the two monkeys seemed to increase. This was apparently due both to Psyche's more frequent acceptance of his advances and to a stronger or more continuous drive in him. From this time on, the mating relations between the pair of monkeys seemed to be mature and entirely normal.

In July, 1926, Topsy and Eva, young females of the same species as Cupid, were secured and taken to the laboratory. When Cupid was admitted to the room in which they were placed, his hair bristled, his tail stiffened and he began to champ his teeth and pull at his leash. His attitude was thoroughly antagonistic, and it seemed best for the sake of future work with the new monkeys temporarily to defer a more intimate meeting. For this reason, Cupid was led quietly from the room and replaced in the outdoor cage with Psyche. A few days later another outdoor cage was prepared about twenty feet from the one occupied by Cupid and Psyche, and the two young females were placed in it. From the time of their first appearance Cupid showed marked antagonism toward them by lunging against the side of his cage with his hair bristling and his teeth showing.

In October, 1926, Psyche was taken from Cupid's cage and Topsy, who a week previously had menstruated for the first time, was led in. Cupid eyed her from a far corner of his cage. Topsy strolled nervously about the cage, never looking directly at Cupid, but frequently stopping with her head away from him, and with her tail up so that her genitals were exposed to him. After about a minute of this behavior, Cupid leaped upon her, seized her by the small of the back and hurled her across the cage. In an instant he was upon her again, and it was with difficulty that she was rescued. Cupid behaved similarly when the other young female, Eva, was brought into the cage. She appeared nervous and frightened, keeping to the far side of the cage and rushing to a top corner of it whenever he showed signs of moving in her direction. Finally he charged after her, and catching her tail in his mouth, bit off about two inches of that member. Eva was immediately removed from the cage and Psyche was returned to it. Cupid greeted her with marked vocalization, copulated with her, and then spent half an hour picking through her fur.

During the following four months, Topsy was placed in Cupid's cage on three occasions. Before each of these, Psyche was removed to the cage with the young females, leaving Cupid alone for from two to three weeks, after which Topsy was placed in his cage. Each time he attacked her, necessitating her early removal.

Cupid's persistent antagonism toward the young females, even when he had been sexually starved for from two to three weeks, suggested that he had built up what was virtually a monogamous attachment for Psyche. With that in mind, in May, 1927, I set about trying to "condition" Cupid to Topsy. Each day she was placed in a small antechamber to his cage, and at the same time Cupid was fed some special delicacy. Topsy was fearful at first but soon became adapted to the new situation. She would play about in the ante-chamber, paying no direct attention to Cupid, although it was evident that her behavior was largely intended for his benefit. Frequently she would take a position such that her genitals were exposed to his view, and there she would stand for several seconds at a time looking back over her own shoulder into space beyond him. He would sit on the opposite side of the separating screen for as much as an hour at a time watching her every movement. Each of them appeared to avoid looking into the face of the other, but whenever by chance their eyes did meet, there was marked emotional response on the part of both. Cupid would rush at the screen, his fur on end and his teeth gnashing, while Topsy would fly in fear to a top corner of her compartment. After ten days of this general procedure, a muzzle was secured for Cupid. With him thus restrained, the two of them were led in company about the campus for an hour or so daily. Following each of these outings they were left together in Cupid's cage for a few minutes. Apparently feeling the restraint of the muzzle, he made no advances either friendly or otherwise, but instead would sit perched in one corner where he would watch her sullenly. On the fourth of the daily outings on the campus, Topsy was running along in front of Cupid when he reached out and touched her. She scampered away in apparent fear, and he made no effort to catch her. A little later he again reached out and this time seized the fur on her side. This time Topsy crouched in the sex position. He mounted her and made ineffectual attempts to copulate. The two were then returned to the cage, his muzzle was removed, and they were left together. Cupid immediately strutted over to Topsy, copulated with her, and then picked through her fur. Beginning at this time the two were friendly and their sex behavior appeared normal.

Cupid and Topsy had been together for five days when the latter was removed to the cage with Eva, and Psyche was returned to the cage with the male. Cupid's behavior with Psyche seemed normal except for the fact that he copulated less often with her than he had in the past, and that much of his attention was directed toward Topsy in the other cage.

Topsy was returned to Cupid's cage after two weeks, and Psyche was taken out again. Cupid mounted Topsy and was about to copulate with her, when he jumped away from her and began biting his hind feet much as he had formerly done in play. This behavior was noted several times during the first three days the two monkeys were reunited. On none of these occasions was Cupid seen to complete the sex act. On the fourth day he was discovered with his hind feet rather badly lacerated. To facilitate examination and medical attention, he was led from his cage by the doorway leading to the area between it and the nearby cage now containing Psyche and Eva. He looked back at the cage where Topsy still remained and then toward the cage containing the other two females. Psyche, who had seemed to be much upset by Topsy's presence in Cupid's cage, was now on the side of her cage shrieking threateningly across at the other female. Suddenly, and with no previous signs of anger or particular emotion, Cupid lurched to the end of his chain and began to bite himself. In a few seconds he tore huge jagged rents in his already lacerated legs. Then, as though in intense pain, he jumped into the writer's arms. He jumped down again and this time tore a three inch gash in his hip, ripped his scrotum open, lacerating and exposing one testicle, and mutilated the end of his tail. In all there were twenty newly made lacerations on his body, and of that number only one was in close proximity to his genitals.

As soon as Cupid could be quieted he was muzzled, then his wounds were treated and his four canine teeth were extracted. Psyche was returned to the cage with him to nurse his wounds—a task she performed remarkably well—and also because it was believed her presence would have a quieting effect upon him. As would be expected, Cupid was weak and sick from loss of blood and from the numerous lacerations. He rapidly recovered, however, and after about three weeks seemed to resume fairly normal sex relations with Psyche. During a period of about four months following the time of his self-mutilation, he frequently seemed to be in a state comparable to the depression of some psychoses. Through many hours of a day he would sit quietly in a corner of his cage or in the nest box, with his head drooped, and only occasionally would he observe the happenings about him through the corner of his eye. During these periods he was highly irritable if approached and he absolutely refused to obey commands. At other times he showed marked hyper-excitability, and would rush wildly about his cage shaking the sides of it and threatening any person or monkey who came in his path.

During Cupid's convalescence there appeared evidence that I was in some manner involved in his abnormal behavior. When greatly excited he tended to seize and bite his still irritated legs or scrotum. The same behavior was called out whenever I appeared and directed my gaze toward him or spoke to him. If I merely passed the cage, or even if I stopped before it without looking at or speaking to him, the biting did not occur. Nor was the presence or speech of other people adequate stimulus for the response. This was verified by numerous trials and always with the results indicated. The same behavior continued throughout the summer and reappeared when Cupid, along with the three females, arrived in New Haven, after having been separated from me for a period of eight weeks.

Immediately prior to and during this eight-week period Cupid was kept caged with Topsy and, according to the reports of his caretakers, his relations with her were entirely amicable during that time. When the group of monkeys arrived in New Haven, Cupid was immediately admitted to the cage with Psyche, whom he accepted and copulated with at once. His tendency to self-mutilation whenever I looked at or spoke to him still persisted. Judging that time alone would not be sufficient to break up this tendency, I first resorted to verbal and physical threats and then finally gave him a severe whipping. There followed a few occasions when a verbal command served to stop the behavior in its incipiency. Then came a period during which my presence would stimulate him to raise an ankle or wrist to his mouth as though to bite it, but instead of carrying the act farther, he would usually turn to picking through the fur on the same member.

As this report is written, some fourteen months after Cupid's first attack upon himself, he is experiencing what seems to be normal sex relations with Psyche and Eva, the other female, Topsy, having been sacrificed after lead poisoning. Cupid's contact with Eva was gained when he broke into a large cage with her and one of the other females during the night. For some two or three weeks he remained antagonistic toward her, but with her increased strength and agility she was able to successfully avoid him. Gradually the barrier was broken down and he accepted her both socially and sexually. Cupid is now in excellent physical condition. He is not as tractable as he was when younger, and he shows considerable irritability, most of which is directed towards four chimpanzees which occupy an adjoining cage. When, in my absence, he becomes highly excited, he will seize one of his hind feet or the sheath of his penis in his teeth, but he bites them only lightly, and during the past four or five months has inflicted no noticeable injury on himself. The biting of the sheath is apparently not to be confused with masturbation, for neither now nor at any other time has he been observed to masturbate in any manner.

22. Behavioral Abnormalities in Young Adult Pigs Caused by Malnutrition in Early Life[1]

R. H. BARNES, A. U. MOORE and W. G. POND

Journal of Nutrition, 1970, *100*, 149-55. Copyright 1970 by The American Institute of Nutrition. Reprinted by permission.

ABSTRACT   Baby pigs were malnourished for a period of 8 weeks by restricting protein or caloric intake with the objective of studying behavioral changes that remained long after nutritional rehabilitation had been achieved. An apparatus was designed for the measurement of changes in the level of excitement or emotionality under conditions of stress, as well as changes in learning performance in a conditioned avoidance situation. The most striking behavioral change due to early malnutrition was the heightened excitement of the pigs when exposed to aversive stimuli, although there was also an indication of decreased learning ability. Since learning performance can be affected by behavioral factors that influence the level of reinforcement (reward or punishment), impaired learning may be due either to decreased intelligence (capacity) or to elevated excitement and consequent over-reaction to reinforcement. The nutritional condition which caused the greatest change in behavioral development resulted from feeding a diet very low in protein from the third through the eleventh week of life. Behavioral abnormalities were also noted, although in lesser degree, if the low protein diet was initiated later, i.e., seventh to fifteenth week of life or if a diet of normal composition was fed in restricted quantity so as to prevent growth during an 8-week period starting either at birth or at 3 weeks of age.

Previous publications from our laboratories have described behavioral abnormalities observed in rats and pigs several months after nutritional rehabilitation from malnutrition imposed during the immediate postnatal period (1-6). In both rats and pigs protein-calorie malnutrition during early life resulted in poorer learning performance in several types of test procedures. Moreover, it was also noted that these animals had elevated excitatory responses to stressful situations such as anticipated electric shock (2), sudden immersion in cold water (1), or the availability of food for a short period of time when the animal was extremely hungry (4). Furthermore, all of these behavioral differences were found in animals after long periods of complete nutritional rehabilitation. In order to understand and interpret the decreased learning performance of previously malnourished animals it will be necessary to evaluate behavioral characteristics such

Received for publication July 18, 1969.

[1] Supported in part by funds provided through the State University of New York and by Public Health Service Research Grant No. HD-02581 from the National Institute of Child Health and Human Development.

as motivation, drive, frustration, fright and other factors which will affect learning performance. Hopefully, this may lead to the ultimate assessment of the contribution, if any, of impaired capacity as a factor influencing the animal's poor learning performance.

Other features of the malnutrition-behavior interrelationship that can be evaluated in experimental animals are the influence of the age at which protein-calorie malnutrition is imposed and the relative effects of protein deficiency as compared with calorie deficiency. In the present communication these factors are examined utilizing the pig as the experimental animal.

MATERIALS AND METHODS

Male Yorkshire piglets at 3 weeks of age (with the exception of one group which will be described later) were weaned from their dams and divided into five groups according to the schedule: four experimental groups of 4 pigs each and a control group of 6 pigs. Insofar as possible, litter-mates were distributed evenly within the groups. At

Table 1. Diet Composition

	Control 18% casein diet	Low protein 3% casein diet
	g	g
Major components		
Casein[1]	18.0	3.0
Glucose monohydrate[2]	47.6	62.6
Dextrin[3]	25.0	25.0
Corn oil[4]	3.0	3.0
Mineral mixture	5.4	5.4
Vitamin mixture	1.0	1.0
Total	100.0	100.0

Minor components

Vitamin mixture			Mineral mixture		
Vitamin A	572	IU	$CaHPO_4 \cdot 2H_2O$	1.54 g	
Vitamin D	66	IU	$CaCO_3$	1.23 g	
Thiamin	4	mg	KH_2PO_4	1.72 g	
Riboflavin	0.99	mg	NaCl	0.61 g	
Niacin	6.6	mg	$CuSO_4 \cdot 5H_2O$	57	mg
Ca pantothenate	4.0	mg	$FeSO_4 \cdot 7H_2O$	66	mg
Choline dihydrogen citrate	396	mg	$MnSO_4 \cdot H_2O$	18.5	mg
Vitamin B_{12}	6.6	μg	$ZnCO_3$	66	mg
Vitamin E	10	IU	MgO	82	mg
Inositol	22	mg	KI	0.04 mg	
Folic acid	0.22	mg	$CoCl_2 \cdot 6H_2O$	1.1	mg
Menadione	0.44	mg	Na_2SeO_3	0.05 mg	
Pyridoxine	0.33	mg			
Biotin	0.033	mg			
Glucose to make	1.0	g			

[1] Crude, 30-mesh, National Casein Company, Riverton, N.J.
[2] Cerelose, Corn Products Company, Argo, Ill.
[3] Nutritional Biochemicals Company, Cleveland, Ohio.
[4] Mazola, Corn Products Company, Argo, Ill.

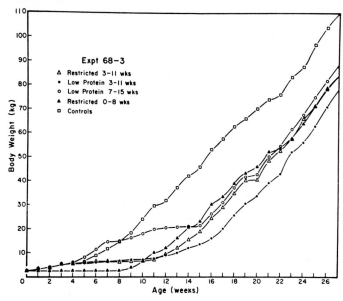

Fig. 1. Growth curves illustrating depletion and rehabilitation for the five dietary treatments.

an early age the experimental groups were subjected to protein or calorie deprivation. Protein deprivation (groups labeled low protein) was achieved by feeding a diet containing approximately 2.5% protein (3% casein). Calorie deprivation (groups labeled restricted) was achieved by restricting the quantity of the control diet in such a manner that the body weight of the piglets remained at the level established at the time of initiating the restricted dietary intake. The one exception to weaning at 3 weeks of age mentioned above was in group 4 (see below). This group was made up of piglets taken from sows at 3 days of age. They were kept in wire screen-bottom chick brooder cages for 3 weeks and were fed 40 ml homogenized, vitamin D-fortified cow's milk four times daily. This amount of food was found to be sufficient to maintain body weight constant and not permit an appreciable gain. At 3 weeks of age these piglets were transferred to pens in the experimental barn and the purified control diet was fed in such an amount as to prevent an appreciable gain in weight over an additional 5 weeks. Dietary deprivations were for 8-week periods according to the schedule: group 1, restricted from 3 to 11 weeks of age; group 2, low protein from 3 to 11 weeks of age; group 3, low protein from 7 to 15 weeks of age; group 4, restricted from 3 days to 8 weeks of age; and group 5 was fed the control diet *ad libitum* from 3 to 11 weeks of age. The composition of the control and low protein diets is given in table 1. Following completion of the experimental periods all pigs were fed a practical pig ration *ad libitum*. This was a corn-soybean meal ration with minerals and vitamins added to meet NRC recommendations. Growth curves presented in Fig. 1 further illustrate the experimental design.

RESULTS

During the depletion period the pigs which were either protein or calorie deprived developed a gaunt, unthrifty appearance. The protein-depleted animals consumed very little food while the calorie-depleted pigs retained their appetite. In fact, it became necessary to remove bedding from the concrete pen floors because the restricted animals ate the wood shavings and one animal in group 4 (restricted 0-8 weeks) died with a large intestinal impaction which was composed of shavings.   Surprisingly, these "marasmic-like" pigs remained active throughout the 8 weeks of depletion and when let out of their pens each morning during a clean-up period, they would run up and down the corridor between the pens. The pigs were kept in pairs in the pens since this has been found to be an important factor in maintaining the young animals during the period of their severe nutritional deprivation. When released in pairs while their pens were being cleaned, the malnourished pigs frolicked and explored the new surroundings during their brief freedom in much the same manner as the control animals. When the experimental animals were switched to the normal commercial swine ration, they were individually penned and remained one to a pen for the remainder of the study. The pens were approximately 180 by 120 cm with solid plywood partitions about 100 cm high.

When the animals were approximately 6 months of age and had been nutritionally rehabilitated for about 3 months, they were subjected to a battery of behavioral tests devised on the basis of several years of studies in our laboratories. The first procedure was an operant test involving a food reinforcement. The pigs were fasted for 24 hours and then placed in a specially designed cage with two devices at one end of the cage. These devices resembled the lids on feeder boxes. They were familiar to the animals since the pigs had been fed from dispensers with these lids during their entire rehabilitation. Under the lids were pans, but only the left pan provided food which was dropped into the pan in very small quantities from an automatic dispenser which was activated by raising the right-hand lid. The animals had to learn that raising the right-hand lid with the snout would cause food to be placed in the pan under the left-hand lid. A fixed ratio of 1 was used and each pig remained in the test pen for 14 minutes without any external stimulation or aid. Complete food deprivation was continued for 2 additional days so that a total of three test sessions was obtained. Contrary to results obtained with both rats and pigs in previous preliminary studies of the same general nature (7), no significant differences between early malnourished and control pigs were obtained.

The animals were then submitted to three behavioral tests. These tests used a 2.5 × 2.5 m room which was divided into 4 smaller squares with partitions extending from the center, but not reaching the outer walls. A passage therefore remained open between each of the smaller sections. A rotating arm extended from the center and the outer end of this arm could be attached to a simple harness fastened behind the front legs and around the chest of the pig. This device could be used either for administering a shock to the animal or to measure the pig's movements from one section of the room to the next. The pig could freely move through the doorways in either direction or move about the floor area within each section. Fig. 2 diagrammatically illustrates this test unit.

Food was removed approximately 18 hours prior to each test period. This was done primarily so as to encourage the animals to walk into the room where the behavioral test would be performed which was adjacent to their home pens. A small amount of food was made available to them in a small stall which facilitated the attachment of the harness. The harnessed pigs could then be put into the testing room and the harness connected to the swivel arm.

The first test with this facility was to place the pigs in the room with wood braces, each 7.5 cm high, placed on the floor in each doorway. This was the animal's first

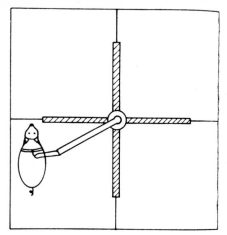

Fig. 2. Diagram of the behavioral testing unit. The doorways joining the four sections contained either minimal obstacles (7.5-cm-high wood braces) or 30-cm-high hurdles.

exposure to the harness and to the room. It was obviously a stressful and frightening experience. All pigs rapidly moved from section to section. They frequently vocalized and exhibited a general attitude of excitement. There were very noticeable differences between the control animals and most experimental groups. With the exception of the pigs that had been restricted from birth to 8 weeks, the experimental animals generally were more difficult to harness, more noisy when isolated in the test room, and as can be seen in Table 2, there were significantly more moves from one section to another during the 14-minute test period. The group restricted from birth to 8 weeks unfortunately had only three animals (one having died earlier), yet uniformly these three pigs and the six controls were easy to harness and were calm and quiet during the test period. The controls moved significantly less than three of the other groups (Table 2). The 0 to 8 weeks-restricted group appeared to be intermediate in activity showing no significant difference from the controls and yet significantly fewer moves than the low protein 3 to

Table 2. Spontaneous Activity in a New Environment

	Number of moves per pig		
Group designation[1]	0-7 min[2]	8-14 min	total[3]
1. Restricted 3-11 wk (4)			55 ± 4.0
2. Low protein 3-11 wk (4)	50 ± 6.2[4]	22 ± 4.5	72 ± 5.7
3. Low protein 7-15 wk (4)			56 ± 6.5
4. Restricted 0-8 wk (3)	28 ± 4.4	21 ± 4.0	49 ± 3.8
5. Controls (6)	18 ± 0.8	15 ± 1.1	33 ± 1.1

[1] Number of pigs shown in parentheses.
[2] Record of movements at short intervals during the test session were unfortunately not made for all groups.
[3] Statistically significant differences for total moves: 5 vs. 1, $P < 0.01$; 5 vs 2, $P < 0.001$; 5 vs 3, $P < 0.025$; 5 vs 4, N.S.; 2 vs. 4, $P < 0.05$.
[4] Mean $\pm$ SEM.

Table 3. Conditioned Avoidance "Acquisition"

Group designation[1]	Avoidances in 9 trials per pig			Avoidance average for 3 days[2]	Inter-trial jumps
	Day 1	Day 2	Day 3		
1. Restricted 3-11 wk (4)	5.2 ± 1.1[3]	7.0 ± 1.2	7.2 ± 1.1	6.5 ± 0.6	14 ± 1.3
2. Low protein 3-11 wk (4)	2.0 ± 0.4	5.5 ± 0.6	4.5 ± 1.5	4.0 ± 0.7	16 ± 1.1
3. Low protein 7-15 wk (3)	5.7 ± 0.4	8.3 ± 0.7	7.7 ± 0.4	7.2 ± 0.5	12 ± 0.6
4. Restricted 0-8 wk (3)	4.7 ± 0.9	7.7 ± 0.9	6.7 ± 0.4	6.4 ± 0.6	11 ± 2.7
5. Controls (6)	4.0 ± 0.4	6.9 ± 0.8	7.1 ± 0.6	6.0 ± 0.5	12 ± 1.8

[1] Number of pigs shown in parentheses.
[2] Controls (group 5) and low protein 3-11 wk (group 2) significantly different. For average of 3 days, $P < 0.005$. No other group differences were significant.
[3] Mean ± SEM.

11 weeks group. Exploratory behavior as manifested by sniffing and licking the floor was seen only during the latter part of the test sessions and was exhibited primarily by the control and 0 to 8 weeks-restricted group.

The day following the spontaneous activity test described above, the animals were returned to the test room with the harness attached. On this occasion and for the succeeding 2 days the animals were subjected to a conditioned-avoidance procedure. The doorways between each of the 4 sections were now equipped with 30-cm-high wood hurdles. The protocol involved the administration of an initial shock when the animal was first isolated in the test room. There was then a 60-second interval followed by 10 seconds of continuous buzzer accompanied by intermittent (1 second) clicking signals. Accompanying the 10th signal and on the subsequent 20, 1-second interval signals, a controlled voltage shock was administered. The pig could interrupt the CS (conditioned stimulus) buzzer signals or the shocks by jumping the hurdle in either direction from one section of the room to the next. Automatic recordings were made of the number of avoidances during 9 tests in which the CS was given, the number of escapes after the US (unconditioned stimulus) had been initiated and the number of moves from one section to another during 10 intertrial periods of 60 seconds each (included 60 seconds before the first signal and after ninth signal). All animals either avoided or escaped the US. Table 3 which shows the results of this study gives only avoidance performance and numbers of intertrial jumps. It can be seen that group 2, the low protein 3 to 11 weeks group, performed more poorly than any of the other groups. However, because of small numbers in the experimental groups the only significant difference was between group 2 and the controls. Although no significant differences existed in the number of intertrial jumps it is interesting that group 2, low protein 3 to 11 weeks, showed the largest number of jumps.

The day following the third conditioned-avoidance session, an "extinction" test was run. The pigs were harnessed, placed in the test room and given an initial shock in the same manner used in the previous 3 days. However, in this session hurdles were removed so that there was only the 7.5-cm-high brace on the floor in each of the doorways. They were given three CS trials; following the 60-second interval after the third trial the CS buzzer signal started with 1-second clicks as in the previous sessions, but this time the CS continued for the entire 10-minute test period regardless of the pig's movements, yet no shocks were administered. The number of movements from one section to another was recorded for each of the 10 minutes of the test. For various reasons, although most commonly due to apparatus failure, a few pigs had to be dropped from this as well as other tests. As a result, three experimental groups and the controls were reduced in numbers by one pig each. Nevertheless, differences in extinction between controls and experimental groups were so large that by statistical analysis they were highly significant. As shown in Table 4 the difference in movements was largely restricted to the second 5-minute period of extinction indicating that the initial level of excitement was not greatly different, but with continuing exposure to the buzzer signal (CS) the experimental groups were generally unable to inhibit the learned responses. The pattern of extinction performance is illustrated more clearly in Fig. 3 in which movements during each minute of the test are plotted against time. By this represen-

Table 4. Conditioned Avoidance ''Extinction''

	Number of moves per pig [2]		
Group designation [1]	0-5 min	6-10 min	total
1. Restricted 3-11 wk (3)	27 ± 5.8 [3]	15 ± 4.8	42 ± 4.0
2. Low protein 3-11 wk (4)	28 ± 6.7	24 ± 1.3	52 ± 2.5
3. Low protein 7-15 wk (3)	36 ± 6.9	15 ± 2.3	51 ± 9.2
4. Restricted 0-8 wk (3)	22 ± 7.2	13 ± 2.2	35 ± 9.0
5. Controls (5)	22 ± 5.2	4 ± 1.5	26 ± 5.1

[1] Number of pigs shown in parentheses.
[2] No significant differences during first 5 minutes. Significance of differences during second 5 minutes as follows: 5 vs. 1, $P < 0.001$; 5 vs. 2, $P < 0.001$; 5 vs 3, $P < 0.001$; 5 vs 4, $P < 0.001$; 2 vs. groups other than controls, N.S.
[3] Mean ± SEM.

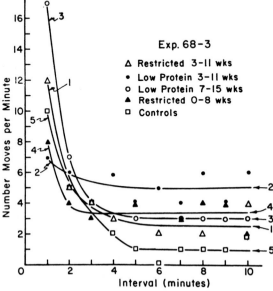

Fig. 3. Extinction of a conditioned response. Pattern of moves per minute for 10 minutes during which continuous conditioned stimulus (buzzer) was provided, but was not accompanied by unconditioned stimuli (electric shocks).

tation of data the experimental groups appear to divide into two classes, each differing widely from the controls. The continued high level of excitement of group 2 (low protein 3 to 11 weeks) is clearly seen in the graph. However, watching and listening to these animals (group 2) during the extinction test was far more dramatic than the data indicate. They snorted and vocalized and continued active movement both between sections and within sections of the test room. They never reached a sufficiently calm state so that excitatory activity became exploratory activity. The control animals behaved in a completely different manner. During the first few minutes of exposure to the continuing buzzer signal they were highly excited, but this excitatory behavior rapidly declined and for the last 5 minutes of the test they were calmly sniffing and licking the floor and, in general, exhibiting exploratory behavior.

DISCUSSION

An extremely interesting feature of these studies is the highly reproducible observation that the marked behavioral abnormalities, which develop as a consequence of a short period of malnutrition during early life, continue to be manifested after complete nutritional rehabilitation has been achieved and months after the initial nutritional insult was imposed. Furthermore, even though learning performance in certain tests may be impaired as a result of early malnutrition, the predominant behavioral characteristics observed in studies with pigs reported here, as well as in previous publications (2, 3, 8), appear to be related to fear of a new environment, elevated level of excitement under conditions of stress and inability to inhibit responses. An increased-hunger drive for food which has been observed in other studies was not seen. These behavioral changes might be categorized as overreaction or heightened emotionality in response to aversive stimuli. These characteristics could affect learning behavior by such mechanisms as altering the degree of reinforcement in operant testing or by increasing the level of distractions or frustrations. The behavioral responses reported above for previously malnourished pigs are remarkably similar to those of rats treated in a similar manner (5, 9).

Certain preliminary indications have emerged concerning the effect of the animal's age when malnutrition was imposed and the relative damaging effect of protein deficiency as compared with calorie deficiency on behavioral development. Although firm conclusions cannot be drawn from this study, two relationships are worthy of comment. First, a critical age in the pig when the initiation of malnutrition has its greatest effect upon behavioral development appears to be prior to 7 weeks. Second, protein deficiency, if initiated sufficiently early, would appear to have a greater effect upon behavioral development than calorie deficiency. A more thorough examination of these factors in future studies will be very important.

LITERATURE CITED

1. Barnes, R. H., Cunnold, S. R., Zimmermann, R. R., Simmons, H., MacLeod, R. R. and Krook, L. 1966, Influence of nutritional deprivations in early life on learning behavior of rats as measured by performance in a water maze, *J. Nutr., 89,* 399.
2. Barnes, R. H., Moore, A. U., Reid, I. M. and Pond, W. G. 1967, Learning behavior following nutritional deprivations in early life, *J. Amer. Diet. Ass., 51:* 34.
3. Barnes, R. H., Moore, A. U., Reid, I. M. and Pond, W. G. 1968, Effect of food deprivations on behavioral patterns, *In: Malnutrition, Learning and Behavior,* N. S. Scrimshaw & J. E. Gordon (Eds.), M.I.T. Press, Cambridge, Mass., 203.
4. Barnes, R. H., Neely, C. S., Kwong, E., Labadan, B. A. and Franková, S. 1968, Postnatal nutritional deprivations as determinants of adult behavior toward food, its consumption and utilization, *J. Nutr., 96,* 467.

5. Franková, S. and Barnes, R. H. 1968, Influence of malnutrition in early life on exploratory behavior of rats, *J. Nutr., 96: 477*.
6. Franková, S. and Barnes, R. H. 1968, Effect of malnutrition in early life on avoidance conditioning and behavior of adult rats, *J. Nutr., 96*: 485.
7. Barnes, R. H., Reid, I. M., Pond, W. G. and Moore, A. U. 1968, The use of experimental animals in studying behavioral abnormalities following recovery from early malnutrition, *In: Calorie and Protein Deficiencies*, R. A. McCance & E. M. Widdowson (Eds.), Churchill Press, London, 277.
8. Barnes, R. H. 1967, Experimental animal approaches to the study of early malnutrition and mental development, *Federation Proc., 26*: 144.
9. Levitsky, D. A. and Barnes, R. H. 1970, Early malnutrition: effect on emotionality in the adult rat, *Nature,* in press.

23. Prenatal Stress Feminizes and Demasculinizes the Behavior of Males

I. L. WARD

Science, 1972, *175*, 82-4. Copyright 1972 by the American Association for the Advancement of Science. Reprinted by permission.

Abstract. Male rats were exposed to prenatal or postnatal stress, or both. The prenatally stressed males showed low levels of male copulatory behavior and high rates of female lordotic responding. Postnatal stress had no effect. The modifications are attributed to stress-mediated alterations in the ratio of adrenal to gonadal androgens during critical stages of sexual differentiation. Specifically, it appears that stress causes an increase in the weak adrenal androgen, androstenedione, from the maternal or fetal adrenal cortices, or from both, and a concurrent decrease in the potent gonadal androgen, testosterone.

The critical role of androgen during perinatal development on the differentiation of adult sexual behavior potentials has been clearly demonstrated. Male rats deprived of androgen prenatally in injection of the antiandrogenic drug, cyproterone acetate, or neonatally by castrating on the day of birth, display less male copulatory behavior and more female lordotic patterns than normal males (1). Conversely, female rats exposed to exogenous androgen during critical perinatal developmental stages show male-like copulatory and ejaculatory patterns while female receptivity is partially or totally impaired (2).

In the normal male, the differentiating androgen is presumably testosterone secreted by the fetal and neonatal testes. There is, however, an alternate source of androgen, namely, the adrenal cortex. Among other androgenic steroids, the adrenals secrete small quantities of testosterone and large amounts of the less potent androstenedione (3). The possible functional significance of this apparently redundant androgen source has not been investigated. However, since the adrenal cortex under certain pathological conditions releases sufficient androgen to virilize human females (4), its role in the differentiation of healthy individuals may have been underestimated. This possibility is worth consideration in view of the large increases in adrenal 17-ketosteroid output during severe stress. The amount and ratio of androgens measured in plasma and urine of stressed animals differ from those of normal subjects. Exposure to a variety of stressors—including shock avoidance, living in overpopulated colonies, and adrenocorticotropin (ACTH)—decreases both testicular size and plasma and urine testosterone concentrations but increases the amount of androgen secreted by the adrenal cortex (5). Presumably the increased adrenal androgen is androstenedione since 80 to 85 percent of adrenal androgen is in this form in the normal organism (3). The fetal adrenal cortices also are highly secretory and respond to stress and ACTH (6), and the placenta is permeable to corticosteroids and ACTH (7); thus the fetus is exposed to maternal hormones as well as its own.

Sexual differentiation in male rats stressed during critical prenatal and postnatal developmental stages appears to take place in the presence of large amounts of the weak adrenal androgen, androstenedione, rather than under the primary influence of testosterone. The resulting behavioral potentials would be expected to resemble those obtained by other experimental manipulations which decrease functional testosterone titers. Male behavior should be reduced and female behavior enhanced. In a study designed to test these proposals, 14 time-mated Sprague-Dawley rats were stressed daily during three 45-minute sessions during days 14 to 21 of gestation by being restrained in 7 by 3 inch (18 by 8 cm) semicircular Plexiglas tubes across which 200 foot-candles (2150 lumens per square meter) of light were directed. This treatment produced piloerection and substantial amounts of urination and defecation. Nine control mothers were housed in an adjacent vivarium and were not handled. Half of the prenatally stressed litters and four of the control litters were then given daily postnatal stress from days 1 to 10 of age; stress consisted of three 30-minute sessions during which each male pup of a given litter was placed in a separate compartment of a plastic ice cube tray mounted on a vibrating metal rack. At about 90 days of age, all males were given 30-minute weekly tests with estrous lure females for spontaneous behavior. Each animal continued to be tested until he had either ejaculated or had failed to copulate for 6 weeks. The number of incomplete and complete intromission patterns as well as of ejaculations was recorded.

The results are presented in Table 1. A marked reduction was obtained in the percentage of prenatally stressed animals capable of showing the ejaculatory response. The postnatally stressed group did not differ from the control group, nor did the combination of prenatal and postnatal stress enhance the effect above that produced by prenatal stress alone. For the most part, the prenatally stressed groups simply did not attempt to copulate. Those animals initiating mating usually did so by the second or third test. Only one male in each group copulated without emitting an ejaculatory response. If the pattern appeared it was normal. Standard measures such as the mean number of copulatory responses emitted preceding the first ejaculation, the time from the first copulation to the ejaculatory response, and the duration of the post-ejaculatory interval were not significantly different among responding animals of the different groups.

The males were then castrated and, after a 10-day recovery period, given 5 weekly injections of 0.1 mg of estradiol benzoate followed 42 hours later by 1 mg of progesterone.

Table 1. Percentage of males which ejaculated or copulated on at least one of six tests with an estrous female. Binomial tests of results against the expected probability of control group gave the following results: prenatal stress, $P < .001$; pre- and postnatal stress, $P < .03$

Stress treatment	N	Percentage	
		Ejaculated	Copulated
Control	11	64	73
Postnatal	12	58	66
Prenatal	19	21	26
Pre- and postnatal	10	30	40

Table 2. Summary of Lordotic Behavior

Stress treatment	N	Mean lordotic responses	Mean times mounted	Tests* receptive (%)	Median[†] highest quality
Control	7	2.7	22.1	36	1
Postnatal	8	4.0	21.1	53	1
Prenatal	14	8.8	25.8	73	2
Pre- and postnatal	8	8.4	22.6	88	2

* Tests on which a minimum of two lordotic responses were emitted.
[†] Median of the highest quality lordotic pattern emitted on the four test days.

Beginning on the second week, female receptivity tests were given before the progesterone injection and 2, 4, 6, and 8 hours after. The number of times each animal was mounted by a vigorous male during a 10-minute period and the number of lordotic responses were recorded. Behavior was rated on a 7-point qualitative scale used in this laboratory with 1 indicating minimal and 7 maximal receptivity (8). Female behavior ratings recorded during the four tests are summarized in Table 2. All groups were mounted about an equal number of times, but the two prenatally stressed groups averaged over 3 times as many lordotic responses as the control group (Mann-Whitney U, $P < .01$). Postnatal stress had no significant effect on this or any of the other measures of female behavior. The enhanced tendency of the prenatally stressed groups to show female behavior is also reflected in the larger mean percentage of tests on which at least two lordotic responses were emitted and by the superior quality measures. Postnatal stress combined with prenatal stress did not increase the effect above that induced by prenatal stress alone.

Close inspection of the quality measure indicates that, although the level of female behavior shown by the prenatally stressed males was higher than that of normal males, it was lower than that of receptive females. No soliciting behavior, darting, or ear wiggling, typical of estrous female rats, were seen; and the males only occasionally held the lordotic posture after the vigorous stud male had dismounted. On the other hand, like estrous females, the males were tense, did not resist being mounted and displayed high-quality lordotic responses which were held as long as the stud remained mounted. Control and postnatally stressed males generally resisted being mounted, but when they permitted it they showed only slight curvature of the neck and back.

With the exception of the group stressed in both ways, responsivity in all groups increased from a low on the first test to a stable level during the last three weekly tests. There was no increase in responding as a function of number of hours after progesterone injection in any of the groups.

The present data support the hypothesis that exposure of pregnant rats to environmental stressors modifies the normal process of sexual behavior differentiation in male fetuses by decreasing functional testosterone and elevating androstenedione levels during perinatal development. During stress conditions plasma testosterone emanating from the gonads decreases while adrenal androstenedione rises (5). The molecular structure of the two androgens being very similar, it is postulated that the two hormones compete for the same receptor sites. Since androstenedione is a less potent androgen than testosterone, the decreased male copulatory ability and increased lordotic potential seen in the prenatally stressed animals of the present study would be expected. The relative difference in potency between testosterone and androstenedione has been repeatedly demonstrated. When injected into intact males, both hormones cause decreased testicular size; they also maintain prostate and seminal vesicle weights in hypophysectomized males. However, testosterone is superior to androstenedione in producing these effects (9). Further, the feminization of behavior of male rats castrated on the day of birth is not blocked by simultaneous injections of androstenedione as it is by administration of testosterone propionate (10).

It is postulated that sexual differentiation occurs under the influence of a dual system. Normally, in males, gonadal steroids would assure the establishment of male copulatory potentials and suppress female lordotic behavior. However, under a variety of unfavorable environmental conditions which have in common the ability to activate the adrenal cortical response to stressors, the normal amount and ratio of testicular to adrenal androgen is altered, and, along with it, the relative potency of androgenic stimuli under which the tissues mediating sexual behavior differentiate. The resulting alterations in sexual behavior provide the basis for an effective population control mechanism, since offspring so affected would not possess the behavioral repertoire necessary to contribute to population growth. Thus, the environment, by triggering or failing to trigger an adrenal stress response, may control the reproductive capacity of successive generations of differentiating fetuses and, thereby, population size. Since male behavior was tested in intact animals, it is not clear whether the modifications in behavior are attributable to stress-induced deficiencies in adult endogenous androgen levels, peripheral sex structures, central nervous system potentials, or some combination of these. Further experiments are in progress to try to delineate the locus of the modification. The female behavior differences, however, were observed in castrated subjects given constant hormone replacement and, therefore, probably reflect central nervous system modifications.

Although sexual differentiation in the rat spans both the prenatal and postnatal periods of development, in the present study, stress was effective only during prenatal differentiation. This is not too surprising since it is known that newborn rats pass through a stress-nonresponsive period for the first 10 days after birth (11). Paradoxically, while the newborn rat lacks the normal adrenal response to environmental stress, its adrenals show an increased sensitivity to ACTH (11). We are currently testing the possibility that by stressing the mother, enough ACTH or adrenal steroids can be transferred to the pup through the milk to influence the process of sexual differentiation which, in the rat, continues to about 10 day of age p. (12).

REFERENCES AND NOTES

1. I. L. Ward, *Physiol. Behav.,* in press; F. Neumann and W. Elger, *Endokrinologie* **50**, 209 (1966); F. Neumann, J. D. Hahn, M. Kramer, *Acta Endocrinol. (Copenhagen)* **54**, 227 (1967); K. L. Grady, C. H. Phoenix, W. C. Young, *J. Comp. Physiol. Psychol.* **59**, 176 (1965); K. Larsson, *Z. Tierpsychol.* **23**, 867 (1966); A. A. Gerall, S. E. Hendricks, L. L. Johnson, T. W. Bounds, *J. Comp. Physiol. Psychol.* **64**, 206 (1967).

2. A. A. Gerall and I. L. Ward, *J. Comp. Physiol. Psychol.* **62**, 470 (1966); I. L. Ward, *Horm. Behav.* **1**, 25 (1969); R. D. Nadler, *ibid.,* p. 53; I. L. Ward and F. J. Renz, *J. Comp. Physiol. Psychol.,* in press; R. E. Whalen and D. A. Edwards, *Anat. Rec.* **157**, 173 (1967); R. A. Gorski and C. A. Barraclough, *ibid.* **139**, 304 (1961); A. A. Gerall, *ibid.* **157**, 97 (1967).

3. R. M. Rose, *Psychosom. Med.* **31**, 405 (1969); H. A. Asakari, *Endocrinology* **87**, 1377 (1970).

4. V. B. Mahesh, R. B. Greenblatt, C. K. Aydar, S. Roy, R. A. Puebla, J. O. Ellegood, *J. Clin. Endocrinol.* **24**, 1283 (1964); J. Money, *Psychol. Bull.* **74**, 425 (1970).

5. J. J. Christian, *Am. J. Physiol.* **182**, 292 (1955); *Ecology* **37**, 258 (1956); C. W. Bardin and R. E. Peterson, *Endocrinology* **80**, 38 (1967). See also reviews by R. M. Rose, *Psychosom. Med.* **31**, 405 (1969); and

K. Milkovic and S. Milkovic, in *Neuroendocrinology*, L. Martini and W. F. Ganong, Eds. (Academic Press, New York, 1966), vol. 1, pp. 371-405.

6. A. Kamoun, C. Mialhe-Voloss, F. Stutinsky, *Compt. Rend. Soc. Biol.* **158**, 828 (1964); S. Milkovic and K. Milkovic, *Proc. Soc. Exp. Biol. Med.* **107**, 47 (1961); *Endocrinology* **71**, 799 (1962); S. Schapiro and E. Geller, *ibid.* **74**, 737 (1964).

7. J. C. Beck, quoted by A. Jost in *The Human Adrenal Cortex* (Little, Brown, Boston, 1967), pp. 11-28; E. Knobil and F. N. Briggs, *Fed. Proc.* **13**, 80 (1954); *Endocrinology* **57**, 147 (1955).

8. I. L. Ward, *Physiol. Behav.*, in press.

9. See review by R. I. Dorfman and R. A. Shipley, *Androgens* (Wiley, New York, 1956).

10. D. A. Goldfoot, H. H. Feder, R. W. Goy, *J. Comp. Physiol. Psychol.* **67**, 41 (1969); R. E. Whalen and D. A. Edwards, *Anat. Rec.* **157**, 173 (1967).

11. S. Schapiro, E. Geller, S. Eiduson, *Proc. Soc. Exp. Biol. Med.* **109**, 937 (1962); also see K. Milkovic and S. Milkovic (5).

12. Supported by grant HD-04688 from the National Institute of Child Health and Human Development. I thank B. Ward and A. Gerall for assistance in the preparation of this manuscript and F. Zemlan and H. Popolow for technical assistance.

Section VII

PSYCHOPHYSIOLOGICAL DISORDERS

24. Learned Asthma in the Guinea Pig

P. OTTENBERG, M. STEIN, J. LEWIS and C. HAMILTON

Psychosomatic Medicine, 1958, *20*, 395-400. Reprinted by permission.

There are few experimental reports substantiating the hypothesis that bronchial asthma can be a learned phenomenon. It has been suggested by French and Alexander[5] and others[18] that one of the psychological factors involved in bronchial asthma is analogous to the conditioned reflex. Stimuli that have been regularly associated with the presence of an allergic substance may precipitate an attack in a susceptible individual.

Conducting allergic studies with humans, Herxheimer[7] observed that merely placing many of the asthmatic subjects in a situation in which on repeated occasions they had been exposed previously to allergens, they developed asthma without the exposure. Dekker, Pelser, and Groen[3] report conditioned asthmatic attacks in a laboratory setting. They followed a procedure similar to Herxheimer's, using a known allergen paired with neutral solvents, and found in two subjects after repeated trials that the inhalation of pure oxygen caused attacks of asthma as demonstrated by clinical signs and vital capacity. The mouthpiece alone was eventually sufficient to cause an attack. These attacks could not be distinguished from those that appeared after the allergen. Dekker and Groen[2] also report psychogenic attacks of asthma using stressful stimuli that have in the past precipitated attacks in their subjects. They concluded that this evidence seemed in line with a conditioning mechanism although it did not follow a classical example.

Liddell[9] has surveyed the literature on conditioning of respiration in animals and its psychosomatic implications in humans. When experimental neuroses are produced in animals by conditioned reflex mechanisms there appear changes in the rate, rhythm, and pattern of respiration. Gantt[6] produced in an experimentally neurotic dog, "loud, raucous breathing with quick inspiration and labored expiration accompanied by a loud wheezing." This respiratory pattern appeared when the dog was brought from the paddock, became more pronounced as the experimental situation was approached, and disappeared in reverse order. This reaction persisted for many years. Examination of this dog showed that there was no true bronchiolar constriction.

Liddell reported that respiratory dysfunction is an invariable manifestation of chronic

From the Department of Psychiatry, School of Medicine of the University of Pennsylvania, Philadelphia, Pa.

Presented at the Annual Meeting of the American Psychosomatic Society, Cincinnati, Ohio, March 30, 1958.

This investigation was supported in part by a research grant (M998C) from the National Institute of Mental Health and a research grant (E1922) from the National Institute of Allergy and Infectious Diseases, National Institutes of Health, Public Health Service.

Received for publication April 20, 1958.

experimental neuroses in animals and resembles the labored breathing of bronchial asthma in some instances.

Another approach to the experimental study of asthma is the use of classical conditioning techniques. Such investigation is feasible since Ratner[14] and others[8] have demonstrated that a finely sprayed antigen produces in sensitized guinea pigs asthmatic attacks which resemble human bronchial asthma. In 1927 Ratner introduced a method for sensitizing and inducing anaphylaxis in guinea pigs solely through the inhalation of dry antigenic dust. The symptom complex produced he called "experimental asthma" because it was comparable to the asthmatic syndrome in the human. Kallos and Pagel[8] concluded from their work that finely sprayed antigen produces in sensitized guinea pigs attacks that clinically, roentgenologically, pharmacologically, and immunologically resemble human bronchial asthma. Ratner[15] has recently concluded that the inhalation of aerosolized liquids and dust results in reactions that are to all intents and purposes similar to human bronchial asthma.

Noelpp and Noelpp-Eschenhagen[11,12] have reported conditioning experiments with guinea pig asthma in which an allergic attack was paired with auditory stimuli. After 5 conditioning trials at irregular intervals, 1 of 8 animals had an asthmatic type of respiration in response to the conditioned stimulus. An additional 5 conditioning trials resulted in conditioned asthmatic responses in 3 more of the animals.

This study deals with the further investigation of experimental and learned asthma in the guinea pig.

METHOD

The experiment was divided into two parts. Part I was concerned with the development of experimental asthma in the guinea pig; Part II was concerned with obtaining information about learned asthmatic responses.

Part I

Thirty young male guinea pigs weighing 200-300 gm., were injected intraperitoneally 3 times with 0.25 ml. of fresh, undiluted egg white in a 1-week period. Following the series of injections 2 weeks were allowed to elapse for sensitization to occur. A special chamber, $10'' \times 16'' \times 16''$ was constructed with a one-way-vision window to permit observation of the animal's respiratory patterns. The chamber had an aperture for a #15 De Vilbiss nebulizer attached to a constant pressure and flow air pump. The nebulizer served to introduce a fine mist of a dilute solution of egg white. The animals were placed individually in the chamber on consecutive days. After 1 minute of observation the egg-white spray was introduced. Duration of the period in the chamber was 15 minutes during the early trials but often of shorter duration in the later trials because the severity of the respiratory distress necessitated removal of the animal. The box was thoroughly cleansed following each trial to remove residual egg white. Four other sensitized animals given only a saline spray served as a control group.

Two judges familiar with the procedure timed these attacks. An attack was marked by use of accessory muscles, gasping, coughing, and pronounced respiratory distress.

Part II

The 6 animals who had attacks on 10 or more consecutive trials were placed daily in the chamber in the absence of the egg-white spray. Independent observers noted the respiratory patterns and judged the presence or absence of an asthmatic attack, as in

Part I. The animals were tested daily until no attacks occurred in 15 minutes on 5 consecutive daily trials, at which time the response was considered extinguished.

RESULTS

Part I

The guinea pigs previously made sensitive to egg white developed respiratory distress when exposed to the nebulized egg-white spray. In producing the respiratory attack it was found that the components developed in a fairly uniform fashion. The

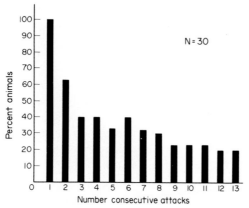

Fig. 1. The percentage of animals and number of consecutive attacks.

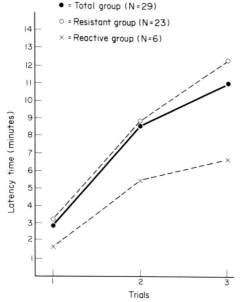

Fig. 2. The mean time between exposure to antigen and onset of attacks for the first 3 trials. The reactive group was composed of the 20 per cent of the animals who had 13 daily attacks. The resistant group composed the remainder.

sequence of respiratory signs was as follows: rapid breathing, restlessness, chewing, ruffling of the fur, then labored breathing with the use of accessory muscles of respiration, prolonged expiration, gasping, coughing, dilation of alae nasi, and finally cyanosis and convulsion. The severity in individual asthmatic attacks varied and all of the animals did not have attacks on each trial. All of the animals demonstrated sensitivity to the egg-white spray in the initial exposure, but after the second trial less than half continued with respiratory distress (Fig. 1).

As the experiments progressed there was an increasing delay between the exposure to antigen and the onset of the asthmatic attack. The difference between the time of the first and the third attack was highly significant ($P < 0.001$). Only 20 per cent of these animals had daily attacks. Mean latency time of the onset of their attacks was much shorter than that of the entire group (Fig. 2). In contrast, the control animals exposed only to the saline spray did not develop any of the signs of respiratory distress.

Part II

During the extinction phase all of this 20 per cent (6 animals) had asthmatic attacks without the presence of egg-white spray. Four animals continued to have attacks through 9 trials. The attacks were milder and did not progress to convulsive trembling or seizures. Figure 3 showing the extinction curve for the animals follows a typical extinction pattern in response to a learned stimulus. Extinction was apparent in all after 13 trials. This we define as learned asthma.

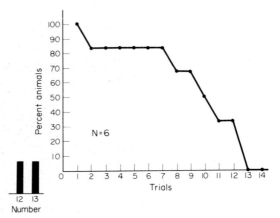

Fig. 3. Extinction curve of learned asthma. The responses are expressed as the percentage of animals who had learned asthmatic attacks on consecutive daily trials.

DISCUSSION

The present study suggests that there may be varying degrees of susceptibility to asthma in different animals, a fact which is important in selecting the most sensitive populations for further psychological experiments. Only 20 per cent of the initial group of animals had consistent daily attacks. The range in the time of onset of attacks also varied, with the most reactive animals having shortest latency periods.

The processes involved in the variability of latency and number of repeated asthmatic attacks is not clear and may be related to immunological changes of desensitization and antianaphylaxis. In another experiment Ottenberg, Stein, and Lewis[13] found that in sensitized guinea pigs single or repeated attacks often lead to a latency time exceeding 15 minutes. Allowing these animals 2-5 days of nonexposure to egg white results in a reduction of the latency period and a recovery of their reactivity.

In a third study 10 animals were exposed to the same procedure with several modifications. A much smaller chamber (15 per cent of the original volume) was utilized to reduce the activity of the animal and to increase the concentration of egg white in the atmosphere. From Fig. 4 it can be seen that all 10 of the guinea pigs had 10 consecutive attacks like the 20 per cent of the group in the larger chamber. The increased reactivity may be due to the higher concentration of antigen; or it could be due to higher susceptibility of the subjects.

It has been suggested that guinea pigs vary in their capacity to become sensitized. Ratner[16,17] has found that 7 per cent of guinea pigs are resistant to the development of experimental asthma and suggests that this may be an innate factor. Zinsser[9] in an earlier study confirmed the finding of resistant strains. Resistance does not appear to be a major factor in the present study, since all of the animals had attacks on the initial trial. Feinberg[4] has demonstrated that the time of onset of asthmatic attacks in guinea pigs is influenced by prior treatment with ACTH, cortisone, and stress.

The difference in the reaction of guinea pigs to the injection and the inhalation of egg-white spray may be related to immunological, genetic, hormonal, local, or psychological variables. Our findings suggest that those that react most quickly to the allergen can be identified very early in the experiment. The findings of differences in the number of repeated attacks and changing latencies in animals are consistent with Mirsky's[10] concept that inherent biological factors play a large role in the susceptibility to disordered function.

This methodology for the production of experimental asthma in a susceptible group afforded an opportunity to investigate learned asthma in the absence of an allergen. Results of the present study indicate that asthma can be learned. Of the 6 susceptible animals, 4 had nine daily attacks in response to the chamber without allergen. The question might be raised that the extinction curve represents merely the physiological process of removal of antigen from the animal's system. The concentration of egg-

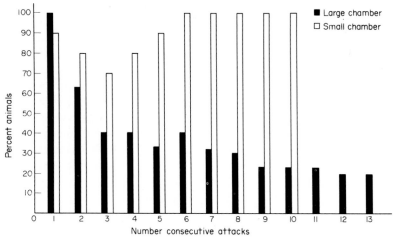

Fig. 4. Influence of chamber size on number of consecutive attacks.

white mist was heavy, and some observers have suggested that allergen may have persisted in the body fur of the animals or in the linings of their respiratory tracts, maintaining a state of autosensitization on repeated trials. This suggests that the asthmatic attacks observed were evidence of a state similar to status asthmaticus.

Although this remains a possibility we have called this response "learned asthma," since it meets the following criteria of conditioning outlined by Andrews:[1] (1) There must exist from the beginning a combination of an unconditioned stimulus and unconditioned response that is dependable, permanent, and not subject to extinction. (2) Then there must be paired with this combination in the proper fashion an extraneous neutral or conditioned stimulus (CS) that thereafter must be presented regularly along with the unconditioned stimulus and unconditioned response. The conditioned stimulus should not in itself induce the response. Our chamber served as the conditioned stimulus. After a sufficient number of trials pairing the conditioned stimulus with the unconditioned stimulus-response combination, the conditioned stimulus by itself must call forth the conditioned response. Four animals in the present study fulfilled these requirements. In addition, 5 of the 10 animals run in the smaller chamber also fulfilled these requirements. They had nine daily attacks in response to the CS.

The extinction of the conditioned reflex lends weight to the finding that this is a learned phenomenon. The question of whether the type of reaction we observed is generalized anxiety or fear also can be raised. In several animals we tried to evoke the response by loud noises, pain, and shock, without producing the pattern of asthmatic breathing we found in the experimental chamber.

The problem of which elements in the experimental situation act as the specific CS to produce the asthma is not clear. Our experimental chamber acted as the CS and could be viewed as a summation of multiple stimuli. It is possible also that internal changes within the animal acted as cues to the respiratory conditioning following the placing in the chamber. It should be noted that the conditioned responses were not as severe as the allergic responses. Such fractional reactions are commonly seen in the conditioning process.

The demonstration that asthma can be learned is of importance not only in relation to allergic phenomenon but also in relation to any agent, physical irritants, odors, or psychological factors, that may produce bronchiolar constriction. The learned responses reported herein bear a striking resemblance to human asthma as well as experimental allergic asthma. Whether the attacks reported are analogous to human bronchial asthma is still subject to much controversy. Asthma must be explained ultimately in terms of the basic pathophysiological change of bronchiolar constriction, which in turn produces the signs and symptoms.

Further studies in progress will enable us to measure quantitatively the physical properties of the lungs as a direct index of bronchiolar function in experimental and conditioned asthma. This will permit a precise definition of asthma in terms of airway resistance and eliminate the dependence on clinical impression of animals' respiratory patterns. This procedure also has considerable importance for further psychological studies of learned asthma and should tell us whether learned asthma is physiologically similar to allergic asthma.

SUMMARY

1. Young male guinea pigs previously made sensitive to egg white responded to a spray of homologous antigen with a respiratory syndrome that bears a marked clinical resemblance to human bronchial asthma.

2. A difference in susceptibility to attacks was found as well as a range of latency time in the onset of attacks in the animal population, suggesting inherent biological differences in disease reaction patterns.

3. Four of the 6 guinea pigs who completed 13 trials and 5 out of 10 in the later study group had learned asthmatic attacks that extinguished rapidly. The role of auto-sensitization, generalized fear, fractional responses, and learning have been discussed.

4. In studies in progress we are eliminating the dependence on clinical signs by measuring quantitatively airway resistance in the guinea pig. The airway resistance reflects the bronchiolar state and should indicate whether conditioned asthma is physiologically the same as experimental asthma.

REFERENCES

1. Andrews, T. G. *Methods of Psychology,* New York, J. Wiley, 1948
2. Dekker, E. and Groen, J. Reproducible psychogenic attacks of asthma: A laboratory study, *J. Psychosom. Res. 1:* 58, 1956.
3. Dekker, E., Pelser, H. E. and Groen, J. Conditioning as a cause of asthmatic attacks. *J. Psychosom. Res. 2:* 97, 1957.
4. Feinberg, S. M., Maikill, S. and McIntire, F. C. The effect of stress factors of asthma induced in guinea pigs by aerosolized antigens, *J. Allergy 24:* 302, 1953.
5. French, T. M., *et al.* Psychogenic Factors in Bronchial Asthma, *Psychosom. Med. Monograph 4,* National Research Council, Washington, D.C., 1941.
6. Gantt, W. H. *Experimental Basis for Neurotic Behavior, Psychosom. Med. Monograph 3,* nos. 3 & 4, National Research Council, Washington, D.C., 1941.
7. Herxheimer, H. Induced asthma in humans, *Internat. Arch. Allergy 3:* 192, 1953.
8. Kallos, P. and Pagel, W. Experimentelle untersuchungen uber asthma bronchiale, *Acta med. scandinav. 91:* 292, 1937.
9. Liddell, Howard. "The Influence of Experimental Neuroses on Respiratory Function", *In* Abramson, H. A., *Treatment of Asthma,* Baltimore, Williams & Wilkins, 1951.
10. Mirsky, I. A. "Psychoanalysis and the Biological Sciences", *In* Alexander, F. and Ross, H., *Twenty Years of Psychoanalysis,* New York, Norton, 1953.
11. Noelpp, B. and Noelpp-Eschenhagen, I. Das experimentelle asthma bronchiale des meer-schweinschens: II. Mitterlung die rolle bedingter reflexes in des pathogenese des asthma bronchiale, *Internat. Arch. Allergy 2:* 321, 1951.
12. Noelpp, B. and Noelpp-Eschenhagen, I. Das experimentelle asthma bronchiale des meer-schweinschens: III. Studien zur bedentung bedingter reflexe, bahnungsbereitschaft and haftfahigkut unter stress, *Internat. Arch. Allergy 3:* 108, 1952.
13. Ottenberg, P., Stein, M. and Lewis, J. Unpublished observations.
14. Ratner, B., Jackson, H. C. and Gruehl, H. L. Respiratory anaphylaxis: Sensitization, shock, bronchial asthma and death induced in the guinea pig by the nasal inhalation of dry horse dander, *Am. J. Dis. Child, 34:* 23, 1927.
15. Ratner, B. "Experimental Asthma", *In* Abramson, H. A. *Treatment of Asthma,* Baltimore, Williams & Wilkins, 1951.
16. Ratner, B. Individual differences in guinea pigs in the development of experimental asthma, *Trans. N.Y. Acad. Sc. 15:* 77, 1953.
17. Ratner, B. Temporal and quantitative factors influencing the development of experimental asthma in the guinea pigs, *J. Allergy 24:* 316, 1953.
18. Wittkower, E. Studies on the influence of emotions on the functions of organs, *J. Ment. Sc. 81:* 533, 1935.
19. Zinsser, H. and Enders, J. F. Variation in the susceptibility of guinea pigs to reversed passive anaphylaxis, *J. Immunol. 30:* 327, 1936.

25. Activity-stress Ulcer in the Rat, Hamster, Gerbil, and Guinea Pig[1,2]

G. P. VINCENT and W. P. PARÉ

Physiology and Behavior, 1976, *16,* 557-60. Copyright 1976 by Pergamon Press.
Reprinted by permission.

If young adult rats are individually housed in running wheel activity cages, allowed continuous access to the wheel, and fed only 1 hr each day, most of these animals will die within 4-16 days and reveal extensive lesions of the glandular stomach [2,8]. Control rats with the same feeding schedule and living in standard laboratory cages will survive and reveal lesion-free stomachs [6,7]. Since the activity variable contributed significantly to these particular lesions, Paré and Houser [8] referred to these lesions as "activity-stress ulcers". The activity-stress ulcer technique used the laboratory rat as the experimental subject and in that sense the technique is similar to the numerous ulcerogenic techniques which have been developed over the past two decades [1]. The extent to which all these techniques can produce stomach lesions in species other than the rat is relatively unknown. One exception to this exclusive preoccupation with the rat is the comparative study conducted by Brodie and Hanson [3] in which they observed the effect of the restraint technique in producing ulcers in mice, guinea pigs, hamsters, rabbits and monkeys as well as in the rat.

Lee and Bianchi [5] propose that one of the criteria for evaluating ulcerogenic techniques is the extent to which the method is capable of producing lesions in a variety of animal species. Activity-stress ulcers have been observed only in the rat. The purpose of the present study was to investigate the interspecies generality of the activity-stress technique by exposing rats, hamsters, gerbils and guinea pigs to this procedure.

METHOD

Animals and Apparatus

Animals included 30 male Sprague-Dawley rats (191-275 g, Sprague Dawley, Madison, Wisconsin). 20 male LHC/LoK hamsters (84-105 g, Charles River, Newfield, N.J.), 20 male DUB/Hart guinea pigs (224-301 g, Dutchland labs, Denver, Pa.), and 20 male gerbils (55-71 g, Tumblebrook Farms, West Brookfield, Mass.).

The activity cages for rats and guinea pigs were the standard Wahmann activity wheels which had an adjoining cage, measuring 25 × 15 × 13 cm. Rats and guinea

[1]Gratitude is extended to W. Love for fabricating the small activity cages, K. Isom, J. Reeves and L. Temple for their technical assistance, and L. Gilliam of the Medical Illustration Service, VA Hospital, Perry Point, Md., for the photographic illustrations.
[2]Veterans Administration Project number 641 6905—10.

pigs which were not housed in activity wheel cages were housed in standard laboratory cages measuring 25 × 17.5 × 17.5 cm. Hardware wire cages were fabricated for the hamsters and gerbils. These cages measured 30 × 15 × 21 cm. Cages in which activity gerbils and hamsters were individually housed each contained a standard pet shop exercise wheel which measured 54 cm in dia. × 7 cm wide. These exercise wheels were attached to the inside surface of the cages' wood covers. Exercise wheels were not installed in cages occupied by control hamsters and gerbils. All wheel revolutions were individually monitored for each activity cage by electromagnetic digital counters.

Procedure

Animals in each species were equated on the basis of body weight into two treatment groups: an activity group and a food control group. Animals assigned to the activity group were individually placed in activity cages. Food control animals were individually housed in cages which did not have activity wheels. All animals were given a 4 day habituation period during which food and water were continuously available. Activity animals also had constant access to the activity wheel in their cages during this period. On Day 5, food was withdrawn from activity rats and guinea pigs. On Day 6 food was withdrawn from food control rats and guinea pigs. Activity rats and guinea pigs were fed for 1 hr between 9-10 a.m. on this and subsequent days. The amount of food consumed by activity rats and guinea pigs was measured and this amount of food was given to food control rats and guinea pigs on the next day. In this sense food control rats and guinea pigs were food-yoked to their experimental mates and lagged behind by 24 hr as far as the experimental protocol was concerned. Because of uncertainty regarding the consummatory behavior of hamsters and gerbils in this situation, the food control animals for these two species were not food yoked to the activity animals. Food was removed from both activity and control hamsters and gerbils on Day 5. On Day 6 and subsequent days, all hamsters and gerbils were fed for 1 hr between 9 and 10 a.m. Body weight and food consumption were recorded daily for all animals. The number of wheel revolutions was recorded daily for each activity animal. If an animal died, the stomach was removed and inspected for ulcers. The number of ulcers was recorded. Because of the difference in stomach size between species, the percentage area of glandular ulceration was determined and recorded. The study was terminated after 21 days of 1 hr feeding and all remaining animals were then sacrificed and stomachs inspected for ulcers.

RESULTS

None of the food control animals died during the study. However, many activity animals died and the comparative cumulative mortalities for the four species are illustrated by Fig. 1. Using a Kruskal-Wallis test, data analysis indicated the existence of a significant differential mortality rate for the four species (x^2 = 245.5, $p < 0.05$). Hamsters died at a significantly faster rate as compared to guinea pigs (x^2 = 13.36, $p < 0.05$), rats (x^2 = 36.90, $p < 0.05$), and gerbils (x^2 = 78.14, $p < 0.05$). Guinea pigs died at a significantly faster rate as compared to gerbils (x^2 = 10.27, $p < 0.05$) and rats (x^2 = 5.14, $p < 0.05$). Rats did not die significantly faster than gerbils (x^2 = 3.16, $p < 0.05$).

Lesions were observed in all four species, and as Fig. 2 illustrates, these lesions were located in the glandular portion of the stomach. Table 1, which summarizes stomach

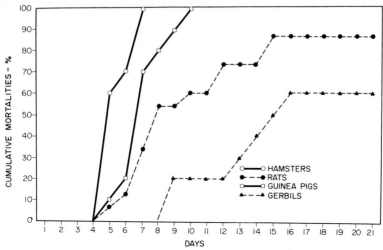

Fig. 1. Cumulative percent mortalities for hamsters, rats, guinea pigs and gerbils for consecutive experimental days.

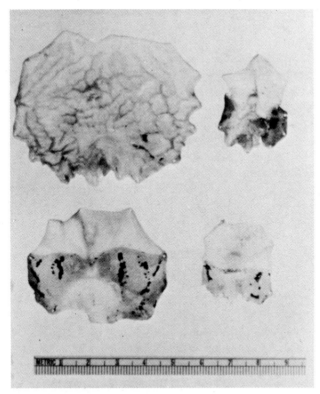

Fig. 2. Ulcerated stomach for a guinea pig (upper left), hamster (upper right), rat (lower left), and gerbil (lower right).

pathology, indicates that practically all activity animals developed lesions, whereas only a few control animals revealed any pathology. When ulcer frequency for the four

Table 1. Summary of Stomach Pathology for Experimental
and Control for Each Species

Species	N	Ulcers	Mean ulcers	% of stomach ulcerated
Rats				
Experimental	15	13	18.3	4.50
Control	15	1	1.5	0.34
Hamsters				
Experimental	10	10	7.5	4.39
Control	10	6	1.4	0.67
Gerbils				
Experimental	10	7*	5.4	4.84
Control	10	0	—	—
Guinea Pigs				
Experimental	10	7	2.1	0.13
Control	10	2	0.4	0.05

* Only 6 animals died in this group, but 1 other had ulcers at autopsy.

activity groups is compared to the four control groups, a significant difference is obtained (x^2 = 25.0, df = 3, $p < 0.0001$) which is attributable to the high degree of ulceration in activity animals.

Because of the difference in size of the stomachs of the four species, differences in extent of ulceration between species were evaluated by comparing the percentage area of the glandular stomach ulcerated between activity animals and their respective controls. Glandular lesions covered a greater portion of the stomach of activity animals as compared to control for rats, $t(1,28)$ = 4.76, $p < 0.001$, hamsters, $t(1,18)$ = 3.37, $p < 0.05$, and gerbils, $t(1,18)$ = 3.32, $p < 0.05$, but not guinea pigs, $t(1,18)$ = 1.01, $p > 0.05$. The difference in percentage of stomach area ulcerated between the four activity groups was significant, $F(3,41)$ = 4.89, $p < 0.01$. This difference was attributed to the guinea

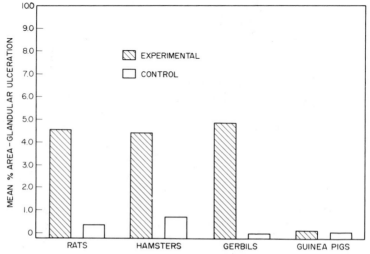

Fig. 3.   Mean percentage area of the glandular stomach which was ulcerated for activity and control rats, hamsters, gerbils and guinea pigs.

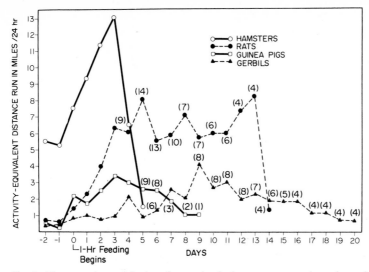

Fig. 4. Mean running activity in miles per day for hamsters, rats, guinea pigs and gerbils. The numbers in parentheses indicate the number of animals represented by a particular data point.

pig which ulcerated significantly less compared to the other three species (Tukey a test, $p < 0.05$). Significant differences in ulcerated area were not observed between hamsters, gerbils, and rats. These data are illustrated by Fig. 3.

In order to correct for the different size activity wheels, all the activity data were converted into distance which an animal ran every day. These data, for each species, are shown in Fig. 4. Because fatalities were recorded after the fourth day of 1 hr feeding in at least one of the species, only the first four days were used for statistical analysis. The four species were significantly different in terms of their daily running activity, $F(3,41) = 124.9$, $p < 0.001$. Hamsters ran significantly more than rats, gerbils and guinea pigs ($p < 0.01$). Rats were more active than gerbils and guinea pigs ($p < 0.01$), while gerbils did not run significantly more than guinea pigs.

An unusually high proportion of hamster control subjects revealed lesions when sacrificed at the end of the 21 day experimental period. Hamsters consumed very little food during the 1 hr feeding periods. Activity hamsters consumed a mean of 0.63 g and hamster controls ate only 0.84 g. This is a small amount of food especially when compared with the mean daily food consumption of a species of comparable size (e.g., gerbils). The smaller gerbils ate more food with activity gerbils and control gerbils consuming a mean of 3.0 g and 4.7 g respectively during the 1 hr feeding periods. Rats consumed an average of 7.1 g while guinea pigs ate an average of 5.2 g during the 1 hr feeding periods.

DISCUSSION

Running activity and ulcer information on interspecies comparisons is rather sparse, but the results of the present study are mostly in accord with the few studies which have been reported. Campbell *et al.* [4] observed that hamsters were more active than guinea pigs both under ad lib feeding and deprivation conditions. This species difference was also noted in the present study. Powell and Peck [9] reported that gerbils were more active than rats, but in the present study the reverse was found to be the case. However, it must be noted that different testing situations prevailed in the two studies.

In the only other study known to the authors on species differences and ulceration, Brodie and Hanson [3] reported that restraining rats, guinea pigs and hamsters for 24 hr resulted in an ulcer incidence of 86, 46, and 4% respectively. This compares with 87, 70 and 100% respectively for rats, guinea pigs and hamsters in the present study. Ulcer incidence was greater in the present study for the species in question, and this may suggest a difference in the ulcerogenic process of activity-stress as compared to restraint.

The most interesting outcome of this experiment was that glandular lesions were observed in all four species exposed to the activity-stress procedure. There are a number of reports that ulcers can be produced in the rat by this technique [2, 6, 7] but this is the first report of ulcers in the guinea pig, hamster and gerbil. In addition, there are no reports, known to the authors, of gastric lesions induced in the gerbil. The high incidence of lesions within species and the interspecies generality of the phenomenon indicates that the activity-stress procedure is a very robust technique for producing gastric lesions. There are, however, a few results in this study which should temper the previous statement. First of all, rats, hamsters and gerbils revealed stomachs with approximately the same amount of ulcerated tissue, whereas a much smaller percentage of the guinea pig stomach ulcerated (re. Fig. 4). This difference between the guinea pig and the other species may be due to the fact that the guinea pig stomach is much larger and is entirely a glandular stomach with no rumen. Since percentage area ulcerated was the index used to compare pathology across species, the absolute size of ulcers in the guinea pig was therefore diminished. A second consideration is the fact that many hamster food control animals had lesions when these were sacrificed after 21 days. In previous studies [6, 7] lesions in food control animals were rare. However, the hamsters in this study ate very little food during 1 hr feeding as compared to the other small species (i.e., the gerbil) and this reduced food intake may have had an inordinate effect on the hamster gastrointestinal system. Obviously, the activity-stress procedure must be repeated with the hamster to determine the relative input of reduced food intake and activity in the development of these gastric lesions.

In spite of the reservations noted above, the present results indicate that the activity-stress ulcer is not a phenomenon specific to the rat and due to its generality to other species, it represents a very useful tool for investigating the etiological dynamics of gastrointestinal ulceration.

REFERENCES

1. Ader, R. Experimentally induced gastric lesions. In: *Advances in Psychosomatic Medicine,* edited by H. Weiner. Basel: S. Karger, 1971, pp. 1-39.
2. Barboriak, J. J. and H. W. Knoblock, Jr. Gastric lesions in food-restricted young rats. *Proc. Soc. exp. Biol. Med.* **141**: 830-832, 1972.
3. Brodie, D. A. and H. M. Hanson. A study of the factors involved in the production of gastric ulcers by the restraint technique. *Gastroenterology* **38**: 353-360, 1960.
4. Campbell, B. A., N. P. Smith, J. R. Misanin and J. Jaynes. Species differences in activity during hunger and thirst. *J. comp. physiol. Psychol.* **61**: 123-127, 1966.
5. Lee, Y. H. and R. G. Bianchi. Use of experimental peptic ulcer models for drug screening. In: *Peptic Ulcer,* edited by C. J. Pfeiffer. Philadelphia: J. B. Lippincott, 1971, pp. 329-348.
6. Paré, W. P. Feeding environment and the activity-stress ulcer. *Bull. Psychon. Soc.* **4**: 546-548, 1974.
7. Paré, W. P. The influence of food consumption and running activity on the activity stress ulcer in the rat. *Am. J. Dig. Dis.* **20**: 262-273, 1975.
8. Paré, W. P. and V. P. Houser. Activity and food-restriction effects on gastric glandular lesions in the rat: The activity stress ulcer. *Bull. Psychon. Soc.* **2**: 213-214, 1973.
9. Powell, R. W. and S. Peck. Running-wheel activity and avoidance in the Mongolian gerbil. *J. exp. Analysis Behav.* **12**: 779-787, 1969.

26. Ulcerative Colitis-like Lesions in Siamang Gibbons

C. Stout and R. L. Snyder

Gastroenterology, 1969, *57*, 256-61. Copyright 1969 by Williams & Wilkins Co.
Reprinted by permission.

A fatal ulcerative colitis-like lesion, occurring in association with socioenvironmental upheaval, is described in 4 Siamang gibbons. Because these animals resided in zoos, it was possible to rule out shigellosis with any degree of certainty in only 1 of the 4 cases. The clinical picture was compatible with acute Shigella dysentery in the remaining 3 animals, but it was remarkable that none of the cagemates or adjacent animals developed diarrhea, and that the apparent precipitating emotional stress was identical in the 3 animals that died.

Although various chronic enterocolitides have been described in dogs, swine, and other species,[1-3] it is generally agreed that a disease similar to chronic idiopathic ulcerative colitis in humans does not occur in animals. Furthermore, although abdominal postganglionic sympathectomy in dogs[4] and manipulation of intestinal flora in guinea pigs[5] have yielded histological alterations which also occurred in a single phase of human ulcerative colitis, it has not been possible to induce the full blown lesion experimentally, despite the use of numerous species and a wide array of techniques.[6]

It is also generally accepted that among members of the animal kingdom, naturally occurring bacillary dysentery, or more specifically, shigellosis, is limited to representatives of the various nonhuman primate species. The acute phase of this illness is readily reproduced in monkeys by injecting Shigella organisms into the gastrointestinal tract.[7-9] The spontaneous disease in these animals is considerably more complicated, however, and is characterized by the presence of a carrier state, with and without colonic mucosal abnormalities, as well as the more familiar acute and often epidemic process.[10-14] Unfortunately, aside from the description of acute outbreaks, the literature contains very few detailed reports of spontaneous shigellosis in monkeys. It is of considerable interest that, in the most extensive of such studies, 12 of 40 dysenteric animals showed evidence of chronic colitis.[15] This process was characterized clinically by intermittent or prolonged diarrhea. Pathologically, the colons contained areas of scarring, alternating with areas of active inflammation and ulceration, and the healed

Received February 11, 1969. Accepted March 18, 1969.
Address requests for reprints to: Dr. Clarke Stout, Department of Pathology, University of Oklahoma Medical Center, 800 N.E. 13th Street, Oklahoma City, Oklahoma 73104.
This work was supported in part by Grants HE-08725, 1-F3-HE-37078, and HE-5690 from the National Heart Institute, United States Public Health Service.
The assistance of Dr. Philip Ogilvie and his staff at the Oklahoma City Zoo, Mrs. Zelma Proctor, Dr. Jacqueline Coalson, and Mr. Ronald Gordon is gratefully acknowledged.

mucosa was often low, containing only a few distorted crypts. Regeneration of epithelial cells into the submucosa and into the lumen in the form of small polyps was seen. The addition of mucosal bridges to this description would render the process morphologically indistinguishable from human ulcerative colitis.[16] The fact that Shigella organisms were isolated from the stools of most of these 12 monkeys does not necessarily establish a cause effect relationship, particularly since Shigella organisms could be cultured from 8% of monkeys without macroscopic colonic lesions in Takasaka's colony,[11] and the elimination of Shigella organisms from the stool did not prevent the continuance or recurrence of diarrheal disease in Cheever's monkeys.[17] The reason for the latter discrepancy was not clear, although it was shown that the enteroviruses were not implicated.[18,19]

The paths of bacterial colitis and idiopathic ulcerative colitis have crossed many times during the last few decades. A prominent role was ascribed to bacteria in earlier investigations of the etiology of human ulcerative colitis,[20] and current ultrastructural studies have shown many morphological similarities between colonic epithelial cells from humans with ulcerative colitis and Shigellosis[21] and from monkeys with experimentally induced acute Shigellosis.[22] It is difficult to avoid the conclusion that bacterial and ulcerative colitis are closely interrelated, and probably share certain pathogenetic mechanisms. Their obvious dissimilarities may simply reflect the differences in genetic composition and response to environmental influences of the colonic epithelial cells of different individuals.

The present report describes the occurrence of a fatal ulcerative colitis-like lesion in 4 Siamang gibbons (*Hylobates syndactylus*). Because these animals were living in zoos at the time of death, it was not possible to obtain sufficient information to ensure an "airtight" diagnosis in all cases. Nevertheless, the extraordinary circumstances which accompanied the final illness in each instance make the description of these cases important, in order that further study of spontaneous colitis in nonhuman primates may be stimulated.

MATERIALS AND METHODS

The Siamang gibbon is a member of the anthropoid ape family, being tailless, with elongated arms and a highly developed central nervous system. In nature these animals live in family groups, maintain definite territorial boundaries, and vocalize frequently with the aid of a large inflatable sac located beneath the chin.[23] They are found only in the forests of Malaya and Sumatra, and, in contrast to macaques and baboons, adjust to captivity with considerable difficulty. Adaptation to the captive state is greatly facilitated by the provision of emotional support, in the form of either frequent interaction with humans or the company of a suitable Siamang gibbon (W. B. Lemmon, *personal communication*). A similar dependence upon interpersonal relationships has been observed in other anthropoid apes and, in one instance, the withdrawal of such support in a young gorilla was associated with the onset of organic illness.[24] For these reasons, Siamang gibbons are usually kept in male-female pairs in zoos, and are noted for the length and compatibility of their relationships. Furthermore, according to "zoo lore," a Siamang gibbon will frequently "pine away" and die following the loss of a long time cagemate. On one such occasion, subsequent postmortem examination disclosed no anatomical abnormality (P. Fontaine, *personal communication*).

Data for the present report were obtained as a consequence of consecutive postmortem examinations of mammals and birds dying in the Oklahoma City and Philadelphia

Zoological Gardens. Studies were conducted at the Institute for Comparative Pathology, which was opened in 1965 by the University of Oklahoma Medical Center and the Oklahoma City Zoo, and the Penrose Research Laboratory, established in 1901 at the Philadelphia Zoo.

CASE REPORTS

In 1960 the Oklahoma City Zoo acquired a pair of prepuberal Siamang gibbons. These animals lived together until the death of the male in December 1967, with extensive acute pyelonephritis. Although apparently healthy prior to this event, the female did not fare well thereafter. She ate poorly, became somewhat lethargic, and within 6 weeks was dead. Although diarrhea or other signs of acute illness were not observed, it is possible that the passage of small amounts of blood or mucus in the stool escaped detection. Postmortem findings were limited to the colon and rectum which showed extensive mucosal ulceration. For the most part, these ulcers were quite shallow, although occasional longitudinally oriented lesions in the transverse segment penetrated almost to the submucosa, with undermining of adjacent mucosa. The unulcerated mucosa was a dark reddish purple color, which in contrast to the whitish yellow ulcerations presented a striking picture (Fig. 1). Microscopic sections revealed exten-

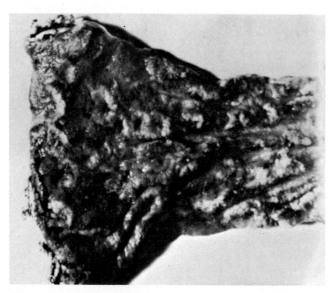

Fig. 1. Z-487, Siamang gibbon, adult female. Rectum and portion of sigmoid colon showing numerous shallow mucosal ulcerations.

sive focal disruption of glandular architecture with frequent crypt abscesses (Fig. 2). The involved mucosa contained remnants of glands and the lamina propria was necrotic and densely infiltrated with polymorphonuclear leukocytes, plasma cells, and lymphocytes. Beneath many of these areas, groups of regenerating glands could be seen pushing into the submucosa, carrying the muscularis mucosa before them (Fig. 3). The lamina propria adjacent to the ulcerated areas was infiltrated with varying numbers of plasma cells, polymorphonuclear leukocytes, and lymphocytes. Goblet cells were increased in these regions and surface mucus was excessive. The submucosa was focally

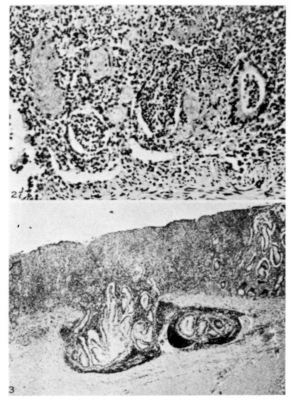

Fig. 2. Microscopic section of colon pictured in Figure 1. Three crypt abscesses in varying stages of development are seen at the base of an ulcerated portion of the mucosa. The muscularis mucosa traverses the bottom of the picture (hematoxylin and eosin stained, × 128).

Fig. 3. Microscopic section of colon pictured in Figure 1. Section through a mucosal ulcer shows extensive disruption of normal architecture, and encroachment of regenerating glands on the submucosa. Distortion of mucosal glands and infiltration of the lamina propria with inflammatory cells is seen adjacent to the ulcer (*right*) (hematoxylin and eosin stained, × 20).

infiltrated with plasma cells, lymphocytes, and polymorphonuclear leukocytes, and occasional large lymph nodules were seen. No large macrophages or granulomata were observed. The muscularis and serosa were only occasionally infiltrated with inflammatory cells, although foci of acute necrosis were seen in several submucosal and serosal lymphoid aggregates. No amoebae or parasites were observed in the many sections. The esophagus, stomach, and small intestine were grossly and microscopically normal, and likewise contained no parasites. A portion of the ulcerated colonic mucosa was cultured for Salmonella, Shigella, and pathogenic coliform organisms; none were found.

Representative sections were sent to several investigators experienced in the field of intestinal pathology. One such expert considered the microscopic changes to be quite similar to those in idiopathic ulcerative colitis (G. Lumb, *personal communication*). A second thought that a diagnosis of Shigellosis was more likely, despite the fact that this organism could not be cultured from the involved tissues (H. Sprinz, *personal com-*

munication.) Unfortunately, serial stool cultures had not been obtained during the period immediately prior to death. Other features of the clinical history were not characteristic of acute shigellosis, e.g., the absence of sudden onset of illness with tenesmus and diarrhea, and the absence of diarrhea among adjacent animals. A third expert thought that a definitive diagnosis could not be made, but favored bacterial colitis (B. Morson, *personal communication*).

Three Siamang gibbons were lost with an ulcerative colitis-like lesion at the Philadelphia Zoo. Death occurred when an attempt was made to introduce a new animal into a cage with one that was thoroughly at home there. Two of the introducees were females and 1 was a male, in each instance introduced into a cage containing 1 animal of the opposite sex. None of the affected animals was overtly injured, but invariably the animal in residence became unusually active and took food away from the introducee which, in each instance, developed bloody diarrhea and died within 5 days. Microscopic sections revealed multiple focal mucosal ulcerations of the colon, similar to, although less advanced than those in the first case. No amoebae or parasites were detected. While cultures for Shigella organisms were not obtained, none of the resident or adjacent animals developed evidence of dysentery during the appropriate period of time.

The immediate cause of death was not clearly apparent in any of the 4 Siamang gibbons studied. No evidence of peritonitis, intestinal perforation, or pylephlebitis was seen. Presumably, dehydration and electrolyte imbalance were important contributing factors.

COMMENT

Because ulcerative colitis in humans has been correlated with feelings of hopelessness and helplessness, often precipitated by real or fantasied losses or separations from loved ones,[25] the occurrence of an ulcerative colitis-like lesion in a nonhuman primate following emotional deprivation is almost too good to be true. Such an occurrence is not beyond the realm of possibility, however, particularly since Brady[26] has shown prolonged alterations in thyroid, gonadal, and adrenal hormonal secretion in monkeys in response to a single 72-hr exposure to experimental stress (Sidman avoidance procedure), and similar avoidance procedures on a 6-hr on-6-hr off schedule have resulted in gastric and duodenal ulcerations and, in 2 monkeys, in chronic colitis.[27] The latter lesions were characterized grossly by areas of mucosal hemorrhage and punctate ulceration. Microscopically, disorganization and erosion of the mucosa were seen, along with marked fibrous thickening of the submucosa. The muscular layers were edematous, and peri-vascular accumulations of lymphocytes and hemosiderin laden macrophages were noted in the mucosa and submucosa. Occasional thrombi were present in the blood vessels. Multiple stool examinations revealed no pathogenic bacteria or parasites. Although the colitis described above and that in the present 4 Siamang gibbons both appear to be related to emotional stress, the two lesions are morphologically dissimilar.

Unfortunately, a definitive diagnosis of ulcerative colitis could not be made in any of the Siamang gibbons here reported and, indeed, the clinical picture in the 3 animals dying in the Philadelphia Zoo was quite compatible with acute shigellosis. The intriguing thing about the latter 3 animals is the fact that a fatal colitis occurred in association with socioenvironmental upheaval, and that none of the cagemates or adjacent animals were affected. No conclusion is warranted on the basis of the material presented. However, it is clear that the Siamang gibbon requires further observation concerning its possible use as an experimental model for the study of the mechanisms involved in the development of acute bacillary dysentery, and possibly idiopathic ulcerative colitis.

REFERENCES

1. Kennedy, P. L., and R. M. Cello. 1966. Colitis of boxer dogs. *Gastroenterology 51:* 926-931.
2. Strande, A., S. C. Sommers, and M. Pelrak. 1954. Regional enterocolitis in cocker spaniel dogs. *Arch. Path. (Chicago) 57:* 357-362.
3. Smith, H. A., and T. C. Jones. 1966. Veterinary pathology, p. 941-946. Lea and Febiger, Philadelphia.
4. Berger, R. L., and R. Lium. 1960. Abdominal postganglionic sympathectomy: a method for the production of an ulcerative colitis-like state in dogs. *Ann. Surg. 152:* 266-273.
5. Sprinz, H. 1966. Discussion of the paper by A. I. Mendeloff. *Gastroenterology 51:* 754.
6. Kirsner, J. B. 1961. Experimental colitis with particular reference to hypersensitivity reactions in the colon. *Gastroenterology 40:* 307-312.
7. Preston, W. S., and P. F. Clark. 1938. Bacillary dysentery in the rhesus monkey. *J. Infect. Dis. 63:* 238-244.
8. Honjo, S., M. Takasaka, T. Fujiwara, M. Nakagawa, K. Audoo, H. Ogawa, R. Takashashi, and K. Imaizumi. 1964. Shigellosis in Cynomologus monkeys (*Macaca irus*). II. Experimental infection with *Shigella flexneri* 2a, with special references to clinical and bacteriologic findings. *Jap. J. Med. Sci. Biol. 17:* 307-319.
9. Formal, S. B., T. H. Kent, S. Austin, and E. H. LaBrec. 1966. Fluorescent-antibody and histological study of vaccinated and control monkeys challenged with *Shigella flexneri. J. Bact. 91:* 2368-2376.
10. Schneider, N. J., E. C. Prather, A. L. Lewis, J. E. Scatterday, and A. V. Hardy. 1960. Enteric bacteriological studies in a large colony of primates. *Ann. N. Y. Acad. Sci. 85:* 935-941.
11. Lapin, B. A., and L. A. Yakovleva. 1963. Comparative pathology in monkeys, p. 11-39. Charles C. Thomas, Publisher, Springfield, Illinois.
12. Ruch, T. C. 1959. Diseases of laboratory primates, p. 79-150. W. B. Saunders Company, Philadelphia.
13. Takasaka, M., S. Honjo, T. Fujiwara, T. Hagiwara, H. Ogawa, and K. Imaizumi. 1964. Shigellosis in Cynomologus monkeys (*Macaca irus*). I. Epidemiological surveys on Shigella infection rate. *Jap. J. Med. Sci. Biol. 17:* 259-265.
14. Ogawa, H., R. Takahashi, S. Honjo, M. Takasaka, T. Fujiwara, K. Audoo, M. Nakagawa, T. Muto, and K. Imaizumi. 1964. Shigellosis in Cynomologus monkeys (*Macaca irus*). III. Histopathological studies on natural and experimental Shigellosis. *Jap. J. Med. Sci. Biol. 17:* 321-332.
15. Yakovleva, L. A. 1958. Pathological anatomical manifestations of dysentery in monkeys, p. 36-48. *In* B. A. Lapin [ed.], Problems of infectious pathology in experiments on monkeys. Abgosizdat: Sukhumi [translated from Russian]. United States Department of Health, Education, and Welfare.
16. Lumb, G. 1961. Pathology of ulcerative colitis. *Gastroenterology 40:* 290-298.
17. Cheever, F. S. 1961. Discussion of paper by J. T. Syverton. *Gastroenterology 40:* 335.
18. Hoffert, W. R., M. E. Bates, and F. S. Cheever. 1958. Study of enteric viruses of simian origin. *Amer. J. Hyg. 68:* 15-30.
19. Heberling, R. L., and F. S. Cheever. 1960. Enteric viruses of monkeys. *Ann. N. Y. Acad. Sci. 85:* 942-950.
20. Weinstein, L. 1961. Bacteriologic aspects of ulcerative colitis. *Gastroenterology 40:* 323-330.
21. Gonzalez-Licea, A., and J. Yardley. 1966. A comparative ultrastructural study of the mucosa in idiopathic ulcerative colitis, shigellosis, and other human colonic diseases. *Bull. Johns Hopkins Hosp. 118:* 444-461.
22. Takeuchi, A., S. B. Formal, and H. Sprinz. 1968. Experimental acute colitis in the rhesus monkey following peroral infection with *Shigella flexneri. Amer. J. Path. 52:* 503-529.
23. Morris, D. 1965. The mammals, p. 159. Harper and Row Publishers, New York.
24. Ratcliffe, H. L. 1967. Report of the Penrose Research Laboratory, Zoological Society of Philadelphia.
25. Engel, G. L. 1961. Biologic and psychologic features of the ulcerative colitis patient. *Gastroenterology 40:* 313-322.
26. Brady, J. V. 1964. Behavioral stress and physiological change: a comparative approach to the experimental analysis of some psychosomatic problems. *Trans. N. Y. Acad. Sci. 26:* 483-496.
27. Porter, R. W., J. V. Brady, D. Conrad, J. W. Mason, R. Galambos, and D. M. Rioch. 1958. Some experimental observations on gastrointestinal lesions in behaviorally conditioned monkeys. *Psychosom. Med. 20:* 379-394.

27. Operant Conditioning of Large Magnitude, 12-hour Duration, Heart Rate Elevations in the Baboon*

A. H. Harris, W. J. Gilliam and J. V. Brady

Pavlovian Journal, 1976, *11*, 86-92. Copyright 1976, J. P. Lippincott Co. Reprinted by permission.

Abstract—Two baboons were prepared with arterial and venous catheters and their heart rate and blood pressure were monitored continously thereafter. Following a 2 to 3 week interval during which baseline cardiovascular levels were determined, the animals were exposed to daily 12 hr conditioning sessions (alternating with 12-hr "rest" or "Conditioning Off" sessions) during which food reward and shock-avoidance were programmed as contingent consequences of pre-specified increases in heart rate. Initially, the criterion heart rate was set at 10-15 bpm above the animal's pre-experimental resting baseline level, with progressive increases programmed to occur at a rate approximating 7 bpm per week over a period of 8-10 weeks. Within this 2-3 month interval, heart rate doubled, reaching levels maintained above 160 bpm for more than 95 per cent of each daily 12-hour "Conditioning On" period. Propranolol selectively eliminated the conditioned heart rate increase but not the blood pressure elevation, indicating the contribution of sympathetic nervous activity to these operantly conditioned cardiovascular changes.

There have now been many demonstrations of heart rate conditioning through the application of "biofeedback" and operant conditioning procedures (Trowill, 1967; DiCara and Miller, 1968; Stephens, Harris and Brady, 1972; Headrick, Feather and Wells, 1971; Well, 1973). For the most part, the reported heart rate changes have been of small magnitude and/or short duration (see Blanchard and Young, 1973 for review), and numerous theoretical and methodological questions have been raised concerning the role of "voluntary mediators" in the development and maintenance of such operant autonomic conditioning effects (Katkin and Murray, 1968). In addition, interpretive analysis of such findings has been difficult because the constraints of indirect measurement techniques have limited the availability of concurrently monitored hemodynamic indices.

The present report describes the effects of food-reward and shock-avoidance pro-

* Supported by NHLI grants HL 06945 and HL 17958.

Mailing address: Division of Behavioral Biology, The Johns Hopkins University School of Medicine, 720 Rutland Avenue, Baltimore, Maryland 21205.

This paper is based upon data presented at the 14th Annual Meeting of the Pavlovian Society held at Sarasota, Florida in October, 1973.

grammed as environmental consequences contingent upon heart rate elevations as these are reflected in both heart rate and blood pressure changes in baboons during repeated daily exposures to 12-hr conditioning sessions.

MATERIALS AND METHODS

Two adult male baboons (*Papio sp.*) each weighing approximately 40 lb (18 kg) served as subjects. Each animal was maintained in a primate restraining chair (Findley, Robinson and Gilliam, 1971a) housed in a sound-reducing experimental chamber provided with stimulus lights and an automatic food dispenser, as previously described (Harris *et al.* 1971, 1973). Brief electric shocks (3-10 ma for 0.25 sec) were administered through stainless steel electrodes applied with conducting paste to a shaved portion of the animal's tail. Each animal was surgically prepared (Werdegar, Johnson and Mason, 1964) with two silicone-coated polyvinyl catheters, one implanted into the femoral artery to a point just above the level of the iliac bifurcation, and the other inserted into the femoral vein and advanced to the inferior vena cava. The distal end of each catheter was tunneled under the skin, exited in the interscapular region, fitted with an 18-gauge Luer stud adapter, and connected to a Statham transducer (P23De) mounted on the outside top of the experimental chamber. Patency of the catheter was maintained by continuous infusion of lightly heparinized saline (5000 USP units/liter) at a constant rate of approximately 4 ml/hour, and by a more rapid "flush" once each day. Periodic blood chemistry determinations established that plasma sodium levels remained within normal limits for the baboon (De La Pena and Goldzieher, 1965) under such saline infusion conditions.

Daily calibration of the system was accomplished without dismantling the components by integration of a mercury manometer through a series of three-way valves (Findley, *et al.* 1971 b). Pressure signals from the transducer were amplified and displayed on an Offner polygraph (type R) which provided continuous heart rate and beat-by-beat blood pressure recordings. In addition, the pressure and rate signals were analyzed by an electronic averager (Swinnen, 1968) which provided on-line printout of heart rate (in beats per minute) and both systolic and diastolic blood pressure (in millimeters of mercury) over consecutive 40-minute intervals. Throughout the experiment, blood pressure and heart rate were measured continuously, 24 hrs each day, and adjustable meter relays integrated with the physiological recording system provided for selection of criterion heart rate levels and automatic programming of contingent food and shock events. Two "feedback" lights, mounted in front of the animal, signalled when heart rate levels were above or below the prescribed criterion.

The conditioning procedure required the animals to maintain prespecified rate levels in order to obtain food and avoid shock. Five 1-g food pellets were delivered to the animal for every 10 min of accumulated time that the heart rate remained above criterion. Conversely, the animal received a single shock for every 60 sec that the heart rate remained below the criterion level. Additionally, each food reward delivery reset the shock time (thus providing an additional 60 sec of accumulated shock-free time), and each occurrence of an electric shock reset the food timer (thus postponing the delivery of food for at least an additional 10 min of accumulated time).

Initially, the criterion heart rate was set at 10-15 bpm above the animal's pre-experimental resting baseline level, with progressive increases programmed to occur at a rate approximating 7 bpm per week over a period of 8-10 weeks. Within this 2-3 month interval, heart rate doubled, reaching levels maintained above 165 bpm for more than

95 per cent of each daily 12-hr conditioning session. During these conditioning sessions, the animal received, on the average, less than 1 electric shock and more than 20 food pellets per hour.

RESULTS AND DISCUSSION

Figure 1 compares the concurrent changes in blood pressure and heart rate during the 12-hr conditioning-on, 12-hr conditioning-off periods with the changes in blood pressure and heart rate during the preconditioning baseline period. The data plot in Figure 1 is in the form of averages for four consecutive 24-hr experimental conditioning sessions (right panel) for each of the two baboons and four consecutive 24-hr pre-experimental baseline sessions (left panel) for the same two animals before conditioning. This figure shows consecutive 40-min-interval average, and summarizes in the right hand panel the response pattern which developed after the baboons had been exposed to at least 40 daily 12-hr conditioning sessions.

Characteristically, the onset of the 12-hr conditioning sessions occasioned a rapid rise in heart rate which was sustained at levels approximating 165 bpm throughout the 12-hour conditioning-on period for both animals. For baboon Andy, heart rate

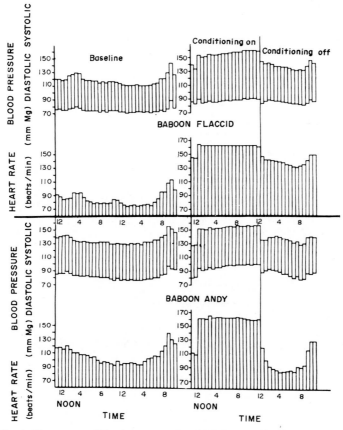

Fig. 1. Heart rate and blood pressure values for baboons "Flaccid" (top) and "Andy" (bottom) averaged over 40-min intervals during four consecutive pre-experimental baseline days (left panels) compared with four consecutive days during the 12-hr ON-12 hr OFF heart rate conditioning program (right panels).

rose from a forenoon level of about 110 bpm to a sustained level (afternoon) of approximately 162 bpm. At midnight, when the 12-hr conditioning sessions terminated, heart rate rapidly returned to baseline levels below 100 bpm. Conditioning-on heart rate levels of similar magnitude were observed with baboon Flaccid though it is noteworthy that the cardiac rate did not return to pre-experimental baseline levels for this animal. As shown in Figure 1, Flaccid's conditioning-off heart rate remained elevated above 130 bpm (compared to a pre-experimental baseline approximating 80 bpm) and the conditioning-on levels of approximately 165 bpm represented an increase of 20 to 30 bpm. For both subjects, blood pressure (both systolic and diastolic) showed a progressive rise of about 12 mm Hg during the course of the 12-hr conditioning-on period and returned to baseline levels during the 12-hr conditioning-off interval.

These results show that marked and durable increases in heart rate can be produced in the baboon through the application of concurrent food reward and shock avoidance conditioning procedures. These heart rate elevations were sustained during daily 12-hr conditioning sessions and were accompanied by modest but progressive increases in blood pressure. The physiological mechanisms underlying these conditioned cardiovascular changes are not as yet determined, but some indications of sympathetic neural influences have been provided by tests with the beta adrenergic blocking drug propranolol (Goodman and Gilman, 1970). Pre-treatment with propranolol (0.5 mg/kg) either prevented or severely limited the conditioned heart rate increase. Figure 2, for example, compared the changes in heart rate occurring at the start of a 12-hr conditioning-on interval in the absence of pharmacological blockade (upper section of Fig. 2) with the markedly attenuated cardiac rate changes observed following administration of propranolol (0.5 mg/kg) 12 minutes prior to session onset (lower section of Fig. 2). In previous work concerned with the neural mediation of conditioned heart rate changes

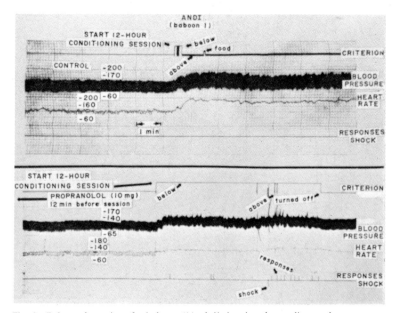

Fig. 2. Polygraph tracings for baboon "Andy" showing the cardiovascular response to the onset of the 12-hour heart rate conditioning session before (upper tracing) and after (lower tracing) pre-treatment with the beta adrenergic blocking drugs propranolol (0.5 mg/kg).

in the dog, Dykman and Gantt (1959) using the parasympathetic blocking drug atropine, emphasized that although both the sympathetic and parasympathetic nerves act together in the elaboration of the cardiac conditional reflex, "the parasympathetic nervous system plays an important role in cardiac acceleration."

Of particular interest would seem to be the chronically maintained tachycardia observed in baboon Flaccid and illustrated in Figure 1 by the elevated heart rate levels recorded during the 12-hr conditioning-off periods. Exposure to a 16-day "vacation" interval (*i.e.*, no heart rate conditioning sessions and *ad libitum* access to food and water) failed to produce a reduction in Flaccid's "resting" cardiac rate below 130 bpm. Though further research will, of course, be required to determine the extent to which the conditioning procedure contributed to this enduring tachycardia, the findings are consistent with the reported effects upon the cardiovascular system of repeated hypothalamic stimulation (Folkow and Rubinstein, 1966), repeated subpressor doses of angiotensin (McCubbin, *et al.* 1965), and long-term exposure to shock-avoidance conditioning (Forsyth, 1969). In this regard, it may also be significant that baboon Flaccid was exposed to a somewhat longer period of heart rate conditioning than baboon Andy over the course of the experiment, and the relationship of such temporal factors to the development of chronic cardiovascular disorders is currently under investigation.

The present findings with the baboon extend the range of potentially useful laboratory models for the analysis of environmental-behavioral influences upon the cardiovascular system, and call for further experimental scrutiny of the physiological mechanisms which mediate this significant alteration of the systemic circulation.

REFERENCES

Blanchard, E. B. and Young, L. D.: Self-control of cardiac functioning: A promise as yet unfulfilled. *Psych. Bull.* **79**: 3: 145-163, 1973.

De La Pena, A. and Goldzieher, J. W.: Clinical parameters in the normal baboon. *In* H. Vagtborg (Ed.) *The Baboon in Medical Research,* University of Texas Press, Austin, Volume 2, 1965; pp. 379-387.

DiCara, L. V. and Miller, N. E.: Changes in heart rate instrumentally learned by curarized rats as avoidance responses. *J. Comp. Physiol. Psychol.* **65**: 8-12, 1968.

Dykman, R. A. and Gantt, W. G.: The parasympathetic component of unlearned and acquired cardiac responses. *J. Comp. Physiol. Psychol.* **52**: 163-167, 1959.

Findley, J. D., Robinson, W. W. and Gilliam, W. J.: A restraint system for chronic study of the baboon. *J. Exp. Anal. Behav.* **15**: 69-71, 1971 a.

Findley, J. D., Brady, J. V., Robinson, W. W. and Gilliam, W. J.: Continuous cardiovascular monitoring in the baboon during long-term behavioral performance. *Common. Behav. Biol.,* Part A, No. 2, June, 1971 b.

Folkow, B. and Rubinstein, E. H.: Cardiovascular effects of acute and chronic stimulations of the hypothalamic defense area in the rat. *Acta Physiol. Scand.* **68**: 48, 1966.

Forsyth, R. P.: Blood pressure responses to long-term avoidance schedules in the restrained rhesus monkey. *Psychosom. Med.* **31**: 300, 1969.

Goodman, L. and Gilman, A. (Eds.): *The Pharmacological Basis of Therapeutics,* 4th edition. New York: MacMillan, Co., 1970.

Harris, A. H., Findley, J. D. and Brady, J. V.: Instrumental conditioning of blood pressure elevations in the baboon. *Cond. Reflex* **6**: 215, 1971.

Harris, A. H., Gilliam, W. J., Findley, J. D. and Brady, J. V.: Instrumental conditioning of large-magnitude daily 12-hour blood pressure elevations in the baboon. *Science* **182**: 175, 1973.

Headrick, M. W., Feather, B. W. and Wells, D. F.: Undirectional and large magnitude heart rate changes with augmented sensory feedback. *Psychophysiology* **8**: 132-142, 1971.

Katkin, E. S. and Murray, E. M.: Instrumental conditioning of autonomically mediated behavior: Theoretical and methodological issues. *Psych. Bull.* **70**: 1: 52-68, 1968.

McCubbin, J. W., DeMoura, R. S., Page, I. H. and Olmstead, F.: Arterial hypertension elicited by subpressor amounts of angiotensin. *Science* **149**: 1394, 1965.

Stephens, J., Harris, A. H. and Brady, J. V.: Large magnitude heart rate changes in subjects instructed to change their heart rates and given exteroceptive feedback. *Psychophysiology* **9**: 283, 1972.

Swinnen, M. E. T.: Blood pressure digitizer. *Proc. Ann. Conf. Engr. Med. Biol.* **10**: 18, 1968.

Trowill, J. A.: Instrumental conditioning of the heart rate in the curarized rat. *J. Comp. Physiol. Psychol.* **63**: 7-11, 1967.

Wells, D. T.: Large magnitude voluntary heart rate changes. *Psychophysiology* **10**: 3: 260-269, 1973.

Werdegar, D., Johnson, D. G. and Mason, J. W.: A technique for continuous measurement of arterial blood pressure in unanesthetized monkeys. *J. Appl. Physiol.* **19**: 519, 1964.

Section VIII

SPECIFIC ANOMALIES

28. Characteristics of Epileptoid Convulsive Reactions Produced in Rats by Auditory Stimulation

E. T. AUER and K. U. SMITH

Journal of Comparative Psychology, 1940, *30*, 255-9. Copyright 1940 by The American Psychological Association. Reprinted by permission.

A number of recent observations have reported the occurrence of a convulsive behavior pattern in rats and mice which has been induced by a jet of air in a conflict situation (1), and, in the absence of specific conflict, by the sound of a bell (2), the jingling of keys (3), or the noise made by an air blast (4). In order to ascertain in some detail the qualitative and quantitative characteristics of this epileptoid pattern of behavior in rats, we have stimulated a large number of rats by a high-pitched whistle and recorded the ensuing activity with a specially devised stabilimeter, which is so constructed that the animal's behavior is observable while its activity is being recorded. Approximately 30 per cent of over 400 rats tested by this method have repeatedly given convulsions.

In Figure 1 are shown typical activity records of rats when subjected to the sound stimulation. The top line in each record represents the activity of the animal as recorded by a tambour connected with the stabilimeter. The middle line is the stimulus line, the deflections of which represent the onset and termination of the sound stimulation. The bottom line indicates the time in ⅓ seconds.

Record A in Figure 1 represents the activity of a normal rat which does not convulse during the sound stimulation, but merely moves about the cage in a more or less haphazard fashion. Record B is that of an animal which, shortly after the beginning of the sound stimulation, starts to run in an excited manner, somewhat similar to that of the convulsive animals. This rat does not display the full convulsive pattern, however, but stops running shortly and behaves thereafter much as do the normal animals. In Record C is shown the nature of a typical full-fledged convulsion as registered by the tambour attached to the stabilimeter. Aspects of behavior which may be correlated with changes in the record include: (*a*) an initial startle pattern occurring at the beginning of the sound; (*b*) a short period of relative quiescence preceding the attack; (*c*) the initial period of convulsive running; (*d*) a second period of quiescence of relatively long duration; (*e*) the second period of convulsive running (usually much more marked than the first); (*f*) a period of rigidity, tremor, falling, squealing, and incontinence, in which the animal's tail is extended, the front feet drawn under, eyes protruded, rear extremities paralyzed, and the whole body shaken by a rigid tremor; (*g*) a period of convulsive jumping accompanied by squealing and the persistence of other features observed during the rigid state. At the end of such a convulsion the animal seems to be partially paralyzed (especially in the hind limbs), completely exhausted, and passive to handling and to pain stimulation. Termination of the sound stimulation during the convulsive jump-

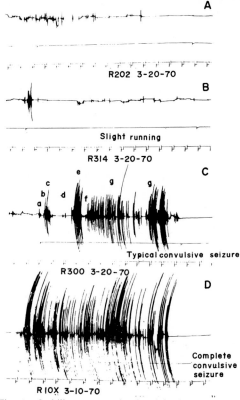

Fig. 1.   Stabilimeter records of activity in (A) A non-convulsive rat, (B) A rat which displays convulsive running alone, and (C, D) Two rats which display the complete convulsive pattern.

ing stage is ordinarily accompanied by the immediate cessation of the jumping, which otherwise may go on until the animal is completely exhausted. Possibly as a result of exhaustion, approximately 0.5 to 1.0 per cent of animals 6 to 7 weeks old in which convulsions are produced by this procedure die within a few hours after the first test. It should be emphasized that the running of the animals seems to be entirely undirected and proceeds without reference to any particular aspect of the environment. Record D shows the convulsion of another rat which differs from the one just described in that there is only a single period of convulsive running.

Table 1 summarizes certain quantitative features of ten typical convulsive seizures which have been recorded by the method described. The data appearing in the table are based on records selected at random from those secured during a second testing of a group of some 75 convulsive animals. The table gives time in seconds for the latency of the initial convulsive running with respect to the beginning of the sound stimulation, the duration of the convulsive running, the duration of the rigid-tremor state, the duration of the convulsive jumping, and the duration of the sound stimulation. In these ten animals the mean latency of the running is 25.5 seconds, with a range of 5 to 50 seconds. The mean duration of the convulsive running is 21 seconds. The duration of the rigid-tremor phase has a range of 5 to 43 seconds, with a mean of 21.3 seconds. The period of convulsive jumping may last until the animal is exhausted. We have usually terminated the stimulation during this phase, so that the times given here for the duration of the jumping are arbitrary. In the ten records under consideration, the maximum duration is 330 seconds. The duration of stimulation used in obtaining the different records is indicated in the last column of the table.

Table 1. Quantitative Characteristics of the Different Phases of the Convulsive Pattern

Subject	Latency of convulsive running	Duration of convulsive running	Duration of rigid state	Duration of convulsive jumping	Duration of stimulus
1	44	15	12	175	246
2	50	40	43	147	278
3	46	14	29	70	289
4	45	7	25	125	220
5	5	43	5	168	213
6	7	29	8	155	239
7	35	23	33	100	213
8	5	18	21	160	211
9	8	11	20	155	400
10	10	10	17	330	373
Mean	25.5	21.0	21.3	158.5	268.2

The present data on convulsive behavior in the rat lead us to believe that this pattern of activity is closely related to the phenomena of fits and epileptic seizures found in other animals, rather than representing a "neurotic" form of behavior arising from "psychological conflict"(5). This interpretation is suggested by the short latency of the convulsion, its uniform characteristics in different animals, as well as its radical form and after-effects. The convulsions elicited in rats have a number of features in common with epileptic attacks in the human individual and epileptoid reactions of other animals, as for example, incontinence, motor aurae preceding the attack, tremor, protrusion of the eyes, and the paralyzing after-effects of the seizure. These similarities suggest that the sound-produced convulsion in the rat is a form of epileptoid reaction rather than a conflict neurosis. The outstanding feature of the convulsive pattern in rats in comparison with human epilepsy is its close relation to the auditory mechanism, a relationship which is frequently noted in cases of epileptic seizures of man.

REFERENCES

(1) Maier, N. R. F. Studies of Abnormal Behavior in the Rat, New York: Harper, 1939, 81.
(2) Humphrey, G. and Marcuse, F. New methods of obtaining neurotic behavior in rats, *Amer. Jour. Psychol.,* 1939, **52**, 616-619.
(3) Dice, L. R. Inheritance of waltzing and of epilepsy in mice of the genus Peromyscus, *Jour. Mammal.,* 1935, **16**, 25-35.
(4) Morgan, C. T. and Morgan, J. D. Auditory induction of an abnormal pattern of behavior in rats, *Jour. Comp. Psychol.,* 1939, **27**, 505-508.
(5) Maier, N. R. F. *Op. cit.*

29. Spontaneously Occurring Forms of Tonic Immobility in Farm Animals

A. F. FRASER

Canadian Journal of Comparative Medicine, 1960, *24*, 330-3. Reprinted by permission.

HISTORY AND INTRODUCTION

In the 17th century Kircher demonstrated the "experimentum mirabile" with a hen (7). He showed that a hen would become temporarily immobile when laid on its back in a certain fashion. At the beginning of the 20th century this type of phenomenon was further investigated. Several workers observed "hypnoidal states" in laboratory animals under experimental conditions (16). Such states, described variously as hypnotic or hypnoidal, have been produced under experimental conditions in a wide variety of animals including bats, mice, guinea pigs, squirrels, rabbits, goats, pigs, and dogs, though the phenomenon is less easily elicited in the higher species (6), (16). The experimental methods producing the condition have usually involved confinement and sudden displacement of the animal and sometimes, as one recent worker states, compression of the thoracic or adjacent regions (3).

Pavlov, in his later years of research, became keenly interested in "the so-called hypnotism in animals" and gave it a very full consideration in terms of an inhibition (13). He encountered the condition in dogs during his well-known conditioned reflex experiments and noticed that it occurred in varying degrees of intensity in different animals at different times. With Petrova he elaborated an intriguing, though complex, theory which implicated inhibitory processes in nervous (cerebral) activity as the underlying mechanism in these cases. Pavlov claimed that the phenomenon represented *"a self-protecting reflex of an inhibitory character"* (which would still seem to be a very acceptable interpretation). The explanation offered for its biological significance was that the reduced mobility in the subject would be less likely to provoke an aggressive reaction by an overwhelming power if the latter were present.

Intensive experimental research on this phenomenon, now usually referred to as "tonic immobility", still continues (9), (10), (12). Although the phenomenon in freely occurring forms outside the laboratory has not received any intensive study, some manifestations are common knowledge. The colloquial existence of the expression "playing possum" is ample proof of this and it would appear that very many species of animals show such immobile behaviour in various circumstances (8). The domestic species are not likely to be exceptions, and it might be that farm animals in particular, with their environment often providing the element of confinement, demonstrate the phenomenon not infrequently. This possibility merits some attention, particularly when there is a strong suspicion that the phenomenon, in many cases, can acquire clinical significance.

MANIFESTATIONS OF THE PHENOMENON

Often the more usual forms can only be induced under experimental conditions but observations here will be focused on farm animals, where the condition appears spontaneously in somewhat variable form under certain common conditions of husbandry. In this seldom considered situation it loses none of its biological and comparative psychological implications and is additionally a matter of some immediate practical account.

In the horse, the behaviour of which has long been generally appreciated, a phenomenon of this same nature has been recognised from an earlier era as "jibbing" or "balking" (2) which a more modern reference describes as a horse vice (11). However, this example in a standing subject is not the best illustration for the more characteristic instances are those in which the subject is recumbent.

One stage towards recumbency in the ruminant is kneeling, and this in fact is an occasional manifestation of the condition. A female goat, currently being used as a "teaser" in semen collections, sometimes shows restiveness and distress when confined in a service crate. A state of "tonic immobility" usually follows which is seen to be expressed in one of two forms. A fixed kneeling posture (Fig. 1) is sometimes maintained for several minutes or until the animal is offered release. At other times the posture adopted by this animal is one of complete recumbency (Fig. 2) which is also maintained in stubborn fashion for periods of varying length. Individual cattle perform a similar kneeling action during various managemental procedures. Such acts are quite commonly observed but are usually of a very transient nature.

In the subject which assumes full recumbency the posture is one of normal recumbency. Here again, the state can be transient and after a short time most subjects rise quite voluntarily to a standing position. Such instances are of minor importance in animal husbandry, but an awareness of them can improve our comprehension of those manifestations which are of greater practical significance—the protracted cases. It is interesting to note at this point that virtually all the experimental workers mention that the state is maintained for widely variable periods of time in different individuals.

As the duration increases so the clinical importance increases, particularly with the heavier farm animals. Spontaneous recovery may occur at any time but physico-pathological conditions can very soon become superimposed and complicate the condition.

The principal characteristic feature of the condition in farm animals is not the subject's inability to move or rise but rather the *unwillingness* of the subject to make a satisfactory rising attempt when strongly urged to do so. However, the greatest caution is required in assuming that a continuous state of recumbency is due to this phenomenon alone since it can exist in conjunction with disabling physical conditions. All possible physical causes must be given full consideration, not only for the obvious reason of appropriate treatment, but also because the absence of a physical condition will tend to support a diagnosis of "tonic immobility".

AETIOLOGICAL FACTORS

It is probable that predisposing factors exist. For example, only the occasional individual goes down when groups of animals are forcefully husbanded, as in shipping. The nature of such predisposing factors is not apparent at the present time. However, certain situations are seen to be closely associated with the appearance of the pheno-

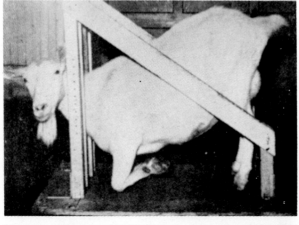

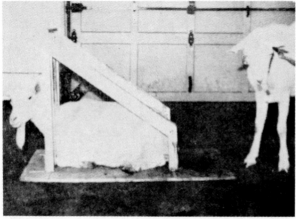

Fig. 1 and 2. Two forms of "tonic immobility" occurring spontaneously in a female goat during routine procedures of semen collection.

menon and it is reasonable to assume that they are, in some measure, causative.

The subject, in virtually all cases, is closely restrained or limited in movement when some stress situation arises. What constitutes a stress situation in one animal may not do so in another and here we see the possible existence of a predisposing factor in the temperament of the subject. Some specific circumstances are fairly frequently implicated. These include:

(a) Transportation of cattle and sheep.
(b) Enforced group movements, such as gathering or droving.
(c) Forceful manipulations on tied stock.
(d) Pain experiences.

Other less commonly associated situations include:

(e) Casting.
(f) Pursuit in enclosed quarters.

It may be that a wider recognition might bring to light a greater variety of situations which can induce the condition but in general it can be said at present that each constitutes a stress situation for the subject.

IDENTIFYING FEATURES

In farm animals, the principal identifying features are briefly as follows:

(1) A history revealing a stress event. The nature of the stress may be variable and of exogenous or, possibly, endogenous origin.

(2) A sudden appearance of a state of locomotor economy in the subject, shown particularly in an unwillingness to make responses which involve complex, co-ordinated, bodily movement.

(3) An apparent absence of any physico-pathological condition likely to create such kinetic deficiences, as are evident in the subject's behaviour.

(4) Associated behaviour includes general alertness as seen in ready, but localised, movements of the head, eyes, and ears. Adjustment limb movements also occur.

(5) Physiological behaviour including excretion, respiration, eating, and drinking continue virtually unimpaired until perhaps secondary pathological conditions, such as retention, hypostasis, necrosis, septicaemia, toxaemia, supervene and affect such activities.

(6) Sensitivity to body surface stimuli e.g. the electric goad, is present and likewise the blink, anal, and other reflexes are present. On the other hand reflexes involving changes in bodily position e.g. some limb movements and righting after lateral rotation, usually show varying degrees of inhibition. A strong persistence of whichever head posture has been adopted is commonly observed.

Reflex behaviour responses which are appropriate to urging stimuli, in recumbent subjects, constitute flight and this latter critical response can be induced fairly frequently under favourable conditions. Urging stimuli, however, might only induce a state of submission (5). This aspect is obviously an important one from a therapeutic point of view.

DISCUSSION ON CLINICAL OCCURRENCE

Even transient forms of the phenomenon can allow physical injury to be superimposed, e.g. during shipping a recumbent subject closely contained in a group can be readily trampled upon by its fellows. Clinical consequences of the phenomenon are more usually seen in protracted cases. Workers on the experimental condition observed that the duration of the phenomenon varied considerably and there is no reason to doubt that, in domestic animals also, the phenomenon can be of variable duration and may in some instances be protracted.

With heavy stock the deleterious effects of persistent recumbency are soon established. Inflammatory lesions usually appear in the region of certain limb joints such as the hocks and elbows. These various sequelae progress insidiously to ensure further recumbency through physical factors. Even when a primary condition has contributed to the recumbency, for example in milk fever, it sometimes happens that recumbency persists for a significant period after the primary condition has been removed.

"THE DOWNER COW"

The downer cow is often one of the large animal practitioner's most difficult problems in differential diagnosis. A wide variety of conditions may be implicated (4), (14), (15) and Roberts even includes "malingering" as a possible cause of protracted recumbency in these cows (14). Blood considers the condition as a precise entity, stating that the true downer cow is one which remains down but the recumbency is not due to any of the known causes (1). When clinical authorities accept that the downer cow can exist without any apparent physical cause there is room to advance the theory that here is another example of a spontaneous form of "tonic immobility". Parturition usually precedes the onset of the downer syndrome and this could amply provide the element of stress required to implicate the existence of a state of "tonic immobility". Also thoracic compression may have occurred.

When the downer cow is encountered maintaining recumbency in the face of all manner of stimulation, but apparently physically sound, many clinical workers adopt the trick of transferring the cow to a new situation e.g. from indoors to outdoors, or otherwise modifying the environment (e.g. presence of a dog) and frequently this makes the subject rise often immediately, in other words, the condition was not so much an inability to rise as a strong unwillingness to try to rise. This unwillingness not only simulates a pathological bodily state but, as already stated, soon establishes one. It is possible that the condition of "tonic immobility" in domestic animals is of greatest significance in this context. It would certainly be interesting to see how far large animal practitioners in general could implicate "tonic immobility" in their differential diagnosis of the downer cow syndrome.

CONCLUSION

These miscellaneous examples of locomotor inertia in farm animals show the existence of a special group of behaviour responses which we must recognise by a new concept based on fundamental biology. Is this group a link between some of the catatonic conditions in man and the simple "animal hypnosis" states occurring quite generally in lower forms of vertebrate life? This possibility certainly suggests itself and adds further interest to a basic biological phenomenon which may be presenting itself in earliest pathological form to the veterinary practitioner as a challenge to his clinical ingenuity and to the veterinary profession as a challenge to its ability to fill the role of comparative medical authority.

SUMMARY

"Animal hypnosis" or "tonic immobility" has been recognised for some time in very many species of animals and it has been the subject of much interest and a certain amount of experimental research. Sometimes the experimentally induced forms of the phenomenon are seldom if ever evident under other circumstances. By employing a concept of this basic biological phenomenon many examples of locomotor inertia occurring spontaneously in farm animal husbandry are seen to belong within the framework of "tonic immobility" states. Some inadequately understood veterinary clinical problems are held to be examples. The relative biological position of such states in farm animals is tentatively suggested.

ACKNOWLEDGEMENTS

Discussions with Dr. C. A. V. Barker and other members of the faculties of the Ontario Veterinary and Ontario Agricultural Colleges have been most helpful in assembling much of the material in this contribution.

Dr. N. D. MacRorie of the Creedmoor General Hospital, New York provided some illuminating information.

Thanks are expressed to the Department of Extension of the Ontario Veterinary College for assistance given in obtaining the photographs.

REFERENCES

(1) Blood, D. C. (1959) Personal communication.
(2) Dwyer, F. (1969) *The Prevention and Cure of Restiveness in Horses,* Lippincott & Co., Philadelphia.
(3) Foley, J. P. (1938) Tonic Immobility in the Rhesus Monkey, *J. Comp. Psych.* **26**, 515.
(4) Fraser, A. F. (1952) Some Observations on Post Parturient Paralysis in Cows, *Vet. Rec.* **64**, 400.
(5) Fraser, A. F. (1957) The State of Submission in Cattle, *Brit. Vet. J.* **113**, 4, 167.
(6) Gilman, T. T. and Marcuse, F. L. (1949) Animal Hypnosis, *Psychol. Bull.* **46**, 151.
(7) Gilman, T. T., Marcuse, F. L. and Moore, A. U. (1950) Animal Hypnosis: A study in the induction of tonic immobility in chickens, *J. Comp. Physiol. Psych.* **43**, 99.
(8) Hartman, C. G. (1950) Playing Possum, *Scientific American,* **182**, 1, 52.
(9) Hoagland, H. (1928) On the Mechanism of Tonic Immobility in Vertebrates, *J. Gen. Physiol.* **11**, 715.
(10) Holmes, S. J. (1929) A Note on Tonic Immobility, *J. Gen. Psych.* **2**, 378.
(11) Miller, W. C. and Robertson, E. D. S. (1936) *Practical Animal Husbandry,* Oliver & Boyd, Edinburgh, London.
(12) Munn, N. L. (1956) *Psychology,* Houghton Mifflin Co., Boston.
(13) Pavlov, I. P. (1957) Trans. *Experimental Psychology,* Philosophical Library, New York.
(14) Roberts, S. J. (1954) *Parturient Paresis Complex,* J.A.V.M.A., **124**, 368.
(15) Rosenberger, J. H. (1958) *The So-called Downer Cow Syndrome,* J.A.V.M.A., **132**, 76.
(16) Warden, C. J., Jenkins, T. N. and Warner, L. H. (1936) *Comparative Psychology,* Ronald Press Co., New York.

30. On the Phenomenon of Sudden Death in Animals and Man

C. P. RICHTER

Psychosomatic Medicine, 1957, *19*, 191-8. Reprinted by permission.

"Voodoo" Death—that is the title of a paper published in 1942 by Walter Cannon.[1] It contains many instances of mysterious, sudden, apparently psychogenic death, from all parts of the world. A Brazilian Indian condemned and sentenced by a so-called medicine man, is helpless against his own emotional response to this pronouncement—and dies within hours. In Africa a young Negro unknowingly eats the inviolably banned wild hen. On discovery of his "crime" he trembles, is overcome by fear, and dies in 24 hours. In New Zealand a Maori woman eats fruit that she only later learns has come from a tabooed place. Her chief has been profaned. By noon of the next day she is dead. In Australia a witch doctor points a bone at a man. Believing that nothing can save him, the man rapidly sinks in spirits and prepares to die. He is saved only at the last moment when the witch doctor is forced to remove the charm. R. Herbert Basedow in his book *The Australian Aboriginal*[2] wrote in 1925:

> The man who discovers that he is being boned by an enemy is, indeed, a pitiable sight. He stands aghast with his eyes staring at the treacherous pointer, and with his hands lifted to ward off the lethal medium, which he imagines is pouring into his body. His cheeks blanch, and his eyes become glassy, and the expression of his face becomes horribly distorted. He attempts to shriek but usually the sound chokes in his throat, and all that one might see is froth at his mouth. His body begins to tremble and his muscles twitch involuntarily. He sways backward and falls to the ground, and after a short time appears to be in a swoon. He finally composes himself, goes to his hut and there frets to death.

Cannon made a thorough search of reports from many primitive societies before he convinced himself of the existence of voodoo deaths. He concluded:

> . . . the phenomenon is characteristically noted among aborigines—among human beings so primitive, so superstitious, so ignorant, that they feel themselves bewildered strangers in a hostile world. Instead of knowledge, they have fertile and unrestricted imaginations which fill their environment with all manner of evil spirits capable of affecting their lives disastrously . . .

Having, after a painstaking search of the literature, convinced himself of the reality of this phenomenon, Cannon next addressed himself to the question "How can an

From the Psychobiological Laboratory, Johns Hopkins Medical School, Baltimore, Md.

Presented at the American Psychosomatic Society 1956 Annual Meeting, March 25, 1956, Boston, Mass. This work was carried on under contracts with the Office of the Surgeon-General and the Office of Naval Research.

ominous and persistent state of fear end the life of man?'' To answer this question he had recourse to his experimental observations on rage and fear in cats. He believed that while rage is associated with the instinct to attack and fear with the instinct to flee, these two emotions have similar effects on the body. Thus, when either of these instincts is aroused the same elemental parts of the nervous system and endocrine apparatus are brought into action, the sympathicoadrenal system.

> If these powerful emotions prevail, and the bodily forces are fully mobilized for action, and if this state of extreme perturbation continues in uncontrolled posses- sion of the organism for any considerable period, without the occurrence of action, dire results may ensue.

Thus, according to Cannon, death would result as a consequence of the state of shock produced by the continuous outpouring of adrenalin. Voodooed individuals would, therefore, be expected to breathe very rapidly, have a rapid pulse, and show a hemoconcentration resulting from loss of fluids from the blood to the tissues. The heart would beat faster and faster, gradually leading to a state of constant contraction and, ultimately, to death in systole.

Cannon expressed the hope that anyone having the opportunity to observe an indi- vidual in the throes of voodoo influence would make observations on respiratory and pulse rates, concentration of the blood, etc., to test this theory.

I bring this up here not because I have had opportunity to examine human victims— I have not—but because I have observed what may be a similar phenomenon in rats and because our studies may throw light on the underlying mechanisms of sudden unexplained death in man, not only in voodoo cultures. We are still actively at work on the problem and consequently this communication must be considered simply as a report of work in progress.

As so often happens, this phenomenon was discovered accidentally, as it were, during the course of other experiments. The first observation was made with Dr. Gordon Kennedy in 1953 while studying the sodium metabolism of rats on very high salt diets. To determine the amount of sodium excreted, three animals on a diet containing 35 per cent NaCl were kept in metabolism cages over large glass funnels. The urine was collected in a cylinder. To prevent contamination of the urine with this salt-rich food, the food-cup in each cage was placed at the end of a passageway, as far as possible from the neck of the funnel; however, despite our precautions, food was still dragged over the funnel, apparently on the whiskers or hair of the snout. In a further attempt to pre- vent this contamination the whiskers and hair were trimmed away with electric clippers. One of the three rats at once began to behave in a very peculiar manner, incessantly pushing its snout into the corners of the cage or into the food-cup with a corkscrew motion. Although before the clipping procedure it had seemed entirely normal, eight hours afterwards it was dead.

This observation was recalled a year or two later, while we were studying differences in the response to stress of wild and domesticated Norway rats. For these studies we measured endurance by means of swimming survival times, using specially designed tanks—glass cylinders 36 inches deep, standing inside glass jars 8 inches in diameter and 30 inches in depth (Fig. 1). A jet of water of any desired temperature playing into the center of each cylinder precluded the animals' floating, while the collar of the cylin- der itself prevented escape. The study was started with observations in our domesticated rats. Figure 2 shows the relationship between swimming time (drowning) and water temperature. The ordinates show average (7 rats at each point) swimming time in

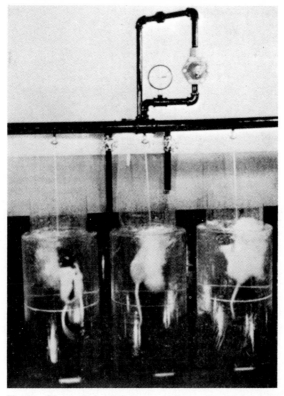

Fig. 1. Glass swimming jars, water jets, cold and hot water faucets, pressure gauge, and pressure regulator.

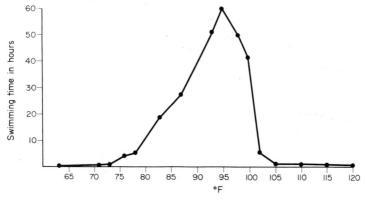

Fig. 2. Curve showing average swimming time (end point, drowning) of unconditioned tame domesticated Norway rats with relation to water temperature. Averages for 7 rats at each point.

hours, and the abscissas water temperature in degrees Fahrenheit. As can be seen, the average survival times were directly related to the temperature of the water; thus, the swimming times ranged from 10-15 minutes at 63-73° F., to 60 hours at 95° F., to 20 minutes at 105°.

The significance of this average curve was greatly reduced by the marked variations in individual swimming times. At all temperatures, a small number of rats died within 5-10 minutes after immersion, while in some instances others apparently no more healthy, swam as long as 81 hours. The elimination of these large variations presented a real problem, which for some time we could not solve. Then the solution came from an unexpected source—the finding of the phenomenon of sudden death, which constitutes the main topic of this communication. On one occasion while I was watching rats swim it occurred to me to investigate the effect of trimming the rat's whiskers on its performance in water. Would a rat swimming without whiskers show the peculiar behavior of the original rat in the metabolism cage?

Our observations were started with twelve, tame, domesticated rats. Using electric clippers, the whiskers and hair of the facial area were trimmed before the animals were placed in water at 95° F., a temperature at which most intact, control rats swim 60 to 80 hours. The first rat swam around excitedly on the surface for a very short time, then dove to the bottom, where it began to swim around nosing its way along the glass wall. Without coming to the surface a single time, it died 2 minutes after entering the tank. Two more of the twelve domesticated rats tested died in much the same way; however, the remaining 9 swam 40 to 60 hours.

Five of 6 hybrid rats, crosses between wild and domesticated rats, similarly treated, died in a very brief time. We then tested 34 clipped wild rats, all recently trapped. These animals are characteristically fierce, aggressive, and suspicious; they are constantly on the alert for any avenue of escape and react very strongly to any form of restraint in captivity. All 34 died in 1-15 minutes after immersion in the jars.

From the results we concluded that trimming the rats' whiskers, destroying possibly their most important means of contact with the outside world, seemed disturbing enough, especially to wild rats, to cause their deaths. However, when we began analyzing the various steps involved in transferring the fierce, wild rats from their cages to the water jars without the use of any anesthetic, it became obvious that a number of other factors had to be taken into account. To evaluate the relative importance of these factors, it became necessary to follow the rats from the time they left their cages until they finally died at the bottom of the swimming jars.

Figure 3A shows the type of metal cage used for the wild rats. The bevelled end contains a hinged door, the flat end a sliding door. Figure 3B shows the black opaque bag used for catching and holding the rat. The open end is held over the sliding door

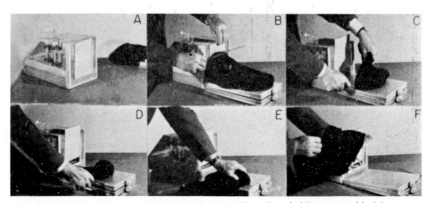

Fig. 3. Various steps involved in transferring wild rat from holding cage to black bag.

at the flat end of the cage. When the sliding door is opened, the rat sees the dark open-ing—an avenue of escape—and usually within seconds, almost "shoots" in. The instant the rat is out of the cage its retreat is cut off by a rod pressed down across the mouth of the bag as shown in Fig. 3C. Figures 3D and E show how, by means of the rod, the rat is then pushed into the end of the bag, where it is firmly but gently prevented from turning. The head is located by palpation and is held between the thumb and fingers, with care not to exert any pressure on the neck, while the body is held in the palm of the hand. Over 2000 rats have been held in this way, and none has ever made an attempt to bite through the bag. The rat is then lifted and the black cloth is peeled back expos-ing its head and body. (See Fig. 3F.) Held in this way the rat can neither bite nor escape; its whiskers can be trimmed, it can be injected, or it can be dropped directly into a swimming jar.

Thus, in evaluating the possible causes of the prompt death of the wild rats in this experiment, account must be taken of the following factors:

1. Reaction of the rat to confinement in the holding bag.
2. Reaction to being held in the experimenter's hand, while being prevented from biting or escaping.
3. Peripheral and cerebral vascular reactions to being held in an upright position. (The upright posture is reported to be fatal to wild rabbits.)[3]
4. Peripheral and cerebral vascular reactions to possible unavoidable pressure on the carotid sinus, carotid body, or larynx, exerted by the tips of the forefinger and thumb in holding the rat. (Prolonged pressure on the carotid sinus can produce syncope and even death in man as well as animals through its effect on vascular and respiratory mechanisms.)[4]
5. Reaction to the process of being clipped.
6. Reaction to confinement in swimming jar, with no avenue of escape.
7. Reaction of the clipped rats to a new situation, determined by the loss of stimula-tion from whiskers.
8. Respiratory reaction to immersion in water. (Diving produces marked slowing in heart rate.)[5]
9. Peripheral and cerebral vascular reactions to immersion in water at a temperature of 95° F. (Immersion in water of this temperature could produce a marked drop in pressure, resulting in cerebral anemia.)
10. Vascular reaction to nearly upright swimming posture. (Similar to, but presum-ably more marked than in No. 3.)

At present it appears that of all these factors, two are the most important: the restraint involved in holding the wild rats, thus suddenly and finally abolishing all hope of escape; and the confinement in the glass jar, further eliminating all chance of escape and at the same time threatening them with immediate drowning. Some of the wild rats died simply while being held in the hand; some even died when put into the water directly from their living cages, without ever being held. The combination of both maneuvers killed a far higher percentage. When in addition the whiskers were trimmed, all normal wild rats tested so far have died. The trimming of the whiskers thus proved to play a contributory, rather than an essential, role.

What kills these rats? Why do all of the fierce, aggressive, wild rats die promptly on immersion after clipping, and only a small number of the similarly treated tame domes-ticated rats?

On the basis of Cannon's conclusions and under the influence of the current thinking about the importance of the part played by the adrenals and the sympathetic nervous system in emotional states, and especially under stress, we naturally looked first of all for signs of sympathetic stimulation, especially for tachycardia and death in systole. Accordingly we were first interested in measuring the heart rate.

Electrocardiographic records were taken by means of electrodes consisting of short pieces of sharpened copper wire, each with a very fine insulated wire soldered to the blunt end. The pointed copper wires were dipped into electrode jelly and inserted under the skin of the two hind legs and one foreleg. They were inserted up the legs and the connecting wires were bent back up over the legs. A piece of plastic adhesive tape wrapped around the leg held the electrode and wire in place, insuring that a force exerted on the connecting wire would pull the electrode further under the skin rather than dislodge it. The connecting wires were brought together over the animal's back. In this way the rat could swim without getting itself entangled. Surprisingly, records taken under water were indistinguishable from those taken in air.

Contrary to our expectation, the EKG records indicated that the rats succumbing promptly died with a slowing of the heart rate rather than with an acceleration. Figure 4

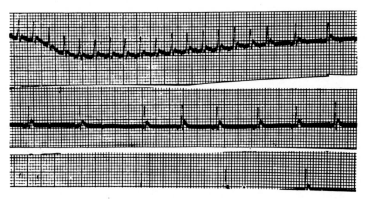

Fig. 4. Part of electrocardiogram on wild rat taken a few minutes after the rat's immersion in the water jar.

shows portions of the underwater EKG record typical of a rat dying promptly after immersion. Terminally, slowing of respiration and lowering of body temperature were also observed. Ultimately the heart stopped in diastole after having shown a steady gradual decrease in rate. As expected, autopsy revealed a large heart distended with blood. These findings indicate that the rats may have died a so-called vagus death, which is the result of overstimulation of the parasympathetic rather than of the sympathicoadrenal system.

It should be pointed out that the first response to stress, whether that of restraint in the hand or confinement in the water jars, was often an accelerated heart rate; only subsequently, with prolongation of the stress situation, was this followed by slowing. In some rats the latter response developed very promptly, in others not for a few minutes.

The following additional facts are in agreement with such a preliminary formulation: (1) pretreatment with atropine prevented the prompt death of 3 out of 25 clipped wild rats. By increasing the dose or by varying the interval between the injections and the test it might have been possible to achieve a higher survival rate: (2) domesticated rats

injected with definitely sublethal amounts of cholinergic drugs (morphine, physostig-
mine, mecholyl), i.e., of parasympathetic stimulants, died within a few minutes after
being put in the swimming jars. Thus, one-tenth of the LD 50 of morphine sufficed to
bring out the sudden death response in these rats, in effect eliminating this distinction
between domesticated and wild rats: (3) so far all the adrenalectomized wild rats tested
still showed sudden-death response, indicating that the deaths were not due to an overwhelming supply of adrenalin. Thyroidectomy likewise did not prevent the appearance
of the sudden-death phenomenon.

The situation of these rats scarcely seems one demanding fight or flight—it is rather
one of hopelessness; whether they are restrained in the hand or confined in the swimming jar, the rats are in a situation against which they have no defense. This reaction
of hopelessness is shown by some wild rats very soon after being grasped in the hand
and prevented from moving; they seem literally to "give up".

Support for the assumption that the sudden-death phenomenon depends largely on
emotional reactions to restraint or immersion comes from the observation that after
elimination of the hopelessness the rats do not die. This is achieved by repeatedly holding the rats briefly and then freeing them, and by immersing them in water for a few
minutes on several occasions. In this way the rats quickly learn that the situation is not
actually hopeless; thereafter they again become aggressive, try to escape, and show no
signs of giving up. Wild rats so conditioned swim just as long as domestic rats or longer.

Another observation worthy of record concerns the remarkable speed of recovery of
which these animals are capable. Once freed from restraint in the hand or confinement
in the glass jars, a rat that quite surely would have died in another minute or two
becomes normally active and aggressive in only a few minutes. Thus, in order to
measure the maximum swimming time, we now try to free the rats of all emotional
reactions to restraint or confinement by successively exposing them to these situations
and freeing them several times beforehand. In this way we have succeeded in eliminating most of the individual variations and are now obtaining quite constant, reproducible, endurance records for both domesticated and wild rats.

It is interesting that a few wild rats have also been protected by pretreatment with
chlorpromazine, without other "conditioning."

That the wild rats as compared to the domesticated rats seem much more susceptible
to this type of death would suggest that they have a higher vagus tone. In agreement
with this thought are the well-known observations that vagus tone is higher in healthy,
vigorous individuals than in weaker ones; also that vagus tone is higher in wild than
in domesticated animals in general.[6]

Other wild animals—rabbits, shrews, and pigeons—as well as some domesticated
animals—ewes—are known to show a sudden-death response; whether of the same
kind as we have described here is not known at present.

How can these results be applied toward the understanding of the voodoo-death
response in man? Apparently the "boned" victim, like the wild rat, is not set for fight
or flight, but similarly seems resigned to his fate—his situation seems to him quite
hopeless. For this reason we believe that the human victims—like our rats—may well
die a parasympathetic rather than a sympathicoadrenal death, as Cannon postulated.

Like the wild rat, primitive man, when freed from voodoo, is said to recover almost
instantaneously, even though he had recently seemed more dead than alive. These
observations suggest that the sudden-death phenomenon may be a one-time occurrence
both in rats and man—in any particular circumstances, ending either in death or in

immunity from this particular kind of death. In human beings as well as in rats we see the possibility that hopelessness and death may result from the effects of a combination of reactions, all of which may operate in the same direction, and increase the vagal tone.

There is the further suggestion that the incidence of this response varies inversely as the degree of civilization, or domestication, of the individual, since it occurs more frequently in wild than in domesticated rats and so far certainly has been described chiefly in primitive man, that is to say, in creatures living in precarious situations.

However, some physicians believe that this phenomenon exists also in our culture. Thus, according to Cannon, Dr. J. M. T. Finney, the well-known surgeon at the Johns Hopkins Hospital, apparently believed in it, since he absolutely would not operate on any patient who showed a strong fear of operation. Many instances are at hand of sudden death from fright, sight of blood, hypodermic injections, or from sudden immersion in water.

During the war a considerable number of unaccountable deaths were reported among soldiers in the armed forces in this country. These men died when they apparently were in good health. At autopsy no pathology could be observed.[7]

Of interest here also is that, according to Dr. R. S. Fisher, Coroner of the City of Baltimore, a number of individuals die each year after taking small, definitely sublethal doses of poison, or after inflicting small, nonlethal wounds on themselves; apparently they die as a result of the belief in their doom.

SUMMARY

A phenomenon of sudden death has been described that occurs in man, rats, and many other animals apparently as a result of hopelessness; this seems to involve overactivity primarily of the parasympathetic system. In this instance as in many others, the ideas of Walter Cannon opened up a new area of interesting, exciting research.

REFERENCES

1. Cannon, W. B. "Voodoo" death, *Am. Anthrop.* *44*: 169, 1942.
2. Basedow, H. *The Australian Aboriginal,* Adelaide, Australia, 1925.
3. Best, C. H. and Taylor, N. B. *Physiological Basis of Medical Practice* (Fifth Ed.), Baltimore, 1950.
4. Weiss, S. Instantaneous "physiologic" death, *New England J. Med.* 223: 793, 1940.
5. Irving, L. The action of the heart and circulation during diving, *Tr. New York Acad. Sc.* *5*: 11, 1942.
6. Clark, A. S. *Comparative Physiology of the Heart,* London, Cambridge, 1927.
7. Moritz, A. R. and Zamcheck, N. Sudden unexpected deaths of young soldiers, *Arch. Path.* *42*: 459, 1946.

31. The Kindling Effect*

J. Gaito

Physiological Psychology, 1974, *2*, 45-50. Reprinted by permission.

Animals subjected periodically to low-intensity electrical stimulation unilaterally to the amygdala or some other brain sites gradually develop automatic behaviors which culminate eventually in convulsions. Characteristic brain wave patterns accompany these behavioral changes. A 60-Hz sine wave with a 24-h interval provides the most optimum condition of stimulation. This kindling effect shows some characteristics similar to learning events, viz, relatively permanent changes, positive and negative transfer effects, involvement of limbic system. The results suggest that two factors are involved in the kindling process: a long-term effect of positive nature (probably due to modified neural circuitry) and a short-term "aftereffect" of negative nature.

If a rat is electrically stimulated unilaterally at a low intensity, e.g., in the amygdala, he will continue to explore his environment as he would normally do. However, after a number of trials with the same intensity of stimulation, he will rear up on his hind paws and the forelimbs will begin to convulse. Apparently, the brain conditions are being modified and the animal's susceptibility to convulsing is being decreased. This procedure wherein an animal's behavior is being modified slowly over a period of trials in response to an invariant stimulus has been termed the "kindling effect" (Goddard *et al.*, 1969; Goddard, 1972). In recent years, this paradigm has been used by a number of researchers with interesting results. The purpose of this paper is to review these efforts, mainly with the amygdala, the tissue which provides the most rapid kindling rate.

HISTORY

Electrical stimulation of the brain was initiated many years ago, e.g., in 1866 by Siminoff and in 1870 by Fritsch and Hitzig (Doty, 1970). However, it is only within recent years that such stimulation has become widespread. Brain stimulation research mainly began in the late 1940's and early 1950's with the discovery that stimulation of certain parts of the brainstem would lead to activation of large portions of the cortex. These results led to interesting theoretical formulations concerning the "reticular activation system" and its role in brain function (Delayfresnaye, 1954).

Other research which gave impetus to the brain stimulation movement was the self-stimulation experiments of Olds and Milner (1954). In these experiments, rats chose

* Preparation of this part was facilitated by support from the President's NRC Fund (Grant 32) from York University and a grant from the Ontario Society for Crippled Children.

electrical brain stimulation over other reinforcers, e.g., food, even when the organism had been deprived.

The reticular formation and self-stimulation research led to a tremendous number of investigators concerning themselves with brain stimulation aspects. However, it is only in recent research, by Goddard and his colleagues, that the changes associated with periodic brain stimulation (e.g., of the amygdala) and the development of seizure forms were the primary concern of the investigation. Previously, these changes were incidental to, and sometimes an embarrassment of, the main purpose of the research.

In 1955 Heath *et al.* reported that stimulation parameters with human amygdala that were initially subthreshold and caused amusement later caused intense fear with an impulse to run.

A few years later, it was shown with cats by Alonso-deFlorida and Delgado (1958) that a few hours of repeated electrical stimulation of the amygdala resulted in lasting electrophysiological and behavioral changes. In one cat, the experimental session resulted in a limited motor seizure which continued independently for 27 days and ended in death. Subsequently, Fonberg and Delgado (1961) observed that amygdaloid stimulation in cats had an inhibitory effect on feeding and learned behavior. The inhibition outlasted the stimulation and became more prolonged when the amygdaloid stimulation was repeated on different days. In one animal, the seizure threshold diminished, motor and electrical manifestations increased, and generalized seizure developed. Also, Delgado and Sevillano (1961) stimulated the cat hippocampus several times a day, eventually producing convulsive behavior.

In 1963, Gunne and Reis (and Reis and Gunne, 1965) found that electrical stimulation of the amygdala in cats initially caused facial twitching, turning, chewing and salivation. By the end of 3 h of intermittent stimulation, the same stimulus resulted in complete rage reactions including clawing, snarling, hissing, and attack. These responses continued after the termination of each train of amygdaloid stimulation.

Yoshii and Yamaguchi (1963) observed the development of a rage reaction in one cat after 40 days of repeated amygdaloid stimulation. The reaction lasted even after the animal returned to the cage, resulting in the destruction of its own electrodes. This result was obtained despite continuous care on the part of the authors to adjust the intensity of stimulation in an effort to avoid after discharge durations of greater than 5 sec. Other cats in their experiment developed more extensive after discharge, progressively more widespread interictal spiking, the emergence of seizure-associated head turning, or tonic-clonic convulsions.

In the self-stimulation studies of Wurtz and Olds (1963), more than half of the rats receiving amygdaloid stimulation developed seizures. It was not reported whether the seizures developed only after repeated stimulation. Bogacz *et al.* (1965) clearly showed that with self-stimulation electrodes in anterior lateral hypothalamus and septal area, the seizure thresholds diminished over time. The authors were surprised to find that the seizure thresholds declined to a greater extent than the self-stimulation thresholds, and in some cases eventually fell below the self-stimulation thresholds.

Stevens *et al.* (1969) and Ervin *et al.* (1969) presented examples of long-latency long-lasting psychological changes in both epileptic and nonepileptic humans. In these cases, as with most studies of electrical stimulation, only one hemisphere was stimulated at a time. The lasting aftereffects may be less noticeable if confined to one hemisphere than if bilaterally represented.

Although the initial brain stimulation research used electrical methods, some research which is pertinent to the kindling event was concerned with the effects of chemicals on brain aspects. In 1961, Morrell indicated that alumina cream on cortical tissue induced an epileptic focus. When the cream stimulated the cortex of one hemisphere, the homologous tissue showed similar activity. At first this activity appeared only when the stimulated cortex was active. Later the tissue of the nonstimulated hemisphere showed spontaneous excitation even when it was isolated from the stimulated one by cutting its connections.

Using cholinergic stimulation of the cat amygdala, Grossman (1963) observed very dramatic changes. A single bilateral injection of carbachol caused seizure activity that continued to reappear two or three times daily throughout the following 5-month observation period. Pronounced changes in disposition, including viciousness and hypersensitivity, were also observed.

Baxter (1967) observed behavioral changes that lasted several hours after cholinergic stimulation of the amygdala. One cat died overnight, possibly as a result of convulsions, and one cat remained resistant to handling on the day after the injection.

Belluzzi and Grossman (1969) reported that bilateral injection of carbachol into rat amygdala was followed by major alterations in avoidance learning which persisted for several weeks after the convulsions subsided. Similarly, other studies with carbachol injected into the rat amygdala (Goddard, 1969) indicated pronounced changes in certain types of avoidance behavior which often lasted for more than 2 weeks after the injection.

Although behavioral changes following electrical and/or chemical changes were reported often, it was Goddard and his colleagues who concentrated on these aspects in a systematic research program. A brief burst of subthreshold electrical stimulation to the amygdala will eventually lead to behavioral convulsions if repeated over a number of trials, separated by at least 20 min (Goddard, 1967; Goddard et al., 1969; McIntyre, 1970; Racine, 1972; Walters, 1970). A number of parametric and anatomical studies in the rat showed that the kindling effect is a relatively permanent transsynaptic change that results from electrical activation of neurons and cannot be explained simply in terms of tissue damage, poison, edema, or gliosis (Goddard et al., 1969).

Although the kindling effect can be obtained from stimulation of areas outside of the amygdala, responsive areas are largely restricted to the limbic system and related structures. Within the limbic system, the amygdala has been found to be particularly responsive. There is also a suggestion that the responsiveness of particular areas is related directly to the extent of their anatomical connections with the amygdala (Goddard et al., 1969).

A number of researchers showed that, attending behavioral changes during the kindling event, there were definite electrophysiological changes as well (Goddard et al., 1969; Racine, 1972; Tanaka, 1972). There is a unique wave form developed in the stimulated site, e.g., the amygdala, which later induces a similar wave in the homologous contralateral site.

Recently, chemical aspects of this phenomenon have been investigated. Tanaka (1972) was concerned with the effects of a number of chemicals on electrical activity and on the kindling rate with rabbits. He found that with some chemicals, e.g., phenobarbital, the usual electrical and behavioral responses during kindling were eliminated or reduced. Gaito and colleagues investigated soluble protein patterns during the kindling process and attempted to determine if kindling facilitation or retardation could be transferred from one animal to another. Negative transfer was reported with intraperitoneal administration of soluble proteins from kindled animals (Gaito and Gaito*). However, no differences were detected in the electrophoretic patterns of soluble proteins of rats at various stages in the kindling process (Gaito *et al.,* 1973).

VARIOUS ASPECTS OF THE KINDLING EFFECT

Behavioral

Goddard *et al.* (1969) reported a three-stage process during kindling. For example, electrical stimulation to the amygdala produced clonic convulsions on the average in about 15 trials. The initial stimulations have little effect on the animal's behavior (Stage 1—normal exploratory behavior); with several repetitions, overt indications of seizure activity can be observed, e.g., eye closure, chewing, salivation (Stage 2—behavioral automatisms); with further stimulations, these automatisms culminate in a complete convulsion (Stage 3—clonic convulsion; see Fig. 1). Although certain behaviors during Stage 2 such as eye closing and chewing are relatively stereotyped and easy to identify, other behaviors can be confused with those observed during Stage 1 (e.g., arrest, head turning to ipsilateral side). However, the clonic convulsions encountered in Stage 3 are relatively the same from animal to animal. The rat stands on its hind paws and bilateral clonic convulsions ensue; these continue after the electrical stimulation is terminated. Thus Stage 3 behavior is less variable and easier to identify than that of Stage 2. This three-stage process has also been reported in other laboratories (Tanaka, 1972; Gaito *et al.,* 1973).

Goddard *et al.* (1969) investigated the conditions under which kindling resulted. A 60-Hz current with a 24-h interval of stimulation provided the most optimum condition of stimulation. Kindling was also induced with intervals of 7 days and with shorter intervals (12, 8, 1, and 1/3 h). Intervals of 10 min or less resulted in adaptation—some

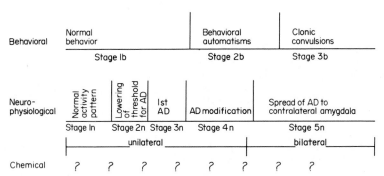

Fig. 1. Diagram to illustrate parallel events during kindling of amygdala unilaterally. First AD (after discharge) is a simple spike and wave form, 1 cps, with duration of from 6 to 50 sec (mean of 17 sec) and amplitude of 702 micro V (mean). AD changes from a simple to a complex wave, 3-5 cps, lasting from about 10 to 100 sec, with a mean amplitude of about 986 micro V. Stimulation of amygdala produces AD in ipsilateral amygdala and induces AD in contralateral amygdala after a number of ADs. ADs during this stage are complex waves, about 5 cps (with some bursts of 14-16 cps), of 50-350 sec duration (mean of 102 sec), with a mean amplitude of 986 micro V. Spikes from contralateral amygdala start at low amplitude and increase until they are equal to, or nearly equal to, those of the ipsilateral site. Complete clonic convulsions occur when the amplitudes of the spikes are about the same in both amygdalae.

---

* Gaito, J. and Gaito, S. Interanimal transfer of the kindling effect. Submitted for publication.

automatic behavior could be initiated but it would not persist. Effective kindling was also produced by other frequencies (25 and 150 Hz). Three hertz was ineffective—it provided neither the characteristic behavioral nor electrophysiological changes. The changes required the electrical stimulation (i.e., no spontaneous convulsions tended to occur), but once initiated, these changes persisted for many seconds after the termination of the current.

An interesting aspect of the kindling phenomenon is the relative permanency of the effect (Goddard et al., 1969). The convulsions occur either on the first trial or within a few trials, even after a 6-week interval of no stimulation (Goddard et al., 1969). Over a longer interval, there is usually the requirement of several trials for convulsions to occur. Thus, there is the suggestion of some loss in strength of the tendency over periods of nonstimulation. Goddard et al. (1969) reported about a 10% loss in rekindling over a 3-month period.

The effect occurs in rats, cats, monkeys (Goddard et al., 1969), and rabbits (Tanaka, 1972).

Neurological

By careful analysis using sine wave electrical stimulation, Goddard et al. (1969) indicated that the behavioral changes were not due to a pathological brain process but were a function of the stimulating parameters. A lesion placed at the site of the area to be stimulated eliminated the behavioral changes.

Many brain regions were not responsive, specifically the majority of the neocortex, the thalamus, and the brainstem. Those that were responsive to electrical stimulation extended from the olfactory bulbs to the entorhinal cortex, including the septal region and the hippocampus. Almost all points in this olfactory-limbic system gave positive effects. The amygdala was the most responsive; all amygdaloid nuclei appeared to be equally responsive. There was a tendency for the number of trials to the first clonic convulsion to correspond roughly with the extent of anatomical connections with the amygdaloid complex. The responsive areas with the number of trials to first convulsion were: amygdala, 15; globus pallidus, 22; pyriform cortex, 24; olfactory area, 29; anterior limbic field, 29; entorhinal cortex, 37; olfactory bulb, 44; septal area, 55; preoptic area, 63; caudate putamen, 74; hippocampus, 77. These areas fall roughly into two systems, the anterior limbic and the olfactory limbic. Stimulation of the first system produced tonic-clonic convulsions; convulsions from the second were clonic-clonic in nature.

Both positive and negative intraanimal transfer effects are possible (Goddard et al., 1969). Kindling one amygdala reduced the number of trials required to kindle the second amygdala. However, having kindled the second amygdala, interference resulted when rekindling the first amygdala. Positive transfer resulted not only from amygdala to amygdala but from amygdala to some other brain structure, e.g., septal region (Goddard et al., 1969).

Gaito and Gaito[1] reported negative transfer when portions of the soluble protein fraction of kindled rats were injected intraperitoneally into naive recipients.

Electrophysiological

A number of investigators have reported electrical changes during the kindling process (Goddard, 1972; Goddard et al., 1969; Racine, 1972). Figure 1 shows these changes in the amygdala of the rat (Racine, 1972). First there is the normal electrical pattern. With repeated stimulation, the threshold for an after discharge (AD) is decreased. Soon the AD appears; it is a simple spike and wave form, 1 cps, with a duration of about 6-50 sec and a mean amplitude of 702 micro V. The first AD appears before behavioral automatisms are observed. Upon further stimulation, the wave form becomes more complex and increases occur in frequency, duration, and amplitude. Then an AD is induced in the contralateral amygdala. At first the amplitude of this wave is lower than the AD in the ipsilateral amygdala. When the two are approximately equal in amplitude, clonic convulsions ensue.

Tanaka (1972) found somewhat similar electrical events with rabbits and indicated that the amygdaloid AD spread not only to the contralateral amygdala but to other parts of the brain as well, usually in an orderly sequence, viz., to the hippocampus first, then to the occipital cortex, and finally to the frontal cortex. (Tanaka recorded only from the amygdala, hippocampus, and frontal and occipital cortices.) The propagated AD usually disappeared concomitantly with or earlier than that of the original AD in the amygdala, although the hippocampus AD continued longer in some cases. Convulsive behavior coincided with the brain wave changes in the frontal cortex.

Chemical

With the changes in behavior and electrophysiology, obviously one would assume that chemical changes were also occurring (Fig. 1). Tanaka (1972) investigated the effects of a number of chemicals on electrophysiology and behavior after the "kindling effect" was complete. When the seizures were inhibited by a drug, amygdaloid stimulations were repeated with the same or stronger intensities every 20 to 60 min until the full seizure reappeared. Diazepam selectively abolished the behavioral responses and the frontal waves, but the amygdaloid AD remained almost unaffected. Acetazolamide modified the amygdaloid AD to an abortive form of short duration; although the convulsive behavior was suppressed, some behavioral automatisms were preserved. Phenobarbital, lidocaine, and methamphetamine eliminated the AD and behavioral responses. Pentetrazol facilitated the full effect, whereas diphenylhydantoin and chlorpromazine had little or no effect on electrographic and behavioral responses.

Gaito et al. (1973) found the same electrophoretic pattern of prealbumin region acidic proteins for amygdaloid kindled rats as for nonstimulated controls and for rats subjected to stimulation for varying periods prior to convulsions. An intraperitoneal injection of soluble proteins from convulsed rats resulted in a retardation in the kindling process with naive recipients if the injection contained the equivalent of two brain amounts. When one brain amounts were used, no effect was noted on the kindling rate (Gaito and Gaito[1]).

Effects on Learning

With some modification of neural tissue occurring during the kindling process, it might seem that other events which depend on this tissue would be affected. Such is the case. Goddard (1964) demonstrated that unilateral electrical stimulation of rat amygdala over a number of trials impaired acquisition of a conditioned suppression when delivered after each CS-US pairing. Pelegrino (1965) found that electrical stimulation of the amygdala in thirsty rats impaired the acquisition of a passive avoidance response to an electrified water spout. The intensity used in both of these studies was probably at a level so as to produce ADs, although this aspect was not indicated.

When the learning task was a one-trial passive avoidance event, Kesner and Doty (1968) obtained amnestic results when retention was tested 24 hr later if the electrical stimulation immediately after the learning event was at sufficient intensity to produce after discharges. Later research (McDonough and Kesner, 1971) showed that similar results occur without the appearance of ADs if bilateral stimulation of the amygdala is used. McDonough and Kesner also reported that unilateral stimulation produced amnesia if a lesion was made in the other amygdala.

McIntyre (1970) reported that convulsions elicited by unilateral amygdaloid stimulation of the amygdala produced two kinds of interference effects on conditioned emotional response learning (CER): retrograde amnesia, for events immediately preceding the convulsion; and prograde effect, an interference in the retention of events occurring at some time after the convulsions. Convulsions produced by stimulation of the anterior limbic field and stimulation of the amygdala not producing convulsions did not have these effects. In later work, McIntyre and Molino (1972) found that bilateral lesions of the amygdala produced the same impairment of CER learning as did the lesioning of one and kindling of the other. They reasoned that the kindled focus acts as a functional lesion interfering with the development of normal processes apparently required for learning to occur.

Bresnahan and Routtenberg (1972) reported that unilateral low-level stimulation did not disrupt acquisition in a repeated trials passive avoidance learning task but did impair retention. With the level of stimulation used, no ADs were present. The site responsible for the impairment was found to be the medial nucleus of the amygdala. Stimulation of the dorsal hippocampus, however, did not affect acquisition or retention.

THEORETICAL POSSIBILITIES

Goddard et al. (1969) and McIntyre and Goddard (1973) indicated that stimulation of one amygdala facilitated kindling in the other amygdala (intraanimal positive transfer), although increased latency resulted. Rekindling of the first amygdala was then impaired (intraanimal negative transfer). To account for these effects, and for the development of convulsions from the initial stimulation, Goddard et al. (1969) maintained that two specific but widespread neural circuits were established. One was developed during stimulation of the first amygdala. During kindling of the other amygdala, the second circuit utilizes and ties into response elements of the first circuit and triggers convulsions in fewer trials than were required with stimulation of the first amygdala. As a result of this utilization, however, the circuits are changed to correspond with the activity of the second region and lose some of their correspondence with the first one. A few trials are necessary to reestablish the original connection with the first circuit.

In the development of convulsions, the modified neural circuits could be limbic-limbic or limbic-motor in nature. Research by Racine et al. (1972) suggested that this development was dependent upon the increased strength of limbic-limbic connections rather than the strengthening of limbic-motor connections.

Goddard (1972) and McIntyre and Goddard (1973) suggested a two-factor model to account for the original kindling and for the transfer effects. These are: (a) a long-term effect of positive nature, due to modified neural circuitry; (b) a short-term "after-effect" of negative nature. The modified neural circuitry are those discussed above. The exact nature and mechanism of the "aftereffect" are not indicated. The "aftereffect'' is able to suppress seizure activity in different parts of the nervous system, is proportional to the number of convulsions, and spontaneously dissipates over time: complete dissipation occurs in 2 weeks or so (Goddard and McIntyre, 1973). It is possible that the ''aftereffect'' is chemical in nature. Thus, the interanimal retardation effect of Gaito and Gaito[1] may be expressing the Goddard and McIntyre intraanimal ''aftereffect''.

IMPLICATIONS OF THE KINDLING RESULTS

An Analogue of Learning

Goddard et al. (1969) pointed out the similarity of kindling to the learning process. For example, each shows relatively permanent changes resulting from repeated experiences, the limbic system is implicated in both, both involve transsynaptic changes in function, both demonstrate positive transfer effects, and in both cases the acquisition of a new response results in retroactive interference with old responses. A number of other individuals have noted the similarity of kindling aspects to learning events (e.g., Kesner and Doty, 1968; McIntyre, 1970; Bresnahan and Routtenberg, 1972). The results discussed above (Effects on Learning) also suggest the similarity of kindling aspects to the learning process.

This paradigm was suggested by Gaito (1974) as a technique which would allow for the evaluation of chemical events underlying a behavioral change in molecular psychobiology research without some of the problems associated with the usual learning task. He emphasized the stereotypy and automaticity of the third stage and relative freedom from factors such as motivation, stress, variability, and other aspects which contaminate usual learning paradigms. Thus, this paradigm could be useful as a ''learning type'' design without some of the extralearning problems.

An Analogue of Epilepsy

The similarity between kindling and epilepsy is quite obvious as a number of individuals have indicated (Goddard, 1972). Kindling appears to be an experimentally produced type of epilepsy. Thus, these procedures would seem to provide an excellent paradigm with which to evaluate various chemicals and agents which affect convulsion susceptibility (Tanaka, 1972; Gaito and Gaito[1]).

Possible Effect During Therapeutic Brain Stimulation

Goddard and McIntyre (1972) pointed out that the kindling results have implications for the use in humans of therapeutic brain stimulation via depth electrodes. Although some positive results may occur with the repeated stimulations that are involved, these repeated trials may induce the development of seizure activity and, eventually, clinical convulsions in response to the stimulating current. Thus, in each individual case, the possible benefits to be obtained via stimulating should be weighed against the possible development of convulsive tendencies.

REFERENCES

Alonson-deFlorida, F., & Delgado, J. M. R. Lasting behavioral and EEG changes in cats induced by prolonged stimulation of amygdala. American Journal of Physiology, 1958, 193, 223-229.

Baxter, B. L. Comparison of the behavioral effects of electrical or chemical stimulation applied at the same brain loci. Experimental Neurology, 1967, 19, 412-432.

Belluzzi, J. D., & Grossman, S. P. Avoidance learning: Long lasting deficits after temporal lobe seizure. Science, 1969, 166, 1435-1437.

Bogacz, J., St. Laurent, J., & Olds, J. Dissociation of self-stimulation and epileptiform activity. Electroencephalography & Clinical Neurophysiology, 1965, 19, 75-87.

Bresnahan, E., & Routtenberg, A. Memory disruption by unilateral low level, sub-seizure stimulation of the medial amygdaloid nucleus. Physiology & Behavior, 1972, 9, 513-525.

Delayfresnaye, J. F. (Ed.) Brain mechanisms and consciousness. Oxford: Blackwell, 1954.

Delgado, J. M. R. & Sevillano, M. Evolution of repeated hippocampal seizures in the cat. Electroencephalography & Clinical Neurophysiology, 1961, 13, 722-733.

Doty, R. W. Electrical stimulation of the brain in behavioral context. In P. H. Mussen and M. R. Rosenzweig (Eds.), Annual review of psychology. Palo Alto: Stanford University Press, 1969.

Ervin, F. R., Mark, V. H., & Stevens, J. Behavioral and affective responses to brain stimulation in man. Proceedings of the American Psychopathological Association, 1969, 58, 54.

Fonberg, E., & Delgado, J. M. R. Avoidance and alimentary reactions during amygdala stimulation. Journal of Neurophysiology, 1961, 24, 651-664.

Gaito, J. A biochemical approach to learning and memory: Thirteen years later. In G. Newton and A. Reisen (Eds.), Advances in psychobiology, Vol. 2. New York: Wiley, 1974.

Gaito, J., Hopkins, R., & Pelletier, W. Interanimal transfer and chemical events underlying the kindling effect. Bulletin of the Psychonomic Society, 1973, 1, 319-321.

Goddard, G. V. Amygdaloid stimulation and learning in the rat. Journal of Comparative & Physiological Psychology, 1964, 58, 23-39.

Goddard, G. V. Development of epileptic seizures through brain stimulation at low intensity. Nature, 1967, 214, 1020-1021.

Goddard, G. V. Analysis of avoidance conditioning following cholinergic stimulation of amygdala in rats. Journal of Comparative & Physiological Psychology, 1969, 68 (Monogr. Suppl. 2, Pt. 2), 1-18.

Goddard, G. V. Long term alteration following amygdaloid stimulation. In B. E. Eleftheriou (Ed.), The neurobiology of the amygdala. New York: Plenum, 1972.

Goddard, G. V., & McIntyre, D. C. Some properties of a lasting epileptogenic trace kindled by repeated electrical stimulation of the amygdala in humans. Paper presented at the Third International Congress of Psychosurgery, Cambridge, 1972.

Goddard, G. V., McIntyre, D. C., & Leech, C. K. A permanent change in brain function resulting from daily electrical stimulation. Experimental Neurology, 1969, 25, 295-330.

Grossman, S. P. Chemically induced epileptiform seizures in the cat. Science, 1963, 142, 409-411.

Gunne, L. M., & Reis, D. J. Changes in brain catecholamines associated with electrical stimulation of amygdaloid nucleus. Life Sciences, 1963, 11, 804-812.

Heath, R. G., Monroe, R. R., & Mickle, W. A. Stimulation of the amygdaloid nucleus in a schizophrenic patient. American Journal of Psychiatry, 1955, 111, 862-863.

Kesner, R. P., & Doty, R. Amnesia produced in cats by local seizure activity initiated from the amygdala. Experimental Neurology, 1968, 21, 58-68.

McDonough, J. H., & Kesner, R. P. Amnesia produced by brief electrical stimulation of the amygdala or dorsal hippocampus in cats. Journal of Comparative & Physiological Psychology, 1971, 77, 171-178.

McIntyre, D. C. Differential amnestic effect of cortical vs. amygdaloid elicited convulsion in rats. Physiology & Behavior, 1970, 5, 747-753.

McIntyre, D. C., & Goddard, G. V. Transfer, interference and spontaneous recovery of convulsions kindled from the rat amygdala. Electroencephalography & Clinical Neurophysiology, 1973, 35, 533-543.

McIntyre, D. C., & Molino, A. Amygdala lesions and CER learning: Long term effect of kindling. Physiology & Behavior, 1972, 8, 1055-1058.

Morrell, F. Electrophysiological contributions to the neural basis of learning. Physiological Reviews, 1961, 41, 442-494.

Olds, J., & Milner, P. Positive reinforcement produced by electrical stimulation of septal area and other regions of rat brain. Journal of Comparative & Physiological Psychology, 1954, 47, 419-427.

Pellegrino, L. The effects of amygdaloid stimulation on passive avoidance. Psychonomic Science, 1965, 2, 189-190.

Racine, R. J. Modification of seizure activity by electrical stimulation: I. After discharge threshold. Electroencephalography & Clinical Neurophysiology, 1972, 32, 269-279.

Racine, R. J., Okujava, V., & Chipashvili, S. Modification of seizure activity by electrical stimulation: III. Mechanisms. Electroencephalography & Clinical Neurophysiology, 1972, 32, 295-299.

Reis, D. J., & Gunne, L. M. Brain catecholamines: Relation to the defense reaction evoked by amygdaloid stimulation in cat. Science, 1965, 149, 450-452.

Stevens, J. R., Mark, V. H., Ervin, F., Pacheco, P., & Suematsu, K. Deep temporal stimulation in man. Long latency, long lasting psychological changes. Archives of Neurology, 1969, 21, 157-169.

Tanaka, A. Progressive changes of behavioral and electroencephalographic responses to daily amygdaloid stimulation in rabbits. Fukuoka Acts Medica, 1972, 63, 152-164.

Walters, D. J. Sporadic inter-ictal discharges in kindled epileptogenic foci. Unpublished MA thesis, Dalhousie University, 1970.

Wurtz, R. H., & Olds, J. Amygdaloid stimulation and operant reinforcement in the rat. Journal of Comparative & Physiological Psychology, 1963, 56, 941-949.

Yoshii, N., & Yamaguchi, Y. Conditioning of seizure discharges with electrical stimulation of the limbic structures in cats. Folia Psychiatrica et Neurologica Japonica (Niigata), 1963, 17, 276-281.

32. "Whirling Behavior" in Dogs as Related to Early Experience

W. R. Thompson, R. Melzack and T. H. Scott

Science, 1956, *123*, 939. Copyright 1956 by The American Association for the Advancement of Science. Reprinted by permission.

In the course of 3 years of experimentation on the relationship of early experience in dogs (Scottish terriers) to their later behavior, there has appeared an interesting phenomenon that is worth reporting separately (*1*). This is the occurrence of "whirling fits" in a number of dogs that were restricted during early life.

Restriction is imposed by rearing the experimental animals from 1 to 8 or 10 months of age in isolation cages (one dog per cage) that are so constructed that the dog inside each can never see any more than the floor of the cage above or the ceiling of the room. By means of a small side compartment adjoining the living space and separated from it by a sliding panel, feeding and cleaning can be accomplished without exposing the restricted animal to the outside environment. After the period of restriction is over, the experimental "Scotties" are compared by means of psychological tests with their littermates which have been reared normally as pets in homes.

Many striking differences have appeared between the normal and the restricted dogs in all phases of behavior, including intelligence, activity, emotionality, and social behavior. These are reported in full elsewhere (*2*). More bizarre than any of these effects of early restriction are the afore-mentioned whirling fits. These have appeared in eight out of eleven severely restricted animals. The three exceptions, while highly active and excitable, have not, to our knowledge, shown the extreme behavior discussed here.

Whirling can be described as follows: very rapid, jerky running in a tight circle; shrill, agonized yelping; barking and snarling; and tail snapping and tail biting. The syndrome may last from 1 to 10 minutes. It is usually heralded by certain characteristic signs. The dog suddenly becomes motionless, cocking its head up and back, as if looking at its own tail. It begins to growl viciously, and its eyes take on a glazed expression. These signs may continue for a minute or two, increasing in intensity until the full-blown fit occurs. To all appearances, whirling does not seem to be under voluntary control but to be "driven". The dog does not seem to be able to control its behavior and cannot usually be distracted even by fairly intense stimuli.

Whatever its nature and causes, whirling is a peculiar and striking form of behavior that is worth further investigation. Several points concerning it should be noted. In the first place, it seems to vary in degree, with respect to both intensity and duration.

Second, although many of the fits appear to occur spontaneously (in that the immediate causes are not known), they usually seem to be set off by some change in the

307

stimulus-environment. This change may be anything from the mere introduction of a food dish into the cage to electric shock or restraint in a harness for a period of time.

Third, all the dogs showing whirling fits shared, to some degree, a common ancestry. All were descendants of three Scotties purchased from Hamilton Station, Bar Harbor, Maine, and bred, within themselves and to outside dogs, for several generations. However, the three animals not showing this behavior were also related to this strain. Consequently, it is difficult to make any obvious inferences concerning the possible genetic origin of the trait.

Fourth, all dogs showing whirling have had a background of severe restriction in early life. None of their normal littermates have shown such behavior. At the same time, since the three exceptions have also undergone restriction, this kind of early experience is not a sufficient condition for the appearance of the symptoms, although it may be a necessary one.

In view of the foregoing points, it is difficult to know what ultimate factors predisposed some animals to whirling fits. Diet is a possible explanation, although it could not be the only cause, since all the animals in the laboratory were fed the same amount and type of ration made up according to the specifications of several experts in dog care. All dogs received, during a typical week, meat (liver, Pard, hamburger), dog biscuits, Purina Dog Chow, vegetables, codliver oil, and milk while they were puppies. The restricted animals showed appetites as good or better than normals. At the same time, we cannot rule out the possibility that this diet might have been inadequate for dogs raised in severe restriction, even though it appeared to be adequate for dogs living in normal environments.

The possibility that whirling was caused by a specific irritation in the tail—thus causing the circling and tail snapping—is unlikely. It does not seem reasonable to suppose that such extreme behavior could be set off so easily and set off only under special conditions involving a change in the sensory environment. When tail injuries did occur, they appeared definitely to be the result rather than the cause of whirling. Consequently, we are inclined to feel that the behavior is central and not peripheral in origin.

Finally, it must be mentioned that the dogs were constantly checked for signs of worms and distemper by examination of their feces and by noting any decline in appetite. There was no evidence of ill health among any of the experimental dogs during their period of restriction. After removal from restriction, they were examined more carefully by a veterinarian, with negative results.

Accordingly, there are considerable grounds for supposing that whirling is dependent, at least partly, on the conditions of restriction imposed during early life. Whether or not it can properly be described as epileptiform is a moot point. None of the parasympathetic components of true seizures were ever observed in the dogs. On the other hand, the gross features of its expression would suggest that it is essentially a related phenomenon.

REFERENCES AND NOTES

1. The observations reported here are part of a project of the McGill Psychological Laboratory supported by a grant-in-aid from the Rockefeller Foundation. The behavior described in the article has been filmed, and the film will soon be available.
2. R. Melzack. *J. Comp. Physiol. Psychol.* 47, 166 (1954); W. R. Thompson and Woodburn Heron, *ibid.* 47, 77 (1954) and *Can. J. Psychol.* 8, 17 (1954).

Section IX

DISORDERS OF CHILDHOOD

33. Toward an Animal Model of Depression: A Study of Separation Behavior in Dogs

E. C. SENAY

Journal of Psychiatric Research, 1966, *4*, 65-71. Reprinted by permission.

INTRODUCTION

Depressive or depressive-like states consisting of anorexia, weight loss, decrease in motor activity, slowing of responses and loss of usual concerns have been observed in a variety of animals. As in the human situation, object loss has been frequently associated with the onset of these states and reunion with the lost object has been noted to be curative. Three sources can be cited to support the contention that such states exist in animals. First there are the observations of naturalists, ethologists, and comparative psychologists. Yerkes,[1] for example, attributed the high death rate of newly captured gorillas to 'psychogenic' factors citing the loss of familiar surroundings and the severance of all meaningful social bonds as antecedent causes of their deaths. Yerkes also observed depression in chimpanzees and again suggested separation as a probable cause. Hebb[2] reported the occurrence of spontaneous depressions in a chimpanzee but did not speculate upon etiology. Scott[3] observed these states in isolated dogs. Kohler[4] observed anorexia in separated monkeys. Lorenz[5] described behavioral changes following object loss in birds and in dogs. Hediger[6] noted 'it is a commonplace among zoo biologists that single animals often lose their appetites and that food intake is materially increased by the so-called social factor, i.e. association with a companion.' A second source of evidence stems from a large body of anecdotes gathered from discussions with veterinarians, animal keepers and people with household pets. These anecdotes indicate that depressive-like syndromes are also seen in domestic animals and that loss of a significant object seems to be related to their appearance. An unexpected suggestion was that reunion behavior might be of interest.

Preliminary observations by the author on domestic dogs undergoing separation constitute a third source. A major depression or withdrawal state was not observed but these observations did confirm that some animals do exhibit behavioral changes following object loss. They also suggested that the factors of temperament and pre-loss levels of gratification would be important variables in separation phenomenon. With respect to temperament it was observed that stable animals exhibited few overt signs in association with object loss; 'nervous' or 'high strung' animals were much more likely to evidence disturbed behavior, e.g. refusal to eat or drink, weight loss, withholding of urine and feces, tremulousness, hyper or hypo activity and increased aggression.

With respect to gratification it was observed that animals who had been infantilized by their owners were more liable to exhibit disturbed behavior in separation periods.

This paper reports an exploratory study of object loss and reunion behavior in German Shepherd dogs. The purposes of this study were to see—in an experimental setting—(1) if object loss would be associated with discernible behavioral changes (2) to see what the nature of these changes might be (3) to see if the 'depressive' syndrome described above might not appear in one or more of the experimental animals and (4) to develop a methodology in this area. Engel[7], Lehman[8], Saul[9] and others have cited the need for such animal models of separation and depression.

METHOD

The author formed a relationship with each of a litter of six three-week-old German Shepherd pups. For the next nine months he was their sole consistent human figure. Feeding, grooming, training, and communal play sessions were centered on the presence of the author during this period. Then for a two month 'separation' period the animals had no contact with the author. During this period a caretaker fed the animals, recorded data from photoelectric counters but did not speak to the animals, touch them or observe them in any formal way. A one-month 'reunion' period followed in which the author assumed again the complete care of the animals and the pre-separation routine of observations and contacts was re-established.

Mode of Initiating Contact and Relating to the Animals

Whenever possible, the author remained passive in the initiation of contact with the animals. This mode of initiating contact was suggested by the work of W. Stanley[10] and the theoretical considerations of T. C. Schneirla.[11] The author's observations tended to confirm the theory that low intensity passive objects evoke approach behavior from infant animals. In both individual and group contacts the author responded to the animals in a warm and friendly manner attempting to maximize the amount of petting and gentle handling.

Measurements

1. *Rankings*. (a) *Temperament*—as operationally defined by the approach-avoidance behavior of the animals with respect to the author when he presented himself in the passive fashion described below. The animals were ranked daily on this scale. The author would enter a pen, get down on one knee and observe the behavior of the animal for a three-minute period. The animal who approached, sought the most contact and displayed the least amount of avoidance behavior was ranked 1. Avoidance behavior consisted of a delay in approach, often in visible back and forth motions on the part of the animal before approaching or withdrawing. The animal who exhibited the greatest amount of avoidance and did not sustain contact (if made) was ranked 6.

(b) *Response to discipline*—ranking here indicates the degree of the disruption of the social bond between the author and any given animal caused by necessary disciplinary measures. A rank of 1 indicates that the animal accepted discipline with the least amount of subsequent avoidance behavior. A rank of 6 indicates that disciplinary action on the part of the author was followed by the most prolonged avoidance patterns in the behavior of the animal.

(c) *Response to training*—again 1 denotes easiest to train—did not exhibit avoidance patterns in response to training procedures; 6 most difficult, exhibited most prolonged avoidance patterns. (The animals were trained to respond to simple commands i.e. sit, come, heel, etc.)

(d) *Approach avoidance behavior in communal play sessions*—the author would remain passive and rank the animals on the frequency and duration of their spontaneous approach and contact behavior.

2. *Independent observations—the behavior rating protocols.* A behavior rating protocol consisting of check lists and an open-ended section for free description was filled out by eleven independent observers in each period of the study. The rating situation was conceptualized as a confrontation between rater and animal with the rater's behavior roughly standardized. The protocols were read to gain an impression of the behavior of the animals in the rating situation during each phase of the study. Scores were constructed for each animal in each period on the following scales:

Scale AG *Aggression*—i.e. the animal reacted to the presence of the observer by exhibiting behavior which showed intent to attack, injure, frighten or which indicated that the animal was angry, generally hostile, or mildly aggressive.

Scale OS *Object seeking*—i.e. the animal reacted to the presence of the observer by exhibiting behavior which would lead to the formation of a positive social bond.

Scale OA *Object avoidance*—i.e. the animal reacted to the presence of the observer by exhibiting behavior which would not lead to the formation of a positive social bond. (This scale does not include aggressive behavior scored on Scale AG.)

Scale GMR *Gross motor-response to the presence of the rater*—this scale attempted to quantify in a rough way the motor component of the animal's response to the presence of the rater.

3. *Activity.* Activity was recorded by means of photo-electric systems beamed across the inside pens. (It was not possible to maintain functioning photo-electric systems in the outside pens and difficulty was encountered in maintaining the inside pen systems, consequently reliable data are available on only three animals.)

4. *Body weight.* Weight was obtained and charted every three days in the pre-separation and reunion periods. During separation the second experimenter observed for signs of anorexia.

RESULTS AND OBSERVATIONS

(1) Temperament and Responses to Training and Discipline: (age 3 weeks–9½ months)

The characterizations of temperament and the rankings of responses to training and discipline are summarized in Table 1. As is evident from inspection of the table, there was consistency and predictability in the behavioral patterns of the animals under varying conditions. Animals of the approach temperament (1, 2) created stable social bonds with the author, were easy to train, and accepted discipline without developing avoidance patterns. Animals of the avoidance temperament (3, 4, 5 and 6) socialized less well, were more difficult to train, and developed avoidance patterns following discipline.

Table 1. Temperament and Response to Training and Discipline

Animal no.	Overall rank:* approach avoidance test		Characterization of temperament		Overall rank: training	Overall rank: discipline	Presence of tachycardia or urination†	
	(months)		(months)		(months)	(months)	(months)	
	0-3	3-9	0-3	3-9	0-9	0-9	0-3	3-9
1	1	3	App	App	2	2	**	
2	2	1	App	App	1	1		
3	3	2	Avoid	App	3.5	3.5	*	
4	4	4	Avoid	Avoid	3.5	3.5	****	*
5	5	5	Avoid	Avoid	5	5	**	
6	6	6	Avoid	Avoid	6	6	****	***
							****	
							**	

* Daily ranks were added and the sum divided by the total number of rankings made. The resulting figure were used for the overall ranks.
† Indicates presence of tachycardia and/or urination on one day.

(2) Pre-separation Behavior: (age 8-9 ½ months) Observations and Scores of the Independent Raters

In the pre-separation rating situation animals of the approach temperament had high scores on the object seeking scale and low scores on the object avoidance and aggression scales while the converse was true for animals of the avoidance temperament. (Table 2 below.) In five of six instances the animals reacted to new objects as one would have predicted from their early behavior in the temperament rating situation (0-3 months). The remaining animal (No. 3) during the course of maturation had developed a stable approach pattern toward the author which it maintained toward the independent raters in this period.

Table 2. Behavior Rating Scales*

Animal	Pre-separation				Separation				Reunion†			
	AG	OS	OA	GMR	AG	OS	OA	GMR	AG	OS	OA	GMR
1	0	13	3	40	0	20	2	46	0	21	0	53
2	0	16	2	48	0	18	0	57	0	20	0	57
3	0	14	3	45	0	2	14	24	0	5	15	36
4	0	3	12	16	0	4	16	23	0	3	19	17
5	7	11	0	61	14	7	0	68	16	4	0	66
6	5	7	6	41	10	10	0	66	15	6	0	67

* The range of possible scores for a given animal on the AG, OS, OA scales was 0 to 22. Each protocol was scored 0, 1, or 2 on each of the three scales (e.g. in the pre-separation period on the AG scale animal No. 5, was scored 2 on two protocols, 1 on three protocols and 0 on six protocols hence his score of seven). It should be kept in mind that these are ordinal scales.[12] The AG score of 14 on animal No. 5, in the separation period does not represent twice as much aggression. (The author scored the protocols. A random 40 per cent sample of the protocols was scored by an independent judge. Agreement was 96 per cent.)
†See reunion period. The total scores do not reflect the differences between the first two weeks and the final two weeks of this period.

Key: AG = Aggression scale   OA = Object avoidance
     OS = Object seeking   GMR = Gross motor response

(3) Separation Behavior: (age 9½-11½ months)

In this period the observations of the raters and the scores on the behavior rating scales indicated that animals of the approach temperament exhibited an increase in object seeking behavior while animals of the avoidance temperament exhibited increases in aggression and/or avoidance behavior. Animal No. 3 reverted as it were to her early mode of avoidance. The gross motor response scores increased with increases in object seeking (1, 2) or aggression (5, 6) and were low in the two animals exhibiting almost total avoidance behavior.

(4) Reunion Behavior: (age 11½-12½ months)

In the first two weeks of the reunion period the scores and the descriptions of the independent raters indicated that there was an intensification of the behavior which had become characteristic for a given animal during the separation period. In the final two weeks of the reunion period pre-separation modes of responding to the raters were re-established.

(5) Activity

The curves of the inside pen activity of nos. 4, 5 and 6 are presented in Fig. 1.

The marked decrease in activity noted during the separation period has to be interpreted cautiously. Inside pen activity alone was measured. The total amount of acti-

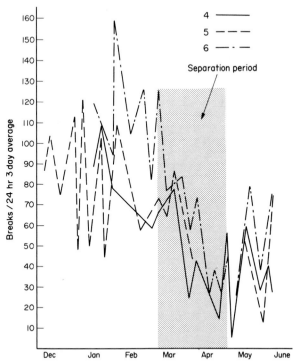

Fig. 1. Friedman two-way analysis of variance performed on the total amounts of activity for successive three-day periods in each condition yields a $X_r = 24.47$ which for 2 degrees of freedom has a $p < 0.001$.

vity may not have changed, for the animals may have been more active in their outside pens. The activity curves indicate that there was a shift in the locus of activity if not a total decrease during the separation period. In two of three instances counts began to increase during the final two weeks of the reunion period.

(6) Appetite and Weight

Anorexia was not observed during the separation period. The animals gained weight as would be expected from the extrapolation of their growth curves.

DISCUSSION

The behavior of the animals in the three conditions of the study can be partially analysed in terms of an interaction between temperament and gratification. With loss of gratification (separation period) dispositions to respond to the presentation of new objects with approach or avoidance were increased. Examination of the pre-separation behavior of the animals in the light of these changes leads to the conclusion that the gratification derived from having an object had a modulating or suppressive effect on temperament; that is, object seeking was less necessary for animals of the approach temperament while the disorganizing aspects of object presentation were less intense for animals of the avoidance temperament. There was also suggestive evidence that re-establishing object relationships in the reunion period called for adjustments in the behavior of the animals which required time for them to accomplish.

It is recognized that these findings and the hypotheses derived from them are highly tentative. A small number of experimental animals was used but there were large numbers of observations on each animal and these observations had a high degree of internal consistency. The results of this study suggest that future attempts to precipitate depressions in animals should involve (a) measures of temperament; that is, longitudinal observations on the quality of responsiveness to objects for separation behavior seems to be strongly influenced by this variable and (b) more gratification for the experimental animals: in order for a profound behavioral change to occur in response to separation gratification from the object probably has to reach a level of intensity which was not possible in this study. The animals had contact with the author for one or two hours a day but were confined to their pens for the balance of each twenty-four hour period.

Some additional observations deserve discussion. The author was impressed by what seemed to be a correlation between intensity of arousal and subsequent approach avoidance behavior in the infant animals. Animals who were highly aroused always displayed avoidance. Animals who were less strongly aroused exhibited approach behavior. (Tachycardia and urination appeared in No. 6 when he was most highly aroused.) Early in life the animals seemed to possess differences in their neurophysiologic arousal systems. These differences seemed to determine whether object presentation would have organizing (approach temperament) or disorganizing (avoidance temperament) effects on the behavioral patterns of the animals. Schnierla made similar kinds of observations on approach withdrawal adjustment in infra-mammalian species. He constructed an 'input theory' to account for them; that is, high intensity stimulation from the object led to withdrawal while low intensity stimulation led to approach, but his theory made no provision for individual variation. The observations made here suggest that with stimulation from the object held constant, animals possess individual differences in their arousal mechanisms and furthermore, that these differences are crucially involved in separation phenomena.

The observations made in this study support the contention that animals exhibit behavioral changes following object loss and indicate that experimental psycho-biologic models of separation can be constructed in animals. Such models should be of interest to many different disciplines in the behavioral sciences.

SUMMARY

Six dogs were raised in an experimental setting by the author who was their sole consistent object. The animals were ranked daily in an approach-avoidance test and their temperament characterized in approach avoidance terms. Eleven independent observers scored the animals on object seeking, object avoiding and aggressive behavior in each of three conditions (1) a pre-separation period in which the animals' relationship with the author was undisturbed (2) a separation condition in which the animals had no contact with the author and (3) a reunion period. Body weight and gross motor activity were also measured.

Separation was associated with increases in object seeking for animals of the approach temperament and increases in object avoidance and aggressive behavior for animals of the avoidance temperament. Activity was significantly decreased in those animals for whom reliable data was obtained. Reunion was associated with further deviations from pre-separation behavior patterns. These results tentatively indicate that models of separation and depression can be constructed in experimental animals.

Acknowledgement—The author wishes to express his thanks to D. X. Freedman for his advice and encouragement.

REFERENCES

1. Yerkes, R. M. *The Great Apes.* p. 298, Yale University Press, New Haven, 1929.
2. Hebb, D. O. Spontaneous neurosis in chimpanzees. *Psychosom. Med.* **9**, 3, 1947.
3. Scott, J. P. Personal communication.
4. Kohler, W. *The Mentality of Apes,* p. 9, Kegan Paul, Trench, Trubner, London, 1927.
5. Lorenz, K. *King Solomon's Ring,* pp. 56, 120, 173, Thomas Y. Crowell, New York, 1952.
6. Hediger, H. *Studies of the Psychology and Behavior of Animals in Zoos and Circuses.* p. 68, Butterworth, London, 1955.
7. Engel, G. L. Selection of clinical material in psychosomatic medicine; the need for a new physiology. *Psychosom. Med.* **16**, 368, 1954.
8. Lehmann, H. E. Psychiatric concepts of depression. *Can. psychiat. Ass. J.* **4**, 1, 1959. Special supplement.
9. Saul, L. J. Psychosocial medicine and observations of animals. *Psychom. Med.* **24**, 58, 1962.
10. Stanley, W. Differential human handling as reinforcing events in the social development of puppies. *Am. Psychol.* **13**, 383, 1958. Abstract.
11. Schneirla, T. C. A theoretical consideration of the basis for approach withdrawal adjustments in behavior. *Psychology Bull.* **36**, p. 6, 501, 1939.
12. Siegel, S. *Non Parametric Statistics.* pp. 23, 166, McGraw-Hill, 1956.

34. Stereotyped Behavior of the Infant Chimpanzee

R. K. DAVENPORT and E. W. MENZEL

Archives of General Psychiatry, 1963 *8*, 99-104. Copyright 1963 by the American Medical Association. Reprinted by permission.

Over the past several years at the Yerkes Laboratories, the authors have engaged in the study of the effects of various kinds of early experience on the psychological, social, and physical development of the chimpanzee. During the course of the study, we have been particularly impressed by the stereotyped behaviors exhibited by chimpanzee infants. These behaviors are characterized by the frequent, almost mechanical, repetition of a posture or movement which varies only slightly in form from time to time, and which to the human observer serves no obvious function.

The purpose of the present paper is to describe these stereotypies, and to indicate the resemblance of chimpanzee stereotypies to some repetitive behaviors which are commonly observed in mentally defective,[1] blind,[2] and psychotic[15] humans. Evidence will be presented to show that stereotypy is related to rearing variables, developmental status, the immediate stimulus situation, and to various forms of ongoing activity. Finally, suggestions will be made regarding the possible mechanisms by which stereotypies develop and are maintained.

MATERIALS AND METHODS

Subjects—The subjects (S) were 19 chimpanzees, divided into 5 groups which differ according to the environment in which they were reared. The study included 4 restricted environment conditions and 1 enriched environment condition.

Restricted Groups: Sixteen S's born at the Laboratories were separated from their mother on the first day of life. They were placed in illuminated gray cribs measuring $48 \times 24 \times 28$ in., where they remained for 2 years. Diapering and feeding were done with a minimum of interaction between caretaker and animal, such interaction amounting to less than 10 minutes a day.[3] At no time did the S see out of the crib.

Five infants (maximum restriction group) were maintained individually in cribs with bare walls, floor, and ceiling. Three other animals (visual added group) were raised in a similar condition with the addition that S was exposed to a wide variety of visual stimuli. The visual stimuli were colored and black-and-white, nonrepresentational paintings, and stationary and moving stereometric objects, none of which could be touched. Four other infants (restricted environment-manipulation added group) were raised in the standard isolation condition except that the cribs were provided with manipulanda in the form of switches and a lever. These manipulanda were exposed

Submitted for publication Jan. 26, 1962.

Support for the major part of this research was provided through Grants M-1005 and H-5691 from the National Institutes of Health and from a grant by the Ford Foundation.

daily throughout the rearing period. Four infants (restricted environment-social added group) were given social enrichment in the form of a companion chimpanzee of similar age. Members of each pair were housed individually in a standard bare crib and the cribs placed end to end so that the animals were separated only by bars. This arrangement prevented complete passage into the adjacent crib but otherwise permitted free interaction between the animals.

Wild-Born Enriched Environment Group: The fifth group consisted of 3 animals that were raised in an environment which, short of home rearing, was as enriched as reasonably could be provided. These infants were wild-born and were procured when between 4 and 7 months old (estimated age). They lived together in a large open cage (88 × 62 × 37 in.) and were provided with toys and exercise equipment. They were handled, disciplined, and played with by laboratory personnel and caretakers.

Procedure—The data presented here were derived from: (*a*) 15-second observations made 3 to 5 times daily, from birth until 21 months; (*b*) data gathered in a battery of some 25 tests that commenced when S was 21 months of age, and continued until he was over 40 months of age; (*c*) laboratory diary records.

RESULTS AND COMMENT

Classification of Stereotypies in Chimpanzee Infants—The stereotypies in infant chimpanzees were topographically similar in form to behaviors exhibited by some normal children[7] and seen in exaggerated and persistent form in humans with certain pathological conditions.[1,15] Three general types of stereotypies were observed: (1) rhythmical rocking, swaying, or turning movements involving the whole body; (2) repetitive movements of individual body parts, e.g., head, hand, or lips; (3) "posturing," or assuming a peculiar stance and holding a limb or limbs in an apparently uncomfortable position. These activities occurred individually or in combination, and the animal might shift rapidly from one to another.

There follows a brief description of the specific stereotypies identified in our chimpanzees. A defining characteristic of the activities is their recurrence in the same S or S's over a period of weeks or months.

1. Rhythmical Rocking, Swaying, and Turning Movements of the Whole Body: The vigor and speed of action varies, a complete cycle lasting from 1 to 10 seconds. Observed patterns include swaying erect, sitting, supine, and on all fours; twirling erect, supine, and on all fours; rocking sitting, supine, and on all fours; pivoting in a prone posture, pelvic thrusts, and chest pounding. In the last behavior the S, while prone, rhythmically and repeatedly strikes his chest on the floor, pushing up with his arms, then falling flat. Individual S's are highly consistent in the posture and form in which they perform these activities. Some S's characteristically grasp their thighs while swaying or rocking; in others the arms hang loosely.

2. Repetitive or Persistent Activities Involving Individual Body Parts: Each may be continued for from a few seconds to several minutes. Some patterns observed are: thumb and toe sucking, lip contortions (folding the upper lip over the nose or protruding a small section of the lower lip and staring at it), exaggerated chewing motions, head banging, scrubbing the chin on the wooden floor, simultaneous head shaking and hand waving, vigorously pressing a finger against the eyelid (eye poking), hand clapping simultaneously shaking the head and rubbing a leg on the floor, vigorously striking the body or cage surface with the end of the index finger as if striking a match, and Parkinson-like rubbing together of thumb and forefinger (pill rolling).

3. Posturing: Stiffly holding a fist against the head, holding a hand within 2 or 3 inches of the eyes, and a complex pattern seen in 1 S in which he stands erect, stiffly holds 1 arm overhead, wrist bent, rolls his head from side to side, and on occasion stamps 1 foot and flaps his elbows.

Group Differences in Stereotypy—All 16 animals in the 4 restricted groups developed stereotyped behaviors during the rearing period, including at least 1 rhythmical activity involving the whole body. These stereotyped behaviors were observed in all of the postrearing tests. Eight restricted animals are presently 4 to 6 years old, and although they have been housed in the relatively enriched environment of the Laboratory outdoor colony for up to 3 years, all of them continue to exhibit stereotyped behavior. The patterns are essentially the same as those manifested during the second year of life. Observation of other laboratory-reared chimpanzees suggests that stereotypies persist to maturity.

Wild-born chimpanzees formed a complete contrast to all restricted animals. The repetitive behaviors they showed were few, infrequent, and different in form from the stereotypies of any restricted animal. Thus when they were placed into an unfamiliar test area (e.g., a 48 × 24 × 28 in. cage, or a large open room) the wild-born S's paced back and forth, or walked in a small circle, as a caged zoo animal might.[6] In some instances they also clutched themselves—that is, crossed the arms on the chest so that the hands were on contralateral sides of the body. No wild-born S developed any rhythmical activity of the whole body or any activity such as thumb-sucking. Moreover, the pacing and circling of wild-born animals were virtually never seen in the familiar home cage. This is different from the tendency of restricted animals to stereotype at nearly all levels of arousal and in almost all situations.

So far as can be determined from the Laboratory records, all chimpanzee infants raised by human caretakers or parent surrogates have engaged in stereotyped movements (see Nissen,[12]; Mason and Green's data on rhesus monkeys[10] similarly reveal a complete dichotomy between laboratory-reared and wild-born, captive animals). This includes several chimpanzees exposed to an unusually enriched social and physical environment (e.g., Hayes[5]). In contrast, no record exists of stereotypies in the mother-reared chimpanzee infants produced at the Laboratories. It seems safe to assume, therefore, that stereotypies are typical of nursery-reared chimpanzees, and are not unique to animals raised under conditions of extreme restriction. Unfortunately, the evidence available does not permit firm conclusions regarding the frequency of established stereotypies as a function of degree of restriction of laboratory environment. There were no obvious or consistent differences in the frequencies or pattern of stereotyped behavior among the 4 restricted groups of the present experiment. It may well be, however, that our restricted S's and open nursery groups did differ in the frequencies and patterns of stereotyped behaviors. Records are not sufficiently complete to make this comparison.

Evidence is also lacking which would enable us to evaluate the role of the mother chimpanzee vs. general environmental enrichment in preventing the development of stereotypy. The Hayes' Vicki, for example, was reared in a human home only after 6 weeks (until that time she was maintained in the laboratory nursery), at which time prone rocking had already been noted. Age factors might be critical both for the establishment and the prevention of rocking and swaying.

Development of Stereotypy in Restricted Chimpanzees—Some of the stereotyped behaviors that have been described commenced very early in life. Characteristically, some repetitive response developed a month or two after birth in restricted animals. However, the motor immaturity of the infants limited the possible patterns of stereotyping. Table 1 presents the patterns observed in 7 animals for whom brief observations were made 3 to 5 times daily from birth to 21 months of age. Thumbsucking occurred in some infants in the first few days of life, and prone pivoting was observed in the second month. The sway pattern was practiced only by older animals who had achieved an erect posture. In general, the infants performed many of the stereotypies possible at the early developmental stages, and it was only as they became older that 1 or 2 stereotypies became dominant.

We have little direct evidence regarding the manner in which specific motor patterns become habitual, but the observed variation from one pattern to another suggests that at some ages and under some conditions many different patterns might serve common functions. One S was observed to switch abruptly from prone chest-pounding to seated rocking when her cage floor was changed from a soft plastic to a hard wood. Seated rocking became this animal's habitual stereotypy, and remained so at the age of 5 years.

To illustrate the frequency and variety of stereotyped behavior observed during the postrearing test battery, Table 2 presents the responses of 18 S's in two 73-minute test sessions in an unfamiliar 48 × 24 × 28 in. test cubicle. Placement in this cubicle was part of the first postrearing test, which was conducted during the week that the S's became 21 months of age. Note that all but 1 restricted S engaged in some stereotypy in more than 60% of the minutes, and all but 3 stereotyped in more than 80% of the minutes. The 4 restricted groups did not differ from each other, but wild-born S's were completely different from restricted animals. In other tests the wild-born S's did show repetitive behaviors, but these were different in type and in frequency from those shown by restricted S's.

The variety and complexity of stereotypies in the restricted animals is noteworthy. In both respects the chimp seems to differ from the rhesus and from the human. The stereotyped behavior of the rhesus can apparently be described in terms of approximately 5 categories of activity: crouching, rocking, swaying, sucking thumb or toe, and rubbing or stroking body parts.[9] On the other hand we have identified at least 25 distinctive patterns in young chimpanzees and adult chimpanzees exhibit additional ones. In human mental defectives, the number of identifiable patterns is limited only by the perceptiveness of the observer.[2]

Relationships to Stimulus Conditions and to Other Behaviors—Table 2 is characteristic of behavior during most of the postrearing tests.

An important feature of stereotypies in the restricted S's was the high proportion of time in which they were manifested. Frequency of stereotypy did, however, vary from time to time; obviously, S's could not rock or sway while they slept. If very frightened, an S whose habitual stereotypy was erect swaying occasionally fell prone or supine, and no stereotypy was recorded. Or again, vigorous activity in some cases replaced stereotypy. Thus, in tests where S's were confronted with novel inanimate objects, stereotypy was related to object-contact (eta = 0.88, N = 15, $p < 0.01$).

Experiments reported elsewhere[11] illustrate the relationships between stereotypy and stimulus novelty, stimulus quality, and object-contact activity.

Animals given new objects to play with initially avoided the objects and spent the entire observation period in repetitive behavior. With time, the animals approached the objects and stereotyping decreased. During periods when they played freely with the objects stereotyping seldom occurred. Then, with prolonged exposure to and

Table 1. Time of Occurrence of the 4 Most Frequently Observed Classes of Stereotypies

													Weeks of Age															
	4	8	12	16	20	24	28	32	36	40	44	48	52	56	60	64	68	72	76	80	84	88	92	96	100	104	108	112
No. 200																												
Sway			X	X	X	X	X	X	X	X	X	X	X	X		X	X	X	X	X	X	X	X	X	X	X		
Rock			X	X	X	X		X	X	X	X	X	X			X	X											
Pivot															X		X		X							X		
Thumb suck					X		X			X				X										X			X	X
No. 169																												
Sway		X	X	X														X		X	X			X	X	X	X	X
Rock		X																X		X	X							
Pivot	X	X				X			X		X	X		X		X	X	X	X		X	X	X	X	X	X	X	X
Thumb suck					X		X																					
No. 171																												
Sway								X	X	X	X	X	X	X		X		X	X	X	X	X	X	X	X	X	X	X
Rock					X	X		X	X	X	X	X	X	X	X	X	X				X		X	X	X	X	X	
Pivot				X	X	X		X	X	X	X	X	X	X			X	X										
Thumb suck		X	X	X	X	X	X	X	X	X	X	X	X	X	X	X	X				X				X	X	X	
No. 190																												
Sway													X			X					X							
Rock																X	X	X										
Pivot			X	X	X	X	X	X	X	X		X	X	X	X	X	X	X	X	X	X	X	X	X	X	X	X	X
Thumb suck		X	X	X	X	X	X	X	X	X	X	X	X	X	X		X	X	X									
No. 173																												
Sway								X	X	X	X	X	X	X	X	X	X	X	X	X	X	X	X	X	X	X	X	X
Rock						X	X	X	X	X	X	X	X	X	X	X	X	X	X	X	X	X	X		X	X	X	X
Pivot															X													
Thumb suck		X	X	X			X		X																			
No. 196																												
Sway						X		X	X	X	X	X	X	X		X		X	X	X	X	X	X		X			
Rock					X	X		X	X	X	X	X	X	X	X	X	X	X	X	X	X	X	X					
Pivot		X	X																									
Thumb suck																								X				
No. 188																												
Sway			X	X		X		X	X	X	X		X	X	X	X	X	X	X	X	X	X	X	X	X	X	X	X
Rock												X		X	X		X			X	X			X		X		
Pivot			X		X	X		X	X	X	X										X							
Thumb suck		X		X		X		X			X		X	X						X	X	X		X				

Table 2. Percentage of Minutes in which Selected Stereotyped Movements Occurred during 146 Minutes of Test Day 1

	Rearing Condition																	
	Restricted																	
Stereotypy	Maximum Restriction S's				Visual Added S's			Manipulation Added S's				Social Added S's				Wild-born Enriched S's		
	159	167	182	169	186	188	173	163	165	196	200	176	178	171	190	Peck	Su	Saki
Any Stereo	99	32	89	91	99	98	86	87	82	86	99	66	100	66	94	0	0	0
Sway	98	10	6		95	94		68		79	92							
Rock													98					
Pivot		18	86	90	76		86		82	16		65	36	66	88			
Suck thumb				3	1		3	2		10	58			16				
Chewing motions			3				11							8				
Eye poking					3	32												
Chin scrubbing			12		2							29						
Hand to head								25										
Head bang								1										

exploitation of the object, play decreased and stereotyping again became the predominant activity.

Thus, stereotypy can be reliably related to stimulus conditions and also to other modes of behavior. It seems that in the 2-year-old chimpanzee stereotypy serves no single function, for it tends to appear *whenever* S is not actively engaged in "externally-directed" behavior (locomotion and object contact).

Stereotyped behavior has been accounted for in terms of "movement restraint,"[8] substitute behavior,[4] infantile emotional dependence,[14] and lack of mothering.[13] In our view the development of stereotyped behavior in the chimpanzee is related to the absence or insufficient amount of stimulation that the mother ordinarily provides her infant as she grasps, hugs, rocks, and carries him during the early months of life. It is not possible at this time to specify the stimulus characteristics of "mothering," the lack of which results in stereotyped behavior. It is conceivable that these stimulus characteristics might be provided by general environmental enrichment and that hence the mother *per se* is unnecessary. It is certain, however, that maternal care is sufficient to prevent stereotyped behavior from appearing in the chimpanzee. Deprived of the factors which enter into normal maternal care, the artificially-reared infant apparently stimulates himself with activities which, when repeated over a period of time, we have termed stereotyped behavior. With time the stereotypies achieve more diverse functions and possibly functional autonomy.

SUMMARY

The present paper is concerned with stereotypies in infant chimpanzees. Evidence is presented to show that stereotypy is related to rearing variables, developmental status, immediate stimulus situation, and various forms of ongoing activity. Most strikingly, stereotypies are phenomena unique to infants raised in restricted environments. They commence within the first few months of life and persist into adulthood. These behaviors show marked resemblances to behaviors of human beings with certain pathological conditions.

The authors wish to recognize the assistance of our colleague, Charles M. Rogers.

REFERENCES

1. Berkson, G., and Davenport, R. K., Jr.: Stereotyped Movements of Mental Defectives: I. Initial Survey, *Amer. J. Ment. Defic.* 66: 849-852, 1962.
2. Davenport, R. K., Jr., and Berkson, G.: Unpublished study, 1961.
3. Davenport, R. K., Jr.; Menzel, E. W., Jr., and Rogers, C. M.: Maternal Care During Infancy: Its Effect on Weight Gain and Mortality in the Chimpanzee, *Amer. J. Orthopsychiat.* 31: 803-809, 1961.
4. Foley, J. P., Jr.: Second Year Development of a Rhesus Monkey (*Macaca mulatta*) Reared in Isolation During the First 18 Months, *J. Genet. Psychol.* 47: 73-97, 1935.
5. Hayes, C.: *The Ape in Our House,* New York, Harper & Brothers, 1951.
6. Hediger, H.: *Wild Animals in Captivity,* London, Butterworths Scientific Publications, 1950.
7. Kravitz, H.; Rosenthal, V.; Teplitz, Z.; Murphy, J. B., and Lesser, R. E.: A Study of Head-Banging in Infants and Children, *Dis. Nerv. Syst.* 21: 203-208, 1960.
8. **Levy, D. M.: On the Problem of Movement Restraint: Tics, Stereotyped Movements, Hyperactivity,** *Amer. J. Orthopsychiat.* **14: 644-671, 1944.**
9. Mason, W. A.: Socially Mediated Reduction in Emotional Responses of Young Rhesus Monkeys, *J. Abnorm. Soc. Psychol.* 60: 100-104, 1960.
10. Mason, W. A., and Green, P. C.: The Effects of Social Restriction on the Behavior of Rhesus Monkeys: IV. Responses to a Novel Environment and to an Alien Species, *J. Comp. Physiol. Psychol.* 55: 363-368, 1962.

11. Menzel, E. W., Jr.: The Effects of Cumulative Experience on Responses to Novel Objects in Young Isolation-Reared Chimpanzees, *Behaviour,* to be published.
12. Nissen, H. W.: Individuality in the Behavior of Chimpanzees, *Amer. Anthropol.* 58: 407-413, 1956.
13. Ribble, M. A.: *The Rights of Infants: Early Psychological Needs and Their Satisfaction,* New York, Columbia University Press, 1943.
14. van Wagenen, G.: The Monkey, in Farris, F. J., Editor: *The Care and Breeding of Laboratory Animals,* New York, John Wiley & Sons, Inc., 1950.
15. White, R. W.: *The Abnormal Personality,* New York, The Ronald Press Company, 1948, p. 524.

35. Mother-infant Separation in Monkeys: An Experimental Model

I. C. KAUFMAN

In J. P. SCOTT & E. C. SENAY (Eds), *Separation and Depression: Clinical and Research Aspects*, Washington: Westview Press for American Association for the Advancement of Science, 1973, 33-52. Copyright 1973 by the American Association for the Advancement of Science. Reprinted by permission.

The focus of this symposium is on the relationship of separation to depression; but, since depression does not *always* follow separation, I wish to consider some conditions under which it *does*, what it may then mean—that is, its sense or function—and the conditions under which depression does not follow separation, and the possible reasons why it does not. My comments are based on studies of mother-infant separation in macaques.

For higher organisms that begin life with a long period in which independent functioning is not possible, normal development depends on continuous parental care. Accordingly, considerable theoretical and practical interest has centered on the dramatic and deleterious effects that are often seen in young children who are separated for varying periods of time from the mother figure (Deutsch, 1919; Bakwin, 1942; A. Freud and Burlingham, 1944; Spitz, 1945; Spitz and Wolf, 1946; Robertson and Bowlby, 1952; Schaffer and Callender, 1959; Heinicke and Westheimer, 1965).

Although it is generally agreed that such separation is fateful for the child, there is still a lack of clarity about the interrelationships among separation, the related experience of loss, and the two powerful affective states with which they appear to be related, namely, anxiety and depression. For example, although many observers would agree that brief separations may lead to anxiety and that longer separation—that is, loss—may lead to depression, there is considerable disagreement about the mechanisms involved (S. Freud, 1926; Bowlby, 1960; A. Freud, 1960; Schur, 1960; Spitz, 1960).

For these reasons, I decided to study the reaction of young individuals to separation from the mother. Since experimental study of this problem in the human being is generally impossible for ethical reasons, I chose to study nonhuman primates as have other investigators. Implicit in this approach is the idea that, despite all the apparent discontinuities in evolutionary development, there is, nevertheless, an obvious continuity, and that knowledge of the principles, mechanisms, and apparatuses of nonhuman behavior is bound to allow some valid extrapolations to the human, especially if the experimental animal chosen shares with the human being relevant behavioral and central-nervous-system characteristics. On the basis of these considerations, I chose to study macaques, the Old World monkeys that are known to show close mother-infant relationships of considerable duration.

327

REACTION TO SEPARATION IN PIGTAIL INFANTS

My studies were focused first on ontogenetic development under relatively undisturbed conditions (Kaufman and Rosenblum, 1966, 1969a) and then on the reactions of infants when they were bereft of their mothers. For 10 years, my colleagues and I have been studying numerous groups of two macaque species, pigtails (*Macaca nemestrina*) and bonnets (*M. radiata*). Each group has typically consisted of a wild-born adult male, four or five wild-born adult females, and their laboratory-born offspring. More than 75 infants have been born, and their ontogenetic development, for many into adulthood, has been carefully observed. The separation experiments were made by removing the mother and leaving the infant with its home group. The mother was later returned.

First, I describe the reaction that was seen in most of the pigtail infants, which were separated when they were between 19 and 24 weeks old (Kaufman and Rosenblum, 1967a, b). The immediate reaction to physical separation of mother and infant consisted of loud screams by both and massive struggling to regain each other. When the infant was replaced in the pen, it was highly agitated (Fig. 1). Pacing, searching head

Fig. 1. An agitated pigtail infant flees from rebuff by adult female it had approached. Note fear grimace during screaming. (From Kaufman and Rosenblum, 1967b, Fig. 2, p. 654.)

movements, frequent trips to the front door and windows, sporadic and short-lived bursts of erratic play, and brief movements toward other members of the group seemed to be constant. No adult attempted to comfort the infant. Cooing, the rather plaintive distress call of the young macaque, and intermittent screeching were frequent. This reaction persisted throughout the first day, during which the infant did not sleep. All observers were struck by a sense of intense acute distress.

After 24-36 hours, the pattern changed strikingly. The infant sat hunched over, almost rolled into a ball with its head often down between its legs (Fig. 2). When the face could be seen, it seemed that the facial muscles had sagged, which, together with the configuration of forehead and mouth, created the same appearance of dejection and

Fig. 2. Depressed pigtail infant shows characteristic posture including head between legs. Note the slightly opened eyes as it sucks its penis. (From Kaufman and Rosenblum, 1967b, Fig. 4, p. 655.)

Fig. 3. Depressed pigtail infant shows characteristic posture and dejected face. (From Kaufman and Rosenblum, 1967b, Fig. 5, p. 655.)

sadness that Darwin described and believed "to be universally and instantly recognized as that of grief" (Fig. 3). Movement virtually ceased except when the infant was actively displaced. The movement that did occur appeared to be in slow motion, except that the movement could be quick at feeding time or in withdrawal from aggressive behavior. The infant appeared to be moping much of the time and rarely responded to social invitation. Also, it rarely made a social gesture, and play behavior virtually ceased. The infant seemed to be largely disengaged from the environment and appeared to derive little comfort from the presence of others (Fig. 4). Occasionally, the infant would look up and plaintively "coo." To all observers there was communicated a strong feeling of dejection, withdrawal, and social isolation. The infant's reaction can be characterized only as the expression of a state of severe depression.

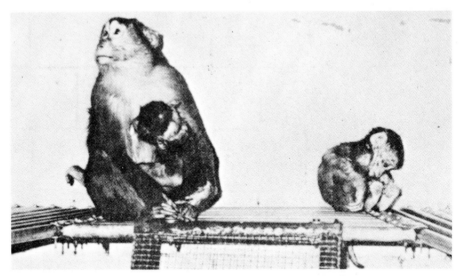

Fig. 4. Depressed pigtail infant shows characteristic hunched-over posture with flexion throughout. It is completely disengaged from the mother and infant nearby in ventral-ventral contact. (From Kaufman and Rosenblum, 1967b, Fig. 3, p. 655.)

After it had persisted unchanged for 5 to 6 days, the depression gradually began to lift. The recovery started with the resumption of a more upright posture and a resurgence of interest in the inanimate environment (Fig. 5). Gradually, the motherless infant also began to interact with its social environment, primarily with its peers, and there was then a reemergence of play activity. The depression continued but in an

Fig. 5. Depressed infant shows tentative exploration of bedding during early stage of recovery. (From Kaufman and Rosenblum, 1967b, Fig. 7, p. 655.)

abated form. Periods of depression alternated with periods of exploration of inanimate objects and play. By the fourth week of separation, play levels were approaching those of preseparation, movement increased in amount and tempo, and the infant appeared to be alert and active a great deal of the time.

COMPARISON WITH HUMAN DATA: ANACLITIC DEPRESSION

Before I compare these data with human data and consider some of the implications, I should mention that other observers, at the University of Wisconsin (Seay, Hansen, and Harlow, 1962; Seay and Harlow, 1965) and at Cambridge University (Hinde, Spencer-Booth, and Bruce, 1966), found roughly comparable reactions in another macaque, the rhesus. The human data offer problems for comparison, because they come from studies made under varied conditions, with separations of varying length, and with children of various ages with varied previous experience.

The first observer who drew attention to the problem of separated human children was Spitz, who described two syndromes in institutionalized infants. One syndrome, which he called "anaclitic depression," arose in the second half of the first year of life when the mothers, who had reared the infants from birth, were removed (Spitz and Wolf, 1946). After an initial period of apprehension and weepiness, the infants showed withdrawal, rejection of the environment, retardation of reaction to stimuli, slowness of movement, loss of appetite, increased finger-sucking, insomnia, "an obvious distaste for assuming an erect posture or performing locomotion" (p. 326), and a "physiognomic expression . . . difficult to describe . . . [which] would, in an adult, be described as depression" (p. 316). If the mother returned within 3 to 5 months, there was an immediate dramatic effect. The infants "suddenly were friendly, gay, approachable" (p. 330) and subsequently recovered fully.

If the mother did not return, the other, more malignant syndrome developed. The latter, which Spitz (1945) called "hospitalism," was first seen in infants who lost their mothers permanently and were cared for by very busy nursing personnel. It was characterized by massive failure in development, both mental and physical, frequent illness, marasmus, cachexia, and often early death. Spitz commented on the importance of locomotion and motility after 6 months of age and thought that, among other things, the loss of mother interfered with the opportunities for locomotion and its important role in development.

I think it is clear that the pigtail infant's reaction is strikingly similar to the "anaclitic depression" of human infants described by Spitz. The studies by all other observers— for example, Robertson and Bowlby (1952), Schaffer and Callender (1959), Bowlby (1960), Provence and Lipton (1962), Heinicke and Westheimer (1965)—have been confounded by the fact that the separation was not only from the mother but from the usual homesite as well. Even so, it seems to be clear from the relevant studies that, from about 6 months of age on, separation from mother is disturbing to children and the initial response is agitation; and, *if there is no alleviation,* as by substitute mothering, this gives way after awhile to depression. Thus, it may be safely concluded that the reaction of human and pigtail infants to separation is phenomenologically comparable.

The similarity is found not only in the form of the behavior but also in the succession of stages: an initial agitation followed by depression. In older children, Bowlby (1960) described a third stage—detachment—in which the child becomes detached from, and hostile to, the mother. This was not seen by Spitz or other observers with younger children, nor has it been seen in monkey infants. Heinicke and Westheimer (1965), in their study of older children, delineated five stages of reaction, which I have not seen in monkeys, but their conceptualization is very apt and fitting. They called the stages "successive efforts at adaptation." Here it is appropriate to consider further the reaction to separation in terms of stages of adaptive response.

ADAPTIVE ASPECTS OF THE STAGES OF REACTION

In a theoretical paper, Frank (1954) offered "the thesis that the depression-elation responses constitute part of the inherent adaptive machinery available to the individual. They are employed automatically, unconsciously, and directly as adaptive measures under conditions when, either in actuality or fantasy, a relatively helpless individual is threatened with the loss of suitable care, protection, and sustenance" (p. 52).

Engel and Reichsman (1956), in their classical study of the child Monica, described how she would withdraw in the presence of a stranger and even go to sleep. Drawing on the thesis offered by Frank, they labeled Monica's response as "depression-withdrawal"; "depression" because of the "impact on the observer of the facial expression, posture, and inactivity, all of which call to mind a mood of dejection, sadness, or depression"; and "withdrawal" because of the "turning away, the closing of the eyes, and the eventual sleep. The immobility and hypotonia may be seen as part of the withdrawal pattern as well as part of the affect disturbance" (p. 439).

In subsequent publications, Engel (1962a, b) elaborated this thesis further. Incorporating observations on infants and young children and the theorizing of Bibring (1953), he wrote (1962b, p. 93); "When we couple such observations with the recognition of the fact that even the most intense crying fit eventually terminates and the infant becomes quiescent, falls asleep, or even becomes comatose, even though the underlying needs have not been fulfilled, we are drawn to the conclusion that the central nervous system is organized to mediate two opposite patterns of response to a mounting need . . . the first, broadly subsumed under the heading of flight-fight, involves activity, energy expenditure, and engagement with the environment to control sources of supply and avert danger. The second, conservation-withdrawal, involves inactivity, energy conservation, raising of the stimulus barrier, and withdrawal from the environment. Each of these is seen as an inborn system, each with its own underlying mediating neural organization. The conservation-withdrawal system is a second biological defense organization which comes into play if and when the energy expenditures of the first (flight-fight) reaction threaten the organism with exhaustion before supplies are secured . . . ." He considered the first system to be the biological anlage of anxiety and the second, of depression-withdrawal, these being in his view the two primary affects of unpleasure.

I believe that my data strongly corroborate Engel's theory. The young of every species that is not independent at the beginning of its existence has been born or hatched preadapted to early life in many ways, including having behaviors that are calculated (by evolutionary adaptation) to maintain closeness to the mothering figure. The eliciting causes of these behaviors in the beginning are varied and are related to the infant's need for dry warmth, food and so forth. The behaviors are frequently vocal. The monkey infant has at least two calls that are distress signals, the screams and the "coo." These location calls match reciprocal mechanisms in the mother to ensure her closeness and thus increase the likelihood of the infant's survival.

In the pigtails described here, distress calls were quite frequent in the first stage after separation. In the wild, had the infant become separated from the mother, the calls would surely have had the effect of bringing her back, if she were able. The monkey infants also showed restless pacing and searching, which, in the wild, would have been over a wider area and very likely would have assisted in reuniting the infant with its mother. However, this calling, searching reaction is not the kind of behavior that could profitably go on indefinitely, for at least two reasons. First, the incessant movement and vocalization increase the risk of provoking aggression, either from conspecifics or from predators. Second, the markedly heightened activity is exhausting. Hence, the agitated distress reaction came to an end after a relatively short period of time.

The second stage of the reaction to the continued absence of mother or a substitute, the depressed response, also appears to have survival value. First, there was an obvious conservation of energy and resources. Depletion of energy or massive fatigue did not occur, because, under certain circumstances, the infant moved quite rapidly and appropriately—for example, when food was put into the pen, or when an act of aggression was directed at it. Conservation is achieved through the marked inactivity as well as by the posture (body rolled almost into a ball with flexion throughout, including the head between the legs), which probably cuts down heat loss by reducing the exposed body surface. The posture also makes the infant literally smaller, so that it presents less of a visual stimulus to the other animals. The paucity and extreme slowness of movement also minimize notice of it by others. It is thus less likely to provoke aggression. Furthermore, the posture would reduce exposure to adverse elements—for example, wind and rain. Finally, the reduction in exposure of body surface and the hiding of the face markedly reduce sensory input to the infant.

Just as the stage-one reaction has time-limited survival value, the depressive reaction, if it continued unabated and indefinitely, would have a host of deleterious effects. This state of minimal action and interaction sharply curtails experience of the outside world and would virtually bring further development to an end. An animal that grows physically larger but otherwise does not acquire the personal and social skills of its species would not long survive, or would survive only as an outcast with no possibility of reproductive success.

The consequences of prolongation of this depressive reaction were tragically evident in the human babies with the hospitalism syndrome described by Spitz (1945). Not only did further development cease, but there was regression and ultimately no fitness for survival. This illustrates the fact that, in the human being, evolutionary adaptation has accentuated the role of the mothering figure to an exquisite degree.

The human infant cannot survive without a mother. The monkey infant, on the other hand, from an early age, *is* capable of surviving without mother, and this was illustrated in my experiments by the third stage of reaction: the recovery from the depression. This, I believe, the monkey infant was able to do because of its locomotor ability.

As Spitz and Wolf (1946) noted, the human infant for a long time has no locomotor ability, and, even when he begins to acquire it, he is very much dependent on other figures in the environment to provide the opportunities to use it. The monkey, however, after the first few weeks of life is able to move about and, within a relatively short time, has very considerable locomotor ability. This provides the mechanism that enables the monkey on its own to reengage its environment to find new sources of comfort, with a reasonable likelihood of success, not only in survival, but also in the resumption of development, acquisition of new knowledge and new skills, and achievement of social growth through interaction with peers and adults.

I am suggesting, then, that the reaction to continued, unrelieved separation consists of successive efforts at adaptation on the basis of available response systems, and that the first two stages are similar in human and monkey infants. In so doing, I am aware of the fact that any attempt to explain both monkey and human behavior must limit the complexity of the explanatory hypothesis necessary for the human case. I believe that an explanation is possible in this instance, because in the young of both species the mediating neural mechanisms are similar and relatively undifferentiated. In fact, there is evidence that the same kinds of neural mechanisms may be present throughout the vertebrate order (Riss and Scalia, 1967).

RELATIONSHIP OF STAGES TO AFFECTS

An important part of Engel's thesis (1962b) is that these two biological response systems are the anlagen of the affects anxiety and depression. The problem of affects is a difficult and complex one, being in the first place a biological problem that Darwin, Freud, and many others attempted to clarify. Affects are regulators of social living as well as of inner, ultimately psychic, life. The behavioral manifestations of an affect serve to communicate to others the organism's needs and states. Affects also include systems of internal regulation. These functions of outward communication and inner regulation, which apparently were selected for their survival value, occur automatically, without necessary psychic participation, at least in the first instances, in response to the conditions for which they were evolved. Earlier I detailed, in line with Engel's hypothesis, the survival value of the agitation and conservation-withdrawal reactions in terms of their communicative and regulatory aspects.

There is one other critical characteristic of affects, namely, the subjective aspect, the felt emotion, regarding which my data must be examined in terms of Engel's hypothesis. Since subjective reports from monkeys are unavailable, as they are also from human infants, my interpretation of the data is limited to what can be seen in the monkeys and what can be felt empathically by observers.

In the first stage, agitation, restless seeking, repeated crying vocalizations, and an anguished face are observed and communicate a sense of panic and distress to the observer. It is difficult not to associate this organismic state with anxiety.

In the next stage, withdrawal, rejection of the environment, retardation of reaction to stimuli, slowness of movements, a collapsed posture, minimal locomotion, and the face that Darwin associated with grief are observed, and a sense of dejection and sorrow is felt. It is difficult not to associate this organismic state with depression.

In the human being, these powerful feeling states, once they are discriminated by the developing ego, then function as signals, as indicators of the total psychic situation, and as calls for appropriate regulation. With further experience, maturation, and learning, many and diverse alterations occur in the gross response patterns as repertories of behaviors and plans emerge and provide new coping and regulating mechanisms, which include differentiation of the affects and their utilization as *internal* communicative signals. In both human beings and monkeys, however, relatively undifferentiated response patterns are seen in the young infant that is separated from its mother.

In describing the reactions of these pigtails, I tried to make it clear that the conservation-withdrawal response, with its subjective aspect of depression, arose only when the agitation response threatened exhaustion in the face of *unrelieved stress*. It is a response available under such conditions, but it need not be called upon, as is illustrated by some of my other data.

REACTION TO SEPARATION IN BONNET INFANTS

My colleagues and I have also performed a series of experimental separations of bonnet dyads, under conditions and using techniques that were quite comparable to those used with the pigtails (Kaufman and Rosenblum, 1969b). In no instance has a bonnet infant showed anything that remotely resembled the severe depressive reaction observed in the pigtail infants. Although some degree of agitation was manifest in bonnet infants during the separation period, with increases in vocalization, there never occurred the marked withdrawal of interest in the inanimate and, particularly, the social environment.

The bonnets showed an overwhelming increase in interaction with other adults that seemed to provide quite adequate substitution for their mothers. They achieved sustained ventral-ventral contact with adults, even the father, equal in amount to what they had had with their mothers before separation, and in many instances they were suckled. In one experiment, a female with her own infant cared for and suckled two separated infants at the same time (Fig. 6).

Fig. 6. A bonnet female with her own infant and two separated infants that she adopted. She nursed, carried, and protected these two infants throughout their separation.

SOME DIFFERENCES BETWEEN BONNETS AND PIGTAILS

It seems reasonable to conclude that in the bonnets the adoption by other adults relieved the stress imposed by the mother's absence and obviated the depressive conservation-withdrawal response. It also seems reasonable to assume that this difference in behavior reflects a genetic difference between the two species. Even so, my data suggest that the difference may be in large part ontogenetically realized under the influence of a difference in temperament, which is reflected in a difference in social structure and differing patterns of mothering (Kaufman and Rosenblum, 1969a).

Although the pigtails and bonnets are taxonomically close and share many behaviors and social characteristics, some striking differences between the two species were found. Bonnet adults tended to remain physically close, often in huddles, but the pigtails did not usually make physical contact with neighbors except to engage in a dynamic social interaction such as grooming, mating, or fighting. At night, the pigtails tended to sleep lying down, and the bonnets tended to sleep sitting up, maintaining physical contact with one another. Since this difference has been manifested by every group that my colleagues and I have formed, utilizing animals captured at different times and probably in different places, we must assume that this is a species difference. How this difference arose is not known at this time, but its consequences on social organization and on infant-rearing are of considerable interest.

The tendency to propinquity among the bonnets continues during pregnancy and after delivery of the young, when bonnet females return to close contact (Fig. 7), but pig-

Fig. 7. A group of bonnet females in a huddle, including a mother and her young infant, who is the center of interest. (From Kaufman and Rosenblum, 1969b, Fig. 3, p. 683.)

tail females with infants tend to remain apart from other females (Fig. 8). Both provide their infants with the intensive maternal care that characterizes most of the primates; the bonnet mother provides this care alongside her peers, but the pigtail mother gives it in relative isolation.

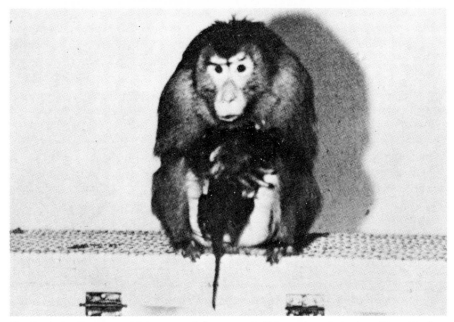

Fig. 8. A pigtail mother, with her young infant, on a shelf shows threat behavior. (From Kaufman and Rosenblum, 1969b, Fig. 4, p. 683.)

The tendency toward closeness among bonnet adults seems to be reflected in a relatively relaxed maternal disposition. Bonnet mothers are less likely to retrieve or otherwise protect their infants, yet bonnet mothers seem to be more tolerant of the continued closeness of their growing infants, weaning (denying access to the nipple) and punishing them less often. As a consequence, bonnet infants appear to be more secure: they are less dependent on their mothers than pigtails, in that they leave them more often and go farther away, and they spend more time than pigtails in social play; pigtails spend more time than bonnets in nonsocial play. The mothers' behavior and the infants' development may indicate a mechanism of great consequence in the perpetuation of the species-characteristic difference in temperament and spatial patterning. This difference was dramatically evident in the separation experiments: mother-deprived bonnet infants were comforted and adopted, but pigtail infants were usually left to their own resources or even harassed.

INFANTS' RESOURCES

This brings up another aspect of the separation situation, namely, the infant's own resources and ability to cope with the stress of the mother's absence. My data on this are less systematic to date. I saw one pigtail infant that did not show the depressive response (Kaufman and Rosenblum, 1967b). During the initial stage of agitated searching, this infant succeeded in securing some attention and comfort from the other adults, although not adoption. Rather than withdraw, this infant remained active in exploration of the inanimate environment and in nonsocial play, and then later in social play. In other words, this infant entered the recovery phase directly after the initial agitation. There was a greater ability to cope through its own resources; perhaps it was aided by the partial comfort provided by the remaining adults. In this case, the explanation may be that the infant was the offspring of the dominant female in the group. There is evidence that the infants of dominant females tend to be more secure, to have greater freedom of movement, to have had more varied and greater experience, and to have built up a greater repertory of behaviors and plans of action, so that the loss of mother may not be a completely shattering experience.

Some data from bonnets that bear on this issue have been collected (Kaufman, Rosenblum and A. J. Stynes, unpublished). I have seen bonnets deal with separation from mother *and* the absence of a substitute without showing the depressive conservation-withdrawal response. Four were infants between 6.5 and 13 months of age, which were left with their groups but did not achieve very considerable ventral contact with adults. At these ages, it should be noted, ventral contact with mother is normally *not* very considerable. These four all showed initial agitation with searching and calling, but then they resumed their exploration and play. Three others, 19 to 24 weeks old, were taken from their mothers and each was placed alone in a cage. They also showed agitation for about a day, and then they resumed exploration and nonsocial play. All of the infants that did not show the depressive response *did* show an increase in self-directed oral behavior.

It appears that the bonnet infant, at least by 19 weeks of age, has developed sufficient security and coping ability to remain engaged with the environment, animate or inanimate, even in the absence of mother or a substitute. This may be a consequence of the bonnet's particular developmental history as I outlined it earlier. These data also point out the likely importance of the age variable in influencing the type of response pattern that is elicited by stress.

To recapitulate, my suggestion is that infants respond to the loss of mother, a major crisis, by using whatever they have available. This includes, to begin with, in line with Engel's thesis (1962a), two biological response systems that are based on the structure of the vertebrate nervous system. The first one is likely to lead to reunion with mother. If it does not, the second one is likely to tide the infant over and help it to avoid injury until comfort can be regained. Alternative coping strategies, largely acquired in early development, may also be available if mother is not found. One is to find a substitute mother. The other is to use already developed plans and repertories and accommodate them to the new situation of a motherless existence

REACTION TO REUNION

So far I have discussed what may be learned from the experimental separation of a monkey mother and infant while the separation continues, but perhaps the aftereffects are even more important. The first aftereffect to consider is the reaction to reunion with mother. The data are variable and suggest that age of infant, duration of separation, the previous mother-infant relationship, and species all play roles. I have in mind not only my studies but also those made by Seay, Hansen, and Harlow (1962), Seay and Harlow (1965), and Hinde, Spencer-Booth, and Bruce (1966).

The common element in all the studies is that, initially, reunion is intense with a marked increase in closeness between mother and infant. The primary variant is the duration of the effect; it is less in older infants, after shorter separations, and in bonnets and rhesus; it is greater in mother-infant dyads that showed greater closeness before separation, and in pigtails. I found the greatest durability in the 19-24-week-old pigtails. All measures of increased closeness, such as ventral-ventral contact, nipple contact, and enclosure of the infant by mother, remained higher for several months after reunion than before separation; but play and exploration remained lower, and departures from mother were briefer and to shorter distances. These observations are striking, since all these measures normally go in the opposite direction at these ages.

What is the explanation of this increased closeness and reluctance to part from mother? It does not appear to be a consequence of the depressive reaction, since it appeared in all the separated infants, whether or not they became depressed. Since all the infants did become agitated and experienced some degree of anxiety, however, I believe that the experience resulted in a heightened degree of apprehension to the possibility that it might happen again. Anxiety then functioned as a signal to keep the infants close to mother and minimize the danger of another loss. This may still be considered adaptive but not if it persists in excessive degree or occurs inappropriately. There is evidence from Hinde's studies (1972) that proneness to anxiety persists even after apparent recovery from separation. He found in the rhesus that, even after 2 years, previously separated animals, which in all other ways appeared to be normal, showed more evidence of anxiety than nonseparated controls when they were confronted by strange objects in a strange cage, although not in their home cage. This may indicate maladaptive development of the anxiety response.

LONG-TERM EFFECTS OF SEPARATION

More information is needed about the long-term effects of separation with respect to depression. This is a different problem from the short-term response of depression to separation, although it is obviously related. The short-term response in infants is a form of available adaptation that is used if necessary. The question now is whether the organism is permanently changed as a consequence. For example, after a separation experience, does the organism remain depressed? Or does it have a readier tendency to respond with depression; and if so, under what conditions? Also, with respect to later depressions, how much is the subjective state of depression tied to the rest of the total conservation-withdrawal response?

In the human being, there is considerable clinical evidence that adult depressions result from actual, fantasied, or symbolic separations, and that these are often modeled on earlier responses to separation. Even if this is so, there are still many unanswered questions, and some are difficult to investigate: What is it about the early separation that changes the organism so that the proneness to depression is produced? It could not be simply the fact of separation; it has to be some aspect of the response to separation. If the infant responds only with anxiety, as I indicated many do, will there be a later proneness to depression? I do not think so. I believe that the anxiety response affects only the further development of anxiety. To develop proneness to depression, the infant, I think, has to experience the depressive response. Actually, there are not many data on this question. It will be necessary to compare the proneness to depression in individuals who responded to early separation only with anxiety with the proneness in those who also showed the depressive response. Doing repeated separations without attention to this distinction will not answer the question.

Another important question, if I am correct in my speculation, is—what is it about experiencing the depressive reaction that leads to a greater proneness, and how is this activated at a later date? I have no definitive answers, but I can report an experiment that bears on this whole issue (Kaufman, Rosenblum, and Stynes, unpublished).

Two pigtail mothers were removed simultaneously from a group. The infants of both showed initial agitation and then depression, but the depressive phase was mild in

one infant and severe in the other. Each proceeded to recover, as I previously described.
Then the mothers were put back for 30 minutes, one at a time, but inside a cage so that
the mother and her infant could not reunite. Each infant ran immediately to the cage
when it contained its mother but not the other mother. Each vocalized and tried unsuc-
cessfully to get to its mother. The infant that had had a mild depression then stopped
trying and resumed playing, but the infant that had had the severe depression now
again collapsed into a ball, showing the typical face of grief, and remained withdrawn
and immobile until the cage with its mother was removed, whereupon it got up and
resumed playing.

On many days during the next 8 weeks, the mothers were each reintroduced for 30
minutes. Each time, the first infant, after a cursory look, continued what it was doing;
but each time, the second infant, after looking at its caged mother, collapsed into a ball
and remained withdrawn and immobile until its mother was removed, whereupon it
quickly resumed playing. For 23.5 hours of each day, it explored and played and ate
and slept like the other infants, but during the half-hour of its mother's caged presence
it showed the depressive response.

An identical experiment was done with two bonnets. The infants showed the agitation response and then each was adopted. Later, when the caged mothers were returned,
each infant ran to its *adopted* mother and remained with her until the cage was removed.

How are these results to be interpreted? It seems to be clear that the return of the
caged mother was a stressful stimulus to all infants, a reminder of the separation from
mother. For the bonnets, I suggest that they felt anxiety and ran for security to their
new mothers. The first pigtail tried to return to its mother, but, when it could not, it
resumed playing. I assume that it responded to its anxiety by using the coping technique it had learned in her absence. The second pigtail had originally shown a deep
and protracted depressive response to the loss of mother, but it seems to be unlikely
that each day the conservation-withdrawal response in its biological entirety was turned
on and off at the mother's appearance and reappearance. It is more likely that her
every reappearance was a reminder of the infant's *helplessness,* inducing the feeling state
of depression with some of its behavioral correlates. This experiment leads me to suggest that it is the feeling state of helplessness that is critical in the original experience
and in the situation that again produces the depressive response.

Acknowledgements. The research reported in this paper was supported by grants MH-
04670 and MH-18144 from the National Institute of Mental Health, U.S. Public
Health Service, Bethesda, Maryland. I am indebted to several colleagues, in particular
L. A. Rosenblum and A. J. Stynes, who aided me in this work.

REFERENCES

Bakwin, H. 1942. Loneliness in infants, *American Journal of Diseases of Children,* vol. 63, pp. 30-40.
Bibring, E. 1953. The mechanism of depression, In *Affective Disorders,* P. Greenacre (Ed.), pp. 13-58, Inter-
    national Universities Press, New York.
Bowlby, J. 1960. Grief and mourning in infancy and early childhood, *Psychoanalytic Study of the Child,* vol. 15,
    pp. 9-52.
Deutsch, H. 1919 (1959). A two-year-old boy's first love comes to grief. In *Dynamic Psychopathology of Child-
    hood,* L. Jessner and E. Pavenstedt (Eds.), pp. 1-5. Grune & Stratton, New York.
Engel, G. L. 1962a. *Psychological Development in Health and Disease.* Saunders, Philadelphia, Pa.
Engel, G. L. 1962b. Anxiety and depression-withdrawal: the primary affects of unpleasure. *International
    Journal of Psychoanalysis,* vol. 43, pp. 89-97.
Engel, G. L., and F. Reichsman. 1956. Spontaneous and experimentally induced depressions in an infant
    with a gastric fistula. A contribution to the problem of depression. *Journal of the American Psychoanalytic
    Association,* vol. 4, pp. 428-452.

Frank, R. L. 1954. The organized adaptive aspect of the depression-elation response. In *Depression,* P. H. Hoch and J. Zubin, (Eds.), pp. 51-65. Grune & Stratton, New York.

Freud, A. 1960. Discussion of Bowlby. *Psychoanalytic Study of the Child,* vol. 15, pp. 53-62.

Freud, A., and D. Burlingham. 1944. *Infants without Families.* International Universities Press, New York.

Freud, S. 1926 (1959). *Inhibitions, Symptoms and Anxiety,* standard ed., vol. 20. Hogarth, London.

Heinicke, C. M., and I. J. Westheimer. 1965. *Brief Separations.* International Universities Press, New York.

Hinde, R. A. 1972. Social behavior and its development in subhuman primates. *Condon Lectures.* Oregon System of Higher Education, Eugene.

Hinde, R. A., Y. Spencer-Booth, and M. Bruce. 1966. Effects of 6-day maternal deprivation on rhesus monkey infants. *Nature,* vol. 210, pp. 1021-1023.

Kaufman, I. C., and L. A. Rosenblum. 1966. A behavioral taxonomy for *Macaca nemestrina* and *Macaca radiata:* based on longitudinal observations of family groups in the laboratory. *Primates,* vol. 7, pp. 205-258.

Kaufman, I. C., and L. A. Rosenblum. 1967a. Depression in infant monkeys separated from their mothers. *Science,* vol. 155, pp. 1030-1031.

Kaufman, I. C., and L. A. Rosenblum. 1967b. The reaction to separation in infant monkeys: anaclitic depression and conservation-withdrawal. *Psychosomatic Medicine,* vol. 29, pp. 648-675.

Kaufman, I. C. and L. A. Rosenblum. 1969a. The waning of the mother-infant bond in two species of macaque. In *Determinants of Infant Behaviour,* B. M. Foss (Ed.), vol. IV, pp. 41-51. Methuen, London.

Kaufman, I. C., and L. A. Rosenblum. 1969b. Effects of separation from mother on the emotional behavior of infant monkeys. *Annals of the New York Academy of Sciences,* vol. 159, pp. 681-695.

Provence, S., and R. C. Lipton. 1962. *Infants in Institutions.* International Universities Press, New York.

Riss, W., and F. Scalia. 1967. *Functional Pathways of the Central Nervous System.* Elsevier, Amsterdam.

Robertson, J., and J. Bowlby. 1952. Responses of young children to separation from their mothers. *Courrier du Centre Internationale de l'Enfance,* vol. 2, pp. 131-142.

Schaffer, H. R., and W. M. Callender. 1959. Psychologic effects of hospitalization in infancy. *Pediatrics,* vol. 24, pp. 528-539.

Schur, M. 1960. Discussion of Bowlby. *Psychoanalytic Study of the Child,* vol. 15, pp. 63-84.

Seay, B., and H. F. Harlow. 1965. Maternal separation in the rhesus monkey. *Journal of Nervous and Mental Disease,* vol. 140, pp. 434-441.

Seay, B., E. Hansen, and H. F. Harlow. 1962. Mother-infant separation in monkeys. *Journal of Child Psychology and Psychiatry,* vol. 3, pp. 123-132.

Spitz, R. A. 1945. Hospitalism. An inquiry into the psychiatric conditions in early childhood. *Psychoanalytic Study of the Child,* vol. 1, pp. 53-74.

Spitz, R. A. 1960. Discussion of Bowlby. *Psychoanalytic Study of the Child,* vol. 15, pp. 85-94.

Spitz, R. A., and K. M. Wolf. 1946. Anaclitic depression: an inquiry into the genesis of psychiatric conditions in early childhood, II. *Psychoanalytic Study of the Child,* vol. 2, pp. 313-342.

36. The Development of Head Banging in a Young Rhesus Monkey[1]

C. A. LEVISON

American Journal of Mental Deficiency, 1970, *75,* 323-8. Reprinted by permission.

This report describes the development of head banging in a rhesus monkey which had been reared under conditions of early social and visual deprivation, but which had, after release from deprivation, exhibited no stereotyped behaviors. Head banging developed as a consequence of a particular set of interactions with the experimenter and subsequently generalized to other related areas of behavior. Head banging has been observed in several diverse clinic populations: mentally deficient children, psychotic children, and blind children. The head banging pattern typically includes repeated and rhythmic blows of the head against a surface. There is little agreement among clinicians or experimentalists on the questions of origin of this behavior or its treatment.

Monkeys and apes separated from their mothers at birth show stereotyped behaviors similar to the stereotyped behaviors exhibited by abnormal humans (c.f. Davenport and Menzel, 1963; Berkson, 1968; Mason, 1968). These stereotypes include non-nutritive sucking, crouching, self-clasping, body rocking, and head banging. The same behaviors are also seen in animals raised with their mothers, but are not present to any significant degree (Berkson, 1968).

Observational studies of head banging in humans have been conducted by deLissovoy (1962) and Kravitz, Rosenthal, Teplitz, Murphy and Lesser (1960) describing the behavior in noninstitutionalized infants. Onset is generally in the last half of the first year (Kravitz *et al.,* 1960). In the majority of the cases, the head banging occurred at bedtime. In the 28 cases of the Kravitz *et al.* study in which electroencephalograms (EEGs) were given, the EEGs were normal. In the total population which they studied (N = 123), there were no cases of brain injury or other severe trauma as a result of head banging. A higher incidence of head banging was noted in males than in females. Rocking often preceded the onset of head banging and continued after head banging had ceased.

Very little head banging is reported in the animal literature, in contrast to the child literature. As opposed to such behaviors as sucking, crouching, and self-clasping, an activity such as head banging appears to be less general and more individual in its expression (Berkson, 1968). Berkson (1968) reports that head banging may occur incidental to rocking. Davenport and Menzel (1963) found that head banging was very

[1] This work was supported by a General Research Support Grant from the University of Chicago and PHS Grant No. HD 02477-01 from the Department of Health, Education, and Welfare. With special thanks to Peter K. Levison and Linda Crnic for their contributions to this work.

infrequent in their animals, occurring in only 1 percent of the minutes of their test condition (this consisted of being placed in an unfamiliar test cubicle). None of the other five animals in our laboratory who were similarly reared exhibited head banging.

Since very little information is available in the clinical literature about the specific development of particular types of stereotyped behavior, the observations made on the animal in this report are considered to be relevant in the development of increased understanding about the onset of such behaviors. Although human behavior related to stereotyped acts is more complex and variable than that of nonhuman primates, observations and experiments with nonhuman primates may provide fresh perspectives into the problems of stereotyped behaviors found in institutions, inadequate homes, and problem families. In the monkey which is the subject of this report, the experimenter was able to observe the development of head banging and, subsequently, to manipulate conditions in the environment which appeared related to the incidence of head banging.

DEVELOPMENT OF HEAD BANGING IN A RHESUS MONKEY

Early Rearing Conditions and Previous Experimental History

The subject, a male rhesus monkey (*Macaca mulatta*), was born in an established breeding colony on March 11, 1968, and was immediately separated from the mother. He was a subject in an experimental sequence investigating the effects of differential early rearing conditions on early stimulation-seeking, or curiosity-motivated behavior. All rhesus monkeys in the experiment were separated from their mothers at birth and installed in a surrogate rearing apparatus on the first day of life. The mother-surrogate chair functionally approximates many of the features of natural mother monkey (Held and Bauer, 1967)—the infant is held in an upright position, is firmly supported around its trunk by a padded cylinder, has a furry substance attached to a sturdy frame for its hands and feet to grasp, and has continuous access to milk from a nipple. The chair was enclosed in an air-filtered and heated plexiglass cubicle. One group of subjects was restricted from access to patterned visual stimulation for the first 60 days. Restriction was accomplished by a translucent plexiglass chamber which enclosed the monkey's head. A second group was reared in identical conditions in the mother-surrogate chair, except that these monkeys had unrestricted visual access to the laboratory. All monkeys were removed from the chairs once daily for cleaning, an operation requiring from 5 to 10 minutes. The head of the restricted subject was covered with a porous bag during this operation to prevent patterned vision. The subject was reared in the total restriction condition. (For a fuller description of similar rearing conditions used for an earlier group of animals, see Levison, Levison and Norton, 1968.)

Testing began on the first day of life. For 1 hour daily, the subject had the opportunity to supply patterned visual stimulation for himself. In the test session, a lever was fastened onto the surrogate structure at hand-level; the visual pattern deprivation box was converted to a test chamber with a projection screen facing the animal. Lever presses resulted in the projection of patterned stimuli onto the screen from the rear. The stimuli were: (a) unpatterned white light, (b) a black cross on a white background, (c) a set of six black lines randomly placed in a white background, and (d) a colored, abstract modern painting. On Days 60 through 75, restriction of pattern vision was terminated and the deprivation chamber was absent except during testing. Deprivation conditions were then resumed until Day 100. On Day 100, the animal was removed from the surrogate rearing apparatus and placed alone in a cage. The subject's stimulation-seeking behavior during this experiment did not differ from that of the other animals in the restricted group.

A relevant aspect of the subject's early experience, in addition to the experimental conditions, was that on his fourteenth day of life, his arm was injured accidentally when it became jammed in the padded cylinder which enclosed the midsection of his body. The injury became infected and gangrene eventually developed, despite medication. His fingers self-amputated on Day 54. During this time, because of the additional medical treatment required, he was removed from the chair two to three times daily (rather than once daily as were the other animals), thus receiving 10 to 30 minutes of additional handling each day. His behavior at this time was not observably different from that of the other animals in the restricted group.

After he was removed from the experimental situation and placed in a cage, the subject's behavior was noticeably different from that of the other pattern-deprivation animals in the same situation. He did not exhibit any of the usual deprivation stereotypes. He did not rock, crouch, bite himself, or clasp himself. Restricted monkeys tended to be excitable and fearful in the postexperiment cage compared with the visually nonrestricted subjects. However, the subject's emotional behavior resembled that of the latter animals. At least one other study (Harlow, Dodsworth and Harlow, 1965) has reported an absence of stereotyped behaviors following rearing under conditions of total social isolation, but the animals were highly fearful. In this instance, the extra handling which the subject received as a consequence of his injury may have effected the subsequent lack of stereotypes and the relatively less fearful behavior. No interaction occurred between subject and caretaker except for the routine care given to all of the animals, which consisted of twice-daily feeding and watering, and cage cleaning and changing of bedding every other day. All of the animals were isolated from other human contact.

Development of Head Banging

When the subject was 1 year old, the experimenter began training him to enter a transfer cage, in preparation for daily removal to an experimental chamber for a new experiment. The subject quickly learned the following sequences for food rewards: (a) to run into the cage for food, (b) to sit, and (c) to let the door close. The cage training took about 10 minutes each day. However, on 2 subsequent days, the door of the transfer cage accidentally dropped on the subject, glancing off his head and shoulders. This was apparently very frightening to him; his response was to race away from the transfer cage and crouch in the left rear corner of the cage, where he sat huddled in the corner. After this, the introduction of the transfer cage into his home cage was correlated with very emotional behavior: refusal to enter the transfer cage, even when very hungry; biting of the cage door; racing out of the cage; crouching, rocking, and head banging. He would sit in the left rear corner of the cage and rhythmically bang his head against the plastic wall of the cage. The subject was never observed to rock without also head banging. He would also bang his head when the experimenter was transfer-cage training other animals. An attempt was made to desensitize him to the transfer cage by extended, benign, and careful handling by a second experimenter, with little success.

At this point, for various reasons, it was decided to test the animals in their home cages and transfer-cage training stopped. The subject was occasionally seen to be head banging in the early part of the next 2-month period; toward the end, head banging was not observed at all.

After this 2-month period, the experimenter introduced some variations into the handling of the subject's feeding routine to determine the conditions under which head banging might reoccur, if at all. All observed instances of head banging are reported. The following observations were made, starting in his fourteenth month of age:

14 months, 20 days: The subject was fed last, rather than in his usual position in the feeding sequence. Before he was fed he drank half his water, then, crouched and started head banging. The experimenter gave him a few pieces of monkey chow (considerably less than the regular portion) and left the animal room. The subject resumed head banging after eating the small portion of food.

14 months, 21 days: The subject was fed last. When the experimenter began feeding the other animals, he immediately began banging his head. Head banging occurred earlier in the feeding sequence than on the previous day.

14 months, 22 days: The subject began head banging when the experimenter entered the animal room and opened the food canister, preparatory to feeding the animals. Then he stopped, but resumed head banging when the experimenter fed the animals on either side of him.

On the next 3 days, the subject was fed in his previous position in the sequence; on the fourth day, delay in feeding was again introduced.

14 months, 26 days: The subject did not head bang until the experimenter fed animals on either side of him.

14 months, 27 days: Banged head briefly when the experimenter put in new bedding in an adjacent cage, but did not resume head banging until the experimenter left the room without feeding him, having fed the other animals.

14 months, 28 days: Same sequence and behavior as previous day.

14 months, 29 days: The subject head banged until the experimenter passed out sugar cubes (which conatined their daily dose of isoniazid); this was usually done before feeding the animals. The subject was then fed first and he stopped head banging.

On the following 5 days, he was given his food in his usual sequence; no head banging was observed. On the sixth day following, delay in feeding was again introduced, and the training cage was reintroduced into his home cage.

15 months, 4 days: The other animals were fed first; after they were fed, he head banged. The transfer cage was placed in his home cage to retest his reactions to it. He became upset when the transfer cage was inserted, and sat in his usual head banging posture, as if to head bang, but did not. He turned his head and became interested in exploring the cage and finally entered it. He allowed the experimenter to partially close the door of the transfer cage before running out, which was unusual because, in previous cage training subsequent to his being hit by the door, he had run out as soon as he saw the experimenter's hand approaching the door of the transfer cage. After running out, he returned into the transfer cage, but would not eat there.

15 months, 5 days: Banged head when not fed in the usual sequence. When the training cage was put in, he was more apprehensive than on the previous day, made unusual vocalizations, and sat in the rear left corner of the cage (the usual place) and banged his head. He did enter the transfer cage to obtain his food, but was very upset and remained upset throughout the feeding routine.

Following this, the subject was always fed in the usual sequence and head banging was observed in the following instances:

16 months, 11 days: When holes were being drilled in his cage front.

16 months, 12 days: When a stranger was in the doorway of the animal room.

16 months, 18 days: When animal on left was fed.

A second set of experiments with the entire group of animals was begun at this time. In this sequence, testing was conducted in the home cage. Every lever response produced a visual stimulus on a screen immediately in front of the cage.

Following the beginning of the new experiment, head banging was noted in the following instances:

16 months, 23 days: When the door to his cage was closed (i.e., when the experimenter finished cleaning cage and he no longer could grab at sponge, etc.).

16 months, 30 days: As the experimenter cleaned adjacent animal's bedding (usually done by animal caretaker).

17 months, 2 days: As the experimenter repaired lever box on front of cage to the left of subject's cage.

17 months, 3 days: When the experimenter stopped washing the subject's cage (signaling end of opportunity to snatch at sponge, etc.).

17 months, 7 days: When the experimenter withdrew glove and sponge from the subject's cage. (The subject had been attacking them.) When the experimenter worked on apparatus on cage on left.

17 months, 9 days: Head banging on this day occurred in a different location: on the top of the cage. He also ran into the wall of the cage and hit his head.

17 months, 10 days: As equipment was moved into place in front of cage.

17 months, 22 days: When the experimenter fixed equipment on cage to left of the subject's cage.

Head banging was not observed to occur when a person was not in the room except under the conditions noted previously, i.e., when he had not been fed.

DISCUSSION

In this monkey, head banging appeared as a response to a negative situation (cage door glancing off his head and shoulders) and subsequently was exhibited in other negative situations. The first three observations indicate that when the regular feeding schedule was disrupted, the subject very quickly began to anticipate not being fed, and head banging appeared progressively earlier in the feeding sequence, finally starting with the first act of the sequence: the experimenter opening the food container. However, after he was fed in the usual sequence, head banging did not occur. When delay in feeding was again introduced, he appeared to learn quickly that he eventually would be fed, and would then head bang only after all the others had been fed or after the experimenter left the room without feeding him. However, after the delay in feeding procedure was terminated, head banging continued to be observed in the following three general kinds of situations: (*a*) disruption of the customary environment; (*b*) in response to strangers; (*c*) at the termination of his interactions with the experimenter at cage cleaning time. All three might globally be described as negative situations, the third being the termination of an apparently positive sequence.

Although the number and variety of stereotyped behaviors increase with the complexity of the organism (c.f. Davenport, Menzel and Rogers, 1966), head banging does occur in both human and nonhuman primates, although apparently at lower frequencies in the nonhuman primate. Even in humans the incidence is, however, variable depending on the population. In what proportion of the population head banging occurs is indeterminate, but Escalona (1968) found a very low incidence in the population of intellectually-average children whom she studied. Incidence is high among mental retardates, and low in the institution children described by Province and Lipson (1962).

Two relatively well-established and related ideas about the development of stereotyped behavior in nonhuman primates do not seem to apply to head banging. The first is that the frequency of particular patterns are related to the length of time of isolation. Berkson (1968) separated groups of crab-eating macaques from their mothers at 0, 1, 2, 4, or 6 months of age. Abnormal stereotyped behaviors developed in all groups, but the frequencies of different patterns were related to the length of time of isolation. Stereotyped behaviors developed more rapidly and to a higher frequency in animals separated in the first 2 months. However, frequency of head banging was not systematically related to length of time of isolation.

The stereotyped behaviors present in animals have also been described in terms of substitute behavior (e.g., Foley, 1935). The development of the stereotyped behavior is believed to be related to the lack of stimulation usually provided by the mother during normal maternal care. Care of the infant by the mother during a critical early period seems permanently to meet certain of the infant's needs so that stereotyped behaviors do not develop later in life, even under conditions of extreme monotony and social deprivation (Davenport et al., 1966, p. 137).

Mason (1968) suggests that behaviors such as digit-sucking and self-clasping have their counterparts in the contact-seeking behavior which is present in the normal relation of mother to infant. Berkson (1968) describes non-nutritive sucking, self-grasping, crouching, and the stereotypy of location as homologous respectively to sucking, grasping the mother's fur and skin, maintaining contact, and remaining with the mother either for sleeping or for safety when there is a disturbance in the environment.

In an experimental analysis of the relationship between early experience and later development of stereotyped behavior, Mason and Berkson (c.f. Mason, 1968) manipulated the early environment of the rhesus and showed a relationship between self-rocking and the quality of "maternal" stimulation. Two groups of animals were reared on a cloth-covered surrogate. One group was reared with a surrogate that moved freely about the cage on an irregular schedule; the other with an identical but stationary surrogate. Animals reared with the stationary surrogate developed stereotyped rocking, while those with the moving surrogate did not.

Head banging in animals does not appear to be related either to length of deprivation experience or to characteristics of the early maternal stimulation provided. Similarities in form to early behaviors are not obvious in the case of head banging, nor are homologous behaviors readily identified. The head banging in the animal described in this report was clearly related to immediate antecedent environmental events. It may well be that head banging can appear in normal human infants or in mental defectives as a result of a specific set of events.

The suggestion that head banging may be situation-specific is supported by reports in the literature on human infants. Two of the mothers in the study by deLissovoy (1962) noted that if their children started head banging during the night, it was a signal that they needed changing; after the diaper change, head banging ceased in both of these cases. deLissovoy (1963) found a higher incidence of otitis media in a group of head bangers as compared to a control group of subjects. He also noted that in four of six cases where head banging was associated with otitis media, head banging appeared after the onset of otitis. The most severe cases of otitis media also showed the most severe head banging. In several cases studied by Kravitz *et al.* (1960), head banging had stopped, but started again with the eruption of a new set of teeth. Levy (1944) reports a case of a child head banging in an orphanage; the head banging stopped when the child's favorite toys were restored to him. The observation by Kravitz *et al.* (1960) that head banging also occurred in siblings in 20 percent of the observed cases also suggests that particular patterns of interaction present in the relationship between either mother and child, or mentally deficient child and caretaker, are of relevance.

Head banging, a low frequency behavior in nonhuman primates, developed in a rhesus monkey with no previous stereotyped behaviors as a consequence of a particular set of interactions with the experimenter. It is suggested that onset of head banging in infants and mental retardates may similarly be a consequence of specific relatively immediate antecedent conditions.

REFERENCES

Berkson, G. Development of abnormal stereotyped behavior. *Developmental Psychobiology*, 1968, 1 (2), 118-132.

Davenport, R. K., & Menzel, E. W. Stereotyped behavior in the infant chimpanzee. *Archives of General Psychiatry*, 1963, 8, 99-101.

Davenport, R. K., Menzel, E. W., & Rogers, C. M. Effects of severe isolation on "normal" juvenile chimpanzees. *Archives of General Psychiatry*, 1966, 14, 134-138.

deLissovoy, V. Headbanging in early childhood. *Child Development*, 1962, 33, 43-56.

deLissovoy, V. Head banging in early childhood: A suggested cause. *Journal of Genetic Psychology*, 1963, 102, 109-114.

Escalona, S. K. *The roots of individuality*. Chicago: Aldine Publishing Company, 1968.

Foley, J. P., Jr. Second year development of a rhesus monkey (Macaca Mulatta) reared in isolation during the first 18 months. *Journal of Genetic Psychology*, 1935, 47, 73-97.

Harlow, H. F., Dodsworth, R. O., & Harlow, M. K. Total social isolation in monkeys. *Proceedings of the National Academy of Science*, 1965, 54, 90-97.

Held, R., & Bauer, J. A., Jr. Visually guided reaching in infant monkeys after restricted rearing. *Science*, 1967, 155, 718-720.

Kravitz, H., Rosenthal, V., Teplitz, Z., Murphy, J. B., & Lesser, R. E. A study of head banging in infants and children. *Diseases of the Nervous System*, 1960, 21, 203-208.

Levison, C. A., Levison, P. K., & Norton, H. P. Effects of early visual conditions on stimulation-seeking behavior in infant rhesus monkeys. *Psychonomic Science*, 1968, 11, 101-102.

Levy, D. M. On the problem of movement restraint: Tics, stereotyped movements, hyperactivity. *American Journal of Orthopsychiatry*, 1944, 14, 644-671.

Mason, W. A. Early social deprivation in the nonhuman primates: Implications for human behavior. In D. C. Glass (Ed.), *Environmental influences*. New York: The Rockefeller University Press and Russell Sage Foundation, 1968.

Province, S., & Lipton, R. *Infants in institutions*. New York: International Universities Press, 1962.

Section X

ENVIRONMENTAL CONTROL OF ANOMALOUS BEHAVIOUR

37. Stereotyped Behavior and Cage Size[1]

W. A. DRAPER and I. S. BERNSTEIN

Perceptual and Motor Skills, 1963, *16,* 231-4. Reprinted by permission.

Zoologists have long been concerned with the problem of caging animals in such a manner that the confining space is adapted to the animals' capacity for movement. Frequently this involves only manipulation of the size of the animal's cage (Hediger, 1950; Hediger, 1955). It appears that changes in the physical dimensions of the spatial environment can be accompanied by a marked change in the form of behavior as well as the frequency of occurrence of various activities that are generally common in cages. Levy (1944) has observed that chickens and horses restrained by small cages or stalls, show stereotyped locomotor and or nonlocomotor activities, the latter occurring under the more severely restricted conditions. Hediger (1950) has noted that stereotyped behavior occurs in a wide range of animals and is a "sure sign of wrong treatment," one aspect of which can be overrestriction of physical space. Feral rhesus monkeys also exhibit stereotyped patterns of behavior both in their home cage and when introduced to novel situations (Mason and Green, 1962). However, the degree to which stereotyped behavior is influenced by spatial determinants is not known. Thus, this experiment was designed to study changes in rhesus monkey activity that accompany systematic variation of cage size.

METHOD

Subjects

*S*s were 12 adolescent wild-born rhesus monkeys (three males, nine females). They were approximately 3 yr. old at the time of testing, having spent the previous 2 yr. housed at Yerkes Laboratories either individually or in small groups in outdoor cages each of which was 3 ft. by 2 ft. by 7 ft., equipped with a shelter hutch located 5 ft. above the floor. Prior to participation in the present study, *S*s had been trained on various discrimination learning tasks but they had had no contact with the specific cages used in this experiment.

Apparatus

Three outdoor cages were used: small (3 ft. by 3 ft. by 3 ft.), medium (4 ft. by 3 ft. by 8 ft.), and large (48 ft. by 24 ft. by 8 ft.). All cages were of wood construction with

[1] This investigation was supported in part by a grant to Dr. A. J. Riopelle by the U.S. Army Medical Research and Development Command, Department of the Army, under Contract No. DA-49-193-MD-2095. Dr. I. S. Bernstein was supported by a U.S.P.H.S. postdoctoral fellowship (MF-11,006) from the National Institutes of Health.

2-in. by 4-in. welded wire sides. The small cage was supported by 18-in. legs and had a metal grille floor; the other cages had concrete floors. An observation post with a one-way screen was used during observations.

Procedure

All animals were tested 10 times in each of the three different cages. On every experimental day a given animal was observed for 5 min. in each cage. Test order was counterbalanced with regard to Ss and days. Simultaneous recordings were made by two Es. For each 30-sec. interval in the 5-min. period, one E recorded on a check list the occurrence of 22 selected types of behavior (see Table 1); the other E recorded the total number of feet traveled and the total duration of periods during which no locomotion occurred.

Observations were made outdoors in a relatively isolated part of the Laboratory grounds. With few exceptions they took place between 8:30 a.m. and 12:00 noon. Testing occurred only when the temperature was between 50° and 80° F. and cloud cover was less than 50%.

Each behavior category was analyzed for over-all differences among the three cage sizes using the Friedman analysis of variance, and where these differences proved significant beyond the .05 level of confidence, subsequent comparisons were made between all pairs of cages with the Wilcoxon test (Siegel, 1956).

RESULTS

Table 1 shows the mean values and significance levels of intercage comparisons for the behavior categories. The following activities occurred less than 1% of the time in any cage, hence they were not included in the table: lie down, urinate, defecate, yawn, teethgrind, squeal, and lipsmack.

Table 1. Mean Incidence of Behavior and Level of Significance of
Differences between Cages

Behavior categories*	Cage size			p**	
	Small	Medium	Large	.05	.01
1. Stereotyped behavior	5.5	1.4	0	c	a,b
2. Cage shake	1.2	.3	0	c	a,b
3. Manipulate cage	1.7	.9	.1		b,c
4. Bite cage	1.5	.7	.1		b,c
5. Travel—1 ft. any direction	9.9	9.5	9.9		
6. Hang—from side or roof	1.7	4.8	.8		a,c
7. Sit	2.7	4.9	3.1	c	a
8. Self-directed activities	.5	1.1	1.7	b	
9. Feeding	.3	.7	1.4	c	a,b
10. Vocal—coo	6.3	5.7	3.5		b,c
11. Vocal-bark	2.7	2.6	1.7		
12. High—off floor	3.4	9.7	8.8	c	a,b
13. Low—on floor	10.0	7.6	6.7		a,b
14. Total time stationary (sec.)	10.5	11.2	5.3	b	c
15. Total distance traveled (ft.)	39.7	34.3	75.5		b,c

* 1 to 13: Max. value = 10.0, 14: Max. value = 300.0, 15: No Max. value.
** Cage comparisons: (a) Small-Medium, (b) Small-Large, (c) Medium-Large.

Stereotyped behavior was most prevalent in the small cage, markedly less frequent in the medium cage, and was never observed in the large cage (intercage differences all significant beyond the .05 level). Ten of the 12 monkeys showed clearly identifiable stereotypies which, in some cases, occupied up to 90% of the time the animal was in the small cage. It is important to note that, although all stereotypies are by definition repetitive, even ritualistic, the exact form that they take differs from one animal to another, and it was possible to differentiate animals in terms of the stereotypies displayed. Common stereotypies included: rapid bouncing on the floor with all four feet, bouncing using only the front legs, predictable circular pacing, pacing with a head thrust at regular intervals, regular pacing and recoiling from one corner of the cage, rapid pacing developing into an exceedingly fast spin or twirl on the hind legs in the center of the cage, twirling holding onto the roof, backward somersaults, unique awkward vertical jumping, and touching one leg to a particular place on the side of the cage as the animal traveled in a fixed pattern. The clearest example of the effect of cage size on stereotyped behavior was seen in a female which exhibited continuous backward somersaults in the small cage. When placed in the medium cage, she displayed regular pacing that involved throwing up the forelegs and tossing back the head as if to begin the somersault, but it was rarely completed. No indication of a stereotypy was seen in the large cage.

Cage-oriented behavior was also related to cage size. One type, shaking the side of the cage, which is of shorter duration but similar in form to bouncing, showed the same relationship as did stereotypies to cage size. Other forms of cage-oriented behavior, such as manipulating and biting the cage, also occurred significantly less often in the large cage than in either of the other cages.

Although the amount of time the animals traveled was the same in all cages, the total distance traveled was much greater in the large cage. Hanging and sitting on the cage—activities which are commonly observed in the home cage—were seen most in the medium cage which is closest in actual size to the home cage. The same was true with regard to self-directed behaviors which included: self-grooming, self-clasping, self-biting, and manipulating the genitalia. Although no food was provided in any of the cages, the animals did eat grass, leaves, or other organic debris in the cages. This type of feeding occurred most in the large cage and least in the small cage, although such debris was equally available in all cages. Vocalization in the form of cooing was recorded during 63% and 57% of the time units in the small and medium cages, respectively, but occurred in only 35% of the time units in the large cage ($P < .01$). Since the vertical distance is much less in the small cage, it is to be expected that more time would be spent on the floor of this cage, and in fact Ss were recorded as being low during all time units. Conversely, Ss entered the upper portion of the small cage during the fewest time units but scores in the medium cage exceeded those in the large cage in this category.

In general, the animals were quite active in all the cages, and although the inactive periods were longest in the small cage, these still occupied less than 5% of the total time. The activity in the small cage is, however, best characterized as excited and frantic. It was also observed that Ss frequently balked on entering the small cage but would rush into the others without hesitation.

DISCUSSION

The results indicate that restriction of rhesus monkeys by decreasing the size of their cage, results in an increased incidence of stereotyped behavior. This effect is specific to the situation; it declines immediately when S is removed to a larger cage and disappears entirely in a very large cage. This suggests that stereotypies under these conditions are a reaction to spatial restriction; when normal expressions of behavior such as locomotion (running, climbing, etc.) are inhibited by the situation, stereotypies appear. Further, stereotyped behavior in the feral monkey is a temporary substitute activity in that it disappears as soon as normal locomotor expressions are again possible. The absence of stereotypies in the largest cage suggests that this size cage exceeds the minimum spatial requirements for the expression of normal rhesus behavior patterns.

The specific spatial dimensions that elicit stereotypies are as yet still unclear. It appears that an increase in vertical space will substantially reduce stereotyped behavior in monkeys, and when this is coupled with greater horizontal space, stereotypies cease. It is likely that the flight reaction of rhesus monkeys involves both upward and outward locomotion away from the source of danger, and some stereotyping remains in the medium-sized cage because of the limitation on horizontal locomotion.

It should be noted that Ss in this experiment were not adapted to the cages, hence when they entered they were excited and hyperactive. It is well known that monkeys housed in laboratory cages show stereotyped behavior more frequently when they are agitated, e.g., in the presence of strangers, before feeding, etc. However, we would expect that, if animals were housed permanently under the conditions used in this experiment, essentially the same differences in behavior would be found. Indeed, subsequent studies of social behavior with the same animals in the largest cage revealed no stereotyped behavior with the exception of extremely rare (less than 1% of the time) instances of bouncing by the dominant male and his female consort, and this occurred only when the animals were agitated, e.g., threatened by people or fighting in the group. The other elaborate ritualistic stereotypies were never observed in any animal.

Finally, it is important to distinguish the stereotyped behavior of feral rhesus monkeys from that observed in monkeys reared in the laboratories without their mother (Mason and Green, 1962). For the most part the stereotypies in laboratory-reared animals are relatively persistent, nonlocomotor part-body movements (head-rocking, self-clasping, etc.), whereas feral monkeys show gross locomotor acts that are substantially modified by changes in the physical environment. It is possible that the physiological mechanisms underlying stereotyped behavior are the same in both cases, and the differential rearing conditions affect the form and direction of motor behaviors.

SUMMARY

12 feral adolescent rhesus monkeys were observed individually during 10 5-min. periods in each of three different-sized cages. Stereotyped and cage-oriented behavior occurred most frequently in the small cage, sometimes in the medium cage, and never in the large cage. It was concluded that spatial restriction which does not permit "normal" locomotor behavior, e.g., running, climbing, etc., results in substitute motor expression which frequently takes the form of repetitive stereotyped movements.

REFERENCES

Hediger, H. *Wild animals in captivity.* London: Butterworths Scientific Publ., 1950.

Hediger, H. *Studies of the psychology and behavior of captive animals in zoos and circuses.* New York: Criterion, 1955.

Levy, D. M. On the problem of movement restraint. *Amer. J. Orthopsychiat.,* 1944, 14, 644-671.

Mason, W. A., & Green, P. C. The effects of social restriction on the behavior of rhesus monkeys: IV. Responses to a novel environment and to an alien species. *J. comp. physiol. Psychol.,* 1962, 55, 363-368.

Siegel, S. *Nonparametric statistics for the behavioral sciences.* New York: McGraw-Hill, 1956.

38. Some Effects of Different Test Cages on Response "Strategies" during Leverpress Escape[1]

H. Davis and S. Kenney

Psychological Record, 1975, *25,* 535-43. Copyright 1975 by the *Psychological Record.*
Reprinted by permission.

Rats were exposed to a leverpress shock escape procedure in each of two commercially available "Skinner boxes." Identifiably different response topographies emerged in each chamber, although both of these "strategies" led to rapid shock escape latencies. In one chamber Ss tended to hold the lever depressed throughout the intertrial interval and escape shock by making a reflexive lurch and return to the lever at shock onset. In the second chamber Ss typically crouched mid-cage and leapt at the lever at shock onset. The observation that all Ss, regardless of test chamber, attempted to leverhold during initial escape training suggests that this strategy, which appears to have been suppressed by the second chamber, may be the more "natural" basis for leverpress escape responding insofar as it is derived from freezing, a species specific defense reaction.

Unless one adopts the view that "a Skinner box is a Skinner box" regardless of size, shape, or manufacturing features, then it is unlikely that these differences in design would not have some behavioral consequences. The possibility that cage topography may affect response topography is more immediately understandable when one deals with shuttleboxes, runways, or mazes in which relatively gross motor behaviors are involved. Nevertheless, it is also conceivable that behavioral differences might result from variations in the design of a test cage which involves only some combination of lever, feeder, and whatever additional features a manufacturer includes in his definition of a "Skinner box."

The purpose of the present experiment was to explore possible interactions between test cage topography and the behaviors which emerge during a leverpress shock escape procedure. In contrast to appetitive conditioning or to other aversive control procedures, a number of aspects of leverpress escape suggest that this procedure might yield behavior which is relatively sensitive to subtle differences found between commercially available Skinner boxes. For example, previous research has indicated that despite the fact that only a single leverpress response is required for escape, subjects typically

[1]The authors thank H. M. B. Hurwitz, John E. Tong, Hugh W. Kirby, and J. D. Keehn for their critical assistance. This research was supported in part by a grant from the University of Guelph Research Advisory Board to the first author and Grant No. A 8264 to H. M. B. Hurwitz from the National Research Council of Canada. Requests for reprints should be addressed to Hank Davis, Department of Psychology, University of Guelph, Guelph, Ontario, Canada N1B 2W1.

spend the majority of session time in contact with the lever emitting what have variously been referred to as "extra responses" or "leverholding" (e.g., Dinsmoor, Matsuoka and Winograd, 1958; Migler, 1963).

A survey of the escape literature, as well as extensive work with rats in the authors' laboratory (e.g., Davis and Burton, 1974, 1975; Davis, Hirschorn and Hurwitz, 1973), points to the existence of at least two distinct "strategies" which may underlie the lever-press escape response. Will (1974) has defined "strategies" within an instrumental conditioning situation as behavior patterns which "enable the subject to obtain, in a defined manner, a certain number of reinforcements within a given period." Will concluded that "despite their different efficiencies, each one of these 'strategies' can be considered as 'correct' [1974, p. 370]." The first behavior pattern which emerges in the present experiment suggests that escape, like other aversive control procedures, is essentially an operant situation. That is, subjects emit a discrete leverpress response in the presence of shock (which functions as a discriminative stimulus) and are reinforced by shock termination. According to this analysis, the "extra" responses which typically occur between trials may be viewed as discriminative failures, "rehearsals," or gener-ally inappropriate behavior (e.g., Dinsmoor and Hughes, 1956; Keller, 1941).

A second behavior pattern which may underlie the leverpress escape response involves the subject's freezing, a species-specific defense reaction (SSDR) while in contact with the lever (Bolles, 1970). Once the subject is "leverholding" in this manner, the next shock causes a "reflexive lurch," which throws the rat momentarily from the lever and causes the response which terminates shock. This analysis of escape behavior in terms of SSDRs stresses its innate or reflexive nature (Bolles and McGillis, 1968). According to this analysis, "extra" behaviors, such as leverholding, are actually an essential com-ponent of successful escape and do not represent discriminative failures or general experimental "annoyances" [cf., Feldman and Bremner, 1960].

A subsidiary question in the present study is whether it is possible for a subject to maintain both of these "strategies" simultaneously (viz., "discriminated" operant responding and leverholding/"reflexive lurch"), but show each in the presence of a different test cage. This being the case, the question would then be raised as to which features of the cage environment make the occurrence of a particular escape behavior pattern more probable.

The present experiment involved a two-group, within-subject design in which sub-jects were exposed, either in A-B-A or B-A-B sequence, to two different commercially available rodent test chambers. Half of the subjects in each treatment sequence were run under a lever *press* and half under a lever *release* requirement. This manipulation has previously been used in escape conditioning to affect the probability of intertrial lever holding (see survey by Dinsmoor, 1968).

METHOD

Subjects

Twelve experimentally naive male Wistar rats, approximately 120 days old at the beginning of the experiment, served. The animals were individually housed and were maintained on ad lib food and water.

Apparatus

Subjects were run in test chambers manufactured by Campden Instrument Co. and

Lehigh Valley Electronics (LVE).[1] A comparison of the dimensions of essential features of the two cages appears in Table 1.

The Campden chamber contained two retractable levers, only one of which was operational during the experiment. A minimum downward force of 12 g was required to activate the lever microswitch. None of the cage lights was lit during the experiments. An exhaust fan monitored at 76dB (ref.: .0002 dynes/cm^2) provided ventilation as well as background masking noise.

The LVE chamber contained a single lever which required 12 g downward force to operate. An exhaust fan monitored at 76dB (ref.: .0002 dynes/cm^2) provided ventilation as well as background masking noise.

A constant current shock generator (Campden Instrument Co.) calibrated at 0.8ma delivered scrambled current to the grids, lever, and three metal walls of both chambers. The fourth wall of both chambers was made of Plexiglas.

Standard relay programming and recording equipment were located in an adjoining room. Subjects' behavior throughout the session was recorded on video tape. An

Table 1. Summary of Essential Features of Campden
and LVE Test Chambers

	Campden	Lehigh Valley
Cage interior:		
length	25.4 cm	30.5 cm
width	25.4	22.8
height	20.3	19.1
Floor grids:		
diameter	0.3	0.6
spacing between grids	1.0	1.3
Lever:		
total length	5.1	5.1
width	3.8	4.5
thickness	1.9	1.0
extension into cage	1.6[a]	2.5
height above grid	5.1	5.4
distance from lever edge to nearest adjacent wall	2.3	8.9
Lever lights:		
height above lever	2.5	none
distance from nearest adjacent wall	3.2	none
Feeder tray light:		
height above grid	13.3	none
distance from adjacent walls	10.2	none

[a] In an attempt to affect "leverholding" behavior during the initial experimental phase, several changes were made to the Campden chamber. For consecutive three session periods, lever extension was temporarily increased to 2.5 cm, and the light above the left lever was removed and covered with a metal plate. Neither manipulation had an appreciable effect on the amount of leverholding and both were discontinued.

[1]Campden Instrument Company products are distributed in the USA and Canada by Stoelting Company, Chicago, Illinois. Lehigh Valley products are distributed by Tech. Services, Inc., Beltsville, Maryland.

event recorder marked the distribution and duration of lever contacts and shock occurrences.

Procedure

Subjects were randomly assigned to one of four specific treatment conditions, which are summarized in Table 2. All subjects were run in both the Campden and LVE test chambers, differing only in the sequence in which cage experience occurred. Subjects in Group 1 (n = 6) were exposed to the test chambers in a LVE-Campden-LVE sequence. For Group II subjects (n = 6) the test cage sequence was reversed.

Half the subjects in each experimental group were trained either to press or to release the lever in order to escape shock. Prior to the experimental sessions, each subject was trained according to the lever requirement and test chamber it would initially encounter. To train the escape response, each subject received approximately 60 shocks with an intertrial interval (ITI) of 30 seconds (shock offset to onset). The duration of each shock was initially controlled by the experimenter, who terminated shock by means of a hand switch according to the subject's successive approximations to the leverpress or lever-release response. Preliminary training was discontinued after the subject made 10 consecutive low-latency (less than 1 second) escape responses.

Subjects were run for an average of 10 sessions in each experimental phase. Each experimental session was terminated after 100 escape trials with ITI = 30 sec.

RESULTS

As indicated by the escape latencies given in Table 2, all subjects, regardless of test chamber, responded in order to escape shock. The leverpress vs. lever release

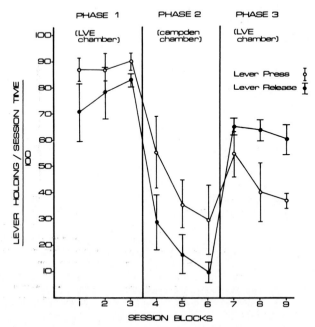

Figure 1. Percentage of session time spent leverholding by subjects in Group I during exposure to leverpress or lever release shock escape procedure in LVE-Campden-LVE test chamber sequence. Vertical bars represent standard error of the mean.

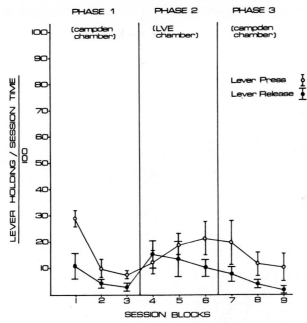

Figure 2. Percentage of session time spent leverholding by subjects in Group II during exposure to leverpress and lever release shock escape procedure in Campden-LVE-Campden test chamber sequence. Vertical bars represent standard error of the mean.

Table 2. Mean Escape Latency during Final Three
Sessions of Each Experimental Phase

	Phase 1	Phase 2	Phase 3
Group 1	(Campden chamber)	(LVE chamber)	(Campden chamber)
leverpress	0.56 sec.	0.56 sec.	0.50 sec.
lever release	0.81 sec.	0.71 sec.	0.59 sec.
Group II	(LVE chamber)	(Campden chamber)	(LVE chamber)
leverpress	0.59 sec.	0.55 sec.	0.85 sec.
lever release	0.50 sec.	0.85 sec.	0.80 sec.

manipulation did not significantly affect either escape latency or the amount of lever-holding behavior (see Figures 1 and 2).

There was a clear relationship between the topography of the escape response and the chamber in which testing occurred. In general, Ss tested in the LVE chamber continued to leverhold throughout the majority of the ITI. When shock occurred, they made what has previously been described as a "reflexive lurch" from the lever, thereby terminating shock. Escape behavior in the Campden chamber, however, generally involved the subject's remaining off-lever during the ITI. At the moment of shock onset, Ss typically leapt towards the lever and made the discrete response which terminated shock. These two escape response "strategies" are illustrated in Figures 3 and 4.

The chamber in which escape behavior initially occurred affected the form of the

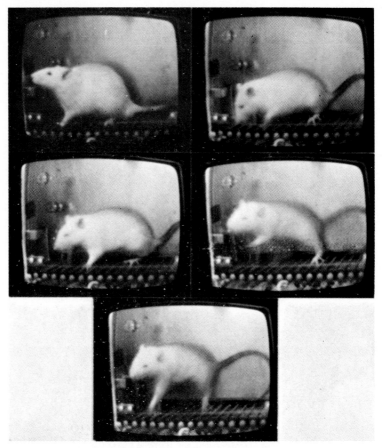

Figure 3. Illustrative escape response "strategy" used by subject in Campden test chamber. Subject typically remained motionless facing lever throughout intertrial interval. At shock onset, subject moved backward slightly and leapt foward toward lever, terminating shock with extended right front paw.

escape response observed throughout the experiment. For example, Phase I experience with leverholding in the LVE chamber appeared to establish this strategy in the repertoire of Group I Ss so that despite a decrease in leverholding during Phase II exposure to the Campden chamber, leverholding was again reestablished as the dominant escape strategy when the subject returned to the LVE chamber in Phase III (see Figure 2). In contrast, Group II Ss which learned the off-lever "discriminated operant" strategy during exposure to the Campden chamber in Phase I, showed only slight increases in the degree of leverholding during Phase II transfer to the LVE chamber (see Figure 1).

It is essential to note that all subjects in both the Campden and LVE test chambers attempted to leverhold during Session 1. Although this behavior was maintained in the LVE chamber, it was rapidly reduced to near zero incidence in the Campden chamber (see Figure 5). This disruptive effect on leverholding by the Campden chamber appeared either in Phase I or, in the case of Ss initially exposed to the LVE chamber, upon exposure to the Campden chamber in Phase II.

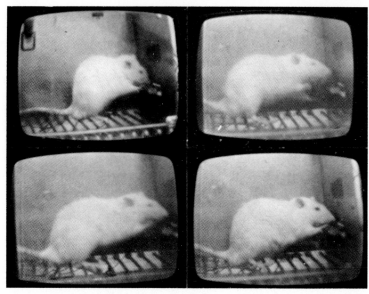

Figure 4. Illustrative escape response "strategy" observed in LVE chamber. Subject typically leverheld throughout the shock-free intertrial interval. At shock onset, subject made brief "reflexive lurch" from and return to the lever, thereby terminating shock and beginning the next leverholding sequence.

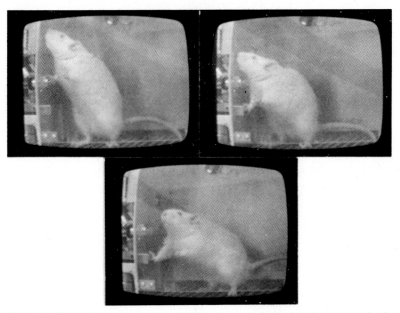

Figure 5. Illustrative attempts at leverholding observed during initial escape session in Campden chamber. Note awkwardness of leverholding posture in lower photographs and displacement of lever contact to light bulb above lever in upper photo. In subsequent sessions intertrial lever contact was reduced to near zero in Campden chamber.

DISCUSSION

The present results provide information not only about the behavior sequences or "strategies" which underlie leverpress escape behavior but also about the constraints which the experimental environment may place upon this class of behavior.

Despite folklore to the contrary, many investigators have reported clear behavioral effects resulting from changes in such test cage features as lever size and position, as well as the location of cage lights (e.g., Davis, Hirschorn and Hurwitz, 1973; Flint, 1969; Schwartz, 1975; Thomas, Appel and Hurwitz, 1958). In the present experiment it is clear that some aspect of cage design affected the form of the escape response either during original learning or after this behavior had been established in another environment.

The critical difference between the LVE and Campden test chambers appears to have been the location of the lever. Because the lever was positioned in the center of the front wall in the LVE chamber, Ss were able to "brace" themselves against the corner or side wall while leverholding and during the "reflexive lurch." In contrast, the corner front wall location of the lever in the Campden chamber did not permit subjects to brace themselves while leverholding. Thus subjects were thrown backward by shock onset, necessitating a return from the rear of the chamber across electrified grids in order to reach the lever. Following several such experiences, all subjects in the Campden chamber learned to position themselves near but out of contact with the lever. At shock onset they moved, often leaping, forward and terminated shock.

The present data, especially those of Group II, suggest that the initial interactions which occur between instrumental responding and the experimental environment may set limits upon the behavior patterns or "strategies" which may be learned later. Moreover, the observation that all subjects attempted to leverhold during the initial escape session suggests that this "strategy" may, as Bolles (1970) and Bolles and McGillis (1968) have argued, be more "natural" insofar as it is derived from *freezing* an SSDR. It may, in fact, be argued that whenever leverpress escape behavior involves any "strategy" other than leverholding/reflexive lurch, it is likely that this alternative behavior pattern has developed only after some aspect of the experimental situation has suppressed its more naturally occurring rival.

REFERENCES

Bolles, R. C. 1970. Species specific defense reactions and avoidance learning. *Psychological Review,* 77, 32-48.

Bolles, R. C., & McGillis, D. B. 1968. The non-operant nature of the bar-press escape response. *Psychonomic Science,* 11, 261-262.

Davis, H., & Burton, J. 1974. The measurement of response force during a lever-press shock escape procedure in rats. *Journal of the Experimental Analysis of Behavior,* 22, 433-440.

Davis, H., & Burton, J. 1975. An analysis of two extinction procedures for lever-press escape behavior. *Bulletin of the Psychonomic Society,* 5, 201-204.

Davis, H., Hirschorn, P., & Hurwitz, H. M. B. 1973. Leverholding behavior during a lever lift shock escape procedure. *Animal Learning and Behavior,* 1, 215-218.

Dinsmoor, J. A. 1968. Escape from shock as a conditioning technique. In M. R. Jones (Ed.), *Miami symposium on the prediction of behaviour 1967: Aversive stimulation.* Coral Gables: University of Miami Press. Pp. 33-75.

Dinsmoor, J. A., & Hughes, L. H. 1956. Training rats to press a bar to turn off shock. *Journal of Comparative and Physiological Psychology,* 49, 235-238.

Dinsmoor, J. A., Matsuoka, Y., & Winograd, E. 1958. Bar-holding as a preparatory response in escape-from-shock training. *Journal of Comparative and Physiological Psychology,* 51, 637-639.

Feldman, R. S., & Bremner, F. J. 1963. A method for rapid conditioning of stable avoidance bar pressing behavior. *Journal of the Experimental Analysis of Behavior,* 6, 393-394.

Flint, G. A. 1969. Bar orientation in operant escape training. *Behavior Research Methods and Instrumentation,* 1, 231-232.

Keller, F. S. 1941. Light aversion in the white rat. *The Psychological Record,* 4, 235-250.

Migler, B. 1963. Barholding during escape training. *Journal of the Experimental Analysis of Behavior,* 6, 65-72.

Schwartz, B. 1975. Discriminative stimulus location as a determinant of positive and negative behavioral contrasts in the pigeon. *Journal of the Experimental Analysis of Behavior,* 23, 167-176.

Thomas, D. G., Appel, J. B., & Hurwitz, H. M. B. 1958. Studies in light reinforced behavior: V. Effects of lever size, shift in lever size and light position. *Psychological Reports,* 4, 411-413.

Will, B. 1974. Development of 'strategies' utilized by albino rats in operant conditioning. *Animal Behavior,* 22, 370-375.

39. Circadian Susceptibility to Animal Hypnosis

J. W. Ternes

Psychological Record, 1977, *1,* 15-19, Volume 27, Special Issue. Copyright 1977 by the
Psychological Record. Reprinted by permission.

Biological rhythms, with periods which correlate with major cyclic environmental events, have frequently been reported (Brown, 1959; Halberg, 1960a, 1960b). In the absence of environmental stimulation, these rhythms persist and thus are considered to be spontaneous and self-sustaining. Nonetheless, environmental stimuli may serve to entrain or to synchronize their phasing and frequency (Halberg, 1960a, 1960b). Entrainment simply means that a certain agent in the environment may be used by the organism to adjust the phase or period of one or more of its biological rhythms. Common entraining agents are the 24-hr. light-dark cycle, day length, and temperature (Aschoff, 1962).

The most prominent, i.e., easily identifiable due to their relatively high amplitude, are the circadian (nearly 24-hr.) rhythms, such as the circadian temperature rhythm. The cyclic fluctuations of most physiological variables are not readily apparent to us, however. They are essentially invisible unless repeated measurement is accomplished at several diverse times within each 24-hr. interval. Nonetheless, throughout any 24-hr. period, many physiological variables undergo changes in amplitude which are both rhythmic and biologically significant.

Rhythms of susceptibility and the implied concept of *hours of changing resistance* have recently been given increasing attention. Biological and behavioral response to agents such as ionizing radiation, drugs, medicines and poisons have been reported to be a function of the time of exposure (Haus, Halberg, Locken and Kim, 1974; Reinberg, 1967; Reinberg and Halberg, 1971; Ternes, 1974). Basically, these results indicate a circadian differential in responsiveness to stimulation, and imply that circadian variations in responsiveness involve significant fluctuations around a daily mean value or level. The reciprocal of resistance is susceptibility. Thus, for a number of organisms, the difference between health and disease or, for that matter, between life or death, may depend upon the stage of an individual's circadian rhythms at which a stimulus is presented (Halberg, 1969; Mills, 1966).

Animal hypnosis is an area of research in which a frequently used dependent measure, trance duration—i.e., duration of the immobility response—is highly variable. An appreciation of the concept of hours of changing resistance due to a rhythm of susceptibility may be of value in interpreting some of the diverse results which have been

Present address: Department of Psychiatry, University of Pennsylvania, Philadelphia, Pennsylvania 19104.

reported. The purpose of the present experiment was to demonstrate that there are circadian rhythms of susceptibility to the immobility response. The hypothesis tested was that, where trance duration is the dependent variable, the values observed for any individual subject change predictably and significantly within the span of each 24-hr. period.

Two different species, *Bufo marinus* and *Cyrtopholis portoricae,* were used as experimental subjects in an attempt to demonstrate the generality of the phenomenon studied. *Bufo,* the giant Surinam toad, was introduced to Puerto Rico to combat the white grub, an insect pest which fed on the root of the sugar cane plant as well as on other crops. Now a very common animal in Puerto Rico, *Bufo* can attain a weight of up to 500 g. It is found at all lower elevations in Puerto Rico. *Cyrtopholis,* the Puerto Rican tarantula, is actually only one of six indigenous species. It is brown in color, and attains a size of approximately 45 mm in length. *Cyrtopholis* normally lives in small mud caves, which it constructs on the ground. Both *Bufo* and *Cyrtopholis* are nocturnal insectivores.

METHOD

Subjects

Bufo marinus

Subjects were 16 giant Surinam toads collected in Rio Piedras, Puerto Rico, just prior to the start of the experiment. All subjects were marked for identification with colored leg bands at the start of the experiment. Subjects ranged in weight from 100 to 490 g. Initially they were housed out of doors in two 24-gal. fish tanks. Under these crowded conditions, seven individuals died within 48 hr. Subsequently, they were set free in an 8 ft. x 10 ft. (2.5 x 3 m) covered patio with several concrete building blocks, the hollow interior chambers of which served as sleeping quarters for the subjects during the day. Of the surviving subjects, five were males and four were females. Although they were free to capture and eat any insects they could find in their quarters, their diet was supplemented at 3-day intervals with live cockroaches.

Cyrtopholis portoricae

Subjects were eight adult females, individually housed in 12-oz. (400 ml) Mason jars with perforated lids. These jars were kept under cover, but out of doors. Subjects were fed cockroaches at 3-day intervals. Water was provided by means of a moist wad of cotton introduced to the jar at feeding time.

Procedure

Bufo marinus

All subjects were tested individually four times in each 24-hr. period, at 6:00 a.m., 12:00 a.m., 6:00 p.m., and 12:00 p.m. Each subject was immobilized by rapid inversion and application of constant light pressure to the thorax while holding the front legs in a flexed position against the body. The hind legs were not restrained. Pressure was discontinued after 5 sec., and a timing device was started. As soon as a subject initiated attempts to bring itself to an upright position, usually by kicking with its hind legs, the timer was stopped. The elapsed time was recorded as the duration of the trance state. Testing was continued for 30 days.

Cyrtopholis portoricae

All subjects were tested individually three times per day, at 7:00 a.m., 3:00 p.m., and 11:00 p.m. The immobilization procedure was as follows: the subject was first transferred from its living container to a standard Petri dish, on top of which a glass pane then was placed. The dish was then rapidly inverted. When the subject became immobile, the dish was removed, and a timing device was started. As soon as the subject initiated righting movements with its legs, the clock was terminated. The elapsed time was recorded as trance duration.

RESULTS

Bufo marinus

A Friedman two-way analysis of variance by ranks was used to test the hypothesis that the four samples (times of day) were representative of the same population of trance durations. The value of Xr^2 was equal to 155. This value was highly significant beyond the .0001 level where, with 3 *df*, the required value is 16.27. These results imply that the size of the scores (trance durations) depends on the condition (time of day) under which it was obtained. Figure 1 shows the group mean trance duration as a function of the time of day when it was induced. The values are plotted twice in succession, to provide a better idea of the shape of the curve. The 6:00 a.m. phase consistently produced the longest trance durations, while the 6:00 p.m. phase produced the shortest durations.

Cyrtopholis portoricae

A Friedman two-way analysis of variance by ranks was used to test the hypothesis that the three samples of trance duration were representative of the same population. The value of Xr^2 obtained was equal to 18.5. This value was highly significant beyond the

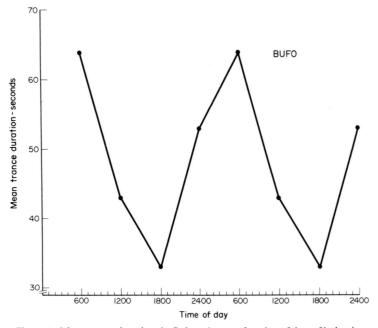

Figure 1. Mean trance durations in *Bufo marinus* as a function of time of induction.

.0001 level where, with 2 *df,* the required value is 12.0. These results imply that the size of the trance duration depends on the phase of the cycle (time of day) at which it was obtained. Figure 2 shows the mean trance duration as a function of the time of induction. The mean values have been plotted in two repeated series to provide a better idea of the shape of the curve. The trances induced at 11:00 p.m. were consistently longer than trances induced at other times of day, while the trances induced at 7:00 a.m. were generally the shortest in duration.

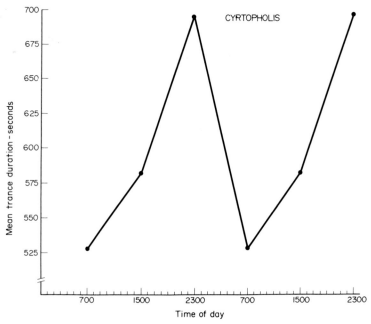

Figure 2. Mean trance durations in *Cyrtopholis portoricae* as a function of time of induction.

DISCUSSION

An accurate description of any periodic function requires a specification of the parameters which characterize the rhythm. Generally, a rhythm may be described by three parameters: (a) its period; (b) a reference measure of temporal phasing, such as the acrophase (time of highest amplitude); and (c) a determination of amplitude, such as the extent of variation around a rhythm-adjusted mean or level. Quantification may include confidence limits for both phase and amplitude, which would allow comparison of the same rhythmic functions between organisms, of several rhythms within the same individual, or of the same rhythm in the same individual under different treatment conditions.

The present paper reports the existence of circadian rhythms of susceptibility to hypnosis, where susceptibility is defined operationally in terms of average trance duration. In other words, short trance durations are considered to be indicative of resistance, whereas longer trances are taken as evidence of susceptibility. No attempt has been made to quantify the present data beyond the point of specifying the period, 24 hr. Such quantification would be premature at this time, due to both the small size of the samples employed and also the small number of phases, i.e., times within the 24-hr. period, for which data were obtained. Such work remains to be done. The reader should be cautioned that, in the absence of such data, very little significance should be attached to the specific times of day at which high and low trance durations were observed; these times of susceptibility and resistance are specific to the two species studied, and to the particular maintenance environment in which they were tested. In the absence of sufficient data and statistical quantification of the parameters described above, generalization at this stage would be premature.

The significance of the present study lies in the demonstration of the circadian rhythm of changing susceptibility to hypnotism. It should serve to stimulate other investigators to determine if such rhythms play a significant role in the species which they employ as subjects.

REFERENCES

Aschoff, J. 1962. Time givers of 24 hour physiological cycles. In K. E. Schaefer (Ed.), *Man's dependence on the earthly atmosphere*. New York: Macmillan.

Brown, F. A. 1959. The rhythmic nature of animals and plants. *American Scientist, 47*, 147-168.

Halberg, F. 1960a. The 24 hour scale: A time dimension of adaptive functional organization. *Perspectives in Biology and Medicine, 3*, 491-527.

Halberg, F. 1960b. Temporal coordination of physiologic function. *Cold Spring Harbor Symposium on Quantitative Biology, 25*, 289-310.

Halberg, F. 1969. Chronobiology. *Annual Review of Physiology, 31*, 675-725.

Haus, E. F., Halberg, F., Locken, M. D. and Kim, Y. S. 1974. Circadian rhythmometry of mammalian radiosensitivity. In C. Tobias & P. Todd (Eds.), *Space radiation biology*. New York: Academic.

Mills, J. N. 1966. Human circadian rhythms. *Physiological Review, 46*, 128-171.

Reinberg, A. 1967. The hours of changing responsiveness of susceptibility. *Perspectives in Biology and Medicine, 11*, 111-126.

Reinberg, A., and Halberg, F. 1971. Circadian chronopharmacology. *Annual Review of Pharmacology, 11*, 455-492.

Ternes, J. W. 1974. Circadian cyclic sensitivity to gamma radiation as an unconditioned stimulus in taste aversion conditioning. In L. E. Scheving, F. Halberg, & J. E. Pauly (Eds.), *Chronobiology*. Tokyo: Igaku Shoin.

40. Schedule-induced Drinking as a Function of Interpellet Interval

J. D. KEEHN and V. A. COLOTLA

Psychonomic Science, 1971, *23*, 67-71. Reprinted by permission.

Two white rats reinforced with 45-mg Noyes pellets on fixed-interval schedules from 15 sec to 5 min exhibited a bitonic relationship between level of polydipsia and fixed-interval value. This relationship depended on three characteristics of drinking: frequency, distribution and duration. At shorter FIs drinks occurred frequently shortly after reinforcement, and drink durations and frequencies varied directly with interval length. At longer intervals, drinking seldom occurred after reinforcement but was more frequent later in the interval. Late drinks were usually brief.

When he first described schedule-induced polydipsia, Falk (1961) reported a typical pattern of postpellet drinking behavior. This observation has since been confirmed many times (e.g., Keehn, 1970; Segal, 1969; Stein, 1964). Falk (1966) has also reported an increase in level of polydipsia as interpellet intervals increase, up to a point. This finding has also been confirmed (Burks, 1970; Colotla, Keehn and Gardner, 1970) and seems to depend more on increased drink durations in longer interpellet intervals than on increased frequencies of postpellet drinks (Colotla *et al,* 1970). However, when interpellet intervals are long enough (e.g., 3 min or more) fluid consumption decreases back to normal levels (Falk, 1966; Hawkins, Everett, Githens and Schrot, 1970). It remains to see how drink durations and postpellet drink frequencies are affected by long interpellet intervals (cf. Segal, Oden and Deadwyler, 1965).

SUBJECTS

Two 300-day-old male albino rats were used. They had previously taken part in studies of polydipsia with and without drugs, but had not been used for experimentation for over a month before the present study. They were maintained at 85% of their free-feeding weights at 100 days of age and were housed in individual cages with tap water always available.

APPARATUS

A standard Grason-Stadler two-bar rat chamber, Type E3125B, was used. The left-hand bar was removed, and its opening covered with a metal plate mounted flush with the wall. A weight of 20 g on the remaining bar served to activate relay programming and recording equipment. A water bottle was attached to the chamber door such that a S could lick at its glass outlet tube through a hole 25 mm above floor level and 90 mm from the wall containing the response bar and food magazine. Licks at this tube were registered on a Gerbrands cumulative recorder via a Grason-Stadler drinkometer. The experimental chamber was housed in a sound-attenuating ventilated chest supplied with a viewing window.

PROCEDURE

Because the animals were experienced, no pretraining was necessary. Experimental sessions were run daily, except at weekends and occasional holidays, and lasted until S obtained 25 reinforcers (100 in Sessions 54-65) scheduled as follows: FI 1 min (Sessions 1-15), FI 5 min (Sessions 16-30), FI 1 min (Sessions 31-33), FI 2 min (Sessions 34-43), FI 3 min (Sessions 44-53), FI 15 sec (Sessions 54-65). Cumulative licking records and water consumption were logged daily.

RESULTS

Major results were clear-cut and are shown in Fig. 1. The familiar bitonic relationship between fluid consumption and interpellet interval was confirmed, although the interval of maximum intake, 1 min, was lower than usual (Colotla et al, 1970; Falk, 1966; Hawkins et al, 1970). The figure also shows that the percentage of pellets followed by drinking within 10 sec (postpellet drinks) bore the same relationship to interpellet interval as did fluid consumption, and that the percentage of interpellet intervals containing interpellet drinks (drinks of six licks or more that occurred at least 10 sec after previous eating or drinking) increased as interpellet interval times increased. The transitions of postpellet drink percentages after reinforcement schedule changes from FI 1 min to FI 5 min and back are shown in Fig. 2.

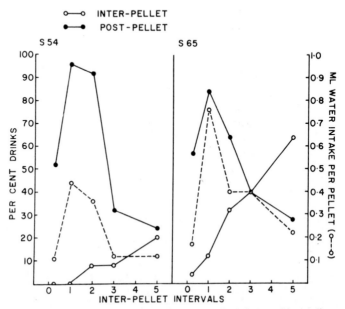

Fig. 1. Median fluid intakes per pellet and median percent of interpellet intervals in which drinking occurred within 10 sec of reinforcement (postpellet drinks) and at least 10 sec after reinforcement or drinking (interpellet drinks) over the final three sessions of each FI schedule. Only one postpellet and/or one interpellet drink was scorable per interval.

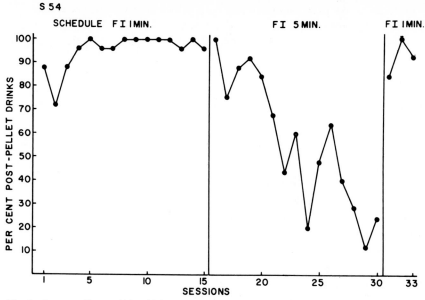

Fig. 2. Percent of intervals in which postpellet drinks occurred on successive sessions under the designated reinforcement schedules. Data of Animal S65 were similar.

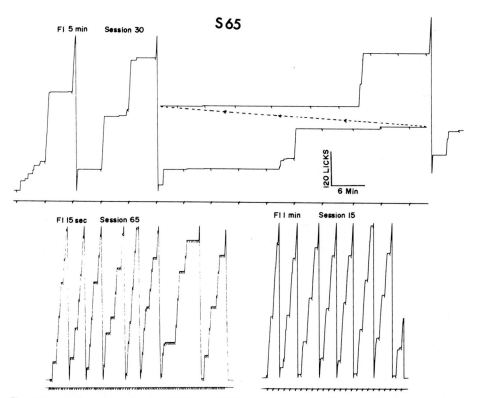

Fig. 3. Cumulative licking records of S65 under FI 15 sec, FI 1 min, and FI 5 min. Data of Animal S54 were similar.

More detailed data are contained in Fig. 3, which shows typical cumulative licking records with interpellet intervals of 15 sec, 1 min, and 5 min. Almost all the drinking with the FI 15 sec reinforcement schedule began within 10 sec of pellet delivery (post-pellet drinking), and lasted for the whole 15-sec interval. Likewise, most of the drinks with the FI 1-min schedule were postpellet; examples of interpellet drinks appear in the figure just before the fourth and final reinforcers. Postpellet drinks rarely lasted for the whole of the 1-min interval, but it can easily be seen that drink durations were longer with the FI 1-min than with the FI 15-sec schedule of reinforcement.

Many fewer postpellet drinks and many more interpellet drinks occurred when reinforcers were scheduled at 5-min intervals. Only six examples of postpellet drinks with this schedule appear in the figure—following the 2nd, 3rd, 4th, 5th, 6th, and 11th pellets. Most of these were of relatively long duration, in contrast to the numerous interpellet drinks, which were usually of short duration and which often occurred as short bursts of licks interrupted by barpresses towards the end of the fixed inter-reinforcement interval.

DISCUSSION

The bitonic relationship between level of schedule-induced polydipsia and inter-reinforcement interval duration appears to depend mainly upon two different behavioral characteristics controlled by the reinforcement schedule: (1) The increasing level of fluid consumption as interpellet interval increases results from an increase in postpellet drink *durations* (Colotla *et al,* 1970); (2) the decreasing level of fluid consumption when interpellet intervals exceed some value stems from a decline in postpellet drink *frequencies*. In both cases complications arise. In the present study, frequencies as well as durations of postpellet drinks increased substantially between 15- and 60-sec interreinforcement intervals, and interpellet drink frequencies increased as postpellet drink frequencies declined in the longer interreinforcement intervals. It is doubtful, though, if these complications much affected the overall shape of the curve relating fluid intake to inter-reinforcement interval.

Drink durations and drink frequencies could be measures of two different types of drinking that contribute to the total amount of fluid consumed. Falk's (1961) original report of schedule-induced polydipsia referred only to drinks that occurred "shortly after a pellet," i.e., postpellet drinking. Since then other drinking by intermittently fed rats has also been reported. Thus, Segal (1969) has described some schedule-induced drinking as operant, i.e., occurring before rather than after reinforcement, Rosenblith (1970) has reported "a second type of drinking" that occurs with second-order reinforcement schedules, and Keehn, Colotla and Beaton (1970) have distinguished between postpellet and interpellet drinking, the latter depending on palatability. In all these cases, the second type of drinking has differed from the first in occurring more remotely in time from preceding feeding or reinforcing events and in being less orderly in terms of duration and frequency of occurrence (Keehn and Colotla, in press; Keehn, Colotla, and Beaton, 1970).

It is, however, questionable whether there is more than one kind of schedule-induced drinking or whether the differences are merely stages of transition to a terminal (unstable) pattern of behaving (cf. Keehn, 1970) that is *maintained* by the proximity of the cessation of drinking to reinforcement (operant drinking, Segal, 1969) and initiated by the onset of nonreinforcement (extinction-induced drinking, Keehn and Colotla, 1970). We have been able to control schedule-induced drink durations by way of inter-reinforcement intervals (Colotla et al, 1970), but this means of control is limited to intervals that maintain high frequencies of postpellet drinking, i.e., those intervals in which reinforcement is available shortly after the cessation of drinking.

REFERENCES

Burks, C. D. Schedule-induced polydipsia: Are response-dependent schedules a limiting condition? *Journal of the Experimental Analysis of Behavior,* 1970, 13, 351-358.

Colotla, V. A., Keehn, J. D., and Gardner, L. L. Control of schedule-induced drink durations by inter-pellet intervals. *Psychonomic Science,* 1970, 21, 137-139.

Falk, J. L. Production of polydipsia in normal rats by an intermittent food schedule. *Science,* 1961, 133, 195-196.

Falk, J. L. Schedule-induced polydipsia as a function of fixed-interval length. *Journal of the Experimental Analsis of Behavior,* 1966, 9, 37-39.

Hawkins, J. D., Everett, P. B., Githens, S. H., and Schrot, J. F. Adjunctive drinking: A functional analysis of water and alcohol ingestion. In *Schedule induced and schedule-dependent phenomena.* Vol. 1, Toronto: Addiction Research Foundation, 1970. Pp. 113-136.

Keehn, J. D. Schedule-induced licking and polydipsia. *Psychological Reports,* 1970, 26, 155-161.

Keehn, J. D., and Colotla, V. A. Prediction and control of schedule-induced drink durations. *Psychonomic Science,* 1970, 21, 147-148.

Keehn, J. D., Colotla, V. A., and Beaton, J. M. Palatability as a factor in the duration and pattern of schedule-induced drinking. *Psychological Record.*

Rosenblith, J. Z. Polydipsia induced in the rat by a second-order schedule. *Journal of the Experimental Analysis of Behavior,* 1970, 14, 139-144.

Segal, E. F. Transformation of polydipsic drinking into operant drinking: A paradigm? *Psychonomic Science,* 1969, 16, 133-135.

Segal, E. F., Oden, D. L., and Deadwyler, S. A. Determinants of polydipsia: IV. Free-reinforcement schedules. *Psychonomic Science,* 1965, 3, 11-12.

Stein, L. Excessive drinking in the rat: Superstition or thirst? *Journal of Comparative & Physiological Psychology,* 1964, 58, 237-242.

Section XI

TREATMENT OF ABNORMAL ANIMALS

41. Animal Clinical Psychology: A Modest Proposal

D. S. TUBER, D. HOTHERSALL and V. L. VOITH

American Psychologist, 1974, *29,* 762-6. Copyright 1974 by The American Psychological Association. Reprinted by permission.

Animals have been intimately associated with man for thousands of years. Although this relationship has been dictated primarily by utilitarian considerations, its character has been greatly influenced by a practical understanding of animal behavior. Attendant upon the domestication of animals as a source of food were the skills that enabled early man to share both labor and leisure with many other species. The dog, for example, has had a particularly protracted and unique relationship with man for almost 10,000 years. Trained for tracking, retrieving, herding, protection, and sport, the dog has also served as a companion. More exotic creatures such as the falcon and hawk were trained for hunting and sport as early as 3,000 years ago. The training of animals solely for the purposes of entertainment has been practiced for at least 4,000 years and has encompassed a wide variety of species both domestic and wild. Thus, the development of the necessary training skills has proceeded in the absence of any formal discipline of psychology and, for the most part, continues to exist apart from it.

Although a seemingly natural ally, the field of experimental psychology shares no common heritage and seldom recognizes or examines this body of independently developed knowledge. In fact, it has been only within the last two decades that the experimental psychologist has emerged into the area of applied animal psychology. In 1951, Keller and Marion Breland used the *American Psychologist* as a forum to enthusiastically announce the founding of a new area of applied animal psychology: commercial animal training. Stating that behavioral technology had now reached a level of development such that the efficiency of the new behavioral techniques would "outstrip old-time professional animal trainers [p. 202]," the Brelands envisioned an area of unlimited opportunities and financial benefits for experimental psychologists. Whereas the Breland's commercial venture, Animal Behavior Enterprises, has indeed flourished, a survey of modern dog training manuals reflects little modernization; the employment statistics for experimental psychologists with animal behavior backgrounds suggest even less improvement and much less hope (cf. the May 1972 issue of the *American Psychologist*).

The assistance of Donn W. Griffith, DVM, and the Ohio State University Veterinary Clinic is gratefully acknowledged. We would also like to thank our colleagues in experimental and clinical psychology for their support and encouragement.

Requests for reprints should be sent to David Hothersall, Laboratory of Comparative and Physiological Psychology, Ohio State University, 1314 Kinnear Road, Columbus, Ohio 43212.

Subsequent reports by other behavioral scientists have described the introduction of applied animal psychology into industrial and military settings. Skinner's (1960) experiences in training pigeons as organic missile control systems for the military are well known. More recently, Cumming (1966) and Verhave (1966) recounted similar experiences concerning the adoption of trained pigeons in industry for use as quality control inspectors. In all of the above cases, the quality of the technology in producing the desired behavior was successfully demonstrated. However, the reception by the military and the industrial reviewers was less than enthusiastic and the projects were terminated. Unfortunately, the optimism of the Brelands has not been borne out.

Ironically, experimental psychology has received acceptance in the extrapolation of behavioral principles to the modification of human behavior. Witness the current use of conditioning therapies in the treatment of phobic reactions (Wolpe, 1958) and in the treatment of retardates and more incorrigible mental disorders (Ulrich, Stachnik and Mabry, 1966).

Considering the outcomes of earlier ventures into the field of applied animal psychology, it is with guarded optimism and a tempered enthusiasm that we come before this readership to describe yet another endeavor: the application of psychological principles to the treatment of behavioral disorders in animals.

For the past two years, we have been engaged in this application of psychology. In this article we report on some of our efforts thus far and on the mechanics of a service which is functionally a clinical psychology for animals. All of our clients (pet owners) have been referred to us by veterinarians and, as such, have had their pets examined to ensure that the behavioral problem was not attributable to any underlying organic dysfunction. In most cases the origin of the behavior and the circumstances under which it first appeared are unknown or obscure. Typically, the problem has been allowed to persist untreated or has resisted treatment by more conventional means. Too frequently, we represent the final resort. Procedurally, we employ a team approach. Our various backgrounds (Hothersall: operant conditioning; Tuber: classical conditioning; Voith: veterinary medicine and conventional training techniques) are combined in the analysis of the behavioral problem, and a training program is developed that often represents a synthesis of these skills. We have found that the most efficient approach is to utilize the owner as the agent of change and the home as the training environment. Consequently, a considerable effort is concentrated on translating the program into an understandable terminology, devising practical analogies to a laboratory situation, and counseling the owner in the implementation of the program. When the owner contacts us concerning an appointment, he is requested to maintain a daily log detailing relevant information regarding the behavioral problem, the circumstances surrounding its occurrence, and any additional information that might be pertinent. The initial interview, attended by the pet and as many family members as practical, is used for obtaining a thorough case history, understanding the domestic environment into which the training program must be interjected, and providing an opportunity to observe the family-pet interactions. At a subsequent session, the owner or the person responsible for the training is presented with a written training program which elaborates on the rationale and describes in detail all relevant manipulations. This is then discussed and may even be rehearsed with the owner. In addition, we provide daily training protocols and behavior records which are to be filled out by the owner as the training progresses. These are useful as training guides for the owner and are indispensable to any evaluation of the effectiveness of the intervention. They may merely confirm a success or identify the source of difficulty, hence affording the basis for a knowledgeable adjustment in either the program or the approach to the problem. All training programs are routinely evaluated with the clients after approximately three weeks of training.

The following case summaries describe the essential points of several pet problems that we have encountered; they are presented to characterize the flavor of our approach and the mechanics of our service.

HIGGINS

Higgins is an affable four-year-old Old English Sheep Dog of Goliath proportions whose tranquil demeanor was breached only by an intense fear of thunderstorms. At the first indication of an impending storm, Higgins would begin an accelerating pattern of aimless pacing, profuse salivation, and marked panting which was rapidly climaxed by the hurtling of his 110-pound body against any obstacle in a futile attempt to escape. A variety of confinement procedures and tranquilizers had been tried without success, and the behavior had continued unabated for two years. The crisis that threatened the relationship between Higgins and his petite owner occurred when they were forced to share the owner's foreign sportscar during a thunderstorm.

Since the fear was elicited by an identifiable and reproducible stimulus, a course of therapy involving counterconditioning in the fashion of Jones (1924) and Wolpe (1958) seemed most appropriate. Having satisfied ourselves that a stereophonic reproduction of a thunderstorm would elicit the fear—Higgins actually overwhelmed the three people in the room with him—the stimulus situation was presented in graded steps along the dimension of intensity. Beginning at an intensity that did not evoke the fear, Higgins was brought under command to lie down, and the subsequent occurrence of thunder was paired with a food reward of chocolate bars. As long as Higgins remained calm and maintained the antagonistic posture, the intensity of the recreated, artificial storm was gradually increased. Training was initiated in the laboratory in daily sessions lasting one hour: The beginning intensity for each session was always slightly less than the terminal level achieved during the preceding session. We had been proceeding gradually with few difficulties; over the course of the first five conditioning sessions we had progressed from a thunder intensity level of a meager 35 decibels to that of a resounding 75 decibels when a typical summer thunderstorm intervened to test our efforts. Happily, the owner reported that Higgins initially exhibited only a mild version of the original fear response, that he was easily brought under control, and that she was able to successfully practice the training as we had done in the laboratory. Subsequent sessions in the home with artificial and real storms have succeeded in the further attenuation of the fear response. Realistically, we do not expect Higgins to ever seek pleasure in thunderstorms, but the change in his behavior has been striking and is at least compatible with his surroundings.

HOOKIE

A more difficult class of problems is concerned with the interruption of established misbehaviors that occur only when the pet is left alone. The behavior appears related inextricably to the absence of the owner, and consequently, any direct control over the behavior is precluded by the absence.

Hookie is an 18-month-old male Afghan whose owner necessarily left him alone for extended periods of time. Upon his return, the owner would find chewed clothing and furniture, a distribution of feces which was described as pernicious, and Hookie, wearing the appropriate expression of shame. The conventional remedy of confinement merely restricted the range of destruction. The punishment, which was necessarily delayed, proved ineffective. The initial interview, supplemented by a daily baseline log, suggested that appropriate manipulations of the prevailing stimuli would modify the behavior considerably. Preparatory to prolonged absences, during which destructive behavior invariably occurred, the owner engaged in an elaborate pattern of ritualistic acts that were intended to secure the house from without as well as from within. No such precautions were required either by absences of short duration or by Hookie's behavior during such absences. Therefore, a necessary part of the training program was to degrade the validity of both contextual and temporal stimuli associated with prolonged absences. By introducing a stable, novel stimulus into the training situation, we provided a manageable cue to which acceptable behavior could become associated and could easily be maintained by training. Further, this training would provide a background against which we could extinguish the undesirable behavior. The new stimulus for Hookie's training was provided by a radio tuned to a local rock station which already had a strong association with the presence of the owner. The new response was simply any behavior other than that of the destructive variety.

Conceptually, the strategy is the expression of the operant reinforcement schedule: differential reinforcement of other behavior under the control of a discriminative stimulus. Viewed as a transfer paradigm, this association between a new stimulus and a new response has been shown by Wickens (1973, pp. 229-231) with cats to be immune to any proactive effects of a prior association. But more remarkable, such a new response appears to have deleterious retroactive effects in that it displaces the response of such a prior association over a long retention interval.

The mechanics of the training were relatively simple. A schedule of training absences was devised such that as training progressed, the average duration of the absences was gradually and variably prolonged. The initial absences were by design very short in order to minimize the occurrence of any misbehavior and to maximize the probability of intercepting and punishing it. During all absences the new stimulus was always present. Later in training, the cues formerly associated with extended absences were systematically introduced into the training situation. Good behavior on Hookie's part following an absence was always reinforced by the owner with an effusive greeting and a brief play session. Misbehavior was to be punished by a stern reprimand followed by a retreat to remedial training at shorter absences with only the novel stimulus. The owner laboriously followed our suggested training schedules, which often required two training absences each day accompanied by tedious cue manipulations. He was duly rewarded for his efforts. In the intervening four weeks between the final interview and the training evaluation, Hookie had violated the house only once despite the occurrence of several unplanned, extended absences by his owner. Accordingly, the training could safely be reduced to a maintenance schedule of several sessions per week.

SANDY AND JENNY

A situation in which the determinants of an undesirable behavior were inherent in the very nature of unavoidable, energetic contact was resolved by the unique modification of the interaction between a small terrier, Sandy, and a three-year-old child, Jenny. Sandy nipped Jenny regularly during play and was becoming increasingly sensitive to all play such that the nipping was beginning to generalize to other children. The interview, which was attended by the parents, the child, and the dog, confirmed that the nipping was elicited by the normal excesses and unsophisticated style of the play itself. A training program was developed which was modeled after the children's game Simon Says. It involved teaching Jenny how to pet an inanimate object—gentle openhanded petting being rewarded with candy. Independently, Sandy was taught to sit on command for a reward of a slice of hotdog. When both were trained satisfactorily, they were brought together and the games were combined. Sandy was required to sit; Jenny was requested to approach Sandy and gently pet him only once. Both were then rewarded immediately. As the training progressed, the game became slightly more detailed in that Jenny was required to pet an ever-increasing number of different areas prior to obtaining her reward, and Sandy, by default, had to tolerate the ever-increasing amount of petting prior to gaining his reward.

The parent was the moderator of the game, the judge of correct responses, and the dispenser of the rewards. Progression to longer and longer schedules of interaction was determined entirely by the comfort and skill of the participants, which were carefully monitored and adjusted by the parent.

The game proved completely effective in eliminating the nipping, and we have suggested that an abbreviated version of the game should be practiced to prevent the recovery of the old play patterns. In addition, we suggested that the game be used as a vehicle for introducing new children to Sandy and ensuring their skill in handling the dog.

CAUTIONS, COMMENTS, AND OTHER CONSIDERATIONS

Transporting the principles and methodologies of a behavioral science beyond the walls of the laboratory is a formidable challenge: refreshing, often rewarding, frustrating, and occasionally intimidating. We have experienced a form of culture shock. Gone are the controlled environments of the experimental chambers and the efficiency afforded by the most fundamental of instrumentations. Absent too are the security offered by group means and the closure provided by the control group.

Whereas in the laboratory one's research methodology is dictated primarily by the problem under investigation, the methodology selected by the animal clinical psychologist is disproportionately influenced by the sensitivities of the owner and his demands, the tenor and routine of an ongoing domestic situation, the physical surroundings, and the pet's relationship to all of these variables. The applied animal psychologist must be aware of, and be particularly adept at incorporating, just those variables that a good research strategy seeks to render ineffectual. What may be the treatment of choice may not be the treatment of convenience—and it is the latter that often determines whether or not a training program, no matter how ingeniously conceived, will be palatable to and consequently implemented by the owner.

Discovering inexpensive analogies of laboratory apparatus demands a similar ingenuity which leads one to explore the shelves of hardware stores and novelty shops. One quickly learns to appreciate the merits of a child's cricket bat; when a conditioned reinforcer is desired. Stereophonic sound effects recordings are another resource when artificially reproducible stimuli are required by a training program.

To all of the preceding must be added the inescapable reality of economics. Overhead expenses dictate fees; fees mean ledgers, billing, and collection. Too often, the fees will be weighed against the cost of euthanasia—a very real consideration for some owners and consequently for the practitioner who must necessarily consider the pet as his primary responsibility. Fees also expose the experimental psychologist to a variety of agonies totally foreign to his academic background which has in fact shielded him or otherwise rendered him contraprepared. There are those clients who expect no fewer guarantees from their pet's psychologist than from their television serviceman, and more than from their family physician. The practitioner must learn by experience to expand the limits of his sensibilities. Fortunately, most clients are concerned, understanding, and often knowledgeably sophisticated about their animals and generally delight in them. Their acceptance of your efforts and their willingness to pursue a sometimes arduous training program are mutually rewarding. The foregoing has been offered, not as a deterrent, but as a caution which must be given thoughtful consideration by any prospective practitioner.

There are an estimated 40 million dogs kept as pets in this country. Although the relative frequency of serious behavior problems is not yet determined, the responses from veterinarians in this area have been encouraging. It does appear that a need for such a service exists and that it is a legitimate extension of experimental psychology. Whether or not such a need can be satisfied by an applied area of animal psychology would seem to be determined largely by the efficacy of our technology and willingness of interested students to pursue such a career. The efficacy of the technology resides partially in the perceptiveness of the applied psychologist, but to a greater extent to the depth of his ties not only to the basic scientist but to his counterpart in the human clinic as well. There is a pleasing irony surrounding the adoption of a therapeutic treatment for a dog which was realized for use with human patients, based on principles generated by experimentation on dogs. The evolution of ideas, reflected in our treatment of Higgins, has been circuitous but advantageous.

We have already alluded to other contributions by the basic scientist to the applied area, but it is important to point out that the advantages of such an alliance are mutual. An example is the article "Misbehavior of Organisms" (Breland and Breland, 1961) which has emerged as a crucial element in the current reexamination of learning theory (Bolles, 1972; Hinde and Stevenson-Hinde, 1973; Seligman, 1970).

Ancillary but very pragmatic considerations have been suggested by Little (1972) regarding remedial measures precipitated by the dismal employment prospects for psychologists. The vulnerability of comparative and experimental psychologists within the academic marketplace might well be attenuated by an area of animal clinical psychology. By expanding the employment opportunities at both the master's and doctoral levels, it would provide a means of maintaining a viable training program without resorting to a reduction in enrolments. In addition, it could also expand the traditional academic roles of psychologists to include schools of veterinary medicine.

We are aware of at least three other groups of psychologists and veterinarians who are currently engaged in behavioral applications similar to our own. Possibly there are more, and we hope that this article will initiate an exchange of information and communication between such groups. We are prepared to act as a clearinghouse for such needed interactions.

REFERENCES

Bolles, R. C. Reinforcement, expectancy and learning. *Psychological Review,* 1972, **79**, 394-409.
Breland, K., and Breland, M. A field of applied animal psychology. *American Psychologist,* 1951, **6**, 202-204.
Breland, K., and Breland, M. The misbehavior of organisms. *American Psychologist,* 1961, **16**, 681-684.
Cumming, W. W. A bird's eye glimpse of men and machines. In R. Ulrich, T. Stachnik, & J. Mabry (Eds.), *Control of human behavior.* Vol. 1. Glenview, Ill.: Scott, Foresman, 1966.
Hinde, R., & Stevenson-Hinde, J. (Eds.) *Constraints on learning.* New York: Academic Press, 1973.
Jones, M. C. A laboratory study of fear: The case of Peter. *Pedagogical Seminary,* 1924: **31**, 308-315.
Little, K. B. Epilogue: Academic marketplace 1984. *American Psychologist,* 1972, **27**, 504-506.

Seligman, M. E. P. On the generality of the laws of learning. *Psychological Review,* 1970, **77**, 406-418.

Skinner, B. F. Pigeons in a pelican. *American Psychologist,* 1960, **15**, 28-37.

Ulrich, R., Stachnik, T., & Mabry, J. (Eds.) *Control of human behavior.* Vols. 1 & 2. Glenview, Ill.: Scott, Foresman, 1966.

Verhave, T. The pigeon as a quality-control inspector. *American Psychologist,* 1966, **21**, 109-115.

Wickens, D. D. Classical conditioning, as it contributes to the analyses of some basic psychological processes. In F. J. McGuigan & D. B. Lumsden (Eds.), *Contemporary approaches to conditioning and learning.* Washington, D.C.: V. H. Winston, 1973.

Wolpe, J. *Psychotherapy by reciprocal inhibition.* Stanford, Calif.: Stanford University Press, 1958.

42. Breaking the Killing Habit in Dogs by Inhibiting the Conditioned Reflex

G. G. MERRILL

Journal of the American Veterinary Medicine Association, 1945, *107,* 69-70. Reprinted by permission.

When dogs develop bad habits, such as killing chickens or sheep, the veterinarian is often consulted concerning treatment. If the dog is valuable or a beloved pet, the owner demands something more than the mere killing of the guilty animal, no matter how quickly and kindly the destruction is carried out. The usual punishments are often ineffectual. By following psychologic principles, much can be done to break the bad habit without injuring the dog.

Pavlov[1] has shown, by extensive experiments with dogs, that the conditioned reflex is the basis of most animal behavior. In its simplest form, this is the eliciting of a given response by a stimulus other than the natural one. Thus, a puppy that has never tasted meat will not begin to drool saliva until meat is placed in his mouth, the flow of saliva being a natural, direct response to the stimulus of taste. But any dog that has been fed meat before will begin to drool saliva at the sight or smell of meat. Here the visual or olfactory stimulus takes the place of the original unconditioned stimulus of taste in evoking the salivary response. Thus, the response to the sight or smell of meat, rather than to its taste, is said to be a conditioned reflex. If a certain noise, such as the ringing of a bell, is made just before feeding, after several repetitions, the noise itself will cause a flow of saliva. It is as if an association of ideas were formed in the dog's mind. Similarly, conditioned reflexes of this type can follow a variety of visual, auditory, olfactory, and cutaneous stimuli, after the conditioned stimulus has been associated with the original unconditioned stimulus often enough for the dog to learn. This type of reaction is important in the behavior of all animals. Many such reflexes develop naturally in the animal's everyday life from natural associations. Thus, the approach of their usual feeder will bring hogs and poultry running expectantly; the rattle of milk pails will cause some cows to drip milk, and many other such examples of animal behavior can be easily recalled by anyone with farm experience. Animal training depends largely on the building up of such conditioned reflexes, so that the stimulus of the trainer's command or gesture will call forth the desired response in the animal. The more intelligent the animal, the more complicated the reflexes that can be built up.

The conditioned reflex enters as much into the formation of harmful habits as it does into harmless ones. When the sight of a chicken or sheep becomes a stimulus for a dog to kill, something obviously must be done to inhibit the undesirable conditioned reflex, if the owner is to keep the dog. Destroying the dog is unintelligent and unnecessary. Any conditioned reflex can be inhibited by repeating the conditioned stimulus a number of times without permitting the reflex to proceed further along its accustomed course. It is as if the dog eventually forgets the association of ideas it has formed. Thus, in a chicken-killing dog, if the dog is surrounded by chickens without being able to kill them, the stimuli of the sight, smell, and sounds of chickens will eventually cease to suggest killing. When the dog is freed, after a few weeks of close association with his former victims, he will no longer be interested in killing them.

Ths principle has been successfully tested under farm conditions. The first case was that of two sheep-killing Great Danes. These dogs killed a stray ewe just after she had dropped a lamb. They overlooked the newborn lamb; it was saved and survived with bottle-feeding. A heavy wire pen was erected for this and another lamb directly in front of the Great Danes' kennel. The dogs were left at large. For the first few days the lambs were in their new pen, there was much excitement on the part of the dogs, with barking, drooling, snapping, and rushing at the wire fence. After a few days, they became gradually less concerned with the lambs and at the end of a few weeks paid no attention to them at all. The fence was then removed. The lambs continued to graze within easy reach of the dogs, but by now the conditioned reflex had been thoroughly inhibited; the dogs had lost all interest in the sheep, and there was never any more sheep killing by those dogs.

The second case was that of a chicken-killing Dalmatian bitch, which had just weaned her first litter of pups. Chickens were killed and brought to the pups as well as eaten by the killer herself. Whippings had no effect on her behavior, the conditioned reflex being too strong to be affected by any fear of punishment. To inhibit this reflex, she was put in a stout pen in a henhouse, so that she could see, hear, and smell chickens all around her without being able to reach them. This also isolated her from her pups. She was kept in the hen-house for one month, being taken out only for regular feeding and daily exercise. At first, she exhibited considerable excitement, but as time went on she lost all interest in the surrounding poultry. On being released after a month, she showed no inclination either to chase chickens or to care for her pups. These pups had started killing poultry for themselves before she was separated from them, so they were similarly confined in another hen-house, and similarly cured of their chicken killing.

These cases are admittedly few, being confined to the writer's own dogs, but the uniformly good results in these cases suggest that it is a method worthy of wider trial. It is to be noted that, under extraordinary circumstances, a recurrence of the conditioned reflex can theoretically happen. Thus it is possible that in the above cases, some extreme excitement in the Great Danes might lead them to kill again, or excessive maternal solicitude when weaning the next litter of pups might lead the Dalmatian to again kill chickens. The owner should, therefore, be warned that vigilance should be maintained, so that if further treatment is necessary it can be instituted without delay. Under ordinary conditions, no recurrence of the undesirable habit occurs.

SUMMARY

A simple, harmless, and effective method of breaking killing habits in dogs is described, based on the fundamental psychologic principle of the conditioned reflex, and illustrated by cases of successful cures among the writer's own dogs.

REFERENCES

1. Pavlov, I. P. *Conditioned Reflexes*, Oxford University Press, 1927.

43. Monkey Psychiatrists

S. J. SUOMI, H. F. HARLOW and W. T. McKINNEY

American Journal of Psychiatry, 1972, *128*, 927-32. Copyright 1972 by The American Psychiatric Association. Reprinted by permission.

Most efforts that have been made to reverse the effects of isolation on monkeys have been unsuccessful. The authors report on successful rehabilitation through the use of "therapist" monkeys. The therapists, three months younger than the isolate monkeys, initiated social contact in a nonthreatening manner. Within six months, the isolates' disturbance behaviors had nearly disappeared and they displayed normal age-appropriate social and play behaviors.

Psychiatric treatment has traditionally been practiced by and upon human beings. Why this should be the case is rather obvious. Prolonged psychopathology is rarely observed among free-ranging animals other than man for a very elementary reason: animals so afflicted are not apt to survive very long (1, 2). Whereas man provides hospitals and clinics for psychologically disturbed members of his species, nature does not. Without psychopathology there can be no psychotherapy.

In recent years, however, investigators working within laboratory settings have devised a number of techniques for the experimental production of profound and prolonged psychopathological abnormalities in nonhuman primate subjects. Undoubtedly, the best known and most well-documented technique has been that of total social isolation, whereby neonatal monkeys are separated from their mothers shortly after birth and placed in isolation chambers (see Fig. 1) where they are deprived of all physical and visual contact with members of any species.

Monkeys so housed for at least the first six months of life exhibit upon emergence from isolation severe deficits in locomotive, exploratory, and social behaviors (3, 4). The appropriate responses of grooming, play, and other social interactions are absolutely minimal in these subjects; instead, they spend the majority of their time engaging in autistic-like self-clasping, stereotypic rocking and huddling, and self-mouthing behaviors. Sexual responses are virtually absent among isolate-reared monkeys (5),

Read at the 124th annual meeting of the American Psychiatric Association, Washington, D.C., May 3-7, 1971.

The authors are with the University of Wisconsin, Madison, Wis. 53706, where Dr. Suomi is lecturer in the Department of Psychology and Research Associate in the Primate Laboratories, Dr. Harlow is Professor in the Department of Psychology and Director of the Primate Laboratories, and Dr. McKinney is Assistant Professor of Psychiatry in the School of Medicine.

This work was supported by Public Health Service grants MH-11894 and MH-18070 from the National Institute of Mental Health and RR-0167 from the National Institutes of Health, by Predoctoral Fellowship MH-47025 to Dr. Suomi, and by Research Scientist Development Award MH-47353 to Dr. McKinney.

and females who have been artificially inseminated typically display inadequate maternal behavior, characterized by indifference and/or brutality (6); see Fig. 2.

Fig. 1. Total-isolation chamber.

Aggressive behavior is primarily either self-directed or, in social situations, inappropriately directed (7). For example, a mature social isolate will readily attack a neonate, an act rarely initiated by a socially normal monkey, or it may attack a dominant adult male, a blunder that few socially sophisticated monkeys are foolish enough to attempt. In summary, total social isolation has a devastating effect on the development of appropriate monkey behaviors.

Attempts have been made to reverse the syndrome resulting from total social isolation since the time when the existence of an isolation syndrome was first recognized. Virtually all of these efforts have been unsuccessful. For example, researches employing aversive conditioning paradigms with isolate subjects have produced only slight behavioral changes, which fail to generalize beyond the highly specific experimental situations (8).

Other experimenters (9, 10), postulating that these effects were due to "emergence trauma," have tried to alleviate the occurrence of such trauma by adapting the subjects during the isolation period to the test situation to be employed following removal from isolation. Any positive effects these adaptation periods may have had were not readily apparent, for "adapted" isolates exhibited social behavior as incompetent as that of isolates denied this experience.

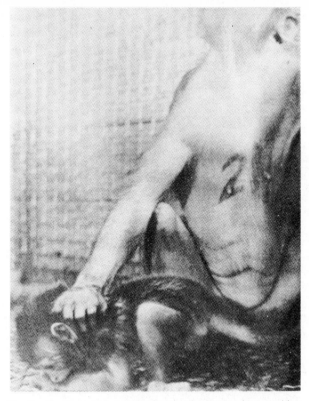

Fig. 2. Abusive total-isolate mother (motherless mother) crushing her infant.

Other efforts designed to rehabilitate isolate monkeys via exposure to socially normal age-mates have also been unsuccessful. When placed in such a social situation, six-month isolates do not readily locomote about, explore the environment, or engage in social interaction with peers. Instead, most of their time is spent self-clasping, rocking, and huddling, usually in a corner of the test area. The typical response of the normal peers is that of continual aggression against the isolates, certainly not the response most likely to elicit positive social behaviors from the disturbed subject (11); see Fig. 3.

Fig. 3. Normal peers attacking isolate monkey.

However, evidence that isolates are potentially responsive to social stimulation of some type has been accumulated in two independent situations. The first involved isolate females who became mothers. As previously mentioned, the initial responses of these females to their own infants were totally inadequate. Some of the infants survived in spite of their mothers' behaviors, and this "survival" was marked by efforts on the part of the infants to maintain maternal body contact. From the fourth postnatal month onward the motherless mothers gradually gave up the struggle against their babies, and the infants eventually achieved near-normative frequency of ventral and nipple contact (6). Some of these isolate females were impregnated again and, contrary to all predictions, exhibited normal monkey maternal behavior toward subsequent offspring. Clearly, for these once maternally inadequate isolate females, rehabilitation had transpired.

Further evidence for the potential of isolate rehabilitation came from a study utilizing heated surrogate mothers (12). Following removal from isolation, six-month total social isolates were individually housed in new cages for a two-week period, during which time behavioral baselines were assessed. Surrogates were then introduced to the isolates in their home cages. Within a few days the isolates began contacting the surrogates with increasing frequency and duration, and their disturbance behavior correspondingly decreased while locomotor and exploratory behavior rose above presurrogate levels. The isolates were housed in pairs after two weeks of individual housing with the surrogates. In this situation they exhibited social play, sex, locomotive, and exploratory behavior almost spontaneously, although the social behavior was clumsy at best and the isolates continued to exhibit disturbance behavior to some degree.

METHOD

These studies led us to believe that rehabilitation of isolates by employment of social stimuli might be possible and that previous failures could probably be attributed at least in part to the type of responses directed toward the isolates by normal stimulus animals. Specifically, it seemed that exposure to "therapist" monkeys who could provide the isolates with contact acceptance rather than aggressive attack might be more likely to promote reversal of the isolation syndrome. Therefore, we designed an isolate rehabilitation study employing a judiciously chosen type of monkey "psychiatrist" for the isolates.

Our therapists were monkeys reared with heated surrogates and given two hours of peer interaction daily, both in pairs within their home cages and as groups of four in a social playroom. They exhibited age-appropriate social development. However, they were three months *younger* than the isolate subjects, and their age when introduced to the isolates was approximately three months, too young to exhibit aggressive responses or social interactions more complex than clinging and the beginnings of simple play. Our prediction, based upon years of research investigating the normal behavioral development of rhesus monkeys, was that the therapist monkeys, when first introduced to the isolates, would approach and cling to rather than aggress against the isolates, would initially play at an elementary rather than a sophisticated level, and would exhibit minimal abnormal behavior themselves.

In this study four males, following six months of total social isolation from birth, were individually housed for a period of two weeks in order to assess postisolation baselines. Like typical six-month isolates, they showed little exploratory or locomotive behavior, but instead exhibited high levels of self-clasping, self-mouthing, huddling, and stereotypic rocking disturbance behaviors (see Fig. 4). These subjects were then placed in individual quadrants of a specially designed "quad cage" (13; see Fig. 5) adjacent to the four three-month-old female therapist monkeys, who themselves had experienced surrogate-peer rearing. The isolates were then allowed to interact with the therapist monkeys for two hours a day, three days a week as pairs (one isolate and one therapist) within the quad cages, and two days a week in groups of four (two isolates and two therapists) in a playroom.

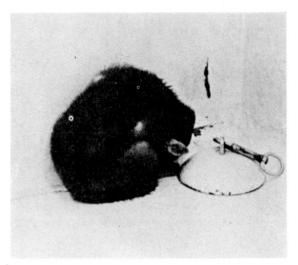

Fig. 4. Disturbance behavior following removal from isolation.

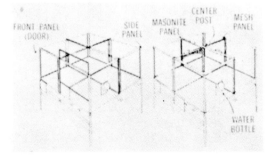

Fig. 5. The "quad cages" for experimental living.

RESULTS

The isolates' initial response to both situations was to huddle in a corner, and the therapists' first response was to approach and cling to the isolates (see Fig. 6). Within a week in the home cage and two weeks in the playroom the isolates were reciprocating the clinging. The therapists were concurrently exhibiting elementary play patterns among themselves and attempting to initiate such patterns with the isolates. Within two weeks in the home cage and a month in the playroom, the isolates were reciprocating these behaviors. Shortly thereafter the isolates began to initiate play behavior themselves and their disturbance activity, which originally had accounted for most of their behavioral repertoire, correspondingly decreased to insignificant levels.

Fig. 6. Therapist monkey clinging to huddled isolate.

By one year of age the isolates were virtually indistinguishable from the therapists in the amount of exploratory, locomotive, and play behaviors, as shown in Figs. 7, 8, and 9. Interestingly enough, the type of play appeared to be sex-specific to a large extent, i.e., the male isolates preferred rough-and-tumble play while the female therapists exhibited play almost exclusively of a noncontact form. The isolates could be identified by occasional lapses into self-clasping and huddling, behaviors that the therapists did

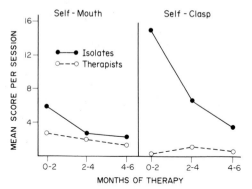

Fig. 7. Self-mouthing and self-clasping behaviors in the therapy period.

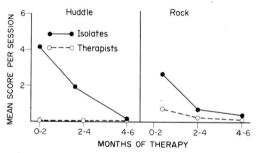

Fig. 8. Huddling and stereotypic rocking behaviors in the therapy period.

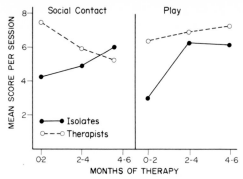

Fig. 9.   Social contact and play behaviors in the therapy period.

not exhibit. These disturbance patterns, however, were infrequent and of short duration. More significant were the intense, complex patterns of play among all subjects (see Fig. 10) as well as the appearance of elementary sexual behaviors in both the isolate and therapist monkeys.

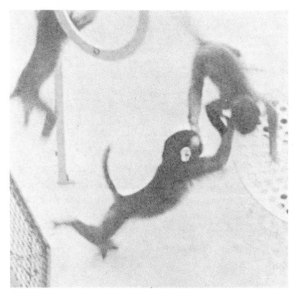

Fig. 10.   Isolates (left, center) and therapist (right) interacting in vigorous play.

At this point the isolates and therapists were removed from their individual home cages and placed together in a large group-living pen, where they have remained to this day. The isolates, now two years of age, show virtually complete recovery. Socially directed behavior characterizes most of their activity and is age-appropriate for normal animals. The earlier forms of play behavior previously observed have now been largely superseded by more mature social activities, such as grooming and sexual mounting. The disturbance behaviors, so predominant before exposure to the therapists, have all but disappeared.

DISCUSSION

We will not consider these isolate subjects to have been completely rehabilitated until they exhibit mature adult rhesus monkey sexual behavior. For this we must wait until the subjects become physiologically mature. However, even at its present state this research has many implications. The data to this point are in direct contradiction to most traditional explanations of the effects of isolation rearing, such as the "critical period" theories (14, 15), and therefore we feel that a reexamination of existing theoretical positions regarding the basis for the effects of social isolation is in order.

Of greater relevance to this group, we feel, are the implications for the process of therapy that these data raise. We are excited by the finding that social recovery can be achieved in subjects whose social deficits were once considered to be irreversible, and we are especially intrigued by the nature of the therapeutic procedure itself. In basic terms, we observed specific behavioral deficiencies in our isolate subjects, postulated specific behavioral patterns that we wished these debilitated subjects to exhibit, and then exposed our subjects to other monkeys who, on the basis of previous knowledge, could be predicted to elicit those particular behaviors.

We did not rehabilitate the isolate subjects ourselves, nor is it likely that we could. The actual therapy was performed by our "monkey psychiatrists." They broke the self-directed isolate behaviors through the initiation of contact;they initiated the first playful interactions and provided a social medium conducive to the recovery that was achieved. We merely sat back and recorded the data while our simian friends performed the actual therapy, an effort truly worthy of more than a footnote. These therapists were not professionals. They had received no formal training, nor were they reimbursed for their efforts by so much as one extra pellet of monkey chow. Rather, they responded to the social situation presented them just as generations of monkeys possessing their approximate age and social history have done for millennia. Their behaviors, so crucial for the therapy, merely represented normal chronological development for them and nothing more.

It is significant that the therapist monkeys in this study were chronologically younger than the isolates. They were thus able to provide a nonthreatening atmosphere in which the isolates could become more socially active. They initially clung to the isolates without aggressing as equal-age peers in previous studies had done. Yet the therapist monkeys were not totally undemanding, since they did approach and initiate social interactions of increasing complexity as the therapy period progressed. The role of gentle physical contact and model-serving exhibited by the therapists was likely of paramount importance for isolate recovery. Many of these principles are not unfamiliar to human psychotherapists.

Compelling as reasoning by analogy might be, we are the first to admit that monkeys are not men. Yet their use as subjects in the controlled study of the production and rehabilitation of psychopathology is of definite merit. Our research group is currently engaged in a major program of developing a monkey model of depression. Encouraging findings on this topic were reported last year (16). In the interim we have accumulated a sizable number of subjects whose behavior patterns could be characterized as depressive, and we are now in a position to determine empirically the relative efficacy of various rehabilitative procedures.

The pharmaceutical approaches currently employed for human patients clinically diagnosed as depressed are obvious candidates. Alternative and/or concurrent therapies could employ other monkeys judiciously chosen for the specific behaviors they exhibit consistently. For example, a number of our monkey depressions can be traced to loss of objects of social attachment. An appropriately affectionate, nonthreatening monkey might become a therapeutic substitute for the depressed subject's loss. Other experimental subjects exhibit withdrawal not derivable from social loss. Continual exposure to peers whose behaviors preclude self-directed social avoidance responses by the isolates conceivably might effect social recovery. Current research will soon permit more definitive judgments on this matter.

In conclusion, we are all aware of the existence of some therapists who seem inhuman. We find it refreshing to report the discovery of nonhumans who can be therapists.

REFERENCES

1. Berkson G: Defective infants in a feral monkey group. Folia Primat 12: 284-289, 1970.
2. Kling A, Lancaster J, Benitone J: Amygdalectomy in the free-ranging vervet (cercopithecus aethiops). J. Psychiat Res 7: 191-199, 1970.
3. Harlow HF, Harlow MK: Social deprivation in monkeys. Sci Amer 207: 136-146, 1962.
4. Rowland GL: The effects of total isolation upon learning and social behavior of rhesus monkeys. Department of Psychology, University of Wisconsin, 1964 (doctoral dissertation).
5. Senko MG: The effects of early, intermediate, and late experiences upon adult macaque sexual behavior. Department of Psychology, University of Wisconsin, 1966 (master's thesis).
6. Harlow HF, Harlow MK, Dodsworth RO, et al: Maternal behavior of rhesus monkeys deprived of mothering and peer associations in infancy. Proceedings of the American Philosophical Society 110: 58-66, 1966.
7. Mitchell GD, Raymond FJ, Ruppenthal GL, et al: Long-term effects of total isolation upon behavior of rhesus monkeys. Psychol Rep 18: 567-580, 1966.
8. Sackett GP: The persistence of abnormal behavior in monkeys following isolation rearing, in The Role of Learning in Psychotherapy. Edited by Porter R, London, J & A Churchill, 1968, pp 3-25.
9. Clark DL: Immediate and delayed effects of early intermediate, and late social isolation in the rhesus monkey. Department of Psychology University of Wisconsin, 1968 (doctoral dissertation).
10. Pratt CL: The developmental consequences of variations in early social stimulation. Department of Psychology, University of Wisconsin, 1969 (doctoral dissertation).
11. Harlow HF, Harlow MK: Effects of various mother infant relationships on rhesus monkey behaviors, in Determinants of Infant Behavior, IV. Edited by Foss BM, London, Methuen, 1968, pp. 15-36.
12. Harlow HF, Suomi SJ: The nature of love simplified. Amer Psychol 25: 161-168, 1970.
13. Suomi SJ, Harlow HF: Apparatus conceptualization for psychopathological research in monkeys. Behavior Research Methods and Instrumentation 1: 247-251, 1969.
14. Dennenberg VH: Critical periods, stimulus input, and emotional reactivity: a theory of infantile stimulation. Psychol Rev 71: 335-351, 1964.
15. Scott JP: Critical periods in behavioral development. Science 138: 949-958, 1962.
16. McKinney WT, Suomi SJ, Harlow HF: Depression in primates. Amer J Psychiat 127: 1313-1320, 1971.

44. Alleviation of Learned Helplessness in the Dog[1]

M. E. P. SELIGMAN[2], S. F. MAIER[3] and J. GEER

Journal of Abnormal and Social Psychology, 1968, *73,* 256-62. Copyright 1968 by The American Psychological Association. Reprinted by permission.

Dogs given inescapable shock in a Pavlovian harness later seem to "give up" and passively accept traumatic shock in shuttlebox escape/avoidance training. A theoretical analysis of this phenomenon was presented. As predicted by this analysis, the failure to escape was alleviated by repeatedly compelling the dog to make the response which terminated shock. This maladaptive passive behavior in the face of trauma may be related to maladaptive passive behavior in humans. The importance of instrumental control over aversive events in the cause, prevention, and treatment of such behaviors was discussed.

This paper discusses a procedure that produces a striking behavior abnormality in dogs, outlines an analysis which predicts a method for eliminating the abnormality, and presents data which support the prediction. When a normal, naïve dog receives escape/avoidance training in a shuttlebox, the following behavior typically occurs: At the onset of electric shock, the dog runs frantically about, defecating, urinating, and howling, until it scrambles over the barrier and so escapes from shock. On the next trial, the dog, running and howling, crosses the barrier more quickly, and so on until efficient avoidance emerges. See Solomon and Wynne (1953) for a detailed description.

Overmier and Seligman (1967) have reported the behavior of dogs which had received *inescapable* shock while strapped in a Pavlovian harness 24 hr. before shuttlebox training. Typically, such a dog reacts *initially* to shock in the shuttlebox in the same manner as the naïve dog. However, in dramatic contrast to the naïve dog, it soon stops running and remains silent until shock terminates. The dog does not cross the barrier and escape from shock. Rather, it seems to "give up" and passively "accept" the shock. On succeeding trials, the dog continues to fail to make escape movements and thus takes 50 sec. of severe, pulsating shock on each trial. If the dog makes an escape or avoidance response, this does not reliably predict occurrence of future responses, as it does for the normal dog. Pretreated dogs occasionally escape or avoid by jumping the barrier and then revert to taking the shock. The behavior abnormality produced by

[1] This research was supported by grants to R. L. Solomon from the National Science Foundation (GB-2428) and the National Institute of Mental Health (MH-04202). The authors are grateful to him for his advice in the conduct and reporting of this experiment. The authors also thank J. P. Brady and J. Mecklenburger for their critical readings of the manuscript.

[2] At the time this work was carried out, the first author was a National Science Foundation predoctoral fellow at the University of Pennsylvania.

[3] National Institute of Mental Health predoctoral fellow.

prior inescapable shock is highly maladaptive: a naïve dog receives little shock in shuttle-box training because it escapes quickly and eventually avoids shock altogether. A dog previously exposed to inescapable shock, in contrast, may take unlimited shock without escaping or avoiding at all.

Aside from establishing the existence of this interference effect, the experiments of Overmier and Seligman (1967) and Seligman and Maier (1967) have pointed to the variables controlling this phenomenon. Three hypotheses concerning the necessary conditions under which this phenomenon occurs have been disconfirmed, and one has been confirmed.

Overmier and Seligman (1967) tested two hypotheses which had been advanced to explain similar phenomena: a competing-motor-response hypothesis (Carlson and Black, 1960) and an adaptation hypothesis (MacDonald, 1946). The competing-response hypothesis holds that, in the harness, the dog learned some motor response which alleviated shock. When placed in the shuttlebox, the dog performed this response, which was antagonistic to barrier jumping, and thus was retarded in its acquisition of barrier jumping. This hypothesis was tested in the following way: Dogs, whose skeleto-musculature was paralyzed by curare (eliminating the possibility of the execution of overt motor responses), received inescapable shock in the harness. These dogs subsequently failed to escape in the shuttlebox. Dogs, paralyzed by curare, but not given inescapable shock, escaped normally. These results disconfirmed the competing-response hypothesis. The adaptation hypothesis holds that the dogs adapted to shock in the harness and therefore were not motivated enough to escape shock in the shuttle-box. Overmier and Seligman (1967) found that dogs failed to escape in the shuttlebox, even when the shock intensity was increased to a point just below which some dogs are tetanized and thus physically prevented from jumping the barrier. These results are inconsistent with the adaptation hypothesis.

Seligman and Maier (1967) presented and tested an analysis of the phenomenon in terms of learned independence between shock termination and instrumental respond-ing. Learning theory has traditionally stressed that two relationships between events produce learning: explicit contiguity (acquisition) and explicit dissociation (extinction). Seligman and Maier (1967) suggested that organisms are sensitive to a third relation-ship: independence between events. In particular, they proposed that, during inescap-able shock in the harness, the dogs learned that shock termination occurred independ-ently of their responses. Conventional learning theory allows that animals are sensi-tive to the conditional probability of shock termination given any specific response, and are also sensitive to the conditional probability of shock termination not given that response. In the special case in which these two probabilities are equal (independence), it is suggested that the animal *integrates* these two experiences. Thus, learning that shock termination is independent of a response reduces to learning that shock termina-tion follows the response with a given probability, that shock termination occurs with a given probability if the response does not occur, and that these two probabilities do not differ. Such an integration could be called an expectation that shock termination is independent of responding. Seligman and Maier (1967) further proposed that one condition for the emission of active responses in the presence of electric shock is the expectation that responding leads to shock termination. In the absence of such an expectation, emitted responding should be less likely. When the dogs are subsequently placed in the shuttlebox, shock mediates the generalization of the initial learning to the new situation, and the probability of escape responding is thereby decreased.

This analysis was tested by varying the dogs' control over shock termination in their initial experience with shock. For one group (Escape), pressing panels located about 3 in. from either side of their heads terminated shock. Another group (Yoked) received the identical shock, but shock termination occurred independently of its responses (since shock duration was determined by the responses of the Escape group). The Escape group escaped normally in the shuttlebox, while the Yoked group failed to escape in the shuttlebox. This result confirmed the hypothesis that the learning of independence of shock termination and instrumental responding is a necessary condition for the interference effect. It disconfirmed a punishment interpretation of interference to the effect that the dogs failed to escape in the shuttlebox because they had been punished in the harness by the onset of shock for active responding. This experiment equated the groups for punishment by the onset of shock; the groups differed only with respect to the independence and nonindependence of shock termination and the head-turning response. This theoretical analysis, as noted below, predicts that failure to escape shock should be *eliminable* by compelling the dog to respond in a situation in which its responses terminate shock. Repeated exposure to the response-relief contingency should replace the expectation that shock termination is independent of responding with the expectation that responding produces shock termination.

Learned "helplessness" was defined as the learning (or perception) of independence between the emitted responses of the organism and the presentation and/or withdrawal of aversive events. This term is not defined as the occurrence of a subjective feeling of helplessness (although such a possibility is not excluded), nor is it to be taken as a description of the appearance of the organism. Such learning seems to be a necessary condition for the occurrence of the interference effect. That such learning occurs, moreover, seems to be a necessary premise for any systematic explication of the concept of "hopelessness" advanced by Mowrer (1960, p. 197) and by Richter (1957), the concept of "helplessness" advanced by Cofer and Appley (1964, p. 452), and the concept of "external control of reinforcement" of Lefcourt (1966).

Overmier and Seligman (1967) found that if 48 hr. elapsed between the inescapable shock in the harness and escape/avoidance training in the shuttlebox, dogs did not show the interference effect. Thus, although experience with inescapable trauma might be a necessary precondition for such maladaptive behavior, it was not a sufficient condition. However, Seligman and Maier (1967) found that the interference effect could be prolonged, perhaps indefinitely. If 24 hr. after inescapable shock in the harness the dog passively accepted shock in the shuttlebox, the dog again failed to escape after further rests of 168 hr. or longer. Thus, chronic failure to escape occurred when an additional experience with nonescaped shock followed the first experience.

Other work with infrahumans also suggests that lack of control (the independence of response and reinforcement) over the important events in an animal's environment produces abnormal behavior. Richter (1957) reported that wild rats rapidly gave up swimming and drowned when placed in tanks of water from which there was no escape. If, however, the experimenter (*E*) repeatedly placed the rats in the tank and then took them out, or if *E* allowed them repeatedly to escape from his grasp, they swam for approximately 60 hr. before drowning. Richter concluded that loss of hope was responsible for the sudden deaths. Maier (1949) reported that rats showed positional fixations when they were given insoluble discrimination problems (problems in which the responses of the rat and the outcome are independent). Making the problems soluble, alone, did not break up these fixations. But the "therapeutic" technique of forcing the

rats to jump to the nonfixated side when the problem was soluble eliminated the fixations. Liddell (1956) reported that inescapable shocks produced experimental "neurosis" in lambs. Masserman (1943, pp. 79-85) reported that cats which instrumentally
controlled the presentation of food were less prone to experimental neurosis than cats
which did not have such control.

The maladaptive failure of dogs to escape shock resembles some human behavior
disorders in which individuals passively accept aversive events without attempting to
resist or escape. Bettelheim (1960) described the reaction of certain prisoners to the
Nazi concentration camps:

> Prisoners who came to believe the repeated statements of the guards—that there
> was no hope for them, that they would never leave the camp except as a corpse—
> who came to feel that their environment was one over which they could exercise no
> influence whatsoever, these prisoners were in a literal sense, walking corpses. In
> the camps they were called "moslems" (*Müselmänner*) because of what was errone-
> ously viewed as a fatalistic surrender to the environment, as Mohammedans are
> supposed to blandly accept their fate.
>
> . . . they were people who were so deprived of affect, self-esteem, and every
> form of stimulation, so totally exhausted, both physically and emotionally, that
> they had given the environment total power over them [pp. 151-152].

Bleuler (1950, p. 40) described the passive behavior of some of his patients:

> The sense of self-preservation is often reduced to zero. The patients do not bother
> anymore about whether they starve or not, whether they lie on a snowbank or on a
> red-hot oven. During a fire in the hospital, a number of patients had to be led
> out of the threatened area; they themselves would never have moved from their
> places; they would have allowed themselves to be burned or suffocated without
> showing an affective response.

It is suggested that an explanation which parallels the analysis of the interference
effect in dogs may hold for such psychopathological behavior in humans. Consider an
individual who has learned that his response and the occurrence and withdrawal of
traumatic events are independent. If a necessary condition for the initiation of responding is the expectation that his responses may control the trauma, such an individual
should react passively in the face of trauma.

The time course of the interference effect found with dogs suggests that such human
disorders may also be subject to temporal variables. Experience with traumatic inescapable shock produces interference with subsequent escape learning. This interference
dissipates over time. Traumatic events must *intervene* if permanent failure to escape
shock is to occur. This suggests that one traumatic experience may be sufficient to
predispose an individual to future maladaptive behavior, producing, perhaps, a temporary disturbance which Wallace (1957) has called the "disaster syndrome." In
order for this experience to be translated into a chronic disorder, however, subsequent
traumatic events may have to occur.

Because the interference effect in dogs and these forms of human psychopathology
may be acquired in similar ways, information about the modification of the interference
effect may lead to insights concerning the treatment of such psychopathological behavior
in humans. Two categories of treatment could be attempted: prevention or "immuni-
zation" against the effects of future inescapable shock (proactive), or modification of
maladaptive behavior after inescapable shock has had its effect (retroactive). Seligman
and Maier (1967) reported that prior experience with *escapable* shock immunizes dogs

against the effects of later *inescapable* shock. Thus, preventive steps have been shown to be effective.

The above analysis of the interference effect predicts that by exposing a dog to the contingent relationship of shock termination and its responses the interference effect established by prior exposure to unavoidable shock should be eliminated. This experiment reports an elimination of learned "helplessness" in dogs that had chronically failed to escape from traumatic shock. Such retroactive treatment resembles the traditional treatment of human psychopathology more than does the preventive procedure.

METHOD

Subjects

The Ss were four mongrel dogs. They weighed 25-29 lb., were 15-19 in. high at the shoulder, and were housed in individual cages with food and water freely available. Each dog chronically failed to escape shock (see Procedure) as a result of receiving inescapable shock in Experiment I of Seligman and Maier (1967).

Apparatus

The apparatus is described fully by Overmier and Seligman (1967). In brief, it consisted of two separate units: a Pavlovian harness, in which initial exposure to inescapable shock occurred, and a dog shuttlebox, in which escape/avoidance training and modification of the failure to escape were carried out.

The unit in which each S was exposed to inescapable shock was a rubberized cloth hammock located inside a shielded white sound-reducing cubicle. The hammock was constructed so that S's legs hung down below his body through four holes. The S's legs were secured in this position, and S was strapped into the hammock. The S's head was held in position by panels placed on either side and a yoke between them across S's neck. Shock was applied from a 500-VAC transformer through a fixed resistor of 20,000 ohms. The shock was applied to S through brass-plate electrodes coated with electrode paste and taped to the footpads of S's hind feet. The shock intensity was 6.0 ma.

The unit in which S received escape/avoidance trials was a two-way shuttlebox with two black compartments separated by an adjustable barrier. Running along the upper part of the front of the shuttlebox were two one-way mirror windows, through which E could observe and which E could open. The barrier was set at S's shoulder height. Each compartment was illuminated by two 50-w. and one 7½-w. lamps. The CS consisted of turning off the four 50-w. lamps which resulted in a sharp decrease in illumination. The UCS was 4.5-ma. electric shock applied through the grid floors from a 500-VAC source. The polarity pattern of the grid bars was scrambled four times a second. Whenever S crossed from one side of the shuttlebox to the other, photocell beams were interrupted, and the trial was terminated. Latency of crossing was measured from CS onset to the nearest .01 sec. by an electric clock. Seventy decibels (SPL) white noise was present in both units.

Procedure

Inescapable shock exposure. Each S was strapped into the harness and given 64 trials of inescapable shock. The shocks were presented in a sequence of trials of diminishing duration. The mean intershock interval was 90 sec. with a 60-120-sec. range. Each *S* received a total of 226 sec. of shock.

Instrumental escape/avoidance training. Twentyfour hours after inescapable shock exposure, *S*s received 10 trials of instrumental escape/avoidance training in the shuttlebox. The onset of the CS (dimmed illumination) initiated each trial, and the CS remained on until trial termination. The CS-UCS onset interval was 10 sec. If *S* crossed to the other compartment during this interval, the CS terminated, and no shock was presented. If *S* did not cross during the CS-UCS interval, shock came on and remained on until *S* crossed. If no response occurred within 60 sec. of CS onset, the trial was automatically terminated, and a 60-sec. latency was recorded. The average intertrial interval was 90 sec. with a 60-120-sec. range.

All four *S*s failed to escape shock on each of the 10 trials. Thus each *S* took 500 sec. of shock during the first escape/avoidance session.

Testing for chronic failure to escape. Seven days later, *S*s were again placed in the shuttlebox and given 10 further escape/avoidance trials. Again, each *S* failed to escape shock on every trial (although one *S* avoided shock once, on the fifth trial). By this time, each *S* was failing to make any escape movements and was remaining silent during shock on every trial. Previous work has shown that when a dog remains silent and fails to make escape movements during shock, this reliably predicts that the dog will continue to fail to escape and avoid.

Treatment. The attempt at behavioral modification consisted of two distinct phases: all *S*s received Phase I; if Phase I succeeded, as it did with one of the four dogs, no further treatment was given, and "recovery" (see Recovery section below) was begun. The other three *S*s received Phase II following Phase I.

Phase I: no barrier, calling. At intervals ranging from 4 to 25 days following the demonstration that the interference was chronic, *S*s were again placed in the shuttlebox. The escape/avoidance contingencies used previously remained in effect during Phase I and II trials. The barrier dividing the two sides of the shuttlebox (formerly set at shoulder height) was removed. Thus in order to escape or avoid, *S* had only to step over the remaining 5-in. high divider. In addition, *E* opened the observation window on the side of the shuttlebox opposite the side *S* was on and called to *S* ("Here, boy") during shock and during the CS-UCS interval. The rationale for such treatment was to encourage *S* to make the appropriate response on its own, thus exposing itself to the response-reinforcement contingency. One *S* responded to this treatment and began to escape and avoid. The remaining *S*s then received Phase II.

Phase II: forced escape/avoidance exposure. Phase II began when it was clear that Phase I would not produce escape and avoidance in the remaining three *S*s since they remained silent and motionless during Phase I. The *S* was removed from the shuttlebox, and two long leashes were tied around its neck. The *S* was put back into the shuttlebox, and escape/avoidance trials continued. The end of each leash was brought out at opposite ends of the shuttlebox. Thus, two *E*s were able to drag *S* back and forth across the shuttlebox by pulling one of the leashes. Phase II consisted of pulling *S* across to the safe side on each trial during shock or during the CS-UCS interval. A maximum of 25 Phase II trials per day were given. The rationale for Phase II was to force *S* to expose himself to the response-reinforcement contingency. Such "directive therapy" continued until *S* began to respond without being pulled by *E*.

Recovery. Following Phase II (for three dogs) and Phase I (for the other dog), each *S* received further escape/avoidance trials. The barrier height was gradually increased over the course of 15 trials until shoulder height had been reached. Ten further escape/ avoidance trials were then given. The last five of these recovery trials (with the barrier at shoulder height) were administered from 5 to 10 days following the first five trials with the barrier at this height. This tested the durability of the recovery.

RESULTS

Figure 1 presents the results of this study. It is clear that the procedures employed in Phases I and II of treatment were wholly successful in breaking up the maladaptive failure to escape and avoid shock. With the single exception of one *S* on one trial, the dogs had not escaped or avoided the intense shock prior to treatment. This is indicated by the mean percentage of escape or avoidance responses present at or near zero during the pretreatment phase. Following Phase I (no barrier, calling) and Phase II (forced escape/avoidance exposure) of treatment, posttreatment recovery trials without forcing or calling were given to determine the effectiveness of the treatment. All *S*s escaped or avoided on every recovery trial.

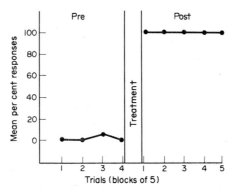

Fig. 1. Mean percentage of escape plus avoidance responses before treatment and during posttreatment recovery trials.

The behavior of one *S* was successfully modified by Phase I of treatment. After sporadic failures to escape shock during this phase, it began to escape and avoid reliably after 20 Phase I trials. With the barrier increased to shoulder height, it continued to avoid reliably. The other three dogs all responded to treatment in a fashion similar to one another: after failing to respond to Phase I, each of these dogs began to respond on its own after differing numbers of Phase II trials on which it had to be pulled to safety. One of the Phase II *S*s required 20 forced exposures to escape and avoid in Phase II before it began to respond without being pulled; the other two required 35 and 50 such trials. During the course of Phase II trials, progressively less forceful pulls were required before *S* crossed to the safe side. With the barrier increased to shoulder height following Phase II, each *S* escaped and avoided efficiently. At this stage, the dogs responded like normal dogs at or near asymptotic avoidance performance.

DISCUSSION

The chronic failure of dogs to escape shock can be eliminated by physically compelling them to engage repeatedly in the response which terminates shock. Solomon,

Kamin, and Wynne (1953) also attenuated maladaptive behavior in dogs by forcing them to expose themselves to the experimental contingencies. They reported that dogs continued to make avoidance responses long after shock was no longer present in the situation. A glass barrier, which prevented the dogs from making the response and forced them to "reality test," attenuated the persistent responding somewhat. Such "directive therapy" is also similar to Maier and Klee's (1945) report that abnormal positional fixations in rats were eliminated by forcing the rat to respond to the nonfixated side, and to Masserman's (1943, pp. 76-77) report that "neurotic" feeding inhibition could be overcome by forcing the cat into close proximity with food.

Seligman and Maier (1967) suggested that during its initial experience with inescapable shock, S learns that its responses are independent of shock termination. They further suggested that this learning not only reduces the probability of response initiation to escape shock, but also inhibits the formation of the response-relief association if S does make an escape or avoidance response in the shuttlebox. That the dogs escaped and avoided at all after being forcibly exposed to the response-relief contingency confirmed the suggestion that they had initially learned that their responses were independent of shock termination and that this learning was contravened by forcible exposure to the contingency. The finding that so many forced exposures to the contingency were required before they responded on their own (before they "caught on") confirmed the suggestion that the initial learning inhibited the formation of a response-relief association when the dog made a relief-producing response.

The perception of degree of control over the events in one's life seems to be an important determinant of the behavior of human beings. Lefcourt (1966) has summarized extensive evidence which supports this view. Cromwell, Rosenthal, Shakow and Kahn (1961), for example, reported that schizophrenics perceive reinforcement to be externally controlled (reinforcement occurs independently of their responses) to a greater extent than normals. Such evidence, along with the animal data cited above, suggests that lack of control over reinforcement may be of widespread importance in the development of psychopathology in both humans and infrahumans.

In conclusion, one might speculate that experience with traumatic events in which the individual can do nothing to eliminate or mitigate the trauma results in passive responding to future aversive events in humans. The findings of Seligman and Maier (1967) suggest that an individual might be immunized against the debilitating effects of uncontrollable trauma by having had prior experience with instrumental control over the traumatic events. Finally, the findings suggest that the pathological behavior resulting from inescapable trauma might be alleviated by repeated exposure of the individual to the trauma under conditions in which his responses were instrumental in obtaining relief. It has been demonstrated that normal escape/avoidance behavior can be produced in "passive" dogs by forcibly exposing them to relief-producing responses.

REFERENCES

Bettelheim, B. *The informed heart.* New York: Free Press of Glencoe, 1960.

Bleueler, E. *Dementia praecox or the group of schizophrenics.* New York: International Universities Press, 1950.

Carlson, N. J., and Black, A. H. Traumatic avoidance learning: The effect of preventing escape responses. *Canadian Journal of Psychology,* 1960, 14, 21-28.

Cofer, C. N., and Appley, M. A. *Motivation: Theory and research.* New York: Wiley, 1964.

Cromwell, R., Rosenthal, D., Shakow, D., and Kahn, T. Reaction time, locus of control, choice behavior and descriptions of parental behavior in schizophrenic and normal subjects. *Journal of Personality,* 1961, 29, 363-380.

Lefcourt, H. M. Internal versus external control of reinforcement: A review. *Psychological Bulletin,* 1966, 65, 206-221.

Liddell, H. S. *Emotional hazards in animals and man.* Springfield, Ill.: Charles C. Thomas, 1956.

MacDonald, A. Effect of adaptation to the unconditioned stimulus upon the formation of conditional avoidance responses. *Journal of Experimental Psychology,* 1946, 36, 11-12.

Maier, N., and Klee, J. Studies of abnormal behavior in the rat: XVII. Guidance versus trial and error in the alteration of habits and fixations. *Journal of Psychology,* 1945, 19, 133-163.

Maier, N. R. F. *Frustration: The study of behavior without a goal.* New York: McGraw-Hill, 1949.

Masserman, J. H. *Behavior and neurosis.* Chicago: University of Chicago Press, 1943.

Mowrer, O. H. *Learning theory and behavior.* New York: Wiley, 1960.

Overmier, J. B., and Seligman, M. E. P. Effects of inescapable shock upon subsequent escape and avoidance responding. *Journal of Comparative and Physiological Psychology,* 1967, 63, 28-33.

Richter, C. On the phenomenon of sudden death in animals and man. *Psychosomatic Medicine,* 1957, 19, 191-198.

Seligman, M. E. P., and Maier, S. F. Failure to escape traumatic shock. *Journal of Experimental Psychology,* 1967, 74, 1-9.

Solomon, R. L., Kamin, L., and Wynne, L. C. Traumatic avoidance learning: The outcomes of several extinction procedures with dogs. *Journal of Abnormal and Social Psychology,* 1953, 48, 291-302.

Solomon, R. L., and Wynne, L. C. Traumatic avoidance learning: Acquisition in normal dogs. *Psychological Monographs,* 1953, 67 (4, Whole No. 354).

Wallace, A. F. C. Mazeway disintegration: The individual's perception of sociocultural disorganization. *Human Organization,* 1957, 16, 23-27.

Author Index

411

Subject Index